A Guide to the Standard EMDR Protocols for Clinicians, Supervisors, and Consultants

About the Author

Andrew M. Leeds, PhD, is a California licensed Psychologist and Marriage and Family Therapist with 34 years of experience in the private practice of psychotherapy. He practices in Santa Rosa, California.

Dr. Leeds received his BA in Psychology with honors in 1972 from the University of California at Santa Cruz, an MA in Clinical Psychology in 1974 from Goddard College, and his PhD in Clinical Psychology in 1983 from International College.

After early training in Gestalt and Somatic psychotherapies, Dr. Leeds served a 2-year internship as program coordinator for an alcohol abuse treatment program in Santa Cruz and received his license as a Marriage and Family Therapist before going on to obtain his doctorate. During his doctoral program, he studied cognitive behavioral therapy, Ericksonian hypnosis, and self psychology.

Dr. Leeds received his initial EMDR training in 1991 and became an EMDR training supervisor that same year. In 1993, he became an EMDR trainer. He has conducted EMDR trainings for 15,000 clinicians at 140 training programs in the United States, Canada, France, England, and Japan.

He has presented papers on EMDR for regional, national, and international conferences. He is the author of a book, book chapters, and several journal articles on EMDR. He served for 2 years on the Standards and Training Committee of the EMDR International Association (EMDRIA) and for 3 years as an elected member of the EMDRIA Board of Directors. He presently serves as a member of the Editorial Advisory Board of the *Journal of EMDR Practice and Research*. He is an EMDRIA-Approved Consultant providing consultation to EMDR clinicians around the world.

Dr. Leeds contributed to the evolution of EMDR by articulating, publishing, and teaching the EMDR procedure he named *Resource Development and Installation* (RDI). In 1999, he received an EMDRIA award for creative innovation in the development of EMDR as well as the Ronald A. Martinez, PhD Memorial Award.

A Guide to the Standard EMDR Protocols for Clinicians, Supervisors, and Consultants

Andrew M. Leeds, Ph.D.

SPRINGER PUBLISHING COMPANY

NEW YORK

Springer Publishing Company, LLC
11 West 42nd Street
New York, NY 10036
www.springerpub.com

Acquisitions Editor: Sheri Sussman
Cover Design: David Levy
Composition: Six Red Marbles

Ebook ISBN: 978-0-8261-1552-2

11/   5   4   3   2

Library of Congress Cataloging-in-Publication Data

Leeds, Andrew M.
    A guide to the standard EMDR protocols for clinicians, supervisors, and consultants / by Andrew M. Leeds.
        p. cm.
    Includes bibliographical references.
    ISBN 978-0-8261-1551-5
    1. Eye movement desensitization and reprocessing. I. Title.
    RC489.E98L44 2009
    616.89'14--dc22

                                                                                            2009021092

Printed in the United States of America by Gasch Printing

Contents

Preface

MY PROFESSIONAL DEVELOPMENT WITH EMDR

Every book has a beginning. This one began when I completed Parts 1 and 2 of the basic EMDR training in 1991. A number of successful early experiences with applying EMDR in my private practice gave me a growing sense of confidence in EMDR. In late 1991, I began serving as a training supervisor for the practice portion of EMDR trainings. The opportunity to supervise the clinical practice of EMDR at trainings deepened my understanding of EMDR, conceptually and procedurally. I observed an incredible number of both common and rare deviations from the standard EMDR procedures. Having to find the words to clarify not only the standard EMDR procedures, but also to be able to offer a rationale from the theoretical model, strengthened my teaching skills and my conceptual understanding of EMDR.

In 1993, I began leading EMDR trainings throughout the United States and Canada and later in Europe and Japan. Through 2008, I led EMDR basic trainings for over 15,000 clinicians. This has been an incredibly rewarding experience. With the help of A. J. Popky, from 1996–2000, I served as the founding moderator of an EMDR e-mail discussion forum. I read over 15,000 e-mails from EMDR-trained clinicians from all over the world and sent over 2,500 e-mails in reply on topics including standard EMDR procedures, treatment planning, and the growing body of EMDR literature. From 2001–2003, I served on the EMDRIA Standards and Training Committee, and from 2003–2005, as elected member of EMDRIA's Board of Directors. Since 2003, I have compiled a summary of recently published EMDR research that appears in each quarterly issue of the *EMDRIA Newsletter*. These many years of service to the EMDR community and with EMDRIA have been essential in strengthening my understanding of EMDR.

Although I am profoundly indebted to all of my colleagues who have helped me evolve in my understanding of EMDR, the flaws, omissions, and other deficiencies in this work are my responsibility alone.

Acknowledgments

I am deeply indebted to all my colleagues who have contributed to my understanding of EMDR. Space does not permit me to name them all. First and foremost, I am grateful to Francine Shapiro for the gift of EMDR. EMDR has transformed my clinical work and opened doorways for professional development that I could never have imagined. I am also grateful for the community of EMDR trainers, training supervisors, and clinicians trained in EMDR. My dear friends and colleagues Carol York, Sandra Foster, and Curt Rouanzoin have been loyal comrades through many adventures. Carol York has been a steady source of support and intellectual stimulation in the evolution of my understanding of EMDR. Deborah Korn and I took turns sitting in each other's conference presentations for many years, finally teaching together in 1998 and coauthoring a paper in 2002. I have matured through their teaching and consultations over these many years. Other colleagues who have supported me directly or indirectly in ways that affect this book include Robbie Adler-Tapia, Nancy Errebo, Ulrich Lanius, Jennifer Lendl, Marilyn Luber, Philip Manfield, and Carolyn Settle.

Masaya Ichii and his colleagues, Masako Kitamura and Masamichi Honda in Japan gave me the opportunity to teach annually in Japan over a span of 10 years. The opportunity to teach with the exceptional translator/clinicians—Tomoko Osawa and Akiko Kikuchi—in Japan challenged me to find the essence of EMDR that would fit in half the speaking time and to develop illustrations for key EMDR concepts. Mark Russell has been an inspiration and a strong supporter to carry this project to completion. Louise Maxfield inspired me with her dedication and scholarship, invited me to serve on the Editorial Board for the *Journal of EMDR Practice and Research*, persistently encouraged me to write, and introduced me to key staff members at Springer Publishing Company. Rosalie Thomas, Wendy Freitag, Mark Dworkin, and many other colleagues with whom I served on the EMDRIA Board and the Standards and Training Committee helped enlarge my perspective about the needs of the larger EMDR community and the future of EMDR. My understanding of EMDR and the global evolution of EMDR have been profoundly affected by the support, teaching, and publications of my European colleagues, Ad de Jongh and Arne Hoffman.

I am deeply indebted to Ted Nardin, President of Springer Publishing Company, who first encouraged me to place this manuscript with Springer when we met in 2006, to Sheri Sussman—an extraordinary editor, raconteur and dancer—who supported me at crucial points and helped me to realize my vision for this book, and to Deborah Gissinger who shepherded me through the challenges of the publishing process of my first book.

I am grateful to my wife, Deborah Taylor-French, and daughter, Alexandra Leeds, who have patiently endured my closeting of myself in my office for so long during the preparation of this book. My wife also gave much helpful feedback at critical junctures in this process, and my daughter contributed the illustration for Figure 7.1.

Introduction

This book is intended to provide an easy to use guide to the standard, research-supported EMDR protocols for graduate students, clinicians, consultants, supervisors, instructors, and researchers. It is intended to supplement the following requirements for all EMDR clinicians: a thorough reading of Francine Shapiro's (2001) text—*Eye Movement Desensitization and Reprocessing, Basic Principles, Protocols, and Procedures;* an EMDRIA-approved basic training in EMDR; and consultation in the use of EMDR from an EMDRIA-Approved Consultant.

Since the publication of the first edition of Francine Shapiro's standard text in 1995 and the founding of the EMDR International Association (EMDRIA), the role of consultation on the use of EMDR has expanded, becoming required in both basic training in EMDR and in EMDRIA's certification program, yet little has been published to offer guidance on the consultative process for EMDR-trained clinicians and consultants. EMDR finds a growing role in organized treatment programs in colleges and universities, nonprofit agencies, and community mental health centers where clinical supervisors need ways to document EMDR treatment planning, process, and outcomes. This book provides an orientation to these issues as well as forms that offer a starting point for documenting the clinical process with EMDR.

THE PLAN OF THIS BOOK

In planning this guide to standard EMDR protocols, decisions had to be made in selecting which areas of application to include and which to exclude. Several factors were considered, including the degree and nature of evidence of empirical validation, congruence with well-accepted principles of treatment in the behavioral literature, content required for EMDRIA-approved basic training in EMDR, and the need to keep the manual to a practical length. A significant number of proposed EMDR procedures and protocols for additional clinical applications that show promise, but did not meet some of these criteria, were omitted.

Section I of the book covers the conceptual framework for understanding EMDR, including the history and evolution of EMDR in chapter 1, the Adaptive Information Processing model in chapter 2; and an overview of the standard eight-phase model of EMDR and the three-pronged protocol in chapter 3. The three chapters in section II cover case formulation, treatment planning, and preparing patients for EMDR reprocessing.

Section III, six chapters in all, covers phases three through eight of the standard protocol for posttraumatic stress disorder (PTSD). The standard EMDR protocol for PTSD can be applied with equal effectiveness for patients who meet partial criteria for PTSD and whose symptoms develop after a range of adverse life events that do not meet criterion A (American Psychiatric Association [APA], 1994; Mol et al., 2005; Wilson, Becker, & Tinker, 1997). These procedural steps and the standard protocol for PTSD apply to patients with primary structural dissociation (van der Hart, 2007), which is always present to some degree in PTSD. Patients with secondary structural dissociation—including those with complex PTSD, borderline personality disorder, or dissociative disorder not otherwise specified (DDNOS)—or with tertiary structural dissociation—dissociative identity disorder (DID)—will need additional interventions and a more complex treatment plan not covered in this text.

Section IV covers the application of EMDR to conditions other than PTSD with chapters devoted to specific phobias and panic disorder. Note that the standard EMDR PTSD protocol can be applied to patients with comorbid substance abuse when sufficient stabilization has been achieved—as described in chapter 6—and when the case conceptualization is that the substance abuse is secondary to the PTSD. When the substance abuse appears to be the primary condition—that is when it began first—and the PTSD appears to be secondary, alternate EMDR approaches may be more suitable as the initial focus of attention needs to be the treatment of the substance abuse itself. The Desensitization of Triggers and Urge Reprocessing (DeTUR) protocol (Popky, 2005; Vogelmann-Sine, Sine, Smyth, & Popky, 1998) continues to be the most promising EMDR approach for treatment of primary substance abuse, but research on DeTUR and other approaches to applying EMDR to substance abuse (Brown & Gilman, 2007; Brown, Gilman, & Kelso, 2008; Hase, Schallmayer, & Sack, 2008) is still at too early of a stage for inclusion in this guide.

Section V addresses issues of professional development in EMDR as clinicians go through the basic training in EMDR and obtain consultation or supervision on their clinical application of EMDR. The three appendices provide sections with fidelity checklists, forms, and resources referred to in the text.

THE PATH TO PROFICIENCY

Over many years of conducting training in EMDR I have at times been surprised at the number of clinicians who returned for the next phase of their training months or years later and who disclosed that they have used EMDR rarely or not at all. When I served on the EMDRIA Board of Directors I supported policies—subsequently implemented—to require inclusion of consultation on trainees' actual clinical use of EMDR as part of basic training in EMDR. As a trainer, I also sought ways to motivate and encourage training participants to get started early and persist in practicing EMDR. While teaching in Japan I developed the following metaphor for the process of learning EMDR. If you have ever seen a student and experienced potter each working with clay at a wheel and throwing a pot, perhaps you have seen what I try to convey in this guide: *EMDR, when done well, looks simple, but it is not easy.*

The student wedges the clay but introduces air bubbles. When fired, the pot made from this clay explodes. The student struggles to center the clay. Instead, it slides off the edge of the wheel. The student becomes frustrated and less able to concentrate. After gaining skills at centering, the student still cannot control the thickness of the pot, which collapses on one side and must be discarded or is too thick and lacks grace.

The experienced potter wedges the clay while avoiding trapping air bubbles. She firmly centers the clay on the turning wheel. Then, she raises the sides, thinning them evenly while retaining stability and grace in the form. In moments, making only simple motions, the pot is done.

It appears simple, but it is not easy. How does the student become proficient? Practice and more practice. Central to learning is the willingness to let others with more experience observe and give feedback on one's work. Only by being willing to reveal one's mistakes, accept feedback and by working together can we find the simplicity that yields graceful and lasting results. Scientific progress, our consultees, our students and most importantly our patients deserve no less.

The Conceptual Framework for Understanding EMDR

The most important fundamental laws and facts of physical science have all been discovered, and these are now so firmly established that the possibility of their ever being supplemented in consequence of new discoveries is exceedingly remote.

—Abraham Albert Michelson, 1903

The more original a discovery, the more obvious it seems afterwards.

—Arthur Koestler,

Whether you can observe a thing or not depends on the theory which you use. It is the theory which decides what can be observed.

—Albert Einstein, 1926

The History and Evolution of EMDR

CONTEMPORARY THEORY AND TREATMENT OF POSTTRAUMATIC STRESS SYNDROMES

Unlike other 20th century psychotherapies, Eye Movement Desensitization and Reprocessing (EMDR) began not from a particular theoretical perspective but from direct empirical observations (Shapiro, 1995, 2001). Nevertheless, other approaches and their theories clearly influenced the evolution of EMDR and its theoretical framework through four main periods from (a) a simple technique (eye movements), to (b) an initial procedure (EMD), to (c) a protocol (EMDR) for treatment of one condition (posttraumatic stress disorder [PTSD]), to (d) an overall approach to treatment. Even though EMDR began from more of an empirical than theoretical origin, an understanding of EMDR's theoretical framework, known as the Adaptive Information Processing model (AIP; Shapiro, 2001), is central to the successful clinical application of EMDR. The AIP model guides case conceptualization, informs treatment planning, supports resolving clinical impasses, and predicts clinical outcomes and potential new clinical applications.

Section I presents the conceptual framework for understanding EMDR. Chapter 1 begins with a review of selected aspects of four models that historically most directly support understanding the evolution of EMDR. These are hypnosis, psychodynamic, behavioral, and cognitive behavioral. An overview of these models and their research base as a treatment for PTSD can be found in *Effective Treatment for PTSD* (Foa, Keane, & Friedman, 2000; Foa, Keane, Friedman, & Cohen, 2009). After a review of these four models, the history of EMDR's evolution is summarized. Next, in chapter 2, the AIP model is presented followed by a summary of the leading proposals to explain EMDR treatment effects.

HYPNOSIS

The history of psychotherapy over the last 125 years begins with the use of hypnosis (Whalen & Nash, 1996) by Charcot, Janet, Breuer, Freud, and Prince (among others). From its early roots in psychotherapy, hypnosis was closely associated with the search to understand and treat the relationship between trauma and dissociation (van der Kolk & van der Hart, 1989; Cardeña, Maldonado, van der Hart, & Spiegel, 2000). The early history and evolution of EMDR in turn has been deeply involved in the search to understand and treat the relationship between trauma and dissociation (Fine et al., 1995; Lazrove & Fine, 1996; Nicosia, 1994; Paulsen, 1995).

The 20th-century models of hypnosis were strongly influenced by Milton Erickson (Lankton, 1987; Rossi, 1980a, 1980b). Hypnosis has contributed key concepts relevant to the theory and practice of EMDR. *Rapport* refers to the qualities of trust, connection, and contingency (Siegel, 1999) needed in the relationship between the person being hypnotized and the hypnotist (Frederick & McNeal, 1999). *Frame of reference* and *narrowing of attention* both refer to phenomena central to hypnotic responses, leading to alternations in perception of the environment and the body. *Hypnotic suggestibility* varies widely in different individuals. Whether there is or is not a consistent, (measurable) altered state of consciousness produced by hypnosis remains a matter of some debate (Kirsch & Lynn, 1995). Preliminary evidence (Nicosia, 1995) suggested that use of standard EMDR procedures—described by Shapiro (1995, 2001) and in this text—do not induce an altered state in the brain similar to brain wave patterns that have been identified in hypnosis. Procedurally, hypnotic phenomena and suggestions are not central to EMDR's main treatment effects (Barrowcliff, Gray, & MacCulloch, 2002; MacCulloch & Feldman, 1996). Suggestibility has been found not to correlate with responses to EMDR treatment (Hekmat, Groth, & Rogers, 1994). While formal trance and suggestion are not central to EMDR treatment, Ericksonian principles, including *utilization*, *naturalistic methods*, and *metaphor*, play an important role in the "preparation phase" and in some strategies for working through *ineffective reprocessing*. In contrast to earlier models of hypnosis based on command suggestion, Milton Erickson was *interactive* and *responsive*, eliciting information and *utilizing* each patient's unique experience and symptoms as a source for solutions. These same principles inform the use of naturalistic strategies in *interweaves* (Shapiro, 1995, 2001) to assist patients in reprocessing intense emotional distress and to foster synthesis between maladaptive and adaptive memory networks.

PSYCHODYNAMIC APPROACHES

Psychodynamic approaches to the treatment of PTSD have a long history with a diverse range approaches and rich tapestry of constructs that have been developed. Of the many concepts and principles found in psychodynamic approaches, a number are relevant to understanding the similarities and differences between psychodynamic approaches and EMDR. Freud (1955) described traumatic events as breaching a *stimulus barrier* leading to a *repetition compulsion* in which periods of intrusive re-experiencing alternate with periods of avoidance. Freud initially explored the structured use of hypnosis pioneered by Charcot and Janet (van der Hart & Friedman, 1989) and advocated by his mentor Breuer (Breuer & Freud, 1955). Their approach focused on using hypnosis to help strengthen patients' abilities to function and then to develop a narrative understanding of traumatic events. For reasons beyond the scope of this overview, Freud literally turned away from his patients and shifted to the technique of *free association* in which he required patients to discuss their concerns without directive guidance while Freud assumed a stance of *neutrality*. This shift in technique was paralleled by a shift in focus from developing a narrative understanding of traumatic events to an exploration of the intrapsychic meaning (defensive purpose) of the patient's symptoms. Frequent sessions and minimal therapist responsiveness served to increase the intensity of the therapeutic relationship. (For the effects of the absence of contingent responsiveness on anxiety, see Siegel [1999].) This also encouraged the *projection of transference material*, which was considered to represent the unresolved *intrapsychic conflicts* of the patient. Interpretation of the defensive meaning of symptoms, verbal and memory lapses, and projected transference material became the primary active intervention.

During the evolution from EMD to EMDR (Shapiro, 1991a), Shapiro incorporated the principle of *free association* and moved further away from a *prolonged exposure model*. However, *interpretation* is normally explicitly avoided in the standard model of EMDR. Rather than pure neutrality, responsiveness to the patient's process is emphasized in EMDR. Transference and counter-transference are recognized, but when transference arises during reprocessing, it is normally addressed by making it the focus of further reprocessing without explicit interpretation or comment. Often, the personal memories that are the sources of projected transference material will emerge spontaneously as reprocessing continues in EMDR treatment sessions. If not, EMDR clinicians can actively encourage patients to explore associations to their personal memories during additional sets of *bilateral stimulation* through affective, somatic, and cognitive linkages.

BEHAVIOR THERAPY

Classical behavior therapy views PTSD through the lens of conditioning in which a powerful *conditioned association* is formed between *specific cues* (external and internal stimuli) that were present at the time of a traumatic event and the intense state of alarm (fear) evoked by the traumatic experience. Systematic desensitization and flooding (implosion) were the two dominant modes of treatment proposed by behaviorists (Wolpe, 1954, 1958; Keane, Fairbank, Caddell, & Zimering, 1989; Stampfl & Levis, 1967). In systematic desensitization, the patient identifies a hierarchy of cues ranging from mildly to highly disturbing. Then the patient is trained to achieve a state of deep relaxation through structured self-control techniques such as *progressive relaxation* or *biofeedback-assisted relaxation training*. Next, the patient is directed to focus on the least disturbing cue and to practice relaxing until a state of calm is achieved again. This is repeated as many times as necessary, working gradually up the hierarchy until the most disturbing cue can be focused on and the patient can remain calm. Only six studies have examined systematic desensitization as a treatment for PTSD. In part, this may be because it is time-consuming and other methods have been shown to be more effective and efficient for most patients (Foa et al., 2000; Solomon, Gerrity & Muff, 1992; van Etten & Taylor, 1998).

Flooding or *implosion therapy* (Stampfl & Levis, 1967) is a form of *imaginal exposure*. Flooding is based on the principle of *extinction*, which proposes that nerves can only continue to produce intense arousal for limited periods of time. Afterward, further exposure to frightening cues no longer produces a fear response. Flooding and related forms of *prolonged imaginal exposure* (PE) have been studied extensively as treatments for PTSD. See reviews in Foa et al. (2000) and Follette & Ruzek (2006). Early reports indicated that PE had a 50% dropout rate in treatment of combat veterans (Cooper & Clum, 1989) and little effect on emotional numbing and social avoidance (Keane et al., 1989). Later reports suggest similar dropout rates for exposure therapy, cognitive therapy, stress inoculation training, and EMDR (Hembree et al., 2003). However, recent reviewers suggest nonresponse and dropout rates vary widely—up to 50% in some behavioral studies—perhaps depending on the population being studied and call for better data in research reports to clarify these rates in treatments for PTSD (Schottenbauer, Glass, Arnkoff, Tendick, & Gray, 2008).

Although PE has been found to be effective for reducing fear-related symptoms, questions remain regarding its effectiveness for resolving feelings of shame and guilt (Adshead, 2000; Pitman et al., 1991; Stapleton, Taylor, & Asmundson, 2006). This has led to approaches such as cognitive processing therapy (Resick & Schnicke, 1993) and stress inoculation training (Meichenbaum, 1985), which combine PE with cognitive therapy. It is possible that the effects of flooding may result in part from patients being unintentionally trained to dissociate (emotional numbing) so that they no longer feel the disturbing material rather than forming new associations to the disturbing cues (Rogers & Lanius, 2001).

COGNITIVE BEHAVIORAL THEORY

Cognitive behavioral theory accepts the paradigm of classical conditioning as a foundation for understanding posttraumatic syndromes (and other anxiety disorders), but turns toward *information processing models* and to the concept of *emotional processing* for models of how to reshape conditioning from these adverse events. Cognitive behavioral models that focus on the intervening variables of irrational beliefs or negative schemas may be more familiar to clinicians from Ellis's (1994) rational emotive behavior therapy (REBT) and Beck's (Beck, Emery, & Greenberg, 2005) cognitive therapy. However, the less widely known cognitive behavioral models of *emotional information processing* are central to understanding the principles that underlie the standard model of EMDR. The key concepts supporting the cognitive model of emotional information processing build on the work of Lang (1977, 1979), Rachman (1980), Bower (1981), Foa and Kozak (1985, 1986), and Foa and Riggs (1995).

COGNITIVE BEHAVIORAL MODELS OF EMOTIONAL INFORMATION PROCESSING

Lang (1968) operationalized the concept of anxiety as involving behavioral responses in the following three systems: physiological activity, overt behavior, and subjective report. Lang proposed a general model (1977, 1979) for treating anxiety

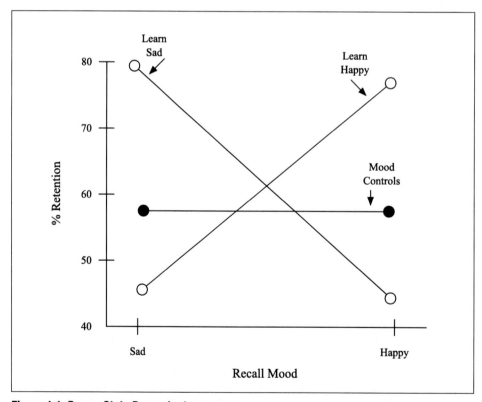

Figure 1.1 Bower State Dependent memory
Percentage retention scores for three groups of hypnotizable subjects tested on recall of lists of happy and sad words. Mood during learning and recall was induced by hypnosis-guided imagery. Mood during testing is shown on horizontal axis. Mood controls were in neutral mood on learning and recall test. Crossing lines with mood reversed on testing from learning show affect-state dependent learning effect. Similar effects were shown for autobiographical recall.

Note. From "Mood and Memory," by G. H. Bower, 1981, American Psychologist, 36(2), pp. 129–148. Copyright 2000. Reprinted with permission.

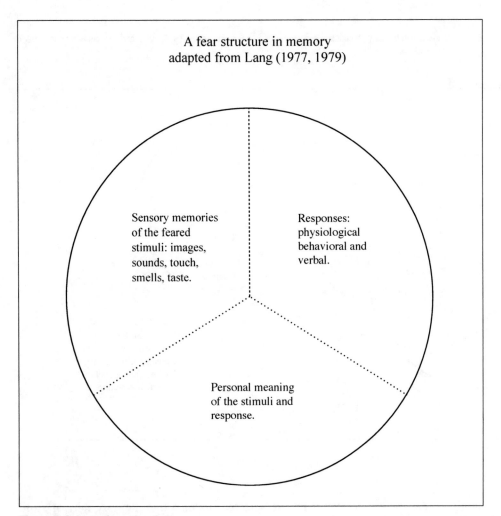

A fear structure in memory
adapted from Lang (1977, 1979)

Sensory memories
of the feared
stimuli: images,
sounds, touch,
smells, taste.

Responses:
physiological
behavioral and
verbal.

Personal meaning
of the stimuli and
response.

Figure 1.2 Lang fear structure

disorders when using *imagery* (in contrast to in vivo treatment). First, some of the response components, holding these emotional memories in *fear structures*, must be activated. The idea that imaginal treatment must first activate *emotionally valenced memory structures* is parallel to Bower's *state specific model* (1981). Bower proposed that access to *recalling* and *modifying emotional information* is dependent on the emotional state (mood) the individual is in at the time.

Lang described fear structures as containing information about the following: (a) the feared stimulus; (b) verbal, physiological, and behavioral responses; and (c) meaning of the stimulus and response. Starting from Mathews' hypothesis (1971, p. 88) that "one of the effects of relaxation may be to increase the vividness of imagery experienced during desensitization," Rachman (1980) proposed that the increased vividness of imagery resulting from relaxation leads to fear reductions by *first producing stronger physiological responses to phobic imagery*. He called this sequence of effects *emotional processing*. Rachman also proposed that repeated *test probes* of phobic imagery were needed to determine the degree to which emotional processing had occurred. These repeated test probes are direct antecedents to the EMDR procedure of returning to target to reaccess the *memory network* and reassess the degree to which reprocessing has occurred. Foa and Kozak (1985, 1986) later proposed that for emotional processing of fear to occur, information—cognitive and affective—incompatible with fear must be available and integrated to modify the fear structure and form a new memory. In EMDR, this concept is described as the need for relevant adaptive memory networks to be present and accessible so that

Figure 1.3
Emotional processing of fear with imaginal exposure based on Foa and Kozak (1985, 1986) and Foa and Rothbaum (1998).

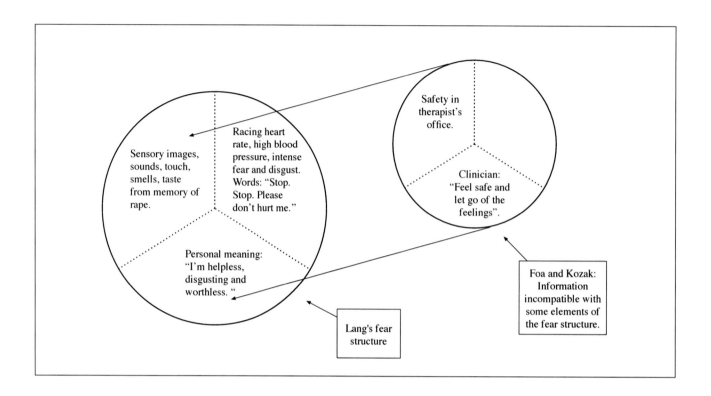

synthesis can take place between the selected maladaptive memory network and adaptive memory networks.

The cognitive behavioral model of clinical anxiety has had a powerful effect on treatment and research. The cognitive behavioral approach to treatment of post-traumatic syndromes, which is still evolving, includes the following: (a) the principle of prolonged exposure derived from the early behavioral models of flooding—that started with the most traumatic memory, (b) some elements of systematic desensitization that started with the least disturbing elements and involve practicing dearousal (relaxation) in the here and now, and (c) some elements of cognitive restructuring. Indeed, there does not yet appear to be agreement on how to manualize treatment of PTSD within a cognitive behavioral model. Different research teams studying models of exposure-based treatment for PTSD have different treatment manuals that change from one study to the next.

Several theoretical questions arise in the cognitive behavioral model of emotional processing as described by Foa and Kozak (1986). First, what prevents or enhances the integration of the information incompatible with fear when fear structures are activated and information incompatible with fear is present? Rachman (1979) suggested that a key element in emotional processing may be relaxation. Is relaxation the only factor? What other factors enhance or inhibit emotional processing? To the degree that relaxation is a factor in facilitating emotional processing, how can relaxation best be evoked when asking a person to focus on a terrifying memory, involving a perception of eminent death or injury to self or other?

Systematic desensitization and stress inoculation training provide patients with training in structured anxiety regulation techniques that are alternated with prolonged exposure to anxiety-provoking imagery. These approaches stand in contrast to EMDR in which patients are challenged to initially simultaneously attend to their anxiety-provoking imagery and to neutral, bilateral sensory stimulation that appears to have a "compelled relaxation response" (Barrowcliff, Gray, MacCulloch, Freeman, & MacCulloch, 2003; Wilson, Silver, Covi, & Foster, 1996, p. 227). However, during EMDR reprocessing, patients are not asked nor required to continue to maintain attention to their anxiety-provoking imagery. Indeed, most patients report that they are unable to maintain persistent attention on their original anxiety-provoking imagery during bilateral sensory stimulation. Instead, most patients begin to report various associations from aspects of their original anxiety-provoking imagery that can lead to other disturbing, neutral, or even positive imagery, sensations, emotions, and thoughts. Thus, psychophysiological arousal tends to move from a zone of hyperarousal to a zone of optimal arousal that facilitates the emotional information processing originally described by Rachman (1979). See Figure 1.5, Yerkes–Dodson later in this chapter.

In cognitive approaches to emotional processing, the two central strategies for integrating information incompatible with a fear response are the following: (a) to have the patient engage repeatedly in daily homework assignments of self-directed imaginal exposure until new, less frightening memories are formed and (b) to have the therapist make statements or ask questions while the patient is engaging in imaginal exposure. These strategies contrast with standard EMDR treatment that requires no patient homework and encourages the patient to reprocess with a minimum of therapist verbalizing during and between sets of bilateral sensory stimulation. Case formulation strategies—described in chapters 4, 5, and 6—call on clinicians to assess before starting EMDR reprocessing, the degree to which patients possess and can access adaptive responses and information *incompatible with a fear response*. When these are absent or difficult to access, EMDR clinicians must take steps both in the preparation phase of treatment and during active reprocessing to assure that this integration can place.

THE PHASE-ORIENTED CONSENSUS MODEL

Nearly all contemporary approaches to the treatment of trauma derive significant elements from the pioneering work of Pierre Janet (1889, 1977). Among Janet's many contributions is the foundational principle of a phase-oriented approach: (a) stabilization and symptom reduction, (b) uncovering and modifying traumatic memories, and (c) personality reintegration. Judith Herman (1992) describes these three phases as (a) safety, (b) remembrance and mourning, and (c) reconnection. Parallel models have been described by Briere (1996), Brown and Fromm (1986), Chu (1998), Courtois (1988, 1999), Gil (1988), Horowitz (1979, 1986), Kluft (1993, 1999), McCann and Perlman (1980), Putnam (1989), Scurfield (1985), van der Hart and Friedman (1989), and van der Kolk, McFarlane, and Weisaeth (1996). Christine Courtois in *Recollections of Sexual Abuse: Treatment Principles and Guidelines* (1999, p 176) described many facets of this evolving *consensus model* of posttraumatic treatment and characterized it as "sequenced, titrated, focused on symptom relief and functioning."

The principles of EMDR (Shapiro, 1995, 2001) situate it within this consensus model. In EMDR, various strategies can be employed to support the goals of stabilization and symptom reduction. Some stabilization strategies commonly used in EMDR were developed in other traditions such as *progressive relaxation* (Jacobson, 1938), self-hypnosis (Eisen & Fromm, 1983; Sanders, 1991), biofeedback (Brown, McGoldrick, & Buchanan, 1997), and meditation (Benson, 1975; Goldstein, 1994). Other stabilization strategies such as the calm or safe place exercise (Shapiro, 2001, pp. 125–127) and Resource Development and Installation (Leeds, 1998; Leeds & Shapiro, 2000) integrate a specific set of stabilization procedures from hypnosis and guided imagery in ways that are unique to EMDR. Regardless of which stabilization strategies are used in treating PTSD, the consensus model recognizes that it is essential to provide adequate stabilization before and during uncovering and resolving traumatic memories to avoid what John Briere calls (1996, p. 11) "overshooting the therapeutic window." This phrase refers to uncovering details about disturbing memories or exposing intense negative emotions at a pace that exceeds the patient's cognitive, emotional, or behavioral coping skills. This problem of *overwhelming patients' coping skills* can occur in both the *history-taking* phases of treatment as well as in the *working-through* phases of treatment. The goal in trauma-informed psychotherapy is to pace the work within "the therapeutic window." Working within this therapeutic window provides sufficient *access* to the maladaptive memory networks that give rise to the patient's symptoms and current functioning while not exceeding the patient's cognitive, emotional, or behavioral coping skills.

A BRIEF HISTORY: FROM EMD TO EMDR

The history of the development of EMDR can be summarized in the following four stages:

1. Discovery and investigation of a simple technique (eye movements).

2. Defining and testing of the EMD procedure.

3. Evolution, clarification, and validation of the standard EMDR protocol as a treatment for PTSD and related syndromes.

4. Extending the theory and application of EMDR to additional clinical syndromes as a general model of psychotherapy. The current status of EMDR is in the process of movement from stage 3 to stage 4.

DISCOVERY AND INVESTIGATION

While walking in a park in 1987, Francine Shapiro (1995, pp. 2–14; 2001, pp. 7–16) noticed a specific effect of saccadic eye movements on certain disturbing thoughts. The emotional component of these thoughts rapidly and spontaneously decreased. She determined to investigate this effect in others. Her first discovery was that most others had difficulty generating sufficient saccadic eye movements to achieve this effect. So she asked others to engage in tracking eye movements by watching her move her hand back and forth about 12–14 inches in front of their faces.

Through her informal investigations with about 70 individuals, Shapiro discovered that several factors assisted different individuals to achieve similar decreases in the emotional component of disturbing thoughts. With some, the pace of the eye movements needed to be faster or slower, or diagonal eye movements were more effective. With others, a wider or narrower range of horizontal eye movements were more effective. Some needed to focus on an image, others on a body sensation, some on a thought, and some on an emotion. Some needed a combination of these elements. By combining several of these factors into a deliberate set of steps, she found that she was able to reliably achieve a decrease in emotional disturbance in a wide range of individuals not suffering from any identified disorder.

She then offered this procedure to a combat trauma survivor with persistent trauma-related symptoms related to a specific incident. A single brief session of this procedure led to a resolution of the emotional disturbances and an extinguishing of the intrusions that had been associated with this memory. The apparent efficacy of this procedure to deal not only with mildly disturbing thoughts in nonpatients, but also with a severely disturbing memory in a combat trauma survivor, encouraged Shapiro to conduct a controlled investigation with a defined population of those suffering from PTSD.

DEFINING AND TESTING EMD

In exploring the literature on the treatment of trauma and anxiety, Shapiro examined Wolpe's (1954) systematic desensitization and flooding (Stampfl & Levis, 1967; Fairbank & Keane, 1982). Wolpe considered *reciprocal inhibition* between relaxation and anxiety to be the primary basis of systematic desensitization—and all effective psychotherapeutic treatments for neuroses. Yet, Wolpe acknowledged that only low levels of anxiety were amenable to treatment with his approach. As in flooding, Shapiro focused her eye movement procedure on the most disturbing aspect of the index trauma. Unlike flooding, this new procedure did not require prolonged exposure or intense abreaction. Instead, Shapiro observed what appeared to be some type of reciprocal inhibition between the conditioned emotional disturbance in the memory of trauma and the specific effects of the eye movements. Years later, in the first physiological study of EMDR, David Wilson (1996, p. 227) would refer to this as a "compelled relaxation response." Since reciprocal inhibition rather than extinction appeared to be the mechanism, in honor of Wolpe's model of systematic desensitization, she decided to name this procedure "Eye Movement Desensitization" or EMD (1989a, 1989b).

DESIGN AND PROCEDURES OF THE EMD PILOT STUDY

In 1980, posttraumatic stress disorder (PTSD) was first explicitly included in the *Diagnostic and Statistical Manual, Third Edition* (DSM III; American Psychiatric Association, 1980; Parrish, 1999). By 1988, there was a widespread and growing recognition of this disorder and of the severe limitations of existing methods for its treatment. Shapiro decided to focus her efforts on a field trial of this new EMD method with individuals who were already in treatment for PTSD. Rather than take on the larger question of whether EMD could resolve all PTSD-related symptoms, her more modest goal in this pilot study was to determine whether intrusive disturbance associated with a single, traumatic memory could be treated to resolution in a single session. She recruited 22 subjects, ages 11–53, from clinicians who were treating them for PTSD symptoms related to rape, sexual abuse, or Vietnam combat trauma.

Half the subjects were randomly assigned to the EMD condition and half to a control group—described by Shapiro (1989a, p. 202) as a "placebo condition"— that received an alternate exposure procedure with no eye movements. All subjects described and quantified their presenting complaints such as intrusive thoughts and sleep disturbances. Each selected a single memory and an image that represented the worst part of the incident or the entire incident. Each subject identified a negative belief such as, "I am helpless" or "I have no control" in response to being asked (Shapiro, 1989a, p. 204), "What words about yourself or the incident best go with the picture?" Subjects were then asked to focus on the traumatic image and their negative words and to assign a Subjective Units of Disturbance level from 0–10 (SUD scale; Wolpe, 1954). Subjects were then asked to say what words they would rather have with their selected picture and to rate these positive self-statements while focusing on their selected image using a Validity of Cognition scale (VoC) (Shapiro, 1989a) from 1–7. Subjects were then advised that they would be asked for their level of disturbance (SUD) periodically during the rest of the treatment session and were told to ". . . let whatever happens, happen" (p. 204).

Subjects in the EMD condition were then asked to imagine their traumatic scene and rehearse their negative statement while Shapiro induced an initial set 10–20 bilateral, rhythmic eye movements. After each set of eye movements, subjects were asked to "Blank it (the picture) out, and take a deep breath." (p. 205) After each set of eye movements, they were then asked to focus on the picture and the negative words and to rate their disturbance from 0–10. Between sets of eye movements, subjects were sometimes asked to report what they were noticing with the question "What do you get now?" (p. 205) Further sets of eye movements were offered until no other traumatic memory or disturbing thought was reported and their SUD level was stated to be 0 or 1. This took from 3–12 sets. Subjects were then asked to rate their preferred statement on the VoC scale from 1–7. Subjects whose VoC was then less than <6 were asked to focus on their selected memory and their positive self-statement and were led in 2–3 more sets of eye movement until a VoC of 6 or 7 was reached.

Subjects in the control group were asked to describe the participants, environment, and events of their traumatic memory in detail. To parallel the number of SUD ratings in the EMD condition, the descriptions in the control group were interrupted seven times at 1- to 1.5-minute intervals to obtain a SUD rating. Subjects were asked if the picture had changed or if anything else had emerged. Then they were instructed to continue their detailed description of their memory. After the seventh SUD rating, subjects' positive self-statements were checked with the VoC rating. After completing this placebo control condition, Shapiro provided all subjects in this group the EMD treatment and then termed this group the "delayed treatment condition" (p. 206).

RESULTS, LIMITATIONS, AND CONTRIBUTIONS OF THE EMD PILOT STUDY

Subjects in both groups were interviewed for 30 minutes at 1 month and 3 months following their single treatment session. SUD and VoC ratings were checked along with each subject's presenting complaints. In most cases (18 of 22 subjects), self-report of changes in presenting complaints were confirmed by referring therapist or a family member.

The design of this pilot study (1989a, 1989b) can be faulted on several grounds. These include the absence of standardized psychometrics or diagnosis, overreliance on self-report measures, incomplete physiological measures (pulse rate only was taken in some conditions), and a nonstandard, combined-treatment control condition. The pilot study did produce significant effects in the experimental (and delayed treatment) condition. In the absence of prolonged exposure or prolonged abreaction, self-reported disturbance (SUD) on the selected traumatic memory decreased significantly ($p < .001$). Belief in the preferred self-statement (VoC) increased significantly ($p < .001$). Nearly all initial presenting complaints were eliminated and the remainder were improved. Results were maintained or improved on follow up.

Given the paucity of treatment outcome studies in existence at that time and the rapidity and size of treatment effects reported, one might have expected a series of follow-up studies. In fact, it took 5 years before a well-designed follow-up study was reported (Wilson, Becker, & Tinker, 1995). Nevertheless, the pilot study did attract considerable attention. Shapiro continued to reevaluate her initial concepts and procedures between 1989 and 1991. This reevaluation led to a series of changes both in conceptual framework and in the standardized procedural steps. It also led to a change in the name of the procedure from EMD to EMDR.

EVOLUTION, CLARIFICATION, AND VALIDATION OF THE STANDARD EMDR PROTOCOL

Between 1989 and 1991, several factors led to evolution in the conceptual model of EMDR and in the standard procedural steps. One factor in the evolution of Shapiro's model was the persistent demand for an explanation of what underlying principles were producing these results. Neither exposure–extinction nor simple desensitization could adequately explain the reported results of EMD (Rogers & Silver, 2002). With prompting from her research assistant, Mark Russell (Russell, 1992; Shapiro, 1995, p iv),

Shapiro turned her attention to the literature on emotional processing and information processing models described by Lang (1977, 1979), Rachman (1980), Bower (1981), and Foa and Kozak (1985, 1986). This culminated in the publication of a paper describing the shift from the desensitization paradigm to an information processing model (Shapiro, 1991a) and the renaming of EMD as EMDR.

Another factor was the result of further reflection on the observed effects of the procedure. Shapiro noted consistent, simultaneous, and parallel changes in arousal, emotion, sensations, and cognitive structures. She was impressed by the remarkable shifts in association to material that was often peripheral to the immediate circumstances of the selected trauma memory. These associations pulled attention away from the selected trauma memory. Yet, Shapiro observed that when she permitted this rapid free association, it led to important, generalized treatment effects on both the selected trauma memory and on related memories and cues. This observation led her to the principle of the "self-healing" paradigm (Shapiro, 1995, p. 31). Her idea was that there is an innate information processing capacity that tends to move disturbing experiences to a state of adaptive resolution by forging new connections between the traumatic memory and existing adaptive memory networks. To accommodate the ways in which this procedure and its evolving theoretical model diverged significantly from both exposure–extinction and from systematic desensitization, she renamed the procedure Eye Movement Desensitization and Reprocessing. During this same period, she made a series of significant procedural changes and clarifications.

In setting up each treatment session, Shapiro extended what she decided to call the "assessment phase" by asking the patient to identify at least one specific emotion – just before obtaining the initial SUD rating – by pairing the memory and the negative self-statement—which was now referred to as the "negative cognition." She also completed the assessment phase by asking the patient to identify a physical location for the perceived emotional or somatic disturbance. During the reprocessing, to permit associative chaining, she no longer returned patients' attention to the picture that represented the worst part of the memory after each set of eye movements. Instead, she instructed patients—and the clinicians she trained—to return to the selected memory only when the associations were reported to be neutral or positive or when the reported contents of the reprocessing were unchanged or became confused.

She decided to make the step focused on the positive self-statement more consistent and named it the "installation phase." After reaching an SUD of 0 or 1 on the target memory, every patient was directed to pair a preferred self-statement with the remaining representations of the target memory until the VoC was rated at 6 or 7 and was no longer changing. She then added a "body scan phase." With eyes closed, every patient was asked to focus on the remaining representations of the target memory, think of the preferred self-statement, and scan sensations from head to toe and to report any "tension, tightness or unusual sensations." (Shapiro, 2001, p. 162) The body scan phase grew out of her observations that the last element to resolve in some patients involved body sensations that represented emotional or somatic resonances with the target memory. Sometimes these sensations represented defensive somatic responses to the target memory. Sometimes, they were links to other, unresolved memories. Other times there were feelings of relief, joy, or other positive experiences that emerged with the resolution of the target memory.

OFFERING RESEARCHERS AND CLINICIANS TRAINING IN EMDR

During this period of evolution in the EMDR procedures, Shapiro began to offer training to qualified clinicians and researchers interested in learning her new procedure. Motivated by a desire to lessen suffering and advance scientific understanding, she provided a series of small training sessions to about 250 clinicians and researchers in 1990. In the interest of advancing research on EMDR, any qualified researcher who stated that they did not have the means to pay for training was granted a complete scholarship. The pace of interest in EMDR training was burgeoning faster than anyone could have predicted.

By late 1990, troubling reports of patients being harmed by EMDR (Shapiro, 1991b) had begun reaching Shapiro. These reports indicated that some recently EMDR-trained clinicians had immediately begun to offer their own EMDR trainings. Patients being treated by the students of these inexperienced EMDR trainers reported significant adverse effects from their treatment. Investigation revealed dramatic deviations from the procedures and principles that Shapiro was teaching. Having originally assumed that professional ethics would protect patients from such practices, she concluded that to adequately protect patients from this danger (Principle 1.16, American Psychological Association, 1992) she would have to institute a written agreement to be required of all participants at her trainings that they would not provide training to others without written permission from her. While compelled by published ethical standards and intended for patient protection, this requirement led to allegations that Shapiro was trying to control the commercial market for EMDR training. This training restriction remained in place until 1995, when Shapiro published the first edition of her basic text (Shapiro, 1995). This text provided a comprehensive reference to which clinicians, patients, licensing boards, and professional associations could turn to evaluate training programs and treatment practices alleging to be EMDR. She then released all who had completed her EMDR training from this restriction and revised the training agreement to ask participants not to offer training to others until qualified to do so. She then encouraged clinicians who had trained with her to start a professional association to establish standards for research, training, and clinical application of EMDR. This led to the founding of the EMDR International Association (EMDRIA, 2008b).

ALTERNATE MODES OF BILATERAL STIMULATION

During this early period (1989–1991) of evolution, variations in technique were developed to address situations in which patients had a medical history of eye problems, blindness in one or both eyes, or adverse responses to the mechanics of engaging in eye movements (such as eye strain). Auditory tones and hand taps were proposed as alternative forms of stimulation. Initially, snapping fingers toward alternate sides of the patient's head or using a clicker would generate alternating left–right tones. Later, electronic tone generators were used with headsets and a control box where speed could be easily changed. Hand (or shoulder) taps were proposed as another variant on eye movements. These were initially offered by having the clinician briefly touch the back of the patient's hands with a finger or with a cork tipped mallet. Later, small paddles connected to a control box became commercially available, which could generate alternating vibrations while held in the patient's hands. A series of electronic devices for generating eye movements were also eventually produced to avoid mechanical injury and fatigue for clinicians. While anecdotal reports have indicated that tones and taps (or vibrations) are often as effective as eye movements (and may be the only practical alternatives for patients with vision problems), there is insufficient controlled research to make definitive statements (Servan–Schreiber, Schooler, Dew, Carter, & Bartone, 2006).

By 1991, nearly all the procedural and theoretical elements of EMDR had evolved to the form in which they appeared in Dr. Shapiro's 1995 text. Researchers trained after 1991 were encouraged to employ the procedural steps that had been presented in EMDR Institute trainings. The training itself had grown from a 1-day workshop in early 1990 to, by mid-1991, 2 weekends comprising 34 hours of training including 13 hours of supervised practice exercises. Part 2 of the training focused on clarifying the basic procedural steps, introducing the *cognitive interweave* and principles for applying EMDR to the treatment of various acute stress and posttraumatic syndromes including phobias with a traumatic origin.

GROWTH IN THE PEER-REVIEWED LITERATURE ON EMDR

The peer-reviewed professional literature on EMDR grew from 2 reports in 1989 to a cumulative total of 79 by 1995 and 257 through the end of 2001 (Baldwin, 2002). It is not possible or appropriate to attempt to review this entire burgeoning literature base here. As of 2002, approximately 16 controlled PTSD treatment outcome studies of EMDR had been completed. The quantity of PTSD treatment outcome data on EMDR has continued to grow rapidly and now represents the largest cohort of individuals studied in PTSD treatment outcome studies and the largest literature on a specific method for the treatment of PTSD. In spite of a robust literature and generally consistently large treatment effect sizes (Maxfield & Hyer, 2002), the status of EMDR remains mixed among some scientists and third-party payors notably in the United States. In European countries, and elsewhere in the world, government health care systems, hospitals, and scholars accept EMDR as an empirically supported and well-tolerated treatment for PTSD. For an excellent review of the controversies and misunderstandings surrounding these issues in the United States, see Perkins and Rouanzoin (2002). Several published meta-analyses (Maxfield & Hyer, 2002; Sack, Lempa, & Lamprecht, 2001; Spector & Read, 1999; van Etten & Taylor, 1998) have reported EMDR to be an efficient and effective treatment for PTSD.

The International Society for Traumatic Stress Studies in its first review of all treatments for PTSD (Foa et al., 2000, p 333) rated EMDR A/B meaning "EMDR was found to be more efficacious for PTSD than wait-list, routine-care and active treatment controls." In its second edition review (Foa, Keane, Friedman, Cohen, & International Society for Traumatic Stress Studies, 2009, p. 575), they stated that "EMDR is rated as a Level A treatment for its use with adults. Quality clinical trials support its use for patients with PTSD." For children and adolescents, they rated it a Level B treatment and noted a need for further studies (p. 576). In a meta-analysis of all published (59) psychological and drug treatment outcome trials for PTSD (van Etten & Taylor, 1998, p 140) concluded that "The results of the present study suggest that EMDR is effective for PTSD, and that it is more efficient than other treatments."

In 2004, the American Psychiatric Association published *Practice Guidelines for the Treatment of Patients with Acute Stress Disorder and Posttraumatic Stress Disorder*, which stated:

> "EMDR appears to be effective in ameliorating symptoms of both acute and chronic PTSD" (p. 35).
> EMDR belongs within a continuum of exposure-related and cognitive behavior treatments. EMDR employs techniques that may give the patient more control over the exposure experience (since EMDR is less reliant on a verbal account) and provides techniques to regulate anxiety in the apprehensive circumstance of exposure treatment. Consequently, it may prove advantageous for patients who cannot tolerate prolonged exposure as well as for patients who have difficulty verbalizing their traumatic experiences (p. 36).

Also in 2004, the U.S. Department of Veterans Affairs and the Department of Defense published *Clinical Practice Guideline for the Management of Post-Traumatic Stress* in which EMDR, along with three other methods, was given the highest rating for level of evidence of efficacy and recommended for treatment of PTSD. Similar conclusions have been reached by several other national and international organizations including the Australian Centre for Posttraumatic Mental Health (2007), the Cochrane Database of Systematic Reviews (Bisson & Andrew, 2007), the Dutch National Steering Committee Guidelines for Mental Health Care (2003), and the National Institute for Clinical Excellence (2005).

Grass roots clinical interest, scholarly recognition, and institutional acceptance of EMDR have grown steadily in European countries. In contrast, in the United States, grass roots clinical interest in EMDR continues to grow at steady pace, while scholarly controversies and inconsistent institutional acceptance of EMDR persist. Misleading and inaccurate descriptions of the status of EMDR and meta-analyses continue to appear in the literature. The most recent of these by the Institute of Medicine (IOM, 2007) has been vigorously rebutted (Lee & Schubert, 2009). A full analysis of the disparity between controversies surrounding EMDR in the United States and the widespread acceptance of EMDR in Europe and other regions—such as Japan, South Korean, and South American—is beyond the scope of this chapter. In part, this disparity in acceptance may relate to issues commonly surrounding scientific revolutions (Kuhn, 1996). A recently published, thorough review of these issues by Mark Russell (2008c) explores both Kuhn's (1996) and Barber's (1961) analyses of resistance by scientists to scientific discoveries. Complicating the picture has been the developer's emphasis on the use of nonstandard and idiosyncratic nomenclature. This shift in nomenclature has served to emphasize the idea that the AIP model is a fundamental departure from earlier information processing models rather than an evolutionary step, building on the work of scholars in earlier emotional processing models.

In addition, early opportunities for U.S. federal recognition of EMDR by Substance Abuse and Mental Health Services Administration (SAMHSA) were not followed in a timely manner. Many state and federally funded clinical programs and research-granting bodies look to the SAMSHA listing of empirically support methods in deciding what methods to permit and to fund. This oversight was finally corrected in 2008 with an application by EMDRIA that remains pending as this book went to press. However, in the meantime, clinicians working in the United States find themselves confronting refusal by some clinical directors to permit the use of EMDR in some community mental health care (CMHC) programs and some Veterans Affairs (VA) treatment centers, while other CMHC and VA clinical directors strongly encourage the use of EMDR. Profound structural barriers have also limited the ability of both active duty and combat veterans to obtain treatment with EMDR (Russell, 2008a), while several regional programs are actively providing EMDR treatment to current and former military personnel. The FBI and some other federal and local law enforcement agencies (McNally & Solomon, 1999; Wilson, Tinker, Becker, & Logan, 2001) have embraced EMDR as part of their critical incident stress management programs, but this is by no means yet a universal or widespread practice.

EXTENDING EMDR TO A GENERAL MODEL OF PSYCHOTHERAPY

Since 2001, EMDR has moved into a transition period from stage 3 to stage 4 of its development. In this period of transition, research continues to extend the evidence of EMDR's efficacy for acute stress disorder for both civilian and combat-related trauma (Fernandez, 2008; Krause & Kirsch, 2006; Kutz, Resnik, & Dekel, 2008; Ladd, 2007; Russell, 2006; Todder & Kaplan, 2007; Zaghrout–Hodali, Alissa, & Dodgson, 2008) and PTSD (Ahmad, Larsson, & Sundelin–Wahlsten, 2007; Brown & Gilman, 2007; Chemali & Meadows, 2004; Chemtob, Nakashima, & Carlson, 2002; Edmond & Rubin, 2004; Elofsson, von Scheele, Theorell, & Sondergaard, 2007; Heber, Kellner, & Yehuda, 2002; Hogberg et al., 2007; Hogberg et al., 2008; Ironson, Freund, Strauss, & Williams, 2002; Jaberghaderi, Greenwald, Rubin, & Zand, 2004; Kelley & Selim, 2007; Kim & Kim, 2004; Konuk et al., 2006; Lamprecht et al., 2004; Lansing, Amen, Hanks, & Rudy, 2005; Lee, Gavriel, Drummond, Richards, & Greenwald, 2002; Lee, Taylor, & Drummond, 2006; Oh & Choi, 2004; Oras, Ezpeleta, & Ahmad, 2004; Pagani et al., 2007; Power, McGoldrick, & Brown, 2002; Propper, Pierce, Geisler, Christman, & Bellorado, 2007; Ricci, Clayton, & Shapiro, 2006; Rothbaum, Astin, & Marsteller, 2005; Sack, Lempa, Steinmetz, Lamprecht, & Hofmann, 2008; Schneider, Nabavi, & Heuft, 2005; Sprang, 2001; Tufnell, 2005; van der Kolk et al., 2007).

Work is also underway on two additional fronts. The first is research to clarify the mechanisms underlying EMDR's effectiveness with empirical studies on the effects of the bilateral stimulation procedures used in EMDR. The second is research to extend the application of EMDR to additional clinical syndromes as a general model of psychotherapy. A full review of the research that has already been done in these areas is beyond the scope of this book. Here is a brief summary for those interested in these areas.

In the area of elucidating the mechanisms contributing to the effects of the bilateral stimulation used in EMDR, a growing number of papers in recent years have proposed psychological, psychophysiological, and neurological explanations for EMDR's well-established treatment effects on PTSD (Barrowcliff, Gray, Freeman, & MacCulloch, 2004; Barrowcliff et al., 2003; Bergmann, 2001; Christman, Garvey, Propper & Phaneuf, 2003; Gunter & Bodner, 2008; Kavanagh, Freese, Andrade, & May, 2001; Kuiken, Bears, Miall, & Smith, 2001–2002; Lansing et al., 2005; Lee, Taylor, & Drummond, 2006; Oh & Choi, 2004; Sack et al., 2008; Stickgold, 2002; van den Hout, Muris, Salemink, & Kindt, 2001). These papers build on earlier studies and theoretical papers from the 20th century (Andrade, Kavanagh, & Baddeley, 1997; Armstrong & Vaughan, 1996; Dyck, 1993; MacCulloch & Feldman, 1996; Merckelbach, Hogervorst, Kampman, & de Jongh, 1994; Nicosia, 1994). Together, this body of research makes it clear that the bilateral eye movements used in the standard EMDR procedures have demonstrated effects that include the following: (a) enhancing the retrieval and reducing the vividness of autobiographical memories, (b) increasing attentional flexibility thereby promoting new associations to old memories, and (c) decreasing psychophysiological arousal associated with negative autobiographical memories. The positive findings from standardized, self-report outcome measures have been confirmed with distinctive findings from SPECT imaging as well as psychophysiological measures in several case reports, case series, and one controlled study cited above.

A growing number of case reports and case series support the view that EMDR can be viewed as a general model for psychotherapy for any condition where environmental factors play a role—that is learning, conditioning, or stress. Notable among the conditions where EMDR is emerging as a potentially helpful treatment are substance abuse (Amundsen & Kårstad, 2006; Besson et al., 2006; Brown & Gilman, 2007; Brown, Gilman, & Kelso, 2008; Popky, 2005; Vogelmann–Sine, Sine, Smyth, & Popky, 1998) and a range somatoform disorders including chronic pain (Grant, 1999; Grant & Threlfo, 2002), phantom limb pain, (Russell, 2008b; Schneider, Hofmann, Rost, & Shapiro, 2008; Tinker & Wilson, 2005; Wilson, Tinker, Becker, Hofmann, & Cole, 2000), epilepsy (Chemali, & Meadows, 2004; Schneider et al., 2005), chronic eczema (Gupta & Gupta, 2002), gastrointestinal problems (Kneff & Krebs, 2004), and body dysmorphic disorder (Brown et al., 1997; Dziegielewski & Wolfe, 2000). In addition, early case reports and strategies have appeared describing the application of EMDR to the treatment of personality disorders (Bergmann, 2008; Brown & Shapiro, 2006; Grand, 2003; Korn & Leeds, 2002; Knipe, 2003). Recent books on EMDR describe additional applications of EMDR to couples and family systems (Shapiro, Kaslow, & Maxfield, 2007), integration of EMDR with a range of well-accepted psychotherapy approaches (Shapiro, 2002b), and a role for EMDR in the treatment of ego-state and dissociative disorders (Forgash & Copeley, 2008; International Society for the Study of Dissociation, 2005).

SUMMARY

In less than 20 years, EMDR has moved rapidly from an observed effect of bilateral eye movements to a standardized procedure, to an internationally recognized method for the treatment of acute stress and PTSD. While some controversies and misleading myths about EMDR's empirical status persist, primarily in the United

States, EMDR has achieved a remarkable global acceptance as an empirically supported treatment offering a new paradigm to alleviate human suffering. More than 150,000 clinicians worldwide have been trained in EMDR. With the help of EMDR treatment, millions of people have recovered from the effects of natural and man-made disasters, motor vehicle, train and airplane crashes, civil war, combat trauma, terrorism, sexual assault, childhood abuse, the trauma of being diagnosed with a terminal illness, phantom limb pain, chronic substance abuse, and a range of somatoform disorders. EMDR professional associations exist on five continents. EMDR conferences are held in at least six countries annually.

These achievements reflect the vision and persistence of Francine Shapiro. She has personally taught EMDR around the world. She encouraged and cajoled graduate students, clinicians, and researchers to conduct and publish case reports, case series, and treatment outcome studies. She has published tirelessly. She fostered the development of Humanitarian Assistance Programs both in the United States and in Europe to bring EMDR training and treatment to people and places where there is no mental health infrastructure or no funding to pay for professional training. She trained a remarkable corps of clinicians in the United States and overseas to become EMDR trainers and consultants. How she has done all this in less than 20 years is a remarkable story that deserves to be told in its own right.

However, the story of EMDR's remarkable evolution and growth is more than the story of what Francine Shapiro has personally achieved. It is a story of the researchers, clinicians, and graduate students who have taken EMDR training and themselves been transformed by the human experience of a change in consciousness. This change in consciousness does not happen to everyone during the practice portion of EMDR training, but it does occur with a significant percentage of those who experience EMDR reprocessing during the training process. For those who experience this transformation, EMDR reprocessing reveals something to us about our human potential to evolve and grow as individuals and as a species. The experience of EMDR's treatment effects awakens something in us that says, "Where did the pain go? Where did the fear, the shame, and the anger go? I thought they were part of me. Without all of that, so much more is possible. I am free to act now." This experience is a compelling one for many. It creates a boundless energy and an excitement to find out what else might be possible.

The Adaptive Information Processing Model

In this chapter, we will review the Adaptive Information Processing (AIP) model, which is the core of the Eye Movement Desensitization and Reprocessing (EMDR) approach to psychotherapy. We will examine how the concept of *memory networks* has evolved from its roots described in chapter 1, to the way it is used in EMDR. We will review research on the specific effects of trauma and early developmental deficits on information processing. Next, we will review some of the research for each leading explanatory hypotheses for EMDR's treatment effects. Finally, we will consider what theory and outcome data suggest to help us predict the effects of different modes of bilateral stimulation during EMDR reprocessing.

THE ADAPTIVE INFORMATION PROCESSING MODEL

Shapiro (1995, 2001) proposed three principles that make up the core of her AIP. First—Principle 1—there is an intrinsic information processing system that has evolved to enable humans to reorganize their responses to disturbing life events from an initial dysfunctional state of disequilibrium to a state of adaptive resolution. When healthy adults are exposed to distressing events—such as being unexpectedly yelled at by a friend or supervisor at work—we normally experience an initial stress response with agitation, fear, shame, or anger; elevations of physiological markers of stress including heart rate, blood pressure, and stress hormones; and irrational thoughts and impulses such as excessive self-criticism, impulses to flee, to harm someone, or to submit. After thinking about the stressor and our responses, dreaming about it, noticing our feelings, writing about it, and talking about it with friends or loved ones, we resolve the distress and learn from it. Our physiological systems return to a healthy, stable baseline. Our emotional state returns to balance. Our cognitive perspective becomes adaptive. Instead of thinking "I did something wrong," or "I shouldn't have said that," we realize, "Oh yes, he's going through a difficult divorce, he's been raising his voice and using that angry tone with just about everyone in the department. I'm okay." Not only are emotions, physiology, and thoughts back in balance, but we have also formed an adaptive template for recognizing the situation should a similar incident occur again and cope with it differently. For example, stating in a warm but firm voice: "I'm sorry you are having

 | Three Principles of the Adaptive Information Processing Model

There is an intrinsic system for adaptation to stressors.	Trauma or persistent stress during a developmental stage causes a blockage.	EMDR restores balance leading to rapid self-healing.
An intrinsic system allows humans to reorganize responses to disturbing life events from an initial dysfunctional state of disequilibrium to a state of adaptive resolution	A traumatic event or a persistent stress during a developmental life stage can disrupt this information processing system leaving the unresolved experience in a state-specific form.	EMDR procedural steps and bilateral eye movements restore balance. Reprocessing continues to an adaptive resolution. Recovery can be as rapid and stable as for physical injuries..

a difficult time. I know what it's like to feel upset about things I can't control, but I am not the source of your problem. I would appreciate you using a calm tone of voice when you're talking with me."

Second, Shapiro (1995, 2001) proposed that a traumatic event or a persistent stress during a developmental life stage can disrupt this information processing system—Principle 2. This second principle is parallel both with Pierre Janet's early hypothesis (van der Hart & Horst, 1989) of vehement emotion as the cause of dissociation and the Yerkes–Dodson law relating performance to level of anxiety (Yerkes & Dodson, 1908). See Figure 2.2. The Yerkes–Dodson

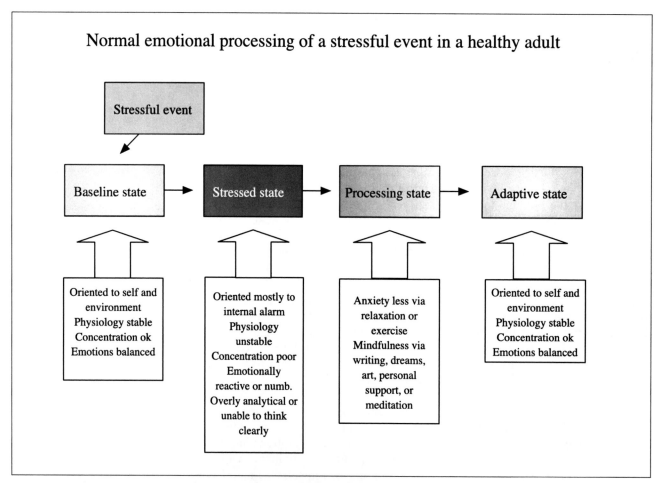

Figure 2.1 Normal emotional processing

law was restated by Ogden and Minton (2000) to reflect concepts of high and low arousal, and an *optimum arousal zone* similar to the therapeutic window described by Briere (1996).

As a result of the disruption of emotional information processing — due to excess arousal from trauma or persistent stress — the information related to the traumatic event or persistent stressor gets stored in a *state-specific* form (Bower, 1981) and fails to reach an adaptive resolution. There is considerable research support for this hypothesis in the literature on the brain's responses

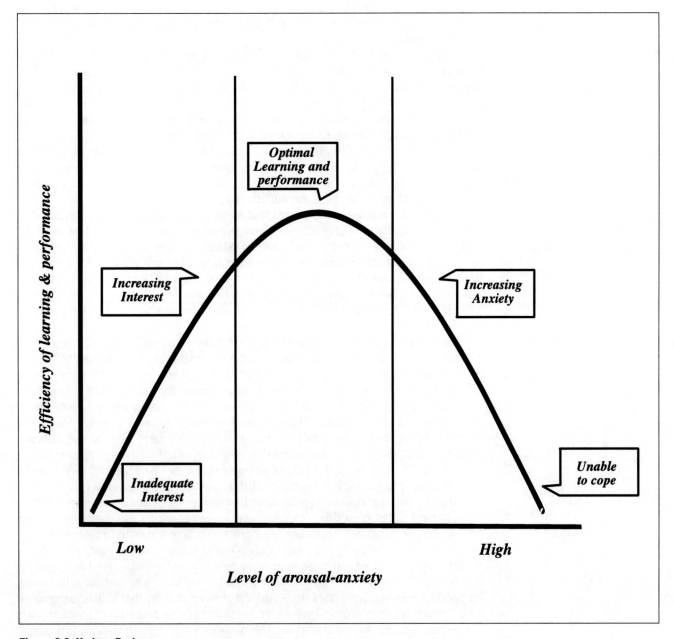

Figure 2.2 Yerkes-Dodson
Note. From "The Relation of Strength of Stimulus to Rapidity of Habit-Formation," by R. M. Yerkes and J. D. Dodson, 1908. Journal of Comparative Neurology and Psychology, 18, pp. 459–482. Copyright 1908 by John Wiley and Sons, Inc. Reprinted with permission.

to trauma and persistent stressors (Joseph, 1998; Osuch et al., 2001; Stickgold, 2002; van der Kolk, McFarlane, & Weisaeth, 1996). This research indicates that traumatic memories are held in an implicit, short-term memory system that holds sensory impressions, and global emotional and physiological stress responses. Nontraumatic, but significant autobiographical and informational memories are gradually shifted from the implicit short-term, right hemisphere-based memory system to the explicit or narrative, long-term left hemisphere memory system (van der Kolk et al., 1996).

Third, Shapiro (1995, 2001) proposed that the combination of the standard EMDR procedural steps and bilateral eye movements *restores balance* to the AIP system resulting in a resumption of information processing, which is then able to proceed until it reaches a resolution that is adaptive for that individual—Principle 3. When dysfunctionally stored experiences have been held in state-specific form for years or decades, the resulting process of reorganization can sometimes be dramatically rapid and comprehensive. However, if the person lacks sufficient *resources* to resolve the experience, the result can be a worsening of the emotional, physiological, and psychological state.

Central to this third principle is the concept of self-healing, which is analogous to what occurs with physical injuries. Surgeons can remove blockages to healing such as foreign objects or tumors, and create conditions favorable to healing, but then they must "let nature take its course." No surgeon can make a wound heal. Only the body itself can do that. This capacity is encoded in our DNA and expressed through the innate reparative systems of the body.

When psychological injuries leave a person with traumatic experiences in an unresolved, state-specific form, the treating clinician cannot make the person heal and cannot direct the details of the process of that healing. The best a clinician can do is to assure that there are sufficient resources and to observe carefully to determine if there are any blockages that need to be removed. When learning to use EMDR, it can be helpful for clinicians to consider the attitude of the midwife, who offers encouragement while avoiding extraneous interventions into the natural processes of birth, unless an intervention is needed when something disrupts the natural process. This stance fits the role of the EMDR clinician better than imitating the role of a traffic safety officer in the middle of a damaged intersection where the signal lights are not working and who is trying to direct cars blocked in a traffic jam.

For clinicians and patients with significant training and experience in models of verbal psychotherapy, initial experiences of optimal responses to EMDR can seem dramatically rapid and comprehensive. Excessive enthusiasm about these effects should be considered a potential impediment for coping with other clinical situations in which such optimal responses do not occur, as well as to wider acceptance of EMDR within the field of psychotherapy. Patients who have been led by mass media reports, lay publications, or rumors to expect they too will achieve dramatic, immediate, and comprehensive results may not be able to engage in the more complex and extended stages of recovery that may be needed when there has been chronic trauma, early neglect, or chronic medical complications.

Clinicians and researchers, who have invested years or decades of professional development based on a different paradigm for approaching treatment, often find wild, overly enthusiastic, or over broad claims a sufficient reason to turn away and simply not to examine the empirical data. On the other hand, in spite of the misleading and dismissive conclusions in some review articles—discussed at length by Perkins and Rouanzoin (2002) and Shapiro (1996, 2002a)—the empirical literature on EMDR treatment outcomes does support the conclusion that EMDR represents a significant breakthrough in rapidity of treatment effects and patient comfort with the healing process over previous models of treatment for posttraumatic stress and related disorders (Altmaier, 2002; American Psychiatric Association [APA], 2004; van Etten & Taylor, 1998).

MEMORY NETWORKS

Shapiro (1995, 2001) has described a model of memory networks that serves to help organize observations of what occurs during EMDR reprocessing as well as recognize *ineffective reprocessing*. There are five elements of Shapiro's model of a memory network: image, thoughts and sounds, physical sensation, emotion, and belief. The first four elements all refer to perceptual aspects of memory. The word *image* refers to the visual element of sensory memory connected to the event. *Thoughts and sounds* represent remembered auditory perceptions. Note that the subcategory of *thoughts* refers to memories of perceived internal self-statements such as "Oh my God" or "He's going to kill me." These are viewed as distinct from presently held self-assessments categorized as "a belief" such as "I am helpless." *Physical sensations* may represent memories of kinesthetic perceptions or the physical correlates of primary affects and are generally identified only by their perceived location rather than by an experiential description. *Emotion* represents the emotions that arise in the present in relation to the target memory. The fifth element is a self-assessment—referred to as a *negative cognition* in the procedural steps—which a person forms in relation to the target memory. Shapiro (1995, 2001) referred to the first four elements as "perceptions" because they involve sensory memory. She referred to the self-assessment as the "meta-perception" (2001, p. 44) because it is an interpretation of the stored perceptions of the experience.

During reprocessing, all five of these elements of a memory network are reorganized simultaneously and in parallel. In contrast to most models of Cognitive Behavioral Therapy (Beck, Emery, & Greenberg, 2005; Ellis, 1994), no special prominence was given in Shapiro's model to the role of the belief statement. If there were to be a central element among these five in Shapiro's model, it would have to be considered affect. "Thus, while a person's beliefs, stated via language,

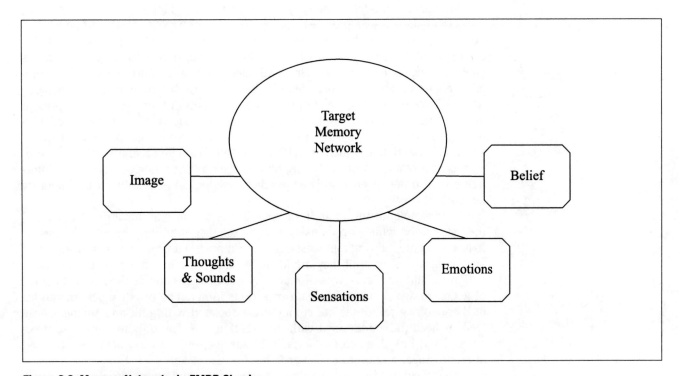

Figure 2.3 Memory Networks in EMDR Shapiro

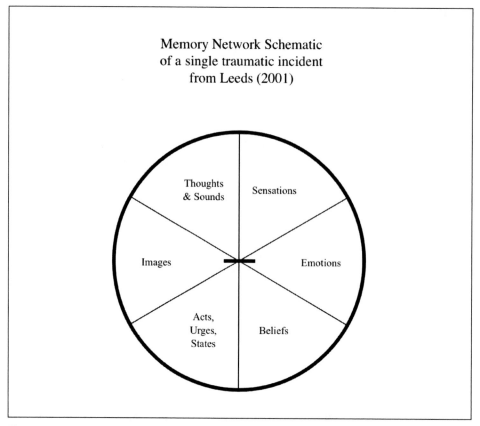

Figure 2.4 Memory Network Schematic Leeds

are clinically useful distillations of experience, it is the affect feeding them that is the pivotal element in pathology" (Shapiro, 1995, p. 43).

An enlarged model of memory networks that includes a sixth element—acts, urges, and states—was proposed in 2001 (Leeds, 2001). This sixth element incorporates the aspect of the fear network described by Lang (1977, 1979) that holds information about the person's *verbal, physiological, and behavioral responses* as well as *unexpressed impulses.* This sixth element of a memory network is included to address issues of theory, neurobiological research, and clinical observations that ineffective reprocessing is often related to aspects of memories that represent impulses not acted upon or of remembered coping actions that may be linked with feelings of shame or guilt and may seem ill considered or inappropriate in retrospect. Lee, Gavriel, and Richards (1996, pp. 169–170) cite several studies that support Lang's emphasis on including descriptions of physiological "response information" in order to elicit greater psychophysiological activation of the memory network.

For example, at the time of an assault, the victim may have first frozen and then submitted while consciously or unconsciously inhibiting impulses to flee or fight back. Later, during reprocessing, these suppressed urges can give rise to ineffective reprocessing until they are identified and are allowed expression in imagination. In addition, survivors of rape may have submission as their wisest course of action to avoid threats of death or serious injury. The physiological memories of these coping responses are commonly associated with guilt and shame. These feelings need to be addressed with interventions first not only to normalize these choices and link them to the decision to survive, but also to liberate suppressed affects of anger and urges to flee or fight off the attacker.

Identification of representations of acts, urges, and states should be incorporated into the history taking and treatment planning for each target memory and cue. Before proceeding to the assessment phase and reprocessing phases, clinicians should have developed an understanding of the behavioral responses of patients during the memory to be reprocessed as well as any inhibited or disavowed impulses for action and their physiological state. Unlike the other elements of the memory network, no specific procedural step is required to access or assess acts, urges and states during the assessment phase of the standard protocol. In general, the elements of the memory network holding representations for acts, urges, and states will be accessed sufficiently through the identification of picture—and other sensory memory—belief, emotions, and sensation to be reprocessed spontaneously. Interventions involving acts, urges, and states will be discussed in chapter 9 to address responses indicating ineffective reprocessing during phases 4, 5, and 6 of the standard EMDR protocol.

EFFECTS OF TRAUMA ON INFORMATION PROCESSING

A traumatic event, as defined in the *Diagnostic and Statistical Manual of Mental Disorders* (*DSM-IV*) (APA, 1994, 2000), involves the experience of "intense fear, helplessness, or horror" in a situation that involves "actual or threatened death or serious injury, or a threat to the physical integrity of self or others." Responses to a single traumatic event are capable of producing dramatic changes in neurological, autonomic, immune, cognitive, emotional, somatic, and social functioning (van der Kolk et al., 1996). However, the same event will produce enduring disruptions of functioning in some exposed individuals, while others will gradually recover "spontaneously" from short-term disruptions in functioning (Kessler, Sonnega, Bromet, Hughes, & Nelson, 1995). The complex set of protective factors involved in the vulnerability to enduring posttraumatic reactions can be grouped into two categories: (a) the ability to make use of external resources and engage in coping behaviors during and after the experience, and (b) the ability to make use of self-capacities for restabilization and self-regulation of internal functioning—physiological, cognitive, and emotional—in the aftermath of the threat (van der Kolk et al., 1996).

  | Effects of Trauma on Information Processing

Hyperarousal	Chronic physiological arousal, related to excess norepinephrine, inadequate serotonin and glucocorticoids; autonomic dysregulation, impaired sleep, and immune response; hippocampal mediated impairments in short-term memory, concentration.
Narrowing of attention	Impairments in prefrontal orbital cortex and anterior cingulate lead to loss of flexibility in attention, inability to sort out irrelevant stimuli, or to sustain complex judgment-based behavioral sequences.
Impaired stimulus discrimination	Lack of habituation to acoustic startle response. Reduced threshold response to sound intensity. Reactivity to neutral stimuli partially similar to the trauma.
Intrusive reexperiencing of state-dependent memory	Excess norepinephrine and vasopressin impair hippocampal function and produce amygdala-mediated over-consolidation of traumatic memories in the right hemisphere leading to reexperiencing instead of remembering.
Avoidance, numbing, dissociative coping, substance abuse	Endogenous opioids and oxytocin continue to be over-produced in response to neutral stimuli—only partially similar to the trauma—and lead to persistent numbing and amnesias.
Loss of meaning	Loss of the assumptive foundation (world as benevolent and meaningful and self as worthy), impaired capacity: (a) to tolerate intense emotions and perceptions of the trauma or (b) to generate a coherent narrative (inhibited Broca's area). Lack of societal response leaves shame-dominant and impaired sense of identity.

Depending on the nature of the event, factors from one or the other of these two groups will be more or less helpful. The paramedic arriving on the scene of a motor vehicle accident, who has the specific emergency responder training and the previous experience to make use of previously developed perceptual and cognitive categories for evaluating the scene, and who has well-rehearsed coping responses, will demonstrate much better organized external coping responses than the well-intentioned driver of a passing vehicle who was first on the scene, who stopped to render aid, but who lacked specific training or experiences. This good-Samaritan driver is soon overcome by the sensory perceptions of grave bodily harm to others and the internal changes in his physiology. He soon starts to go into shock. On the other hand, the survivor of rape or political torture may find that all attempts to use external – flight or fight – coping strategies are not only hopeless or ineffective but also trigger much more dangerous responses from the perpetrator. In such cases, more passive coping strategies that draw on internal self-capacities can be the only pathway to survival (Janoff–Bulman, 1992; van der Kolk et al., 1996).

EFFECTS OF EARLY DEVELOPMENTAL DEFICITS ON INFORMATION PROCESSING

Posttraumatic stress disorder (PTSD) has many effects on information processing in adults. These include problems with attention, concentration, memory, and the breakdown of stimulus discrimination (APA, 1994, 2000; van der Kolk et al., 1996). In addition, early childhood neglect and abuse exert even more profound impacts on information processing and emotional self-regulation. A partial list includes behavioral disinhibition and hyperresponsiveness to stimuli, memories poorly linked to a spatial–temporal map, memories poorly categorized in relation to other memories, and hemispheric suppression, in which the right hemisphere inhibits the left during recall of traumatic memories and the left hemisphere inhibits the right during recall of positive memories (Bremner, Elzinga, Schmahl, & Vermetten, 2008; Bremmer et al., 1995; Rauch et al., 1996; Teicher et al., 1997; van der Kolk et al., 1996). Suppression in the left prefrontal cortex of survivors of chronic early traumatic exposure has been described as "the loss of the witnessing self" (van der Kolk et al., 1996). Schore (1996) describes how inadequate shared positive affect in the first year of life leads both to insecure attachment and to deficits in right hemisphere and right prefrontal mediated capacities for modulating both positive and negative arousal in the amygdala. For a more comprehensive review of these impacts see Schore (1994, 2003a); Teicher (2000, 2002), and Fonagy, Gergely, Jurist, and Target (2002).

Although treatment outcome research clearly shows that the specific impacts of both childhood and adult onset trauma on information processing can be successfully resolved with the standard EMDR PTSD protocol and procedures (van der Kolk et al., 2007), the more pervasive impacts of profound early neglect and chronic abuse require additional, specialized interventions to address issues with severe affect dysregulation (Korn & Leeds, 1998, 2002; Leeds, 2001, 2006; Leeds & Shapiro, 2000; Linehan, 1993) and structural dissociation (Forgash & Copeley, 2008; Putnam, 1989; van der Hart et al., 2006). A discussion of these additional specialized interventions is beyond the scope of this work.

EXPLANATORY HYPOTHESES

In considering explanations of what makes EMDR an effective and well-tolerated treatment for posttraumatic stress and related disorders, we need to consider both the structure of the procedural elements themselves as well as the specific effects of bilateral eye movements, taps, or tones.

DUAL ATTENTION

Central to the EMDR approach to psychotherapy and the treatment of post-traumatic stress syndromes is the principle of a dual focus of attention to the *selected target memory* to be reprocessed and to the *sensory stimulation* provided by bilateral eye movements, taps, or tones. (Corrigan, 2004; Shapiro, 2001, pp. 31, 32, 55, 69, 92, 141–142, 173,177–178, 199, 306, 324). The concept of dual attention can be viewed as a state in which consciousness is in balance, where attention can fluidly shift between current perceptions and relevant memory networks. I illustrate this healthy state of consciousness in balance with the "teeter-totter model of consciousness" in Figure 2.5. When we are in this state of balance, we easily shift attention between changing sensory perceptions and the information, skills, and sense of self stored in memory needed to respond effectively.

During a traumatic experience, people's perceptions of the experience overwhelm their behavioral, emotional, or cognitive capacities to cope with the event, throwing aspects of their attentional system out of balance, as shown in Figure 2.6. As soon as the event is over, these perceptions can return as intrusive re-experiences of the traumatic event. In the aftermath of a traumatic experience, people gradually learn that external and internal cues can stimulate intrusive reexperiencing, as shown in Figure 2.7. This leads to the development of avoidant behaviors in an attempt to avoid known cues restimulating these painful memories, as shown in Figure 2.8.

Dual attention appears to foster a state of mindfulness that has been shown to enhance emotional information processing (Rachman, 1980; Teasdale, 1999). The dual focus of attention, which is essential in facilitating emotional information processing in EMDR, is to be contrasted with an exclusive focus on the elements of the traumatic memory in prolonged exposure (PE)-based behavioral therapy of PTSD. During therapy with PE, patients are asked to "revisit" their traumatic memories.

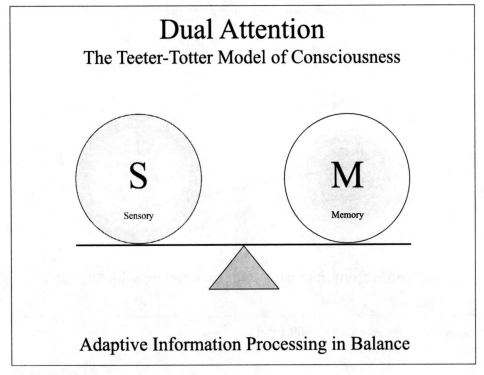

Figure 2.5

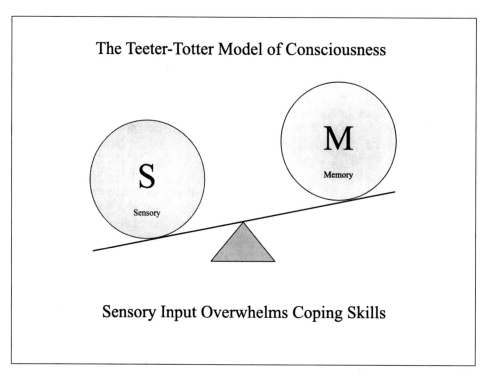

Figure 2.6 AIP during traumatic event

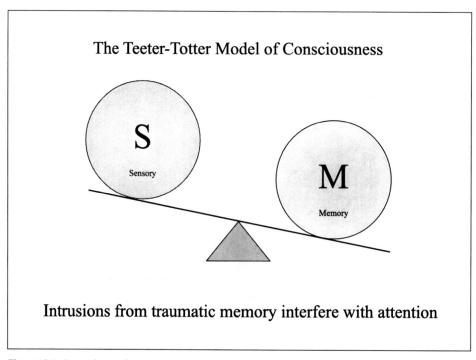

Figure 2.7 Intrusions after traumatic event

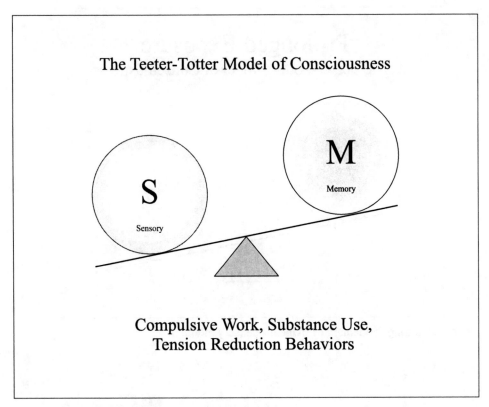

The Teeter-Totter Model of Consciousness

S
Sensory

M
Memory

Compulsive Work, Substance Use,
Tension Reduction Behaviors

Figure 2.8 Avoidant behaviors after traumatic event

They are instructed to close their eyes, to recall their traumatic memories as vividly as possible, and to recount aloud what happened with as much detail as possible, as shown in Figure 2.9. Impulses to stop the exposure because of discomfort are strongly discouraged (Rothbaum, Foa, & Hembree, 2007, p. 49). Thus, therapy with PE appears to foster what Linehan calls the "emotional mind" and what Teasdale refers to as "mindless emoting" (Teasdale, 1999).

In contrast to PE, during EMDR reprocessing the periods of exposure to the traumatic memory tend to be brief and are regularly interrupted by periods of fairly distracting bilateral sensory stimulation. During EMDR reprocessing, patients frequently associate to other positive or negative memories. Frequently they report that they were not consciously aware of their traumatic memory during the periods of bilateral stimulation. Patients may stop the reprocessing at any point if they feel excessively fearful, vulnerable, or overwhelmed. They are taught a stop signal and are reminded that they may use this stop signal at any time. Patients are not required to produce a detailed narrative and indeed, clinicians can assist in reprocessing traumatic memories without having to know the details of patients' traumatic experiences.

As the APA's *Practice Guideline for the Treatment of Patients With Acute Stress Disorder and Posttraumatic Stress Disorder* states, "EMDR employs techniques that may give the patient more control over the exposure experience (since EMDR is less reliant on a verbal account) and provides techniques to regulate anxiety in the apprehensive circumstance of exposure treatment. Consequently, it may prove advantageous for patients who cannot tolerate prolonged exposure as well as for patients who have difficulty verbalizing their traumatic experiences" (APA, 2004, p. 36). Although the APA's *Practice Guideline* and many respected scholars refer to EMDR as a variant of "exposure therapy," there are strong theoretical, observational, and experimental reasons not to view EMDR as an exposure therapy (Rogers & Lanius, 2001; Rogers & Silver, 2002), but as an approach founded on the principles

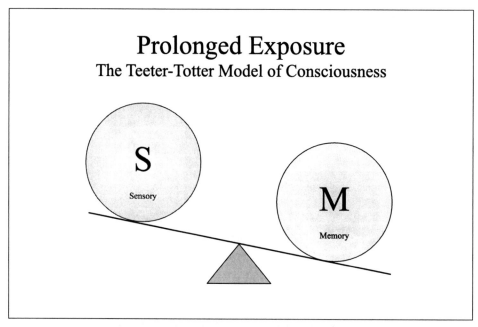

Figure 2.9 During PE Memory overwhelms sensory attention

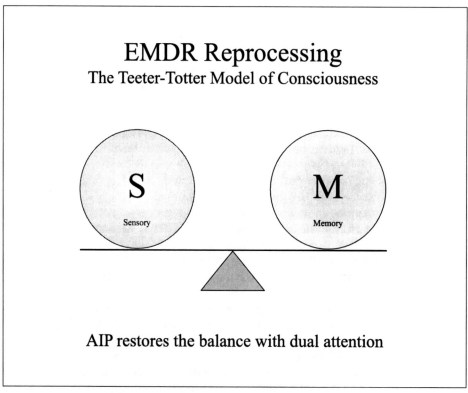

Figure 2.10 EMDR restores AIP balance

of emotional information processing espoused by Lang (1977, 1979), Rachman (1980), and Teasdale (1999) that facilitate a state of mindfulness, which is illustrated in Figure 2.10 and discussed in the next section.

ENHANCING MINDFULNESS, BARE ATTENTION, AND THE WITNESSING STANCE

The sequence of the procedural steps in EMDR is significantly different from any other treatment; even without bilateral eye movements or other bilateral sensory stimulation, it produces a number of therapeutic benefits. Critical aspects of the procedure include the nature of the verbal instructions, deliberately activating all aspects of the traumatic memory network in a counterbalanced sequence in the *assessment phase,* and the limited scope and nature of verbal interaction during the reprocessing (phases 4, 5, and 6). Partly because of *peritraumatic dissociation* (Shalev, 1996) and avoidance processes (Wegner, 1994) in survivors of traumatic experiences, the elements of trauma-related memory networks are often significantly dissociated from each other. The steps of the assessment phase sequence broadly alternate between evocative awareness of sensory, affective, and somatic perceptions mediated in the right hemisphere and evaluative and narrative processes mediated in the left hemisphere and prefrontal orbital cortex. This sequence helps ensure whole brain activation and helps set the stage for mindful awareness. The concept of "mindful awareness" has a long tradition in Buddhist meditation practices (Goldstein, 1994). Teasdale (1999) has operationalized a cognitive model of mindfulness and proposed it as central to fostering *emotional processing* as originally described by Rachman (1980). Teasdale refers to this effective mode of processing emotion as *mindful experience/being* and states it essentially similar to what Linehan (1993), whose work is also derived from Buddhist principles, has referred to as the "wise mind."

Mindful awareness and free association are further fostered by specific instructions given before each EMDR session and between sets of eye movements. Before reprocessing begins, patients are told: "Sometimes things will change and sometimes they won't. Just give as accurate feedback as you can without judging whether it should be happening or not. Let whatever happens, happen." Between sets of eye movement, patients are told: "Just notice that and continue." These instructions appear to support the state of "mindful experience/being" described by Teasdale and are similar to those given in traditional Buddhist meditation to encourage the state of mindful awareness known as "bare attention" (Goldstein, 1994).

2.3 | Three Modes of Processing Emotion (from Teasdale, 1999)

MINDLESS EMOTING	CONCEPTUALISING/DOING	MINDFUL EXPERIENCING/BEING
"Lost" or "immersed" in emotional experience	"Thinking about" experiences/ self as objects; focus on goal-related discrepancies	Directly, intimately, experiencing feelings, sensation, thoughts with awareness in the moment
Linehan: emotional mind	Linehan: reasonable mind	Linehan: wise mind

Note. From "Emotional Processing, Three Modes of Mind and the Prevention of Relapse in Depression," by J. D. Teasdale, 1999, Behaviour Research and Therapy, 37(Suppl 1), pp. S53–S77. Copyright 1999 by Elsevier. Reprinted with permission.

ALTERING NEURAL NETWORKS

Although the sequence of the procedural steps and the instructions and the principles of information processing used in EMDR clearly are significantly different from those used in other psychotherapeutic approaches to treating PTSD, much of the speculation about central mechanisms and component analyses in EMDR treatment has focused on possible specific effects of bilateral, alternating eye movements, auditory tones, and tactile stimulation.

Contemporary models of memory emphasize constructive and reorganizing processes that are affected by the state the person is in and the information available at the time memories are being retrieved (Freyd & DePrince, 2001). Clearly, with the appropriate scientific understanding and technology, observed changes in psychological functioning should be correlated with changes in the functioning and/or structure of the brain. Attempts to explain EMDR treatment effects in terms of cellular or regional changes in brain structure or function must be considered speculative because of the limitations of explicit data and models. Because many of these speculations do not have any immediate implications for clinical practice, they will be touched on only briefly, and the reader will be referred to other sources for an exploration of these models. A model based on the investigatory response will be given somewhat greater attention because of the preliminary data that support it.

SPECT IMAGING OF TRAUMATIC MEMORIES AND EMDR

Not surprisingly, preliminary reports of SPECT imaging before and after effective EMDR treatment for PTSD have identified observable changes in regional blood flow (RBF) when subjects are asked to attend to their standardized trauma script (Lansing, Amen, & Klindt, 2000; Levin, Lazrove, & van der Kolk, 1999; Oh & Choi, 2004; Pagani et al., 2007). Psychological and neurocognitive data show an over consolidation of traumatic memories (van der Kolk et al., 1996). Therefore when a treatment for PTSD is effective, there must be corresponding neural processes and changes that could be correlated with both (a) decreases in the strong associations that have been maintaining hyperarousal and intrusive reexperiencing of the traumatic memory and (b) with increases in the strength of previously weak associations to adaptive responses. Shapiro (1995, pp. 315–319; 2001, pp. 327–332) has speculated about various cellular and regional brain processes that could be correlated with EMDR treatment effects including changes in synaptic potential, inhibition of protein synthesis in the amygdala, and a right hemispheric preference for weak over strong associations. Rossi (1999, 2000) has similarly proposed a role for the activation of immediate-early genes.

REM AND ENHANCING DUAL HEMISPHERIC COMMUNICATION AND INTEGRATION

A related set of models to explain reported EMDR treatment effects on trauma-related symptoms are based on functional neurological changes that result in enhancing communication between the left and right cerebral hemispheres. An early model of bilateral mechanisms was proposed by Russell (1992). This was followed by a single-case EMDR treatment report with quantitative electroencephalographic (QEEG) data by Nicosia (1994). Nicosia reported that a rapid elimination in psychogenic amnesia occurred with an increase in delta and theta band coherence in homologous areas of the left and right hemisphere from 4.99 to 0.1 standard deviations out of phase. He speculated that this increase in synchronous communication between the two hemispheres was partly due to the effect of eye movements in generating synchronizing (theta) pacemaker signals arising in and ascending from the lateral pontine region of the reticular formation. Nicosia pointed out that long-term potentiation (LTP), widely hypothesized to modulate synaptic function underlying memory, is preferentially induced when stimuli are separated by 200 milliseconds (5 hertz), a theta frequency. He made reference to Winson's model (1990, 1993) on the role of REM sleep and theta rhythm in activation of the NMDA (*N*-methyl *D*-aspartate) receptors of the hippocampus. In essence, he hypothesized that EMDR activated a REM-like system for memory reorganization. Bergmann (1998, 2001) also proposed that the repetitive (bilateral) redirection of attention in EMDR turns on the brain's REM sleep system, which leads to the integration of the traumatic memory into general semantic networks by activating (a) a filtering function in the cingulate gyrus, (b) cognitive and language functions supported by the lateral cerebellum, and (c) integrative functions in the left dorsolateral prefrontal cortex.

More recently, a similar model for EMDR treatment effects has been proposed by Stickgold (2002, 2008), a leading researcher on the role of sleep in memory consolidation. Stickgold concluded that, whereas repeated saccadic eye movements might "'push-start' brainstem REM-induction mechanisms" (p. 70), the kinds of tracking eye movements, bilateral tones, and tactile stimulation used in EMDR require a different mechanism to explain how they might induce a REM-like brain state that would facilitate reorganization of traumatic memories. He proposed that the leading candidate for such a mechanism is the orienting response (Pavlov, 1927; Sokolov, 1990) and described research models to test this hypothesis (2002, p. 72).

ORIENTING (INVESTIGATORY) RESPONSE

The orienting (or investigatory) response (OR) was first described by Pavlov (1927) and elaborated by the experimental and theoretical work of Sokolov (1990). The orienting response or "what is it" reflex (Pavlov, 1927, p. 12) can occur with any novel environmental stimulus. It produces a specific set of changes that increase readiness to respond to danger. These changes include body movements to orient the head, eyes, ears, and nose toward the stimulus as well as changes in autonomic responses with increased blood flow, heart rate, and skin conductance. With the OR, there is also a broad desynchronization of electrical activity in the brain. When the stimulus is *milder*, there is an investigatory response that involves a similar but less intense and cortically *more localized* desynchronization response that occurs in a *specific sensory processing region* of the brain. With nonthreatening cues, the OR produces a biphasic response in which there is first an increase in arousal during the initial orientation to the novel stimulus, then a subcortical appraisal in the limbic system (Siegel, 1999). When the subcortical appraisal indicates the absence of danger, the initial readiness to respond is followed by a dearousal response in the autonomic system. With persistent nonthreatening stimuli, the limbic system rapidly habituates to the stimulation, leading to synchronizing slow waves in the brain and a release of beta-endorphins, which decrease pain and increase feelings of safety and well-being.

Lipke (1992, 1999) was the first to propose the OR as playing a role in enhancing information processing in EMDR treatment effects. Armstrong and Vaughan (1994, 1996) also turned to the OR to explain the speed and extent of observed effects with EMDR. They proposed that the OR triggered by eye movements in EMDR (a) prevents avoidance, (b) facilitates continued attention to the traumatic memory, (c) activates emotional processing (central analyzers), (d) facilitates incorporation of new, trauma relevant information, and (e) reduces pain via release of beta-endorphins. Armstrong and Vaughn (1994) clearly distinguish between these information processing effects of the OR, which requires sufficient stimulation to attract attention, and the distracting effects (away from the fear structure) of a defensive response when the level of stimulation exceeds an optimal level. Later, empirical studies organized by Becker, Todd–Overmann, Stoothoff, and Lawson (1998) confirmed the differential effects of optimal versus insufficient or excessive speed of bilateral stimulation. Although the hypothesis of Becker et al. was a cognitive load (distraction) model, their data also appear to support the OR model of EMDR.

An initial theoretical analysis by MacCulloch and Feldman (1996) independently proposed the investigatory response as the primary basis for treatment effects related to bilateral sensory stimulation in EMDR. This was followed by psychophysiological studies that showed not only that the investigatory response was central to EMDR's treatment effects, but also indicated that cognitive load (i.e., distraction) was not the mechanism behind these effects (MacCulloch & Barrowcliff, 2001; Barrowcliff, MacCulloch, Gray, MacCulloch, & Freeman, 2001; Barrowcliff, MacCulloch, & Gray, 2001). Like Wolpe's model (1954) of systematic desensitization, and Rachman's model of emotional processing (1980), the model proposed by MacCulloch emphasizes the role of relaxation in producing desensitization effects. MacCulloch does not examine the implications of his findings in terms information processing models such as those proposed by Rachman (1980) and Foa and Kozak (1986). Thus, the desensitization model proposed by MacCulloch powerfully explains the specific effects of EMDR on intrusive and hyperarousal symptoms of PTSD, but it fails to explicitly address neither spontaneous cognitive restructuring observed in trauma memory reprocessing nor how the investigatory response facilitates greater access to and incorporation of adaptive responses following Resource Development and Installation procedures (Korn & Leeds, 2002; Leeds, 1998a, 2001). When we recall that Rachman (1980) proposed that relaxation (dearousal) is central to producing emotional processing, the capacity to reliably trigger a "compelled relaxation response" (Wilson, Silver, Covi, & Foster, 1996) by activating the investigatory response via bilateral eye movements, tones, or kinesthetic stimulation, then the investigatory response emerges as a compelling candidate to explain the observed efficacy of both EMDR and RDI. It also helps explain other clinical observations such as the effect of varying characteristics of the stimulation on reprocessing and why shorter sets of stimulation are better when using Resource Development and Installation or Calm Place procedures with unstable clients.

DUAL ATTENTION: OVERCOMING SHAME (INHIBITION OF INFORMATION PROCESSING) VIA INTEREST AFFECT DISINHIBITION EFFECTS

In 1998, Nathanson presented an affective model for explaining EMDR treatment effects that is parallel to the investigatory response model. Foa and Kozak (1986) proposed that excess fear itself prevent information processing. Based on earlier work on the innate affects by Tomkins (1962a, 1991), Nathanson (1998) proposed that the inability to modulate or make a sufficiently adaptive response to frightening stimuli induced shame affect, and that shame affect, not fear, inhibited information processing. Because Tomkins's construct of innate shame affect is widely misunderstood as being derived from guilt or humiliation, Leeds (2001) proposed that shame affect be considered equivalent to the more neutrally descriptive term "central inhibition."

In the model of Tomkins (1962a, 1962b, 1991), interest-excitement affect produces a gradual increase in arousal, fear produces a rapid increase in arousal, and shame affect produces a rapid inhibitory effect on arousal. This model may help to explain why flooding produces effects on fear, but not on shame and guilt. It may be conjectured that the stimulating effect of interest-excitement affect on arousal is produced by the release of catecholamines–epinephrine and norepinephrine; fear therefore involves a rapid, larger releases of catecholamines as well as cortisol,

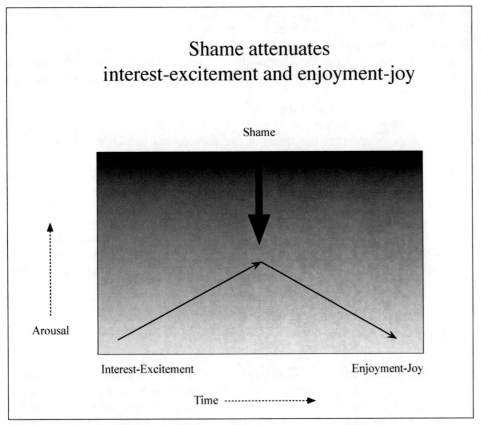

Figure 2.11 Shame attenuates interest

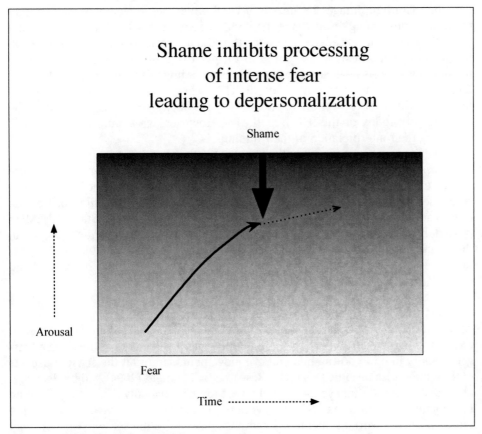

Figure 2.12 Shame attenuates fear

vasopressin, and oxytocin. The inhibitory effects of shame may be produced by correspondingly large, rapid releases of endogenous opioids (van der Kolk, 1996). Thus, in the intense affective states of fear, helplessness, and horror induced by traumatic events, both intense arousal (fear—catecholamines, glucocorticoids and oxytocin) and inhibitory (shame—endogenous opioids) mechanisms are triggered at high levels.

It has been shown that imitating affects via facial expression and posture induce the subjective experience of imitated affects (Nathanson, 1992). Therefore, Nathanson proposed that the tracking eye movements in EMDR reflect an imitation of environmental scanning activity that induce interest-excitement—mild arousal—affect and thereby disinhibits the shame—central inhibition—that had prevented information processing. Shame affect is also induced whenever a person perceives a response that does not match expectations. It is therefore noteworthy that treatment procedures during EMDR reprocessing call for clinicians to scrupulously avoid responses such as interpretations, questions, or suggestions that might interrupt the client's process or fail to match client expectations. Standard EMDR procedures are organized as much as possible to avoid any shame-triggering cues that would disrupt information processing.

WORKING MEMORY

Models of "working memory" (Baddeley & Hitch, 1974) describe a central executive, and two subsystem "buffers" where the central executive can hold information for later use. One of these buffers is the phonological loop, which stores verbal and auditory information. The other is the visuospatial sketchpad (VSSP), which stores visuospatial information. Andrade, Kavanagh, and Baddeley (1997) suggested that during EMDR reprocessing sessions, memories are held in the VSSP, and that the disturbing images become less vivid when eye movements make use of the limited processing resources in the VSSP. A recent study by Gunter and Bodner (2008) provides an excellent review of the EMDR research related to the working memory hypothesis and reports on further experiments to test the working memory hypothesis against other hypotheses including the investigatory reflex and increased hemispheric communication (IHC). They concluded that their experiments provided more support for a working memory hypothesis than either the investigatory reflex or the IHC hypotheses. However, we should be cautious in accepting their interpretation of their findings.

Their research design, like other studies of the working memory hypothesis, made use of nonclinical subjects. In addition, portions of their experiments did not replicate standard EMDR procedures. For example, they tested the investigatory response by having some subjects engage in eye movements while not holding their disturbing memory in mind during bilateral eye movements. Standard EMDR procedures clearly require *accessing* the target memory network *while* engaging in the bilateral stimulation. Therefore, an experiment that calls on subjects to access the target memory *after* engaging in bilateral eye movements does not provide an equivalent condition to actual EMDR sessions.

It seems clear from research by Andrade, Kavanagh, and Baddeley (1997) and Gunter and Bodner (2008) that elements of the working memory hypothesis contribute to EMDR treatment effects. Phenomenologically, patients treated with EMDR routinely report difficulty in maintaining all the elements of the selected target memory in mind during bilateral eye movements, and that the sensory aspects of their memories become less vivid. Research by Maxfield (2004) and by Becker et al., (1998) showed that eye movements need to be sufficiently distracting by being fast enough to disrupt the VSSP, yet without being too fast. However, because the research on the working memory hypothesis uses (a) subjects who do not meet the criteria for PTSD and (b) conditions that do not fully match those used in the standard EMDR protocol, it does not resolve the degree to which these alternate mechanisms contribute to EMDR treatment effects. It may be that each of these hypotheses is correct, and that for different patients, different elements may contribute to treatment effects to different degrees based on modes of bilateral stimulation use and patient characteristics.

DIFFERENTIAL IMPACT OF OPIOD ANTAGONISTS (NALOXONE OR NALTREXONE) ON ENHANCING EMOTIONAL INFORMATION REPROCESSING IN EMDR VERSUS INHIBITION OF EXPOSURE–EXTINCTION

Rogers and Lanius (2001) explored the differential treatment effects produced by opiod antagonists (naloxone and naltrexone) that appear to facilitate EMDR reprocessing (Ferrie & Lanius, 2001; Lanius, 2004, 2005) yet block the effects of exposure-extinction in phobic subjects (Egan, Carr, Hunt, & Adamson, 1988; Merluzzi, Taylor, Boltwood, & Gotestam,1991). Rogers and Lanius (2001) suggested that future controlled studies should explore the impact of pretreatment opiod antagonists on treatment effects of exposure therapy and EMDR on PTSD. Both Rogers and Lanius (2001) and Lanius (2005) highlight the role of dissociation in PTSD in explaining the observed effects of pretreatment with opiod antagonists on EMDR reprocessing. As discussed above in the section on the orienting response, the eye movements used in EMDR appear to activate both synchronizing slow waves and a release of beta-endorphins. Excessive conditioned release of beta-endorphins appears to be a factor in structural dissociation (van der Hart, Nijenhuis, & Steele, 2006) which Lanius (2005) suggests is mediated at least in part via mechanisms of learned helplessness that trigger the excessive release of endogenous opiods (Hemingway & Reigle, 1987). It may be that the therapeutic effects of synchronizing slow brain waves produced by the OR in EMDR on reorganizing memory networks may be blocked in those with excessive conditioned releases of endogenous opiods in tertiary structural dissociation (Lanius, 2005). PTSD patients – with primary dissociation– are clearly able to benefit from EMDR without needing opiod blockade. It appears that those with secondary and tertiary structural dissociation can learn counterconditioning strategies to decrease the severity of structural dissociation and eventually permit synthesis of traumatic memory networks even without the use of medication to blockade excessive opiod releases (Fine et al., 2001; International Society for the Study of Dissociation [ISSD], 2005; Paulsen, 1995). Lanius (2004) has also highlighted the binding role of tonic 40 Hz thalamic waves during successful EMDR reprocessing that may be involved with facilitating neuronal reorganization by overcoming the inhibitory effects of thalamic burst activity.

REDUCING OVERCOHERENCE WITH INCREASING COMPLEXITY

Consciousness—self-reflective, mindful, associative awareness—appears to depend on the activation of in-phase, electrical activity in widely distributed areas of the brain where different aspects of perception, memory, and response set are processed. However, when there is excessive or overcoherence of in-phase electrical activity, the result can be seizure-like or actual partial complex seizures. Childhood abuse, in particular, is known to produce excess coherence of in-phase electrical activity, which leads to increased risk of symptoms suggestive of temporal lobe epilepsy (Teicher, 2000), and pseudoepileptic seizures, which occur as a conversion symptom in those with histories of severe early trauma (Bowman, 2006; Bowman & Coons, 2000). The pace of rhythmic bilateral sensory stimulation in EMDR has been observed to be an essential variable in treatment effects (Becker et al., 1998). Shapiro (1995, p. 178) proposed that when there is ineffective reprocessing of traumatic memories, the first adjustment in the procedure should be changes in the speed, direction, range, and height of eye movements. Although such alterations in speed and other characteristics can be conceptualized as inducing a new orienting—investigatory—response, they can also be viewed as having an interaction with the pace and phase of electrical activity in activated regions of the brain, holding both maladaptive traumatic and adaptive elements of memory and coping responses. Alterations in the rate and other characteristics of the sensory stimulation may induce beat oscillations and other interactions in the rhythm and phase of electrical activity in regions of the brain where maladaptive memory networks are encoded, decreasing overcoherence and increasing complexity of brain wave activity. Such increases in the complexity of brain wave activity may serve to increase the potential for new patterns of association and new coping responses to emerge.

CONTINGENCY: THE ROLE OF THE OTHER

Capacities and patterns for emotional self-regulation are strongly influenced through the degree of contingency between caregivers and the infant (Siegel, 1999). In the earliest phases of development, infants rely on simple sensory cues for evidence of availability of external regulation based on the pacing and changes in the prosody and intonation of the caregiver's voice and changes in facial expression (Schore, 1996, 2001a). In posttraumatic states, when internal self-regulation has failed, the survivor becomes dependent on evidence of the availability of external resources for enhancing self-regulation. The role of bilateral eye movements—as well as auditory and kinesthetic stimulation—is not merely mechanical and rhythmic. An important parallel factor in effective reprocessing of traumatic memories in EMDR is the role of *contingent responses* by the clinician. The clinician must make contingent changes in the duration and pacing of eye movements to encourage maintenance or resumption of eye movements when the patient's eyes stop moving in the middle of a set of eye movements. The EMDR clinician is instructed to make non-specific supportive comments during sets of eye movements such as "That's it," "Good," "Just notice," or to say "Follow, follow, follow" in rhythm with eye movements. The pace of prosodic, vocal encouragement is even more important when the intensity of emotional and somatic re-experiences increases.

Making such statements in contingent response to subtle—or obvious—changes in patient facial expression, breathing patterns, or coloration is widely reported by patients to be extremely helpful in sensing that the clinician is attentive, interested, supportive, and understanding of changes in the patient's internal state. When the patient's degree of arousal strongly increases during more emotionally or physiologically intense memory processing, memory elements can threaten to overwhelm the patient's orientation and access to coping responses. At these times, contingent responses by the clinician provide more than just assistance in maintaining dual awareness of the traumatic memory and the current sensory surround. They provide the experience of a witnessing, supportive other whose full attention and responses are attuned and responsive. These contingent responses recreate the most fundamental aspects of the dyadic regulation of emotion that underlies the emergence of the experience of self.

PREDICTING EFFECTS OF MODES OF STIMULATION FROM THEORY AND OUTCOME DATA

There is extremely limited controlled data on the differential effects of alternating bilateral eye movements, auditory, and kinesthetic stimulation in EMDR treatment. Further, the existing data suffers from a number of problems that limit firm conclusions. These include the use of analogue rather than clinical subjects, small sample and cell size, and the use of bilateral sensory stimulation without full EMDR treatment procedures (Maxfield, 2003; Maxfield & Hyer, 2002). It does appear that across many subjects, these three different modes of stimulation can be equally effective (Servan–Schreiber, Schooler, Dew, Carter, & Bartone, 2006), yet for any given subject, a specific mode stimulation may be less or more effective.

Eye movements appear to exert specific effects on the visuospatial sketchpad of working memory and thereby disrupt vividness and detail in visual components of memory (Andrade, Kavanagh, & Baddeley, 1997). For patients who have not been able to escape intrusive visual aspects of traumatic memories, this effect can be especially helpful. However, for patients who may be more easily distracted by external visual cues and whose abilities to achieve and maintain sufficient access to representations of disturbing memories are more limited, keeping eyes closed during auditory or kinesthetic bilateral stimulation may more easily permit achieving and maintaining sufficient access to salient aspects of memory. For these patients, alternating bilateral auditory or kinesthetic stimulation not only permits having eyes closed during sets of bilateral stimulation, it may also increase a sense of self-control. This increased sense of self-control may be enhanced by decreasing anxiety about clinician–contingent responsiveness—and feared clinician judgments. Increased sense of self-control and decreased anxiety with eyes closed during bilateral auditory or kinesthetic stimulation may facilitate retrieval of additional elements of the selected target memory needed for emotional processing while exerting fewer effects on visual elements of memory. Eye movements have been shown to enhance the additional retrieval of episodic, autobiographical memories and to increase the tendency for new associative linkages (Christman, Garvey, Propper, & Phaneuf, 2003).

For patients who tend to become flooded with excess arousal with high levels of fear and mild to moderate depersonalization, it can be helpful to increase the density of sensory stimulation with kinesthetic stimulation or simultaneous visual and kinesthetic stimulation, or simultaneous auditory and kinesthetic stimulation. This additional density of multimodal sensory stimulation may help patients retain greater dual awareness of their current sensory surround without becoming lost in reexperiencing feelings of fear, helplessness, and freezing responses.

LIPKE'S FOUR-ACTIVITY MODEL OF PSYCHOTHERAPY

In considering the tasks that need to be accomplished during treatment and the problems that can arise during various EMDR procedures, clinicians may find the four-activity model of psychotherapy proposed by Lipke (1996, 1999) useful as a broad conceptual guide. Lipke has identified four types of activity in psychotherapy: category 1 – accessing of information already acquired; category 2 – introduction of new information; category 3 – facilitation of the processing of information; and category 4 – inhibition of accessing. Although many forms of psychotherapy provide different ways of providing activity in categories 1, 2, and 4, EMDR is unique in having a specific method for enhancing activity in category 3. Understanding to what degree different proposed mechanisms contribute to EMDR treatment effects may take another 10 years of research.

An Overview of the Standard Eight-Phase Model of EMDR and the Three-Pronged Protocol

Eye Movement Desensitization and Reprocessing (EMDR) is an integrative approach to psychotherapy that encompasses principles, procedures, and protocols (Shapiro, 1995, 2001). Chapter 2 presented the foundation of the Adaptive Information Processing (AIP) model and the principles for applying EMDR in psychotherapy. The EMDR approach to psychotherapy is described (Shapiro, 1995, 2001; EMDRIA, 2007) as consisting of eight distinct phases. This chapter will provide an overview of the standard eight-phase model of EMDR and the general three-pronged protocol that provides the framework for the specific treatment protocols for diagnostic groups covered in this treatment manual. However, some tasks, described by the standard eight-phase model as occurring in the preparation phase (phase 2) will generally overlap with those described as occurring in history taking (phase 1), and in some cases will extend into later phases. This is primarily because of the wide range of patient needs for stabilizing or resource-building interventions. In the standard eight-phase model of EMDR (Shapiro, 1995, 2001), these skill-building interventions are described as occurring during the preparation phase – phase 2. In actual clinical practice, many patients need preparation before and during history taking and treatment planning – phase 1 – and may need to return to stabilizing interventions during the reprocessing of memories of traumatizing events. In addition, we will briefly touch on clinical situations where the general principle of treatment planning based on the three-pronged protocol must give way to an initially *inverted protocol* (Hoffman, 2004, 2005) for treatment planning that starts with reprocessing on the future, then on the present, and then addresses the past only after significant treatment gains have been achieved.

Later chapters will integrate the principles that support this approach with detailed descriptions of the procedures used in each phase of treatment of the standard EMDR protocols and detailed clinical illustrations. Overall treatment and individual session planning and recording forms will be offered, and decision trees will be presented and discussed to support effective clinical decision making with fidelity to the standard EMDR procedural steps and the standard EMDR protocol for posttraumatic stress disorder (PTSD) specific phobia, and panic disorder.

PHASE	GOALS	TASKS
Phase 1 History Taking	■ Establish therapeutic alliance. ■ Gather psychosocial and medical history. ■ Develop the treatment plan and case formulation. ■ Rule out exclusion criteria.	■ Obtain narrative or structured history. ■ Objective assessment of symptoms. ■ Identify targets for reprocessing: (a) past events etiological to current symptoms; (b) current triggers, and (c) future goals.
Phase 2 Preparation	■ Obtain informed consent to treatment. ■ Offer psychoeducation. ■ Practice self-control methods. ■ Have patient start a weekly log. ■ Strengthen therapeutic alliance.	■ Orient patient to issues in trauma-informed psycho-therapy with EMDR. ■ Provide metaphors for mindful noticing during reprocessing. ■ Verify from log patient is helped by methods for self-control.
Phase 3 Assessment	■ Access primary aspects of the target selected from treatment plan for EMDR reprocessing. ■ Obtain baseline measures on SUD and VoC.	■ Elicit the image, current negative belief, desired positive belief, current emotion, and physical sensation. ■ Record baseline measures for SUD and VoC.
Phase 4 Desensitization	■ Reprocess the target experience to an adaptive resolution as indicated by a 0 SUD.	■ Provide discrete sets of bilateral stimulation and assess changes via brief patient reports. ■ Return to target periodically to assess gains and identify residual material. ■ Use additional interventions only when reprocessing is overtly blocked.
Phase 5 Installation	■ Continue reprocessing target with overt inclusion of preferred belief. ■ Fully integrate preferred belief into memory network as indicated by 7 VoC.	■ Provide discrete sets of bilateral stimulation while patient holds target in awareness with desired positive belief. ■ Continue until patient reaches 7 VoC or "ecological" 6 VoC.
Phase 6 Body Scan	■ Verify any residual disturbance associated with the target is fully reprocessed. ■ Allow patient to reach higher levels of synthesis.	■ Provide discrete sets of bilateral stimulation while patient focuses on reprocessing any residual physical sensations until there are only neutral or positive sensations.
Phase 7 Closure	■ Ensure client stability and current orientation at the close of each reprocessing session.	■ Use self-control techniques if needed to assure stability and current orientation. ■ Brief patient about treatment effects. ■ Request patient to keep a log of self-observations between sessions.
Phase 8 Reassessment	■ Verify whether all aspects of the treatment plan are being addressed.	■ Adjust treatment plan as needed based on patient reports from log. ■ Recheck target(s) to assure stable treatment effects.

Note. From EMDR Institute Training Manual, by F. Shapiro, (Jan, 2008 & Jan, 2005), Watsonville, CA: EMDR Institute. Copyright 2008, 2005 by EMDR Institute. Adapted with permission.

Note. From Handbook of EMDR and Family Therapy Processes (pp. 3–34) by F. Shapiro, 2007, Hoboken, NJ: Wiley. Copyright 2007 by Wiley. Adapted with permission.

PHASE 1: PATIENT HISTORY, SELECTION, AND TREATMENT PLANNING

In phase 1, you begin by gathering as much information as needed to develop a comprehensive treatment plan. This information includes: identifying the patient's treatment goals, presenting complaints, screening for medical, social, financial, legal, and psychiatric issues, and developing an understanding of the patient's history sufficient to prepare a comprehensive and collaborative treatment plan. The scope of screening and history taking will depend on many factors, including life adjustment prior to the *index trauma*, complexity of clinical presentations, quality of childhood experience and development, extent and kind of trauma history, attachment status, and stability of current environment.

As a result of the extensive empirical evidence and the widespread understanding that EMDR is a time-efficient treatment, patients may expect or demand that you rush to begin the reprocessing phases of treatment. It is crucial that you take an adequate history and not be pressured into abbreviating or skipping this phase of treatment. Rushing into reprocessing can lead to overlooking potential contraindications for reprocessing trauma memories, such as:

- The need for referral to a physician for evaluation of medical risk factors or to evaluate for medication to assist with stabilization of psychiatric symptoms
- Indications of an undiagnosed dissociative disorder
- The need to do more extensive patient stabilization to address risks of maladaptive tension-reduction behaviors (e.g., substance abuse, self-injury, high-risk behaviors)
- The need to allow more time to build a therapeutic alliance adequate for the specific needs of a more vulnerable or unstable patient

On the other hand, clinicians who have completed an EMDR International Association (EMDRIA)-approved basic training in EMDR (EMDRIA, 2007) should not withhold EMDR treatment from patients who can benefit from it simply because of their own personal insecurities or doubts about their skills. A controlled study by Edmond, Rubin, and Wambach (1999) demonstrated that EMDR's effectiveness can be greater when clinicians newly trained in EMDR are unsure of their EMDR skills—or are skeptical about EMDR—but demonstrate good fidelity to standard procedures (e.g., by reading from a prepared script when necessary) than when clinicians with more experience and confidence with EMDR apply EMDR reprocessing, but demonstrate lower fidelity. Issues surrounding professional development in EMDR are discussed in Section V in chapters 16 and 17.

Sufficient history must be obtained to ensure that an appropriate treatment plan has been developed. A multimodal assessment is encouraged, such as that described by Lazarus and Lazarus (1991) and McCullough (2001). For a detailed description of history taking and patient screening and selection issues see chapters 4 and 5. A few of the specific cautions to be considered will be introduced here.

DISSOCIATIVE DISORDERS

Screening for a possible dissociative disorder is essential before offering EMDR reprocessing on either traumatic targets or resource installation. Dissociative disorders described in the *Diagnostic and Statistical Manual of Mental Disorders* range from depersonalization disorder and psychogenic amnesia to somatoform dissociative disorder to dissociative identity disorder (American Psychiatric Association, 2000). In patients who meet criteria for a dissociative disorder, but whose diagnoses have gone unrecognized prior to EMDR treatment, the EMDR treatment has been reported to be capable of catalyzing rapid associative chaining that overcomes their amnestic barriers, and of flooding these patients with emotions, traumatic images, and body sensations that overwhelm their defenses (Paulsen, 1995). This is not only retraumatizing to these patients, but can also lead them to potentially dangerous loss of impulse control, acting out, and parasuicidal, suicidal, and aggressive behaviors. EMDR can be successfully incorporated into the treatment of patients with dissociative disorders (International Society for the Study of Dissociation, 2005); however, this should only be done by those with appropriate specialty training and supervised experience in both the use of EMDR and the treatment of dissociative disorders (Fine, et al., 1995; Lazrove & Fine, 1996; Paulsen, 1995).

DEPRESSION

Depressed mood by itself is not a contraindication for use of the standard EMDR protocol, as patients with PTSD are generally subject to cycling between episodes of hyperarousal and avoidance with symptoms of both anxiety and depression (van der Kolk, et al., 1996b). There is substantial evidence from controlled studies that EMDR alleviates symptoms of depression associated with both PTSD and partial PTSD syndromes. See, for example, Wilson, Becker, and Tinker (1995, 1997).

However, not all depressive symptoms are associated with posttraumatic syndromes. Patients with more severe depression often benefit from, and may need, antidepressant medication for stabilization to be able to participate adequately in psychotherapy (Feldman, 2007). Adult survivors of childhood neglect, whose parents were chronically depressed, may exhibit-early onset or lifelong dysthymia or recurrent major depressive disorder. Inadequate attachment experiences, such as with a depressed caregiver, have been shown to be a stronger factor in early onset depression in teens than by genetic factors (Tully, Iacono, & McGue, 2008).

Such individuals may have never experienced an adequate "premorbid" period and may therefore lack many of the adaptive resources needed to respond positively to the standard EMDR–PTSD protocol. Specialized Resource Development and Installation approaches have been reported (Ichii, 2003; Korn, 2002; Leeds, 1997; Wildwind, 1994) to be helpful in some of these patients, but controlled research is needed to assess the efficacy, risks and range of applications of these approaches. Patients who have suicidal risks, including those with a history of hospitalizations to prevent or following suicide attempts, need to be managed conservatively. EMDR reprocessing should only be offered to these patients by clinicians with appropriate training and experience. Hospitalization or residential treatment to permit more intensive work in a safe environment may be a viable option in certain cases.

For some patients with pervasive early neglect and abuse, a treatment approach based initially on reprocessing trauma may be overwhelmingly painful. In such cases, a skills-focused treatment approach based on the development of mindfulness and other self-capacities and reworking of central schemas for self and attachment (Fonagy, et al., 2002; Gold, 2000; Korn and Leeds, 2002; Linehan, 1993; Segal, Williams, & Teasdale, 2002) is more likely to be appropriate at least in the initial stages of treatment. However, clinical experience indicates that for some patients with impaired self-capacities related to early neglect, specific, focal trauma-related symptoms can sometimes be resolved using a modified version of the standard EMDR–PTSD protocol. Criteria for discerning which patients require extended stabilization interventions and which may benefit from early application of EMDR reprocessing are discussed in chapters 5 and 6. Clinicians newly trained in EMDR may need to consult about cases where they are unsure of the patient's stability and readiness for reprocessing.

ADULT ATTACHMENT STATUS, AFFECT CHANGE AND INTENSITY TOLERANCE

The capacity to tolerate changes in affect state and affect intensity is often subsumed under the concept of ego strength (Frederick & McNeal, 1999) or described as a self-capacity (McCann & Pearlman, 1990). Evaluating these capacities needs to be a central aspect of assessing readiness before commencing standard EMDR protocols. Chapter 5 describes the following instruments and principles in more detail. The Trauma Symptom Inventory (TSI) (Briere, 1995) and Inventory of Altered Self-Capacities (IASD) (Briere, 2000) offer self-report measures that can tap these dimensions of concern. Adult attachment status (Cassidy & Shaver, 1999; Main, 1996) tends to vary along with the capacity to tolerate affective intensity and change. Insecure adult attachment, by definition, is associated with specific impairments in core schemas. Treatment goals, strategies, and case formulation will often depend in large measure on clinical assessment of adult *attachment classification*. This should not be confused with adult relationship status, as many patients in stable family or marital relationships show insecure attachment classification (Slade, 1999; Stein, Jacobs, Ferguson, Allen, & Fonagy, 1998).

MALADAPTIVE SCHEMAS, AFFECT PHOBIAS AND RIGID DEFENSES

Schema theory (Young, 1999) is an extension of cognitive behavioral therapy developed for working with patients with pervasive patterns of maladaptive behavior, and beliefs. In Young's model, schemas are comprised of memories, bodily sensations, emotions and beliefs about oneself and relationships with others. There are significant parallels between Schema theory and the concepts of maladaptive memory networks in the AIP model. Schema theory asserts that maladaptive schemas form when specific, core childhood needs are not met. Schema therapy combines cognitive, behavioral, attachment, object relations, and experiential approaches. Several self-report questionnaires have been published for assessing patients' schema profiles. See chapter 20 for how to obtain these questionnaires. Young, Zangwill, and Behary (2002) have described potential benefits from combining schema-focused therapy and EMDR.

When patients have impairments in core schemas, they will be more likely to show rigid defenses and to meet criteria for an Axis II diagnosis (American Psychiatric Association, 2000). As a result, their treatment will tend to be more complex and lengthy. Leigh McCullough's 1996 text, *Changing Character: Short-Term Anxiety-Regulating Psychotherapy for Restructuring Defenses, Affects, and Attachment*, describes a dynamic model for restructuring defenses for patients with Axis II issues that is highly compatible with EMDR. Her text is a remarkable contribution to the psychotherapy literature and includes one of the best summaries of the affect theory of Silvan S. Tomkins. This research-supported approach is more fully described in a treatment manual (McCullough, et al., 2003). When patients show rigid defenses with Axis II features, EMDR treatment planning will need to carefully consider the sequencing of targets in terms of the self-capacities and schemas that the patient needs most and can best tolerate addressing. While we will touch on these issues in later chapters, an in-depth exploration of how to apply EMDR to these more complex cases is beyond the scope of this text.

TREATMENT PLANNING AND THE THREE-PRONGED PROTOCOL

During phase 1—the history taking and treatment planning phase—the clinician identifies suitable foci for treatment, which in the EMDR model are called *targets*. The general plan for organizing treatment in the standard model of EMDR is referred to as the three-pronged protocol (Shapiro, 1995, 2001). The three prongs are the past, present, and future and are addressed in that order in the standard model of EMDR. In selecting targets for the past prong, formative past events, which the clinician and patient view as the foundation for the patient's symptoms, are identified and prioritized to be reprocessed. In the standard model of EMDR, only after the targets from the past have been reprocessed to resolution, does attention turn toward the present prong and reprocessing current stimuli capable of triggering pathological responses.

Baseline information—for cues, situations, frequency, and intensity of maladaptive coping responses—on current stimuli is identified at intake and is monitored during treatment using feedback from the patient's log, which is described in chapter 6. After the targets from the past are resolved, presenting symptoms and the current stimuli will be checked and targets from the present prong will be selected and reprocessed if they remain sources of dysfunction. In the third prong of the protocol, new skills and identity structures that the patient may need in the future will be reprocessed as *future templates* to ensure that they will be integrated into the patient's coping capacity and self-concept.

Not every identified past traumatic event and present trigger will necessarily need to be reprocessed individually. Clinical experience and controlled research have repeatedly shown that generalization of treatment effects often permits related traumatic events and stimuli to be grouped in clusters with representative targets reprocessed to achieve functional resolution of related targets and broad symptomatic relief. Strategies for selecting and sequencing targets for reprocessing are described in chapter 4.

PHASE 2: PREPARATION

In the second phase of treatment the clinician prepares the patient in several ways.

Therapeutic Alliance

The most important is establishing a supportive therapeutic alliance. A truly collaborative relationship permits honest communication between the patient and clinician. The time needed to establish an adequate level of openness greatly varies with the extent to which trust schemas have been violated in the patient's past and with the nature of the issues to be resolved and can take from two to three sessions to many months.

Psychoeducation and Informed Consent to Treatment

The patient is given adequate information to provide informed consent for treatment options, including explanations of procedures, a rationale for treatment, common and uncommon reported reactions to EMDR, and any other potential treatments relevant to the history and risk factors that have been reported.

Metaphors and Models

Helpful metaphors and models of the treatment process are provided to orient the patient and reduce his or her anxiety about being open to a new experience.

Introduction to Bilateral Stimulation

To assure that patients can tolerate the bilateral eye movement normally used in EMDR reprocessing, the clinician introduces bilateral eye movements and tests various speeds and directions. If the eye movement cause discomfort or cannot be used, then bilateral tones or taps are introduced. Usually, the clinician offers the Calm Place Exercise or Resource Installation after this simple testing of bilateral stimulation.

Self Control

Patients are instructed in various self-control procedures to increase (or establish) their stability in current functioning. These may include training in structured breathing, relaxation or grounding exercises, self-observation skills, sensory focusing, and guided imagery. As part of self-control training, and to introduce bilateral stimulation on a positive experience, most EMDR clinicians teach patients the Calm Place exercise or provide Resource Development and Installation during the preparation phase.

Stop Signal

The patient is taught a stop signal (i.e., a hand gesture) to enhance the sense of control during reprocessing of traumatic memories. The stop signal also helps to lessen any confusion over the interpretation of patient verbalizations, such as saying, "Stop" or "It's too painful." Often, these verbalizations do not indicate an actual request to stop the reprocessing, but rather are directed at others involved in the memory or reflect expressions of the level of current distress. The stop signal is an unambiguous cue like the emergency stop cord on the train. It alone signals the patient's request to cease reprocessing with the bilateral stimulation.

The extent of work needed in phase 2 to prepare a given patient for the standard EMDR–PTSD protocol will vary greatly depending on an array of patient characteristics. For patients with a single episode, adult onset trauma with a good premorbid adjustment, this preparation phase may take only one session to assure stability and readiness. Survivors of prolonged adult trauma, such as imprisonment and torture, who suffer from complex PTSD (Herman, 1992) may need more work in the preparation phase to provide sufficient stability and adequate access to self-control and affect modulation skills. For some adult survivors of early childhood neglect suffering from complex PTSD and insecure attachment-related syndromes (Barach, 1991; Gold, 2000; Liotti, 1992; Main, 1996), the preparation phase may need to expand to become the central focus of treatment for an extended period of time. These patients often need extended support in developing basic self-capacities for self-care, tolerating changes and more intensity in the negative and positive affects, and for containing impulses for self-injurious and suicidal behaviors.

PHASE 3: ASSESSMENT

During the assessment phase, the therapist leads the patient in selecting the target to be reprocessed. The principal elements of the selected maladaptive memory network are identified as the most representative: image, belief, emotion(s), and sensation(s). Baseline ratings of the target are also taken during the assessment phase. The components of these procedural steps, the eliciting phrases for each step, and their sequence were optimized into a standard set of procedures (Shapiro, 1995, 2001) based on years of clinician feedback from a wide range of clinical experience. Their value has been confirmed by meta-analysis, which shows that stronger treatment effects are obtained when greater fidelity to the standard procedures is achieved (Maxfield & Hyer, 2002). It is important to bear in mind that each of the procedural steps in the assessment phase that precedes reprocessing with bilateral eye movements—taps or tones—is an integral part of the therapeutic process and contribute to the overall treatment effects in various ways.

Delineation and assessment of the selected treatment target begins with identifying a visual image of the most emotionally painful part of the experience. When there is no visual image, an alternative sensory memory that represents the target is selected, such as a sound or smell. The sensory aspect of an unresolved traumatic memory has been reported to be predominantly stored in the right hemisphere (van der Kolk, Burbridge, & Suzuki, 1997).

Next, the clinician assists the patient with identifying the central personal negative attribution(s) with which the patient is identified as a result of that experience. This is referred to as the negative cognition (NC). In EMDR, the NC is pre-eminently a negative self appraisal, such as:

1) "I am bad."
2) "I am worthless."
3) "I am unlovable."
4) "I am vulnerable."

Psychologically, this step helps the patient to recognize the irrationality of the cognitive interpretation of this experience. Neurologically, this requires the patient to activate Broca's area in the left hemisphere, which has been shown to be functionally inhibited when the traumatic memory is activated (Rauch, et al., 1996), as well as the left prefrontal orbital cortex, where self-reflective, semantic self-statements are organized (Schore, 1994). The negative cognition will be used later in the assessment phase, along with the image, to activate another facet of the dysfunctional memory network—the disturbing emotion.

The next step is to help the patient develop a more adaptive self-attribution in relationship to that painful experience. This more adaptive self-statement is known as the positive cognition (PC). This positive cognition is a positive self appraisal, such as:

1) "I did the best I could."
2) "I am a worthy person."
3) "I am lovable enough."
4) "I can protect myself."

Psychologically, developing the positive cognition introduces corrective information, incompatible with the original assessment. It also represents an expression of the treatment goal for the session that can help encourage the patient to continue through the reprocessing of the emotionally charged material. Neurologically, eliciting the positive cognition requires the patient to activate left hemisphere and left prefrontal- mediated areas of the brain, which provide analytical skills that are less linked to sensory-based experience and provide a more symbolic and categorical mode of information processing (van der Kolk, et al., 1997). Clinically, the process of eliciting and rating the positive cognition helps the clinician assess how much the patient can imagine a positive outcome. In patients with chronic or complex PTSD, the severity of hemispheric suppression (Teicher et al., 1997) can make the identification of an appropriate and ecologically relevant positive cognition a challenging, yet crucial part of the treatment.

The patient is then asked to rate how true the more adaptive statement *feels* on a scale of 1 (feels totally false) to 7 (feels totally true). During the rating of the Validity of Cognition (VoC), the patient is asked to hold the disturbing image—activating right hemisphere—in awareness, along with the positive cognition—activating left hemisphere—and give an affective rating, which requires prefrontal activation. This baseline rating of the VoC provides an additional reference point for assessing treatment effects later in the session. This baseline reference can be especially useful when reprocessing of the traumatic material must be extended over more than one treatment session, even partial increases toward a 7 VoC can provide a validating evidence of the patient's gradual progress through challenging material.

Note that this initial sequence of procedural steps in the assessment phase facilitates the patient's ability to connect the selected visual image with a preferred belief by doing this before the associated disturbing emotions of the traumatic material are explicitly stimulated to reduce potential interference from intense affective arousal.

Next, the patient is asked to focus on the selected image and the NC and to name the emotions presently experienced. Explicitly naming the present emotions establishes further baseline information that can aid in evaluating progress. It is not uncommon for the emotional response to the traumatic memory to change several times during the reprocessing of a traumatic memory. If the overall level of emotional disturbance—see Subjective Units of Disturbance (SUD) scale level below—were to remain unchanged at the end of the session, knowing the baseline emotional response for the session can clarify for the patient and the clinician if progress has been made. For example, the emotional response may have shifted from intense fear and helplessness at the beginning of the session to anger at the end of the session. Knowing the present baseline emotion, in addition to the NC, assists the clinician in being able to give the needed support and to identify potential beliefs that could interfere with effective reprocessing.

After identifying the present emotion, the patient is asked to rate how disturbing the specific memory or situation feels *in the present* on a scale of 0 (calm or no disturbance) to 10 (the most disturbance the patient can imagine). This SUD scale (Shapiro, 1995, 2001; Wolpe, 1958) provides baseline information that can be helpful to both the patient and the clinician in monitoring treatment responses across one or more treatment sessions. For example, in the rare situations where there are few or no reported changes in sensory image, negative self-statement, disturbing affect, and physical sensation, changes in intensity on the SUD scale can sometimes provide the only evidence that reprocessing is, or is not, taking place.

Finally, the patient is asked to report where the present disturbance is felt in the body. This physical location may correspond with elements of the emotion just described, with memories of physical touch or injury, or with memories of bodily responses or impulses for responding to the traumatic memory. Identification of the location of the physical sensations before and during reprocessing assists in further activation of the unresolved aspects of the memory network. Asking for the body location helps assure that the patient is feeling something, and provides a check against the patient arbitrarily naming a likely emotion to merely satisfy the clinician's inquiry. Naming the location also provides another way for the patient to observe, without judging or having to describe in detail, what is being experienced during reprocessing. This shift to an observing stance of mindful noticing, which only requires the patient to note *where* something is felt, furthers the treatment goals. It can help lessen a tendency, which many patients experience, to become caught up in self-judging or overly verbalizing as a way to avoid re-experiencing distressing aspects of traumatic memories.

The location of physical sensations described in this last step of the assessment phase represents quite different aspects of the maladaptive memory network for different patients. The physical sensations, themselves, may represent an aspect of associated emotions. They may be linked to the memory of sensations produced during the traumatic event. Physical sensations may also represent memories of actual physiological or behavioral responses (Lang, 1977, 1979) or action urges that may have been experienced outside of awareness at the time of the event. In some cases, asking about actual responses or action urges during the earlier history-taking phase can be helpful in identifying a crucial aspect of the maladaptive memory network that will need to be addressed during subsequent reprocessing. However, during the assessment phase it is generally neither necessary nor helpful to make a specific inquiry in an attempt to determine which of these categories the location of reported sensations might actually represent. Instead, it is sufficient simply to identify that the patient can localize sensations.

PHASE 4: DESENSITIZATION

The next three phases (desensitization, installation, and body scan) of EMDR involve alternating bilateral stimulation together with other procedural elements intended to enhance information processing (Shapiro, 1995, 2001), and are collectively referred to as reprocessing. Forms of bilateral stimulation include:

1. Bilateral eye movements.
2. Bilateral auditory tones.
3. Bilateral hand, knee, or shoulder taps.
4. Combinations of two or more types of bilateral stimulations.
5. Vertical, circular, and looping eye movements in the shape of the infinity sign.

Throughout these three phases, any or all aspects of the maladaptive memory network may be simultaneously changing—as reported by the patient or observed by the clinician with changes in vividness or content of sensory memory, changes in affect quality or intensity, changes in self-assessment and thoughts about the memory, and changes in the characteristics and location of physical sensations or action urges.

When the target to be treated has been delineated and assessed, just before starting bilateral stimulation, the clinician makes sure the essential elements of the target have been activated by briefly restating them, and then asks the patient to adopt a nonjudgmental attitude and just notice whatever takes place while beginning the bilateral stimulation. The procedures employed throughout the three reprocessing phases of EMDR are intended to enhance the rapidity of treatment effects while maintaining the patient's stability and the sense of safety and control over the treatment process and outcome. For example, the instruction to ". . . let whatever happens, happen. . ." (Shapiro, 2001, p. 145) before commencing bilateral stimulation is intended to reduce demand characteristics and patients' fears of "failure" while enhancing mindful awareness of spontaneous associations to relevant aspects traumatic or other memories. One of the central features of EMDR treatment is the tendency to promote associative chaining through the formation of new associations to memory networks that are adaptive for the patient. Such free associations are both highly meaningful and unpredictable. Patient willingness to permit these associations, without disruptive judgment or avoidant responses, is essential to positive treatment effects.

At the end of each set of bilateral stimulation, the patient is asked to "Rest, take a deeper breath. What do you notice now?" These instructions and the pause called for by the request to "take deeper breath" appear to further the nondemand exploratory stance established at the outset. This helps the patient maintain sufficient dual attention to the present, and then to reaccess the most relevant emerging aspects of the target material.

At the same time, the predictable and minimal clinician statements, between sets of bilateral stimulation, permit the accessing of affective arousal in the maladaptive memory network to continue. Any state-dependent information processing, (Bower, 1981; Demos, 1988) associated with a type or degree of affective arousal, is thereby permitted to continue and resume after the patient provides a brief verbal report. The patient's verbal report need only be sufficient to allow the clinician to determine that emerging material is effectively reprocessing.

Both verbal and nonverbal patient responses during and after each set of bilateral stimulation help inform clinical decisions regarding potential changes in procedural elements, such as length, speed, type, and other characteristics of the bilateral stimulation. The clinician may also offer the patient reminders of relevant information incompatible with the emerging material when it appears that the patient is not attaining or maintaining effective reprocessing with changes in the type of stimulation alone.

Shapiro (1995, 2001) initially labeled phase 4 of EMDR as "desensitization" to reflect the tendency of typical treatment effects to lead to decreases in anxiety, distress, and vividness of sensory recall, along with increasingly adaptive self-attributions. However, in the AIP model, these desensitization effects are hypothesized to be a consequence of emotional information processing. Actually, in what is called the "desensitization" phase, there is commonly an array of rapid changes in insights, organization of memory, associated affect, and self-concept not typical of observations of classical desensitization procedures (Wolpe, 1958). While many patients experience immediate decreases in anxiety, distress, and vividness of sensory memories, for some patients, especially when avoidance processes or dissociation have kept significant material from awareness, the level of disturbance may rise significantly to a much more distressing level as a result of accessing more aspects of painful memories until these elements are also resolved. The desensitization phase is said to be complete when the patient can focus on the target memory or situation, even after doing a set of eye movements and then rate the SUD level as being a 0—or in some situations, to be described in chapter 8, a SUD of 1.

PHASE 5: INSTALLATION

In the installation phase, the focus is on deliberate association of a more adaptive self-appraisal statement with the target memory. Installation involves bringing the target event into awareness at the same time as a more adaptive self-appraisal statement, and adding bilateral stimulation. It is not uncommon for a different statement representing a more appropriate and adaptive belief to emerge during the desensitization phase than the PC, initially selected, during the assessment of the target in phase 3. The VoC on the selected self-appraisal statement is identified and then sets of bilateral stimulations are offered until the rating of the emotional validity of a more adaptive belief rises to a 7 or a 6, if that is ecologically valid for the patient's situation. Procedurally, the installation phase differs from both the desensitization phase (phase 4) and the body scan (phase 6). Rather than inquiring about spontaneous associative linkages after each set of bilateral stimulation, in the installation phase, the VoC is checked after each set of bilateral stimulation.

PHASE 6: BODY SCAN

The body scan is the last reprocessing phase of the standard EMDR procedural steps. The body scan phase has two goals. The first is to identify any residual disturbance associated with the target and make sure that it is fully reprocessed. The second is to allow patient to reach higher levels of synthesis. Sometimes, the body scan phase is brief and merely confirms the absence of any somatic tension or unusual sensation. Other times, it can lead to more extensive reprocessing of residual maladaptive material or to significant clinical gains in a positive dimension of self. Only after completing phases 4 and 5 is the patient asked to:

1. Focus on the selected target memory or situation,
2. Hold in mind the positive cognition (PC) used in the installation phase.
3. Scan from head to toe for any sensations.

If tension or discomfort is found, the bilateral stimulation is continued until the patient reports no unpleasant bodily sensations when pairing the target memory and the positive belief. It is not uncommon for multiply traumatized patients to report unpleasant sensations during the body scan that turn out to have associations with other traumatic memories. Because of time constraints, these unpleasant sensations and their associated maladaptive memory networks may need to be reprocessed in a subsequent session.

Treatment of the originally selected target is not considered complete until the patient reports no further unpleasant sensations, even those that may be associated with other disturbing memories or current stimuli. Not all uncomfortable sensations identified in the body scan can be cleared with bilateral stimulation. For example, uncomfortable sensations from a recent or chronic injury or an uncomfortable chair may not be linked to a maladaptive memory network.

When positive sensations are found during the body scan, the bilateral stimulation is continued until the patient reports that the pleasant sensations are not getting any more pleasant. It is important that clinicians give adequate time to the body scan phase, both in clearing residual unpleasant sensation as well as for enhancing positive sensations. Some of the most significant therapeutic gains take place when the reprocessing on positive sensations during the body scan phase is continued.

PHASE 7: CLOSURE

As described in chapters 1 and 2, to modify maladaptive memory networks, it is essential that the patient access, and to some degree, shifts into the feeling state of the maladaptive memory network. As each reprocessing session moves toward closure, checks are made to confirm that the patient's distress or pain has been reduced and that the patient is fully oriented and able to function well in the present. Before each session comes to a close, the patient is brought back to an adaptive state of emotional equilibrium either through completed reprocessing or through the use of affect regulation and self control methods developed during the preparation phase (phase 2).

After the clinician has confirmed that the patient is comfortable and well-oriented, the patient is asked to remain alert until the next session for indications of further changes, positive or negative, related to the presenting symptoms and targeted memories, emotions and beliefs, and to make a record of observations in a written log. Other homework assignments are given and plans are made for the following appointment or for a telephone check-in. Closure procedures are intended to assure patient stability and coping between sessions.

PHASE 8: RE-EVALUATION

At the beginning of subsequent sessions, the clinician re-evaluates the patient's current level of functioning, together with feedback from the patient's written log. The target addressed during the previous session is re-evaluated to verify stability of treatment effects. Checks are made to determine if any new issues or problems have arisen or if there is a need to develop additional self-care or interpersonal skills. The treatment plan may need to be adjusted based on the observed responses to treatment. It is essential to pace the therapeutic work to the patient's observed capacity to tolerate changes in affect state, behavior, and self-concept, as well as to integrate responses by the patient's primary social systems to the effects of treatment.

Successful treatment can only be determined with sufficient re-evaluation. Within session treatment effects are not considered a sufficient basis for verifying successful treatment. Treatment is considered complete when the patient has reached and is able to maintain treatment goals. These would normally include resolution of the patient's presenting complaints, including: (a) intrusions and re-experiencing of disturbing memories, avoidant behaviors and hyperarousal have been eliminated; (b) current stimuli are no longer able to evoke maladaptive responses; and (c) the patient is prepared for likely future situations with a sense of resilience and confidence.

SUMMARY

The standard eight-phase model of EMDR emphasizes that EMDR is not a simple technique of bilateral stimulation that can be applied indiscriminately; rather, EMDR represents a unique form of psychotherapy with its own approach to history taking, treatment planning, and resolving the impact of adverse life experiences. Because of EMDR's potential to induce rapid changes in associative processes and emotional state, it is essential that clinicians have appropriate education and supervised training from an EMDRIA-approved basic training in EMDR—or one of the other national EMDR professional associations—before offering EMDR treatment to patients.

As discussed in chapter 1, the EMDR approach has been successfully applied to a wide range of clinical issues and patient presentations; however not every patient or every condition can be treated with the standard EMDR protocol for PTSD. Specialized applications often require modifications in the standard EMDR procedural steps or the standard EMDR–PTSD protocol and may require the integration of EMDR with other methods of psychotherapy. In this book, our focus is on applications of standard EMDR protocols supported by research. In section II, we will explore the theoretical and practical aspects of the EMDR approach to case formulation, treatment planning, and selecting and preparing patients with PTSD and other posttraumatic syndromes for EMDR reprocessing.

Case Formulation, Treatment Planning and Preparing Patients for EMDR Reprocessing

Easy is right. Begin right
And you are easy.
Continue easy and you are right.
The right way to go easy
Is to forget the right way
And forget that the going is easy.

—Chuang Tzu

For every complex problem there is an answer that is clear, simple, and wrong.
—H. L. Mencken

Hope is both the earliest and the most indispensable virtue inherent in the state of being alive. If life is to be sustained hope must remain, even where confidence is wounded, trust impaired.

—Erik H. Erikson

... if we wait for the moment when everything, absolutely everything is ready, we shall never begin.

—Ivan Turgenev

Case Formulation and Treatment Planning

OVERVIEW

The Importance of Case Formulation in Treatment Outcome

When using the Eye Movement Desensitization and Reprocessing (EMDR) approach, clinical results depend not only on fidelity and skills in applying the standard procedural steps, but also on good case formulation and treatment planning. It is essential to select the most salient targets for reprocessing in an optimal sequence and, if necessary, persist in reprocessing each of those well-selected targets over multiple sessions to a complete resolution. Inappropriate case formulation or treatment plans can lead to several kinds of complications. These include (a) having to frequently alter the focus of attention as earlier significant memories emerge either during reprocessing or between sessions, (b) increased risk of ineffective responses during reprocessing, or (c) premature termination when patients become discouraged from lack of progress.

Every clinician evolves his or her own approach for getting started with a new patient. Some routinely include psychological testing. Some prefer structured clinical interviews. Some approach each patient differently. Patients vary tremendously in their needs at intake. Some show great overall behavioral stability. Others may present with problems with impulse control, severe anxiety, or dissociative symptoms that lead the clinician to decide to offer stabilizing interventions (discussed in chapters five and six) before conducting any structured history taking. Clinicians have to adjust their approach to history taking and treatment planning to best meet the needs of each patient.

Potential Sources of Information Overload for Clinicians New to EMDR

Clinicians being trained or newly trained in EMDR face significant challenges with the potential for information overload because of the multiple skill sets and wide range of knowledge needed to integrate the EMDR model into their clinical work. For clinicians new to EMDR, the sequence of the standard procedural steps can seem counterintuitive. The need to memorize (or read) standard phrases for the

 | Sources of Potential Information Overload for New EMDR Clinicians

- The sequence of the standard procedural steps can seem counterintuitive.
- The need to memorize (or read) standard phrases for the key procedural steps requires cognitive resources that can feel embarrassing and can detract from thoughtful clinical decision making.
- The rapidity and intensity of clinical material that emerges during reprocessing can be overwhelming.
- The mental effort to monitor and suspend well-established impulses to offer empathic verbal responses, interpretations, or reframing can interfere with the familiar felt sense of competence.
- It can be difficult to choose between what seems like too many choices for what to do next.
- The emphasis on the importance of fidelity in application of the procedural steps can lead to self-judgments that reduce the felt sense of confidence and competence.

key procedural steps initially requires cognitive resources. The rapidity and intensity of material that emerges during reprocessing can seem overwhelming. The mental effort to monitor and suspend well-established impulses to offer empathic verbal responses or interpretations can interfere with the familiar felt sense of competence. It can feel difficult to choose among what seem like too many choices for what to do next. The emphasis on the importance of fidelity in application of the procedural steps can lead to self-judgments that reduce the felt sense of confidence and competence. These and other initial challenges can make it difficult for newly trained EMDR clinicians to be able to also grasp the importance of EMDR case formulation and treatment planning. When these issues are not addressed in an ongoing manner in the training and consultative process of integrating EMDR into clinical application, discouraging treatment issues or complications can result.

Sources of Difficulty in Developing and Following a Treatment Plan

Clinicians come from a wide range of backgrounds before obtaining training in EMDR. Approaches to treatment planning and habits formed by using these other approaches can lead to difficulties in appreciating the importance of central issues in EMDR case formulation and treatment planning. The following examples of potential difficulties are not meant to imply that these specific problems with treatment planning are intrinsic to these other approaches, nor that these problems are found only with clinicians with these backgrounds. They do reflect common observations from EMDR training and consultation sessions.

Those who come from client-centered approaches may be inclined to allow each session to unfold from the issues foremost in the patient's thoughts that week. This can lead to a new target being selected at each session from the "issue of the week." Previous targets that were incompletely reprocessed remain unresolved and continue to be a source of residual symptoms. If the clinician initially develops a treatment plan with an ordered series of targets, this plan can become lost in the pressure of addressing the patient's current concerns.

Those who have been trained in cognitive behavioral approaches may be more intently focused on their patients's predominant maladaptive beliefs than on developing a case formulation-based treatment plan. These clinicians may select targets based primarily on the current stimuli that give rise to maladaptive beliefs. As a result, they may fail to give importance to identifying and reprocessing the etiological events that are the source of the initial onset and early reinforcement of these beliefs. In the same way, those with a behavioral focus may be inclined to reprocess current instances of maladaptive behaviors and not attempt to identify or reprocess the foundational experiences that set the template for these maladaptive behaviors.

 | Common Errors in Treatment Planning New EMDR Clinicians

- Clinicians from client-centered approaches (Rogerian, Gestalt, psychodynamic) may:
  - ☐ Abandon the treatment plan when responding to patients' current concerns
  - ☐ Select a new target from the issue of the week
  - ☐ Leave incompletely reprocessed targets as sources of residual symptoms
- Clinicians from a cognitive behavioral background may:
  - ☐ Formulate cases based primarily on current maladaptive beliefs
  - ☐ Select targets from current stimuli
  - ☐ Fail to identify etiological events as the source of these maladaptive beliefs
  - ☐ Encounter ineffective reprocessing because of unidentified, earlier memories
- Clinicians from a behavioral background may:
  - ☐ Formulate cases based primarily on current maladaptive behaviors
  - ☐ Select targets from current stimuli
  - ☐ Fail to identify etiological events as the source of maladaptive behaviors
  - ☐ Encounter ineffective reprocessing because of unidentified, earlier memories

Essential Elements of Case Conceptualization

Case conceptualization requires thinking beyond the patient's immediate symptoms (maladaptive attitudes, thoughts, behaviors, and defensive emotional responses) to form a mental model of these problems grounded in the Adaptive Information Processing (AIP) model of psychotherapy. This mental model provides a set of hypotheses about the causes of the patient's symptoms. These hypotheses provide the outline for building the treatment plan. If these hypotheses are correct and the methodology is correctly applied, then the patient's symptoms should improve. New information can arise—and often does—during the treatment process that may lead to a need to modify the treatment plan; for example, because additional memories emerge that will need to be reprocessed; or there may be major revisions in the case formulation because the patient turns out to have more complex structural dissociation (van der Hart, Nijenhuis, & Steele, 2006). This also means that lack of treatment progress can either implicate technical errors in the application of the method—the standard EMDR procedural steps—or can suggest that the case formulation is incomplete or incorrect.

A case formulation includes, but cannot be uniquely derived from diagnoses in the Diagnostic and Statistical Manual of Mental Disorders (*DSM-IV*) (American Psychiatric Association [APA], 2000) or the International Statistical Classification of Diseases and Related Health Problems, 10th Revision (ICD-10), (World Health Organization, [WHO] 2004). Most diagnoses, including posttraumatic stress disorder (PTSD), are based on

4.3 | Dimensions of Structural Dissociation

■ Primary Structural Dissociation	■ Acute Stress Disorder ■ PTSD
■ Secondary Structural Dissociation	■ Complex PTSD – DESNOS ■ Borderline Personality Disorder ■ Dissociative Disorder NOS
■ Tertiary Structural Dissociation	■ Dissociative Identity Disorder

(Adapted from van der Hart, Nijenhuis, & Steele, 2007, p. 8)

Note. From The Haunted Self: Structural Dissociation and the Treatment of Chronic Traumatization by O. van der Hart, E. R. S. Nijenhuis, & K. Steele, 2006, New York: W. W. Norton & Company, Inc. Copyright 2006. Adapted with permission.

meeting a minimum number of criteria from within subsets of symptoms. Different patients meet the same diagnosis in different ways. In addition, most patients have one or more comorbid diagnoses. This is especially true with PTSD (Kessler et al., 1995). Patients have different histories and different levels of premorbid functioning, current functioning, and social support. Case formulation is based on a functional analysis of the patient's symptoms, their etiology, their current manifestations, and hypotheses about the underlying functional structure of their adaptive and maladaptive memory networks.

History Taking

The AIP model directs us to identify the experiences that are etiological to the patient's presenting concerns. We begin with identifying the patient's primary treatment goals. These include the aim to lessen overt symptoms (e.g., anxiety, panic attacks, nightmares) and to add new experiences and capacities (overcome avoidance, increase assertiveness, gain mastery or confidence).

A broad model considers the four primary domains of experience: behavioral, affective, cognitive, and somatic. What is the patient doing, feeling, thinking, or experiencing that he or she wants less or wants more? What is the patient unable to do, feel, think, or experience that he or she wants to be able to? What concerns does the patient or the clinician have about these goals? The Treatment Goals and Concerns Chart provides a simple outline to summarize these issues (see Table 4.4).

Patients generally can describe their primary symptoms, but verbal reports can be incomplete for a variety of reasons. Symptoms related to PTSD wax and wane over time. Patients may be reluctant to disclose certain symptoms because of feelings of shame, or because they have come to view these symptoms as normal or not treatable. For this reason, structured interviewing and standardized assessment tools can help provide a more complete picture. During the early phases of treatment, adult survivors of childhood abuse may find reporting their symptoms on a form to be less anxiety- or shame-inducing than responding to verbal inquiries. Two simple forms (see Tables 4.5 and 4.6 below) are included for clinicians to use when requesting patients to report their significant positive and negative life experiences and their current responses to triggers.

The next section reviews three standardized tools to assist in gathering information about patients' histories, presenting complaints, and treatment goals. Additional standardized assessment tools for assessing symptom severity, screening for structural dissociation, and tracking treatment outcomes are described in chapter 5. For information on where to obtain these tools, see appendix C.

Standardized Tools for History Taking and Treatment Planning

The Psychotherapy Assessment Checklist Forms

The Psychotherapy Assessment Checklist (PAC) Forms (McCullough, 2001) provide a comprehensive set of questions to help clinicians gather information about patients including significant positive and negative life events, presenting complaints, and a comprehensive set of symptoms associated with the multiaxial diagnosis system from the *DSM-IV* (APA, 2000). The PAC Forms, a PAC Summary Form (McCullough, 1998), and directions for their use (McCullough, 2003b) are available free of charge at http://www.affectphobia.org/pacforms.html. Patients can complete the PAC Forms at home prior to their initial intake session. Clinicians review the PAC Forms and complete the PAC Summary Form. The PAC Forms and PAC Summary Form can then be used to guide the initial clinical interview and assessment. The PAC Forms and PAC Summary Forms are intended to prepare for treatment based on the *Treating Affect Phobia* manual (McCullough 2003a). EMDR-trained clinicians will also find them invaluable as a starting point for history taking and clinical assessment of patients' presenting complaints and specific treatment goals.

| Treatment Goals and Concerns

Name: _____   Date: _____

BEHAVIORAL: WANTS MORE	WANTS LESS	CONCERNS

AFFECTIVE: WANTS MORE	WANTS LESS	CONCERNS

COGNITIVE: WANTS MORE	WANTS LESS	CONCERNS

SOMATIC: WANTS MORE	WANTS LESS	CONCERNS

4.5 | Patient Handout: List of Memories

Name: _____   Date: _____

Please list your *most significant* life experiences starting with the earliest. Include positive and negative experiences. For each negative experience, see if you can list at least one person, situation, or experience that helped you cope with it.

AGE AT TIME	ONGOING STRESSORS AND TRAUMATIC LIFE EXPERIENCES	SIGNIFICANT ACHIEVEMENTS, PEOPLE WHO SUPPORTED YOU, AND EXPERIENCES THAT HELPED YOU COPE

4.6 | Patient Handout: List of Current Stimuli

Name: _____   Date: _____

PATIENT HANDOUT: LIST OF CURRENT TRIGGERS

LIST IMAGES, SOUNDS, SMELLS, PHYSICAL SENSATIONS, PEOPLE, PLACES, ACTIVITIES, AND DREAMS THAT TRIGGER INTENSE EMOTIONS AND NEGATIVE COPING RESPONSES.	RESPONSES TO THESE CUES.			
	EMOTIONS	LOCATION OF SENSATIONS	URGES	THOUGHTS

Multimodal Life History Inventory

The Multimodal Life History Inventory (Lazarus & Lazarus, 1991) is an adult questionnaire with five sections: general, personal and social history, presenting problems, expectations about therapy, and a modality analysis of current problems covering behaviors, feelings, physical sensations, images, thoughts, interpersonal relationships, and biological factors. Patients need 1 to 2 hours to complete this comprehensive questionnaire, which provides a strong foundation on which to build treatment plans in more complex cases (Lazarus, 1989).

Genograms and the Genogram-Maker Millennium Software

Genograms are a widely used graphical tool for summarizing extensive information obtained on a family system. "By creating a systemic perspective that helps to track family issues through space and time, they [genograms] enable an interviewer to reframe, detoxify, and normalize emotion-laden issues" (McGoldrick, Gerson, & Petry, 2008, p. 2). Clinicians may find the Genogram–Maker Millennium Software, available for both Windows and Mac OS X operating systems, a convenient way to generate clear, legible genograms.

Beginning to Gather Information for Treatment Planning

When patients first enter your office, how do you begin? Each clinician develops his or her own approach. In my work, I have developed a style that begins informally and then moves into more structured interviewing based on each patient's situation. When patients present with complex issues and vulnerability, the first session may need to be less structured to focus on building rapport and starting to establish trust. My first words are often "How can I help you?" My approach adapts and shifts as I learn about a patient's needs and concerns.

If there are forensic issues as in cases of personal injury from a motor vehicle crash or industrial injury, there is objective information that needs to be obtained such as the exact date of injury and the names of other treating professionals. Written permission needs to be obtained for records and to release information to other professionals involved in the case. The standardized assessment tools reviewed in chapter 5, can be invaluable to document symptom severity and objectively establish diagnoses.

With adult survivors of neglect or abuse, there is often a history of multiple previous episodes of psychotherapy. It is important to determine whether those have been helpful experiences and what concerns, if any, the patient has about starting with a new psychotherapist. The question, "What led you to contact me at this time?" may open a discussion of current stressors, recent crises, or episodic resurgence of symptoms. For patients suffering from acute stress disorder or PTSD following a single traumatic incident with good premorbid functioning, the process of history taking and case formulation will generally be simpler and briefer, but still needs to be done in a thorough and careful manner.

Elements of Case Formulation

When formulating cases within the AIP model (Shapiro, 1995, 2001), the central concern is an understanding of the etiology of the patient's symptoms. Because memory networks are viewed as the primary basis for health and pathology, the sequence in which experiences have been encoded into memory networks is the foundation for case conceptualization and treatment planning. Events that meet criterion A for PTSD (APA, 1994) generally produce both vivid and lasting memories as well as immediate overt symptoms of intrusive re-experiencing and hyperarousal. However, many other life events are capable of producing adverse effects

Elements of Case Formulation

EMDR case formulation includes the following elements:
- Looks beyond patients' immediate symptoms to etiological events
- A functional analysis of symptom etiology, symptom maintenance, and current patterns of symptomatic response leads to hypotheses about the adaptive and adverse experiences associated with the patients' symptoms.
- Based on the AIP model
- Identifies key underlying adaptive and maladaptive memory networks
- As new information arises, the case formulation may need to be modified.
- When the case formulation is correct, skillfully applied reprocessing leads to symptom reduction.

(Mol et al., 2005) and dysfunctionally encoded memory networks without appearing to be unusual enough to stand out as meaningful to the individual. These life events, referred to as "small t" events by Shapiro (2001, p. 4) can themselves produce persistent difficulties in living that may or may not lead to meeting a specific diagnosis and may also contribute to vulnerability to additional symptoms or treatment issues when there is later exposure to criterion A events.

Inquiring about both Criterion A and Other Adverse Life Events

Given that both criterion A events and other adverse life events can be etiological to persistent symptoms, clinicians need to inquire about both types of events when exploring the etiology of symptoms. For each significant symptom, the standard question is "When did that begin?" If the patient identifies a significant life event as the start of the symptom, then it can be added to the master treatment plan list of targets for reprocessing (see Table 4.14 later in this chapter). If the patient does not identify a specific significant life event, but does remember the time frame for the onset of the symptom, a useful question is, "What kinds of stressful events were going on in your life or with your family at about that time?"

Searching for Associated Memories by Bridging from Current Memory Networks

Occasionally, patients will not recall discrete events or experiences associated with the onset of one or more of their symptoms. Clinicians should continue to explore patients' current patterns of response for information about responses to perceived *threat cues*. Helpful information to obtain about current patterns of response includes frequency of occurrence, settings, intensity of response, and elements of the associated maladaptive memory network. The maladaptive memory networks linked to current stimuli can be used as a starting point in searching for earlier associated memories. Threat cues can be almost any kind of external stimuli or internal stimuli.

External stimuli can be:

- Other people's facial expressions, gestures, or statements
- Sounds
- Smells
- Tastes
- Scenes in life or in a movie, such as when someone is hurt, abandoned, angry, etc.
- Being touched in a certain way
- The anniversary of a stressful event
- Having a child reach the same as an adverse event that occurred in childhood

Internal stimuli can include:

■ Rapid breathing
■ Rapid heart beat
■ Sweating
■ Being hot or cold
■ Being hungry or thirsty
■ Feeling a specific emotion or physical sensation

The elements of the memory network to be identified for situations that trigger the symptom include:

■ The image or other sensory memory that include the worst part
■ Thoughts and sounds experienced
■ The present negative self-assessment associated with the experience
■ Emotions
■ Location of body sensations
■ Defensive action urges engaged in or inhibited during the experience

The Affect, Somatic, and Defense Urge Bridge Techniques

When a patient has not been able to identify an etiological event for a significant symptom through structured or clinical history taking, elements of the memory network from current stimuli can be used as the starting point to explore for the earliest associated memories using the *affect* or *somatic bridge* (Watkins, 1971, 1990, 1992) or the defensive urge bridge. In the EMDR approach, these techniques have sometimes been referred to as the *floatback technique* (Shapiro, 2001, pp. 433–434; Young, Zangwill, & Behary, 2002, p. 195).

The affect bridge focuses on the emotion(s) and the somatic bridge focuses on the location of physical sensation(s) experienced when accessing an initial memory network to recall an earlier memory network. When a defensive urge, as described in chapters 2 and 7, has been identified in a memory network, it can also be used to bridge back to an earlier associated memory. These techniques are most commonly used in four situations in the EMDR approach to treatment as summarized in Table 4.8.

 | When to Use Bridge Techniques

The affect, somatic, and defensive urge bridge techniques are most commonly used in four situations in the EMDR approach to treatment.

First, during the history-taking phase they can be used to assist in identifying the etiological experiences for patient symptoms when the patient has not identified relevant etiological experiences during clinical history taking or on standardized history taking forms.

Second, they can be used to restore effective reprocessing (as described in chapter 9) when reprocessing has stalled because of unidentified, associated earlier memories.

Third, they can be used during the assessment phase of a Future Template (described in chapter 11) when the SUD level turns out to be significantly elevated.

Fourth, these techniques can also be used to uncover adaptive memories for use in Resource Development and Installation procedures (described in chapter 6) for ego strengthening or performance enhancement purposes.

Bridge Techniques Supplement Clinical History Taking

For treatment planning purposes, the affect, somatic, and defensive urge bridge techniques should be considered a supplement to standard structured and clinical history taking, not the primary approach. There are several reasons why the use of a bridge technique in the history-taking phase will not necessarily lead to the identification of the *actual* foundational adverse experience that is etiological to the symptom. First, there is generally no way to ascertain if a memory identified through an affect or somatic bridge faithfully represents an actual event. Second, there may be several related memories of adverse events in a cluster. A memory identified with an affect or somatic bridge technique may therefore be more representational of a cluster rather than a unique cause of the symptom. Finally, and most importantly, a memory identified using a bridge technique may be linked to a more peripheral aspect of the initial memory network and thus may not always be an efficient target for resolving symptoms. A memory identified through an affect, somatic, or defensive urge bridge technique can be helpful in target identification and selection. Memories identified through a bridge technique support further history taking inquiries surrounding the identified early memory. Thus, when used with clinical skill and judgment, bridge techniques can be a helpful aid in identifying and selecting optimal targets for EMDR treatment plans.

Earlier Targets Generally Make More Effective and Efficient Targets

When it is time to start EMDR reprocessing, it is far more effective and efficient in the standard EMDR PTSD protocol to start from an early, disturbing memory than to start reprocessing from current patterns of response. In cases of single event trauma where patients had excellent health until a singular event, it is not necessary to use an affect bridge to identify an early, disturbing memory. It is important to note that when using the *inverted protocol* (Hoffman, 2004, 2005) in complex and unstable cases, clinicians should avoid these kinds of uncovering techniques in the history-taking phase as well as in the early stages of EMDR reprocessing.

The principle for all three of these bridge techniques is to use one or more of the generalizable components of the initial memory network to "float back" to the earliest associated memory. Starting with a specific incident, generally from current threat cues, the sensory components of the initial memory are set aside to assist the patient in focusing on some combination of the negative cognition, emotion(s), or physical sensations. Defensive action urges associated with the initial memory network can also be used for a bridge to an earlier memory. These defensive action urges can include urges for fight, flight, and submission, as well as depersonalization, and derealization.

Issues Surrounding Recovered Memories and the Use of Bridge Techniques

When using methods such as the affect bridge technique, issues can emerge about the accuracy of recovered memories. This became a contentious issue for much of the last decade of the 20th century and prompted both the APA (Alpert, Brown, Ceci, Courtois, Loftus, & Ornstein, 1996) and the International Society for Traumatic Stress Studies (ISTSS) (Roth & Friedman, 1997) to study the issue and to publish reports that remain available on their respective Web sites. Clinicians interested in exploring this topic further are encouraged to review these documents and the literature that they cite. Lipke's (1995) survey of EMDR-trained clinicians identified a greater tendency for forgotten memories to emerge during EMDR reprocessing

 | The Affect, Somatic, and Defensive Urge Bridge Techniques

The Affect Bridge in EMDR

Ask the patient:

What picture represents the worst part of that experience? _____

What words go with that picture that represent your present negative belief about yourself?

_____

When you focus on that picture and those negative words _____, *what emotions do you feel now?*

_____

Notice those feelings and that thought and just let your mind float back to the earliest time in your life when you had the same thought and feelings. What memory comes up for you now?

The Somatic Bridge in EMDR

Ask the patient:

What picture represents the worst part of that experience? _____

What words go with that picture that represent your present negative belief about yourself?

_____

When you focus on that picture and those negative words _____, *what emotions do you feel now?*

_____

Where do you feel it in your body? _____

Notice that thought and where you are feeling it in your body, and just let your mind float back to the earliest time in your life when you had the same thought and with those same feelings in that part of your body. What memory comes up for you now?

THE DEFENSIVE URGE BRIDGE IN EMDR

Ask the patient the following starting with standard questions from the assessment phase:

What picture represents the worst part of that experience? _____

What words go with that picture that represent your present negative belief about yourself?

_____

When you focus on that picture and those negative words _____, *what emotions do you feel now?*

_____

Where do you feel it in your body? _____

As you focus on that picture, those negative words and where you are feeling it in your body, notice any behavioral impulses or urges to act that come up for you. What do you notice? _____

Notice that behavioral impulse or urge to act and just let your mind float back to the earliest time in your life when you had the same impulse or urge. What memory comes up for you now? _____

Adapted from the *affect bridge* (Watkins, 1971, 1992) and the *floatback* technique (Shapiro, 2001, pp. 433–434; Young, Zangwill, & Behary, 2002, p. 195).

than in other methods previously used by these clinicians. Whether patients arrive for therapy with continuous memories or previously recovered memories, or whether they remember previously forgotten memories while they are in treatment—either between sessions or in session—clinicians are advised to remain completely neutral on the issue of the historical accuracy of these memories (Pope & Brown, 1996).

The Plasticity of Memory

As described in both the APA and ISTSS reports, much is known about the plasticity of memory. Memories are shaped by multiple factors during initial encoding, memory retrieval, and re-encoding after retrieval. Memories can be of events that never happened or combinations of events together with material derived from dreams, narratives overhead or read, and images seen in movies. The result is that, without multiple, independent sources for corroboration, it is impossible to know how factually accurate any memory is. When using bridge techniques, the purpose is not to recover a specific memory, but to assist in identifying a memory that appears to be etiological to the patient's symptoms. Most patients who seek treatment have continuous recall for the memories selected as targets from both history taking and from bridge techniques. The purpose of bridge techniques is to identify a memory that the patient had not previously recognized as etiological to a symptom, not to recover a forgotten memory. The purpose of EMDR treatment is not to recover memories nor to determine their accuracy, but to help patients resolve their presenting complaints. Although the stance of neutrality on the accuracy of memories can be a difficult one to maintain for various reasons, it is essential to the therapeutic enterprise.

Attachment Classification

Another central factor in EMDR case formulation is attachment classification (Slade, 1999). Because of space constraints and the focus of this text on the standard EMDR protocols, this section on attachment classification will serve as an introduction to the role of attachment classification in case conceptualization. A more complete discussion will have to wait for a book that addresses complex cases in more detail.

As discussed below in the section on adult attachment assessment tools, there are no clinically normed and readily accessible standardized, objective instruments for assessing adult attachment classification. This is unfortunate because there are compelling reasons for considering attachment classification as an essential element in EMDR case formulation. Research on the neurobiology of the development of capacities for self-regulations shows that the development of a resilient self depends to a critical degree on early attachment experiences. (Fonagy, Gergely, Jurist, & Target, 2002; Schore, 1994, 1996, 1997, 2000, 2001a, 2001b; 2003a, 2003b; Siegel, 1999; Teicher, 2000, 2002; Teicher et al., 1993; Teicher et al 1997).

Given the emphasis in the AIP model on the potential impact of foundational experiences on responses to later-occurring traumatic exposures, it makes sense to consider adult attachment classification as an important aspect of case formulation issues (Leeds, 2001). Longitudinal attachment research has shown the persistence of childhood attachment patterns into adolescence and adulthood (Carlson & Sroufe, 1995; Demos, 1988). An examination of the attachment literature in the context of the AIP model suggests that patterns of attachment shaped in early caregiver experiences influence all later adaptive and maladaptive coping responses.

Childhood Attachment Status Assessed in the Strange Situation

In the 1960s, Ainsworth developed a laboratory paradigm called *A Strange Situation* for studying the effects of early caregiver separation on infant development (Ainsworth et al., 1978). Twelve-month-old children were observed in a playroom with unfamiliar toys for 20 minutes while their primary caregivers and strangers entered and left the room. Two key aspects of each child's behavior were carefully observed: (a) the child's behavioral and affective responses to the departure and return of a caregiver, and (b) the amount of exploration—playing with new toys—the child engaged in. On the basis of these brief behavioral observations, Ainsworth was able to classify children into three groups: secure, anxious–ambivalent, and avoidant. Later, after finding that some children could not be classified into one of Ainsworth's three groups, Main and Solomon (1986) added a fourth group, disorganized attachment, which unlike the other three attachment classifications indicates the absence of an organized strategy for coping with stress. The primary observations that led to the classification of these four groups by Ainsworth et al. (1978) and Main and Solomon (1986) are summarized in Table 4.10.

Adult Attachment Instruments

Increasing emphasis on attachment-related issues has been reflected in a rapidly expanding literature in recent years on the role of attachment processes in the vulnerability to adult psychopathology (Cassidy & Shaver, 1999; Schore, 1994, 2003a, 2003b; Solomon & George, 1999). However, it is important to recognize that the disorganized attachment and insecure attachment classifications do not, at present, constitute attachment disorders or diagnoses. Because of the complexity of the underlying constructs and the limitations of self-report especially for those in the avoidant insecure attachment classification (Shedler, Mayman, & Manis, 1993), there is no single instrument available to allow clinicians to easily assess the full extent of adult attachment classification. After reviewing just three of the adult attachment instruments, we will consider some strategies that can be used by EMDR-trained clinicians who want to consider adult attachment classification

4.10 | Childhood Attachment Classifications

CHILDHOOD ATTACHMENT CLASSIFICATION FROM THE STRANGE SITUATION

Secure (group B). A majority of infants cry and protest the caregiver's absence during the separation phase in the Strange Situation, and are quickly comforted on reunion. These infants actively explore new toys when their caregivers are present and are able to engage with strangers.

Insecure–avoidant (group A). A minority of infants show little or no overt distress during separation from their caregivers in the Strange Situation. They actively avoid contact on the caregiver's return. They may show fleeting greeting behaviors. These infants often relate to strangers in the same manner as they do to their caregiver. The caregiver actively rejects attachment behavior at home. Physiological studies by Sroufe and Waters (1977) with heart rate monitors indicated that these infants actually experienced prolonged elevated levels of physiological distress during separation and after reunion not revealed in their faces or behaviors.

Insecure–resistant–ambivalent (group C). A minority of infants show high levels of distress during separation. Yet, on reunion they show a mixture of both seeking and resisting caregiver contact. Their caregiver interactions have a distinct angry quality. Observations of their caregivers show them to be unpredictably available, and they excessively intrude into their infants' exploration. Typically, these infants explore little and are often guarded with strangers, even when the caregiver is present.

Insecure: disorganized–disoriented (group D). A subset of infants display odd and conflicting behavior patterns in their caregiver's presence such as approaching the caregiver with head averted suggestive of contradictions in intention or sudden immobility accompanied by a dazed expression indicating a lack of orientation to the present environment. Such infants may show another, more oriented and organized, pattern in the same situation at the same period in life with a different caregiver. Main and Solomon (1986), Barach (1991), and Liotti (1992) have suggested that these infants experience their caregiver's facial expressions and behaviors as either frightening or frightened or both, putting them into a paradox of approach–avoidance as the source of both safety and alarm. This paradox may be the source for "stilling" behaviors and dazed expressions observed in these infants.

Summarized from Ainsworth et al. (1978) and Main and Solomon (1986).

when developing a comprehensive case formulation. For a more systematic review of adult attachment instruments, see Stein, Jacobs, Ferguson, Allen, & Fonagy (1998). For a discussion of the limitations of self-report measures of adult attachment and of dimensional versus categorical models of assessing attachment, see Crowell, Fraley, & Shaver (1999) and Waters et al. (2002). Waters et al. commented, (p. 7), "But we found few correlations between the AAI and self report attachment style measures and none substantial enough to suggest that the measures were interchangeable or even parallel." Here, we will focus primarily on just two adult attachment instruments: The Adult Attachment Interview and The Relationship Questionnaire.

The Adult Attachment Interview

The Adult Attachment Interview (AAI) has been the primary research tool for developing adult attachment classification (George, Kaplan, & Main, 1996). It is remarkable in the way it reveals the relationship between adult attachment status and the structure of the narratives adults produce when speaking about their attachment experiences. However, the AAI is a research tool that is not normed for individual administration; it requires extensive training for learning the interview methodology as well as coding, scoring, and interpretation of the syntax in the narratives produced in response to the 20 structured questions. A review of these 20 questions is useful for clinicians, but clinicians need to keep in mind that the AAI is scored on a syntactical analysis of the narrative, not on a content analysis.

The syntactical analysis of the AAI narrative can show gaps, internal inconsistencies, answers that are not responsive to the question, vague responses with an absence of details, excessive details, emotionally intense responses, and responses that appear disconnected from the emotional characteristics of the narrative. The AAI is able to identify adult attachment classification from such syntactical characteristics, because they reflect the neural organization of the prefrontal region of the brain that was shaped by attachment experiences in the first few months of life. See chapter 4 of *The Developing Mind* by Siegel (1999) for an overview of the AAI and a list of most of the questions from the AAI. Appendix C provides a link for how to obtain Main's "Adult Attachment Interview Protocol." Table 4.11, "Attachment Classification as a Continuum of Affect Regulation and Structure," shows a summary of the relationship between narrative structure and affect regulation in adults with insecure avoidant/dismissing, secure, and insecure resistant/preoccupied attachment classifications as described by Slade (1999).

4.11 | Attachment Classification as a Continuum of Affect Regulation and Structure

AVOIDANT/DISMISSING	SECURE/AUTONOMOUS	RESISTANT/PREOCCUPIED
Minimal free expression of both negative and positive affect	Structure and affect are in balance.	Heightened free expression of especially negative affect
Structures for suppressing affect are rigid and highly organized.	Affects can be represented and acknowledged with a flexible, coherent narrative.	Absence of structures for regulating affect

Summarized from Slade (1999)

The Adult Attachment Projective

The Adult Attachment Projective (AAP) is an adult attachment classification system (George & West, 2001) that uses the same four classification groups as the AAI. The AAP is based on an analysis of verbal responses to a set of attachment-related drawings. It retains a focus on mental representation and defensive process central to adult attachment theory. The AAP provides researchers and clinicians with a construct validated measure of adult attachment that avoids many, but not all, of the limitations of administration and analysis of interview measures like the AAI. The AAP requires significant training for administration, scoring, and interpretation, although not nearly as much as the AAI. See appendix C for more information on the AAP.

The Relationship Questionnaire

The Relationship Questionnaire (RQ) is based on a categorical model of attachment classification developed by Bartholomew (1990, 1997) that differs fundamentally from the original adult attachment literature in how adult attachment classification is determined. Bartholomew extended the earlier work of Hazan and Shaver (1987), who developed a set of three brief statements summarizing adult analogues to Ainsworth's "secure," "avoidant," and "ambivalent" attachment patterns from the strange situation (Ainsworth, Blehar, Waters, & Wall, 1978). They asked adults to classify themselves into one of these three patterns. Bartholomew and Horowitz (1991) identified two subgroups of avoidant individuals: "fearful" and "dismissing." This led to a four-category model based on two dimensions—the model of self and the model of other—each of which could be positive or negative. Although the Bartholomew categorical model does not address the issue of disorganized attachment and depends on self-report, it has the distinct advantage that it can be quickly administered and interpreted.

Here are the four statements of the RQ from Bartholomew and Horowitz (1991, p. 244):

> Secure: "It is easy for me to become emotionally close to others. I am comfortable depending on others and having others depend on me. I don't worry about being alone or having others not accept me."

> Preoccupied: "I want to be completely emotionally intimate with others, but I often find that others are reluctant to get as close as I would like. I am uncomfortable being without close relationships, but I sometimes worry that others don't value me as much as I value them."

> Fearful: "I am uncomfortable when getting close to others. I want emotionally close relationships, but I find it difficult to trust others completely or to depend on them. I worry that I will be hurt if I allow myself to become too close to others."

> Dismissing: "I am comfortable without close emotional relationships. It is very important to me to feel independent and self-sufficient, and I prefer not to depend on others or have others depend on me."

Clinical Assessment of Adult Attachment Status

For clinicians who want to consider adult attachment classification in case formulation, several informal approaches can be useful. First, clinicians can consider the pattern of interaction with attachment figures in the patient's reported history. Table 4.12, "Clinical Assessment of Adult Attachment Status Based on Childhood and Adult Attachment Patterns," provides a summary of the patterns of interaction with significant attachment figures and the associated suggestive attachment classifications. Questions from the AAI can be incorporated into the history taking and treatment planning process. See appendix C for how to easily obtain access

4.12 | Clinical Assessment of Adult Attachment Status based on Childhood and Adult Attachment Patterns

Reported history	Consistent contingent supportive behaviors	Inconsistent contingent supportive behaviors mostly not supportive	Consistent absence of contingent supportive behaviors	Prolonged periods of frightened or frightening behaviors	History suggestive of disorganized attachment with periods of physical or sexual abuse
Attachment classification with that attachment figure	Suggestive of secure attachment	Suggestive of insecure preoccupied	Suggestive of insecure avoidant	Suggestive of disorganized	Suggestive of secondary or tertiary structural dissociation
Mother or other primary childhood maternal figure					
Father or other primary childhood maternal figure					
Significant attachment figure from primary family unit					
First adult romantic attachment figure					
Second adult romantic attachment figure					
Most recent adult romantic attachment figure					

to the AAI questions. Clinicians can subjectively assess the quality of a patient's narrative itself in a manner similar to that used in the formal assessment of the AAI as discussed above (Main, 1996; Cassidy & Shaver, 1999) and in the resources listed in appendix C. Table 4.11, "Attachment classification as a continuum of affect regulation and structure," may assist in thinking about how patients' narratives are organized in terms of affect regulation and structure.

Holding the Big Picture: Why Patients Come for Treatment

Even when patients present themselves at your office specifically because they are seeking treatment with EMDR, it is essential to keep your responsibilities to the big picture in mind. Why do patients present for treatment in the first place? As important as procedural fidelity (Maxfield & Hyer, 2002) is to EMDR treatment effects, the aim of psychotherapy is not determined by methods and models. The big picture is about helping patients achieve what they are seeking.

Patients approach psychotherapists for treatment for quite different reasons. Some hope to change. Others hope to prove that no one can change them. Some want to end or at least reduce their pain. Others want someone to console them while they hold on to the pain that has come to define who they are. Some want comprehensive changes. Others want to avoid central issues and to make modest gains with quite specific symptoms.

A patient may flatter the clinician with statements about their reputation as being skilled with hypnosis, psychoanalysis, cognitive behavioral therapy, or EMDR.

A patient may claim that this is the reason why he or she is entering treatment. This is not the reason. The methodology of the clinician is not the aim of psychotherapy. The reason for entering treatment is always about something the patient wants to change, to have more of or less of in life, or to keep from changing.

A patient who presents with a limited goal, and who achieves it, may later decide to return to address larger issues. During initial discussions of the treatment contract, the clinician may explicitly encourage the patient to agree to a different or larger treatment contract from the outset. A patient may agree or decline. The clinician may decline to offer treatment when it is not possible or ethical to help a patient with a limited goal that ignores glaring symptoms or clinical issues that warrant treatment—such as severe substance abuse. What needs to be guarded against is a clinician forgetting the patient's stated goals and allowing the methods or theories of treatment to gradually shift the treatment contract and the aim of the therapy from what the patient was seeking to something that serves the clinician's preferred theories or techniques.

Keeping in mind the "big picture" of what the patient is seeking is doubly important when considering the use of EMDR reprocessing. One important reason is that with some patients, it can be more difficult to limit the scope of psychotherapy with EMDR reprocessing. For some patients, EMDR reprocessing may tend to open up the central issues in a person's life so they can be resolved. Some patients may not want to address family of origin or other central life issues. Although clinicians can take some steps to assist patients in limiting the scope of material that emerges during reprocessing, what emerges is not something that clinicians can control. Associations to other issues and other memories can emerge no matter how skillful the clinician is. EMDR tends to unlock patients' own unconscious resources and concerns. When patients are not seeking such comprehensive results, EMDR reprocessing may not be indicated for them.

When Treatment Goals are Incompatible with EMDR Reprocessing: The Case of Julie

Here is a case example where a patient had limited treatment goals that made EMDR reprocessing not suitable for this specific course of treatment. Julie presented for treatment in early spring after struggling with progressively worsening symptoms of anxiety, nightmares, insomnia, panic attacks, and agoraphobia. During our initial session, she told me that she had been severely mistreated as a young child and had experienced both physical and sexual abuse at the hands of her parents. She explained that after years of being free of debilitating anxiety, her symptoms had resurfaced when she had reestablished contact with her parents after many years of avoiding them.

Ten years earlier, shortly after she married, she had finally mustered the courage to enter treatment for the many psychological and emotional problems that resulted from these adverse events. It was very hard for her to trust anyone, but she endeavored to put her trust in her psychotherapist. Her therapist explained that the only way for her to recover from the damaging effects of her childhood abuse was to tell every detail until her symptoms abated. Julie attempted to do what her therapist asked her to do. Unfortunately, when she began to tell the details of what she had experienced, more details and more memories that she had dissociated began to surface. Her anxiety worsened and she began to have small dissociative fugue episodes, losing track of time and developing difficulty coping with the demands of daily life. She became severely depressed.

To help her through this crisis, her psychotherapist increased the frequency of their sessions to twice a week. As her symptoms continued to worsen, her psychotherapist referred her for a medication evaluation. Her psychiatrist placed her on one medication, then a second. When she developed side effects, she was prescribed a third and then a fourth medication. Her symptoms and her functioning continued to deteriorate. She finally reached a decisive moment when she realized if she continued in therapy she would end up being hospitalized. She dropped out of psychotherapy, and over the next few weeks she weaned herself off all her medications. When she was no longer in psychotherapy and no longer on medication, she found that the remaining intrusive memories, nightmares, and other symptoms were much more manageable. She discovered that an active lifestyle helped her to suppress her symptoms. She was in a stable, loving marriage. She got more involved in work that took her out of doors, and her symptoms gradually subsided to a tolerable level.

She had done reasonably well until the previous November when she had the thought that she might attempt to reestablish contact with her parents for the first time in more than 10 years. She imagined that her parents might finally be willing to admit what had happened in her childhood. When she visited them, she was shocked to discover that nothing had changed. Her parents continued to deny the worst of the abuse and blamed her as the cause for the few instances that they admitted had happened. Following this visit her symptoms began to return. She started to have nightmares about her childhood abuse every night. She developed insomnia and seldom slept more than 4 or 5 hours a night. She started to have panic attacks up to three or four times a day. She avoided leaving the house. When she and her husband decided that she had to get help, she needed him to drive her to my office.

After she told me her story, I apologized to her for the retraumatizing experiences she had suffered in her first course of psychotherapy and psychiatric treatment. I asked her what her goals were in coming to me for psychotherapy. She stated clearly that she just wanted to reestablish the level of functioning she had been enjoying before her decision to recontact her parents. She wanted the panic attacks to stop. She wanted to be able to leave the house and travel freely without debilitating anxiety. She wanted to achieve this without having to work through her memories of childhood abuse.

I told her that I could help her to achieve her goals and that we would do so within 6 to 8 weeks and without delving into her traumatic memories. I added that after she had achieved stable functioning, she could decide to stop or to make a larger contract to work through the adverse events of the past in a different way than she had attempted before—with EMDR rather than having to recount the details of her abuse. I reassured her that she would be under no obligation to focus on the past after her symptoms had subsided.

I asked Julie to promise me that while she was in treatment with me that she would never answer any question I might ask her unless she truly wanted and felt ready to. I asked her to be in control of whatever we might discuss. She readily agreed to this. She was greatly reassured that she would not have to revisit the past. There were several points in our sessions when I interrupted Julie as she started to delve into childhood memories to check and to see if she really wanted and needed to tell me those details. I made certain that she was the conscious gatekeeper of her past. She appreciated my confidence and my predication of rapid symptom improvement, but was quite skeptical that her symptoms would abate so quickly.

I then taught her a series of self-control exercises such as square breathing, covered in chapter 6, and did a safe place imagery exercise but without the eye movements we typically use in EMDR. I instructed her in the fundamentals of sleep hygiene and gave her a graded series of behavioral homework assignments that involved initially going for walks near her home and later at greater distances. Over the next few weeks, I continued to help her gain mastery over her anxiety and her nightmares. We discussed her disappointment, hurt, and anger at her parents' denials, but without delving into the memories or the details of the traumatic experiences of her childhood. Within a few weeks, she was driving her car increasing distances and had decided to return to college to pursue course work toward completing a bachelor's degree she had long abandoned. By the eighth week, she was free of intrusive and avoidant symptoms or anxiety that could interfere with her functioning. She had few residual nightmares and those did not disrupt her sleep. She was sleeping well nearly every night.

She raised the possibility of continuing in psychotherapy and doing EMDR reprocessing. However, she ultimately decided that she was too busy with her schoolwork. She asked me if she could return to see me should her symptoms resurface. I reiterated my open door policy. I told her I was delighted with her progress and that she was welcome to return should there ever be a need.

Julie's case illustrates the importance of holding the big picture in mind when developing a treatment plan. As an experienced EMDR clinician I knew that *in principle,* I could help Julie reprocess her memories of childhood trauma and permanently resolve her symptoms. Because symptoms of untreated PTSD can resurface in response to current stressors, I was concerned that not treating the core of Julie's PTSD itself and only managing her anxiety symptoms behaviorally left her vulnerable to further episodes in the future. However, in Julie's situation it was more important to empower her to be in charge of her treatment goals and to achieve what she wanted for herself. Just because I had EMDR skills in my toolbox did not define the role her psychotherapy with me was to play in her life. I don't know if she will ever return, but if she does, her goals and not my methods will still be the determining factor in what treatment approach I offer her.

A Symptom Informed Model of Treatment Planning

The AIP model (Shapiro, 2001) informs the EMDR approach to treatment planning. Symptoms are viewed as expressions of perceptions and coping responses encoded in maladaptive memory networks in need of reprocessing. EMDR has been extensively researched as a treatment for posttraumatic stress disorder, and has shown promising results for other Axis I disorders. When focusing on treatment of PTSD, a symptom-focused approach to treatment planning has been found to be effective (Korn, Weir, & Rozelle, 2004). The sequence for selecting targets is based on several foundational principles.

First Principle of Treatment Planning: Start with the Earlier Memory

The first principle is that earlier experiences set the foundation for responses to later events. This leads to first reprocessing memories for earlier traumatic events before memories of later events. After past etiological events have been fully resolved, some maladaptive responses to current stimuli can remain. The next focus for reprocessing is on current stimuli. After current stimuli no longer give rise to maladaptive responses, we can explore additional treatment goals with imaginal rehearsal to expand the scope of future behaviors, integrate new skills, and instill a new self-image.

Beginning with the past, if there are multiple traumatic events of a similar kind, such as many instances of physical abuse by a parent, we group these events into a cluster. Within a cluster of related events, we begin reprocessing with the earliest event within that cluster and continue reprocessing the memory of that event to completion. Selecting the earliest event in the cluster as the first target reduces the chance of ineffective responses because of earlier material being triggered from outside of the patient's awareness. The coping responses to this first event may have been limited by the developmental stage, physical size, knowledge, and coping capacities of the patient. Therefore, it is essential to normalize and realize the factors that are limiting perceptions and coping capacities encoded in memory, and facilitate synthesis of these early memories with other later acquired adaptive memory networks.

After the first event in the cluster has been successfully reprocessed to completion, we shift our focus to the worst event within that cluster of events and continue reprocessing the memory of that event to completion. If there is no worst event, we select a representative memory to reprocess. Then, we should focus on the last occurrence in that cluster of events and reprocess the memory of that event to resolution. Finally, we should ask patients to scan their memory for any other events within that cluster of events that still hold a felt sense of disturbance and reprocess those to full resolution.

Second Principle of Treatment Planning: Start with the Worst Symptom

The second principle is that by first reprocessing the memory (or cluster of memories) associated with the most debilitating of patients' symptoms, we can improve their functioning to the greatest extent. After the most debilitating symptom has been alleviated, we can shift attention to the memory (or cluster of memories) associated with the next most debilitating symptom.

Third Principle of Treatment Planning: Selected Activated Memories

The third principle is that we should focus on adverse and traumatic events that are clearly distressing to the patient. These have been described as "activated" memories (Korn et al., 2004). Clinicians may hypothesize that certain memories for adverse events are etiological to current symptoms, but if these memories are not overtly disturbing to the patient they need not be included in the initial treatment plan.

Fourth Principle: Treatment Planning is a Collaboration

The fourth principle is that a treatment plan must be a collaboration between the clinician and the patient. Although it is well tolerated by most patients, psychotherapy focused on trauma resolution can be a fairly stressful process. Many patients approach it with some trepidation. Patients can have fears and concerns about addressing their traumatic past. They may want to begin with a recent traumatic memory when overt symptoms first appeared rather than reopen early childhood memories. These early childhood memories may have contributed to the patient's symptom profile in ways that may be obvious to the EMDR clinician but are less obviously linked in patients' awareness. Therefore, it may be necessary to begin with reprocessing the most recent trauma and only address foundational memories after patients realize that their symptoms can only be fully alleviated when they deal with these early memories.

Deciding How to Address Treatment-Related Concerns and Fears

Sometimes, treatment-related fears or concerns intrude into the development of the treatment sequence. Until these fears are addressed, patients will not be able to begin reprocessing memories of etiological events. Clinicians can consider four strategies for coping with these treatment-related concerns and fears: (a)psychoeducation, (b) problem solving, (c) RDI, or (d) memory reprocessing.

Psychoeducation, informed consent, and problem solving

When concerns or fears are based on lack of information, psychoeducation and informed consent are often indicated first. Examples include religious concerns that EMDR is a form of hypnosis which is prohibited in certain sects, fear of being controlled by the therapist, fear of having to disclose details the patient would rather not, fear of going crazy, fear of being rejected as hopeless, or fear of losing positive memories. Some fears call for a combination of psychoeducation and informed consent. Examples include the fear of having less vivid recall in forensic cases and the fear of remembering other even more disturbing events. See chapter 6, "The Preparation Phase" for how to address these concerns and fears. Some concerns are reality based. These often require problem solving before reprocessing can be started. Examples include not having sufficient funds to pay for a complete course of treatment or being in danger from additional criminal assaults by a domestic partner.

Reducing fears with Resource Development and Installation (RDI)

When patients have not yet achieved sufficient stability for reprocessing, and fears or concerns persist after appropriate psychoeducation and problem solving, RDI can often provide a way of decreasing fears or resolving concerns while helping to increase stability and prepare for reprocessing. See chapter 6 "The Preparation Phase" for the RDI protocol. One example would be installing resources to foster self-worth, courage, and assertiveness to support asking for a well-deserved and overdue increase in pay, or seeking alternate employment, to enable the patient to afford a full course of treatment. Another example is a patient with a history of some early neglect who shows ambivalence about engaging in treatment and presents a fear of being rejected by the clinician as hopeless. When this fear persist after appropriate psychoeducation, to lessen the risk of premature termination that could be triggered by attempting to process early experiences of abandonment or neglect, consider installing resources for unconditional acceptance and validation.

Reprocessing Conditioning Events Associated with Present Fears

When patients meet adequate criteria for current stability, fears that persist after appropriate psychoeducation, informed consent, and problem solving can be directly addressed with EMDR reprocessing. Identify events associated with the fear and reprocess those events to alleviate the fear to sufficient resolution to permit reprocessing of the events associated with the presenting complaints. One example is a patient who had been terminated after 4 months of treatment by a previous clinician after revealing she had begun to remember episodes of childhood sexual assault by her grandfather. This patient was afraid that if she recalled other disturbing memories, as she was told is common in EMDR, her EMDR clinician would also reject her. Another example is a patient with a presenting complaint of flying phobia who feared becoming distraught in reprocessing and having to be hospitalized. This patient's mother was treated for postpartum depression in a psychiatric hospital for several weeks when the patient was 8 years old. The patient recalled the mother crying and crying before being taken away. The patient's belief was, "If I cry or get upset, I'll lose control and have to be hospitalized."

Identifying memories associated with the origin of these fears and making them the first target for EMDR reprocessing reduces the current fear. Patient can then feel ready to redirect attention to the primary etiological targets the clinician has helped them identify for the recommended treatment plan.

Selecting and Sequencing Targets for EMDR Reprocessing

The following outline describes a research-supported (Korn et al., 2004) model for selecting and sequencing targets for EMDR reprocessing for patients with Axis I trauma-related symptoms. This is the treatment planning model that was used in a recent large National Institute of Mental Health-funded study comparing treatment effectiveness of EMDR with Fluoxetine, brand name Prozac, and a placebo (van der Kolk et al., 2007). This symptom-informed model needs to be modified when secondary or tertiary structural dissociation has been identified (van der Hart, Nijuenhuis, & Steele, 2006). See chapter 5 for assessment of dissociative disorders. A different model is needed when the focus of attention is symptoms related to an Axis II disorder. Figure 4.1. "Schematic EMDR Treatment Planning," shows this same model as a flow chart.

1. Past

A. Starting with the worst symptom, reprocess completely the earliest accessible disturbing memory associated with the most disruptive, intrusive, avoidant, fight–flight, somatic, or dissociative symptom. This earliest accessible disturbing memory may be unique or may be one in a sequence or cluster of events associated by affect, belief, behavior, or impulse. The earliest memory is generally found through history taking, but this can be supplemented by using an affect or somatic bridge as described in Table 4.9 earlier in this chapter.

B. If clinically indicated during reprocessing of the 1A event, shift to—and complete reprocessing—other associated events *if they are earlier* or if they are linked to a defensive belief. Then return to the memory in 1A. Postpone reprocessing of other associated events when they are more recent until the earlier events have been fully reprocessed.

C. Continue with and complete reprocessing subsequent and still disturbing memories in that sequence or cluster of related experiences. The worst symptom, by this point, should have significantly decreased in severity.

D. Continue on to the next most disturbing symptom. Continue reprocessing all other still disturbing memories associated by affect, belief, behavior, or impulse with the next most disruptive, intrusive, avoidant, fight–flight, somatic, or dissociative symptom.

E. Continue in this manner to address remaining symptoms by starting reprocessing with the earliest memory associated with the onset of each symptom. Then, continue reprocessing with subsequent associated memories.

2. Present

After all past events are resolved, check and reprocess as needed memories of recent events and current stimuli revealed during history taking or that have been revealed in the patient's log (described in chapter 6) that remain disturbing or are associated with presenting complaints. Start with those that are the most disturbing or disruptive.

3. Future

Continue with reprocessing future templates—imaginal rehearsal—for all future behaviors, events, or stimuli that are still associated with maladaptive responses, anticipatory anxiety, or for which the patient needs to develop greater confidence

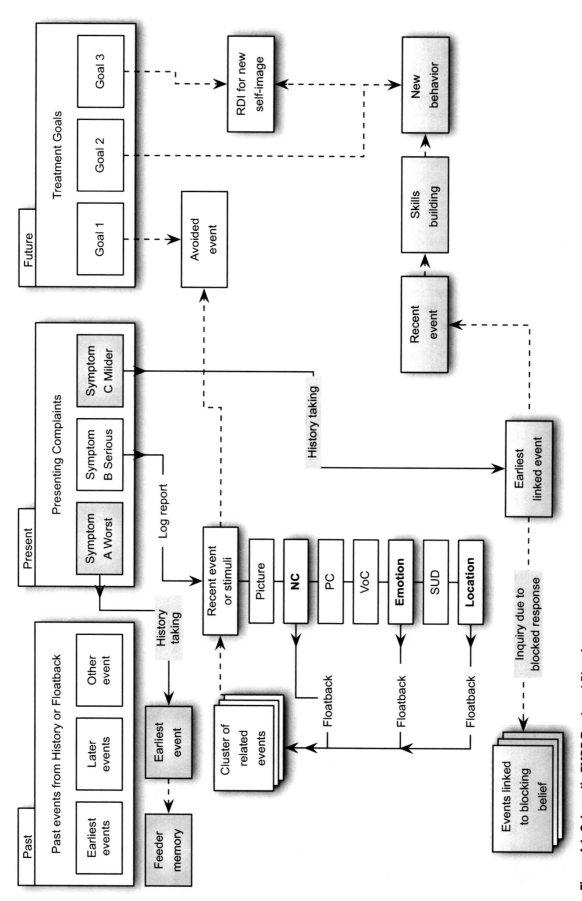

Figure 4.1 Schematic EMDR Treatment Planning

4.13 | Elements of Treatment Planning

- ■ Identify patients' presenting complaints and treatment goals.
- ■ Identify patients' current symptoms:
  - ☐ When current symptoms began?
  - ☐ How symptoms have changed or evolved over time?
- ■ Obtain a complete history:
  - ☐ Childhood patterns of attachment
  - ☐ Adverse and traumatic events in childhood, adolescence, and adulthood
  - ☐ Overview of family history and constellation.
- ■ Identify past and current health and medical issues:
  - ☐ Early surgeries and any life threatening illness
  - ☐ Current health issues that could be risk factors to EMDR reprocessing
  - ☐ Current or potentially needed psychiatric medication
- ■ Consider impact of military service
- ■ Identify mastery experiences (such as past successes with school, work, and special interests)
- ■ Screen for past and present legal problems
- ■ Identify history of any alcohol or substance abuse
- ■ Assess patients' current coping skills and social supports:
  - ☐ Adult attachment classification
  - ☐ Ego-strength
  - ☐ Affect tolerance
  - ☐ Capacities for emotional and behavioral self-regulation
- ■ Screen for presence and nature of structural dissociation
- ■ Consider presence and impact of Axis II issues
- ■ Consider secondary gain or loss issues and resolve if present

or skills. If clinically indicated, consider installing a new self-image using the RDI protocol (described in chapter 6) to consolidate the gains achieved during treatment.

Essential Elements of EMDR Treatment Planning

EMDR treatment planning begins with gathering information on the patient's presenting complaints. It is essential to learn when current symptoms began—and how they have changed or evolved over time—and treatment goals. Treatment planning continues with obtaining a complete history. This history needs to consider early childhood patterns of attachment, any adverse or traumatic events in childhood, adolescence, and adulthood, and a basic overview of the patient's family constellation. Past and current health and medical issues need to be identified including early surgeries, any life threatening illness, current health issues that could be risk factors to EMDR reprocessing, and current or potentially needed psychiatric medication. Military service, mastery experiences (past successes with school, work, and special interests), legal problems, and history of any alcohol or substance abuse need to be identified. Treatment planning requires an assessment of the patient's current coping skills, social supports, ego-strength, affect tolerance, and capacities for emotional and behavioral self-regulation. The presence and nature of structural dissociation needs to be clarified (van der Hart et al., 2006). The presence and impact of Axis II issues needs to be considered (APA, 1994). Secondary gain or loss issues need to be explored and, if present, addressed with problem solving.

Each clinician develops his or her own approach to gathering the information needed for treatment planning derived from educational background, training, and clinical experience. Some always include psychological testing, some rarely or never. Some use standardized structured clinical interviews. Some use the genogram

4.14 | Master Treatment Plan List of Targets

MASTER TREATMENT PLAN CHART

List memories and resources from earliest (top) to most recent (bottom)

Name: _____   Page: _____ of _____

ID	AGE	TRAUMA MEMORY OR PERSISTENT STRESSOR DATE(S) OF TREATMENT AND POST-TX SUDS	ID	AGE	RESOURCE MEMORY DATE(S) OF TX AND POST RDI VOR
1			A		
2			B		
3			C		
4			D		
5			E		
6			F		
7			G		
8			H		
9			I		
10			J		

List symptoms and associated current stimuli with Frequency (F) and Severity (S) 0–7

ID	SYMPTOMS	CURRENT STIMULI	INTAKE F AND S	DESIRED F AND S	DISCHARGE F AND S
a					
b					
c					
d					
e					
f					
g					

system for identifying the family history and constellation (McGoldrick, Gerson, & Petry, 2008). We will review some of standardized assessment tools that can be helpful for treatment planning and for assessing patient readiness for EMDR reprocessing in chapter 5.

Once all this information is gathered, how is it used to create a treatment plan? Cases vary greatly in complexity. Some patients have limited traumatic exposures and stable family histories. In cases like this, it is relatively easy to keep track of the available information and establish a plan. In other cases, because of the extent of the traumatic exposures at different ages, clinicians can become overwhelmed and unclear regarding where to focus attention.

Table 4.12, "Master Treatment Plan List of Targets," can help clinicians keep information from the patient's history available in an abbreviated form and be able to localize the work being done at particular points in therapy within the overall treatment plan. We will look at clinical case examples that make use of the master treatment plan list of targets in chapter 12.

Next, in chapter 5 we will examine how to assess patient readiness for EMDR reprocessing.

Assessing Readiness
for Reprocessing

OVERVIEW

In this chapter, we list and examine essential criteria to consider when assessing patient stability and readiness for Eye Movement Desensitization and Reprocessing (EMDR). We will also review standardized assessment tools that can assist clinicians in assessing symptom severity, screening for dissociative disorders, and monitoring treatment progress and outcomes.

ASSESSING STABILITY AND READINESS FOR REPROCESSING

At the same time clinicians are gathering the patient's history, they need to be assessing potential concerns for the patient's suitability for EMDR reprocessing. In considering a patient's suitability and readiness for EMDR reprocessing, five kinds of issues need to be considered: (a) medical concerns, (b) social and economic stability, (c) behavioral stability, (d) mood stability, and (e) comorbid axis I and axis II diagnoses with particular attention to secondary and tertiary structural dissociation, substance abuse and severe (i.e., organic) mental illness, such as bipolar disorder, obsessive compulsive disorder, and schizophrenia. Clinicians need to develop their own strategy and sequence for reviewing and assessing all five of these areas. The worksheet "Assessing Stability and Readiness for Reprocessing" and the accompanying notes are offered to aid clinicians in documenting that they have completed this review for each patient. The notes summarize the material presented in the following section.

SECONDARY GAIN AND SECONDARY LOSS

Issues of potential secondary gain and loss that may be associated with presenting complaints can sometimes be easily identified at intake, but may only emerge in later stages of treatment. In some cases, the presence of secondary gain or loss issues at intake may require early identification and problem-solving interventions before reprocessing is considered. One example is when patients are cur-

Assessing Stability and Readiness for Reprocessing

Name: _____   Date: _____

For *history* indicate severity of worst episode.
For *current situation* indicate severity on date of assessment.
Impact of factor on stability: 0 absent; 1 minimal; 2 moderate; 3 severe.

Issue	History includes	Severity	Current situation	Severity
Secondary gain/loss		0 1 2 3		0 1 2 3
Trust or truth absent		0 1 2 3		0 1 2 3
External crises		0 1 2 3		0 1 2 3
Financial instability		0 1 2 3		0 1 2 3
Health risk		0 1 2 3		0 1 2 3
Bipolar Depression		0 1 2 3		0 1 2 3
Suicidal ideation		0 1 2 3		0 1 2 3
Suicide attempts		0 1 2 3		0 1 2 3
Self-injury		0 1 2 3		0 1 2 3
Injury to others		0 1 2 3		0 1 2 3
High-risk behaviors		0 1 2 3		0 1 2 3
Denial of diagnosis		0 1 2 3		0 1 2 3
Accident-prone self		0 1 2 3		0 1 2 3
Substance abuse		0 1 2 3		0 1 2 3
Compulsive sex		0 1 2 3		0 1 2 3
Compulsive acts ($)		0 1 2 3		0 1 2 3
Alexithymia		0 1 2 3		0 1 2 3
Flooded by affect		0 1 2 3		0 1 2 3
Depersonalization		0 1 2 3		0 1 2 3
Amnesia or fugue		0 1 2 3		0 1 2 3
DID or DDNOS		0 1 2 3		0 1 2 3

rently receiving disability payments because of their mental health symptoms. If patients lack skills for employment and fear becoming homeless should disability payments end, problem-solving interventions to help patients gain awareness of and access to rehabilitation, educational and job retraining resources may need to precede treatment for trauma-related symptoms. In other cases discussed below, issues of secondary gain or loss may emerge later in treatment and after being recognized, may require a combination of problem solving and further reprocessing.

Another frequent concern and occasional source of confusion for some clinicians is when there is a pending civil law suit for damages, such as following a

Secondary gain/loss	When current secondary gain is moderate or severe, reprocessing is more likely to be incomplete and may require problem solving. Reprocessing may be attempted unless incomplete reprocessing would lead to premature discontinuation of treatment.
Trust or truth absent	When the patient lacks sufficient trust to be truthful *and* there are other dangerous or therapy-interfering behaviors, reprocessing may need to be postponed. Even without overt evidence of dangerousness, attempts to reprocess targets with inadequate trust or disclosure (truth telling) can lead to dangerous acting out or complications that might prevent future consideration of reprocessing.
External crises	When external work, personal, or family crises require patient's full attention, reprocessing may need to be postponed. Other patients may benefit from prompt reprocessing of associated early memories.
Financial instability	Inability to complete treatment or realistic fears of impending loss of basic financial security may need to be addressed before reprocessing.
Health risk	Any life threatening health risk that could be exacerbated by emotional reprocessing, and any history of eye problems should be evaluated and cleared by a physician before starting reprocessing. (Examples: risk of stroke, heart attack). Also potential risk to pregnancy requires informed consent and physician ok.
Bipolar depression	Bipolar depression carries greater risk of suicide attempts.
Suicidal ideation	Suicidal ideation requires careful assessment and ongoing monitoring for intent, plan, and lethality.
Suicide attempts	Past suicide attempts need to be fully understood to assess current risk. Risk factors need ongoing monitoring during treatment. When risk remains present, clinicians should be cautious in considering reprocessing. Clarify treatment contract and mandated actions to protect patient.
Self-injury	Self-harming behaviors need to be carefully assessed for dangerousness to life and risk of self-mutilation. Dangerous self-harm should be fully stabilized before reprocessing and carefully monitored during reprocessing. Clarify treatment contract and mandated actions to protect patient.
Injury to others	Past and current acts and urges need to be carefully assessed and monitored for risk and lethality. Clinicians should be cautious in considering reprocessing when risks factors are present. Clarify treatment contract with patient and that mandated reports may become necessary.
High-risk behaviors	Current vulnerability to high-risk behaviors should be carefully assessed and addressed to protect patient from dangerous self-injury, revictimization, or harm to others.
Denial of diagnosis	Attempts to proceed with reprocessing when the patient is in denial of a major diagnosis—such as substance abuse, dissociative identity disorder, bipolar disorder, or any psychotic disorder—can put the patient at risk.
Accident-prone self	Accident proneness can indicate unconscious acts of self-injury or assault and should be assessed carefully for current risk.
Substance abuse	For types of substance abuse that can be threats to life or health, reprocessing should be postponed until stable recovery is achieved. With limited published EMDR research for this population, clinical issues require careful consideration and informed consent.
Compulsive sex	Dangerousness to self and others needs to be carefully considered.
Compulsive acts ($)	Compulsive spending or gambling could remain unstable or be worsened by emotional reprocessing. Absence of controlled research needs to be part of informed consent. Stabilizing interventions should be considered.
Alexithymia	Mild alexithymia (such as problems naming emotions) should not interfere with reprocessing. Moderate to severe alexithymia—no access to affect—is more likely to interfere with reprocessing and may require modifications in procedure. Alexithymia by itself is seldom a reason to withhold EMDR, but it may be when present with other factors.
Flooded by affect	Prolonged intense weeping, anger, terror, or shame during verbal therapy may predict inability to reprocess. Affect tolerance and management skills building may need to be the focus. Standard reprocessing should not be withheld unless a failure at reprocessing would lead to a refusal to consider reprocessing in the future.
Depersonalization and derealization	Depersonalization and derealization experiences can be intensely painful, frightening, and shameful for some patients. Patients who frequently experience depersonalization or derealization in verbal therapy are more likely to do so and more intensely during reprocessing. Strategies for self-control and affect management may need to be practiced before reprocessing can succeed.
Amnesia or fugue	Evidence of past or current fugue or current amnesia episodes—loss of time—indicates a need for more complete assessment of dissociation before reprocessing to avoid risk of harm to patient.
DID or DDNOS	A possible current diagnosis of dissociative identity disorder or dissociative disorder not otherwise specified indicates a need for more careful assessment of dissociation before reprocessing to avoid risk of harm to patient. Lack of stabilization in DID or DDNOS such as uncontrolled rapid switching, uncontrolled flashbacks, and poor cooperation and communication among parts of the personality indicate a need to postpone reprocessing. ISST-D and EMDR Treatment Guidelines should be followed.

Please note: This checklist and notes reflect only the most common issues that need to be considered. Clinicians need to remain alert to other issues that would provide reasons to be cautious or to postpone reprocessing based on common sense, specialty education, training, or clinical experience.

motor vehicle crash or unresolved issues regarding an industrial injury. In such cases, it is possible that the patient may continue to show significant emotional distress until the legal and financial issues are satisfactorily resolved. This is not a reason to postpone or withhold EMDR. There are additional issues of informed consent to be considered in forensic cases, such as the possibility that the vividness of intrusive memories may be lessened. These issues will be addressed in chapter 6. Even when there are pending issues of financial compensation, EMDR reprocessing should be offered, but the clinician should realize that because issues of social recognition are still engaged, patients may show less complete resolution of all emotional issues until the satisfactory resolution of legal or financial issues.

Clinicians need to be clear about their own thoughts on the differences between so-called negative emotions (e.g., anger or shame that is maladaptive and debilitating) where there are excessive self-blame or rage episodes that threaten loss of self-control, and those that are normal and adaptive (e.g., resentment at the adversarial nature of legal proceedings). EMDR reprocessing will only be able to resolve maladaptive aspects of negative experiences; however, *contributory experiences* (e.g., past injustices in high school) unrelated to the index trauma, can sometimes inflame the degree of response to current stressors. EMDR reprocessing of these contributory experiences can often make current stressors much more tolerable.

While some issues of secondary gain and loss can be identified at intake and considered during initial treatment planning, others may emerge later as secondary symptoms as a result of treatment gains. Patients with long-standing symptoms can also become identified with these symptoms. Effective reprocessing of etiological experiences can lessen the severity of presenting complaints, leading to secondary anxiety over the loss of the symptoms or grief over the time lost to the symptoms. These emerging secondary loss issues can then become the targets for further reprocessing in subsequent sessions.

One example of emerging secondary loss issues is what occurred with Brianna, an adult survivor of childhood sexual abuse who had long-standing social anxiety and isolation. Her only social support and connection had been a peer-led group of other women survivors of abuse and neglect with similar issues of recurrent nightmares, somatic flashbacks, loss of sense of meaning or belonging, and a strong aversion to romantic relationships. After 2 months of successful EMDR reprocessing of her traumatic memories of childhood sexual abuse, Brianna's recurrent nightmares and somatic re-experiencing had ceased. She developed an emerging sense of hope and optimism. Paradoxically, she began to experience a confusing sense of alienation and guilt in her relationships with the other women in her support group whose symptoms had not abated. Brianna started to feel ambivalent about doing more EMDR reprocessing, but she was unsure about the source of her ambivalence.

Such emerging secondary loss issues need to be identified for possible solutions to develop. The survivor may want to rescue others or motivate them to find effective help in psychotherapy. When not all her peers want such help or do not respond as positively as she did, she may feel increasing guilt. Some survivors may be willing to develop new support systems that foster a larger sense of self through groups that are based on current interests (school or art) or religion (by becoming active in a church). Others may be able to reduce their guilt by reprocessing background issues thematically linked to survivor guilt, such as not having been able to protect a younger sibling from the same perpetrator.

THERAPEUTIC ALLIANCE: TRUST AND TRUTH TELLING

The therapeutic alliance has consistently been found to be a powerful predictor of outcome in psychotherapy (Hovarth, Gaston, & Luborsky, 1993; Summers & Barber, 2003). The therapeutic alliance is also a frequent source of challenge to clinicians working with traumatized patients because of the significant potential for countertransference (Dalenberg, 2000; Pearlman & Courtois, 2005). At a minimum, clinicians need to establish a therapeutic alliance strong enough to permit the degree of honest and accurate patient self-disclosure, which is needed to assess and monitor patient stability and responses to treatment. For patients with excellent premorbid functioning before a single traumatic incident, it is often possible to establish an adequate therapeutic alliance to begin EMDR reprocessing within one or two sessions. On the other hand, when patients' backgrounds include betrayals of trust by caregivers, teachers, or other authority figures, it can be much more challenging to determine when a sufficient alliance has been achieved. It can take weeks or months to establish sufficient trust and truth telling and a therapeutic alliance sufficiently strong to start EMDR reprocessing. Proceeding to attempt EMDR reprocessing of traumatic memories in advance of an appropriate degree of trust and truth telling can put patients at risk for a range of adverse outcomes including mood instability, increased suicidal ideation or urges, self-harming and other tension reduction behaviors, and relapse into substance abuse. Starting reprocessing in advance of an adequate therapeutic alliance puts patients with histories of betrayals of trust at greater risk of ineffective reprocessing, which increases the risk of premature termination of treatment or a decision to reject further treatment with EMDR.

Clinicians should be alert both to direct demands from patients who insist on EMDR reprocessing at the first visit and to subtle pressures such as countertransference fears that the patient will leave treatment unless there is rapid symptom reduction. Clinicians should only commence reprocessing after a sufficiently strong therapeutic alliance has been established to assure accurate and comprehensive assessment and monitoring of patient stability and responses to treatment.

EXTERNAL CRISES

At intake, some patients face external crises, such as a marriage on the verge of divorce, threats of violence from domestic abuse, imminent loss of employment or housing, or financial security. It may be necessary to defer EMDR reprocessing until these crises have passed and the patient is safe and secure. Other environmental stressors can include upcoming deadlines or presentations at work, major family events, or a move to a new residence. Note that some patients may benefit quickly from prompt reprocessing of associated early memories. A careful consideration of these stressors and patient's current strengths and resilience is essential to avoid either needlessly postponing EMDR reprocessing or subjecting the patient to excessive stress from starting trauma resolution work at an inopportune time.

FINANCIAL INSTABILITY

Patients need to have sufficient financial stability to cope with their economic needs. This generally includes the ability to pay for psychotherapy. When a patient's ability to pay for a complete course of treatment or to meet basic economic needs is in doubt, this issue must be addressed before EMDR reprocessing is started to avoid premature termination in the middle of treatment. Sometimes, a combination of problem solving, Resource Development and Installation (RDI), or EMDR reprocessing on the issues related to the financial problems can lead to a stable course of treatment.

For example, Rita was a survivor of early childhood sexual abuse who presented with an episode of recurrent depression and stated that she could only afford a limited course of treatment. Clinical assessment indicated that she would need more extensive treatment than she could afford on the minimal salary she received from her employment in a nonprofit agency. It also emerged that Rita was being underpaid for her skills and contributions, but she lacked the self-confidence to apply for a better paying position for which she was qualified. Over the initial six sessions, while obtaining her history and developing the therapeutic alliance and a treatment plan, I offered Rita a combination of RDI, graded behavioral task assignment, and cognitive restructuring to help her apply for and obtain better employment.

I paradoxically predicted the problem that Rita would face would not be the inability to obtain a suitable job offer, but the need to select wisely from the numerous offers she would receive, the position offering the best combination of pay, benefits, job duties, and opportunities for advancement. After preparing a suitable resume and applying for the first three low-paying open positions she could identify, Rita obtained three job offers, none of which was a dramatic improvement over her current position. However, getting three job offers gave Rita the confidence to apply for better paying, more challenging positions. She soon obtained an excellent position that paid more than 150% of her former pay with excellent benefits—including better mental health coverage. During this time Rita obtained a prescription for an SSRI-type antidepressant that had been helpful in the past. With Rita's mood stabilized from medication and enhanced from taking a series of empowering and self-affirming steps and a stable economic situation, it was then possible to make a successful transition in focus to EMDR reprocessing of the sexual abuse and other adverse events from her childhood that she had wanted to address, but had never been addressed in her previous therapy.

Occasionally, there are no immediate solutions to patients' financial issues and a more limited treatment goal may need to be selected. With problem solving, other patients may be able to secure offers from their family members to pay for the therapy or to find other assistance through a period of financial hardship. In some cases, patients may be engaged in "retail therapy" spending beyond their means while protesting that they cannot afford to pay for their treatment. Regardless of the nature of the financial difficulty, when present, these issues need to be assessed and addressed with appropriate interventions.

HEALTH RISK

EMDR has been employed with a range of comorbid medical issues and generally found to be safe and well tolerated. Common sense and prudent treatment dictate that clinicians consider their patients' health status and medical concerns that may indicate a need to have them and/or their patients consult with their physician. Obviously, when there is a history of or current eye problems, eye movements should not be employed without clearance from a physician. The general health question to be considered is whether a treating physician would consider the degree of psychophysiological arousal that can be stimulated by reprocessing traumatic memories to be a medical risk. Examples of situations that call for consultation with the treating physician include diagnosed heart disease, elevated blood pressure, and being at risk for or with a history of stroke or heart attack.

EMDR and Pregnancy

The question of the safety of EMDR for pregnant women has not been explicitly addressed in the scientific literature. There are no published reports that indicate any danger from EMDR, but isolated anecdotal reports indicate some women have complained of unstable pregnancies after EMDR sessions and believed EMDR was a factor in the need for rest and medical intervention. Such reports cannot be considered scientific evidence of risk, but they should not be casually dismissed either. An appropriate informed consent would probably be to indicate that the risk to pregnancy may be low, but may not be zero and that EMDR reprocessing should only be employed with pregnant women after consultation with the woman's physician.

EMDR and Seizure Disorders

Questions about using EMDR in seizure disorders have been explored in several studies (Lipke, 1995, p. 382; Schneider, Nabavi, & Heuft, 2005). From the available data, it appears that EMDR can be safely applied without increasing the likelihood of genuine epileptic seizures. Patients with pseudoseizures—conversion disorder—have been successfully treated with EMDR (Chemali & Meadows, 2004; Kelley & Selim, 2007), but clinicians should have appropriate education, training, and experience in the diagnosis and treatment of dissociative disorders before offering EMDR reprocessing to patients with potential pseudoseizures (Bowman, 2006; Bowman & Coons, 2000), and should follow the relevant treatment guidelines (Fine, Paulsen, Rouanzoin, Luber, Puk, & Young, 2001; International Society for the Study of Dissociation, 2005).

BIPOLAR DEPRESSION

There have been some reports suggesting that unrecognized bipolar disorders or certain bipolar disorders present with a greater risk of suicide attempts (Muzina, Colangelo, Manning, & Calabrese, 2007; Schneck, 2006). See the section below for more on suicidal ideation and history.

SUICIDAL IDEATION AND ATTEMPTS

There is an extensive literature on assessment of suicide risk and prediction (Bryan & Rudd, 2006; Jacobs & Brewer, 2006; Rudd, Berman, Joiner, Nock, Silverman, Mandrusiak, van Orden, & Witte, 2006). Clinicians should be familiar with procedures for assessing suicide risk and should keep in mind that the single greatest predictor— but by no means the only one—of future suicide attempts is past attempts (Oquendo, Currier, & Mann, 2006; Oquendo, Galfalvy, Russo, Ellis, Grunebaum, Burke, & Mann, 2004). Suicidal ideation by itself is not a strong predictor of suicide attempt, but does call for a more comprehensive assessment. When suicide risk factors are present and elevated, clinicians should postpone EMDR reprocessing and make use of appropriate clinical interventions (Comtois & Linehan, 2006; Jobes, Wong, Conrad, Drozd, & Neal-Walden, 2005) including collaborating with primary case physicians and psychiatrists. When risk factors are present, clinicians should clarify their treatment contract and indicate under what circumstances they must take mandated actions to protect their patients. After the patient has made gains with reduced depression and lower risk of suicide and the clinician has developed a stronger working relationship with the patient, it may be possible to proceed with standard EMDR reprocessing of adverse events or with further ego-strengthening and mood-enhancing applications of RDI (Korn & Leeds, 2002; Spector & Kremer, 2009; Wildwind, 1994).

SELF-INJURY

Self-injurious behaviors exist on a continuum of dangerousness and can serve quite different purposes for different patients. Self-injury is often not suicidal in intent, but even when not suicidal in intent it can lead to self-mutilation and even fatal outcomes (Brown, Comtois, & Linehan, 2002; Hyman, 1999). Self-injury is more common in cases meeting criteria for borderline personality disorder (BPD). The treatment of BPD is beyond the scope of this book. (Clarkin, Levy, Lenzenweger, & Kernberg, 2007; Giesen-Bloo, et al., 2006; Linehan, 1993).

In cases where risk of serious self-injury is low (e.g., in light fingernail scratching on the forearms), it may be possible to proceed directly to EMDR reprocessing.

In other cases of more serious self-injury (e.g., cutting or burning), where there is a risk of mutilation or life threatening injury, initial interventions must focus on bringing the self-injurious behaviors under control before considering EMDR reprocessing (Walsh, 2006). Dangerous self-harm should be fully stabilized before reprocessing and carefully monitored during reprocessing. When self-injury is identified, clinicians should pay additional attention to the degree of the therapeutic alliance to make sure that they will be able to accurately monitor urges and current self-injurious episodes. Clinicians should clarify their treatment contracts and indicate under what circumstances they are mandated to take action to protect the patient. Preliminary evidence of effectiveness of RDI for stabilization of tension-reduction behaviors including self-injury is described by Korn and Leeds (2002).

INJURY TO OTHERS

Patients who have a history or may be at risk of assaultive behaviors need to be assessed and monitored for current risk (Connor, Melloni, & Harrison, 1998; Crouch & Behl, 2001; McEwan, Mullen, & Purcell, 2007; Piquero, Brame, Fagan & Moffitt, 2006). Clinicians should postpone beginning EMDR reprocessing until they have a sufficient working relationship and understanding of patients who are found to be at risk of assaultive behavior to determine whether initial interventions should focus on stabilization and skills development, or whether reprocessing of etiological events would likely resolve memory networks that have contributed to making the patient vulnerable to loss of control. Clinicians should clarify their treatment contract with the patient and that mandated reports may become necessary. See Stowasser (2007) for a discussion of EMDR and family therapy in the treatment of domestic violence.

HIGH-RISK BEHAVIORS

Patients who engage in high-risk behaviors should be assessed for risk of danger to self and others and possible comorbid disorders before clinicians offer them EMDR reprocessing. The term "high-risk behavior" is used broadly here and encompasses a range of behaviors from relatively controllable activities, such as enjoying extreme sports (e.g., rock climbing, white water kayaking, and bungee jumping) to more pathological aggressive high-speed driving, unprotected promiscuous sexual encounters, and drinking games that involve extremely rapid consumption of alcohol. High-risk behaviors can represent a form of self-punishment associated with histories of traumatic exposure, trauma reenactments, or impaired judgment related to a dissociative disorder, attention deficit hyperactivity disorder (ADHD), or other disorders.

DENIAL OF DIAGNOSIS

It is best to postpone EMDR reprocessing when the patient remains in denial of a major diagnosis including bipolar disorder, dissociative identity disorder, any psychotic disorder, or any substance abuse disorder.

ACCIDENT-PRONE SELF

While accident-prone patients may have brain injuries or coordination problems, their accidental injuries may represent intrusions from emotional parts (EP) of their personality (van der Hart, et al., 2006) and may be associated with secondary structural dissociation as found in BPD or dissociative disorder not otherwise specified (DDNOS), or tertiary structural dissociation as found in dissociative identity disorder (DID). Clinicians should make careful assessments and develop hypotheses about the dynamics of their accident-prone patients' behavior before proceeding with EMDR reprocessing.

SUBSTANCE ABUSE

For types of substance abuse that can be threats to life or health, EMDR reprocessing should be postponed until stable recovery is achieved. In the absence of published EMDR treatment outcome research for this population, clinical issues require careful consideration and appropriate informed consent. In cases of chronic relapsers with histories of traumatic exposure that precede onset of substance abuse, clinicians may view the substance abuse as a form of self-medication. For dual-diagnosis cases where the primary diagnosis is viewed as PTSD and prior attempts at treatment of substance abuse as the focus of attention have repeatedly failed, clinicians may decide to offer EMDR reprocessing with appropriate informed consent. However, for dual diagnosis cases where substance abuse preceded and may have led to an increased risk of traumatic exposure, the substance abuse appears to be the primary diagnosis. Preliminary research suggests a specific cognitive-behavioral approach—"Seeking Safety"—may be helpful for these patients (Najavits, Schmitz, Gotthardt, & Weiss, 2005; Najavits, Weiss, Shaw, & Muenz, 1998; Zlotnick, Najavits, Rohsenow, & Johnson, 2003). This research supports an emerging model that for some dual-diagnosis patients, a combination of stabilization and trauma-focused treatment may be helpful (Najavits, Gallop, & Weiss, 2006). Alternative investigational procedures for using EMDR with patients with primary substance abuse issues have been described by several authors (Popky, 2005; Vogelmann-Sine, Sine, Smyth, & Popky, 1998), but have only been subjected to limited formal investigations (Brown, Gilman, & Kelso, 2008; Hase, Schallmayer & Sack, 2008).

COMPULSIVE SEX

Compulsive sexual behavior can be associated with various psychiatric diagnoses (Carnes, 2000; Mick & Hollander, 2006). Dangerousness to self and others needs to be carefully considered. As described above in the section on substance abuse, clinicians need to carefully develop hypotheses about the etiology and dynamics of the compulsive sexual behavior before deciding whether to offer EMDR reprocessing.

COMPULSIVE ACTS: SPENDING AND GAMBLING

Compulsive spending (Black, 2007) or gambling (Dannon, Lowengrub, Gonopolski, Musin & Kotler, 2006) have various etiologies, dynamics, subtypes, and comorbid diagnoses and could remain unstable or be worsened by EMDR reprocessing. Limited treatment outcome research and the absence of EMDR treatment outcome research need to be part of informed consent. Stabilizing interventions should be considered.

ALEXITHYMIA

Mild alexithymia (e.g., problems naming emotions) should not interfere with reprocessing as long as patients can identify the location of sensations associated with the reprocessing of the target material (Sifneos, 1975, 1988; Taylor, Ryan, & Bagby, 1985).

Moderate to severe alexithymia, which interferes with access to affect, is more likely to lead to ineffective reprocessing and may require modifications in procedure. (see chapter 9). Alexithymia by itself is seldom a reason to withhold EMDR, but may be an issue of concern when present with other factors.

FLOODED BY AFFECT

Prolonged intense weeping, anger, terror, or shame during verbal therapy may predict inability to reprocess because of the need for patients to maintain dual attention to both internal experiences and external stimuli with a stance of mindful noticing of whatever material emerges. Affect tolerance and management skills building may need to be the initial focus of attention. Standard reprocessing should not be withheld unless a failure at reprocessing would lead to a refusal to consider reprocessing in the future.

DEPERSONALIZATION AND DEREALIZATION: PRIMARY STRUCTURAL DISSOCIATION

Depersonalization and derealization experiences can be intensely painful, frightening, and shameful for some patients. Depersonalization and derealization, as expressions of primary structural dissociation (van der Hart et al., 2006) are frequently the only dissociative symptoms in patients with PTSD. Patients vary in their willingness and ability to tolerate re-experiencing depersonalization or derealization episodes during psychotherapy. Patients, who frequently depersonalize in verbal therapy are more likely to depersonalize, and sometimes, more severely during reprocessing. Strategies for affect management and self-control—and for decreasing severity of dissociation—may need to be practiced to prepare the patient before reprocessing can succeed.

When more severe secondary and tertiary structural dissociation (van der Hart, et al., 2006) have been ruled out, and patients have been properly prepared and have given informed consent to the possibility of re-experiencing episodes of depersonalization or derealization during reprocessing, these symptoms by themselves are not a reason to withhold EMDR reprocessing. When depersonalization or derealization episodes are identified, clinicians need to be sufficiently thorough in history taking and treatment planning, so they can carefully consider the possible role of early foundational and attachment-related experiences in developing a vulnerability to depersonalization and derealization. However, depersonalization and derealization occur frequently as part of peritraumatic dissociation. Their recurrence during EMDR reprocessing does not always reflect the presence of adverse foundational experiences in need of attention in the treatment plan. Depersonalization and derealization that emerged only after a recent index trauma can frequently be resolved during reprocessing using standard interventions covered in chapters 8 and 9.

AMNESIA, FUGUE, DID, AND DDNOS: SECONDARY AND TERTIARY STRUCTURAL DISSOCIATION

Evidence of past or current fugue or current amnesia episodes—loss of time (American Psychiatric Association, 1994) and other symptoms suggestive of secondary and tertiary structural dissociation (van der Hart, et al., 2006)—indicates a need for more complete assessment of dissociation before considering starting EMDR reprocessing to avoid risk of harm to patient (Paulsen, 1995; Shapiro, 1995, 2001).

A possible current diagnosis of DID or DDNOS (American Psychiatric Association, 1994) indicates a need for more careful assessment of dissociation before reprocessing to avoid risk of harm to patient. Minimum screening procedures to rule out a more severe dissociative disorder include the use of the Dissociative Experiences Scale-II (DES-II; Carlson & Putnam, 1993), the DES Taxon calculator (Waller & Ross, 1997), the SDQ-20 (Nijenhuis, Spinhoven, Van Dyck, Van Der Hart, & Vanderlinden, 1996) or SDQ-5 (Nijenhuis, Spinhoven, van Dyck, van der Hart, & Vanderlinden, 1997) and a focused mental status exam (Lowenstein, 1991). The DES Taxon calculator scores the DES-II—the average of the 28 DES items—using a Microsoft Excel-compatible file and computes the probability that the patient falls into a diagnostic category of a dissociative type. The SDQ-20 and SDQ-5 screen for somatoform dissociation, which is not well covered by the DES-II. Richard Lowenstein's 1991 article, *An Office Mental Status Examination for Complex Chronic Dissociative Symptoms and Multiple Personality Disorder,* remains the most cited introduction for how to conduct a diagnostic interview to screen for symptoms of a dissociative disorder. See the section below on *Dissociative Symptom Instruments* for additional screening tools including structured clinical interviews and Appendix C for how to obtain these tools.

Any unresolved doubts about the presence of a dissociative disorder indicates a need to conduct further assessment and screening and to consider consultation from a clinician with training and experience in diagnosis and treatment of patients with a dissociative disorder. Lack of stabilization in DID or DDNOS, such as uncontrolled rapid switching, uncontrolled flashbacks, or poor cooperation and communication among parts of the personality, indicates a need to postpone reprocessing. Treatment guidelines of both the International Society for the Study of Trauma and Dissociation (ISST-D; International Society for the Study of Dissociation, 2005) and the EMDR task force (Fine, Paulsen, Rouanzoin, Luber, Puk & Young, 2001) should be followed. The ISST-D treatment guidelines are freely available on their Web site as listed in appendix C.

USE OF STANDARDIZED ASSESSMENT TOOLS

Standardized assessment tools can provide additional information for multiaxial symptom identification not easily or efficiently obtained through clinical interviews. Some patients will more easily disclose the full range of their symptoms and concerns when reporting them initially with paper and pencil. However, clinicians need to be aware that self-report instruments have limited abilities to detect symptoms in some patients (Shedler, Mayman & Manis, 1993); thus, they should never be considered a substitute for skilled clinical assessment. Standardized assessments can be helpful in screening for dissociative disorders. They are essential when tracking treatment outcomes both for quality assurance purposes and when making formal reports for either forensic or scientific purposes. This next section summarizes standardized assessment tools that clinicians may find helpful for the range of applications of EMDR covered in this volume. Information for obtaining these instruments is listed in appendix C.

OBJECTIVE SELF-REPORT SYMPTOM ASSESSMENTS

The Symptom Checklist 90-R (SCL90R) is a widely used 90-item comprehensive screen for symptoms with specific subscales and global scales. The Brief Symptom Inventory (BSI) is a shorter 18-item version of this instrument. Both have excellent test–retest reliability and, thus, are useful for measuring progress during treatment, as well as for tracking treatment outcomes for research and reports.

TRAUMA SYMPTOM ASSESSMENT

There are many adult PTSD self-report instruments (see Carlson, 1997). A summary of many of these instruments is available through the National Center for PTSD. Qualified clinicians may obtain copies of many of these instruments for a nominal fee by completing a request form at http://www.ncptsd.va.gov/ncmain/assessment/

The Posttraumatic Checklist—Civilian (PCL-C)

The PCL-C is a 17-item self-report, paper and pencil test based on *Diagnostic and Statistical Manual of Mental Disorders (DSM-IV)* criteria for PTSD. It is a US government document in the public domain. Research shows internal consistency, test–retest reliability, convergent validity, and discriminant validity (Walker, Newman, Dobie, Ciechanowski, & Katon, 2002). It is brief enough to be used for test–retest and, thus, is helpful for tracking treatment gains and outcome. It can be downloaded directly from the Web site of The Georgetown Center for Trauma and the Community in the tool kit area.

The Impact of Events Scale (IES and IES-R)

The Impact of Events Scale (IES) is widely used 15-item self-report scale for assessing the intrusion and avoidance symptoms of PTSD (Horowitz, Wilner, & Alvarez, 1979). IES-R is a revised 22-item—with 7 hyperarousal items added—self-report scale for assessing the intrusion, avoidance, and hyperarousal symptoms of PTSD (Weiss & Marmar, 1997). Both have been available from various Web sites. While the IES-R and IES are not intended to diagnose PTSD without further clinical assessment, various cutoff scores have been cited in the literature (Coffey, Gudmundsdottir, Beck, Palyo, & Miller, 2006) ranging from 27 to 29 for the IES and 33 to 35 for the IES-R for a preliminary diagnosis of PTSD.

The Trauma Symptom Inventory (TSI)

The TSI is a 100-item commercial instrument that provides a thorough screen for trauma symptoms with 3 validity scales (Briere, 1995). While it is not a formal *DSM*-based diagnostic test of PTSD, the TSI shows trauma-related symptom severity in several symptom subscales. Its validity scales help assess response style for forensic reports. It includes three subscales that assess impaired self-capacities often affected by repeated or prolonged trauma exposure.

The Clinician Administered PTSD Scale (CAPS)

The CAPS provides a structured PTSD diagnostic interview that evaluates both long-term and current PTSD symptoms and diagnostic status (Blake et al., 1995). Depending on the extent of patients' symptoms, the CAPS requires 40 to 60 minutes to administer. It is available on request from the National Center for PTSD and for a fee from Western Psychological Services.

The Inventory of Altered Self Capacities (IASC)

The IASC is a 63-item self-report assessment tool that measures seven types of "self-related" difficulties, such as identity problems, affect dysregulation, and interpersonal conflicts that are features of BPD (Briere, 2000). With a history of repeated or prolonged trauma exposure, these altered self-capacities are considered part of "complex PTSD" (Herman, 1992; Pelcovitz, van der Kolk, Roth, Mandel, Kaplan, & Resick, 1997).

The Trauma Assessment Packet

The Trauma Assessment Packet includes four test instruments, along with three research and clinical articles, which together provide a comprehensive assessment of trauma histories at different ages. Using an optional Microsoft Excel-based scoring system clinicians can track patient progress. The four test instruments described below are the Traumatic Antecedents Questionnaire (TAQ), the Modified PTSD Symptom Scale, the Structured Interview for Disorders of Extreme Stress (SIDES) and Self-Report Instrument for Disorders of Extreme Stress (SIDES-SR), the and Trauma-Focused Initial Adult Clinical Evaluation. The Trauma Assessment Packet is available from The Trauma Center at Justice Resource Institute (see appendix C).

The Traumatic Antecedents Questionnaire (TAQ)

The TAQ is a self-report assessment tool that gathers developmental information about lifetime experiences in 10 domains: (a) competence, (b) safety, (c) neglect, (d) separations, (e) family secrets, (f) conflict resolution, (g) physical trauma, (h) sexual trauma, (i) witnessing trauma, and (j) exposure to drugs and alcohol. These domains are assessed at four age periods: birth to 6 years, 7 to 12 years, 13 to 18 years, and adulthood. The TAQ provides crucial developmentally based information for organizing case formulation and treatment planning.

The Modified PTSD Symptom Scale

The Modified PTSD Symptom Scale is a 17-item scale that asks patients to rate the frequency and intensity of *DSM-IV* PTSD symptoms in the past 2 weeks regarding intrusions, re-experiencing, avoidance and numbing, and increased arousal.

The Structured Interview for Disorders of Extreme Stress (SIDES)

The SIDES and the Self-Report Instrument for Disorders of Extreme Stress (SIDES-SR) are both 45-item scales that assess the presence and severity of the proposed diagnosis disorders of extreme stress not otherwise specified (DESNOS), which is found in the Associated Features of PTSD (American Psychiatric Association, 1994). The clinician-rater version was used in the *DSM-IV* Field Trials for PTSD, and has been validated as a measure of DESNOS diagnosis. The self-report version has good behavioral anchors and good internal reliability as a measure of current DESNOS severity. Both versions of the SIDES consist of six major scales with related subscales indicating alterations in: (a) regulation of affect and impulses, (b) attention or consciousness, (c) self-perception, (d) relations with other, (e) somatization, and (f) systems of meaning.

The Trauma Focused Initial Adult Clinical Evaluation

The Trauma-Focused Initial Adult Clinical Evaluation is a structured clinical interview that can be used to facilitate a comprehensive intake for new patients. It explores trauma history, associated symptoms, current internal resources, social supports, substance abuse, and treatment history.

DISSOCIATIVE SYMPTOM ASSESSMENT

The Dissociative Experiences Scale (DES-II)

The DES-II is 28-item self-report assessment tool for screening primarily cognitive dissociative symptoms (Bernstein & Putnam, 1986). It is copyrighted and placed in the public domain. Because it contains a mixture of items that address nonpathological constructs as well as those that are symptomatic of structural dissociation, clinicians are strongly encouraged to score not only the global DES-II average score, but also to compute the DES Taxon score (DES-T; Waller & Ross, 1997) by using the DES Taxon calculator—an Microsoft Excel 97 compatible spreadsheet—which is freely available for download from http://www.isst-d.org/education/des-taxon-portal.htm.

The Somatoform Dissociation Questionnaire (SDQ-5 and SDQ-20)

The SDQ-5 and SDQ-20 addresses somatoform manifestations of dissociative processes and can detect aspects of structural dissociation that are not addressed in the DES II (Nijenhuis, et al., 1996, 1997). The 20-item SDQ-20 evaluates the severity of somatoform dissociation. The five-item SDQ-5 screens for *DSM-IV* dissociative disorders. They are both available without charge at: http://www.enijenhuis.nl/sdq.html

The Multidimensional Inventory of Dissociation (MID)

The Multidimensional Inventory of Dissociation (MID) is a 218-item, self-report, multi-scale instrument that assesses pathological dissociation and diagnoses the dissociative disorders (Dell, 2006a, 2006b). Those who request a copy of the MID receive: (a) the MID, (b) its Excel-based scoring program, (c) the directions for using that scoring program, and (d) the MID Mini-Manual. The MID is useful for both clinical research and diagnostic assessment of patients with a mixture of dissociative, posttraumatic, and borderline symptoms. The MID is the most comprehensive measure of pathological dissociation that has been developed to date (Dell & Lawson, 2009). It has shown internal reliability, as well as temporal, convergent, discriminant, and construct validity as well as incremental validity over the DES. When brief screening with the DES-T, the SDQ, or clinical observations suggests that a more comprehensive assessment is needed; the MID is extremely useful for clarifying the diagnosis. The MID is in the public domain; it is freely available upon request—without charge—to all mental health professionals from the members' area of the International Society for the Study of Trauma and Dissociation at: http://www.isst-d.org/ or by request from PFDell@aol.com.

The Structured Clinical Interview for DSM-IV

The Structured Clinical Interview for *DSM-IV* Dissociative Disorders-Revised (SCID-D-R) (Steinberg, 1994) has been reported in several studies in the United States and other countries (Steinberg, 2000) to have a good-to-excellent reliability and validity. It is widely accepted in forensic evaluations and is useful for treatment planning and differential diagnosis. It is commercially available.

The Dissociative Disorders Interview Schedule (DDIS)

The DDIS is a structured interview intended to assist in the *DSM-IV* diagnosis of somatization disorder, BPD and major depressive disorder, as well as all five dissociative disorders (Anderson, Yasenik, & Ross, 1993; Ross & Joshi, 1992). It includes questions about positive symptoms of schizophrenia, secondary features of DID, extrasensory experiences, substance abuse, and symptoms relevant to the dissociative disorders. It is available from the Web site of the Ross Institute at: http://www.rossinst.com/dddquest.htm

THE ROLE OF PATIENT RECORD KEEPING AND FEEDBACK

In developing and adjusting their treatment plans, clinicians depend on accurate information from patients about their current symptoms, stressors, and responses to treatment. While some patients may be capable of providing concise and accurate summaries when they present for their next session, most patients offer incomplete information, which can be significantly influenced by their emotional state at the time of the session. Therefore, having patients keep a brief written record of their current symptoms and their responses to current stressors is extremely helpful.

Unlike prolonged imaginal exposure, which requires extensive daily homework assignments (for example, Foa & Rothbaum, 1998), the EMDR approach to psychotherapy does not require patients to do extensive self-directed homework. Instead, all that is needed in EMDR is for patients to do simple self-monitoring and brief documenting of current issues. Two kinds of self-monitoring can be useful. The first is tracking frequency and severity of a selected, primary symptom such as nightmares or panic attacks. This type of self-monitoring is generally done daily with a 1- to 2-minute recording of the selected symptom's occurrence and severity. The second type of self-monitoring is a simple log for documenting responses to current stressors and any current symptoms. Both types of self-monitoring can be done using a brief log entry. A simple patient log based on the elements of the memory network is described in the next chapter.

ASSESSING STABILITY AND READINESS FOR TRAUMA REPROCESSING

In this chapter, we examined essential criteria to consider when assessing patient stability and readiness for EMDR Reprocessing. Table 5.1 "Assessing Stability and Readiness for Reprocessing" provides a single-page summary of these essential criteria with rating scales. This form is intended to assist clinicians in organizing their clinical assessments of patients' readiness for EMDR reprocessing for their own records and for presentation to clinical consultants or supervisors. The rating scales for each item indicate relative severity of specific items, but are not intended to be scored or totaled. While bold items are generally considered more critical in the assessment of patient stability, an "Assessing Stability and Readiness for Reprocessing" form with zeros on all of the bold, critical items does not necessarily indicate readiness for reprocessing. Any one of the items listed, such as financial instability, denial of diagnosis, or trust or absence of truth, could be an indicator of a need to postpone EMDR reprocessing and to focus on stabilization. Good clinical judgment will always be the final guide for determining when patients are ready to begin EMDR reprocessing. While some patients will present with sufficient stability to begin EMDR reprocessing during the second treatment session, others will require more extended preparation. In chapter 6, we will turn our attention to the preparation phase (phase 3) and explore a range of basic strategies for preparing patients suffering from PTSD for EMDR reprocessing.

The Preparation Phase

OVERVIEW PHASE 2

In this chapter, we will examine how to prepare patients for the reprocessing phases of EMDR. The essential elements of the preparation phase covered in this chapter include providing patients the essential information needed for informed consent; offering guidance and metaphors to orient patients to standard EMDR reprocessing procedures and that foster an attitude of mindful noticing that supports effective reprocessing. Other essential tasks include introducing patients to bilateral stimulation to verify their tolerance for bilateral eye movements or alternate forms of bilateral stimulation and providing additional skills building as needed to assure that patients have the skills and capacities needed to cope with their current symptoms and the process of treatment with EMDR.

STABILIZATION AND THE CONSENSUS MODEL

The preparation phase in the EMDR approach to treatment corresponds with the initial stabilization or ego-strengthening phase of treatment in the consensus model of treatment for trauma discussed in chapter 1 (Briere, 1996; Brown & Fromm, 1986; Chu, 1998; Courtois, 1988, 1999; Gil, 1988; Horowitz, 1979, 1986; Kluft, 1993, 1999; McCann & Pearlman, 1990; Putnam, 1989; Scurfield, 1985; van der Hart & Friedman, 1989; van der Kolk, McFarlane, & Weisaeth, 1996). The consensus model of treating trauma is informed by the work of Pierre Janet (1889, 1977) and emphasizes the importance of providing sufficient stabilization before and during uncovering—history taking—and resolving traumatic memories with EMDR reprocessing. In addition to stabilization, primary tasks in the preparation phase include the following:

- Forming a therapeutic alliance
- Psychoeducation on the EMDR approach to resolving traumatic experiences
- Assessment of responses to bilateral stimulation procedures

Patients vary widely in the extent to which they need different kinds of preparation for EMDR reprocessing. For example, some patients need only basic information about trauma and EMDR to make an informed choice to move forward with EMDR treatment. Other patients want extensive information about EMDR's research base, theories of EMDR's mechanism, and case illustrations to develop a sense of understanding EMDR and to make an informed decision to consent to treatment.

Most patients with single incident posttraumatic stress disorder (PTSD) have some anxiety, mood, or dissociative symptoms, but require only limited stabilization interventions in one or at most two sessions. However, patients with multiple and complex trauma histories with serious anxiety, mood, or dissociative symptoms need a different kind of preparation. They may require extensive stabilization interventions before and during history taking and treatment planning as well as occasionally during the reprocessing phases of treatment. To be ready to participate in clinical bilateral stimulation procedures, most patients need only 2 to 3 minutes of practice with bilateral eye movements, taps, or tones. However, for others, there can be medical issues—a history of eye problems—or difficulties with accommodating to the mechanics of bilateral stimulation that require greater flexibility and time before the patient is ready.

THE THERAPEUTIC ALLIANCE

The therapeutic alliance is the foundation for all psychotherapy (Hovarth, Gaston, & Luborsky, 1993; Pearlman & Courtois, 2005; Summers & Barber, 2003). Research consistently indicates that the degree of therapeutic alliance is more strongly associated with a positive outcome in psychotherapy than the method or years of experience of the clinician (Seligman, 1995). There have not yet been formal studies of the role of the therapeutic alliance in EMDR treatment outcome among patients suffering from PTSD, but there has been a lively debate within the EMDR community on the assertion that the therapeutic alliance may be less important than fidelity in application, especially in cases of single episode trauma exposure. As case complexity increases, the role of the therapeutic alliance becomes more central (Pearlman & Courtois, 2005; Spinhoven, Giesen–Bloo, van Dyck, Kooiman, & Arntz, 2007).

While some may mistakenly consider EMDR to be a "technique" less dependent on the therapeutic alliance, EMDR is an approach to psychotherapy where successful outcomes depend on meeting the unique needs of each patient. Accurate empathy, appropriate pacing, and responding to moments of expressed concern or misattunements are just as important in achieving successful outcomes in structured EMDR treatment plans as in any other form of psychotherapy. The amount of time and attention that must be given to establishing the therapeutic alliance varies more based on patient characteristics and needs than on the specific methodology or approach.

The time needed to establish a sufficient therapeutic alliance before beginning reprocessing can vary from a few minutes to months. In disaster response and urban terrorism situations, a modified EMDR protocol is used with an abbreviated approach to the therapeutic alliance appropriate to acute care settings (see Fernandez, 2008; Kutz, et al., 2008). In the context of cases where the standard EMDR protocol will be used, clinicians should generally plan to allow a minimum of two sessions to accomplish the essential tasks for phases 1 and 2 before starting reprocessing of the first target memory. In cases where there is a history of chronic betrayal of trust, clinicians will need to allow considerably more time to establish an adequate therapeutic alliance and develop an appropriate treatment plan. Additional issues related to establishing and maintaining the therapeutic alliance are discussed further in the sections below.

CLINICAL SKILLS AND BEHAVIORS THAT ENHANCE THE THERAPEUTIC ALLIANCE

Elements of clinician skill and behavior that enhance the therapeutic alliance include the following:

- Accurate empathy
- Communicating a clear case conceptualization that makes sense to the patient
- Pacing of interventions to patient readiness

■ Cultural sensitivity and appropriateness
■ Willingness and ability to repair patient experiences of misattunement

At a minimum, before commencing EMDR reprocessing, clinicians need to assure that there is a sufficient therapeutic alliance to be confident of current and accurate reporting of patient symptoms and responses to treatment. If the patient cannot disclose urges or actual relapse into substance use, self-injury, or dangerous acting out, then it is not safe to begin reprocessing. The greater the presence of risk factors, as described in chapter 5, the greater the need to assure a sufficient therapeutic alliance. The number of sessions needed to forge a therapeutic alliance adequate to the needs of the patient before offering EMDR reprocessing varies from as little as one session to several months. The more patient histories involve experiences of betrayal of trust, insecure attachment, and social manipulation, the greater the time needed to form an adequate therapeutic alliance.

PATIENT EDUCATION

An essential aspect of the preparation phase is patient education. Patients need to understand the following:

■ Their diagnosis
■ Their symptoms
■ The impact of trauma
■ The stages of the treatment plan
■ What to expect during EMDR reprocessing

These elements are essential both to legally required informed consent to treatment and to prepare patients for the experiences they are likely to encounter during treatment with EMDR.

A wealth of online and print resources is available to assist in patient education about the impact of trauma, its treatment, and specifically EMDR. A selection of these resources is listed in appendix C. The EMDR International Association (EMDRIA) produces brochures intended to help orient patients to EMDR treatment. The EMDR Humanitarian Assistance Programs (EMDR HAP) online store provides some helpful audiovisual materials on EMDR. A helpful book for many patients is *EMDR: The Breakthrough Therapy for Overcoming Anxiety, Stress, and Trauma* by Francine Shapiro and Margo Silk Forrest (1997). This book provides a clear overview of EMDR and its development written for patients and their families. It includes a wide range of stories of clinical successes where the EMDR approach has helped survivors of many different kinds of traumatic experiences. Another helpful introduction to EMDR with additional patient resources on ways to treat anxiety and depression can be found in *The Instinct to Heal: Curing Depression, Anxiety, and Stress Without Drugs and Without Talk Therapy* by David Servan-Schreiber (2004).

INFORMED CONSENT TO TREATMENT WITH EMDR

EMDR is an empirically supported treatment for disorders that develop after exposure to traumatic and other adverse life experiences. Extensive published case reports, as described in chapter 1, suggest that it can be useful in a wide range clinical case. Informed consent to treatment with EMDR should touch on at least three main issues discussed in this section. These are reexperiencing aspects of the traumatic event, remembering suppressed or dissociated material, and changes in the ways memories are experienced. Additional broader issues of informed consent and psychoeducation will be explored throughout this chapter.

REEXPERIENCING ASPECTS OF TRAUMATIC AND ADVERSE MEMORIES

The first issue with informed consent, as with any trauma-informed and trauma-focused approach, is that patients need to be prepared for a certain amount of reexperiencing of central aspects of the memories of traumatic and adverse events that are addressed with EMDR reprocessing. This can lead to emotionally intense reexperiencing of painful feelings. If the original experiences included physically painful sensations from injuries, these may be reexperienced. If the original experience included unwanted sexual arousal, the patient could reexperience these sensations again during reprocessing. Generally, the period of reexperiencing is a matter of a few minutes at most. It is essential that patients be made aware of and adequately prepared to face this possibility. Failure to discuss and prepare patients for the kinds of reexperiencing that they are most likely to encounter exposes patients to being caught off guard and experiencing needless additional shame, distress, or fear. After successful reprocessing, patients will be at dramatically less risk of such reexperiencing ever occurring again at such a vivid level.

REMEMBERING FORGOTTEN, SUPPRESSED, AND DISSOCIATED MATERIAL

Second, as discussed in chapter 4, there is a significantly greater tendency for forgotten, suppressed, and dissociated material to reemerge into awareness during EMDR (Lipke, 1995). Patients must be prepared to accept the possibility that they will recall disturbing aspects of memories that had minimized or forgotten or other memories may emerge that they had forgotten. For guidance on how to address this issue, see the discussion in chapter 4 on reports from the APA and International Society for Traumatic Stress Studies (ISTSS) on the nature of memory and the plasticity of memory.

VIVIDNESS OF SENSORY INTRUSIONS TENDS TO FADE

Third, sensory aspects of memories for traumatic and adverse life experiences tend to fade after reprocessing, as they normally tend to do with ordinary memories. After successful reprocessing, patients who have always had intrusive scenes, smells, or physical sensations associated with certain memories may be unable to retrieve them as vivid sensory experiences. Contrary to myths that some patients may have formed, EMDR does not erase memories. Patients do not lose their memories, but after successful reprocessing, they will be experienced as "just an old memory," not as a form of reexperiencing

This tendency for fading of sensory vividness may be a concern in some forensic situations where the patient may be called on to give testimony after EMDR reprocessing. This may be due in part to uninformed assumptions about possible similarities between hypnosis and EMDR. Hypnotically, enhanced recall and hypnotherapy can legally "contaminate" eyewitness testimony in some jurisdictions (Webert, 2003). However, scholars do not view standard EMDR reprocessing as a form of hypnosis (Nicosia, 1995).

Before commencing EMDR reprocessing, it can be prudent in criminal and some civil cases to request the patient to provide a written release to discuss these issues with the prosecuting or civil attorney. In high-profile legal cases, depositions can be given and videotaped before EMDR reprocessing and psychotherapy sessions can be videotaped or audiotaped to provide further documentation that no hypnotic or other suggestive interventions were used to alter the contents of the patient's memory.

Informed consent in such forensic situations should not become refusal to treat on the part of clinicians. The patient with a broken leg gets an x-ray, and then the leg is properly set and put into a cast. The orthopedic physician does not postpone appropriate medical care until after the trial. Similarly, we provide relevant information about EMDR treatment, obtain informed consent, clarify issues and procedures as needed with the relevant attorney, and then proceed to provide appropriate treatment.

Another potential issue that can arise with the tendency of memories to become less vivid is that some patients may fear losing their only memories for highly meaningful experiences. This can be the case with patients with recent traumatic losses of a family member and with combat veterans with the loss of a member of their unit. See Silver & Rogers (2002, p. 84, pp. 111–114) for a discussion of addressing these and other fears with combat veterans. While EMDR does tend to make traumatic memories less vivid and intrusive, these memories are not forgotten. More importantly, with traumatic loses, there can be an inability to access the positive memories. With successful reprocessing, these positive memories tend to resurface and to become more accessible as patients move out of the mood state associated with their traumatic losses. Providing this information can help assuage these fears.

ESTABLISHING THE FRAMEWORK FOR TRAUMA-INFORMED PSYCHOTHERAPY

The first and most important issue in psychoeducation is for patients to understand that what they experience as debilitating symptoms are normal responses to adverse life events. Patients suffering from PTSD may or may not be aware of their diagnoses when they enter treatment. Of those who are aware that their symptoms are the result of exposure to traumatic experiences, many blame themselves as defective and weak for not recovering on their own and "just getting over it." Many others who are suffering from chronic PTSD who enter treatment are unaware of or not able to fully realize the cause of their symptoms. This is true of both adult survivors of childhood abuse and those with combat-related PTSD. These patients may privately believe that they are intrinsically defective or "crazy" in part because they do not fully realize the connections between the adverse events in their pasts and their symptoms. In particular, many survivors of chronic childhood abuse do not enter treatment, viewing themselves as "victims of abuse." They are unaware of the nature of their status. Before they can enter into the recovery process (Hansen, 1991) and progress from "victim" to "survivor" and finally "thriver," they must first learn to recognize the cause of their condition.

NORMALIZING THE ONSET OF PTSD AFTER EXPOSURE TO TRAUMATIC EXPERIENCES

For those with histories of exposure to traumatic life experiences, normalizing the development of PTSD is essential. Psychoeducation can be an essential element of preparing these patients even before starting a detailed exploration of their history and assessment of their current functioning and symptoms. The 1995 National Comorbidity Survey showed rates of exposure to traumatic events to be 60% for men and 50% for women, with the majority being exposed to multiple traumatic events (Kessler et al., 1995). For those exposed to childhood abuse or neglect the risk of developing PTSD was found to be over 30% for men and nearly 60% for women (Kessler et al., 1999). The risk of developing PTSD for men exposed to combat trauma was reported at nearly 30%, whereas after rape, the rate was over 45% for both men and women. (Kessler et al, 1999). The much more common exposures of witnessing someone being seriously injured or killed and being in a life-threatening accident, fire, flood, or natural disaster carried lower but still significant rates of risk ranging from 10%–23% (Kessler et al., 1999). The actual risks of developing PTSD may be even higher than these numbers indicate, as they do not reflect the cumulative effect of a history exposure to multiple traumatic experiences that is common in clinical settings.

Exposure to adverse life events is not just a risk factor for developing PTSD, but increases vulnerability to all the most common premature causes of death. This has been described in a remarkable series of studies (Felitti, et al., 1998) on the effects of adverse childhood experiences (ACE) on adult health. The ACE studies are an ongoing collaboration between Kaiser Permanente's Department of Preventive Medicine in San Diego, California, and the U.S. Centers for Disease Control and Prevention. See the Resources section on Childhood Trauma in Appendix C.

"SEEING IS BELIEVING": BRAIN IMAGES OF PTSD PATIENTS BEFORE AND AFTER TREATMENT

Often, a brief explanation of how the brain's defensive systems respond to adverse and traumatic events can help patients realize that posttraumatic stress responses reflect real neurochemical injuries to the brain. Summaries and images from single photon emission computed tomography (SPECT) brain imaging research on trauma survivors demonstrate to patients that they are suffering from real injuries. These injuries, while they are not visible to the unaided eye, are visible with modern technology. More importantly, SPECT images of PTSD patients before and after effective treatment—such as those in Lansing, Amen, Hanks, and Rudy (2005)—help reassure patients that treatment can make an effective difference in their recovery.

THE NEUROBIOLOGY OF TRAUMA AND MEMORY

Some patients may also benefit from basic information about the differences in how normal memories are stored in the brain versus how traumatic memories are stored. See van der Kolk (1996) for a summary of the neurobiology of trauma. Normal memories are encoded primarily in the left cerebral hemisphere and in the hippocampus as coherent narratives of the experience. The hippocampus is located in the brain stem and is the indexing center for complex memories. The hippocampus also holds information about the "where" and "when" experience occurs.

Trauma memories are encoded primarily in the right hemisphere as sensory memories and in the amygdala. The amygdala is the defensive center in the brain where fight, flight, and submission responses (among others) take place. Sensory threat cues (sights, sounds, body sensations, and smells) are encoded in the amygdala. The amygdala retains a database of all threat cues to allow us to respond quickly, and *without thought*, to danger. A breakdown in the discrimination of threat cues in trauma survivors leads to persistent, recurring overly defensive reactions and intrusions from relatively innocuous stimuli. Stress hormones secreted by the amygdala lead to inhibitions in the function of the hippocampus in trauma survivors and, if untreated, to actual shrinkage in the size of the hippocampus. The excessive activation in the amygdala tends to dampen activation in the orbital prefrontal regions of the brain, just above the eyes in the forehead, inhibiting the normal executive function of exercising thoughtful control over impulses. Thus, when memories of trauma intrude, they tend to produce a state of "speechless terror" (van der Kolk, 1996) in which they are not really "remembering," but instead are helplessly re-experiencing their traumatic experiences.

The Adaptive Information Processing (AIP) model parallels what is known about the neurobiology of how the brain moves memories of traumatic and adverse life experiences from this maladaptive, temporary storage system—sometimes referred to as implicit memory—into adaptive long-term storage in the narrative—or explicit memory system (Schacter, 1987). This reorganization and consolidation occurs during dreaming or rapid eye movement (REM) sleep. It may well be one of the mechanisms behind the effectiveness of EMDR (Stickgold, 2002, 2008).

While many contemporary forms of psychotherapy rely primarily on getting the patient to consider or rehearse new thoughts, EMDR depends on stimulating the brain's intrinsic capacity for adaptive information processing. This capacity is not driven by deliberate thought, but by deeper, intrinsic structural capacities in the brain to adapt to and learn from experience. *Indeed, during periods of bilateral stimulation with eye movements, taps, or tones in EMDR reprocessing, most patients are not capable of holding specific thoughts in mind.* This inability to deliberately retain images or thoughts in awareness is normal and needs to be explained to patients as part of the preparation phase to prevent patients from judging themselves as somehow failing or not doing EMDR correctly. On the other hand, during reprocessing some patients will experience a wealth of vivid images, body sensations, emotions, associations to other memories, insights, disturbing or pleasant thoughts, and even smells.

RIDING A TRAIN: A METAPHOR FOR MINDFUL NOTICING

One of the most effective ways of conveying a helpful orientation to patients is with the metaphor of riding a train. This metaphor helps patients take on a stance of mindful noticing without pressuring or judging themselves. It provides clinicians a rich opportunity to provide the essential information patients need about what to expect and how to prepare for the experience of EMDR reprocessing.

 | The Train Metaphor

A helpful way to approach EMDR reprocessing is to think of what it is like when you ride a train. You get on the train in the station and find a seat. Looking out of the window of the train, you notice what you can see out of the windows before the train starts the journey. This is how your trauma memory may seem to you before you begin. There are parts of your memory that you may be aware of or have feelings about, but there may be other parts that may be hidden at this point. As the train pulls out of the station, the scenery may appear to be quickly changing and flickering past the window of the train like it does in the city with nearby buildings, trees, and vehicles. At times, the scenery may appear to be barely changing as it does when you have a distant view of the mountains. Other times, it may be like you are in a tunnel where you can no longer see any scenery and you just have a sense of movement.

We will do the eye movements (or taps or tones) for about 45–60 seconds and then stop. That is like when the train pulls into the next station and stops. At that point, I will ask you to rest, take a deeper breath, and tell me what you are noticing. You do not need to try to describe what you noticed while the train was going down the tracks, just let me know whatever you're aware of as you are in the train at the station. If things seem to be changing, then I will just tell you to start with what you are noticing at that point and go forward again. If they appear not to be changing, I may change the direction of the eye movements or the speed of the stimulation. When the train starts down the track, you do not have to try to hold in mind where you were or try to think about anything in particular.

From time to time, I will ask you to bring your attention back to your memory and I may ask you to rate how disturbing it seems to you now. Sometimes, it may have changed or it may not have changed. It could be more disturbing or less disturbing. Just give as clear feedback as you can without judging what should be happening. There are no "should's" or "supposed to's" during EMDR reprocessing. Just notice whatever happens without judging whether it should be happening or not. You cannot do EMDR incorrectly. Whatever happens will allow us to move forward through the material that is emerging.

If at any point you feel you need to stop the reprocessing just raise your hand like this or this. (First, show one palm up, facing patient; then show the "time out" signal with tips of fingers of one hand touching palm of other hand.) Show me how you would do that please. Good. Do you have any questions or concerns?

6.2 | Explaining the Three Phases of Treatment

The standard EMDR treatment plan applies EMDR reprocessing in three stages. These stages focus in turn on the past, the present, and the future.

In the first stage, reprocessing is applied to the memory of traumatic events. For patients with one or a few traumatic memories, it typically takes between one and three reprocessing sessions to fully resolve a single memory. For patients with chronic traumatic experiences in early childhood, some traumatic memories may require a little more work, but most individual memories will be resolved in one to three sessions. When there are repeated traumatic experiences of a similar kind, not every individual memory needs to be reprocessed separately. Generally, it is only necessary to reprocess the first, worst, and last time it happened and then check to see if there are any other residual disturbing memories in that cluster. We might also reprocess nightmares along with any intrusive memories. In a systematic, but flexible way, we will work through all the memories that need attention until they are no longer disturbing.

Then we will turn our attention to current cues that still are capable of stimulating distressing thoughts, feelings, or behavioral impulses. These persistent tendencies to respond defensively are encoded during traumatic experiences in a part of the emotional brain called the *amygdala*, also known as the fight, flight, and submission center. The amygdala evolved to always remember past threat cues and react quickly without conscious thought. These defensive responses can persist even after the trauma memories have completely faded. So in the second stage of treatment, we will reprocess external cues (e.g., images, sounds, or smells) and internal cues (e.g., a fast heartbeat or rapid breathing) that still provoke distressing thoughts, feelings, or behavioral impulses. Keeping a simple written record of those kinds of reactions can help us monitor your responses to treatment and help us plan what needs attention in the second stage of treatment.

After we have reprocessed current cues and they no longer provoke distress, we will turn our attention to the future. Together, we will mentally rehearse coping with any future situations that are likely to arise. We can resolve remaining anticipatory anxieties and rehearse new skills for coping effectively until you feel well prepared for what lies ahead.

PHASES OF TREATMENT

In the preparation phase, in addition to psychoeducation about the nature of trauma and what to expect during EMDR reprocessing, clinicians should offer an overview of the phases of treatment for the treatment plan they recommend to the patient. In most cases, the treatment plan will follow the three-pronged model of past, present, and future described in chapter 3. Explaining this model of treatment is not only part of appropriate informed consent to treatment, but it also helps to prevent any sense of failure or inadequacy in patients.

A significant percentage of patients will continue to experience reactivity to current cues even after successful reprocessing of their memories of traumatic experiences. Even after both past disturbing memories and current cues have been fully reprocessed, patients may still have a need to address anticipatory anxieties or to strengthen new skills with mental rehearsal in the future template. Briefly explaining the three phases of treatment in the preparation phase helps to normalize expectations for what will take place over the course of a series of treatment sessions. When this psychoeducation has been provided in the preparation phase, then later in the midst of treatment, if patients become troubled at the persistence of certain symptoms, it is much easier to remind them of the three phases of treatment and how their concerns will be fully address by the treatment plan.

INTRODUCING AND TESTING BILATERAL STIMULATION

For patients who meet readiness criteria and do not require extended stabilization, clinicians will introduce patients to bilateral stimulation without initially focusing on a memory. Once a mode of stimulation has been selected, clinicians will generally offer patients the calm place exercise—described below in Table 6.6—to confirm that this method of bilateral stimulation is well tolerated and effective.

MODES OF STIMULATION

There are three modes of alternating bilateral stimulation employed in EMDR treatment sessions, which include the following: (a) eye movements, (b) auditory tones, and (c) tactile stimulation. The aim in incorporating alternating bilateral stimulation, along with the other procedures in EMDR, is to enhance information processing by engaging the patient's attention with the external stimulation in a way that is safe, well tolerated, and enhances the formation of new, adaptive associations. Most published EMDR research involves the use of the eye movement condition alone. Of studies examining different modes of stimulation, most were with nonclinical subjects where the results may not be generalizable to clinical treatment. These analogue studies do suggest that the eye movements may be more efficient at generating increased cognitive flexibility and novel associations (Kuiken, Bears, Miall, & Smith, 2001–2002) and thus tend to favor the use of bilateral eye movements. With few studies investigating clinical outcomes with specific types of stimulation, it is premature to conclude that methods of bilateral stimulation other than eye movement are as effective. Therefore in general, when patients can tolerate eye movements, they should be considered the primary method for bilateral stimulation. However, patient safety, comfort, and treatment response should guide clinical choices in the mode of stimulation. When patients cannot tolerate eye movements due to dizziness, nausea, or any eye discomfort, alternate forms of bilateral stimulation should be used.

OPTIONS

The original method described by Shapiro (1989a, 1989b, 1995) for generating tracking eye movements begins by placing the clinician's chair slightly to the side of the patient's chair. The clinician does not sit directly in front of the patient to avoid having the clinician's face in the center of the patient's field of vision and to avoid the strain of a "straight arm" position for generating eye movements. Next, the clinician's hand is positioned within a comfortable distance of the patient's face—about the same distance as for reading a book. Then starting—and ending—at the center of the patient's field of vision, the patient begins tracking eye movements while observing the clinician's hand moving from side to side. If necessary, the patient should be instructed to keep the head still so that only the patient's eyes are moving. Generally, the width of the eye movements should cover two-thirds to three-fourths of the patient's horizontal field of vision. The extent of arm movements needed to generate these eye movements will depend on how close the clinician's hand is to the patient's face.

To facilitate ease of visual pursuit and avoid an intrusive quality, the clinician should refrain from pointing the fingers of the moving hand toward the patient's eyes. Instead, to ease observation of the movements, the clinician should hold several fingers or the entire palm perpendicular to the patient's face while the forearm is elevated 30–45 degrees. The resulting hand movements should approximate a straight line. Semicircular or "windshield wiper" type movements should generally be avoided as these can generate considerable eye strain for the patient and have been observed to be less effective than more linear eye movements. To avoid excessive strain, fatigue, or self-injury, the clinician should generate the hand movements from the elbow by moving the forearm as though the fingertips were sliding along a smooth railing, rather than by locking the elbow and generating movements from the shoulder. It will generally be easier to do this with both feet squarely on the floor rather than with one leg crossed over the other. To help approximate this type of arm movement, clinicians can practice the forearm movements by placing an elbow on the top of a chair back or a table.

For some patients, the need to sit considerably closer than is likely to be customary in most psychotherapy settings may require some advance discussion to address any concerns about such physical proximity. To further reduce arm strain or to accommodate patient discomfort with physical proximity, it is possible to use a simple mechanical aid to lengthen the forearm such as an extensible pointer, a ruler, or other lightweight object that can be held in the hand and moved in front of the patient's face. This permits the clinician to sit further away from the patient and to make relatively smaller arm or wrist movements while still generating tracking eye movements of sufficient width.

Smooth pursuit eye movements can be difficult to establish with some patients using the basic method described above. To reduce any incipient struggle over these mechanics, clinicians may encourage patients to "Imagine pushing my fingers with your eyes and I'll follow you." Another option is to ask patients to switch the direction of gaze from side to side by placing the clinician spreading their arms apart and placing one hand on either side of the patient's face and alternately raising one or more fingers on each hand.

Alternating auditory tones may be easily generated by side by placing the clinician's hands toward the sides of the patient's face and gently snapping fingers, using a small clicker or the taping the bottoms of two small paper cups. Some clinicians have described using long-handled, cork-tipped mallets to alternately tap on the arms of the patient's chair as a way to generate alternating tones.

Prior to the advent of technological aids, alternate touches on the hands had been the most common form of kinesthetic stimulation. For this option, the clinician must sit close enough to touch the patient. The patient's hands are generally placed palm down on the arms of the chair or on the patient's knees. The clinician then uses one or two fingers to gently touch the back of patient's each hand in turn. The clinician can administer this bilateral touching or gentle tapping two hands or one. The two-handed method requires the clinician to sit in front of the patient. The one-handed method can be done from slightly to the side. To avoid directly touching the patient, a light mallet with a soft head or a small soft object such as a cloth ball can be used to touch the back of the patient's hands. If the patient is wearing shorts or a short skirt, the clinician may offer the patient a small blanket, scarf, or clean towel to cover the patient's knees and thighs.

TECHNOLOGICAL AIDS FOR ADMINISTERING BILATERAL STIMULATION

A growing number of technological aids are now available to assist EMDR-trained clinicians in generating bilateral stimulation. These options may be helpful to avoid clinician fatigue, overcome a clinician's physical handicaps, or to address a patient's special needs. In the absence of controlled data on the effects of different technologies on clinical outcomes, the primary factors driving the selection of technological aids seem to involve cost, the availability of simultaneous multimodal options, and clinician preferences.

The Neurotek Corporation was the first to offer such products and markets the most widely used devices for assisting with EMDR treatment. The EyeScan 4000 provides a tripod mounted, rectangular bar with 24 green (or blue) LED lights in a line. These can be set to sequentially light up and down the length of the device or to alternately light up at each end of the bar. The speed can be adjusted before or during eye movements using a wireless remote control. At the end of bar, a display screen automatically keeps track of the number of repetitions per set. The EyeScan 4000 can also provide alternating auditory tones via an optional headset and kinesthetic stimulation via two small tactile probes. Again, the speed and number of repetitions are easily monitored and regulated via the remote control. These three modes of stimulation may be used separately or in any desired combination. Neurotek also provides simpler and less expensive devices that can be held in the lap or to provide only kinesthetic and auditory or auditory-only stimulation.

Several other companies offer audiotapes and CDs that feature varied types of alternating auditory stimulation from tones, to nature sounds to music. Advertisements for these products can generally be found in the EMDRIA Newsletter and in the display hall at the EMDRIA annual conference. It can be difficult or impossible to alter the speed of the stimulation with prerecorded sounds and it may be difficult or impossible to monitor the number of repetitions except by timing the length of exposure to the alternating sounds. Prerecorded alternating sounds have been used by some clinicians to provide continuous bilateral auditory stimulation throughout treatment sessions via headphones or speakers or for home use by patients. There are no published studies on the effects of listening to these types of prerecorded, alternating sounds either as an adjunct to psychotherapy or for self-use to indicate whether or not they are helpful. The use of continuous bilateral auditory stimulation would have to be considered a significant deviation from the standard EMDR procedural steps not yet supported by published studies.

Several companies and individuals have also developed software to generate tracking eye movements and alternating sounds or tactile stimulation. These software approaches can provide technology that may be less expensive for those who already have the necessary computer hardware available. Software can offer varied options for visual and auditory stimulation and for automating record keeping of treatment sessions. However, to provide the optimal width of eye movements typically used for EMDR, it can be necessary to sit quite close to the computer monitor or to obtain a fairly expensive, large monitor. Of these available technological options, only the EyeScan 4000 is known to have been extensively field-tested by EMDR training supervisors and observed to be as effective and well accepted by patients as manually generated eye movements. Clearly, controlled research is needed to evaluate patient variables and responsiveness to the use of modes, frequencies, and duration of alternating stimulation as part of EMDR treatment.

VERBAL FEEDBACK AND RESPONSES TO MODES AND TYPES OF STIMULATION

Clinicians should initially inquire about patient tolerance for different speeds or modes of stimulation before any positive or negative memory has been accessed. Then, after selecting an initial mode of stimulation, clinicians should evaluate patient responses to the mode of bilateral stimulation selected during the calm place exercise or Resource Development and Installation (RDI). Clinicians must continue to monitor patient responses to the selected mode and speed of bilateral stimulation during initial reprocessing of disturbing memories in the desensitization phase. Any indications of change in the sensory content, affect, physical sensations, and thoughts of the patient are indications that the mode of stimulation is effective.

STABILIZATION OF ANXIETY, MOOD, IMPULSE CONTROL AND DISSOCIATIVE SYMPTOMS

Patients with serious anxiety, mood, impulse control, or dissociative symptoms require additional stabilization interventions before they are ready for EMDR reprocessing. We will consider each of these kinds of instability in turn.

Patients suffering from severe anxiety episodes or panic attacks need to develop skills to reduce their anxiety before starting EMDR reprocessing. When patients suffer from PTSD, their severe anxiety symptoms most likely will not be fully eliminated through self-control skills until EMDR reprocessing is offered, but it is still important that patients have some sense of control over anxiety states. If initial EMDR reprocessing sessions are incomplete or if they experience additional intrusive symptoms between sessions, patients need to be able to shift their state to a calmer state using the methods that were practiced during the preparation phase.

Patients are generally anxious about starting EMDR reprocessing of their traumatic memories. Practicing methods for reducing anxiety can help them to feel ready to make the transition to reprocessing. One metaphor for explaining this is that when you know that the brakes are working well in your automobile, you can confidently drive fast knowing you are in control and can slow down or stop safely. If you know that the brakes in your automobile are not working well at all, you are not fully in control even when going slowly, and you certainly do not feel safe driving at high speed. Practicing methods for self-control "repairs the brakes" and provides enough sense of self-control to enable patients to begin reprocessing. Practicing the calm place exercise or RDI can be particularly helpful because their use of bilateral stimulation makes them seem like reprocessing has already begun.

Patients vary in their response to different methods for regulating anxiety, so it can be important to offer several methods until patients have sufficient tools to manage current anxiety. Methods for regulating anxiety fall into the following two broad categories: active methods (such as progressive relaxation) and passive methods (such as mindfulness meditation). Active methods show a lesser risk of paradoxical anxiety responses (Heide & Borkovec, 1983) and generally produce positive effects more quickly than passive methods.

METHODS FOR REDUCING ANXIETY

Progressive muscle relaxation (PMR) is a technique for stress management widely described in the behavioral literature (Conrad & Roth, 2007; Lehrer, Woolfolk, & Sime, 2007) developed by American physician, Edmund Jacobson, in the early 1920s (Jacobson, 1938). While there is some evidence that progressive relaxation has greater effects on muscular tension than on autonomic function such as hyperarousal or anxiety (Lehrer, Carr, Sargunaraj, & Woolfolk, 1994) many patients find it quite helpful. Progressive relaxation involves deliberately and gently tensing small groups of muscles in one part of the body at a time and then deliberately relaxing this increased tension. This gentle tensing and releasing is applied progressively, generally starting from the feet and working up to the head. Clinicians can provide patients direct training in progressive relaxation in session or can chose to just discuss the rationale for progressive relaxation, explain it in session and then have patients practice at home using a prerecorded audiocassette or CD.

Autogenic training is a stress management technique first developed by the brain physiologist, Oskar Vogt, and later expanded by the German psychiatrist, Johannes Schultz (Schultz & Luthe, 1959). Autogenic training is based on observations of hypnotic subjects who reported heaviness and warmth, especially in the arms and legs. It involves six standard exercises of visual imagination and verbal cues that make the body feel warm, heavy, and relaxed. It requires regular daily practice over an extended period of 4–6 months. Therefore, it is best suited for patients who are sufficiently motivated and disciplined to practice it diligently. Autogenic training may be more useful for patients with autonomic dysregula-

 | Progressive Muscle Relaxation

- Progressive muscle relaxation (PMR) involves deliberately and gently tensing specific muscle groups and releasing the tension. Practice PMR about 10 minutes a day for 10–14 days. Finish each practice session with a relaxation cue—see below.
- Practice PMR in a quiet place free of distractions including background music. Remove your shoes and wear loose clothing. Practice before meals rather than after. Avoid using alcohol or drugs before practicing.
- Practice sitting in a comfortable chair or lying down—if you can do so without falling asleep.
- Tension–Relaxation

    a) Step 1: *Tension.* First, focus on the muscle group. Then inhale and simply squeeze the muscles firmly for about 6 seconds. For example, starting with your right hand, make a firm fist with your hand.

    b) Step 2: *Releasing the Tension.* After about 6 seconds, as you simultaneously exhale, let go. Let all the tension flow out of the muscles as you feel your breath going out. For example, imagine the tension flowing out of your hand through your fingertips as you exhale. Feel the muscles relax and become loose.

    c) Step 3: *Rest during the next breath cycle.* Notice the difference in this area of your body between tension and relaxation.

- As you practice, you may notice that you are tensing other muscles than just the intended area. When you notice this, just do the best you can. For example, you might be tensing muscles in your right arm and shoulder, not just in your right hand. As you continue to practice, you will learn to make increasing discriminations among muscles.
- Work with all the major muscle groups in your body in a systematic progression from your feet upward in the following recommended sequence:

    ☐ Right foot
    ☐ Right lower leg and foot
    ☐ Entire right leg
    ☐ Left foot
    ☐ Left lower leg and foot
    ☐ Entire left leg
    ☐ Right hand
    ☐ Right forearm and hand

    ☐ Entire right arm
    ☐ Left hand
    ☐ Left forearm and hand
    ☐ Entire left arm
    ☐ Abdomen
    ☐ Chest
    ☐ Neck and shoulders
    ☐ Face

- Relaxation cue: When you have completed the PMR sequence, notice the state of relaxation of your muscles. Then pair a relaxation cue with the state of relaxation. For example, touch the thumb and forefinger of your nondominant hand together gently. You can also use a word or phrase as a relaxation cue. By practicing the relaxation cue each day for at least 10 days, you will establish a conditioned response. You can then use the relaxation cue as a quick physiological cue to relax when needed.
- When you finish a practice session, remain relaxed with your eyes closed for a while, and then get up *slowly.* Lowered blood pressure from deep relaxation can lead to orthostatic hypotension, a sudden drop in blood pressure due to standing up quickly, and could cause you to feel dizzy or even to faint.

tion as research shows it to have positive effects on several stress-related health problems (Lehrer, Woolfolk, & Sime, 2007). Prerecorded CDs are readily available to assist patients for whom autogenic training would be helpful.

Breathing exercises provide brief, easily learned interventions that can rapidly decrease anxiety and increase the sense of self-control.

Diaphragmatic breathing has been found to be helpful in improving self-regulation with anxiety disorders (Telch, et al., 1993) and idiopathic epilepsy (Fried, Fox, & Carlton, 1990). However, for stable, long-term treatment of anxiety symptoms, studies indicate that breathing retraining must be combined with cognitive–behavioral methods (Craske, Rowe, Lewin, & Noriega–Dimitri, 1997; Eifert & Heffner, 2003; Schmidt et al., 2000) or EMDR (Fernandez & Faretta, 2007; Goldstein & Feske, 1994). Diaphragmatic breathing is generally easily learned and produces benefits relatively quickly.

Square breathing is another easily learned method that appears to help rapidly reduce anxiety and increase patients' sense of well-being (McCraty, Atkinson, Tomasino, & Bradley, 2001). Square breathing is derived from ancient yoga breathing exercises known as *pranayama* (Iyengar, 1981). The name is based

 Diaphragmatic Breathing

- The diaphragm is a large, dome-shaped muscle at the base of the lungs.
- Practice diaphragmatic breathing for 5–10 minutes about two to three times per day.
- To practice while lying on a flat surface:

1) Lie on your back on a flat surface, with your knees bent. You can use a pillow under your knees. Place one hand on your upper chest. Place the other just below your rib cage to allow you to feel your diaphragm move as you breathe.
2) Breathe in slowly through your nose so that your stomach moves out against your hand. The hand on your chest should remain as still as possible.
3) To exhale, gently tighten your stomach muscles, letting them fall inward as you exhale through your nostrils or through pursed lips. The hand on your upper chest should remain as still as possible.

- To practice while sitting in a chair:

1) Sit comfortably, with your knees bent and your shoulders, head, and neck relaxed.
2) Place one hand on your upper chest and the other just below your rib cage. This will allow you to feel your diaphragm move as you breathe. Breathe in slowly through your nose so that your stomach moves out against your hand.
3) To exhale, gently tighten your stomach muscles, letting them fall inward as you exhale through your nostrils or your mouth. The hand on your upper chest should remain as still as possible.

on equalizing the length of the different components of the breath cycle. I favor this method in my own practice, as it appears to be helpful to the widest range of patients by both age and presenting complaint. It can be taught in just a few minutes and provides immediate self-control benefits without requiring long periods of practice.

Heart rate coherence training is a form of biofeedback training that has been shown helpful in the treatment of a large number of stress related disorders including depression, fibromyalgia, test-taking anxiety, and panic (Bradley, McCraty, Atkinson, Arguelles, & Rees, 2007; Hassett et al., 2007; Karavidas et al., 2007; McCraty, Atkinson, Tomasino, & Stuppy, 2001). Thus, heart rate coherence training appears to provide both cognitive and autonomic benefits. Clinicians can obtain a heart rate coherence training system from the Institute of HeartMath (http://www. heartmath.org) that they can use to help patients develop increased self-control over their internal states. Dr. David Servan–Schreiber (2004) has written a marvelous introduction to both EMDR and the role of heart rate coherence training in health that both patients and clinicians may find useful.

THE CALM PLACE EXERCISE

The calm place exercise, originally known as the safe place exercise (Shapiro, 1995, 2001), was developed by Neal Daniels in 1991 (Shapiro, 1998b) to address paradoxical anxiety responses (Heide & Borkovec, 1983, 1984) in combat veterans

 Square Breathing

- Breathe in through the nose, filling the lower lungs by extending the belly for a count of 3 or 4. Hold the breath for the same count. Then exhale completely for the same count, emptying the lungs by pushing with the belly. Finally, rest while holding your lungs empty for the same count. Repeat for 2–3 minutes.

to structured relaxation training in the stabilization phase of treatment. Because a significant portion of patients struggle to or simply cannot identify a place associated with a sense of "safety," it is easier to simply ask patients to identify a "calm place." In the calm place exercise, the patient is asked to focus on imagery and feelings related to a place associated with feelings of being calm and engage in several sets of bilateral stimulation—with eye movements, taps, or tones. To lessen the risk of attention shifting via spontaneous association to a traumatic memory, a more limited number of repetitions and sets of eye movements are employed in the calm place exercise than when engaging active reprocessing of a traumatic memory.

The calm place exercise serves as both a stabilization exercise and an assessment tool. Widespread clinical experience has led to the consistent observation that patients who respond well in session to the calm place exercise are generally good candidates for EMDR reprocessing. Patients who respond well to the calm place exercise show simple, positive shifts in state and an absence of any negative associations. They are also able to make use of it in between session to help regulate moments of intrusion and anxiety. On the other hand, patients who have complex or adverse responses to the calm place exercise are likely to require both more complex treatment plans and more sophisticated EMDR skills from clinicians.

Difficulties with the calm place exercise can involve not being able to even think of a calm place or thinking of places with both positive and negative associations. After identifying a calm place, adverse responses can include having negative associations within that scene or to another disturbing scene. These negative

 | Calm Place Exercise

---

When patients cannot identify a calm place, suggest that they focus on a place that is beautiful or peaceful or focus on remembering being with a person or people with whom they feel at ease or secure.

1) **Image:** Say, "Think of a place (real or imagined) you connect with feelings of being calm and peaceful."
2) **Emotions and sensations:** Say, "Notice the image that goes with your calm place. Notice what you hear, see and feel in this place." Ask, "What do you notice?" Write down the descriptive words and phrases the patient says.
3) **Enhancement:** Enhance the patient's access to the memory network of the calm place by repeating the patient's key descriptive sensory words and phrases and emphasizing the positive feelings and sensations. Then ask, "What are you feeling and noticing now?" If the patient continues to report pleasant feelings and images, go to the next step.
4) **Bilateral stimulation:** Offer three to four sets of bilateral stimulation with 4–6 passes per set. Say, "Focus on your calm place and notice where you are feeling the pleasant sensations in your body." Begin the first set of bilateral stimulation. Then ask, "What do you feel or notice now?" If the patient reports positive feelings and sensations, repeat two to three more times. Say, "Focus on that and follow again."
5) **Cue word:** Ask, "What word or phrase represents your calm place." After the patient identifies a cue word or phrase say, "Notice the positive feelings as you think of that word and follow again." Offer 4–6 passes of bilateral stimulation. Then ask, "How do you feel now?" Repeat this sequence with the cue word about three times.
6) **Self-cuing:** Direct the patient to access the calm place with the cue word. "Now I'd like you to say that word and notice how you feel." After the patient reports accessing the sensations of the calm place again, offer 4–6 passes of bilateral stimulation.
7) **Cuing with disturbance:** Ask the patient to, "Imagine a minor annoyance from the last few day and how it feels." Pause and listen to the patient's report. Then say, "Now focus on your calm place and your cue word and notice what happens in your body." If the patient is able to access the positive emotions and sensations, offer 4–6 passes of bilateral stimulation. Repeat once or twice.
8) **Self-cuing with disturbance:** Say to the patient, "Now, I'd like you to think of another mildly annoying incident. Then shift back to focusing on your calm place by yourself. As you do this, notice the changes that happen in your body. Let me know when you have done this and are back to your calm place."

Homework: "I'd like you to practice using your calm place, between now and our next session at least once a day and any time you feel it would be helpful. We'll talk about it next time we meet.

Adapted from multiple sources including Shapiro (2001, pp. 125–126) and Greenwald (2007, pp. 106–108).

associations can occur during the initial eliciting of more sensory details about the calm place or during bilateral stimulation. The calm place exercise can be viewed as a projective assessment tool in which both the content of the calm place imagery as well as the visual and verbal associations provide information about the patient's construction of narrative and structure of self.

As discussed in chapter 5, it is essential to screen patients for a dissociative disorder before offering any clinical bilateral stimulation procedures including before offering the calm place exercise. If the patient were to turn out to have an undiagnosed dissociative disorder, potential complications can include the sudden accessing and emergence of an emotional part of the personality (van der Hart et al., 2006) also known as an *alter personality* (Putnam, Zahn, & Post, 1990). Conceptually, this breach of an amnestic barrier between discrete states of structural dissociation can be viewed as the result of the tendency of the bilateral stimulation used in EMDR procedures to induce increased associations between memory networks. Clinically, this leads to potentially disruptive shifts in which part of the personality is active, from an apparently normal part of the personality, known as ANP, to an emotional part of the personality, known as EP (van der Hart et al., 2007).

An example is the clinician who asked a 32-year-old mother of three children to identify a calm place at their first session. The clinician had not administered the Dissociative Experiences Scale, Version II (DES-II) and had not conducted a mental status examination to screen for a dissociative disorder as described in chapter 5. For her calm place, she described a bench where she used to sit by a pond as a young child with her grandfather and feed the ducks. After the third set of bilateral stimulation, the patient shifted in her chair, tucking her legs underneath her, and started looking fearful and confused. Speaking in a childlike voice she said to the therapist, "I don't want to be here anymore. Can I go home now?" When the therapist asked if she knew how to drive, her response was, "No. Will you drive me home?" This is not the best way to discover that your new patient is suffering from dissociative identity disorder. While such unexpected discoveries are rare, they have been reported even by experienced EMDR clinicians (Leeds, 1998b) who had omitted screening for a dissociative disorder before doing the calm place exercise. For what to do in such circumstances, see the section below on managing dissociative states in the preparation phase.

When selecting memories and images to use in the calm place exercise, it can be helpful to ask for memories of adult experiences especially if the patient has reported a history of chronic adverse childhood events. While patients can successfully use purely imaginary scenes, such as a patient who has never been there who imagines walking on the beach in Hawaii, it is still important to assure that imaginary scenes were not originally the focus of a fantasy escape from inescapable fear and anxiety. One patient said that her calm place was floating in the clouds, listening to the angels sing. Asked when she first remembered using that calm place for self-soothing, she replied, "When I was 7 years old, I hid in the closet, afraid of being beaten when my alcoholic father would come home from work." While patients may occasionally believe such imaginary places to be appropriate for the calm place exercises, clinicians should set aside any image or memory that is inextricably linked by historical association to a state of fear or anxiety. Rehearsing imagery historically associated with the use of dissociative defenses while offering bilateral stimulation not only risks strongly negative associations but also could lead to reinforcing the use of maladaptive dissociative defenses. Instead, ask for a real memory or select a new imaginary place that has only positive associations for all parts of the personality.

After doing the full calm place exercise in session with the patient, clinicians should follow up in subsequent sessions to verify that the patient is able to make use of the calm place exercise at home to achieve at least some sense of self-control over intrusive recollections and states of anxiety (hyperarousal) before moving on to starting EMDR reprocessing. See the section on the use of a written log below, near the end of this chapter.

Distraction and dispersal methods of self-control temporarily shift attention away from intrusive re-experiencing. These approaches take many forms such as guided imagery exercises (Rossman, 2000) and hypnosis derived interventions (Fromm & Kahn, 1990; Hammond, 1990). Shapiro has encouraged the use of various imagery methods for self-control such the "light stream technique" (Shapiro, 2001, p 244–246) that attenuate tension by shifting focus across sensory channels. The "light stream technique" is extremely helpful in the closure phase, as described in chapter 10, for patients with residual physical disturbance at the end of incomplete reprocessing sessions.

METHODS FOR MANAGING DEPRESSIVE MOOD STATES

Patients who suffer from moderate to severe symptoms of depression sometimes reprocess less effectively than those whose depressions are partially controlled. The presence of depressive symptoms does not rule out the use of EMDR reprocessing. Indeed, EMDR treatment outcome research of subjects with PTSD who had clinically significant depressive symptoms showed marked reductions or elimination of clinical depression (Wilson, Becker, & Tinker, 1995, 1997). RDI may also turn out to be an effective intervention in some cases of depression as suggested by preliminary research (Ichii, 2003; Korn & Leeds, 2002). In those cases where depressive symptoms are more severe and may interfere with reprocessing effects or may warrant initial stabilizing interventions, clinicians should consider a referral for medication evaluation. However, many patients are averse to accepting psychiatric medication and are justifiably concerned about the potential for negative side effects. Further, there are simple alternatives to medication that can be highly effective in reducing depressive symptoms for most patients.

Moderate exercise reduces symptoms of major depression quickly and without the risk of side effects (Dunn, Trivedi, Kampert, Clark, & Chambliss, 2002). Both aerobic and nonaerobic forms of exercise are equally effective (Martinsen, Hoffart, & Solberg, 1989). Moderate exercise has been shown to be an effective treatment for chronic depression even in the face of chronic medical conditions and additional adverse life events (Harris, Cronkite, & Moos, 2006).

In 2007, the American College of Sports Medicine (ACSM) and the American Heart Association (AHA) updated physical activity guidelines for physically healthy adults less than the age of 65 (Haskell, et al., 2007). The ACSM and AHA recommendations state (p. 1423) the following:

> To promote and maintain health, all healthy adults aged 18 to 65 years need moderate-intensity aerobic (endurance) physical activity for a minimum of 30 minutes on five days each week or vigorous-intensity aerobic physical activity for a minimum of 20 minutes on three days each week.

Moderate-intensity aerobic activity is defined (p. 1423) as "equivalent to a brisk walk and noticeably accelerates the heart rate." Vigorous-intensity activity (p. 1423) is "exemplified by jogging, and causes rapid breathing and a substantial increase in heart rate." They add (p. 1423), "In addition, every adult should perform activities that maintain or increase muscular strength and endurance a minimum of two days each week."

Patients who start or resume exercise following these guidelines will obtain benefits of reduced symptoms of depression while promoting general health. In addition, since most patients who suffer from depression and PTSD experience significant sleep disturbances, these patients can also benefit from moderate to vigorous intensity exercise through its positive effects on sleep quality (Merrill, Aldana, Greenlaw, Diehl, & Salberg, 2007; Santos, Tufik, & De Mello, 2007). Sleep deprivation has direct effects on prefrontal activity and leads to impairments in mindfulness, mood, learning, executive decision making, and moral judgments (Curcio, Ferrara, & De Gennaro, 2006; Ferreira, et al., 2006; Killgore, Kahn-Greene, et al., 2007; Killgore, Killgore, et al. 2007; McEwen, 2006; Yoo, Hu, Gujar, Jolesz, & Walker, 2007). The neurological benefits of improved sleep from regular exercise on prefrontal activity directly support greater ability to benefit from psychotherapy in general and EMDR in particular by enhancing mindfulness and the ability to "just notice" disturbing components of trauma targets in a nonreactive manner during EMDR reprocessing. Improving sleep hygiene has important stabilizing influence on current functioning. For more information on improving sleep hygiene see Foldvary–Schaefer (2006). One of the simplest ways to improve sleep quality in depressed patients is through starting or resuming regular moderate to vigorous exercise.

When there are concerns that depressive symptoms may temporarily preclude effective responses to reprocessing, clinicians should also consider other cognitive and behavioral interventions. Extensive evidence indicates that cognitive behavioral therapy (CBT) provides effective, rapid treatment effects on symptoms of depression in adults (Brunstein Klomek & Stanley, 2007; Feldman, 2007). However, component analysis suggests the behavioral components have the greatest effects on mood state change (Jacobson, et al., 1996; Jacobson & Gortner, 2000) and treatment effects may not be stable in children and adolescents (Watanabe, Hunot, Omori, Churchill, & Furukawa, 2007). Clinicians and patients need to consider all these factors in making informed, collaborative decisions on the right combination of cognitive, behavioral, and pharmacological interventions to manage acute symptoms of depression in the preparation phase.

Mindfulness training (Kabat–Zinn, 1994) has attracted increasing attention in recent years as a treatment to improve the stability of treatment effects for patients with recurrent depression (Segal, Williams, & Teasdale, 2002). Mindfulness training is a more passive form of self-control and thus is associated with a greater risk of paradoxical anxiety responses (Heide & Borkovec, 1983, 1984) in some patients. Manualized mindfulness training programs require a significant time commitment from patients, produce benefits gradually, and are not available in all areas. While manualized mindfulness training may not be appropriate as a stabilization intervention in most cases of PTSD, it may be helpful for complex PTSD cases with more chronic and recurrent depressive symptoms.

METHODS FOR DECREASING DISSOCIATION

Dissociative symptoms can be highly disturbing and disruptive for patients suffering from PTSD and other disorders of structural dissociation (van der Hart et al., 2007). Symptoms of depersonalization and derealization may appear for some patients only during times of heightened anxiety, intrusive re-experiencing, or in response of specific threat cues. In other patients, these symptoms may be chronic aspects of daily living. In the *Diagnostic and Statistical Manual* (*DSM*) (American Psychiatric Association, 1994) PTSD and acute stress disorder (ASD) are considered anxiety disorders while depersonalization disorder, DDNOS, and DID are considered dissociative disorders. However, in the model of structural dissociation (van der Hart et al., 2007), these disorders are conceptualized in a spectrum where the degree of structural dissociation varies from primary to secondary to tertiary structural dissociation. See Table 4.3 in chapter 4. After screening for the presence of depersonalization disorder, dissociative disorder not otherwise specified (DDNOS), and dissociative identity disorder (DID), as described in chapter 5, clinicians must consider whether patients need to develop skills to decrease the severity of dissociative symptoms and to move out of dissociative states as part of the preparation phase of treatment before beginning EMDR reprocessing. Practicing skills in the preparation phase to control dissociative symptoms is not likely, or intended, to eliminate these symptoms permanently. Dissociative symptoms, which are associated with ASD and PTSD, can only be fully and permanently resolved by directly addressing etiological events and residual threat cues. For that, EMDR reprocessing or another effect method of resolving the etiological experiences is needed.

THE BACK-OF-THE-HEAD SCALE

It is helpful to ask patients to rate their degree of dissociation, depersonalization, and derealization before and after practicing exercises intended to decrease dissociation using the Back-of-the-Head Scale (BHS) developed by Jim Knipe (Knipe, 2002; Knipe & Forgash, 2001). The BHS is a subjective self-rating based on the reported sense of location of self. In severe states of depersonalization, patients report perceiving their sensory perspective as being from out the back of the head. These perceptual alternations appear to be due to deficient multisensory integration (i.e., dissociation) at the temporoparietal junction in the brain (Ehrsson, 2007; Lenggenhager, Smith, & Blanke, 2006; Lenggenhager, Tadi, Metzinger, & Blanke, 2007). The BHS goes from 0, meaning fully present in the body with the sense of self right behind the eyes, to 10, meaning fully depersonalized and out the back of the head watching the scene from outside the body. Five would be an intermediate state of depersonalization and derealization with a sense of being "spacey," pulling back from being fully embodied, and being partially disconnected from bodily feelings. This BHS can also be used to help patients monitor the degree of depersonalization and derealization they experience during history taking, during assessment of the target to be reprocessed, and during reprocessing. If the degree of dissociation exceeds a previously agreed upon amount, the focus can shift to decreasing dissociation before returning to the previous task. Knipe (2002) described several simple methods for decreasing dissociation and increasing sensory focus in the here-and-now. Additional methods are described below.

Increasing sensory focus in the here-and-now helps to decrease dissociative withdrawal from sensory awareness and increase presentification. I use a simple "external sensory focusing exercise" for this purpose. For this and other dissociation decreasing exercises, ask patients to rate their perceived degree of dissociation before and after the exercise. This exercise is somewhat similar to the "5-4-3-2-1 Technique" taught by Yvonne Dolan (1991) and Betty Alice Erickson, daughter of Milton Erickson, but is not intended to decrease anxiety. Rather, the aim is to shift the patient's attention from a dissociative, internally focused awareness of self-generated voices and images to here-and-now externally perceived images and sounds. I use a quick, matter-of-fact tone during this exercise intended to increase alertness. If the exercise proves helpful in decreasing depersonalization and derealization, I ask patients to practice this exercise at home when they notice they are entering or have entered states of dissociation.

Structured tension to increase tone in extensors is another simple set of exercises I developed to increase activity in the postural reflexes and decrease somatic aspects of dissociation. Conceptually, these exercises emerged from the intention to reverse the paradigm found in a child or young adult who has gone into a posture of submission curled up in the fetal position. In such a stuporous state of withdrawal, the postural reflexes are inactivated. I selected the term *structured tension* in relationship to the behavioral technique of "applied tension" (Öst & Sterner, 1987; see chapter 13) in which a seated blood phobic patient tenses lower body muscles to gain control over the decreased blood pressure of the vasovagal response to decrease faintness and increase blood supply to the brain. In a parallel manner, structured tension is intended to reverse the loss of tonic reflex in the postural system and to shift somatic activity from the defensive system of submission to the orienting system of alert and upright posture.

 External Sensory Focus Exercise

EXTERNAL SENSORY FOCUS EXERCISE TO DECREASE DISSOCIATION

Visual – Phase 1 – find objects in the room with certain characteristics.
   Look around the room and find a red object. Let me know when you find it.
   Look around the room and find a blue object. Let me know when you find it.
   Look around the room and find a shinny object. Let me know when you find it.
   Look around and find the largest object in the room. Let me know when you find it.
   Etc.
Auditory – Phase 1 – sounds inside the room.
   Listen for sounds in room and notice direction of sound. Let me know what you hear.
Visual – Phase 2 – name objects seen in the room.
   Notice and say the name of several objects you can see.
Auditory – Phase 2 – listen for sounds from outside the room.
   Listen for sounds from outside the room.
   Notice the sound that seems to come from furthest away.
   Notice from what direction the sound appears to come.
   Notice a sound outside the room that is closest.
   Notice from what direction the sound appears to come.

 Structured Tension Exercises

STRUCTURED TENSION EXERCISES TO DECREASE DISSOCIATION

Suggested sequence:
1) Rate dissociation with the BHS from 0—*none* to 10—*full* depersonalization, derealization.
2) Practice structured tension while seated and/or standing.
3) Rate dissociation 0 to 10 with BHS.
4) Next, identify and access a current dissociation cue.
5) Rate dissociation 0 to 10 with BHS.
6) Then, practice this sequence again.
7) Rate dissociation 0 to 10 with BHS.

Seated structured tension:

1) One arm pushes outward elbow against hand; repeat on other side of body.
2) One knee pushes upward against elbow; repeat on other side of body.
3) While looking up and back, and leaning back slightly, back of head presses gently back against overlapping palms.

Standing structured tension:

1) Put one leg forward and one back in the "runner's stretch." While looking up, with elbows slightly bent, press both palms firmly against wall at shoulder level. Press rear heel down. Press wall with both arms. Then reverse legs.
2) Stand with feet hip width apart. Shift hips as far back over heels as possible. Extend arms straight overhead. Press palms toward the ceiling and reach fingers back. Look back as far a possible. Then stand in a normal posture and notice how you perceive the room and yourself in the room.

METHODS FOR DECREASING SELF-INJURIOUS AND MALADAPTIVE TENSION–REDUCTION BEHAVIORS

Many patients with chronic PTSD and those with early histories of exposure to adverse life events experience maladaptive tension–reduction urges that can lead to efforts at self-medication with alcohol or drugs, compulsive sexual behavior, compulsive gambling, shopping, or exercise, overworking, and to impulses for self-injury (Black, 2007; Connors, 1996; Henry, 1996; Kessler, et al., 1995).

Seeking safety is a 25-session manualized safety and stabilization treatment for patients with PTSD and comorbid substance abuse that has shown significantly better outcomes than treatment as usual for substance use, beliefs related to substance abuse and PTSD, some trauma-related symptoms, as well as anorexia and somatization (Najavits, 1998, 2002, 2005, 2006). Seeking safety can be delivered in individual or group sessions by a professional or paraprofessional clinician, making it a cost-effective alternative for populations traditionally incapable of paying for therapy privately and often not covered by insurance.

Brown & Gilman (2007; Brown, Gilman, & Kelso, 2008) studied seeking safety in combination with EMDR for drug court referred cases (*N* = 30) with dual diagnosis substance abuse and PTSD. They found 68% of referred cases met or nearly met criteria for PTSD. Of those who completed seeking safety, 66% accepted further treatment with EMDR, receiving an average of 14 sessions of EMDR, and 83% of this group went on to complete drug court successfully. Of those completing the initial seeking safety treatment and who declined further treatment with EMDR, only 33% completed drug court. From this preliminary study, it appeared that seeking safety functioned as an effective stabilization intervention successfully preparing a significant portion subjects to benefit from EMDR reprocessing and that the combination of seeking safety and EMDR reprocessing led to greater success in completing drug court requirements.

Dialectical behavior therapy (DBT) is a manualized treatment for borderline personality disorder (BPD) that has been widely validated in treatment outcome research (Linehan, 1993). BPD has been increasingly viewed as a posttraumatic syndrome (Herman & van der Kolk, 1987; Liotti & Pasquini, 2000; Trull, 2001) and appears to significantly parallel the proposed diagnosis of disorders of extreme stress not otherwise specified (DESNOS) (American Psychiatric Association, 1994; Pelcovitz, et al., 1997) that Judith Herman termed *complex PTSD* (Herman, 1992a). DBT shows benefits for most symptom domains of BPD, but it does not specifically treat or resolve the disturbing memories from traumatic exposures found in BPD patients. Newer comparison research suggests DBT may not produce as comprehensive a reduction in symptom domains as a structured form of transference-focused psychotherapy (Clarkin, Levy, Lenzenweger, & Kernberg, 2007). DBT is delivered through a combination of individual and group psychotherapy that requires significant specialized training for a treatment team. While there have not yet been formal studies of using DBT as a stabilization phase intervention before offering EMDR treatment, there is one case report (Brown & Shapiro, 2006) that successfully followed this paradigm and reported stable, positive treatment outcome. Hopefully, future controlled research will clarify what combinations of treatment are most beneficial for patients suffering from BPD–DESNOS.

Resource Development and Installation is a method of ego strengthening that has been proposed as a stabilization intervention within the EMDR approach to the treatment of PTSD (Leeds, 1997; Leeds, 1998a; Leeds & Shapiro, 2000; Shapiro, 2001 pp. 434–440). RDI is also used in EMDR approaches for substance abuse (Popky, 2005) and performance enhancement (Foster & Lendl, 1995, 1996; Lendl & Foster, 2003). While there is as yet no controlled treatment outcome research on these uses of RDI, preliminary published case reports (Korn & Leeds, 2002) and widespread use within the EMDR community suggest RDI may be helpful in decreasing intense shame, depersonalization, angry outbursts, self-injurious behaviors, compulsive eating, obsessive self-critical thoughts, persistent negative emotional states (misery), and sexual acting out.

When patients cannot identify a calm or safe place, RDI provides a broader set of options to introduce patients to bilateral stimulation procedures with a positive experience that also serves an assessment role in a manner similar to the calm place exercise. In addition to its use as an alternative to the calm place, RDI may be helpful for several kinds of clinical challenges that are described in more detail below: (a) patients who do not meet standard readiness criteria for standard EMDR reprocessing for impulse control or affect regulation, (b) patients with fears of starting EMDR reprocessing, (c) clinician concerns over risks of premature termination if EMDR reprocessing were started, (d) indications patients experience episodic depersonalization, (e) patients who lack any narrative capacity for describing recent stressful events, (f) patients who become so flooded with affect, memories, or maladaptive urges after starting standard EMDR reprocessing that their day-to-day functioning is adversely impacted, and (g) patients who have chronically incomplete EMDR reprocessing sessions.

The same cautions apply to RDI as to the calm place exercise. Clinicians should always screen for a dissociative disorder before offering any bilateral stimulation procedures, including RDI. In addition, patients with dismissing (Main, 1996) or fearful (Bartholomew & Horowitz, 1991) insecure attachment status may have limited or adverse responses to the RDI protocol and may need a modified RDI approach or a focus on developing positive affect tolerance (Leeds, 2006). While

 | Clinical Indications to Start With RDI

CLINICAL INDICATIONS TO CONSIDER RDI BEFORE STARTING STANDARD EMDR REPROCESSING FOR PTSD INCLUDE:

1) Patients who cannot control tension reduction, avoidant or aggressive behaviors that involve:

    a) Risk of serious self-injury, mutilation, death
    b) Life-threatening abuse of dangerous substances
    c) Harm to others
    d) Loss of economic stability, housing or essential social support with no acceptable alternatives

2) Patients who are afraid or unwilling to start EMDR and

    a) Standard self-care and self-regulation methods, such as structured relaxation and guided imagery methods (such as calm or safe place) do not alleviate patient distress in the office or are not useful to the patient between treatment sessions.
    b) This inability to regulate anxiety (or other affects) leaves the patient vulnerable to emotional flooding or acting out during and between treatment sessions.

3) Although the patient has indicated an interest in starting trauma resolution with EMDR, the clinician may determine there is a substantial risk the patient would abruptly terminate treatment if the clinician proceeded to use EMDR due to:

    a) Poor ego strength.
    b) Inability to tolerate suppressed or dissociated material.
    c) Already observed Borderline shifts from idealization to devaluing the clinician.
    d) Intolerable shame if they were to resume acting out in non-lethal ways or if they were to reexperience certain painful memories.

4) Patients who have episodes when they cannot speak or can barely articulate their thoughts. These patients appear confused or overwhelmed by emotional states at these times.

5) Patients who cannot give coherent narrative accounts of events of the week (even with clinician prompting) such as stressful interactions with family members or coworkers. Instead, these patients give fragmentary accounts of these situations and then lapses into vague self-critical comments.

6) Patients who become so flooded with affect, memories or maladaptive urges after starting standard EMDR reprocessing that their day-to-day functioning is adversely impacted.

7) Patients who have chronically incomplete EMDR reprocessing sessions

there is widespread acceptance and recognition of the benefits and risks associated with RDI, there is no controlled research yet on RDI. Appropriate informed consent should be obtained before offering RDI to patients.

While providing RDI is nearly always an extremely positive experience for patients and clinicians, there have been concerns (Korn, Weir, & Rozelle, 2004; Shapiro, 2004) that some clinicians use RDI inappropriately or excessively. In part, this may be because some clinicians find exposure to their patients' traumatic memories aversive due to lack of sufficient training, experience, or skills in using EMDR. It may also be due in part to clinicians having their own personal unresolved experiences restimulated by offering EMDR reprocessing to patients with PTSD (Dalenberg, 2000).

When clinicians who have completed training in EMDR offer patients with PTSD RDI over significantly more sessions than needed to meet readiness criteria for EMDR, they may convey the message the patient is too weak to tolerate the traumatic material thereby increasing avoidance and anxiety about EMDR reprocessing. They may also deplete the patient's financial resources and thus prevent the patient from being able to complete medically necessary effective treatment for their PTSD.

When patients are clearly suffering from symptoms of PTSD and meet readiness criteria, there are several invalid reasons to use RDI before starting standard EMDR reprocessing. These include situations when the clinician has a *vague sense* that the patient is "unstable," has anxiety about possible patient abreaction, has aversion to the content of patient memories, has a preference for helping the patient to "feel good," or has fears of not being able to "complete" the session. In circumstances like these, the clinician should obtain additional education, training, consultation, or EMDR to resolve their issues and make appropriate use of EMDR.

What percentage of those with PTSD needs RDI before starting standard EMDR reprocessing? There are no definitive studies to answer this question. Korn and Leeds (2002) suggested that RDI might be needed in the stabilization phase of treatment in a substantial portion of cases of complex PTSD–DESNOS subjects meeting criteria for BPD. Korn et al. (2004) reported that in a large well-controlled, eight-session, study of EMDR treatment <5% of adult PTSD subjects, even those with childhood onset PTSD, needed RDI and then they generally only needed one session of RDI. EMDRIA Approved Consultants generally report only a small percentage of patients presenting with PTSD need RDI before standard EMDR reprocessing of disturbing memories. Therefore, it appears that most patients who meet criteria for PTSD, and *do not* meet criteria for BPD, or any other serious comorbid disorder that affects stability, will need one session of RDI before they are ready for standard EMDR reprocessing.

Several different written versions of RDI scripts have been published, as well as those distributed through EMDRIA and EMDR Europe conference presentations and in various EMDR training manuals. The standard EMDR procedural steps have been formally operationalized with precise steps and have been subjected to repeated empirical evaluation with fidelity tests. In contrast, RDI has not been subjected to controlled studies nor has it been uniquely linked to one specific procedural description with precise steps. As the person recognized as the developer of the name for RDI and the earliest versions of standardized RDI procedural steps, I do not believe that the effectiveness of RDI depends on the wording of the script so much as it does adherence to a series of seven essential steps in its application. As long as clinicians follow these seven steps, they may chose to use their own language or to follow any of the available scripts that adhere to these essential steps. For clinicians who want to use a script for administering RDI, two RDI scripts are included in Appendix B.

The focus for applying RDI begins with a behavioral chain analysis (Koerner, Miller, & Wagner, 1998; Linehan, 1993; Shearin & Linehan, 1994) of current

6.10 | Seven Main Procedural Steps for Resource Development and Installation

1) Identify a target situation from a behavioral chain analysis.

2) Select a mastery, relational, or symbolic memory or image that:
   ✓ Represents a needed capacity, and
   ✓ Is associated with positive affect.

3) Access (through guided inquiry) and enhance (through repetition of patient's descriptors) as many aspects of the memory as possible.

4) Add several short sets (6–12 repetitions each) of eye movements (taps or tones).
   ✓ If needed to retain access to the positive memory, it can be helpful to repeat patient's descriptors before each set.

5) Repeat steps 2–4 for as many memories and qualities as needed until

6) The patient can imaginally rehearse (in a future template) making use of these adaptive capacities in the target situation.

7) Verify stability in the target situation with feedback from patient log and repeat steps 2–6 if needed on this or other target situations.

maladaptive coping behaviors. A behavioral chain analysis identifies in detail the specific environmental cues, personal antecedents and consequences of dangerous or maladaptive behaviors. When eliciting and selecting resources, clinicians should simultaneously consider both the current stimuli and the original childhood experiences in which resources were lacking. Well-selected resources will be helpful both in enhancing current behavioral, emotional, and cognitive stability, and when the patient is ready, in reprocessing the original childhood experiences that underlie adult maladaptive responses.

Resources are naturally developed and can be drawn from three broad domains of experience: mastery memories, relational resources, and symbols. Mastery experiences are memories of past successes and achievement, effective boundary setting, assertiveness, and self-care. Relational resources are of two varieties: supportive others and role models. *Supportive others* have provided direct care, empathy, support, validation, mentoring, or guidance. There is a certain degree of implied dependence, trust, and direct relationship with supportive others. *Role models* demonstrate ways of being and capacities that the patient wants to emulate. There need not be any direct contact or relationship with role models who can be historic or fictional figures, as well as individuals from the patient's community or extended family. Symbols can be derived from cultural, religious, and metaphysical sources as well as those that are generated directly by the patient from dreams, guided imagery, or art therapy. Care should be taken in selecting resources when working with those from backgrounds of pervasive emotional neglect. Those with avoidant insecure attachment (Main, 1996) often have a pronounced counterdependent stance and can have adverse reactions to attempts to install resources that imply any trust in others or dependency on others. In contrast, those with anxious–ambivalent insecure attachment who may show borderline traits, generally respond extremely well to installation of supportive others.

The intent of this section on RDI has been to offer a brief introduction to its use in cases that fit within the scope of this text. A full description of the use of RDI in cases of secondary and tertiary structural dissociation such as complex PTSD, BPD, DDSNOS, and DID is beyond the scope of this text. Additional information on RDI

 | Behavioral Chain Analysis for RDI

Using RDI with a Behavioral Chain Analysis in the Stabilization Phase of Treatment for Complex PTSD:

1) Establish a contract for patient to stop the behavior and to log and report all further instances of urges to engage in and actual self-harming behavior.
2) Conduct a behavioral chain analysis that identifies in detail the specific environmental cues, personal antecedents and consequences of dangerous or maladaptive behaviors based on the following hierarchy of importance:

   a) Life-threatening, suicidal, and parasuicidal behaviors
   b) Behaviors that interfere with treatment (i.e., noncompliance, canceling appointments, premature dropout)
   c) Patterns that have a severe effect on quality of life (i.e., drug abuse, failure to maintain employment)
   d) Coping skills development (See Koerner et al., 1998; Linehan, 1993; Shearin & Linedhan, 1994.)

3) Identify the purpose(s) of the behavior.
4) Identify and list external and internal cues, emotions, and beliefs that precede or are associated with the maladaptive behavior. Rate the pretreatment level of urge for the maladaptive behavior for each target cue.
5) Identify needed resources and alternative coping responses.
6) Install these and practice with future template until validity of resource(s) (1–7) reaches 6 or 7 when focused on target situations from the behavioral chain.
7) Reprocess current stimuli (rather than earliest memory) with resources as cognitive interweaves as needed until the SUD or level of urge (0–10) falls to 2 or less and is no longer being acted on in response to current stimuli.

---

with a range of clinical examples is available in published and forthcoming books and journal articles.

MEDICATION

In assessing the role of medication in cases where EMDR is to be used, the general rule of thumb is that any psychiatric medication that enhances the stability and functioning of patients will enhance their responses to EMDR. Patients who are too severely depressed, once stabilized with appropriate medication and therapeutic interventions, will reprocess more effectively. Patients who are too anxious will reprocess more effectively when their anxieties have been reduced with appropriate medication and therapeutic interventions.

The primary exception to this general observation involves patients on high doses of tranquilizers in the benzodiazepine class. Common medications in this class include alprazolam (Xanax), chlordiazepoxide (Librium), clonazepam (Klonopin), diazepam (Valium), flunitrazepam (Rohypnol), flurazepam (Dalmane), lorazepam (Ativan), and temazepam (Restoril). When prescribed at moderate to high doses, these medications can inhibit patients' abilities to access enough of their emotional disturbance to block effective reprocessing. This does not occur in all or even most patients taking benzodiazepines. Clinicians do need to be alert to this possibility when considering intervention to address blocked responses during reprocessing. As patients develop more effective self-control strategies, it is often possible to work collaboratively with prescribing physicians to explore adjusting or changing patient prescriptions. Other classes of medications can sometimes be considered that enhance prefrontal activation—such as low doses of atypical major tranquilizers like olanzapine (Zyprexa), risperidone (Risperdal), quetiapine (Seroquel), ziprasidone (Geodon), and aripiprazole (Abilify). Unfortunately, some medications in this class have been linked to increased risk of both weight gain and type II diabetes, so patients need to explore these issues carefully with their prescribing physician.

Patients diagnosed with bipolar I, bipolar II, schizophrenia, and other psychoses who have been appropriately stabilized on medication have been reported to reprocess effectively. In offering EMDR to patients with these diagnoses, the intention is not to resolve a bipolar disorder or schizophrenia, but to reprocess memories of traumatic and other adverse events that contribute to current maladaptive responses. Early reports suggest that some trauma-related psychoses can be directly treated successfully with EMDR (Miller, 2007).

6.12 | Log

Making brief log entries provides important information on your experiences and your responses to treatment. Your log helps us monitor and adjust your treatment plan. Write a word or two or a short phrase in each box to summarize your experience.

Name: _____ Week of: _____

Date	Trigger or incident	Image or sound or smell	Belief or self-statement	Emotion	Location of sensation	SUD 0–10	Notes

THE LOG

One of the most helpful ways of monitoring patient responses to EMDR reprocessing is for patients to keep a written log of their symptoms. It is helpful to start keeping track of symptoms and responses to sessions during the preparation phase to help determine whether patients have sufficient self-control over states of anxiety, depression, and maladaptive tension–reduction urges. Keeping a written log is not considered a mandatory homework assignment: rather, it is intended for monitoring treatment responses and adjusting treatment plans. When patients have difficulty keeping a written log, it can be useful for patients to record their log reports by calling in to the clinician's telephone answering machine.

The amount of information needed in a log entry is quite minimal, consisting of just a few key words. The format for log entries is based on the elements of the memory network. While making regular written log entries is difficult for some patients, many patients will bring their written log entries to session. Log entries help clinicians determine whether the patient is able to make use of the calm place exercise and other stabilization interventions practiced during the preparation phase. Log entries can help identify additional current triggers that the patient may not have been aware of or been able to remember to tell the clinician during history taking. Log entries can sometimes help identify additional disturbing memories that need to be added to the treatment plan. Changes in the frequency and severity of log entries give patients a written record of their changes and progress over time that can help them keep a larger perspective through an occasionally difficult week.

COORDINATION OF CARE WITH PHYSICIANS AND OTHER HEALTH CARE PROFESSIONALS

A final element of the preparation phase to review is coordination of care with physicians and other health care professionals. It is always a good policy to establish contact with other treating health care professionals involved with the case to coordinate care and exchange helpful information, of course, after obtaining written permission for release of information. Some additional issues may need to be considered when clinicians are providing EMDR treatment. While some health care professionals will already be aware of EMDR and may be supportive of patients receiving EMDR treatment, others may be unaware of EMDR or may have misinformation that could be detrimental to patients' understanding. This misinformation can include overly limiting or overly broad expectations of what kinds of conditions EMDR may be able to help and how long treatment is likely to take. See chapter 16 for additional discussion of educating and correcting misinformation with other health care professionals.

Most psychiatric medications are prescribed by primary care doctors. It can be helpful to consult with these physicians about adjusting prescriptions, additional medication options, or the need for a referral to a psychiatrist. Sending treating physicians and other health care professionals a letter informing them of your assessment, diagnosis, and treatment plan during the preparation phase is courteous, helpful for coordination of care, and is good business practice, as is sending a brief discharge report. When treatment is likely to extend over several months, it can be extremely helpful to send summary reports once a month to other specialists who are involved in the case especially a psychiatrist or other physician who is managing any psychiatric medications. EMDR reprocessing can easily lead to changes in patterns of soft tissue tension that may be no noticeable to chiropractors, physical therapists, and other bodywork professionals. So, consider coordinating care with these providers as well.

6.13 | History Taking, Treatment Planning, and Preparation Overview

TASKS	SINGLE INCIDENT	MULTIPLE INCIDENT
Identify goals and concerns.	First session	Several sessions. Careful attention may be required to decide how to address concerns.
Screen for exclusion criteria.	First session	May require several sessions when history of betrayal makes trust and disclosure more difficult.
Develop therapeutic alliance sufficient to patient needs before reprocessing.	First session	May require several sessions. Repair of moments of misattunement and acknowledgement of any technical errors may be needed.
Objective testing	First or second session	May require multiple sessions to select and complete assessment battery.
Inquire about life history of adverse events, medical history, and assess patterns from family of origin.	First session. Previously asymptomatic early or adult adverse events may need to be addressed for symptom resolution.	Several sessions. Being alert to quality of narrative about family of origin may help identify attachment related issues.
Offer psychoeducation on trauma treatment and EMDR.	First session	May be important to continue to normalize symptoms and concerns over several sessions.
Practice stabilization methods.	First session or second session. Calm or safe place exercise may be sufficient.	Often essential to offer multiple methods to address different issues and verify effectiveness from log. Calm or safe place response may be complex or absent. Resource installation may be more helpful.
Assign log and obtain reports.	Generally in compliance	May require repeated encouragement.
Assign homework to obtain more complete history: life events list and/ or multimodal life history inventory.	Not needed	May require 1 to 3 weeks to complete and may need follow-up encouragement.
Develop case formulation and treatment plan.	Generally by first or second session	May require several sessions.
Verify readiness from log to begin reprocessing.	Generally by second or third session	May require several sessions.

SUMMARY

In this chapter, we examined how to prepare patients for EMDR reprocessing. It is essential that clinicians provide patients the information needed for informed consent. Patients need guidance and metaphors to help them understand standard EMDR reprocessing procedures and to develop the attitude of mindful noticing that supports effective reprocessing. In the preparation phase, we introduce patients to bilateral stimulation to verify their tolerance for bilateral eye movements or alternate forms of bilateral stimulation and offer them the calm place exercise or RDI. We provide additional skills building when needed to assure patients have the skills and capacities to cope with their current symptoms and the process of treatment with EMDR. Once we have completed the tasks of the history taking and preparation phases, we are ready to begin EMDR reprocessing on the first target in the treatment plan. This takes us to phase 4, the assessment phase.

Phases Three Through Eight of the Standard Protocol for PTSD with the Standard Procedural Steps for EMDR Reprocessing

Confusion is a word we have invented for an order which is not yet understood.
—Henry Miller

In the beginner's mind there are many possibilities, but in the expert's there are few.
—Shunryu Suzuki, 1970

No one can persuade another to change. Each of us guards a gate of change that can only be opened from the inside. We cannot open the gate of another, either by argument or emotional appeal.
—Marilyn Ferguson

The mind can assert anything and pretend it has proved it. My beliefs I test on my body, on my intuitional consciousness, and when I get a response there, then I accept.
—D. H. Lawrence

The Assessment Phase

OVERVIEW PHASE 3 OF THE STANDARD PROTOCOL

Chapter 7 describes the assessment phase (phase 3) of the standard Eye Movement Desensitization and Reprocessing (EMDR) protocol for treating posttraumatic stress disorder (PTSD). Before proceeding to phase 3, you have already achieved the following tasks:

- Establishing a good therapeutic alliance
- Obtaining informed consent to treatment
- Determining that the patient meets readiness criteria
- Formulating a case conceptualization
- Developing a written treatment plan with clearly identified memories and current stimuli that will be the primary targets for EMDR reprocessing
- Assuring that the patient has sufficient skills for managing anxiety, depressive and dissociative states, and maladaptive tension reduction urges

With all of these elements in place, you are ready to begin the assessment of the target memory you selected from your master treatment plan list of targets to be reprocessed.

The Two Main Purposes of the Assessment Phase

The two main purposes of the assessment phase are to *access* key aspects of the maladaptive memory network and to *establish baseline measures* for the level of disturbance in the target, rated with the Subjective Units of Disturbance scale (SUD), and the felt confidence in a positive self-appraisal, rated with the Validity of Cognition scale (VoC). The procedures to accomplish both of these purposes are described below. You will nearly always start reprocessing immediately after completing the assessment phase. However, in some circumstances, it may be possible or necessary to complete the assessment phase in one session and then begin reprocessing in the next session. In these cases, it is best to recheck the VoC and SUD before starting reprocessing, because the tasks accomplished in the assessment phase *access* and *organize* the elements of the maladaptive memory network, and thus may begin some reprocessing. If several days or a week have passed since the assessment of the selected target, VoC and SUD measures may have changed.

Following Your Treatment Plan when Patients Present the "Issue of the Week"

Similar with the sessions in the history-taking and preparation phases, you begin each reprocessing session with a brief review of patient's current functioning to confirm stability and appropriateness of proceeding to reprocessing. Review information from the patient's log and, if necessary, consider adjustments to the treatment plan. However, clinicians should not allow themselves to be easily distracted from their established treatment plan by the "issue of the week."

As you learn to think within the Adaptive Information Processing (AIP) model, you increasingly perceive maladaptive responses to current stimuli as reflecting adaptations to past adverse events. These past adverse events need to be reprocessed to lessen the patient's symptoms. Reprocessing of these etiological events will not happen if discussion of current issues persistently distracts attention away from commencing reprocessing early in the session. See chapter 16 for a more extensive discussion of session length. When clinicians are working within a 50-minute session, it is essential to start reprocessing by 10 minutes into the sessions to have at least 30 minutes for reprocessing. This is possible if clinicians limit the check-in to 5 minutes and complete the assessment of the target in 5 minutes. Even with extended 75- or 90-minute sessions, the time available for reprocessing can quickly be consumed by an extended discussion of the latest manifestations of the patient's difficulties. Therefore, clinicians who are newly trained in EMDR need to restrain habitual impulses to respond to every patient statement with a summary, an interpretation, an alternate perspective, problem solving, or a probing inquiry. Instead, for patients who meet readiness criteria, clinicians should move forward to the assessment phase of the selected target as simply and as directly as possible.

Taking Process Notes

When developing skills in EMDR in clinical setting as well as in research settings, it is extremely helpful to keep detailed process notes of the assessment, reprocessing, and closure phases of EMDR reprocessing sessions. These process notes can be kept on a standard legal pad, on a laptop computer, or using the procedural steps script or the session summary form. See appendix B for the complete versions these forms. Having process notes available significantly enhances the learning process in case consultation as required by the EMDR International Association (EMDRIA) during the training process, in clinical supervision required of prelicensed clinicians, and for clinical review before subsequent sessions. Some clinicians may experience note taking as diminishing their ability to retain the degree of rapport and attention to the patient to which they are accustomed. In these cases, to document process issues for professional development, consultation, or supervision, more limited note taking in just the assessment and closure phases may be sufficient when combined with audio taping or videotaping of sessions.

Image (Sensory Memory)

The assessment phase begins with the identification of the image that represents the target. The most efficient question to ask is generally: "What image represents the worst part of the incident?" Most—perhaps 70% of patients—will be able to access and describe a scene that represents a sensory image of the target memory. However, some patients will not be able to identify any visual sensory memory. Some patients simply did not encode any personally significant visual sensory memory at the time of the event. Examples include those who received tragic news of the serious injury or death of a loved one on a telephone call or who were surprised by a traumatic event in the dark or were asleep at the time of a traumatic event. Other patients may have focused more intensely at the time of the event on

| Procedural Steps Script—Assessment Phase

PROCEDURAL STEPS SCRIPT

TARGET SELECTED FROM MASTER TREATMENT PLAN LIST TARGETS:

Phase 3: Assessment of the Target Image:

"What image represents the worst part of the incident?"

If the patient has no image, elicit another aspect of *sensory* memory: *"When you think of the incident, what part of the incident do you notice?"*

Negative Cognition:

"What words go best with that image" (if there is no image, say *"with that incident"*) *"that express your negative belief about yourself now?"*

Positive Cognition:

"When you think of that image, what would you like to believe about yourself now*?"*

Validity of Cognition (VoC):

"When you think of that image" (if there is no image, say *"with that incident"*), *"how true do those words* _____ *"*
(repeat the positive cognition as an "I" statement) *"feel to you now, on a scale of 1 to 7, where 1 means they feel completely false and 7 means they feel completely true?"*

1   2   3   4   5   6   7
completely false   completely true

Emotions:

"When you focus on that image," (if there is no image, say *"on that incident"*) *"and think of those words* _____ *"*
(repeat the negative cognition as an "I" statement), *"what emotions do you feel now?"*

SUD scale:

"On a scale from 0 to 10, where 0 is no disturbance or neutral and 10 is the highest disturbance you can imagine, how disturbing does the incident feel to you now?"

0   1   2   3   4   5   6   7   8   9   10
(no disturbance or neutral)   (highest disturbance)

Location of Body Sensation:

"Where do you feel it in your body?"

Note. From EMDR Institute Training Manual, by F. Shapiro, (Jan, 2008 & Jan, 2005), Watsonville, CA: EMDR Institute. Copyright 2008, 2005 by EMDR Institute. Adapted with permission.

Note. From Eye Movement Desensitization and Reprocessing: Basic Principles, Protocols, and Procedures by F. Shapiro, 2001, NY: Guilford Press. Copyright 2001 by Guilford Press. Adapted with permission.

physical sensations, sounds, or smells than on visual threat cues. Examples include those who are knocked to the ground by the air blast in an explosion, the force of an earthquake, or the smell of smoke, and the sound of alarm bells signaling a raging fire in a tall office building.

What to do When Patients Offer an Answer That is Not an Image

If the patient's response to the standard question, "What image represents the worst part of the incident?" is to offer an emotion, "fear," or a thought, "I'm stupid," you should accept this response as helpful and use it to further the assessment of the image if possible. You should avoid suggesting that this initial response is incorrect, thus triggering shame or a sense of failure in the patient. Instead, merely ask, "When you remember the "fear" or the thought "I am stupid," which part of the memory is connected with that?" Listen for any sensory memory in the patient's report.

If the patient responds to the standard question, "What image represents the worst part of the incident?" by asking "What do you mean by an image?" offer the more general question: "When you think of the incident, which part of the incident do you notice?" Listen for any sensory memory in the patient's report. Examples include: "When I felt him slap my face." "The sound of the metal scraping in the crash." "The smell of the alcohol and the cigar smoke on his breath." "When I realized I couldn't feel my legs at all anymore." "The sound of her scream."

The Term "Image" and its Details are Generally Used Only in the Assessment Phase

Once you have identified some aspect of perceptual memory, for the rest of the assessment phase you will use the image, sound, smell, or physical sensation as the primary reference point for eliciting the negative and positive cognitions and the specific emotion. Note that once you have completed the assessment phase and have started reprocessing, you will generally avoid using any specific reference to a particular image, sound, smell, or physical sensation to refer to the selected target memory network. In part, that is because all these elements of the memory network are likely to be changing during reprocessing. They may be diminished, modified, or replaced by other perceptual memories. When you need to refer or return to the target, you will instead use a more general question that refers to the "incident" or "memory" rather than to "the image." Additional reasons for this will be clarified when we get to that part of the standard procedural steps.

A Detailed Image is Not Needed

Note that in the assessment phase, it is not necessary to have a detailed description of the incident. The primary time for clinicians to develop an understanding of the context and nature of the target to be reprocessed is during initial or subsequent history taking and treatment planning. Delving into these details during the assessment phase will consume excessive session time needed for reprocessing.

During the assessment phase, it is also not necessary to repeat the patient's description of the "image," "emotion," and "location." It is useful to write down the patient's description on the session summary form or in your process notes. The purpose of obtaining the image is not to generate a narrative or to help the clinician develop an understanding of the details of what happened in the target experience. The primary purpose is to assure that the patient can internally access some sensory memory for the target incident. Thus, extremely brief statements for the image are both acceptable and generally preferable. Examples include: "The look of rage on his face." "The headlights of the truck coming at me." "Seeing her stumble and fall." Immediately after obtaining the image, or any other sensory memory, go on to elicit the negative cognition.

Selection of Statements for the Negative and Positive Cognitions

Many clinicians with a background in cognitive behavioral therapy (CBT) (Beck, Emery, & Greenberg, 2005) are familiar with the strategies and importance of identifying negative belief statements, often referred to as *automatic thoughts* However, in the AIP model, the roles of the negative cognition (NC) and positive cognition (PC) are viewed significantly differently than the "automatic thoughts" identified in CBT. In EMDR, NC are not viewed as the cause of the patient's symptoms, but as merely one element of the maladaptive memory network. In the AIP model, the patient's symptoms are viewed as emanating from the entire memory network. The focus of the therapeutic work in EMDR reprocessing sessions is not on the identification and restructuring of the "automatic thoughts" through verbal dialogue, but on the reorganization of the memory network.

Two Primary Purposes of the Negative Cognition

The NC in EMDR serves two primary purposes. The first is to assist in accessing and activating the disturbing emotion(s) in the memory network. The second is to assist in identifying the PC. Although we will consider several additional selection criteria for the identification of appropriate NCs, these two primary purposes should always be kept in mind. The primary exclusion criterion for statements offered as NCs is that if they may be accurate or rational assessments. As long as the statements offered as NC are not potentially accurate, and they meet these two basic criteria, it is generally preferable to use the patient's own initial statement rather than spend inordinate amounts of time trying to get just the right NC.

Eliciting the Negative Cognition

After identifying the image, the standard inquiry to elicit the NC is: "What words go best with that image" (if there is no image, say, "with that incident") "that express your negative belief about yourself *now*?" Clinicians who are learning EMDR will find it useful to write down whatever the patient says in response to this question. This gives you time to quietly evaluate the appropriateness of the NC and then decide what to do next.

There are five selection criteria that apply to most statements offered as NCs. First, these statements are negative, irrational, self-referencing self-assessments. They are generally an "I" statement. For a listing of the most common NC and PC statements, see Table 7.4. Second, these negative statements are presently held self-appraisals that are relevant when focusing on the picture or incident. Third, they accurately focus the patient's presenting issue. Fourth, they are generalizable to related events or areas of concern. Thus, any details that are descriptive of the perceptual memory can be omitted. "I am in danger from trucks," can be simplified to "I am in danger." Fifth, and most importantly, they resonate with the patient's associated disturbing emotion in the target maladaptive memory network. Thinking, saying, or hearing the NC statement will tend to activate the associated disturbing emotion(s) in the maladaptive memory network.

If we think of the "image" as a scene in a picture frame, we can view the statements selected to be the NC and PC as captions written under the scene on the picture frame. The woman in Figure 7.1 is a wounded survivor of a domestic shooting incident. In the thought bubble, she is talking to herself in a state of shock about what has just happened. Her memory of what she thought at the time is not her presently held self-appraisal. This past thought, "Oh God. . . This can't be

Selection Criteria for Negative Cognitions

A statement selected as the negative cognition generally meets the follow criteria:
1) A negative, irrational, self-referencing, self-assessment: an "I" statement
2) A presently held self-appraisal when focusing on the picture or incident
3) Accurately focuses the client's presenting issue
4) Generalizable to related events or areas of concern
5) Resonates with the patient's associated disturbing emotion in the memory network

The statement selected as the Negative Cognition must not be:
1) A possibly accurate description of disturbing circumstances, past events, negative attributes of others or the patient

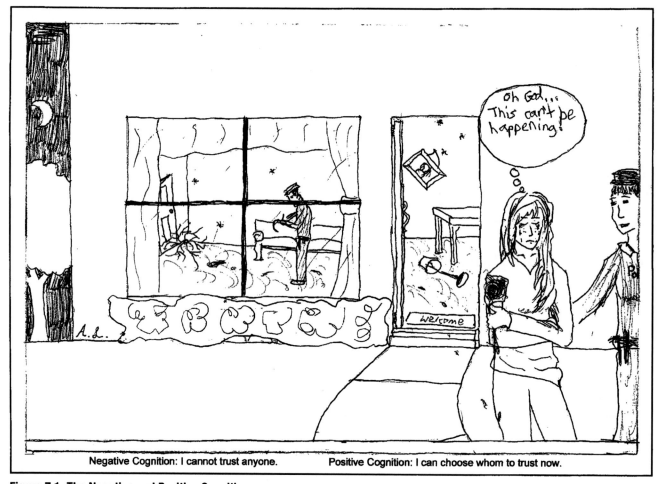

Figure 7.1 The Negative and Positive Cognitions

happening!" is a perceptual memory. It is part of what she remembers happening. Looking back on the memory weeks after she has recovered from her wounds, she is no longer in physical pain. She is no longer feeling numb or in shock. However, the experience has left her with feelings of hurt, fear, and doubts about her judgment. When asked, "What words go best with that image that express your negative belief about yourself now?" she replies, "I cannot trust anyone." Her preferred belief is, "I can choose whom to trust now." The negative belief she identifies now is not what she was thinking or feeling at the time of the incident, but instead signifies how she has encoded the experience. The point to remember here is that the statement selected as the NC should not reflect merely the thoughts a person may have had at the time of the original event, but must instead reflect the presently held self-appraisal.

Four common patient responses can lead clinicians into difficulties with eliciting an appropriate statement for the NC. These are when patients offer a statement that is (a) an emotion, (b) a sensation, (c) a possibly accurate or an actually accurate description, (d) or say there is no negative belief or statement that goes with the image or incident.

When the patient offers a simple statement of emotion such as "terror," you can simply ask: "What belief about yourself goes with that terror?" Similarly, when the patient offers a simple statement of sensation such as "tension" or "tightness in the chest," you can simply ask: "What belief about yourself goes with tightness in the chest?" When the patient offers a potentially accurate or an actually accurate description, incorporate the description into your follow up inquiry. "When you think of (repeat description), what do you believe about yourself?" For example, one patient had been trapped in a burning building because of a badly designed emergency escape. When asked for her self-appraisal, she made the statement "I'm too short." The clinician was concerned that because of the design flaws in the emergency escape, her height may have been a factor in her being trapped. Rather than discuss this issue, the clinician pressed for a more irrational self-assessment. When asked, "When you hold in mind that image not being able to reach the exit and the thought 'I'm too short,' what do you believe about yourself now?" she replied, "I am inadequate." This second statement clearly fits the nature of the event and the tendency of survivors to take on excessive self-blame.

In response to a possibly accurate description, you can also ask: "What does that say about you as a person?" A police officer referred for EMDR treatment after his partner was seriously wounded in a line of duty shooting initially offered the statement, "It's my fault." If the captain making the referral indicated that the wounded officer appeared to have violated standard procedures, thereby exposing himself to greater danger and being wounded, we might accept this statement as irrational. But if we do not know the circumstances or if the captain indicated that the patient, recently out of the police academy, is suspected of having violated standard procedures, we would have to further inquire, "When you think 'It's my fault,' what does that say about you as a person?" If the patient offers a second or third description to these initial inquiries, merely repeat the follow up question a second or a third time. So for example, if this rookie officer said, on follow up, "I failed," we would not accept this statement because it appears to be a factual description in the past tense. Instead, we ask again, "When you think 'I failed,' what does that say about you as a person?" Then we would accept, "I am a failure," or "I cannot succeed." In cases where a fourth or fifth descriptive statement is offered, it may be more expedient to offer one or two potential common statements of NCs that might fit the memory network. Then ask the patient to indicate which is linked most strongly to the disturbing feelings connected with the image or incident. See Table 7.4, "Most Common NC and PC Statements," for a list of common NCs.

Occasionally, patients may say that there is no negative belief or negative statement about themselves that goes with the image or incident. It is a fundamental human trait to construct meaning around our most intense experiences. In the EMDR approach to psychotherapy, we assume that there are always interpretative statements to be elicited. When patients claim not to have a self-appraisal, we need to be flexible in our approach. Several strategies can be used to address this situation. First, we may need to shift to initially asking about assessments of the incident.

One example comes from the work of Roger Solomon, Ph.D. a specialist in critical incident stress. As described in the *Diagnostic and Statistical Manual of Mental Disorders,* 4th edition (American Psychiatric Association, 1994) definition of PTSD, criterion A events induce feelings of "intense fear helplessness, or horror." Early in my work with EMDR, I learned from Dr. Solomon that for many highly trained emergency responders the response to these overwhelming events is not fear or helplessness, but horror. For them, the negative appraisal statement may initially be more about the nature of the event than about their coping responses. We can ask, "What words go best with that image that express your negative belief about yourself or *that incident*?" The answer may be, "It's horrible." Clinicians may be inclined to think that this is too much of a literal description to be irrational and too much about the event to serve as the statement of the NC. We may suspect that there is survivor guilt and we may want to push for some deeper self-statement like, "I am inadequate (because I didn't do enough)." However, in assessing target memories of critical incidents, we should think of statements such as "It's horrible" as *a frozen moment in time* from which the patient cannot escape. Such statements do link to the disturbing emotion in the memory network and do allow for the identification of a PC, "It's over now. I can let it go." During the reprocessing or in reassessment of the target incident in later sessions, issues of survivor guilt may later emerge spontaneously. It is not necessary to push for them at the start when they are not initially apparent.

In a similar vein, some clinicians are initially reluctant to accept the statement, "I am going to die" as an NC because they view it as rational and descriptive. These clinicians say, "But it's true, we're all going to die." However, this is not what the statement means to the survivor of a high-speed, head-on motor vehicle collision or a witness to the murder of fellow hostages in a school shooting incident. These patients are describing not their ultimate mortal fate, but the frozen moment of time in which they foresaw their imminent death. The statement "I am going to die" for these patients is linked to their disturbing affect and allows us to elicit a statement for the PC such as "It's over. I survived" or "I am safe now." Therefore, we accept "I am going to die" as the NC, and simply go on to elicit the PC statement.

Sometimes, it may be difficult to elicit a statement for the NC when patients are not sufficiently accessing their disturbing emotions to connect with a negative self-appraisal. These patients may initially insist that they do not have any negative self-statement that fits their image. It may be helpful to remind these patients that they are seeking treatment, because they have been continuing to report intrusive reexperiencing of the traumatic event and then ask, "In your worst moments, when you are re-experiencing some aspect of this event, what negative thoughts or beliefs do you have about yourself?" It may be as simple as, "At that moment I think, 'I can't stand it'." The preferred belief statement may be along the lines of "I can cope" or "I can deal with it now."

Finally, for patients who protest that they have no negative thoughts about themselves related to the memory, it may be helpful to include details of the image when eliciting the NC. "When you focus on that image of (repeat the key descriptive words), what negative words go with that image that express what you believe about yourself, not in your head, but in your gut?" The last option is to ask the patient to read over the list of the most common NCs and PCs, listed in Table 7.4, and to select one statement from each column.

Eliciting the Positive Cognition

Once you have identified and written down the statement for the NC, go on to elicit the PC. "When you think of that image, what would you like to believe about yourself *now*?" Selecting a statement as the PC in the assessment phase serves two primary purposes. The first is to access adaptive memory networks in which the PC is encoded prior to starting the reprocessing. The second is to assess the degree of ease or difficulty the patient experiences in locating an appropriate statement as an alternative to their NC statement. The implication of asking the patient to select what they would rather be able to believe when thinking of the target situation is that by the end of the reprocessing, they might be able to believe that statement. This instills some hope, some confidence in the patient that change is possible. The matter-of-fact stance that you, the clinician, take in asking for the statement to serve as a PC is based both on the script of the standard EMDR procedure steps and on your own past experiences of seeing patients reach high levels of felt confidence in their PC statements at the end of reprocessing.

It is remarkable how frequently survivors of recurrent traumatic exposures struggle to find a preferred belief to replace common NC statements such as: "I am helpless," "I am unlovable," or "I am in danger." As clinicians, it seems such a simple exercise to think of rational opposites to these statement: "I am in control now," I am lovable," and "I am safe now." Yet, patients struggle precisely because they are not engaged in a rational exercise of thought substitution, but are accessing and, to a large degree immersed, in a state-specific memory network (Bower, 1981) in which they cannot easily locate a simple opposite statement. Asking them to do so begins the process of stimulating the adaptive memory network(s) that

 Selection Criteria for Positive Cognitions

A statement selected as the positive cognition generally meets the follow criteria:

1) A positive self-referencing, self-assessment—an "I" statement
2) Accurately focuses the patient's desired direction of change
3) Is initially at least somewhat believable as a desirable, hoped-for goal
4) Generalizable to related events or areas of concern
5) Addresses the same issue or theme presented in the negative cognition

The Positive Cognition is not:
1) The negation of the negative cognition such as: "I am not helpless."
2) An absolute statement. Avoid the use of "always" or "never."
3) A magical thought about changing past events, negative attributes of others or the patient.

need to be integrated into the maladaptive memory network of the selected target memory. Their degree of ease or difficulty in doing so gives us some initial clinical insight into the availability and accessibility of the needed adaptive memory network(s). We will also get further information about this when we ask for a rating using the VoC.

In addition to these two primary purposes for eliciting a statement for the PC in the assessment phase, we use five positive criteria and three exclusion criteria in selecting a statement for the PC. First, with the NC, statements selected as PCs are generally positive self-referencing self-assessments—an "I" statement. Second, they accurately focus patient's desired direction of change. Rather than merely negating an NC statement—"I am no longer helpless," statements selected for the PC offer a positive direction for change—"I am in control now."

Third, they are initially at least somewhat believable as a desirable, hoped-for goal. Thus, any PC statement that was rated below "1" on the VoC scale that runs from 1–7 would need to be modified or replaced with one that is more believable. If a patient rates the statement "I am ok as I am" with a VoC of less than "1," the clinician should ask the patient, "What positive statement can you make that would be more believable?" This might lead to the statement, "I can learn to accept myself as I am." Fourth, statements selected as the PC are generalizable to related events or areas of concern. To enhance generalizability, any details that refer to elements of the image or other perceptual memory should be omitted from the statement selected as the PC. Thus, "I am in control when driving" should be simplified to "I am in control now." This can be done by writing down the patient's complete statement, putting parentheses around the words "when driving," and then reading back only the essential words. "So when you hold in mind that image of what happened when you were driving, the positive words you want to believe are 'I am in control now'."

Fifth, the statement selected for the PC must address the same issue or theme presented in the statement selected as the NC. If the patient offers "I am worthless" as the statement for the NC and "I am competent" as the statement for the PC, we must investigate to determine which theme to address. To decide, we will use the principle that the statement of the NC helps stimulate the disturbing emotions in the memory network. First, transform the PC statement—"I am competent" into the corresponding NC statement—"I am incompetent." Then ask, "Which of these two statements is more strongly linked to the disturbing feelings you have in this memory: 'I am worthless' or 'I am incompetent'?"

As mentioned above, there are three exclusion criteria to keep in mind when selecting statements for the PC. First, statements selected as PCs are never in the double negative form such as, "I am not helpless." Instead, we must elicit a positive

| Most Common Negative and Positive Cognition Statements

NEGATIVE COGNITION STATEMENTS	POSITIVE COGNITION STATEMENTS
Responsibility: defectiveness, shame	
I am worthless.	I am worthy.
I am not loveable.	I am loveable.
I do not deserve. . .	I deserve. . .
I am a bad person.	I am a good person.
I am defective.	I am fine as I am.
I am a failure.	I am a success. (I am worthy.)
I am terrible.	I am ok.
I am not good enough.	I am good enough.
I am permanently damaged.	I am whole. (I am healing.)
I am ugly.	I am attractive. (I am fine as I am.)
I am stupid.	I am smart.
I am invisible.	I matter.
I am a disappointment.	I am ok as I am.
I deserve to die.	I deserve to live.
I deserve to be miserable.	I deserve to be happy.
I am different.	I am ok as I am.
I don't belong.	I belong.
Responsibility: actions, guilt.	
I should have. . .	I did the best I could.
I should not have. . .	I learned from it. (I can learn from it.)
I did something wrong.	I do the best I can.
I should have known better.	I did OK.
Safety: perception of danger	
I am in danger.	I am safe.
I will be hurt.	I am safe now.
I am going to die.	I survived. I am safe now.
I cannot trust anyone.	I can choose whom to trust now.
It's not OK to show my emotions.	It's OK to show my emotions.
I cannot let it out.	I can let it out.
It's horrible.	It's over. It's in the past now.
Control: choices, self-efficacy.	
I am not in control.	I am in control.
I am powerless.	I am powerful. (I have choices.)
I am helpless.	I have choices. (I am capable.)
I am weak.	I am strong.
I cannot get what I want.	I can get what I want.
I cannot succeed.	I can succeed.
I have to be perfect (please everyone).	I can be myself. (It's ok to make mistakes.)
I cannot protect myself	I can protect myself.
I cannot stand up for myself	I can stand up for myself.
I cannot be trusted.	I can be trusted.
I cannot trust myself	I trust myself.
I cannot trust my judgment	I trust my judgment.

statement such as "I am in control now" by asking, "How would you say that in positive terms?" Second, we want to avoid absolute statements that use words like "always." Finally, we do not accept as the PC statements that are magical thoughts about changing past events, negative attributes of others, or the patient.

One survivor of chronic childhood verbal abuse initially offered the statement "My father didn't love me" as her NC. After being asked, "What does that say about you as a person?" she replied, "I am not lovable." For the PC she initially offered, "My father does love me." Because the aim of EMDR reprocessing is not to change the father's behavior or beliefs about the father's behavior, but to change the patient's self-appraisal linked to the memory network, she was asked, "And if he did love you, what would you be able to believe about yourself?" She replied, "Then I could believe, 'I am lovable'." This statement was selected as the PC.

Ultimately, the goal of reprocessing is not just to metabolize the specific memories related to verbal abuse by the father but also to help the patient develop a new self-concept. By reprocessing the emotional information contained in the memory networks related to these adverse early life events, we support a reorganization and reappraisal of the way these experiences are encoded in the brain. Even before we begin active reprocessing with bilateral stimulation, eliciting an appropriate statement for the PC is already a step toward transforming her self-image from that of a person who doubts that she is worthy of love to one who can be confident she is.

Validity of Cognition

As soon as you have elicited an appropriate statement to serve as the PC, the next step is to assess the VoC. "When you think of that image" (if there is no image, say "with that incident"), "how true do those words _____" (repeat the positive cognition as an "I" statement) "feel to you now, on a scale of 1 to 7, where 1 means they feel completely false and 7 means they feel completely true?" This initial VoC rating establishes a baseline rating prior to starting reprocessing of the target. This will enable you to monitor treatment effects when you reach the installation phase.

To obtain an accurate VoC rating, four separate conditions must be met. First, the patient must be accessing and referencing the target memory network. You do this by asking the patient to "think of the image" or "hold the incident in mind." Second, the patient must be thinking about the statement of the PC. Third, the patient must understand the direction of the rating scale—from 1, completely false, to 7, completely true. It can help lessen confusion for some patients to visually anchor this rating scale by holding one hand at the level of your belly when you say "1" and then holding the other hand at the level of your head when you say "7." Fourth, the rating must be a felt rating, not a cognitive rating. If the initially offered VoC rating is a 6 or 7, repeat the question emphasizing the need for a felt rating. "As you hold that image in mind" (or if there is no image, say "as you hold that incident in mind"), "using a scale of 1 to 7, where 1 means they feel completely false and 7 means they feel completely true, how true do those words _____" (repeat the positive cognition as an "I" statement) "feel to you now on a gut level?" Often, this second inquiry will yield a lower and more accurate rating that reflects a felt rating rather than how true the patient thinks the statement should be.

Specific Emotion

One you have elicited statements for the NCs and PCs and obtained a valid VoC rating, use the image and the NC to access the current specific emotion(s) in the maladaptive memory network. "When you focus on that image," (if there is no image, say "When you focus on that incident") " and think of those words _____" (repeat the negative cognition as an "I" statement) "what emotions do you *feel now*?" As with the NC, the specific emotion is not necessarily what the person felt at the time of the original incident. Instead, you are seeking the emotion that emerges when you access the *current contents* of the memory network. If the patient offers more than one specific emotion, that is fine. Merely write down each named emotion. If the patient offers only one emotion, that is also fine. There is no need to prompt for more emotions.

Identifying the specific emotion(s) serves two purposes. First, it helps the patient to access a central and crucial element of the maladaptive memory network. The specific emotion is not only central to the specific selected target memory network. Specific patterns of emotional response are also a central organizer of associated memory networks, and thus help open channels for associations to any related maladaptive memory networks that needs to be addressed (Reiser, 1990). Second, the specific emotion establishes baseline information about how the maladaptive memory network is encoded and accessed before starting reprocessing. Later, in the middle of reprocessing, when you return to probe the target memory, if the patient reports similar negative self-appraisals or the same SUD rating, the patient may report different specific emotions. Thus, establishing specific emotions in the assessment phase allows you to monitor whether there are changes in the maladaptive memory network through reported changes in the specific emotion associated with the target memory.

Subjective Units of Disturbance

One you have established the specific emotion(s), you obtain a rating on the Subjective Units of Disturbance scale most commonly referred to as the SUD. Wolpe (1958) first developed this self-report scale for use in systematic desensitization. The SUD scale is commonly used in several behavioral treatments, including prolonged exposure (Foa, Hembree, & Rothbaum, 2007). For a review and investigation of the psychometric validity of the SUD demonstrating evidence of convergent and discriminant validity, concurrent validity, and predictive validity in a treatment sample, see Kim, Bae, and Park (2008).

The SUD rating is elicited immediately after the patient names the specific emotion. However, the SUD is not a just a rating of the specific emotion, but is rather a rating of the overall sense of disturbance associated with the entire memory network. "On a scale from 0 to 10, where 0 is no disturbance or neutral and 10 is the highest disturbance you can imagine, how disturbing does the incident *feel* to you *now*?" Note that the SUD is not a rating of how disturbing the event *was*. A "historic rating" generally will not change. An event that the patient believes deserved a 9 rating for *how disturbing it was* will always have been a "9." Rather, the SUD is the *felt rating* of current subjective disturbance while focusing on the memory.

Generally, the initial SUD rating will be significantly elevated. Occasionally, patients will initially report surprisingly low SUD ratings for events that would be disturbing to most people. An initial low SUD rating can reflect an accurate rating of an incident that is no longer significantly disturbing. It can also reflect limited accessing of the true level of disturbance in the memory network because of the activation of various defenses ranging from intellectualization to various levels of structural dissociation. In the later case, this can lead to significant or even dramatic increases in the subjective rating of disturbance in the middle of reprocessing as the patient moves through these dissociative defenses to fully access what is contained in the maladaptive memory network. The potential for the patient to experience a dramatic increase in perceived level of disturbance again underscores the need for appropriate informed consent prior to starting EMDR reprocessing.

Location

The last step in the standard assessment phase of the selected target is identifying the location of physical sensations associated with the maladaptive memory network.

The standard question is: "Where do you feel it in your body?" The patient may offer one location or several. Again, one location is enough. There is no need to prompt the patient for more locations. If the answer is "in my head," just write this down and proceed to the next step. "In my head" is a valid location. An answer of "nowhere" calls for follow up. A response of "nowhere" for the felt location raises the possibility of an inaccurate statement of accessing specific emotion or an inaccurate SUD rating possibly due to an attempt to "please" the clinician. It also may merely reflect a need for assistance to access a relevant sensation due to excessive anxiety about the procedure, fear of giving the wrong answer, defenses against feeling sensations or emotions, or other issues. More complex issues of defenses against feeling sensations or emotions should normally be identified when assessing readiness for reprocessing (see chapter 5) and addressed in the preparation phase (see chapter 6) before proceeding to the assessment phase.

A Simple Method to Help Patients Locate Their Sensation

A simple method to address an answer of "nowhere" is to ask the patient to "close your eyes." "As I direct you to notice aspects of this incident, just notice where anything changes in your body. Notice where anything changes in your body as you focus on the image that represents the worst part of the incident. (Pause.) Notice where anything changes in your body, as you think of the words _____." (Repeat the statement of the negative cognition). (Pause.) "Now notice the _____." (Repeat the specific named emotion(s). (Pause.) "Where do you notice anything change?" This structured follow-up inquiry will often yield some physical sensation linked to the maladaptive memory network.

Defensive Action Urges

Defensive action urges are the natural patterns of response to life threatening experiences and are always present to some degree in maladaptive memory networks for traumatic and adverse life events. A limited number of action tendencies exist within the human (mammalian) system for defense against threats to life. (Panksepp, 1998; van der Hart et al., 2006 pp. 37–38). These include hypervigilance and scanning the environment, the separation cry, flight, freeze with analgesia, fight, total submission with anesthesia, recuperative states of rest, and isolation from the group. The standard EMDR procedural steps do not explicitly call for the identification and accessing of which defensive action urges were most activated and which were most inhibited by the circumstances of the selected target memory. However, as discussed in chapter 1, the psychophysiological and behavioral responses to the original experience form an important part of the memory network as conceptualized by Lang (1977, 1979) whose work on emotional information processing provides an essential foundation to the AIP model later developed by Shapiro. In the model of structural dissociation (van der Hart, et al., 2006) these action tendencies for defense become the central organizers for the *emotional part of the personality*, which is present in PTSD and acute stress disorder (primary structural dissociation) and the multiple *emotional parts of the personality* in complex PTSD and dissociative disorder NOS (secondary structural dissociation) and in dissociative identity disorder (tertiary structural dissociation).

Korn and Leeds (1998) noted that defensive action tendencies may contribute to ineffective reprocessing of memories of childhood abuse and neglect. Leeds (2001) proposed that these defensive action urges need to be viewed as an additional discrete element of the memory network in addition to the five elements identified by Shapiro—image, thoughts and sounds, emotion, body sensation, and belief. This would help draw attention to their tendency to be the source of ineffective reprocessing and the frequent need to identify them and to make brief interventions during reprocessing to explicitly address these sources of blockage. Although Shapiro (2003) views these defensive action urges as implicit within the element of sensation—identified as a bodily location—I follow Lang's view that the overall psychophysiological and behavioral, defensive responses to the threatening situation are encoded in the memory network as a discrete and meaningful element. The perceived bodily location of felt sensation may be linked to these defensive action urges or the sensation may be linked to the affective state or even to simple memories for physical sensations from the traumatic experience. I believe clinicians should at a minimum be alert in listening for an expression of defensive action tendencies overtly expressed within the memory network as well as those that may have been blocked by the circumstances or the fears of the patient in the original experience.

For example, one survivor of rape, when asked, "When you focus on that image and think of those words, 'I am helpless' what emotions do you *feel now*?" responded, "Fear." Then she added, "I felt like screaming for help and fighting back, but he threatened to kill me if I did. At first I believed he might. Then, when I realized he wouldn't, it was too late." She reported that she had submitted with anesthesia and ever since had experienced persistent feelings of shame, lack of sensation in sexual situations, and a sense of being frozen in her life. In this case, the patient volunteered both the defensive action tendency that was activated—submission with anesthesia—and the tendency that was inhibited—calling out for help and fighting to get free. In most cases, patients do not volunteer descriptions of either the activated or inhibited defensive action tendencies when initially describing their memories. To help lessen later uncertainty about how to facilitate effective reprocessing, clinicians may want to explore and identify the activated and inhibited defensive action tendencies in the history taking phase or in the assessment phase before starting EMDR reprocessing.

When treating patients with more complex histories that include early childhood traumatic exposures, some defensive action urges may have been overly reinforced while others may have been overly inhibited. The combination of (a) insecure or disorganized attachment, (b) secondary or tertiary structural dissociation, and (c) overly reinforced and inhibited defensive action urges is a potential source of significant difficulties in EMDR reprocessing. Whether these overly reinforced or inhibited defensive actions tendencies are identified in advance or not, in chapter 9 we will explore several ways for clinicians to facilitate effective reprocessing of shame or guilt about what is encoded in memory networks regarding both the activated and inhibited defensive action tendencies.

SUMMARY

In the assessment phase, you begin working with the target memory you selected from your master treatment plan list of targets to be reprocessed. The two main purposes of the assessment phase are (a) to *access* key aspects of the maladaptive memory network and (b) to *establish baseline measures* for the level of disturbance in the target. In the assessment phase, you identify, in this order, the *image* or other sensory memory, *the NC, the PC, the specific emotion*, and *the body location* of the felt disturbance. You obtain baseline measures for the VoC and the SUD. Once you have accomplished these steps, you are ready to begin reprocessing with the desensitization phase.

The Desensitization Phase: Basic Procedures

OVERVIEW PHASE FOUR: BASIC PROCEDURES

Chapter 8 describes the basic procedures used in the desensitization phase—phase 4 of the standard Eye Movement Desensitization and Reprocessing (EMDR) protocol for treating posttraumatic stress disorder (PTSD). These basic procedures are generally sufficient for those who are optimal responders to EMDR. Typically, these basic procedures may be sufficient for single-incident trauma cases in individuals who have not previously experienced significant trauma or other adverse life experiences. Many patients have more complex histories and may experience ineffective reprocessing at some stage in their treatment. In these cases you will need to apply some of the additional procedures for ineffective reprocessing described in chapter 9. During initial training exercises in an EMDR International Association (EMDRIA)-approved basic training in EMDR, it can be helpful to first practice just the basic procedures without having to consider the more extensive choices offered by the additional procedures described in chapter 9.

Phase Four: Desensitization

Standard EMDR reprocessing begins with the desensitization phase. The goal of the desensitization phase is to foster spontaneous emotional information processing that leads to synthesis between the maladaptive memory network of the selected target memory and other adaptive memory networks. You do this by maintaining a balance of dual attention between the associations that arise from the selected target and the alternating bilateral stimulation (BLS)—as shown in figure 2.10 in chapter 2. During the desensitization phase, you continuously assess treatment effects based on evidence of adaptive shifts in (a) the brief patient verbal reports between sets of BLS, (b) your observations of nonverbal indications of adaptive emotional and psychophysiological change, (c) and by occasionally returning to refocus on the target and check on how the patient's perception of the memory of the incident has changed. Therefore, during reprocessing your verbal interactions tend to be brief. During reprocessing, rapport is maintained more by the pacing of the sets of BLS and the periodic brief pauses for patient reports than by the verbal interaction between clinician and patient.

 | Procedural Steps Script—Desensitization Phase

PROCEDURAL STEPS SCRIPT

ORIENTATION TO REPROCESSING:
"We'll start reprocessing now. As we do sets of eye movements (taps or tones), *sometimes things will change and sometimes they won't. You may notice other images, thoughts, emotions or body sensations. Other memories may come up. Other times you may not be aware of anything but the eye movements* (taps or tones). *Remember what we discussed with the metaphor of riding the train. There are no right or wrong responses. Just notice whatever happens. If you need to stop at any point, just show me the stop sign we rehearsed."*

PHASE FOUR: DESENSITIZATION
"I'd like you to focus on that image (if no image—'on that incident') *and those negative words* _____ _____ (repeat the negative cognition – as an 'I' statement). *Notice where you are feeling it in your body, and follow my fingers* (or *'notice the lights'*, *'the taps'*, or *'the sounds'*). *"*
After a set of 24 to 30 complete movements:
"Rest. Take a deeper breath. Let it go. What do you notice now?"

AFTER PATIENT REPORTS, CONTINUE REPROCESSING:
"Focus on that and notice what happens next."

Continue sets of eye movements down a channel of associations using the instructions above as long as patient reports indicate reprocessing is occurring. If the patient reports the same content without change after two sets of BLS, change the direction, height, speed and/or width of the eye movements. If using auditory stimulation, change the speed or type of sound. If using kinesthetic stimulation, change the speed, intensity or location of the stimulation.

RETURNING TO TARGET:
Continue additional sets of bilateral stimulation until the patient reports no further disturbing material and reports only neutral or positive material. Also return to target if associations become so remote from the original target that clinical judgment suggests reprocessing of the selected target is no longer occurring. Then, to return to the target, say:
"When you bring your attention back to the original experience, what do you notice now?"

If the patient reports additional disturbing material:
"Focus on that and notice what happens next."

When you return to target, if the patient reports ambiguous, or apparently neutral or positive associations on the target, check the SUD rating.

CHECK SUD SCALE:
"Focus on the original experience. On a scale from 0 to 10, where 0 is no disturbance or neutral and 10 is the highest disturbance you can imagine, how disturbing does it feel *to you* now?*"*

AFTER CHECKING THE SUD SCALE:
If the SUD rating is a 1 or higher, say:
"What's the worst part of it now?" _____.
Then say: *"Focus that, and notice what happens next."*

Or

"Where do you feel that in your body?" _____.
"Focus that, and notice what happens next."

If the SUD rating is 0, say:
"Focus on how the incident seems to you now, and notice what happens next."
When the patient reports a SUD rating of 0 a second time, continue to the installation phase.

Orientation to Reprocessing

Before starting reprocessing, you should reinforce the patient's orientation to dual attention. The standard instructions are as follows:

> *We'll start reprocessing now. As we do sets of eye movements (taps or tones), sometimes things will change and sometimes they won't. You may notice other images, thoughts, emotions, or body sensations. Other memories may come up. Other times you may not be aware of anything but the eye movements (taps or tones). Remember what we discussed with the metaphor of riding the train. There are no right or wrong responses. Just notice whatever happens. If you need to stop at any point, just show me the stop sign we rehearsed.*

Accessing the Target Before the First Set of Bilateral Stimulation

You start reprocessing by directing the patient to access the target just before the first set of bilateral stimulation. The standard statement is: *"I'd like you to focus on that image* (if no image say—*'on that incident') and those negative words _____ _____* (repeat the negative cognition—as an 'I' statement). *Notice where you are feeling it in your body and follow my fingers* (or *'notice the lights,' 'the taps,' or 'the sounds').*"

Nonspecific and Contingent Verbal Encouragement During Bilateral Stimulation

You then begin the first set of bilateral stimulation. At least once or twice during each set of bilateral stimulation, give nonspecific verbal encouragement such as *"Just notice"* or *"Follow."* Also offer contingent, but nonspecific verbal encouragement when you observe nonverbal changes in facial expression, breathing patterns, or eye movement such as *"That's it,"* or *"Just notice."* After a set of 24 to 30 complete movements, you pause and say, *"Rest. Take a deeper breath. Let it go. What do you notice now?"*

Standard Clinician Phrases After Every Set of Bilateral Stimulation in Phase Four

This simple set of phrases should be used consistently after each set of bilateral stimulation. Each phrase has a specific purpose. *"Rest. Take a deeper breath."* means in effect, "Pause and briefly shift your attention away from everything that occurred during that set of bilateral stimulation to the here-and-now by taking a deeper breath." Notice you should *not* say, *"Relax"* instead of *"Rest"* because this would direct the patient to try to deliberately change their psychophysiological state perhaps at a moment of strong fear, shame, anger, or grief. Saying *"Rest"* allows the patient to continue to experience whatever psychophysiological state has emerged together with any emotions, thoughts, images, or sensations that are most prominent. *"Let it go"* signifies both to let go of the deeper breath as well as to let go of any attempt to hold onto or to try to express all that may have occurred during that set of bilateral stimulation.

You then make the inquiry *"What do you notice now?"* The form of this general inquiry permits the patient to make a report of whatever is most present in conscious awareness. What is most salient could be a change in the image, other perceptual memories, body sensations, emotional intensity, or state. It could be a shift in the self-appraisal or a different memory emerging. It could be a concern, a fear, or a judgment about the reprocessing.

Therefore it is important *not* to inquire *"What do you feel now?"*, *"What do you notice about the picture now?"* or *"Did the fear change?"* Such specific questions narrow and direct the patient's attention to material that may not be germane to the spontaneous and effective reprocessing of the maladaptive memory network. You will only use such specific inquiries in order to address evidence of ineffective reprocessing.

You listen to the patient's verbal report. It can be helpful to write it down, especially when learning EMDR reprocessing skills, when you are conducting research, or when you are working under supervision or obtaining consultation. Writing down the patient's verbalization tends to inhibit habitual clinician tendencies for excessive verbal responses and allows a few more seconds to silently assess what the patient just said. There is no need to repeat or rephrase whatever the patient said. Unless the patient's report indicates the need to make an intervention to deal with ineffective reprocessing, just give the standard instruction: *"Focus on that and notice what happens next,"* or just, *"Go with that."*

Channels of Association

You continue sets of bilateral stimulation using the instructions above as long as patients' reports indicate that effective reprocessing is occurring until they report material that is neutral or positive. How to discern that effective reprocessing is occurring is described in the next section below. Generally, patients will experience some changes in their focus of attention from one set of bilateral stimulation to the next. Patients may report changes in the intensity, characteristics, and specific aspects of the target memory or they may associate to another memory.

Shapiro (2001, p. 35) describes these changes as occurring in "channels of association." These "channels" vary tremendously in length and number. In length, a channel of association can vary from a few sets of bilateral stimulation to more than 20 or 30 sets. The number of times that you need to return to target and identify another channel containing additional material will also vary from a few to a great many. When effective reprocessing is taking place, you will typically continue down a channel of association for between approximately 6–14 sets of bilateral stimulation *until the patient begins to report neutral or positive material.* However, keep in mind that channels can be much briefer or much longer. After two or perhaps three sets of bilateral stimulation focusing on neutral or positive material, you will generally return to the target to identify any additional disturbing material in need of reprocessing. How to return to target is described further below.

Changing the Bilateral Stimulation

If the patient reports the same disturbing content without change after two consecutive sets of bilateral stimulation, the first intervention is to change the direction, height, speed, or width of the eye movements. If you are using auditory stimulation, change the speed or type of sound. If you are using kinesthetic stimulation, change the speed, intensity, or location of the stimulation. Because most clinicians have been so thoroughly trained to think about altering their verbal responses when patients' experience "no change," it is counterintuitive for many clinicians to remember first to change the nature of the bilateral stimulation. However, a significant portion of EMDR's effectiveness seems to derive from its direct impact on the limbic system via neurologically mediated stimuli as much if not more than from psychologically mediated interactions with the neocortex (Servan-Schreiber, 2004). As you are learning to use EMDR, remember that more than 50% of the time, merely changing the characteristics of the bilateral stimulation will be enough to restore effective reprocessing.

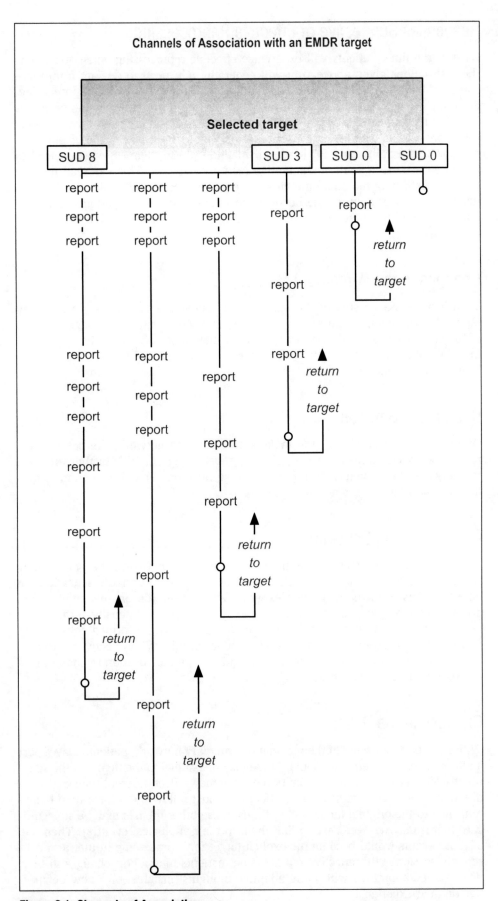

Figure 8.1 Channels of Association
Note. From Eye Movement Desensitization and Reprocessing: Basic Principles, Protocols, and Procedures by F. Shapiro,
2001, NY: Guilford Press. Copyright 2001 by Guilford Press. Adapted with permission.

Responses Suggestive of Effective Reprocessing

Most of the time, patients will experience effective reprocessing when you follow the instructions given above. You will generally only need to deviate from these standard instructions when there is evidence of lack of effective reprocessing. So a key question is how can you tell that effective reprocessing is taking place? Most changes in the content of the patient's verbalization are suggestive of effective reprocessing. This includes decreases as well as increases in the level of disturbance. Especially early in the desensitization phase, reprocessing can lead to increased accessing of the maladaptive memory network. This can lead initially to more disturbing material emerging. Further below, we will explore what to do when the level of disturbance becomes so intense that *you* experience concerns about continuing. First, here are additional indications suggestive of effective reprocessing.

Changes in the Perceptual Memory

With increased accessing of the maladaptive memory network, the patient may report that the image is closer, more intense, or a more disturbing image or series of images associated with the target incident may arise. With effective reprocessing, the patient may report that the image is further away, blurrier, less distinct, losing color, smaller, or gone.

Changes in Emotion

With increased accessing of the maladaptive memory network, the patient may report increased intensity of fear, shame, anger, or grief. With further effective reprocessing, the patient may report a change from one emotion to another or a decrease in intensity of emotion.

Changes in the Sensation

With increased accessing of the maladaptive memory network, the patient may report increased intensity of physical sensations or uncomfortable sensations in new locations. With patients who experienced intense pain or unwanted sexual arousal in the original experience, the potential for increased intensity of the sensations needs to be addressed in the preparation phase with informed consent and with psychoeducation. See chapter 6 for how to do this. With effective reprocessing, the patient may report a change in sensation from one location to another or a decrease in intensity of sensation.

Changes in the Belief

With increased accessing of the maladaptive memory network, patients may report additional negative self-statements. These may be parallel to the theme in the statement selected as the negative cognition or they may reflect different themes. When different themes emerge, it may be effective to just follow them for a time before returning to the original target. Other times, these other themes may be so significant that it may be necessary to link them to their etiological event(s). Then one of those events would become the explicit target for reprocessing in that or a subsequent session. With effective reprocessing, patients may report changes in their negative self-appraisals with more adaptive thoughts, insights, or a new perspective on their experience.

Changes in Defensive Action Urges

With increased accessing of the maladaptive memory network, patients may report awareness of a new defensive action urge or an increased awareness of a previously identified defensive action urge such as the urge to flee. Sometimes patients will report awareness of two competing defensive action urges, such as the urge to submit and the urge to flee. Initially, *as long as effective reprocessing continues*, you should not attempt to select among these multiple defensive action urges any more than you would attempt to narrow patients' awareness to only one of several physical sensations. Instead, encourage the patient to continue by saying, *"Just notice both and follow again."* With effective reprocessing, patients may report a shift to a different defensive action urge, such as a shift from the urge to flee to the urge to fight.

Shifts to Another Memory

With effective reprocessing, patients can make reports that remain focused primarily on shifts within the selected target. However, many patients will report shifts to other memories within a cluster of similar events—such as other episodes of physical abuse by a stepsibling. Or they may report earlier or more recent memories that may or may not initially appear to you, the clinician, to be related—such as a memory of a parent dismissing the patient's protest over maltreatment. However, there will always be significance to these associated memories. They can be related by belief, participant, sensation, emotion, defense, or coping response. Sometimes these emerging memories will reflect resources that contain solutions or adaptive material to assist in the reprocessing of the selected target memory—such as a favorite aunt who provided steady maternal warmth and protection.

Sometimes these other memories will reflect additional concerns that need to be given priority over the initially selected issues in the target memory. In these cases, the treatment plan may need to be modified to include a focus on the additional concerns reflected in the other memory. Sometimes these other memories will reflect spreading activation across one or more divergent clusters or sets of issues that may threaten to overwhelm the patient with too much material. In these cases, you may need to limit the focus of attention and help structure the reprocessing. When and how to do this will be discussed in chapter 9.

When and How to Return to Target

In the desensitization phase, the purpose of returning to target is to determine if there is more material that needs to be reprocessed. When do you know to return to the target? Normally, you will continue with additional sets of bilateral stimulation down a channel of association until the patient reports no further disturbing material and reports only neutral or positive material for two to three sets of bilateral stimulation. Then you return to target. Also return to target if the patient's associations become so remote from the original target that your clinical judgment suggests reprocessing of the selected target may no longer be occurring. Early in your experience in learning to use EMDR, you may initially doubt how a new association could be linked to the original target. However, if you allow one or two more sets of bilateral stimulation on this emerging material, you may then discover that the patient is making an important connection. It can take quite a bit of clinical experience to discern when new material is supporting effective reprocessing and when you are metaphorically wandering around at the end of a channel of association without sufficient engagement with the selected memory network. When you decide it is appropriate to return to the target, say: *"When you bring your attention back to the original experience, what do you notice now?"*

If, because of associations to other disturbing memories in that channel of association, the patient is uncertain to which event you are referring when you say, *"the original experience,"* then reference something objective about the event—such as saying, *"That first time you remember him threatening your brother."* Notice that when you return to target, the aim is to determine what spontaneously emerges in the patient's awareness. Therefore whenever you return to target do so in a completely neutral way. *When returning to target, do not repeat the negative cognition, the details of the image, the original emotions, or original location of physical sensations.* Just say: *"When you focus on the original experience, what do you notice now?"*

When the Patient Reports Clearly Disturbing Additional Material

If the patient reports additional material that is clearly disturbing, you do not have to check the Subjective Units of Disturbance (SUD). The only two essential times to check the SUD are in the assessment phase and again at the end of desensitization phase when you confirm the SUD is stable at a zero. So when there is additional, clearly disturbing material in the target, it is often enough to just say: *"Focus on that and notice what happens next."* If you are concerned that the patient is reporting primarily cognitive material and may be becoming too distant from residual disturbance in the target experience, after the patient's report you can ask *"Where do you feel that in your body?"* Then after the patient reports a location you can say *"Focus on that."*

Checking the SUD When the Patient Reports Ambiguous, Neutral, or Positive Material

When you return to target, if the patient reports ambiguous or apparently neutral or positive associations on the target, you may need to check the SUD rating. The standard way to check the SUD scale is to say: *"Focus on the original experience. On a scale from 0 to 10, where 0 is no disturbance or neutral and 10 is the highest disturbance you can imagine, how disturbing does it* feel *to you now?"*

When the SUD is a 1 or Higher

If the patient reports that the SUD rating is a 1 or higher, ask: *"What's the worst part of it now?"* After the patient reports the worst part, say: *"Focus that, and notice what happens next."* Or you can ask: *"Where do you feel that in your body?"* Then say, *"Focus that, and notice what happens next."*

When the SUD is a 0

If the SUD rating is 0, say: *"Focus on how the incident seems to you now and notice what happens next."* If nothing clearly disturbing emerges after the next set of bilateral stimulation, check the SUD rating again. When the patient reports a SUD rating of 0 a second time, you have completed the desensitization phase. Then continue to the installation phase.

Maintaining and Restoring Effective Reprocessing in the Desensitization Phase

OVERVIEW

Chapter 9 covers a wide range of strategies for maintaining and restoring effective reprocessing in the desensitization phase—phase 4—of the standard Eye Movement Desensitization and Reprocessing (EMDR) protocol for treating posttraumatic stress disorder (PTSD). We begin with clarifying standard sequences and decision trees that guide clinical work. We continue by examining the issues and strategies for supporting patients experiencing prolonged, intense emotional responses. Finally, we explore when and how to use interventions to deliberately stimulate an adaptive memory network to encourage synthesis with the selected target memory, which Shapiro (1995, 2001) refers to as "cognitive interweaves."

Clinicians preparing for initial training exercises do not need to master all the material in this chapter before starting to use the standard procedural steps in training or clinical settings. Your training instructor may suggest you skim this advanced material or skip ahead to the installation phase and the rest of the standard procedural steps covered in chapter 10. However, mastering this material is essential to applying the standard EMDR PTSD protocol with high fidelity.

Coping With Feeling Overwhelmed by the Range of Possible Clinical Responses While Learning EMDR

Clinicians actually face a relatively small number of decisions at each moment during EMDR reprocessing. Yet, when learning EMDR it is normal to feel overwhelmed with what to do next. It is analogous to the experience of learning to drive a car. There are relatively few controls required to operate modern automobiles. Each operates simply. Yet, after having studied the function of each control, when you finally get behind the wheel to sit next to your driving instructor, it is easy to become confused and overwhelmed, especially if anything unexpected happens. Only with practice does the conceptual knowledge of all the elements of driving a car gradually become procedural knowledge. Only with practice do the many skills of driving become automatically available to you so that your focus shifts away from the mechanical aspects of driving to simply enjoying getting safely and efficiently to where you are going.

Until you have had enough practice to integrate the principles and procedures you have learned with actual clinical experience to generate a sense of mastery, you need to accept that feeling a certain degree of uncertainty, confusion, hesitancy, and doubt is normal. In chapters 16 and 17 we will explore the process of professional development in EMDR and the role of consultation in supporting the development of clinical skills and mastery. It is helpful to make good process notes, write down your questions, and consult regularly. While you are integrating EMDR into your clinical skills, remind yourself that the standard EMDR procedural steps are quite robust. Most patients will still obtain significant benefit from reprocessing sessions in which you felt uncertain or made technical mistakes.

Standard Sequences and Decision Trees During the Desensitization Phase

In this first section, we will clarify a number of standard sequences and decision trees that guide clinical work in the desensitization phase.

When "Nothing" Changes Early in Reprocessing

One of the first confusing responses you will encounter during the desensitization phase is when in response to your inquiry, "What do you notice now?", a patient reports "Nothing." The first time you elicit this report, just make your usual response, "Focus on that and notice what happens next." Often after the next set of bilateral stimulation (BLS), the patient will report changes in the material. Occasionally, the patient may offer the response of "nothing" again, perhaps adding, "I was just watching your fingers going back and forth." The standard response when you get the same report after two consecutive sets of BLS is to change the direction or other characteristics of the BLS. After changing the stimulation, the third report may again be, "Nothing." At this point you might be thinking that nothing is changing in the memory network; that is possible. However, the repeated verbal report of "*nothing*" early in reprocessing is not necessarily an indication that nothing is changing in the memory network. Next, change direction for the second time. At this point the patient may begin to report other material that indicates actual shifts in the content or intensity of the memory network or may again report "nothing." After the fourth report of "nothing," and having changed direction twice, return to target with the standard phrase, "When you bring your attention back to the original experience, what do you notice now?" A significant portion of the time, you will be surprised to discover that the material being reported in the target is different in content or intensity from the material that was reported before you started reprocessing. How is this possible? It may reflect differences between verbal reports from the stream of awareness in the prefrontal regions of the cortex and where change is occurring in the limbic system and other areas of the brain.

The verbal report of "nothing" can signify many different experiences across a series of sets of BLS. Here are a few examples: (a) "Changes are occurring, but I don't know how to put them into words"; (b) "Something is happening but I'm too distracted by you waving your fingers to be able to explain it"; (c) "I'm too afraid of doing this wrong and I'm just too focused on your hand moving back and forth to notice how different I'm really starting to feel"; (d) "I'm afraid to admit this might be working. Nothing else has worked, and I don't feel like I'm really doing anything on purpose, so I'll just say I'm noticing nothing." The take away lesson is do not assume the first, second, or even the third time you hear "nothing" that nothing is changing. You, the clinician, are not failing when the patient reports "nothing" after several sets of bilateral stimulation. Often, material will begin to emerge after two or three sets of bilateral stimulation. If not, after changing direction, just return to target, reaccess the memory network, and assess whether the selected target has shifted. Persistent patient reports of "nothing" with little or no change reported when returning to the selected target may also indicate (a) insufficient accessing of the maladaptive memory network; (b) specific fears interfering with reprocessing; (c) dissociative, intellectualizing, or other defenses; (d) issues of secondary gain or loss; or (e) insufficient trust in the therapeutic alliance. We will explore how to respond to each of these possibilities in this chapter.

Responding to Transference Material During Reprocessing

Another challenge for clinicians new to EMDR is responding to transference material that emerges during reprocessing. Transference is defined in *Webster's New World Dictionary of the American Language* (Guralnik, 1970) as "a reproduction of emotions relating to repressed experiences, esp. of childhood, and the substitution of another person . . . for the original object of the repressed impulses." Patients who were raised with unrelenting standards by one or both parents may express doubts such as, "I'm wondering if I'm doing this correctly." Patients who developed parentified aspects of their personality as young children and who came to believe they were responsible for their parents' needs may become concerned, "Isn't your arm getting tired?" Patients who felt emotionally abandoned in their early life experience may protest, "I'm used to you talking more. You're not saying very much. I'm feeling very alone in this."

Staying Out of the Way

There are two principles to keep in mind as transference issues emerge. The first is that whatever issue the patient is addressing in the selected memory will tend to manifest itself in the process; that is, in the nature of the material being reported and the clinical interactions during reprocessing. The second is that most transference issues will resolve themselves if you *stay out of the way* and allow the material to move through *without any additional comments, interpretations, or reassurances*. Inhibiting your usual clinical responses to transference material may feel awkward or may bring up countertransference issues for some clinicians. However, experience has shown that working within the framework of the Adaptive Information Processing (AIP) model and avoiding intruding into the patient's material generally lead to the best outcomes.

When Earlier Memories Are Accessed

As you move through channels of association, earlier memories may spontaneously surface. Based on the principle from AIP model that earlier experiences set the patterns of response for later events, when earlier events emerge, you will generally stay with and complete reprocessing of the earliest material before returning to the originally selected target. The earlier material may resolve within that session or may require additional sessions. Unless there are indications that the earlier material is linked to a different theme, it is generally not necessary to start over with a new assessment phase for this earlier target.

When More Recent Memories Are Accessed

Often, memories of more recent disturbing events compared to the selected target will emerge during the desensitization phase. Although these more recent disturbing events may be similar to the selected target in terms of content, participants, nature of event, or other characteristics, it is generally best to limit the number of sets of BLS given to more recent disturbing events to just one or two sets before returning the focus to the earlier, selected target memory. The principle for this is again based on the AIP model, which emphasizes that unresolved, maladaptively encoded earlier experiences set the framework for responding to later occurring experiences. Therefore, until the earlier, selected target memory has been fully reprocessed, it is generally more clinically efficient to limit the extent of reprocessing on associations to more recent disturbing memories. Note that when patients associate to more recent *adaptive* memories, you will generally limit the number of sets of bilateral stimulation to two or three before returning to target to probe for additional disturbing aspects of the selected target memory.

If you had not been aware of these more recent disturbing memories, you should notate them in your process notes to be added to your master list of targets to be addressed in a subsequent session. You might comment to the patient along the lines of "It is clear that these memories are related for you. We can return to this more recent incident in another session. For now, let's continue and complete our work on the earlier memory." Even if, when returning attention to the selected target, the Subjective Units of Disturbance (SUD) is considerably lower, even close to a zero, it is generally more efficient to complete the desensitization, installation, and body scan phases on the earlier memory before going on to reprocessing a more recent event. Otherwise, the incompletely resolved earlier memory may continue to generate maladaptive material as you attempt to work on a more recent memory. Often, the more recent memory will be partially, substantially, or completely resolved by completing reprocessing on the earlier memory.

Responding to Prolonged Intense Emotional Responses

When reprocessing target memories that are strongly emotionally charged, it is not unusual for patients to experience intense emotion responses during reprocessing. Howard Lipke's early survey (1995) indicated that this is more common in EMDR than in most traditional forms of verbal psychotherapy. It is important that both patient and clinician have sufficient affect tolerance skills, are properly prepared, and have an appropriate stance toward these episodes of intense emotion.

Starting first from the theoretical perspective, in EMDR, unlike with prolonged exposure, the duration and the intensity of emotional reexperiencing are not the essential elements in therapeutic change. In EMDR, effective reprocessing is viewed as a result synthesis between maladaptive and adaptive memory networks. Although intense emotional responses may be more likely to occur in EMDR reprocessing than in many types of verbal psychotherapy, their duration and intensity are not considered essential for therapeutic change. Indeed, research indicates EMDR is *more effective* when reprocessing trauma in a detached manner compared with vivid reliving (Lee & Drummond, 2008; Lee, Taylor, & Drummond, 2006). Thus, EMDR should not be viewed as an *exposure extinction*-based treatment but as a method of enhancing emotional information processing.

The traditional psychoanalytical term invented by Sigmund Freud for moments of intense emotional responses in psychotherapy is *abreaction*. Abreaction refers to a kind of reliving of an experience in order to purge it of its emotional intensity ("Abreaction," 2007). In EMDR, we do not emphasize the need to *relive*. The focus is on establishing *dual attention*. This requires both *accessing* the maladaptive memory network and *attending* to BLS, thereby allowing the brain to reorganize the way the memory is held. Still, reexperiencing aspects of the maladaptive memory network at a significant level of disturbance is a common and often unavoidable occurrence during reprocessing.

When effective reprocessing is taking place, the appropriate stance during intense emotional responses should be one of compassion and support rather than trying to prolong, abbreviate, or distort the patient's movement through the material that is emerging. There are several standard procedural elements that clinicians should bring into play as part of this supportive stance, but you should generally avoid interventions to address your own discomfort with the nature of the content or intensity of the material that emerges. The key issue during moments of intense emotional responses is monitoring whether there is evidence that effective reprocessing is taking place.

Good Preparation Is Essential Before Dealing With High-Charged Material

Before commencing EMDR reprocessing on clearly, intensely charged material, you should be sure that patients are appropriately prepared with psychoeducation and affect tolerance and containment skills. See chapter 6 for a detailed discussion of procedures to prepare patients for EMDR reprocessing. Psychoeducation for patients includes information about what to expect during reprocessing, together with metaphors that support an appropriate stance of mindful noticing toward the experience. Patients should know first of all that they are in control and can stop at any time by showing you the prearranged stop signal. Let patients know that they can always pause from the reprocessing if they feel the need. Remind patients that you have practiced the calm place exercise and other methods that help control anxiety and other intense emotional states. Let patients know that these interventions can be used at any point, if needed, to help them regain a sense of control over their emotional state.

Second, patients should know that continuing the sets of BLS is the best way to both move through the emotional states that emerge and to ensure that memory networks producing these intense emotional states are reorganized into a form in which they are no longer capable of giving rise to future experiences of intrusive, painful reexperiencing. At the time of traumatic experiences, the sensory and emotional systems in the brain encoded these intense sensory and emotion experiences into traumatic memory storage (van der Kolk, McFarlane, & Weisaeth, 1996, chap. 12). During EMDR, reprocessing the elements that make up these traumatic memory networks are reorganized into the same type of narrative memory storage as normal old memories (Levin, Lazrove, & van der Kolk, 1999; Lansing, Amen, Hanks & Rudy, 2005).

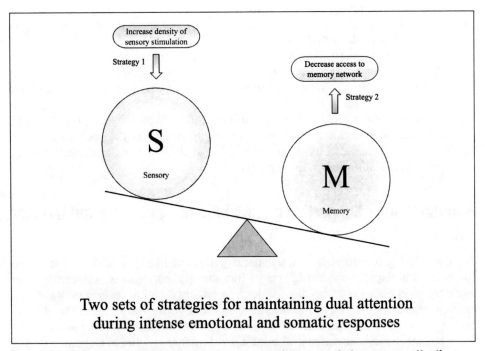

Two sets of strategies for maintaining dual attention during intense emotional and somatic responses

Figure 9.1 Two sets of strategies when intense emotions overwhelm sensory attention.

Two Sets of Strategies for Maintaining Dual Attention During Intense Emotional and Somatic Responses

During episodes of intense emotional responses, consciousness will tend to shift away from the point of balance toward greater attention to the highly distressing material stored in memory with less attention to the bilateral sensory stimulation. To help the patient maintain the balance of dual attention, it is helpful to increase the intensity of the bilateral stimulation. You can do this in several ways.

Increase the Number of Movements Per Set of Bilateral Stimulation

First, the number of movements per set of bilateral stimulation should be increased from the standard 24 to 30, 40, or 50 or more movements per set. Instead of relying on a set number of movements, you should be more focused on changes in facial expression, breathing patterns, skin color, characteristics of eye movements, and other nonverbal cues that indicate level and quality of affect experiencing. If possible, extend the number movements in a set of bilateral stimulation until there are nonverbal indications of a softening in the intensity or a shift in the characteristics of the emotional state.

Increase the Frequency of Verbal Encouragement

Second, in order to support the maintenance of dual attention, increase the frequency of your nonspecific verbal encouragement to the patient by saying these phrases more frequently: "that's it" and "just notice." Third, consider reminding the patient of the metaphor of being on the train. "You're on the train. It's just a memory passing by. Just notice." If they seem frightened you can remind them: "You are here with me in the office. You're safe now. Just notice what's happening in your memory and watch it go by." When you see shifts in facial expression that suggest the patient is accessing other material you can comment "That's it. Just notice." These nonspecific but *contingent responses* (Siegel, 1999) serve to maintain the strength of the therapeutic alliance and help the patient to *regulate arousal* by feeling connected with you as they move through their material.

Fourth, in more intense portions of sessions, you can use your voice in rhythm with the BLS echoing: "That's it. Follow. Follow. Follow. Follow." Most patients will not find this distracting or intrusive but rather will feel that you are matching their intensity. They will feel supported and retain a stronger sense of being able to both stay with the memory and be present with you. Fifth, if you are using the Eye Scan 4000 for bilateral stimulation (see chapters 16 and Appendix C), you can consider adding a second mode of bilateral stimulation such as adding auditory tones or kinesthetic stimulation to eye movements.

Remain Calmly Supportive and Mindful of Options as You Monitor Evidence of Effective Reprocessing

After increasing the number of movements per set of BLS, you continue to monitor nonverbal expression during sets of BLS and patient reports between sets for evidence of effective reprocessing. As long as patients' verbal reports indicate continuing evidence of effective reprocessing, continue to move from one set of bilateral stimulation to another with minimal dialogue between sets. Perhaps two of the most crucial elements to successful resolution of intense emotional responses during EMDR reprocessing are (a) your confidence in the reprocessing, and (b) your ability to remain calmly supportive and mindful of all the tools and options you have at your disposal to assist the patient through this material. Maintaining a stance of detached compassion is essential to your ability to perceive clearly what is occurring and to be reflective on whether or not there is any need to intervene to assist the patient.

Monitoring Your Own Affect Tolerance

Doing less at such moments and allowing the reprocessing to move through can be extremely challenging for clinicians who are learning to use EMDR. Certainly, if there is evidence of ineffective reprocessing, you need to be prepared to intervene. However, some clinicians intervene not because the patient needs the intervention, but because their own affect tolerance limits are being exceeded and they are experiencing anxiety or countertransference material from their professional or personal past that is being reactivated. If this occurs with you, first consider getting additional education and consultation from a consultant approved by the EMDR International Association (EMDRIA). Show videotapes of sessions with intense emotional responses to an EMDRIA Approved Consultant to get feedback on these issues. If feedback indicates that your patients are responding optimally at times you find difficult to tolerate, consider having EMDR sessions to address your own emotional responses to your patients' intense emotional material. Often, a relatively small number of EMDR sessions can be enough to resolve the material that is activated at these moments of emotional intensity.

Recognizing and Responding to the Four Causes of Ineffective Reprocessing

Although it is important to do less and stay out of the way when effective reprocessing is taking place, it is essential to intervene when reprocessing is ineffective. The key characteristics for recognizing effective versus ineffective reprocessing were detailed in the section of chapter 8 on "Responses Suggestive of Effective Reprocessing." These characteristics provide cues to clinicians of the need to make an intervention, but they do not always indicate which type of intervention is needed. To be able to select the type of intervention, you need to conceptualize the nature of the difficulty in terms of the Adaptive Information Processing model. Fortunately, there are only four broad categories of difficulty in reprocessing from which to choose: (a) under accessing the maladaptive memory network; (b) over accessing the maladaptive memory network; (c) the need to shift the focus to access a different, earlier maladaptive memory network; and (d) lack of spontaneous synthesis between the maladaptive memory network and an appropriate, adaptive memory network. (See table 9.1 - Four Categories of Ineffective Reprocessing.) Once you recognize which of these four categories of difficulty is contributing to the ineffective reprocessing, it is much easier to select from the various interventions to restore effective reprocessing. So let us examine each of these in turn.

 | Four Categories of Ineffective Reprocessing

1) Under accessing the maladaptive memory network
2) Over accessing the maladaptive memory network
3) The need to shift focus to access a different, earlier maladaptive memory network
4) Lack of spontaneous synthesis between the maladaptive memory network and an appropriate adaptive memory network

| Procedures for Increasing Access to the Maladaptive Memory Network

1) Changing the direction, speed, or number of repetitions of the bilateral eye movements or the mode or other characteristics of the bilateral stimulation.
2) Before each set of bilateral stimulation ask the patient, *"Where do you feel it in your body?"* Then say, *"Focus on that,"* with the next set.
3) Return to target and remind the patient of visual or other sensory threat cues from the memory.
4) Return to target and remind the patient of the selected negative cognition to stimulate more of the disturbing emotion in the target memory.
5) Inquire about unspoken words: *"With this next set of eye movements* (taps or tones), *notice any words that you wished you had said, or now wish to say, even if you would not actually say them out loud."*
6) Inquire about unacted impulses: *"With this next set of eye movements* (taps or tones), *notice any impulses to act that had then, but didn't act on, or any impulses you have now, even if you would not actually act on them in real life."*
7) Invite giving a voice to physical sensations: *"With this next set of eye movements* (taps or tones), *notice where you have that feeling in your body and imagine part of your body could speak or express the feeling that is there."*
8) Explore specific fears that may be interfering with accessing. *"What fears or concerns do you have now that might prevent this memory from being resolved?"* Resolve the identified fear with psychoeducation, RDI, or reprocessing the life experience associated with acquiring that fear.
9) Teach patients skills for decreasing depersonalization and derealization described in Chapter 6 before resuming reprocessing.

Under Accessing

The first situation that can produce ineffective reprocessing is when there is insufficient accessing of the appropriate maladaptive memory network. Table 9.2, "Procedures for Increasing Access to the Maladaptive Memory Network", lists nine types of interventions to address under accessing. We will examine each in turn.

Changing Characteristics of the Bilateral Stimulation

The first set of interventions for patients who are under accessing the maladaptive memory network—in the absence of significant psychological defenses—involves simply changing the characteristics or mode of the bilateral stimulation. The options include increasing or decreasing the speed; increasing or decreasing the width of the movements; raising or lowering the height of horizontal movement; and changing to a left or right diagonal, circular, or infinity sign movements. Finally, consider changing the mode of stimulation to auditory or kinesthetic bilateral stimulation.

Changing the Mode of Bilateral Stimulation

Some patients have difficulty adequately accessing the emotions, sensations, and defensive action urges associated with their maladaptive memory networks. Some of these patients may show some general signs of *alexethymia*. Others may only have difficulty when attempting to reprocess maladaptive memories. Some of these patients come from families where there were many and frequent visual and auditory threat cues that were signals of impending danger of injury to self or others, verbal abuse, or threats of abandonment. These patients experience residual visual hypervigilance to subtle threat cues during EMDR reprocessing sessions, which serves as a barrier to their accessing of their maladaptive memory network during reprocessing with bilateral eye movements. To assist them in reducing the distraction they experience when scanning for threat cues, you can ask them to switch from eye movements to auditory bilateral stimulation and close their eyes.

"Where Do You Feel It in Your Body?"

The next intervention is to refocus the patient to the felt location of disturbance. Before each set of BLS, ask the patient, "Where do you feel it in your body?" Then say, "Focus on that," when you start the next set of BLS.

Emphasize Threat Cues in the Target Memory

To help increase access to elements of the maladaptive memory network, return to target and remind the patient of visual or other sensory threat cues from the memory. Repeat the sensory details the patient reported about the incident during history taking or the assessment phase.

Use the Negative Cognition to Stimulate the Disturbing Emotion

Because the negative cognition tends to stimulate the disturbing emotion in the maladaptive memory network, you can use the to help increase access to the maladaptive memory network. Return to target and remind the patient of the selected negative cognition.

Unspoken Words and Unacted Impulses

Three powerful and related ways to increase access to aspects of the maladaptive memory network are to invite one of the following: (a) *unspoken words*, (b) *unacted impulses*, and (c) *giving a voice to physical sensations*. The need to inquire about unspoken words may be identified by visible clenching of the jaw, a band of white or red coloration around the throat, or verbal reports of tightness in the throat. An invitation for unspoken words goes like this: "With this next set of eye movements (taps or tones), notice any words that you wished you had said, or now wish to say, even if you would not actually say them out loud." Then offer the next set of BLS. Often, after the next set of BLS, the patient will begin to report appropriate dialogue with the other significant person in the target memory.

The need to inquire about *unacted impulses* may be identified by noticing muscle clenching, tapping, or holding parts of the body, verbal reports of discomfort, or suppressed defensive action urges. An invitation for *unacted impulses* goes like this: "With this next set of eye movements (taps or tones), notice any impulses to act that you had then, but didn't act on, or any impulses you have now, even if you would not actually act on them in real life." In a similar vein, uncomfortable physical sensation that persists even after changing the direction of eye movement can be addressed by an invitation to give a voice to them. You can invite the patient to give *a voice to physical sensations* by saying: "With this next set of eye movements (taps or tones), notice where you have that feeling in your body and imagine that part of your body could speak or express the feeling that is there."

Explore and Resolve Fears That May Be Interfering With Accessing

In chapter 6, we discussed the importance of developing an adequate therapeutic alliance. Patients need to feel sufficient trust and rapport to be able to honestly report whatever is occurring. Sometimes, under accessing of the maladaptive memory network reflects insufficient trust in the therapeutic alliance. Patients may have fears of loss of control, being judged, failing, or other specific fears that they have not disclosed during the history taking or preparation phases or that they may not have realized.

When such concerns or fears are based on lack of information, psychoeducation is often indicated first. Examples include religious concerns that EMDR is a form of hypnosis that is prohibited in certain sects, fear of being controlled by the therapist, fear of having to disclose details that the person would rather not, fear of going crazy, fear of being rejected as hopeless, and fear of losing positive memories. Some fears call for a combination of psychoeducation and informed consent. Examples include the fear of having less vivid recall in forensic cases and the fear of remembering other even more disturbing events. Some concerns are reality based. These often require problem solving before reprocessing can be effective. Examples include not having sufficient funds to pay for a complete course of treatment or being in danger from additional criminal assaults by a domestic partner.

Addressing Fears by Reprocessing Contributory Experiences

Other fears may derive from life experiences other than the selected target memory. These can include contributory experiences from childhood, such as a caregiver's failure to protect or provide needed support or an adverse prior therapy experience. Even though these contributory experiences may be less disturbing than or may have seemed peripheral to the selected target memory, they can interfere with accessing and reprocessing. Initially refocusing the treatment plan to reprocessing one or more contributory memories associated with the identified fear may be all that is needed to allow successful reprocessing of the originally selected target memory.

One example is a patient who had been abruptly terminated after 4 months of treatment by a previous clinician when she revealed she had begun to remember episodes of childhood sexual assault by her grandfather. This patient became afraid during reprocessing that if she were to recall other disturbing memories—as she was told is common in EMDR—her EMDR clinician will also reject her. This was resolved with a combination of psychoeducation about her current clinician's practice philosophy and professional standards and then reprocessing the memory of being rejected from her previous treatment. In the next session, they were able to successfully reprocess the original target memory.

Another example is a patient who was reprocessing the memory of being the victim of a physical assault. After some initial successful reprocessing on the assault memory, he experienced ineffective reprocessing partway through the session. When asked, "What fears or concerns do you have now that might prevent this memory from being resolved?" he reported that he feared crying, becoming distraught, and having to be hospitalized. He was then asked, "What experience is connected to the fear that crying could lead to having to be hospitalized?" He then identified a childhood memory. His mother was treated for postpartum depression in a psychiatric hospital for several weeks when the patient was 8 years old. The patient recalled his mother crying and crying before being taken away. The patient identified the associated belief as, "If I cry or get upset, I'll lose control and have to be hospitalized." The patient's symptoms had begun directly after the adult assault. He had not identified this childhood separation from his mother during history taking. Once this contributory experience was reprocessed, he was able to successfully complete reprocessing the memory of the adult assault.

Addressing Fears by Enhancing Self-Capacities With RDI

Sometimes fears are based more on the absence of a self-capacity than from an adverse experience. Examples include confidence in the strength to cope with painful memories and being worthy of the resources being used for therapy. In these cases, using the Resource Development and Installation (RDI) (see exhibits 6.10

in chapter 6, and B5 and B6 in appendix B) procedure to develop and install one or more resources for strength of self-worth may allow successful accessing and reprocessing the selected target memory.

Addressing Dissociative and Intellectualizing Defenses

A range of psychological defenses can interfere with accessing. Two commonly encountered are dissociative and intellectualizing defenses. In the absence of a full dissociative disorder, many patients with PTSD will experience significant depersonalization with numbing, confusion, or disorientation during reprocessing. This will be more likely to occur in those with early childhood or prolonged adult exposures to adverse or traumatic experiences. Strategies for helping to decrease these dissociative responses are described in chapter 6. It may be necessary to shift from reprocessing to teaching and practicing strategies for decreasing dissociation until these patients can tolerate accessing their traumatic memories without excessive depersonalization. In some cases, installing resources for self-nurturing, safety, or protection has been helpful for patients with mild to moderate depersonalization. Patients with mild intellectualizing defenses can generally be assisted to achieve effective reprocessing with the strategies described above for under accessing.

Over Accessing the Maladaptive Memory Network

During over accessing of the maladaptive memory network, the patient is unable to maintain dual attention with the external bilateral stimulation because of the intensity or nature of the material being accessed in the maladaptive memory network. You will generally recognize this category of difficulty from patient reports between sets of bilateral stimulation, from observing displays of persistently high levels of patient affective distress, or from the patient resorting to the stop signal. However, you should be alert to the possibility that some patients will move into a persistent state of ineffective reprocessing because of over accessing aspects of the maladaptive memory network without reporting it verbally, without showing easily observable affective

 | Procedures for Decreasing Access to the Maladaptive Memory Network

---

1) Change the direction, speed or number of repetitions of the bilateral eye movements or the mode or other characteristics of the bilateral stimulation.

A) Slow the speed of bilateral stimulation.

B) Use the minimum number of repetitions per set—24.

C) Use vertical eye movements—anecdotally reported to be calming.

D) If eyes have been closed to help access the memory network with auditory or kinesthetic stimulation, instruct the patient to keep eyes open during bilateral stimulation.

E) Add a second or third mode of stimulation.

2) Use interventions to decrease the degree to which the patient is accessing the maladaptive memory network.

A) Imagine disturbing images are farther away. Use an imaginary "remote control" to alter vividness, remove color, pause, or fast-forward.

B) Imagine disturbing sounds are further away or decreasing volume with an imaginary "remote control."

C) Focus on just on sensation.

D) Focus on just one emotion.

E) Focus on just one defensive action urge.

F) Offer a natural essential oil to help reorganize high disturbing memories of taste or scent.

signals of distress, and without displaying the stop signal. This may be more likely when working with individuals from some indigenous or other cultures—such as some Asian cultures—who were trained not to protest or overtly display the level of their distress to their elders or authority figures. It also is more likely when working with individuals with a dismissing or avoidant insecure attachment classification, who often may not detect or display overt signs of excessive distress until they are on the verge of panic, or flight, or have begun to experience severe depersonalization. When working with individuals with these tendencies, it is essential to work in the preparation phase with psychoeducation and skill building to increase their skills at detecting and signaling when their distress is reaching the point when they begin to lose dual attention to both the bilateral stimulation and to their connection with you.

There are two main sets of strategies for responding to patients who experience ineffective reprocessing because of over accessing of a maladaptive memory network during reprocessing. These are illustrated above in Figure 9.1, "Two Strategies for Intense Emotional and Somatic Responses." The first set of strategies is to increase the density or to change characteristics of the bilateral stimulation. The second set of strategies focus on decreasing the degree to which the patient is accessing the maladaptive memory network.

Changing Bilateral Stimulation for Patients Who Are Over Accessing

When you are using eye movements for BLS, the first intervention for ineffective reprocessing is always to change the speed and the other characteristics of the BLS. As described earlier in this chapter, in the section on "Responding to Prolonged Intense Emotional Responses," when there is a lack of change in patients' reports during intense emotional processing, you can switch from one mode of BLS to a different mode of BLS. If you had initially selected auditory BLS to allow a patient to lessen visual distraction by having eyes closed during the BLS, you can request the patient to open his or her eyes during the BLS to help strengthen dual attention to visual cues in the present sensory surround. Another very helpful intervention for patients who are over accessing is to add a second mode of BLS. This is easiest to do when you are using technology such as the EyeScan 4000 to generate BLS.

When patients are able to remain in touch with their physical sensations and emotions, but are flooded by disturbing images, you might try first adding auditory tones to eye movements. When patients are starting to experience some depersonalization and numbing, with decreased ability to feel sensations, you might first try adding kinesthetic stimulation to eye movements. In rare situations of primary structural dissociation and more commonly for patients who have secondary or tertiary structural dissociation, you may find that using all three modes of BLS may restore reprocessing.

You can shorten the number of repetitions in each set of BLS to the basic 24 repetitions and then take longer to refocus patients into the here-and-now between sets of BLS. You can ask patients to take several slower, deeper, diaphragmatic breaths. You can ask patients to practice grounding exercises such as moving their feet and ankles and noticing the contact their bodies make with the chair and the floor. If you have had patients close their eyes initially during BLS with taps or tones to assist with accessing the maladaptive memory network, ask them to keep their eyes open during sets of BLS to retain a greater focus on current sensory stimulation and bring more balance to in dual attention. You can switch to vertical eye movements, which have been reported anecdotally to be calming.

Limiting Accessing With Narrowing of Attention or Suggestion

The next set of strategies use narrowing of attention or suggestion to decrease the degree of accessing the selected target memory network. Each of these strategies focuses on one of the elements of the selected target memory network—the image or other sensory perceptions, physical sensations, emotions, beliefs, and defensive action urges. For some patients this may enable them to move through high levels of disturbance and reach a point of some resolution for some aspects of the selected target memory network. However, because these interventions distort spontaneous accessing, it is important to recheck the selected target memory network in subsequent sessions. When rechecking the selected target memory network, avoid interventions that would distort accessing of the selected target memory network to assure that all aspects of the target memory network have been fully resolved.

Distancing Images and Other Sensory Memories

When patients report highly disturbing images, you can suggest they imagine the images are further away. One way to do this is to imagine the images are on a television screen and to imagine being able to move further back from the screen to make the image both more distant and smaller. You can suggest that color can drain out of the images so that they are just black and white. Asking patients to imagine using controls on an imaginary remote control, you can suggest making the image dimmer and less distinct. If patients report a series of many disturbing images or a mental movie of events, you can suggest freezing the images using the "pause button" so that there is just one image.

In the same way with sounds, smells, and other sensory perceptions, you can suggest that the sounds can appear to be coming from farther away or to use the remote control to turn down the volume so the sounds can barely be heard. With physical sensations, patients sometimes report awareness of sensations in several parts of their bodies. You can suggest they focus on just one sensation rather than remaining aware of all of the sensations. When there are multiple emotions, you can suggest that the patient focus on just one emotion until it resolves. In the same way, when patients are accessing multiple defensive action urges, you can suggest that they focus on just one of these. When patients are flooded by memories of a terrible smell or taste, you can offer them a selection of natural essential oils such as vanilla, mint, or lavender. Allowing patients to smell a pleasant smell during reprocessing can help reorganize the scent memory by simultaneously having the disturbing scent memory activated while taking in a pleasant scent during BLS.

Earlier Memories That Contribute to Ineffective Reprocessing

The third situation that can lead patients to have ineffective reprocessing is when different, earlier maladaptive memory networks need to become the initial focus of attention. After trying the strategies listed above, whether patients appear to be over accessing or under accessing the selected target memory network, they may need assistance to refocus attention to an earlier maladaptive memory network. As described above when discussing issues of informed consent, many patients will spontaneously associate to earlier memories after you have started reprocessing on a selected target memory. When this does not happen spontaneously, you may need to simulate what often occurs spontaneously. You can do this with either a simple one- or two-step intervention to redirect attention to the appropriate maladaptive memory network.

These earlier maladaptive memory networks can be associated with the same theme as in the original selected target memory network. Shapiro (2001, p. 189–192) refers to these as "feeder memories" because they hold the disturbance and "feed" it forward into later occurring experiences. Earlier memories with the same theme can be the source of difficulty when patients appear to be either over accessing or under accessing the selected target memory network. These memories can generally be quickly identified as described below with history taking or one of the somatic or affect bridge strategies discussed in chapter 4.

Alternately, this earlier memory network can be linked to a different theme. These have been described by Shapiro (2001, 192–193) as "blocking beliefs." We can also conceptualize earlier maladaptive memory networks with different themes as "defenses" in that they represent earlier attempts to adapt to an adverse life event or situation and have not yet been replaced or reorganized with more adaptive coping responses. To identify these defensive or "blocking belief" maladaptive memory networks, you will need to engage in some exploration before you use an affect or somatic bridge to identify the earlier memory network. In either case, shifting attention to these earlier maladaptive memory networks allows reprocessing to engage directly with the source of the material that needs to be addressed.

Accessing an Earlier Maladaptive Memory Network With the Same Theme

When patients continue to have ineffective reprocessing after trying the strategies discussed above, you should consider that there might be earlier memories that are the primary source of disturbance and need to be targeted directly. When earlier memories do not emerge spontaneously and there is ineffective reprocessing, you can explore for an earlier memory using the affect or somatic bridge. See Exhibit 4.8, "The Affect, Somatic and Defensive Urge Bridge Techniques."

In the middle of reprocessing, you already know the patient's negative cognition. When you suspect that ineffective reprocessing may be caused by an earlier associated memory network, use that negative cognition as the starting point of a bridge. You may decide to do this after returning to target and determining that there has not been significant change or in the middle of a channel of associations with a persistent, disturbing, but unchanging response. You can tell the patient, "Let's do an experiment. Notice that thought _____"—repeat the negative cognition in the first person—"and where you are feeling it in your body. Now just let your mind float back to the earliest time in your life when you had the same thought and with those same feelings in that part of your body. What memory comes up for you now?"

Depending on the material that the patient has been reporting, instead of floating back on the somatic bridge, you may use the affect or the defensive action urge. For example, perhaps the patient is not progressing in the reprocessing and is reporting the urge to run away. You can say, "Notice that urge to run away and where you are feeling it in your body and just let your mind float back to the earliest time in your life when you had the same impulse to run away in that same part of your body. What memory comes up for you now?" If the patient is able to identify an earlier associated memory, there is no need to do a full assessment on this maladaptive memory network. Instead, just continue reprocessing on the earlier memory until it is fully reprocessed—through desensitization, installation, and body scan phases—before returning to the originally selected target memory network to complete reprocessing on it.

Accessing an Earlier Maladaptive Memory Network With a Different Theme

When you return to target and determine that the SUD level has not gone any lower than it was the last one or two times you checked, you should consider exploring for an alternate maladaptive memory network linked to a different theme. Such an earlier maladaptive memory network may be linked to an earlier acquired defense or a "blocking belief" that must be directly identified, accessed, and reprocessed before the initially selected target memory can be resolved.

The Case of Sharon: Finding Earlier Memories on the Same and Different Themes

Here is a clinical example that illustrates how earlier memories on the same theme and on different themes can cause lack of change in the level of disturbance. Sharon was a college student who sought treatment at the student-counseling center for concentration problems and insomnia that were affecting her ability to complete her bachelor's degree. History taking determined that these problems had worsened over a period of nearly 3 years and were linked to an episode of sexual assault by a stranger. She had not disclosed the incident to anyone and had not sought help. She met full criteria for PTSD with nightmares, avoidance of any close contacts with a male, and sleep disturbances. Her clinician offered her EMDR reprocessing. She had mentioned in the history taking that there had also been a "date rape" episode 1 year before the sexual assault but said that she had not developed any of these symptoms after that incident. Therefore, the clinician and she had selected the target of the sexual assault from 3 years previously.

Her image was of turning her head away to stare at the wall at the moment the assault took place. Her negative cognition was "I am helpless." Her positive cognition was "I can protect myself now." The Validity of Cognition (VoC) was 2. Her emotion was fear and shame. Her SUD level was 9. The felt location was her chest and face. After a few sets of BLS, she began to report scenes from the date rape memory. They shifted attention to this earlier memory of the date rape by a man who had been her study partner for two semesters.

After more than 15 minutes of additional reprocessing, the SUD level was still only down to an 8. The clinician then asked Sharon to scan for an earlier memory using an affect bridge. What emerged were memories of two incidents of sexual abuse one summer by a visiting, older male cousin that took place in her home when she was 11 years old. As with the adult incidents of sexual assault, she had never disclosed these two experiences to anyone. They continued reprocessing on the first of these two incidents that was linked to the same negative cognition, "I am helpless," as the initially selected adult memory of the sexual assault by a stranger. However, after another 10 minutes of reprocessing, the SUD level on this childhood memory remained unchanging at an 8 as well.

At this point the clinician asked her, "What keeps the disturbance from going any lower?" The patient replied, "Well, you know, boys will be boys. It's a man's world. You just have to learn to deal with it." The clinician then asked, "Where did you learn that?" She replied, "That's what my mother always said when I was a little girl. I'd go to her for help when my older brothers would play too roughly with me and humiliate me. That's what she'd always say." They then selected and did a full assessment on a scene where she had sought protection from her mother. Sharon identified the negative cognition for that memory as, "I am worthless." Reprocessing proceeded much more effectively with this memory and the SUD level began to drop. Her feelings of shame and fear soon shifted to anger at her mother's lack of support. They ran out of time before they were able to complete reprocessing in that session. In the next two sessions, she made rapid progress and completed the entire series of memories they had uncovered.

The defensive beliefs Sharon formed in learning to cope with her mother's failure to protect or support her in coping with her older brothers led her to believe "I am worthless." It also led her to expect no support or comfort when a man physically assaulted her. Perhaps a more thorough history taking might have revealed these key childhood experiences. An expanded initial treatment plan that started with the mother's failure to protect might have avoided the ineffective reprocessing. The patient had not forgotten any of these key incidents, but she had not considered them to be relevant to her symptoms. No matter how thorough you are in history taking and case conceptualization, you will still encounter situations where earlier material will turn out to be the source of difficulty in ineffective reprocessing.

How to Identify Earlier Memories Linked to a Different Theme

To identify an earlier memory that is linked to a different theme, the key question to ask is, *"What keeps the disturbance from going any lower?"* If the patient comes up with a new statement representing a different negative cognition, then use that as the starting point for history taking, an affect or somatic bridge to locate an earlier memory on the new theme.

Lack of Spontaneous Synthesis Between the Maladaptive Memory Network and an Appropriate Adaptive Memory Network

The fourth situation that can produce ineffective reprocessing is when there is a lack of spontaneous synthesis between the maladaptive memory network and an appropriate adaptive memory network. In EMDR, we generally stay out of the way to permit spontaneous reprocessing. Deliberately stimulating an adaptive memory network during reprocessing can be appropriate or essential in four types of situations—(a) for responding to prolonged intense emotional responses, (b) for bridging a lack of synthesis with adaptive memory networks, (c) for assuring generalization of treatment effects, and (d) when limited progress has been made over the course of the session.

In these situations, you will need to offer one or more interventions to assist the patient to access an appropriate adaptive memory network. Shapiro (1995, 2001) refers to these interventions as "cognitive interweaves" because they involve making some kind of verbal interaction with the patient. However, this choice of terminology can be somewhat misleading, especially for those with previous training in cognitive behavioral therapy (CBT). Although EMDR *interweaves* bear some superficial similarities to interventions used in CBT, they differ in a number of crucial ways.

In CBT, the aim of the clinician's interaction with the patient is to modify the tendency to accept automatic (negative) thoughts. This is done through various confrontations to restructure the patient's thoughts such as challenging the evidence that supports or assumptions underlying an automatic, negative thought (Beck, Emery, & Greenberg, 2005; Ellis, 1994). These verbal interactions constitute the primary portion of treatment sessions and involve many back and forth exchanges. In an EMDR *interweave*, the aim of the interaction is generally to help the patient to access an adaptive memory network. Occasionally, the clinician may offer new information, but most interweaves merely stimulate already existing memory networks. The best interweaves are generally quite brief, lasting 15 to 30 seconds and often involve a single question.

Another difference between cognitive restructuring in CBT and interweaves in EMDR is the broader range of the aspects of a memory network that the clinician can address in EMDR. Adaptive memory networks consist not only of beliefs, but also include images, sounds, physical sensations, emotions, and action tendencies. Therefore, clinicians can direct patients' attention toward any of these aspects of an adaptive memory network to facilitate reprocessing—that is, synthesis between an adaptive memory network and the selected target maladaptive memory network.

Depending on the patient's needs and accessible adaptive memory networks, the brief interactions you use for EMDR interweaves may focus not only on accessing another belief but also on accessing an image, a memory of another person or the patient in a positive memory, a current life situation, sounds, poetry, or a metaphor. Once the patient gives a response suggestive of having accessed an appropriate adaptive memory network, you promptly begin the next set of BLS. After that set of BLS, you listen to the patient's report to evaluate whether effective reprocessing has resumed.

Appropriate and Inappropriate Use of Interweaves

Deliberately stimulating an adaptive memory network during reprocessing can be essential to avoid prolonged ineffective reprocessing, yet it can also distort patients' clinical work in the service of an agenda set by the clinician's theoretical perspective or countertransference. Carefully reviewing your own psychotherapy notes or video tapes and consulting with an EMDRIA-Approved Consultant are indispensable in finding the right balance in deciding how soon and how often to use interweaves. Because most clinicians are trained to use restructuring interventions, make interpretations, or otherwise offer their clinical wisdom, it can be tempting to use interweaves in a manner similar to traditional verbal therapy. However, this would be contrary to the AIP model, which posits a "self-healing" paradigm. Deliberately stimulating an adaptive memory network should only be done in the service of supporting the patient's own process and should stay as close as possible to spontaneous reprocessing.

There are several kinds of situations during reprocessing where you will be cued to consider using an *interweave*. Note that it is extremely helpful to be mindful of whether patients have appropriate and accessible adaptive memory networks during history taking and treatment planning. With experience, you will be able to identify potential tendencies for ineffective reprocessing before you begin reprocessing by being alert to evidence of excessive self-blame, intense fears, and lack of control during treatment planning and assessment of the target. In a sense, you will often be able to preconfigure potential interweaves before they are needed and then find it is easier to select the most apt interweave from among several options that you had already considered.

Four Situations Where Interweaves Can Be Used

Interweaves are used in four kinds of reprocessing situations: (a) when patients experience intense levels of emotional reexperiencing with slow or marginal movement in the material being accessed, (b) for ineffective reprocessing—at any level of emotional disturbance—where no new material is being accessed, (c) to probe for generalization and assure that a maladaptive memory network has been fully synthesized with an adaptive memory network, and (d) when limited progress has been made over the course of the session to test if the remaining material can be shifted to a more adaptive state. Examples of each of these situations will be covered in the case examples described in chapter 12. In this chapter, we will focus on two main aspects in the use of interweaves during EMDR reprocessing. First, we will explore the relationship between the themes represented by the negative cognition selected in the assessment phase, the issues that are emerging in the patient's reports between sets of bilateral stimulation and the three thematic domains from which interweaves are selected—responsibility, safety, or choices (Shapiro, 2001, pp. 252–260). Second, we will look at the most commonly used varieties of interweaves.

Responsibility

The first theme we will consider is taking on of excessive responsibility for what happened. Across a wide range of traumatic experiences, survivors have a tendency to take on excessive responsibility. This happens with survivors of childhood physical and sexual abuse who blame themselves for the bad behaviors of their caregivers. Instead of realizing that the caregiver's behavior reflected the caregiver's limitations, they identify themselves as defective. In part, this may be a protective mechanism to retain an image of their attachment figure as positive while developing a cause and effect explanation for why they are mistreated. In younger children, we can view this self-blame as reflecting a developmentally early narcissistic perspective, where *self* and *other* are not yet fully differentiated. This same excessive assumption of responsibility also happens in survivors of combat trauma who use hindsight to second guess what they should have done in the midst of chaotic situations where they made snap judgments based on their training and experience. Rape survivors likewise tend to blame themselves, perhaps to preserve at least one element of their "assumptive world"—the idea that they have control (Janoff-Bulman, 1992).

Two Types of Responsibility Interweaves

We can sometimes anticipate the potential need to use a *responsibility interweave* when the negative cognition identified in the assessment phase reflects shame or guilt. Examples include the following: "I am worthless," "I am bad," "I am a failure," "I am not good enough," "I should have known better." There are two types of responsibility interweaves. The first type seeks a memory network with adaptive perspective that appropriately externalizes the responsibility for the other's bad behavior. The second type of *responsibility interweave* seeks to access a memory network representing the capacity for a soothing, nurturing response to validate the intrinsic worth of the patient.

The Paradox of Terror Linked to Self-Blame

During reprocessing, excessive taking on of responsibility can lead not only to persistent experiencing of defectiveness, shame, and guilt, but also of terror. Survivors of early childhood sexual or physical abuse, at times, may show prolonged intense emotional responses with terror during reprocessing. You may be tempted to view this terror as reflecting the perception of danger in the environment and have an urge to offer an *interweave* for current safety. However, a *responsibility interweave* may be needed first. It is easy to think of the urge to seek safety when the danger is from the outside such as a speeding car, a bank robber waving a gun, or a violent caregiver. But survivors of early abuse perceived the source of their vulnerability to danger in their own nature because they came to see themselves as defective. You cannot run away from yourself. So in clinical situations where there is persistent terror in a survivor of early childhood abuse, it may be more effective to ask: "Who was responsible for what he did to you that day, the little child or the adult?"

Interweaves That Shift Responsibility Can Lead to the Emergence of Resentment

This first type of responsibility interweave seeks to access an adaptive adult perspective that externalizes responsibility to the "other." Here are two examples of this type of interweave.

- "If the same thing happened to _____ (your child, your best friend, or your sister), whom would you hold as responsible, _____ (your child, your best friend, or your sister) or _____ (the perpetrator)?"
- "Is there a law against small children hitting (or sexually abusing) their caregivers or only a law to protect small children from being hit (or sexually abused) by their caregivers?"

After a successful interweave that shifts appropriate responsibility from the self to the other, it is common to see anger or disgust at the other begin to emerge.

Compassionate Interweaves Increase Self-Soothing

A second variety of responsibility interweave is accessing an adaptive memory network that enhances compassion for the self. When we think of a young child who has been maltreated, we readily imagine how a nonoffending caregiver learning of the maltreatment would have impulses to reassure the child: "You're not to blame. It wasn't your fault. He shouldn't have done that to you. You are good person. What he did was wrong." Unfortunately, in many cases, nonoffending caregivers were absent or impaired in their capacities to offer protection soothing or reassurance. When these adaptive memory networks for reassurance and support were not encoded in early childhood, it may be necessary to help patients during reprocessing by deliberately accessing other, later adaptive memory networks representing a "compassionate" interweave by a soothing figure. In some cases, when survivors have become parents and can readily offer appropriate nurturing responses to a child, you can access a compassionate "internal parent." "If this happened to your daughter, what would you say or do to let her know she is not to blame for what happened and that you still love her?" After the next set of bilateral stimulation, patients may report internal dialogue of having remembered a moment of reassuring daughter or holding her hand or offering a reassuring hug. In some cases, you will need to access a memory network holding the image of a compassionate other from the present or the past such as a member of the extended family, an adult friend, or a trusted figure such as a minister, teacher, or a member of a peer support group. "If your Aunt Rose knew of what happened to you, how would she respond to that little girl? Would she blame the little girl or would she offer reassurance?" "No, she wouldn't blame me. She'd hold me and tell me I deserved to be protected and treated with kindness." "Notice that."

After an Interweave Do a Standard Length Set of Bilateral Stimulation

If, before offering an *interweave*, you have extended the number of repetitions because of the presence of intense emotions, when you offer an interweave, the first set of BLS should be closer to the standard length of 24 repetitions. That way, you will not continue to extend the BLS should the first interweave not lead to an adaptive shift. If the first interweave does not lead to effective reprocessing, you can offer a second or a third until you access an appropriate adaptive memory network that restores effective reprocessing.

Safety

The second domain from which you can select interweaves is the domain of safety. The negative cognitions from the assessment phase that will alert you to the potential need for a safety interweave are those reflecting the external perception of danger: "I am in danger." "I will be hurt." "I am going to die."

In some cases, you may begin with a responsibility interweave and then later need to offer a safety interweave. For example, with patients where you know from history taking that the danger represented in the memories of childhood abuse is safely past, you may initially offer a responsibility interweave and get adaptive shifts from terror with self-blame—"I'm worthless. I can't get away."—to fear with the perception of danger and the need for flight—"He's bad and I need to get away." Then if the sense of danger still being present does not quickly pass after a few more sets of BLS, you can offer a safety interweave by asking, "Where is he now?" "He's old and senile in a nursing home now." "Notice that."

Safety Interweaves Can Lead to the Emergence of Defensive Action Urges

Successful safety interweaves often lead to the emergence of instrumental defensive action tendencies to flee, fight, maim, injure, or kill the perpetrator. Clinicians should not fear or suppress the emergence of these urges, but rather see them as a way to work through the defensive impulses from the emotional brain that need to be discharged so they are no longer being held in abeyance. It is much better that patients should resolve these suppressed impulses during reprocessing them than have them remain in a suppressed form where they are capable of emerging as defensive reactions to perceived threat cues or even as factors leading to reenactments (Ricci, Clayton, & Shapiro, 2006). In survivors of childhood abuse, some of these defensive action urges may have been suppressed since early childhood and can retain the developmentally immature form in which they often occur in young children. With further reprocessing, these urges can resume the process of developmental maturation away from primitive impulses and toward insight and capacities for verbalization. In some cases, you may need to normalize such strong defensive impulses when they first emerge or at the end of the session after patients reflect back on what happened in their reprocessing.

Finding Safety After a Critical Incident

For many patients whose traumatic memories were singular critical incidents such as a motor vehicle crash or a criminal assault, you may ask a similar question to access evidence of current safety. When the patient keeps reporting having the image of the other vehicle about to crash into their car and the words, "I am going to die," you can ask, "Where are you now?" The first response may be, "In the driver's seat." So then offer a second interweave, "Where are you sitting today?" "In your therapy chair in your office." "Ok, notice that." In this way the patient is accessing both the memory network with the threat cues from the traumatic memory active and at the same time is accessing evidence of current safety.

Many times, survivors of critical, life-threatening incidents have a "frozen moment" of terror or horror that seems locked in place in their memory. It might be the moment just before the motor vehicle crash or the moment they saw the gun barrel of the bank robber pointed at their chest. Another way to offer a safety interweave is just to ask the patient to "Notice what happened next." One patient had been driving alone in a small car and was hit when a driver of a large truck failed to stop at a stop sign. Over several sets of BLS, she kept reporting the large expanse of the white truck looming before her with a sense of terror and imminent danger. "It's so large and coming so fast. I'm going to die." Then the interweave was offered, "Notice what happened next." (BLS followed by the standard inquiry.) "There was the sudden impact. The airbag exploded in my face. I couldn't see anything." "Ok, notice that and notice what happens next." (BLS followed by the standard inquiry.) "The car stopped moving and I realized I survived." "Ok, notice that and notice what happens next." (BLS followed by the standard inquiry.) "I was in shock, but I remember thinking with amazement, 'I'm ok. I'm not seriously hurt.'"

Choices

The third domain from which you can select an *interweave* is that of choices. You may be cued in the assessment phase for the potential need for choice interweaves by negative cognitions such as "I am not in control." "I am powerless." "I am helpless." "I am weak." "I cannot get what I want." In other cases, it will only become apparent from the content of patient reports during the reprocessing that a *choice interweave* is needed. In a sense, these interweaves help the patient shift from an external locus of control—with external safety—to an internal locus of control—"I am in control now." Choice interweaves also represent the adaptive capacity to learn from the past and to make new choices. "I can protect myself." "I can stand up for myself." "I trust my judgment."

Sometimes a choice interweave simply involves rehearsing alternate potential responses within the memory of the past event. In this sense, the responses for "unspoken words" and "unacted defensive action tendencies"—described above—

can both be considered forms of choice interweaves because they invite patients to imagine integrating new choices into the selected maladaptive memory network. For survivors of childhood sexual abuse who were threatened with dire consequences if they ever revealed the nature of the abuse to anyone, being able to imagine disclosing the abuse to a sibling or a trusted authority figure represents the reclaiming of the truth, of learning to trust their own perceptions and judgments, and being able to act on what they know to be true. For survivors of physical abuse where it was too dangerous to fight back, being able to imagine saying "stop," leaving, fighting back, or reporting the abuse to the authorities represents a newfound ability to access potentially more adaptive coping responses.

Working With Appropriate Guilt and Responsibility

Sometimes patients have guilt over poor choices made in the past such as those who have been violent with a spouse or a child or engaged in sexual assault or abuse. During reprocessing, these patients may move through any last denial or minimization to feel a tremendous sense of guilt and remorse. Although some clinicians may believe that it is important for these patients to retain this guilt in order to maintain their motivation to avoid reoffending, in the EMDR model, we work from the hypothesis that reprocessing cannot "erase" or lessen appropriate negative emotions such as shame or guilt. Reprocessing can only modify maladaptive responses. Treatment plans for patients who became involved with sexually abusing children after having been sexually abused as children would normally begin with any preoffending experiences of having been abused themselves (Ricci & Clayton, 2008; Ricci et al., 2006). These initial reprocessing sessions reorganize patients' awareness of the impact of the abuse on themselves and increase empathy for victims. After those earlier events have been resolved, reprocessing can be focused on the memories of patients' offenses. At this point, should the reprocessing become stalled and ineffective, you could invite patients to imagine what they would do if in those situations again.

A Choice Interweave Helps Erik End the Cycle of Physical Abuse

Erik, a survivor of childhood physical abuse by an alcoholic father, had repeatedly become violent toward his wife whenever she would demean him for his limited education and his inability to earn enough money to support the family. He had completed a court mandated group domestic violence program in which he had had learned anger management and assertiveness skills. He shared with his individual EMDR clinician the group leader's praise to him in the group for his participation and how his disclosures, learning, and feedback had been helpful to other participants in the group. During EMDR reprocessing, he was flooded with feelings of shame, anger, and confusion. None of the new skills he had learned seemed to come into his awareness as he focused on the first incident in which he had been violent with his wife. He kept reporting hearing her disturbing words and having the image of hitting her to make her stop. His clinician asked him, "If one of the members of your domestic violence group was telling you about an incident like this one, what would you say to him about how to cope with his wife's upsetting words?" He immediately replied, "I'd say, 'It's not worth going to jail over it.' I'd tell him to just walk away. You can't control what your wife says or does. You can only be in control of yourself." The patient couldn't access an adaptive perspective when thinking about his own past responses to his wife, but could immediately access them in support of another man in a similar situation. Then the clinician said, "Notice that," and offered him the next set of BLS. After that set of BLS Erik reported, "She can't control me with her insults anymore. I know when she says those things, it's just because she's afraid. I've started night school to improve my job skills. Things will be better soon." "Notice that." After the next set he said,

"I imagined telling her that. She calmed down and apologized. She admitted she was afraid we would be evicted from the house because we'd been late with the rent again. I reminded her about the overtime pay I had been getting and that we'd have enough to get by." In this example, the patient reprocessed a past event and spontaneously imagined alternate coping responses that would lead to a different outcome. When they returned to target to probe for residual disturbance Erik said, "I still feel guilty for what I did, but strangely, the memory doesn't bother me like it did anymore. I know what I can do now if that happens again. I can walk away until I'm calm or I can listen to my wife's words. I know she only talks that way when she's scared. I'm not limited by the choices my father made. I know I can treat my wife with respect even if she forgets herself."

Choice Interweaves Can Help Patients Rehearse New Coping Strategies

Choice interweaves help patients rehearse alternate coping choices in past memories. Later, when attention shifts to current stimuli and the future template, these alternate responses will be further strengthened and reinforced. Helen had been verbally demeaned and exploited in a management position where she eventually found herself pressured to ignore evidence of improper financial actions by the owner of the business. She had been raised in a household where her father kept denying and lying about his gambling problems to her mother. Her mother had never confronted her father. Helen had tremendous difficulty trusting her perceptions of the business owner's unethical and illegal actions. In reprocessing a memory of one of her father's many lies to her mother, she remained focused on how confusing it was for her as a young girl that both her mother and father really seemed to believe the promises he made. Her clinician offered her a choices interweave, "From what you know now as an adult about your mother's and father's actions, what would you tell that little girl to help her understand what happened?" Helen replied, "I'd tell her that momma was too weak to confront poppa and that poppa was a compulsive gambler who never got the help he needed. I'd tell her that by facing financial problems there's always a way to make things better." "Notice that and follow again." After the next set of bilateral stimulation Helen reported a sense of a veil of confusion lifting away from her head, neck, and shoulders and a weight lifting off her chest. The rest of the material from that memory reprocessed smoothly over several more sets of BLS without the need for further interweaves. She was able to integrate the words "I can trust and act on my perceptions now" with complete confidence and had a clear body scan with feelings of calm and strength.

Varieties of EMDR Interweaves

There are several ways to offer interweaves. With practice, you will find that a few simple variations will work in most clinical situations you encounter. You will also be able to be creative in finding new variations to make use of the unique capacities and situation of each patient. Here is a listing of some of the most common and frequently used varieties of interweaves.

Missing Information

In offering interweaves when working with adults on early adverse life events, you are looking for an adaptive adult perspective. Generally, an appropriate adult perspective will be available, but occasionally you will encounter patients who were never exposed to the appropriate information. One example is with survivors of childhood sexual abuse who blame themselves for the fact that the abuse happened but who may never have considered how they came to hold such irrational beliefs. In the responsibility section above, we discussed ways that this self-blame may occur spontaneously; however, there is evidence that sexual offenders induce cognitive distortions in their victims as a result of their own cognitive distortions (Salter, 1995). Anna Salter describes how nonsadistic pedophiles work to stimulate sexual responses in their victims to create the illusion that the child really was interested in and wanted the sexual act. Often, they will then turn cause and effect around and say, "See, your body is saying you wanted this to happen." During reprocessing a memory of childhood sexual abuse, patients may be stuck with feelings of shame and self-blame. You can offer the "missing information." "Did anyone ever tell you that with enough stimulation, any child is capable of becoming physically aroused even at a young age?" "No, I didn't know that." "Just notice that."

In this example, the psychoeducation needed is offered in the form of a question that evokes a brief moment of a new perspective with just a glimmer of acceptance. That's all that is needed before offering the next set of bilateral stimulation, then listen to the patient's report to find out whether that one brief intervention is enough to allow effective reprocessing to resume before you offer a more extensive discussion. Where it is needed, you can go on to mention Dr. Salter's research on pedophiles to offer more extensive psychoeducation.

In a similar way, many adult survivors of childhood abuse and neglect were not offered healthy modeling of basic communication skills, assertiveness, boundary setting, recognizing, and responding to subtle danger cues in the environment, money management skills, and so on. Sometimes a brief question is all that is needed to make the connection to a healthy adult perspective. Other times, patients will need more extensive psychoeducation or resource development to acquire missing knowledge and skills before they can resolve some adverse life experiences.

"What If It Happened to Your Child?"

When patients are parents, they often will have an appropriate perspective when thinking about how their children deserve to be cared for while continuing to hold an excessive sense of responsibility for their own adverse early life events. In these cases, we can ask, "What if it happened to your child? Who would you hold responsible, your child or the adult?" If they don't have children, perhaps we can ask about their adult perspective by asking about a favorite nephew or their neighbor's child.

"I'm Confused."

One of the most effective varieties of *interweave* starts with "I'm confused" and ends with a direct question. Patients are often motivated to be helpful to their clinician when the clinician appears briefly unable to understand. This creates a moment of receptivity where the patient wants to help resolve the clinician's "confusion." So when the patient keeps saying, "It's my fault I was beaten as a child," you can respond, "I'm confused. Are you saying that a 4-year-old child can do something that deserves being beaten?" "Well, no?" "Notice that." Here the interweave shifts from the autobiographical memory of the patient to the general fund of knowledge by referencing "a 4-year-old child." Most adults know that no child deserves to be beaten. That's one of the reasons we have child protective service agencies and laws against child abuse. You can even use that fact as an interweave. "I'm confused. I'm wondering why there are laws in this country against child abuse?" "Because no child deserves to be physically abused." "Notice that."

Stimulating Adaptive Visual Images

You can deliberately stimulate adaptive memory networks with visual images. A common example is to ask the patients to imagine their adult self stepping into the memory with their child self and holding the hand of their child self or holding, comforting, or encouraging their child self. When patients cannot imagine their adult selves doing this, consider asking them to imagine a supportive family member, friend, or mentor to step into the memory to do this.

Stimulating Adaptive Somatic Responses

When one defensive coping urge, such as submission, has been so strongly conditioned from an early age or prolonged adverse experiences, and alternate, adaptive coping responses are not readily accessible through spontaneous reprocessing, verbal, or imaginal interweaves, you can consider inviting patients to practice an alternate response by changing their physical stance in the therapy office and engaging in a new somatic response. An example would be standing and pushing away with both arms while saying, "Get away from me!" or saying "No! Leave me alone," in a firm, strong voice.

Metaphors, Stories, and Fables

Fables and fairy tales endure as important forms of literature because they represent succinct expressions of human wisdom in a form that the youngest child can understand and internalize. Teaching stories have been incorporated into therapy by many clinicians (McLeod, 1997; Pearce, 1996). When patients are stalled in their reprocessing, one of the most interesting ways to elicit an adaptive perspective is to remind the patient briefly of a familiar fable or to share a teaching story or a metaphor. This can be especially helpful when more straightforward interweaves have not worked to restore effective reprocessing. This is the most challenging and perhaps least often used type of interweave for two reasons. First, it brings the attention of the patient to another perspective, one that is selected by the clinician. Second, it requires creativity to select a metaphor, story, or fable that is structured to fit what the patient needs at that moment. Although not all clinicians will be comfortable with the use of metaphors, stories, or fables, these interventions often seem capable of stimulating a patient's capacities to locate additional, relevant resources.

Nick had sought EMDR treatment after a series of unanticipated deaths in his family. Having lost his mother to cancer in childhood, these recent losses had reactivated the traumatic loss of his mother. After initially experiencing effective and complete reprocessing in the first session on the memory of how he and his family had been affected by his mother's death, in his second session, he began to experience ineffective reprocessing while addressing the memory of the recent loss of the aunt who had become a substitute maternal figure for him. He was experiencing a strong sense of hopelessness and despair with doubts that he could ever recover again. After trying several interventions, the clinician told him a teaching story from Milton H. Erickson (Rossi, 1980a).

A man sought treatment from Dr. Erickson. While the man was in a deep trance, Dr. Erickson gave him the task of taking a walk up the trail of nearby mountain. He was to notice what he saw on this hike and then come back and tell Dr. Erickson in a few days. On his return the man went back into a trance and spoke of his walk. At first, he just walked and noticed nothing unusual. But finally he became winded and, stopping to catch his breath, he realized he was looking at a tree, split and blackened by multiple lightning strikes. At first he just saw where the blackened trunk had been torn apart. Then he noticed how the tree had sealed up its wounds and that there was new growth and leaves even in the damaged areas of the tree. The clinician finished telling the story and then asked Nick to just notice what happened with the next set of bilateral stimulation. After the second sets of bilateral stimulation, the man reported memories of what he had experienced a few years after his mother's death at a series of high school cross country races. At each of several races, he reached the point of exhaustion and then felt her spirit come to him. Each time, he felt as though he was suddenly free of the exhaustion. "When that happened, I realized she had not left me but was always with me. This flood of images would come to me of all the times she had been there for me when I had doubts. She would always smile and tell me that I could do whatever I decided I needed to do." Light on his feet and open in his breathing he had gone on to set new school records. After remembering those experiences Nick was able to resume effective reprocessing of his aunt's death.

Other Times to Consider Deliberating Stimulating Adaptive Memory Networks

Two other times to consider deliberating stimulating adaptive memory networks are: (a) to assure generalization of treatment effects, and (b) to support a shift to a new but accessible perspective when limited progress has been made over the course of the session. When themes of excessive self-blame, fearfulness, or helplessness have been persistently evident in the history taking and treatment planning phase, a positive response with renewed effective reprocessing from a single intervention is encouraging. However, before completing the desensitization phase, you may want to probe for generalization of treatment effects on returning to the target. After using the standard question, "When you bring your attention back to the original experience, what do you notice now?" before beginning the next set of bilateral stimulation, probe with a brief version of the same type of interweave you used earlier. For responsibility you might ask: "And who was responsible for what happened that day?" Or for choice you could ask, "And what would you do now if that happened again?" Because this theme had been chronically impaired, probing for the adaptive perspective again when the level of disturbance is low may either reveal (a) that it has been fully addressed or (b) that there is a need for further integration of the adaptive perspective.

Finally, when it is clear that there will not be sufficient time to complete reprocessing of the selected target memory in that session, before time would require, moving toward closure an interweave can be offered to support the patient in shifting to a more adaptive perspective. If there is a clinical sense that appropriate anger at the perpetrator is close at hand but hidden, an interweave to externalize responsibility can help move the patient from shame and self-blame to an appropriate sense of anger at maltreatment. On the other hand, if the patient seems overwhelmed by feelings of hurt or grief, offering a compassionate interweave before moving to closure can help end the session on a soothing note. "What would Aunt Rose say to reassure you?" "She'd hold me and tell me I deserved to be protected and treated with kindness."

Use of Previously Installed Resources as Interweaves

When you have developed and installed resources during the preparation phase of treatment, these resources can be reaccessed as interweaves during ineffective reprocessing to assist patients in locating adaptive memory networks. Supportive others who have been previously installed can offer soothing encouragement or a healthy perspective. An example is the grandmother who showed the first genuine interest in the boy's mind and feelings during his occasional summer visits. "What would Grandma Clara say?" Previously installed imaginal and symbolic resources, such as "the wise woman," "coyote," or "the hidden spring in the cave," can offer ways to access needed self-capacities contained in other memory networks that merely need a slight reminder to be accessed.

Summary

In this chapter we clarified standard sequences and decision trees that guide clinical work in the desensitization phase of the standard EMDR protocol for treating PTSD. We examined strategies for supporting patients during prolonged, intense emotional responses. We then explored the creative use of interweaves to deliberately stimulate an adaptive memory network to encourage synthesis. Next, we return to the standard sequence of the protocol to pick up with phase 5—the installation phase.

The Installation, Body Scan, and Closure Phases

PHASES 5, 6, AND 7

Chapter 10 describes the installation, body scan, and closure phases—Phases 5, 6, and 7—of the Standard EMDR Protocol for treating posttraumatic stress disorder (PTSD).

PHASE 5: INSTALLATION

As described in chapter 8, The Desensitization Phase: Basic Procedures when you return to target and the patient reports a Subjective Units of Disturbance (SUD) rating of 0 a second time, you have completed the desensitization phase. You then continue to the installation phase. The aim of the installation phase is to extend reprocessing and assure generalization of treatment effects with a complete integration of a new perspective on the target memory network. The installation phase is the second of the three reprocessing phases of the standard procedural steps. In all three reprocessing phases, you use at least 24 complete movements in each set of bilateral stimulation (BLS) at a similar speed. However, compared with either phase 4 (desensitization) or phase 6 (body scan) you will notice an important procedural difference during phase 5 (installation). After each set of BLS, instead of asking the patient "What do you notice now?" you check the Validity of Cognition (VoC) scale. Unless the patient were to spontaneously report new negative associations in the installation phase, there are no "channels of association." In this way, the installation phase is more similar to the original version of Eye Movement Desensitization (EMD; Shapiro, 1989a, 1989b) in which you would return to target after every set of BLS.

START BY CHECKING FOR A BETTER POSITIVE COGNITION

The first step in the installation phase is to check to see if there is a better, more appropriate positive cognition (PC). Ask the patient, "Do the words _____ " (repeat the positive cognition as an "I" statement) "still fit, or is there another positive statement

10.1 | Procedural Steps Script – Installation Phase

PHASE 5: INSTALLATION
Check for a better positive cognition.
"Do the words _____ *"* (repeat the PC as an *"I"* statement) *"still fit, or is there another positive statement that would be more suitable?"*

Check the VoC on the selected positive cognition.
"Think about the original experience and those words _____ *"* (repeat the selected PC in the first person). *"On a scale from 1 to 7, where 1 means they feel completely false and 7 means they feel completely true, how true do those words feel to you now?"*

1 2 3 4 5 6 7
completely false   completely true

Before each set of BLS in the installation phase, link the original experience and the positive cognition.
"Focus on the original experience and those words _____ *"* (repeat the selected PC in the first person) *"and follow."* Offer another set of BLS.

After each set of BLS in the installation phase, check the VoC again.
Check the VoC on the selected positive cognition.
"Think about the original experience and those words _____ (repeat the selected PC in the first person). *On a scale from 1 to 7, where 1 means they feel completely false and 7 means they feel completely true, how true do those words feel to you now?"*

1 2 3 4 5 6 7
completely false   completely true

When the VoC is rising
Continue the installation phase as long as the patient continues to report growing confidence in the selected PC or other more positive material.

When the VoC does not rise to a 7
After several sets of BLS, if the reported material is not getting more positive and rising up to a VoC of 7, change the direction or type of BLS. If the patient continues to report a VoC of 6 or less—even after changing the direction or type of BLS—check for a blocking belief.
   "What thought or concern keeps these words from feeling completely true?"
   This blocking belief can sometimes be directly targeted and resolved in a few more sets of BLS. Then, return to standard installation phase instructions above to complete the installation phase.
   In other cases, starting from the patient's expressed blocking belief, you may need to use an *affect bridge* or *somatic bridge* to identify an associated memory and target that for reprocessing in this session or in the next session. This generally will mean the originally selected target will remain incomplete for this session until the source of the blocking belief can be reprocessed.

Completing the Installation Phase
When the patient reports a VoC of 7 and the material is no longer becoming more positive, go on to the body scan phase.

Note. From EMDR Institute Training Manual, by F. Shapiro, (Jan, 2008 & Jan, 2005), Watsonville, CA: EMDR Institute. Copyright 2008, 2005 by EMDR Institute. Adapted with permission.

Note. From Eye Movement Desensitization and Reprocessing: Basic Principles, Protocols, and Procedures by F. Shapiro, 2001, NY: Guilford Press. Copyright 2001 by Guilford Press. Adapted with permission.

that would be more suitable?" About 50% of the time, there will be a better PC. Make certain that any revised PC meets the selection criteria, and then check the VoC on the selected PC. "Think about the original experience and those words _____" (repeat the selected PC in the first person). "On a scale from 1 to 7, where 1 means they feel *completely false* and 7 means they feel *completely true*, how true do those words feel to you now?"

Write down the VoC rating. In most cases, the VoC will have risen several points higher than the initial VoC rating. It often will be a 5, 6, or 7. Then access the original experience and the selected PC and offer a series of sets of BLS until the VoC has risen to a "7" and is not getting any better. You do this before each set in the installation phase by saying, "Focus on the original experience and those words _____" (repeat the selected PC in the first person) "and follow." Then offer another set of BLS. After each set of BLS, check the VoC again.

In most cases, the VoC will rise smoothly to a 7 over several sets of BLS. As long as it continues to become more positive, continue to offer additional sets of BLS. The rating of 7 is just a number. In some cases, the subjective sense of how true the PC feels can continue to improve even after the first VoC rating of a 7. Continuing to offer additional sets of BLS as long as the felt sense of validity improves is essential to obtaining optimal clinical benefits from EMDR reprocessing. EMDR reprocessing is not merely about the resolution of disturbing feelings associated with a selected target memory. Comprehensive reprocessing leads to a restructuring of the sense of self. In the installation phase, the VoC captures only a limited aspect of the gains patients can make. Fully integrating the PC as long as it continues to improve is essential to allowing patients the opportunity to go as far as they can go.

WHEN THE VOC DOES NOT RISE TO A 7

After several sets of BLS, if the reported material is not getting more positive and rising up to a VoC of 7, change the direction or type of BLS. If the patient continues to report a VoC of 6 or less even after changing the direction or type of BLS check for a defensive belief or remaining issues by asking, "What thought or concern keeps these words from feeling completely true?" In some cases, the thought or concern that the patient expresses can be directly targeted and resolved in a few more sets of BLS. Then, return to standard installation phase instructions above to complete the installation phase. In other cases, the thought or concern may come from another memory network that needs to be identified and targeted for reprocessing.

An example of a residual concern that was resolved simply comes from a patient who was reprocessing a memory of domestic violence. Her husband had been arrested, charged, and convicted of several counts of assault. At the time of the session, he was currently in prison. During the installation of the PC, "I am safe now," the VoC rose to a 5 and was not going any higher. After changing directions, the clinician asked, "What thought or concern keeps these words from feeling completely true?" The patient replied, "Some day he will be released. He could hurt me again." Her clinician asked to "Hold that thought in mind and follow again." After two more sets of BLS, she laughed and said, "Yes, he could possibly hurt me again someday, years from now. I also could get cancer or be in an automobile crash. There are no guarantees in life. But right now, today, 'I am safe now.' I won't live in fear of him anymore." After this the clinician returned to the standard installation procedure and the VoC rose to a 7. So in this case, just asking for the thought or concern was enough to allow it to resolve.

USING AN AFFECT BRIDGE TO RESOLVE AN ISSUE IN THE INSTALLATION PHASE

In other cases, the expressed thought or concern may reflect an unresolved issue from another memory network that needs to be identified and directly targeted.

Starting from the patient's expressed concern or belief, you may need to use an *affect bridge* or *somatic bridge* to identify an associated memory and target that for reprocessing in the same session or in the next session. This will sometimes mean that the originally selected target will remain incomplete for that session until the source of the blocking belief can be reprocessed.

An example is an EMDR reprocessing session with a gay professional whose career had been badly damaged by a homophobic supervisor. After the desensitization phase, the memory of the supervisor's undermining behaviors was no longer disturbing. At the start of the installation phase, the patient confirmed the original PC, "I am competent." The VoC had risen from an initial 3 to a 5, but did not rise further during the installation phase. After trying changing directions without any gains on the VoC, the clinician asked, "What thought or concern keeps these words from feeling completely true?" The man replied, "I don't know. When I hear those words I just have this sense of feeling defeated." The clinician asked, "Where do you feel that in your body?" He replied, "In my face and chest." The clinician asked him to, "Focus on where you feel that and let yourself drift back to the first time you can recall having that same feeling." After a few moments, the man recalled a disturbing incident from his adolescence where a priest had shamed him when he had hinted that he had homosexual yearnings. This experience was quite pivotal for the man and had influenced his decision to keep his sexual orientation hidden throughout most of his 20s. The NC connected to this incident was, "I am unworthy." They spent the next two sessions reprocessing that incident to completion before returning to successfully complete reprocessing the more recent adult incident with the supervisor.

WHEN TO ACCEPT A VOC LESS THAN A 7

In some cases, it may be clinically appropriate to accept a VoC rating of a 6 as indicating completion of the installation phase. When asked what keeps it from being a 7, some patients will make a statement that expresses a cultural or personal value rather than evidence of additional dysfunctionally stored material or a defense. Shapiro (1995, 2001) refers to these statements as "ecological" meaning that they are an appropriate stopping place given the individual's values and the personal and social context. Some examples of such statements express a general cultural or religious value. "I'm a Quaker. We don't speak in such extremes." Other statements might express a personal value. "I won't know it is completely true until I see how I feel in the future."

It is important to offer at least one additional set of BLS even when you hear a statement that seems to make a VoC of 6 seem acceptable. This needs to be done sensitively and without any pressure or expectation of further change in the VoC. Sometimes, the belief in the PC will increase. Sometimes it will not. Here is an example where it did not. One victim of a school-shooting incident had selected the PC, "I'm safe now. I can let it go." The VoC rose to a 6 and did not go higher. When asked, "What keeps it from being a 7," this patient said, "'I'm safe now,' is a 7, but 'I can let it go' may never be completely true. This experience changed my life. This community will never be the same. The media will never let us forget what happened. So, a 6 is probably as true as it can ever be." "Focus on that." After another set of BLS, there was no change. They moved on to the body scan phase.

Another patient had struggled all her life to be able to act decisively. She was reprocessing the memory of her father abandoning the family when she was a child. In the installation phase, the PC was "I can trust my judgment." The VoC rose to a 5 and did not go higher. The clinician asked, "What keeps it from going any higher?" The patient responded, "You know in my culture, many men are often not trustworthy. It's probably not wise to trust my judgment completely." The clinician had a

10.2 | Procedural Steps Script – Body Scan Phase

PHASE 6: BODY SCAN

"Close your eyes. Hold in mind the original experience—as it seems to you now—and those words _____ " (repeat the selected PC). *"Then bring your attention to all the different areas of your body, starting with your head and continuing down to your feet. Any place you feel any tension, tightness, or unusual sensations, tell me."*

For any reported negative sensations, offer additional sets of BLS until the patient reports only neutral or positive sensations. Then return to target again, and use the instructions above to do the body scan again to check for any new, residual sensations.

For reported positive sensations, continue BLS to enhance the positive sensations until they are no longer getting more positive. In the body scan phase, use the same standard directions between sets of BLS as in the desensitization phase.

"Rest. Take a deeper breath. Let it go. What do you notice now?" _____

"Focus on that and notice what happens next."

_____

Note. From EMDR Institute Training Manual, by F. Shapiro, (Jan, 2008 & Jan, 2005), Watsonville, CA: EMDR Institute. Copyright 2008, 2005 by EMDR Institute. Adapted with permission.

Note. From Eye Movement Desensitization and Reprocessing: Basic Principles, Protocols, and Procedures by F. Shapiro, 2001, NY: Guilford Press. Copyright 2001 by Guilford Press. Adapted with permission.

history of a betrayal by a man. This statement stimulated the clinician's own memory and she was tempted to stop the installation phase there because the statement had a ring of truth to it. However, she remembered the caution she had heard in her EMDR training to add more BLS even to statements that initially sound plausible. As an experienced clinician, she knew that she should not permit her own personal or cultural experiences to limit her patient's growth. So she said, "Focus on that and follow again." Over the next few sets of BLS, the patient made further gains. She said, "You know just because some men are not trustworthy does not mean all men are. If I cannot trust my judgment, I may reject a good man out of false suspicions. Even if my judgment is not perfect, to live well, I have to rely on it. It is wise not to trust blindly, but it is foolish not to trust my own judgment completely." The VoC then rose to a 7.

PHASE 6: BODY SCAN

Once the VoC has reached a 7 and is not getting any better, go on to the body scan phase. There are two purposes of body scan phase. The first is to confirm that there is no residual material left unaddressed in the selected target memory. The second is to extend the gains that have been made in the desensitization and installation phases.

In the body scan phase, you ask the patient to: "Close your eyes. Hold in mind the original experience—as it seems to you now—and those words _____ " (repeat the selected PC). "Then bring your attention to all the different areas of your body, starting with your head and continuing down to your feet. Any place you feel any tension, tightness, or unusual sensations, tell me."

For any reported negative sensations, offer additional sets of BLS until the patient reports only neutral or positive sensations. In the body scan phase, use the same standard directions between sets of BLS as in the desensitization phase. "Rest. Take a deeper breath. Let it go. What do you notice now?" After the patient reports any change, say, "Focus on that and notice what happens next." Continue reprocessing any residual sensations until the patient reports only neutral or positive sensations. Then, return to target and use the same instructions to do the body scan again to check for any new, residual sensations.

When the patient reports only positive sensations, continue BLS to enhance the positive sensations until they are no longer getting more positive. The aim of EMDR reprocessing is not just about resolving dysfunctionally stored material. It is equally about enlarging a person's sense of self. In some cases, the most profound work occurs in the body scan phase when the patient reports no negative sensations and a positive sense of relief. "I feel like a weight has been lifted from my shoulders." Focusing on such positive sensations and adding BLS can lead to profound experiences of well-being and even to transpersonal states (Krystal et al., 2002).

PHASE 7: CLOSURE

The closure phase serves several purposes. The first is to provide a structured sense of completion to each EMDR reprocessing session. The second is to assure patient stability before the patient leaves the session. The third is to give the patient guidance about being alert to observing and documenting emerging issues and changes

 | Procedural Steps Script—Closure Phase

---

PHASE 7: CLOSURE
Procedures for an incomplete session
An incomplete session is one where the SUD rating is above a 1; the VoC rating is less than a 6; or there are residual negative sensations reported in the body scan that were not reported before the session began and that appear to be linked to the targeted material.

Explain the need to stop. Offer encouragement for the patient's work in the session. When the desensitization phase is incomplete, skip the installation of the PC and the body scan. Explore the patient's somatic, emotional and cognitive state. Assess the patient's need for structured containment or stabilization procedures.

"We are almost out of time and we will need to stop soon. You have done good work today. I appreciate the effort you have made. How are you feeling?"

If needed, offer one or more containment, calming, or sensory orienting exercises.
When the patient is in a stable state, review the briefing statement below.

Closure procedures for a complete session
Offer acknowledgment for the patient's work in the session. If time remains, encourage the patient to discuss their observations about what occurred in the session. If appropriate, briefly mention any significant observed shifts or gains the patient does not mention.

You have done good work today. How are you feeling?"

Brief the patient and request a log report.
"The processing we have done today may continue after the session. You may or may not notice new insights, thoughts, memories, or dreams. You may notice changes in how you are functioning. To help us evaluate your responses to today's session, notice what you experience and make entries in your log. Remember to practice the _____ exercises we worked on to help you manage disturbances this week. We will review your log report and continue our work next time. If you have something urgent to report or need additional support before our next session, call me."

Note. From EMDR Institute Training Manual, by F. Shapiro, (Jan, 2008 & Jan, 2005), Watsonville, CA: EMDR Institute. Copyright 2008, 2005 by EMDR Institute. Adapted with permission.

Note. From Eye Movement Desensitization and Reprocessing: Basic Principles, Protocols, and Procedures by F. Shapiro, 2001, NY: Guilford Press. Copyright 2001 by Guilford Press. Adapted with permission.

that may occur following each EMDR reprocessing session. Some EMDR reprocessing sessions reach completion with a SUD of 0, a VoC of 7, and a body scan with only neutral or positive sensations. Other sessions will be incomplete to varying degrees. We will first consider the situation where a session is incomplete and then the simpler case of a completed treatment session.

PROCEDURES FOR CLOSING AN INCOMPLETE SESSION

An incomplete session is one where the SUD rating is above a 1, the VoC rating is less than a 6, or there are residual negative sensations reported in the body scan that were not reported before the session began and that appear to be linked to the targeted material. Tension in the neck and shoulders that emerged during the installation phase and was reported in the body scan phase is likely to be linked to the targeted material. If this tension were not cleared in the body scan phase, the session would be classified as incomplete. A simple sensation of eye fatigue from repeated sets of bilateral eye movements that were not present before the session is probably not linked to the targeted material. Even with this residual sensation of eye fatigue, the session could be classified as complete.

To bring an incomplete session to a close, explain the need to stop the reprocessing and end the session. Offer acknowledgment and encouragement for the patient's work in the session. When stopping during the desensitization phase, you should skip the installation of PC and the body scan phase. You should avoid returning to target and asking for information about the selected target memory, as this would tend to increase disturbance. Therefore, you should not check the SUD or the VoC, as both of these require focusing on the target memory.

PRESERVING TIME FOR PATIENTS WHO NEED ASSISTANCE WITH MENTALIZATION

Explore the patient's somatic, emotional, and cognitive state. Assess the patient's need for structured containment or stabilization procedures. "We are almost out of time and we will need to stop soon. You have done good work today. I appreciate the effort you have made. How are you feeling?" In some cases, it can be helpful to stop early enough to have time for a brief discussion of the patient's insights and perceptions of gains and any additional material that emerged into awareness through the session. This is especially helpful for patients with limited capacities for mentalization and for putting feeling states into an organizing frame of reference (Fonagy, Gergely, Jurist, & Target, 2002).

PRESERVING TIME FOR PATIENTS WHO NEED STRUCTURE CONTAINMENT

Some patients will need structured assistance with containment, calming, or sensory orientation. When such interventions are needed, just offering the calm place exercise may be enough. However, other patients will need a series of stabilization, containment, and sensory orienting exercises. These interventions should include those that were useful in the preparation phase. A series of interventions could begin with the calm place exercise, followed by the light stream visualization exercise (Shapiro, 2001, p. 244–246) then finish with sensory orientation. When the patient is in a stable state, review the briefing statement below.

However, just because a session is incomplete does not mean that such interventions are routinely needed. Many patients were distressed about the unresolved memory or presenting issue before the incomplete session but were able to cope adequately. While reprocessing can lead to patients accessing greater levels of disturbance, this is not the most common occurrence. Stabilization interventions are clearly needed when patients are in danger of succumbing to dangerous, tension–reduction impulses for self-injury or remaining stuck in states of excessive anxiety, depression, or dissociation. Clinical discernment is required to assess the need for structured containment, calming or sensory orientation procedures.

PROCEDURES FOR CLOSING A COMPLETE SESSION

When a session is complete, there is generally no need for stabilization, containment, or sensory orientation procedures. However, as described in the section above on incomplete sessions, some patients may benefit from or may need a brief discussion of the gains they experienced in the session. Therefore, you should allow sufficient time for the closure phase based on the individual needs of each patient. In most cases, you can just brief the patient about being alert to post session treatment effects and request a log report at the next session by reading the statement below.

Brief the patient and request a log report.

"The processing we have done today may continue after the session. You may or may not notice new insights, thoughts, memories, or dreams. You may notice changes in how you are functioning. To help us evaluate your responses to today's session, notice what you experience and make entries in your log. Remember to practice the _____ exercises we worked on to help you manage disturbances this week. We will review your log report and continue our work next time. If you have something urgent to report or need additional support before our next session, call me."

LOG REPORTS

Obtaining log reports from patients is a helpful way to monitor patient responses to treatment sessions, emerging issues, and environmental stressors. If you have introduced the log in the preparation phase, you will find it easier to continue to obtain log reports from patients when you begin reprocessing. See Table 6.12 – "Log." While purely verbal reports can be helpful, many patients will tend to forget details of distressing and positive moments due to state specific memory effects (Bower, 1981). Brief written log reports not only provide more specific details but also help the patient to reflect on their experiences both when they write them down and when they share them with you.

Occasionally, patients will have fears or concerns that interfere with their willingness to make written log reports. They may fear family members or friends will read their log entries. They may fear that you will judge them for how well or poorly they are progressing in treatment. They may have unrelenting standards and tend to judge themselves harshly. They may find it too painful to record certain nightmare or intrusions of traumatic memories. They may have too much shame about avoidant or compulsive behaviors to record them.

Normally, these issues will surface early in the preparation phase when you introduce the importance of keeping a simple log of their significant experiences during treatment. However, when issues with keeping a writing log emerge during reprocessing, it can be quite helpful to confront these issues directly with both a frank discussion and with interventions to address concerns. Supportive discussion, psychoeducation, and problem solving may resolve these concerns. Occasionally, instead of a written log, patients may prefer to make brief verbal reports by calling in log entries to your telephone answering machine. In other cases, emerging issues or fears about making and reporting log entries can lead to modifications in the treatment plan by highlighting the need for additional resource installation or reprocessing of current concerns and any associated life experiences. We will discuss how to review log reports and when to consider modifying the treatment plan in the next chapter on the reevaluation phase.

The Reevaluation Phase and Completing the Treatment Plan

OVERVIEW

Chapter 11 describes the reevaluation phase (phase 8) and completing the treatment plan of the standard Eye Movement Desensitization and Reprocessing (EMDR) protocol for treating posttraumatic stress disorder (PTSD).

PHASE 8: REEVALUATION

Reevaluation is a continuing aspect of the EMDR approach to psychotherapy. Reevaluation begins during the history-taking and preparation phase in which we consider the impact of patients' disclosure of information, perceptions of the clinician's responses, as well as the impact of skill-building and stabilization exercises on patients' stability, symptoms, and functioning. Once EMDR reprocessing has begun, reevaluation continues to be essential—to assure stability of treatment effects from apparently complete reprocessing sessions, confirm the appropriateness of continuing reprocessing on incomplete target memories or switching to an earlier target, and monitor the effects of reprocessing. It may be useful to think of reevaluation as taking place on two levels: a *micro* level and a *macro* level. On the *micro* level, you need to reevaluate the specific impact of the previous session. On the *macro* level, you need to consider the implications of what you have learned from reevaluation in making adjustments to the overall treatment plan.

MONITORING THE TREATMENT PLAN WITH "MACRO" REEVALUATION OF PATIENT RESPONSES

Monitoring patient responses to treatment is essential to the *macro* level of reevaluation. For this reason, you will generally ask for feedback from patients' logs at the start of each session. Pay attention to reports of changes in dreams, reactions to current stimuli that may represent threat cues, additional memories, and new thoughts or insights. You should actively inquire about changes in any of the primary symptoms that were associated with the selected target memory that you reprocessed in the previous sessions, including intrusive reexperiencing, avoidant behaviors, agitation, hyperarousal, somatoform symptoms and states of anxiety, depression, dissociation, and maladaptive or tension-reduction urges and behaviors. In cases in which these issues were present at intake, you should monitor basic activities of daily living, such as regular eating, sleeping, exercising, working, and family life. If you are using standardized assessment tools before each session described in chapter 5, you may also note changes in symptom severity based on test scores. Occasionally, patients will report that new and disturbing aspects of the selected target memory have emerged since the previous session, or that they have been thinking about other earlier-associated memories. These would then be selected for additional reprocessing.

When patients' log reports indicate that successful reprocessing has led to some reduction in their current symptoms, this suggests that it is appropriate to continue the treatment plan and to move on to reprocessing the next target. However, when reprocessing leads to the emergence of additional disturbing memories, increased intrusions accompanied by less stable mood states, greater anxiety, or increased urges for maladaptive or tension-reduction behaviors, you may need to consider adjustments to the treatment plan. Ask yourself, *"Should we continue with reprocessing past incidents, or do these increasing symptoms signal that we need to return to stabilizing interventions that focus on building needed self-capacities?"* Mild regression in functioning may be acceptable to some patients and may not necessarily lead to any serious consequences. In many cases, pressing forward with further reprocessing will often be the most effective course of action for patients with sufficient self-capacities and accessible resources. An example of this kind is described in the section below on "When to Continue Reprocessing After Mild Regressions in Symptoms or Functioning." However, even though some patients may report that a regression in their functioning with increasing symptoms is acceptable to them and state that they want to press ahead with more and more reprocessing, this does not always indicate a wise course of action.

SOME SURVIVORS OF EARLY NEGLECT OR ABUSE LACK SKILLS IN SELF-MONITORING

Survivors of early neglect or abuse do not always have sufficient self-knowledge or skills for self-monitoring to accurately assess their capacities to tolerate the continuing impact of uncovering and reprocessing. They often are in a hurry to get reprocessing "over with." They imagine that pressing forward will somehow "magically" resolve their issues quickly. Clinicians recently trained in EMDR may have had initial experiences with EMDR reprocessing with other patients that led directly to consistent and perhaps dramatic reductions in symptoms. However, EMDR reprocessing, as well as any trauma-focused method (e.g., prolonged exposure), can lead to gradual or rapidly worsening symptoms for survivors of chronic or complex traumatic exposures (Cloitre, Koenen, Cohen, & Han, 2002; Gelinas, 2003; Korn & Leeds, 2002; Pitman et al., 1991).

Clinicians therefore need to consider not only patients' stated preferences, but also their own clinical judgment regarding what course of action is needed. Sometimes, further reprocessing will improve temporarily worsening symptoms. Other times, further skills building and stabilizing interventions will avoid a decline into a regressed state that could slow down patient progress or lead to a crisis. Key elements to consider in making this determination are the patients' capacities to maintain normal self-care and the daily activities that sustain their mental energy and efficiency. If these adaptive action tendencies begin to degrade, it is essential to for clinicians to focus their attention on restoring them before resuming reprocessing on traumatic memories. See the discussion on promoting adaptive action in chapter 12 of *The Haunted Self* (van der Hart et al., 2006).

WHEN TO CONTINUE REPROCESSING AFTER MILD REGRESSIONS IN SYMPTOMS OR FUNCTIONING

In other cases, mild regressions in functioning, especially after a session in which a traumatic memory was incompletely reprocessed, can be quickly overcome by resuming reprocessing to fully resolve the memory. For example, consider a case in which, in the previous session, you reprocessed an adult patient's memory of witnessing one of few domestic violence episodes during adolescence, involving a parent who had temporarily discontinued taking medication for bipolar disorder. This patient generally has a high level of functioning, has no substance abuse or tension-reduction problems, and has presented for treatment because of mild anxiety that started after a new relationship with a partner who is more asser-tive and more emotionally expressive than those in previous relationships. On the next session after the first reprocessing session of an adolescent memory, the patient reports a week of having frequent awakenings after a series of disturbing dreams all clearly related to these episodes of domestic violence. Given the overall stability and excellent coping skills of this patient, it would generally make sense to view the disturbing dreams and sleep problems as temporary side effects of incompletely reprocessed material from these memories. Therefore, you would most likely continue reprocessing on the incompletely resolved memory without further delay.

THE "MICRO" LEVEL: REEVALUATION OF REPROCESSING FROM THE PREVIOUS SESSION

While the *macro* level of reevaluation considers adjustments to the overall treat-ment plan, the *micro* level focuses on reevaluation of the specific impact of repro-cessing on the target memory from the previous session. Let us first consider cases in which the previous session was incomplete and you moved toward closure dur-ing the desensitization, installation, or body scan phases.

RESUMING REPROCESSING AFTER INCOMPLETE DESENSITIZATION

If desensitization was incomplete, reprocessing generally stopped in the middle or near the end of a "channel of association." First, you need to check feedback from the patient's log. Unless additional earlier material has emerged, just con-firm if the patient is ready to continue reprocessing and then "return to target" to continue reprocessing it. It is not necessary to redo the entire assessment phase. It is not necessary to recheck the Subjective Units of Disturbance scale (SUD) level, although you may choose to do so. Your primary aim should be to resume reprocessing. Ask the patient, "When you bring your attention back to the experi-ence we worked on in our last session, what do you notice now?" If the patient reports additional disturbing material say, "Focus on that and notice what hap-pens next."

After resuming reprocessing, when you return to target, you return to target, if the patient reports ambiguous, or apparently neutral, or positive associations on the target, you will need to check the SUD rating. You may also choose to check the SUD to clarify the patient's progress. "Focus on the original experience. On a scale from 0 to 10, where 0 is no disturbance or neutral and 10 is the highest disturbance you can imagine, how disturbing does it feel to you now?" If the SUD rating is a 1 or higher, say, "What's the worst part of it now?" Then say: "Focus on that, and notice what happens next."

 | Target Reevaluation Worksheet

For a previously incomplete target

When the previous reprocessing session was incomplete, first check feedback from the patient's log. Unless additional, earlier material has emerged, just confirm whether the patient is ready to continue reprocessing and then *"return to target"* to continue reprocessing. It is not necessary to do a complete assessment of the incomplete target memory. It is not necessary to check the SUD level, but it may be useful to do so in some cases.

"When you bring your attention back to the experience we worked on in our last session, what do you notice now?"

If the patient reports additional, disturbing material say: *"Where do you feel that in your body?"* Then, *"Focus on that and notice what happens next."*

If the patient reports ambiguous, or apparently neutral or positive associations on the target, check the SUD rating. You may also choose to check the SUD to clarify patient progress. *"Focus on the original experience. On a scale from 0 to 10, where 0 is no disturbance or neutral and 10 is the highest disturbance you can imagine, how disturbing does it feel to you now?"*

If the SUD rating is a 1 or higher, say: *"What's the worst part of it now?"* Then say: *"Notice where you feel that in your body, and notice what happens next."* Then resume bilateral stimulation.
If the SUD rating is a 1, ask: *"Where do you notice it in your body?"* Then say: *"Focus on that, and notice what happens next."* Then, resume bilateral stimulation.

For a previously complete target

When reprocessing on the previous target was complete, first check feedback from the patient's log. Unless additional, earlier material has emerged, first access the previous target memory network. Then check the SUD on the previous target memory.

"When you bring your attention back to the experience we worked on in our last session, what do you notice now?" You can also probe the target with questions that are more specific: *"When you focus on the experience we worked on in our last session, what images comes up? What thoughts do you notice about yourself and the incident? What emotions do you notice? What sensations?"*

After listening to the patient report, check the SUD level again: *"As you focus on the original experience, on a scale from 0 to 10, where 0 is no disturbance or neutral and 10 is the highest disturbance you can imagine, how disturbing does it feel to you now?"*

In most cases, the SUD will remain a 0. You can then check the VoC: *"Think about the original experience and those words _____ "* (repeat the positive cognition that was installed in the first person). *"On a scale from 1 to 7, where 1 means they feel completely false and 7 means they feel completely true, how true do those words feel to you now?"*
In most cases, the VoC will remain a 7. You can then go on to the next target in your treatment plan.

If the SUD has increased above a 0, ask, *"What makes it a _____?"* (State the SUD rating.) Then ask, *"When you notice those disturbing _____ (images, thoughts, emotions, or sensations), do they feel more connected to that incident or to another related incident?"*

Unless you and the patient conclude that residual disturbance relates to an associated memory, resume reprocessing on the incomplete target as described above for an incomplete target. If you and the patient conclude that residual disturbance relates to an associated memory, then consider whether to make that associated memory the next target in your treatment plan.

If the SUD remains a 0, but the VoC has dropped below a 7, ask, *"What keeps it from being completely true?"* After the patient's report, ask the patient to, *"Notice that and follow."* Then resume bilateral stimulation and follow standard procedures for the installation phase.

RESUMING REPROCESSING AFTER INCOMPLETE INSTALLATION

If reprocessing stopped in the installation phase, you should first verify that the SUD remains a 0, then resume the installation phase. "Think about the original experience and those words _____" (repeat the selected PC in the first person). "On a scale from 1 to 7, where 1 means they feel completely false and 7 means they feel completely true, how true do those words feel to you now?" Then resume installation. "Focus on the original experience and those words _____," (repeat the selected PC in the first person) "and follow." Then resume BLS.

RESUMING REPROCESSING AFTER INCOMPLETE BODY SCAN

If reprocessing stopped in the previous session during the body scan phase, first review the feedback from the log. Then, verify that the SUD remains a 0 and the Validity of Cognition (VoC) a 7. Then do the body scan again. "Close your eyes. Hold in mind the original experience—as it seems to you now—and those words _____" (repeat the selected PC). "Then bring your attention to all the different areas of your body, starting with your head and continuing down to your feet. If there is any place you feel tension, tightness, or unusual sensations, tell me." Reprocess any residual disturbance. Keep in mind that any residual negative sensations that have persisted during the time since the previous reprocessing session in spite of the SUD being a 0 and the VoC a 7 could well be linked to a different memory than the identified target memory. If these negative sensations do not resolve even after changing directions of BLS, be prepared to scan for a different or earlier memory using history taking or an *affect, somatic*, or *defensive urge* bridge as described in Exhibit 4.9, "The Affect, Somatic, and Defensive Urge Bridge Techniques".

REEVALUATION AFTER A COMPLETED REPROCESSING SESSION

Next, let us consider cases in which the prior EMDR reprocessing session resulted in a *completed reprocessing session*. At the next session, it is important, at least briefly, to check the feedback from the patient log and to reassess the SUD and VoC on the selected target memory. To check the SUD, ask, "When you bring your attention back to the experience we worked on in our last session, what do you notice now?" You can also probe with questions that are more specific: "When you focus on the experience we worked on in our last session, what images come up? What thoughts do you notice about yourself and the incident? What emotions do you notice? What sensations?" After listening to the patient report, check the SUD level again: "As you focus on the original experience, on a scale from 0 to 10, where 0 is no disturbance or neutral and 10 is the highest disturbance you can imagine, how disturbing does it *feel* to you *now*?" In most cases, the SUD will remain a 0. You can then check the VoC: "Think about the original experience and those words _____" (repeat the PC that was installed in the first person). "On a scale from 1 to 7, where 1 means they feel completely false and 7 means they feel completely true, how true do those words feel to you now?" In most cases, the VoC will remain a 7. You can then go on to the next target in your treatment plan.

EXPLORING FOR THE NEXT TARGET WITH SUD OR VOC CHANGES AFTER A COMPLETED SESSION

Occasionally, the SUD or VoC shifts and you then need to consider whether this is because of the additional material within that specific memory, or because of an associated memory from within a cluster of similar experiences. With single-incident trauma survivors, you can simply resume reprocessing on the previously selected target memory. In survivors with a cluster of closely related traumatic experiences, your original case formulation and reevaluation may lead you to hypothesize that any small regressions in the SUD or VoC are related to other associated memories already listed in your treatment plan or that these patients revealed in their log reports. A direct question to the patient can sometimes clarify this. "When you notice those disturbing _____ (i.e., images, thoughts, emotions, or sensations), do they feel more connected to that incident or to another related incident?" If you and the patient conclude that the residual disturbance appears more related to a closely associated memory, it will often be more efficient to shift the focus of reprocessing to the associated memory. Note that this general guidance applies to cases in which the case formulation and treatment plan focus on *Diagnostic and Statistical Manual of Mental Disorders* Axis I diagnoses. Different factors would come into play if the case formulation and focus of attention were on characterological or Axis II issues.

THE PAST: ASSESSING AND TARGETING OF DISTURBING MEMORIES

As you move through reprocessing the memories originally selected for the treatment plan, the patient's symptoms will generally improve. The pace of improvement will vary greatly depending on the degree to which the clinical presentation is chronic and complex. Continue to refer back to the master treatment plan list of targets (Exhibit 4.14 in chapter 4) in chapter 4. Ideally, you will be able to reprocess all of the significant memories that were identified in the treatment plan. In some cases, patients will improve so significantly that they will not want or need to address every memory identified at intake as potentially related to current symptoms. In many cases, there will be a generalization of treatment effects from memories that were reprocessed to memories that have not yet been directly targeted. When you return to the master treatment plan list of targets, you will find that some of these memories simply no longer appear to hold any residual disturbance for some patients. For most patients, it is a good idea to check these memories for level of disturbance and to reprocess those that may still be contributing to symptom maintenance.

In many cases, symptoms will persist even after all of the significant memories, identified both at intake, and during the course of treatment, have been completely reprocessed. This is consistent with the Adaptive Information Processing (AIP) model and the basic three-pronged protocol of past, present, and future. Even after all etiological memories have been reprocessed, symptoms often persist in response to current stimuli because of the tendency of the brain to retain threat cues from past adverse life events (LeDoux, 1996; LeDoux, Romanski, & Xagoraris, 1989). Therefore, to achieve further symptomatic gains, attention will have to shift to reprocessing current stimuli that remain capable of evoking symptoms.

THE PRESENT: ASSESSING AND TARGETING OF CURRENT STIMULI

In the second "prong" of the three-pronged standard EMDR–PTSD treatment plan, attention shifts to reprocessing current stimuli that are still capable of evoking maladaptive perceptions, attitudes, and behaviors. In the AIP model, these symptoms are viewed as expressions of maladaptively encoded aspects of patients' traumatic experiences. These may appear as intrusive reexperiencing, such as nightmares, flashbacks, and somatoform symptoms. Patients may continue to experience residual urges to avoid situations that might evoke intrusive reexperiencing or they may engage in actual avoidant behavior. Finally, there may be residual agitation, hyperarousal, anxiety, or unstable mood states. All of these can be addressed with further reprocessing to continue the treatment plan and resolve these residual symptoms.

ASSISTING SURVIVORS OF PERSISTENT TRAUMATIC EXPOSURE TO RECOGNIZE TREATMENT GAINS

While it is essential to monitor patient feedback for signs of residual symptoms, it is also important to be alert to treatment gains and to actively acknowledge these gains. When traumatic exposures have been limited to one or a few episodes and when these have been more recent, patients are often able to accept the rapid and comprehensive gains they tend to make during EMDR reprocessing without needing a great deal of confirmation or validation from their treating clinician. They may need to be reminded that the treatment plan predicted the need to address current stimuli during the second part of treatment. However, when the number of traumatic exposures is greater and when patients have had to adapt to their symptoms over a much longer period of time, patients sometimes make more gradual and less even gains. These patients may need more recognition of their gains to help build their confidence that they will be able to overcome issues that may initially appear to be more intractable or that are more strongly linked to a sense of self. So before turning to the resolution of residual maladaptive responses in the present, let us first examine ways to strengthen and extend the gains made by patients with more complex and long-standing traumatic exposures.

BUILDING ON TREATMENT GAINS

With a minority of patients, it may be sufficient to note evidence of treatment gains in your written record without the need to discuss these gains at length. However, for most patients, the course of treatment can be uneven. It can be extremely helpful to acknowledge their gains verbally. When you comment on their gains you strengthen both the therapeutic alliance and patients' sense of their progress. As you continue the treatment plan, and especially when there are mild regressions or new targets that have emerged, acknowledging these gains helps patients feel the confidence they need to address additional traumatic material. With complex cases, these gains can be hard-won and may merit further attention as targets for Resource Development and Installation (RDI) as described in chapter 6 and appendix B to strengthen patients' abilities to access these positive states at later points in their treatment. In the two following sections on consolidation dreams and new adaptive behaviors are case examples in which RDI was employed when these gains emerged. However, in many cases, a brief discussion of such gains is all that is needed.

CONSOLIDATION DREAMS

Just as recurrent nightmares are symptoms of PTSD, so changes in these dreams after EMDR reprocessing of the memories are sometimes signs of shifts in the way information about traumatic experiences has been modified (Wittmann, Schredl, & Kramer, 2007). Nightmares can become less frequent or can shift from reexperiencing to more symbolic forms. Another kind of change is the emergence of positive dream content or a different, more positive ending to a dream. One woman survived a life-threatening motor vehicle crash with her sports car in an intersection that left her with temporary postconcussive cognitive impairments. At intake, she reported being awoken every night by recurrent dreams of the crash. After her third EMDR session, she reported a dream of driving her sports car on her favorite winding mountain road. That week, she went to take delivery of her replacement car and had a pleasurable drive home.

When positive dream content emerges in survivors of chronic traumatic exposures, it can be useful to target the positive dream content for resource installation. A few brief sets of bilateral stimulation can enhance the patient's access to the positive aspects that emerge in dream content. My first dramatic experience of the benefits of installing consolidation dreams is described in *"Lifting the Burden of Shame: Using EMDR Resource Installation to Resolve a Therapeutic Impasse"* (Leeds, 1998a). Meredith was a survivor of chronic adverse early childhood experiences who had presented for treatment of dysthymia, impaired self-esteem, and a chronic tendency to emotionally collapse in the face of interpersonal stressors. After her third incomplete EMDR reprocessing session, she reported a remarkable positive dream of a Sphinx-like being in the sand. *"With his presence I felt like I could do anything I needed to do."* We targeted this positive dream image and enhanced it with a few short sets of bilateral stimulation. This led to a series of several additional resource installations in that session. The next week, Meredith was free of long-standing chronic pain and was able to sleep through the night for the first time in her memory. She also began to show resilience and assertiveness in social situations. In subsequent sessions, EMDR reprocessing was more productive, generally leading to completed treatment sessions. There were two keys to resolving what had been an impasse in attempting to use EMDR with Meredith. The first was recognizing the consolidation of self-capacities represented in the positive dream content she reported. The second was choosing to spend two sessions applying RDI on this emerging positive material.

NEW ADAPTIVE BEHAVIORS

In a similar manner, when patients are able to engage in new adaptive behaviors, it can be helpful not only to acknowledge their reports of new coping behaviors, but also to enhance these with resource installation. Such gains can come in the form of overcoming avoidance of settings that have previously triggered intrusive memories or in the form of new adaptive behaviors. An example comes from the case of Natalie who had developed chronic avoidance of confrontations with authority figures. After several reprocessing sessions on memories of verbal abuse and being cutoff from normal social events by an overly controlling and highly punitive stepfather, Natalie reported at the start of the next session that she stood up to her employer that week when he asked her to change her long-established and agreed-upon vacation plans to cover for another employee who was unexpectedly out because of an extended illness.

When Natalie reported her firm and assertive response to her clinician, they both realized this represented an important treatment gain. After listening to her narrative of the key assertive moment, her clinician asked Natalie to identify where she felt the positive feelings in her body and then added several short sets of bilateral stimulation. The positive feelings were strengthened. She reported an increased sense of having the right to protect her enjoyment of good things happening in her life and not having to be valued just for what she does for others. She then added that 2 days later, her employer apologized to her for having asked her to forgo her vacation plans. He not only acknowledged what a valued employee she was, but also that she deserved the time off.

Natalie said, "You know, unlike my stepfather, my employer wasn't being mean. He was just frantic and reacting when he was worried about being understaffed. Once he thought about it and settled down, he was able to acknowledge that it was his problem and not mine and that I deserved the time off that I had earned." In this statement, she was able to verbalize an increased sense of self-worth and stimulus discrimination. She was now able to recognize a situation that initially reactivated aspects of her stepfather's responses to her, to clearly delineate appropriate responsibility and to gain the freedom to act on her own perceptions. The clinician enhanced her statement with two more sets of BLS. They then went on to discuss the next step in their treatment plan.

Several weeks later, they were reprocessing a memory of an abusive and demeaning boyfriend who had been overly controlling of her during high school. At a critical point in the reprocessing, Natalie recalled not only this moment of assertiveness with her employer, but his subsequent apology and validation of her entitlement to her vacation. Spontaneously reaccessing this previously installed resource helped her move through the reprocessing of the memories of this abusive relationship in which she had never received any support or validation.

These examples illustrate how, in selected cases, brief enhancement of treatment gains with RDI can extend these gains and make the emerging adaptive memory networks more accessible both in daily life and when needed during subsequent reprocessing sessions. In the next section, we will examine how to continue reprocessing on current stimuli after all identified targets from the past have been appropriately resolved.

ADDRESSING UNRESOLVED SYMPTOMS

Nightmares

Nightmares are commonly used targets in the second "prong" of the standard EMDR–PTSD treatment plan. Nightmares tend to come in two forms. They can be in the form of reexperiencing or reliving a somewhat realistic narrative of elements of the patient's traumatic memory. Nightmares can also take the form of symbolic expressions of one or more aspects of the traumatic experience that capture emotions and situations from the index trauma, but with dramatically altered context or participants. As you reprocess the traumatic memories themselves, nightmares will tend to lessen in frequency and intensity. Nightmare content will also tend to shift from the reexperiencing form to the more symbolic form (Raboni, Tufik, & Suchecki, 2006). Regardless of their realistic or symbolic content, after the traumatic memory or memories are no longer perceived to be disturbing, recurring or occasional nightmares should be near the top of your list of targets for further reprocessing.

The procedure for targeting nightmares for reprocessing is essentially the same as for any memory. Some patients may want to describe the nightmare in detail. This can be useful when monitoring dream content or for various forms of dream work or dream interpretation. However, a complete narrative of the nightmare is not essential to be able to target the nightmare for reprocessing anymore than a complete narrative is required before a memory is reprocessed with EMDR. Once the nature of the nightmare has been reported, it is sufficient to ask, *"What image represents the worst part of the incident?"* From that point, you continue and complete the standard assessment phase of the target and then begin the reprocessing. Continue reprocessing through the desensitization, installation, and body scan phases.

When targeting symbolic dream content, there may be a slightly greater tendency for memories earlier than the index trauma to emerge during reprocessing. If there is any evidence of ineffective reprocessing of symbolic nightmares, be alert to the need to scan for earlier material—using an *affect, somatic,* or *defensive urge bridge* as described in Exhibit 4.8.

FLASHBACKS AND OTHER FORMS OF INTRUSIVE REEXPERIENCING

Intrusive reexperiences are often referred to as flashbacks. However, these painful intrusive experiences do not always take the form of visual intrusions. Emotional, somatic, and olfactory reexperiences are common and just as disturbing (van der Kolk & Fisler, 1995). While EMDR reprocessing is generally effective at reducing the vividness and frequency of all forms of reexperiencing, such intrusive experiences can and often do continue in response to current stimuli. Continued intrusive reexperiencing after initial memory reprocessing is more common in patients with chronic exposures including combat trauma and adult survivors of childhood abuse. Because emotional, somatic, and olfactory intrusions are as common as visual intrusions, clinicians should actively solicit patient feedback for evidence of the full range of possible reexperiencing or should use standard assessment tools to reassess for intrusions as treatment progresses.

Procedures for targeting intrusions are simple and straightforward. After obtaining a patient report of an intrusion, simply ask, *"What image or other sensory memory is the worst part of that?"* Continue and complete the standard assessment phase. Then continue with reprocessing through the desensitization, installation, and body scan phases. As with targeting nightmare content, clinicians should remain alert to the possibility that other previously unrecognized memories may turn out to be linked to reported instances of intrusive reexperiencing.

Hank was a veteran police officer who successfully reprocessed a series of initially vivid and horrific memories of crime scene incidents. After reprocessing these incidents, he reported significant gains in sleep quality and freedom from visual intrusions that had haunted him for many years. However, he had begun to notice a recurring sense of deep sadness and helplessness that would come over him at seemingly random moments. The most vivid and recent of these *emotional intrusions* occurred while visiting the house of a friend who had a 4-month-old daughter. The officer was puzzled by this experience because he should have been happy for his friend who was enjoying fatherhood for the first time.

When asked to identify the worst part of the experience, Hank reported it was when they put the infant down in her crib for a nap. With this as the starting point, he focused on the location of the sensations and emotions, which he experienced in his chest and arms. Bridging back from these sensations, he quickly retrieved a memory he had briefly mentioned during history taking, but that had been set aside for several weeks. The incident involved a sudden infant death investigation. While nothing suggested foul play, standard department procedures had required him to take the dead infant from the grief-stricken parents for an autopsy to rule out accident or intentional injury as the possible cause of death. After taking the infant from the parents into his arms, he was later required to be the investigating officer to witness the autopsy of the dead infant. He had received prior training to cope with such a situation. He recalled the sense of grief and helplessness he had felt during the autopsy.

This memory was selected as the next target for reprocessing. During the reprocessing, the sensations and emotions associated with holding the dead infant in his arms faded away, as did the smell of the autopsy room. After completing the reprocessing of this experience, the officer reported a tremendous sense of relief and a sense of a burden having been taken from him. In subsequent sessions, he reported that the smell of rubbing alcohol no longer disturbed him as it had ever since the infant's autopsy. The next time he visited his friend's house, he noted that he felt at ease around his friend's daughter and was able to freely share in his friend's enjoyment of his infant daughter.

AVOIDANT BEHAVIORS

While intrusive reexperiencing generally resolves quickly during EMDR reprocessing of single incident and limited duration-related PTSD, anticipatory anxieties and avoidant behaviors can persist even after successful reprocessing of memories of discrete traumatic events. In part, this may be because avoidance develops over time in the weeks, months, or years after traumatic incidents and is self-reinforcing as an overlearned defensive coping strategy. Thus, after successful reprocessing of all identified and associated traumatic memories, residual avoidant behaviors and anticipatory anxieties may need to be reprocessed with a focus on current stimuli and future templates. Compared with residual intrusions, residual avoidant behaviors are somewhat less likely to be linked to unresolved traumatic memories.

Procedures for reprocessing recent occurrences of avoidant behaviors are essentially the same as for old memories. When patients report residual intense anxiety to reminders of a natural disaster or feelings of wanting to avoid tasks of daily living, such as settings or situations similar to those in a motor vehicle crash or criminal assault, your first question is, *"What image represents the worst part of the incident?"* From that point, you continue and complete the standard assessment phase of the target and then begin the reprocessing. Continue reprocessing through the desensitization, installation, and body scan phases.

One recently hired young police officer had been first on the scene of an incident reported in an apartment building. Assuming at first that it was a domestic violence incident, the officer was not mentally prepared to walk in to discover a completed suicide by hanging. Not knowing how long the body had been hanging there and believing the hanging to have just taken place, the officer broke standard procedure by disturbing the scene to attempt resuscitation. After the memory of the incident had been successfully and completely reprocessed, at a subsequent session, the officer expressed some apprehension during recent experiences driving past that particular apartment building, as well as concerns if there were to be future calls to that building. This led to the decision to make the recent experience of anxiety about driving past the building the target for further reprocessing. During reprocessing of recent stimuli, the officer further reworked the memory of what did happen. This led to spontaneously and calmly reexamining the sensory information available in the original scene and imagining following standard procedures. The next week, the officer reported having driven past the building without anxiety and being able to easily imagine calmly and confidently entering the premises again in the future should there be another call for police response there.

In this case illustration, targeting and reprocessing the recent occurrence of an urge to avoid exposure to stimuli reminiscent of a traumatic experience led to the resolution of both urges to avoid such exposure, and to the elimination of anticipatory anxiety about confronting a similar scene in the future. In other cases, even after successfully reprocessing current cues associated with avoidance, some anticipatory anxieties can remain. These can be addressed with the future template.

11.2 | Three Types of Future Templates

After successful reprocessing of identified targets from the past and present, reprocessing focused on the future can resolve remaining issues to achieve treatment goals.

Standard Future Template: overcoming residual anticipatory anxiety and avoidance by reprocessing images of the future with low to moderate SUD ratings.

The Positive Template: combines mental rehearsal of new skills and adaptive behaviors to potential challenges with bilateral stimulation to improve self-confidence and skills.

Fostering a New Self-Concept: consolidating a new sense of self by gathering mastery memories representing treatment gains and images that symbolize a new identity defined by current values, capabilities, and goals.

THE FUTURE—USE OF FUTURE TEMPLATES

The third prong of the standard EMDR–PTSD protocol addresses the future. This use of the EMDR procedural steps has generally been referred to as the "future template" (Shapiro, 2001). There are at least three basic types of future templates. The first involves confronting likely situations in the future to lessen residual anticipatory anxiety and enhance behavioral freedom (Sartory, Rachman, & Grey, 1982). The second involves the mental rehearsal of new skills and adaptive behaviors in the future to improve self-confidence and skills (Allami, Paulignan, Brovelli, & Boussaoud, 2008; Foster & Lendl, 1995, 1996). This is also referred to as the "positive template" (Shapiro, 2001, pp. 211–214). The third involves the fostering of a new sense of self no longer defined by the impact of traumatic experiences (Herman, 1992b). In the standard PTSD–EMDR protocol, the future template is usually applied in the later phases of treatment. However, situations that may call for the use of the future template can arise before there has been time to fully address all past adverse events. An example of this appears in chapter 12. In addition, several EMDR interventions focused on the future self or alternate coping responses before patients have even started to address past adverse events have been described in cases of complex PTSD (Hoffman, 2004, 2005; Korn & Leeds, 2002) and in working with substance abuse (Popky, 2005).

COPING WITH PREVIOUSLY AVOIDANT STIMULI

As mentioned in the section above on addressing recent and current stimuli in the present, avoidant behaviors are generally overlearned. Persistent anticipatory anxiety over long-avoided or essentially new behaviors is a frequently occurring symptom that may need to be targeted specifically, even after resolving past traumatic and conditioning events. The first type of use of the future template is to help patients address residual anticipatory anxiety, anger, fear, or shame over confronting stimuli associated with past adverse experiences.

If past adverse and conditioning events and current stimuli have been appropriately addressed with EMDR reprocessing, the level of disturbance as measured by the SUD in the assessment phase for a future template should be relatively low—in the range of 0 to 4. When the residual SUD rating obtained during the assessment phase for a future template is moderate to high—in the range of 5 to 10—this suggests that more work may be needed on other aspects of the past. In these cases, before reprocessing the future template, clinicians should probe for additional past targets by using the affect or somatic bridge technique described in chapter 4. After spontaneous reprocessing of the future template is complete, clinicians may assist patients to go further by suggesting additional stimuli to challenge any possible residual material that has been previously avoided.

As an illustration of the use of the future template for residual anticipatory anxiety, here is a case vignette. Shirley had successfully reprocessed memories of several instances of childhood sexual abuse by her maternal Uncle Gilbert. She had also reprocessed the hurt and anger she had felt over her mother's initial inability to accept that this had happened and to be appropriately protective and supportive. During Shirley's early childhood, Uncle Gilbert had been abusing alcohol. Shortly afterward, he went into treatment. He had been in stable recovery from alcohol dependence for many years. When Shirley was in her 20s, he had written letters of acknowledgment and apology to both Shirley and her mother. However, Shirley did not seek treatment for the residual effects of these adverse early experiences until her daughter was about the same age as she had been at the time of the abuse.

After EMDR reprocessing, the memories of the sexual abuse no longer held the emotional pain they had when she entered treatment with EMDR. Her recurrent nightmares had ceased. Her general background anxiety had gone away for the first time in her adult life. She felt better about herself and much happier in her relationship with her husband.

During the intake process, Shirley had also mentioned a pattern of avoidance as one of the issues she wanted to address in her therapy. She had not visited her cousin's family for several years to avoid the feelings of shame she had always experienced there. She felt shame because her cousin knew of the abuse; however, she and her cousin had never directly discussed her experiences. She also wanted to avoid the possibility of encountering her Uncle Gilbert, who lived outside the area but occasionally visited her cousin.

When she and her EMDR clinician discussed this residual issue, Shirley stated her distress was not as great as before, but she still felt some uneasiness over the idea of planning a trip to her cousin's house. Her first concern was the idea that, were Uncle Gilbert's name to come up in conversation, her cousin would be thinking about Shirley's experience of having been sexually abused. They agreed to target an imagined future scene in which his name did come up in conversation.

Her negative cognition was, "I am dirty." Her positive cognition was, "I am ok." Her initial VoC was a 5. Her emotion was shame. Her initial SUD was between 3 and 4. Her initial body location, where she felt tension, was in her face and chest. Because the SUD was in the low to moderate range, they proceeded to reprocess this target. The reprocessing was uneventful. The level of discomfort fell with each set of eye movements and soon went to 0. The installation phase went smoothly. Shirley stated she had a better positive cognition to install, "*I am a good person.*" The VoC rose steadily to a 7. In the body scan, she reported feelings of ease and acceptance as warmth in her chest that remained stable after adding additional sets of eye movements.

To further probe for comprehensive resolution of these issues, the clinician asked Shirley to imagine her cousin asking her about how she would feel bringing her family to a combined holiday dinner where Uncle Gilbert would be present. Shirley had previously attended only one family get together that had included Uncle Gilbert. She felt in control and only mildly anxious at the time, but she focused a great deal of attention on monitoring her children around Uncle Gilbert. The week after that encounter, she experienced a more intense series of nightmares and felt a greater strain in her interactions with her husband.

When asked to imagine discussing with her cousin a family get-together that would include Uncle Gilbert, Shirley reported feeling some tension in her solar plexus and chest and an SUD of 4. Reprocessing led to increased feelings of trust in her perceptions and a desire to be protective of her children. She was able to spontaneously rehearse telling her cousin, "It would be wonderful for our families to get together more often. Even though Uncle Gilbert has appeared to be appropriate since he went into recovery, I am not willing to have him alone around my children ever. Until our children are older, I want my husband or me to be present whenever Uncle Gilbert is in the same area as my children. As long as that's understood, I would be happy to make plans for all of us to get together." After rehearsing making this statement, her SUD soon went to 0. Shirley then identified a new positive cognition, "I can protect myself and my children." She was able to install this PC to a 7 and again had a clear body scan.

On follow-up several weeks later, Shirley described her family's visit to her cousin's house for the holiday dinner. She said, "It went really well. Before we went, my husband and I discussed how we would supervise our children at my cousin's house. All the children got along well. While I was there, I was alert, but at ease. I felt in control. I spoke briefly with Uncle Gilbert. He told us that he *understood and supported my request to have* my husband or me to be present whenever he was near our children. So, that part went well too. The following week, I didn't have any nightmares or disturbing thoughts about the past, the way I did after the previous time I saw him. It was a sad chapter in my life that affected me for so long, but it no longer haunts me. I'm so grateful for being able to release all that through the EMDR."

In this vignette, the patient was able to successfully complete reprocessing anticipatory anxiety in the future template without needing to address any residual material from the past. To assure comprehensive results, the clinician deliberately probed with an issue—contact with the perpetrator—that the patient had previously identified as being capable of eliciting residual symptoms. Follow-up reports from the patient's log confirmed the absence of both anticipatory anxiety and any residual intrusions. Further, Shirley was able to actively assert her need to be protective of her children in discussions with her husband, her cousin, and Uncle Gilbert. She experienced these conversations as supportive and they helped her to confirm a new sense of herself as in control and a good parent.

REHEARSAL OF NEW SKILLS

The second type of future template used in EMDR focuses on the mental rehearsal of new skills and adaptive behaviors in the future to improve self-confidence and skills. It is similar to the installation phase and also related to RDI procedures. This type of future template can be used in clinical cases to assist in mental rehearsal of social skills, such as assertiveness and active listening. It can also be used for performance enhancement in executive and athletic coaching (Foster & Lendl, 1995, 1996). Both of these applications are also referred to as the "positive template" (Shapiro, 2001, pp. 211–214). There is significant evidence that such mental rehearsal has a measurable effect on skill enhancement (Allami, Paulignan, Brovelli, & Boussaoud, 2008).

Public speaking is perhaps the most common form of social phobia (Barlow, 2002). In treating patients who fear public speaking, it is important to assess patients' level of skills and assure that patients have been exposed to appropriate education, training, and modeling in good public speaking skills. Then, after reprocessing adverse past experiences and current stimuli associated with public speaking anxiety, in the future template, attention turns to mental rehearsal of future public speaking. This mental rehearsal provides opportunities for patients to imagine experiencing positive experiences and build mental models of skillfully coping with various challenges that can arise in public speaking settings.

Survivors of early childhood abuse and neglect may never have been exposed to healthy models of communicating needs and resolving conflicts over family issues, such as budgeting or planning a family event. It is important that patients with such background have adequate skill-building experiences through reading books and attending classes, and have opportunities to rehearse new skills through roll playing or family therapy. The positive template provides another structured format for supporting patients in rehearsing and integrating new skills and coping behaviors.

When using the positive template, the focus of mental rehearsal is on building mental models of effective future performance. In these situations, it is not useful to carry out the standard assessment of the target. Instead, the positive template begins by asking patients to visualize the essential elements of their presentation from beginning to end as a series of positive scenes. Then patients can be asked to imagine this rehearsal while thinking of a suitable positive self-statement, such as "I am competent," "I am successful," or "I am in control." Then you can add several sets of bilateral stimulation as patients rehearse their positive scenes with their positive self-statement.

Patients should have already been exposed to education and training on how to cope with these kinds of situations before being challenged to mentally rehearse coping with additional stressors. After patients report positive responses to mental rehearsal of positive scenes and positive statements with bilateral stimulation, they can be challenged to imagine successfully coping with typical stressors they may encounter. With public speaking issues, these can include problems with audiovisual equipment, interruptions of various kinds, and difficult questions or comments from the audience. Survivors of childhood exposure to domestic abuse and neglect who are learning more effective conflict resolution skills would first imagine positive scenes of being able to request time for a conversation devoted to the unresolved issue, asserting their own preferences and actively listening to their partners' preferences, proposing workable compromises, and finding resolution. Then they can be asked to imagine coping with their partner's responses of disinterest, irritation, lack of flexibility, or voice raising.

When patients can imagine themselves coping effectively with these challenges, continue with additional sets of bilateral stimulation on their positive experience. If patients begin to feel any tension or anxiety, have them notice the location of these sensations and reprocess the negative sensations with bilateral stimulation until they dissipate. Finish the future template by, again, linking their positive scenes of performing well together with their positive self-statement and adding a few more sets of bilateral stimulation.

INTEGRATING A NEW IDENTITY

Survivors of traumatic and adverse life events who develop persistent symptoms often modify their self-concept as a result of the adaptations they have made to cope with lingering effects of these experiences. While most overt symptoms of PTSD quickly diminish during EMDR treatment, some aspects of the impact of adverse life events on a person's sense of self can persist and continue to affect quality of life and distort choices for the future. To assure the most comprehensive treatment results, in the later phases of treatment, clinicians may decide to offer selected patients the opportunity to work on their self-concept through a different type of future template intended to foster a new self-concept.

While some patients may recognize their self-concept as needing work, others may not be able to either recognize or articulate this need precisely because of the degree to which their sense of self has become adapted to these adverse life experiences. These patients may have begun to exhibit new adaptive behaviors that suggest more positive self-concept, such as greater assertiveness, improved self-confidence, healthy boundary setting, selecting more supportive relationships, and pursuing more fulfilling goals. Yet, in many cases, these patients have yet to consolidate these emerging self-capacities into a new sense of self. This occurs most commonly in adult survivors of prolonged early childhood trauma and chronic exposures to adverse life events that span at least one developmental stage of life. It also occurs after prolonged exposure to combat trauma, as well as after major disasters (e.g., the 9/11 attacks and hurricane Katrina) that affect whole communities and disrupt the social fabric. The extent of personal losses can be so great in these cases that survivors need directed work to help them consolidate emerging elements of a new sense of self.

This can be thought of as a process similar to quilt making. Each of the targets that has been reprocessed has been transformed from being held as a dysfunctional memory network to being an adaptive memory network. New adaptive behaviors have emerged. Each of these positive gains may be thought of as a separate "patch" of fabric that has already been successfully rewoven. However, these disparate elements have yet to coalesce into a complete "quilt" as a new sense of self. The clinical task begins with guiding patients to identify the gains they have made. Often, these have been individually reported over the period of many weeks or months of psychotherapy. Patients may have read them aloud from their log entries or personal journals. Clinicians can assist patients to gather these separate gains together in a written list, a collage, or they can merely help them summarize these gains in mastery verbally.

Each adaptive gain can then be briefly targeted for installation with the image that represents it, a positive self-statement, and any emotions and sensations linked to this experience. A few sets of bilateral stimulation can be offered to enhance the associations and access to each adaptive gain. This can be repeated for as many areas as indicated. Patients can then be asked to allow an image to emerge that represents the integration of a set of these gains. This can be done in a manner similar to what was described in the Resource Development and Installation procedure described in chapter 6. Because all identified targets from the past and the present have already been reprocessed, there is little concern that extending the number of repetitions per set could lead to negative associations. So a moderate number of repetitions per set—14 to 20—can safely be used. This process can be combined with imaginal rehearsal by asking the patient to imagine being in a new setting in the future, either alone or with one or more significant others. Examples of the use of the future template for consolidating a new self-concept are included in chapter 12.

THE OPEN DOOR

The process of completing treatment ideally involves discussion and review of the treatment process, gains, possible future issues, and scheduling of any follow-up visits or posttreatment assessment. Occasionally, these steps do take place in an orderly manner. Other times, patients may abruptly decide they no longer need further treatment even when the clinician may think otherwise. Patients may discontinue treatment abruptly because of financial crises, a change in insurance coverage, or having to relocate or spend time away from home for an ill family member. Sometimes, probing discussions will reveal that such decisions are based on issues that warrant clinical attention and sometimes circumstances simply cut short treatment. Whether treatment comes to an abrupt end or an agreed-upon closure, my philosophy has always been the "open door policy." I have always let my patients know that my door will always be open to them. I would rather have patients know they can discontinue treatment and resume when indicated than to try to keep patients in long-term psychotherapy when that is not needed. Each case is unique and most often we do not have continuing contact with former patients. When follow-up care is warranted, it can be scheduled in advance. Patients may want to decide for themselves when to reestablish contact or a reminder can be sent to the patient.

## 12

Cases Illustrating EMDR Treatment of PTSD

To illustrate Eye Movement Desensitization and Reprocessing's (EMDR) treatment principles, two composite cases are summarized in this chapter. The first case presented initially as a single-incident adult trauma. The patient, Gladys, is a 32-year-old married woman who became fearful while driving and at home after a recent motor vehicle crash in which she sustained physical injuries. However, her history included a single traumatic incident in her childhood that had never been discussed in her family and that had to be addressed as part of her treatment. The patient in the second case, Eva, is a 23-year-old college student who decided to take a break from school after episodes of drinking to the point of blacking out and having sex with men she didn't know. Her history included childhood sexual abuse by her father that had never been addressed.

To save space and avoid needless repetition in the session transcripts that follow, nearly all of the standard EMDR phrases actually used during the reprocessing sessions are omitted. For example, the standard phrase spoken by the clinician after each set of bilateral stimulation "Rest. Take a deeper breath. Let it go. What do you notice now?" is omitted from the transcripts. Words spoken by the clinician and nonverbal observations are placed in square brackets [like this]. Unspoken annotations from within the session or added later for the reader, are placed in curly brackets {like this}. Also, a single word is often used to indicate a standard phrase or EMDR procedure. For example, the word [Location] replaces, "Where do you feel that in your body?" The word [Install] replaces "Focus on the original experience and those words _____" (the selected positive cognition) "and follow." The phrase "When you bring your attention back to the original experience, what do you notice now?" is replaced with a "T" in the left column to indicate a return to target.

GLADYS: A SINGLE INCIDENT ADULT TRAUMA RECRUITS HIDDEN ISSUES FROM THE PAST

Gladys was a 32-year-old married woman who presented for treatment 4 months after she was injured in a motor vehicle crash. She had been driving on a winding country road on a sunny afternoon with her young niece in the backseat. She looked back for a moment to say something to her niece. When she faced forward again, she realized too late that the car ahead of her had unexpectedly slammed on its brakes for something out of sight around the curve ahead. She tried to stop too late to avoid crashing into the

12.1 | Gladys Treatment Plan

MASTER TREATMENT PLAN CHART

List memories and resources from earliest (top) to most recent (bottom)

Name: _____ Gladys _____   Page: _1_ of _1_

ID	AGE	TRAUMA MEMORY OR PERSISTENT STRESSOR DATE(S) OF TREATMENT & POST-TX SUDS	ID	AGE	RESOURCE MEMORY DATE(S) OF TX & POST RDI VOR
1	32	Rear-ended other MV after sudden stop. Arms cut on windshield. 10/31: 0.	A	32	"Tranquility corner" in home. I deserve to be at peace. 10/24: 7.
2	7	Dad hit Mom on head. He left home forever. Never discussed. 12/12: 0.	B	30	Last session: Beach. I can face my fears & deal with them. Heart & mind clear. 1/30: 7.
3	7	Aftermath of #2: Running to grandma's house for help barefoot in lightning storm. 12/19: 0.	C		
4	32	Log: last 3 weeks anxious at stop sign to cross highway. 11/14: 0.	D		
5	32	Log: anxious at stop sign to cross highway at night & rain. 1/16:0. 1/23: 0.	E		
6	32	Future template of driving to LA with husband on I–5. 12/04: 0.	F		
7			G		
8			H		
9			I		
10			J		

List symptoms and associated current stimuli with Frequency (F) and Severity (S) 0-7

ID	SYMPTOMS	CURRENT STIMULI	INTAKE F & S	DESIRED F & S	DISCHARGE F & S
a	Fearful of driving	Alone on winding roads, and at night in the rain.	5/6	0/0	0/0
b	Fearful at home	Only when alone, worst when in shower.	6/7	0/0	0/0
c	Insomnia	Depends on Ambien. Reluctant to deal with this "on her own"	7/6	0/0	0/0
d	Fearful of father	His location is and has been unknown for many years.	4/5	0/0	1/1
e					
f					
g					

 | Gladys Record of Treatment

RECORD OF TREATMENT

List symptoms by name or letter from Master Treatment Plan. Indicate worsened: –3, –2, or –1. Unchanged 0 or improved: +1, +2, to +3.

For each session code activities with this key

Hx = History taking
Mem = Target Memory
IVE = in vivo exposure
IM = Imagery

RE = Reevaluation
CrS = Current Stimuli
CBT = Cognitive

SC = Structured Calming
Fut = Future Template
Art = Art Therapy

RDI = Calm Place or Resource
VT = Verbal Therapy
Hyp = Hypnosis

For RDI and EMDR sessions, you can list selected target memory, stimuli, or resource by ID # from Master Treatment Plan.

Name: _____Gladys_____   Page: __1__ of __1__

SESSION	DATE	GAF	SYMPTOMS		ACTIVITY TARGET	PRE-SUD VOC	POST-SUD VOC	SELECTED NEGATIVE COGNITION FINAL POSITIVE COGNITION	OUTCOME HOMEWORK
1	10/24	60	a=0 c=0	b=0 d=0	Intake, history, safe place.	Tried EM	HT best.	MVA 5 months before. At fault. She alone in car injured. Arms cut.	Diagnosis PTSD. Good response to RDI.
2	10/31	60	a=0 c=0	b=0 d=0	Mem: 1 MVA	6 3.5	0 7	I'm weak. I'm strong. I can get over it.	Clear BS.
3	11/07	61	a=+1 c=0	b=0 d=0	RE: 0.5 Hx: Dad	N/A	N/A	Mem 1 stable. Log CrS: in rain SUD 5. Sudden stop: SUD 4.5.	CrS identified. More early Hx obtained.
4	11/14	61	a=+1 c=0	b=0 d=0	CrS: 4	8 4	0 7	I'm not safe. I'm safe. BS sense of pressure on right side.	Completed except for BS
5	11/21	62	a=+2 c=0	b=0 d=0	Sleep hygiene	N/A	N/A	Wants to reduce use Ambien.	Sleep hygiene. Self-control methods.
6	12/04	63	a=+2 c=+1	b=0 d=0	Fut: 6 Drive to LA	3.5 1	0 7	I'm not safe. I'm safe. BS clear.	Ready to curl up like a cat.
7	12/12	63	a=+2 c=+1	b=0 d=0	Mem: 2 Dad hit mom.	7.5 1	0 7	I'm not safe. I'm OK. I'm calm. BS clear. 18 sets. 2 CI resp.	Completed Mem
8	12/19	65	a=+2 c=+2	b=+1 d=+2	Mem: 3 Running for help in rain.	9 1	0 7	I'm helpless. I can't cope. I can handle this. I am powerful.	BS clear. Completed.
9	01/09	67	a=+2 c=+3	b=+2 d=+2	Mem: 3. Run for help with thunder	5 2	0 7	I'm not OK. I'm OK.	BS clear. Completed.
10	01/16	69	a=+2 c=+3	b=+2 d=+2	CrS: 4	7 1	0 7	I'm going to get hurt. I'm OK. BS clear. (Early Mem: lightening fear)	CrS linked to Mem.
11	01/23	74	a=+3 c=+3	b=+3 d=+2	CrS: 5 MV Anx in rain + early Mem	6 1	0 7	7 y/o: I can't deal with this. I can. CrS: I'll be hurt. I am in control.	Both Mem and CrS completed
12	01/30	76	a=+3 c=+3	b=+3 d=+2	RE: RDI to consolidate gains	N/A	N/A 7	Beach. I can face my fears and deal with them.	Heart & mind clear. Treatment complete.

car ahead. Her airbag deployed, protecting her face and head, but her arms were thrown forward and badly cut on the smashed windshield. Her niece was shaken up but not injured. No one was injured in the other car, a large SUV. She was taken to the hospital, treated, and released. By the time she came to see me, she had gone through physical therapy. She had regained full use of her arms. The scars on her arms were fading, and she had no residual physical symptoms. However, she had developed several psychological and behavioral issues for which she was seeking treatment with EMDR.

Until a few months before the crash, Gladys had been employed as a professional at a large company. She had worked extremely long hours for years and had decided to stop working to lower her stress level and take time for herself. She had been journaling, taking yoga classes, and exploring options for part-time self-employment in preparation for wanting to get pregnant. Her husband was a well-paid professional and shared her desire to have children. Gladys was a slender, attractive woman, who was soft spoken and conveyed an almost childlike sense of innocence and gentleness.

Prior to the crash, Gladys had never had a depressive episode or anxiety symptoms. She had no history of substance use and seldom drank. After the crash, Gladys developed a driving phobia, insomnia, and several anxiety symptoms, including nightmares and fear of being home alone. In fact, she met full criteria for posttraumatic stress disorder (PTSD). During our initial visit, I explored the nature of her current driving anxiety. Not surprisingly, her driving anxiety was worse on curving roads where the view ahead was hidden, but I was surprised to find out that her greatest driving anxiety was at night when she had to drive across a four-lane highway at a stop sign, and was worst when it was raining. I was also surprised by her fear of being home alone, which was most disturbing if she was in the shower "because then I couldn't hear if someone was trying to break into our house." She had not had such fears before the crash and there was no history of break-ins in their gated community.

After gathering information about the crash and her presenting complaints, I asked about her history and early family life and whether there were any other traumatic events in her life. She said that their mother had raised her sister, brother, and herself after her father left home when she was young. They had a simple and quiet life. Gladys said that her life had been free of trauma until this recent motor vehicle crash, then added that there had been just one prior trauma that had led to her father's leaving when she was 7 years old. One night during dinner, her father had become agitated and assaulted her mother, hitting her in the head with a large glass vase. There had been no prior incidents of domestic abuse. This incident was completely unexpected and shocking. Her mother was knocked unconscious to the ground and was bleeding from the scalp. She and her sister fled the house and ran two blocks in a thunder and lightning storm to their grandmother's house. Grandma called for an ambulance. Gladys' mother was treated for her injuries at the hospital for a few days and then released. Her father fled their home. They never saw him again and they never spoke of the incident.

While she was describing this childhood memory, Gladys' demeanor changed. While her voice remained almost calm and matter of fact, her face showed fear and pain and a sense of this memory being too overwhelming to confront. I expressed surprise that the family had never spoken of this dramatic incident. Gladys confirmed that her mother had never spoken about it. Her mother was forced to work throughout their childhood to support them, but with their grandmother living nearby, they managed. The story of this incident did a lot to explain some of the additional symptoms that Gladys had developed after the crash. Her fears of driving at night and in the rain, especially if having to drive across a larger road, suddenly made sense as did her fears of being home alone and of someone breaking in to their home. Her father's whereabouts were unknown. There had been a couple of newspaper reports of her father being involved in altercations and bizarre incidents in another state. She had concerns that he might show up unexpectedly someday. Gladys speculated that her father might have suffered from a bipolar disorder. It would explain his sudden atypical behavior and her brother had developed a bipolar disorder but did not like taking stabilizing medication. Unlike her sister and she, who had both gone on to college and had stable lives, her brother was emotionally troubled and led an unstable life.

In that first session, I provided information to Gladys about what she could expect from EMDR and told her that I believed that to fully resolve her symptoms; we would need to include addressing the childhood memory with EMDR. I suggested her treatment might go more quickly if we started with the childhood memory. Gladys agreed that if it proved necessary, she would reprocess that memory but that she wanted to see how much improvement she could get from just focusing on the motor vehicle crash. We then reviewed the mechanics of the bilateral stimulation. She found the eye movements uncomfortable, but she responded well to the hand paddles attached to the EyeScan. Her calm place was her "tranquility" corner in her house where she lit candles and incense and meditated. She found the calm place exercise soothing and calming after telling me about the traumatic memory of her early family history. She left the session eager to start EMDR at our next visit.

GLADYS: SESSION 2

During a brief check-in at the start of the second session, Gladys reported that she continued to sleep poorly and remained completely dependent on her prescription for Ambien. She was anxious about trying to sleep without it. She was still troubled by nightmares a few times during the week. When I asked for the image that went with her memory of the crash, Gladys said, "It's seeing my blood on the shattered windshield and the smell from the airbag." When I asked what negative belief about herself went with this image, her initial reply was, "It's painful and scarier than crap! It's the scariest thing I've ever been through. The sight of all that blood. . . is so scary." Here, I silently noted the echoes of the vision of her mother's blood on the dining room floor when she was 7 years old. When I asked, "What does that say about you?" she replied, "I'm not invincible," and then added, "I'm vulnerable and weak." Her preferred belief was, "I'm strong and powerful. I can get over anything." Her initial Validity of Cognition (VoC) was 3 or 4. Her emotion was "sad." Her Subjective Units of Disturbance (SUD) was 6. For location, she said, "My heart beats faster. My stomach feels shaky."

REPROCESSING TRANSCRIPT WITH GLADYS FROM SESSION 2

# SET	PATIENT REPORT AND [CLINICIAN RESPONSE]
27	Can they [the pulses in the paddles] be faster? At first, my tears welled up. The images got stronger and then faded. I'm not about to cry now. [Here, I increased the speed setting slightly.]
22	I'm calmer. [Coughs.] I feel pretty warm, comfortable. Can I have some water? [There was a short break while I got a glass of water for Gladys.]
T	It's not as bad. It's still something that happened. [What's the worst part of it now?] I blame myself for not paying attention. . . 2 seconds before. . . I could have prevented it if only. . . I could have hurt someone else instead of just myself. {Here I silently noted the self-blame and began to consider the need for an interweave for addressing "responsibility."}
28	Just the same. [Did you know what was going to happen?] I'm angry and I blame myself. My niece was in the car. She is 7. {Here, I silently noted the odd parallel with Gladys' trauma at age 7.} [If a friend were in a crash, what would you say if she kept blaming herself?] It's ok. You can't be perfect. It's going to be ok. . . These things happen.
31	It's ok. Things happen. You can't just beat yourself up. I'm human. . . Things will happen. I try to be perfect. . . Sometimes things just happen. [Where do you feel it now?] My heart is calm.
23	I'm calm.

T	It was something that happened to me, but I'm ok with it. It was painful. . . I'm healing. Things happen and you get through it. [SUD] 3. [Worst.] I was startled and scared. I looked down and saw all that blood. I was in and out of consciousness. I didn't know what had happened.
33	It's a memory. I'm safe now. I'm warm and toasty. My heart got a little bit fluttery, but it's calm now.
26	I'm ok. . . It's nice to be validated and to talk about it.
T	I still notice I'm upset by all the blood. I don't like to focus on it. {Here, I decided to do a two-step "safety" interweave, first probing the cue of the blood for connections with the past and then accessing safety information.}[Do you know why?] I was hurt? {Then I soften my voice and ask again.}[Do you know why?] Oh, because of my mom. [Look of surprise on Gladys' face. She starts to cry.] [Is your mom ok?] Yes. [Are you ok?] Yes. [Notice that and tell yourself how it turned out.]
34	I got anxious and then I calmed down. I'm ok. [When you talk about the blood, you know your niece was 7 too.] She was ok until she saw me covered in blood. Then she lost it, just like I did when I was girl.
31	Sad. I feel bad. She shouldn't have had to see it. [Have you seen her since the crash?] Yes. [Is she afraid in the car?] I'm not sure. I don't think so.
26	I am a more cautious driver now.
T	I'm not having any tears now. I'm not anxious. It's a memory. [SUD] 0. It's not disturbing at all. [PC: I'm strong and powerful. I can get over anything.] I'm courageous. I can get over anything. [VoC] 6 or 7.
27	[VoC] 7. [Body Scan.] Nothing. [Standard closure for completed session.]

GLADYS: SESSION 3

At her third session, Gladys confirmed that the memory of the crash remained no more disturbing than between 0 and 0.5. She told me that she was amazed by what had happened in the first session. She discussed residual symptoms of driving anxiety, which were better during the day, unless the car in front stopped quickly, and remained unchanged at night and in the rain. Her husband was going to be out of town for a week and she was feeling anxious about "my father finding me." She gave me more information about the childhood incident and the little that was known about her father. It was clear that her fears about her father finding her were primary related to unresolved issues from the childhood memory. She revealed that she had seen him actually one time when she was 18 years old and he showed up unexpectedly where she worked. There had been no contact over the last 14 years and their home phone number was unlisted.

GLADYS: SESSION 4

At her fourth session, Gladys reported on a recent visit with her mother and her strategies to avoid getting caught up in her mother's "negativity." She discussed her thoughts about her father and the possibility of determining his whereabouts. We touched on the idea of reprocessing her childhood memory. She asked to postpone that for a few weeks until after a long driving trip she and her husband had planned. She described the most disturbing recent experience of driving anxiety on a very windy day. During this session, this recent experience was selected as the next target and reprocessed completely with basic EMDR procedures.

GLADYS: SESSION 5

At her fifth session, Gladys requested that we focus on her insomnia. This session was devoted to behavioral strategies to improve her sleep hygiene. We reviewed her nighttime routine and self-control methods for managing sleep onset anxiety. We established a plan for her to practice these and report back.

GLADYS: SESSION 6

At her sixth session, Gladys requested EMDR to help her prepare for her upcoming long drive out of town with her husband. The childhood material remained in need of attention and several current cues were still capable of evoking considerable anxiety. Normally, I would not use a future template with these other issues in need of attention. However, she wanted to postpone work on these targets until her return from this trip. As indicated in Table 12.2, I applied the future template to the upcoming trip with a positive outcome. At that time, I was experimenting with using a heart rhythm coherence device from the Institute of HeartMath to monitor sessions. It was interesting to note how her heart rate changed over the course of the session when focusing on the upcoming long drive from an initial rate of 88 beats/min to 72 beats/min by the end of the future template, but there were no significant changes in her heart rhythm coherence in that session.

GLADYS: SESSION 7

At her seventh session, Gladys was ready to reprocess the memory from age 7 of her father's assault on her mother. During the check-in, she reported increased driving comfort with fewer "flinches" at the approach of other cars. She reported continuing sleeping problems, but added she had begun tapering down on the amount of Ambien she was taking 1 week at a time. She was already down to one fourth the dose she had been initially prescribed. She said that she knew logically it was not doing much medically, but it gave her some confidence to take this small dose.

For the image of her memory, she described her father bashing her mother in the head with a large glass vase. Her negative cognition was, "I am helpless." Her positive cognition was, "I can handle this and everything is ok now." Her VoC was 1. For emotion, she said, "Hurt, anger, and fear." Her SUD was "7 or 8." For location, she reported feeling it in "My heart and eyes."

REPROCESSING TRANSCRIPT WITH GLADYS FROM SESSION SEVEN

# SET	PATIENT REPORT AND [CLINICIAN RESPONSE]
25	My heart is heavy. I want to cry. I feel really scared. I'm scared to talk about this scary time in my life.
29	I'm relaxing a little. [Location.] My heart is not as fast.
26	I'm really sad.
26	I'm really upset. I'm really hurt they let this happen to me.
35	I'm calming down. [Location.] My heart and my hands.
25	I'm calmer.
T	[Cries.] It's very painful. {Here I offer a responsibility interweave.} [And whose responsibility was it to protect you and your mother, yours or your mother's?] My mother's.

26	Tightness in my heart. Feeling uncomfortable.
24	The tightness in my heart went down a little. I'm calming.
24	Still tight in my heart. [What feeling is that?] Fear. {Next, I try a safety interweave.}[After your mother was treated at the hospital, was she ok?] [Nods, yes.].
30	My heart is still scared, tight. My palms are sweaty. When you ask if she was ok afterward, I thought about the extent of her injury. Glass in her head. Broken jaw. How serious it was. She's ok now. {Here I offer an interweave for both safety and choice.}[Is it safe to talk about it now?] Yes. It's safe now. [Can you?] Yes. [Can she?] No. [Notice that.] You mean that I can and she can't? [Yes.]
30	I'm calmer. My heart doesn't hurt as much.
25	I'm ok.
26	Calmer. It's ok that I can talk about this. It doesn't have to be a secret anymore. I wonder how you can listen to people talk about things like this and not have it affect you. I'm recalling other parts of what happened now. On the way to get help, I slammed my legs rushing out the door. Then I ran to grandmother's house. {Based on how long Gladys had avoided confronting this memory, I decided to consider this other scene to be another closely related target and to leave the next part of the memory for the next session. To keep the focus on the first part of the memory, we returned to the assault.}
T	Wow. I don't get totally freaked out. It happened and I can deal with it. A little heart rate increase, but not much. [SUD] 1. [Location.] A little pain in my heart.
24	Calmer. [For containment of focus, I returned to target again.]
T	It's different. It's like a movie, not like I am there. It's like I'm far away from it, not like I'm there.
25	I'm OK, calmer. My body's warm. [SUD] 0. [Original PC: "I can handle this and everything is ok now."} {Here she revised her PC.} I'm safe and it's not my fault. [VoC] 7. [Install]
24	[VoC] 7. I'm pretty proud of myself. Wow. It's not that hard. I'm proud of myself. I can deal with this like an adult. I'm ok. [Install]
26	[VoC] 7. I'm ok. I'm calm. [BS] Nothing. I'm warm and calm. [Standard closure and briefing for a completed session.]

GLADYS: SESSION 8

At her eighth session, Gladys reported her driving was going well and that she was still taking a small amount of Ambien. She was now only slightly restless at night and was getting 7.5 to 8 hours of sleep with no nightmares. The memory of the motor vehicle crash remained a 0. The scene from the previous session remained not disturbing, between a 0 and 1. In this session, we reprocessed the aftermath of the memory from the previous session with the decision to run from the house. Even though Gladys described this aspect of the memory as being about "the running part," nothing in her narrative for this session indicates memories of running. Instead, it appears to be localized with the sense of being frozen in terror, afraid to leave the house, and a desire to be comforted.

The image for this memory started with being caught at the doorway with a sense of responsibility to get help for her mother. Gladys spontaneously reported how the scene was "Scary. Very disturbing." Her negative cognition was, "I'm helpless. I can't cope." Her positive cognition was, "Everything is ok. I can handle this." Her VoC was 1. The emotions were, "Sad. Frightened." The SUD was 9. The location was again in her heart and her palms. Note, we continued to use hand taps with the paddles attached to the light bar. As we started the session, the light bar was turned at a different angle than in previous sessions, so that the end of the bar showing the number of repetitions per set was initially visible to Gladys.

REPROCESSING TRANSCRIPT WITH GLADYS FROM SESSION EIGHT

# SET	PATIENT REPORT AND [CLINICIAN RESPONSE]
19	I was distracted by the counter on the light bar. [Maybe it's easier to be distracted than focus on the memory!] Yes, I'm anxious about it, but I can do it. [You have a choice. It's up to you.] I want to.
30	My heart started racing a little. My palms are sweaty. I want to cry.
26	It's the same. [As an adult woman today, imagine the words you could say to the little girl who is so sad and scared.]
29	My palms are sweaty. My heart is pounding. I feel pressure in my chest. I'm sad. {Interweave – choices.} [As an adult in that situation, how would you respond differently?] I wouldn't be as scared. I would know what to do and that it would be ok.
27	I'm calming down. I still feel the pain in my heart. My hands are still sweaty. [Let yourself really notice the pain in your heart to really feel it and understand it.]
30	I'm calmer. The pain is still there. I don't understand it. I'm sad. It's overwhelming. I need answers. [Allow the pain in your heart to have its own voice and to speak inside you.]
23	The voice said I was such a little girl, totally frightened for my life. Unprotected. I wish an adult could just scoop me up and say, "You're ok." No one should have to deal with that kind of fear.
27	I feel better. I'm pretty safe right now under my raincoat.
27	I'm ok.
T	It still bothers me. It's not as intense. It still bothers me being helpless, small, unprotected. [SUD] 6. {Interweave for safety and choices with an adult resource.} [What would you need to feel protected now?] My husband. [Imagine having him with you as you continue with the memory.]
34	He's there, calming me down. It's fine now. It's all that I needed. I didn't have anybody to do that.
25	I'm calming down. If only I had someone there to hug me and tell it would be ok. It would have been easier. My parents didn't. My mom was in the hospital. She didn't. She couldn't deal with it. She couldn't stand the pain. {Interweave for responsibility.}[How do you feel about that?] What? [Her refusal to talk about it.] I'm angry.
28	I'm very angry with my mom. She hasn't ever been as supportive as I need. It really hurts me and makes me angry. I'm so angry. I was robbed. It's not fair.
23	I'm calming down. That isn't as heavy now. [She whispers the next phrase.] It's always the mother.
26	I'm calmer. I'm strong and powerful. I'm not going to be a victim like my mom. I don't have to hide my anger.
T	[SUD] 1.5. {Even though the SUD was not a 0, due to the time for the session being nearly over, I moved to installation.} [PC: I can handle this.] I can handle this; I'm powerful. [VoC] 7. [Install.]
24	I'm doing it. I'm getting through this. I'm pretty proud of myself. [BS] I'm calm. [Standard closure and briefing.]

GLADYS: SESSION 9

At her ninth session, Gladys reported that her driving anxiety continued to lessen, but she still felt fear about being home alone. She asked to continue her work on her memory from age 7 on the experience of running through the lightening and thunder. Her negative cognition was, "I'm not ok." Her positive cognition was, "I'm ok." Her VoC was 2. The emotion was "Fear." Her SUD was 5. She felt it in her heart and palms.

REPROCESSING TRANSCRIPT WITH GLADYS FROM SESSION 9

# SET	PATIENT REPORT AND [CLINICIAN RESPONSE]
28	Calmer.
28	Pretty relaxed. [Go through the memory again like watching a movie. When you get to a part that's upsetting, tell me.] The running part. My heart rate increases.
33	I'm ok. Calmer. A bit of a headache. I had a little one coming in today.
30	It's not as sharp on the right side. {Here I increased the speed setting one step.}
30	Still not on the right temple. {I again increased the speed setting one step.}
36	Still not here. I'm tired. [Yawns.] It's sad, very sad, that my father did this to my mom. I had no control over it. [Tears.] [And who was responsible for what happened?] My father.
34	Just that I'm sad about that. I couldn't do anything to prevent this.
31	Just scared that this will happen to my brother because he has some similar characteristics. I'm tired of trying to take care of everyone else. Just overwhelmed. {Her brother occasionally showed up at her house unexpectedly, on the verge of homelessness asking for money.}
25	I'm calming down. It pisses me off that I can't control this. [You can choose to come to terms emotionally with what happened. You have that choice now.]
31	Thinking about my brother. He's only on meds erratically. It scares the crap out of me. What power do I have to prevent something like that happening? He gave up pot and alcohol a year ago. He was delusional.
T	[SUD] 0. [PC: I'm ok.] Still fits. [VoC] 7. [Install]
22	[VoC] 7. [BS] I still have something in my heart, but I think it's more about my issues with my brother today than about the memory. I'm calm.

GLADYS: SESSION 10

In her tenth session, Gladys spent quite a bit of time discussing concerns about her brother and issues with struggling with her limits and boundaries with him. I reviewed some principles and strategies for assertiveness with her. Near the end of the session, she requested to do a little more work on the cues of being in the dark and the rain as she had experienced another episode of some residual anxiety driving in the rain at night. In spite of the time being limited, we set up the target to reprocess the current cue at the stop sign waiting to cross a four-lane highway. Her negative cognition was "I'm going to get hurt." Her positive cognition was "I'm in control." The mismatched themes were a clue to residue of her fear in her childhood memory. Her VoC was 1. The emotion was sadness and fear of pain in her arm. Her SUD was 7. The location was her heart, her palms, and her arm.

REPROCESSING TRANSCRIPT WITH GLADYS FROM SESSION 10

# SET	PATIENT REPORT AND [CLINICIAN RESPONSE]
29	Sweaty palms.
29	I'm really scared and sad. [I want you to notice where you feel that in your body and remember being afraid, running to your grandmother's house in the dark with the rain and the lightning.]
37	I don't remember being scared of the lightning. My sister told me it was dangerous. I remember running. [Maybe it wasn't the lightning you were afraid of. Maybe it was. . .] If he would hurt her more. [Did he?] No. [Remember that.]
35	I was scared she would be killed, but she recovered and was fine.
T	[SUD] 0.5 [PC: I'm in control now.] [VoC] 7. [Install.]
31	It's not really the rain and the dark that was scary. It was not knowing what was happening to my mom and if she would be ok.

GLADYS: SESSION 11

In her eleventh session, Gladys completed reprocessing on both her current cues of driving anxiety and her memory. She had returned from a long driving trip out of state with no significant driving anxiety. She asked to return again to check on the memory of running in the dark and the rain just to see if there was anything there that still needed more work. The image was running in the dark and the rain. Her negative cognition started as, "I'm afraid I'll be hit by the lightning." Then it was, "I'm not going to get there in time." Finally it was, "I can't deal with this." Her positive cognition was, "I can deal with this." Her VoC was 7. The emotions were her heart beating and remembering feeling scared. Her SUD was a 0. To probe this further, we did a set of bilateral stimulation. She reported, "Nothing. I'm calm, relaxed." We did a second set of bilateral stimulation. She again reported, "Nothing." Her VoC was still 7. We then installed her positive statement, "I can deal with this." Her VoC was still 7.

To recheck current cues, we then focused on her being in her car at the stop sign at the four-lane highway with people driving by. Her negative cognition was "I'm not safe." Her positive cognition was, "I am safe." The VoC was 6. Her emotion was, "Scared." The SUD was 1. She felt it in her stomach.

# SET	PATIENT REPORT AND [CLINICIAN RESPONSE]
29	Just my heart beating a little faster. My palms feel warm.
22	My heart slowed a bit. I'm here. I'm safe. I'm ok.
24	I'm fine.
T	I'm ok. I can handle it. [SUD] 0. VoC 7. [Install]
22	I'm ok. [VoC] 7. [BS] Heart feels a little faster.
24	Not much. I'm fine.

We then reevaluated Gladys' traumatic memories from childhood, the motor vehicle crash, and the current cues she had reported. None were disturbing. She recalled a memory from when she was 18 falling asleep while her sister was driving and waking up when her sister had lost control of the car and it was doing a 360-degree spin. That memory was not disturbing either.

GLADYS: SESSION 12

At her twelfth session, we again reviewed Gladys original presenting complaints. Except for some mild anxiety about the whereabouts of her father, all of her original symptoms had remitted. She had stopped taking Ambien and was sleeping normally. She was able to drive at night and in the rain without anxiety. More importantly, she had begun to have a new sense of herself as a person who, perhaps unlike her mother, could face her fears. To support further consolidation of this self-image, I asked Gladys to select an image that represented her new sense of self. She described herself on the beach lying on a blanket with her feet in the sand, looking at the water with the sounds of kids playing nearby and a foghorn in the distance. The statement that went with this was, "I can face my fear and deal with them." She felt this in her heart. Her mind was quiet and clear, easy. I then did three sets of bilateral stimulation. After each set, she just said, "I feel relaxed and at peace."

GLADYS: SUMMARY

While the sequence of targets used with Gladys may not have been optimal in terms of treatment efficiency, it was necessary to respect for her need to first develop greater confidence in her ability to confront a central life-changing event that had never been discussed in her family of origin. At intake, her initial image of herself was that of a person too vulnerable to face emotionally painful material. Her treatment with EMDR did more than resolve her PTSD symptoms. It helped her generate a new self-concept and a greater sense of resilience. During the course of her treatment, she revealed that she had decided to become a life coach and to help other people with their life transitions. The case of Gladys illustrates the use of interweaves for responsibility, safety, and choices, which helped Gladys at crucial moments in her reprocessing to move through challenging material within the framework of a standard length treatment session. Her treatment ended with the use of resource installation to consolidate her new self-image as a woman able to confront life's challenges and overcome them.

EVA: RESOLVING ALCOHOL ABUSE AND REENACTMENT OF CHILDHOOD SEXUAL ABUSE

Eva was a 23-year-old college student who had moved to my community temporarily and was living with a supportive relative. She had decided to take a break from school after episodes of drinking to the point of blacking out and having sex with men she didn't know. She was quite embarrassed by these episodes as she considered herself a moral person. A family member had suggested that she get treatment with EMDR.

Eva wore a baseball cap to her first half-dozen sessions with the bill pulled down low, hiding her face. Except for her last session, she wore baggy sweatshirts that hid her torso. At her first session, she did not maintain eye contact with me as she told me about her life, but glanced up to see if I was watching her. Eva told me that she believed her father had sexually abused her, perhaps before she was 4 years old. She had reported this abuse to her mother and her mother reported the abuse to child protective services (CPS). The investigators, however, did not believe her report, and her father was not charged with sexually abusing her. He was charged with sexually abusing an older sister and was found not guilty by a judge. Her father had been sexually unfaithful to her mother. When Eva was older, perhaps about 12 or 13, her mother revealed to Eva that her two older siblings had both also disclosed episodes of sexual abuse by her father and that her father had been found not guilty. By then, Eva had forgotten her early childhood disclosures, the investigation by CPS, and the trial. Her mother also told her the story of what had happened to her when she was younger.

Eva told me that she did not have distinct memories of her abuse except for some scenes of being given a bath by her father that were too upsetting for her to think about. Eva also told me that she had many positive memories of her father from summer visits after the divorce. Her father would take her to her softball games. When she was a teenager, she recalls happy memories playing with her stepsiblings from her father's second marriage.

When I asked Eva how she had been affected by the sexual abuse and the divorce, she told me that one way was that she started drinking heavily when she was 13 years old. "I only had one relationship in high school. I had an eating disorder and drank a lot and smoked weed. In high school, I was a size zero. I didn't eat except if I was at home and had to eat. That changed when we moved out of state. I worked more. Not having a boyfriend helped. I didn't want to eat in front of him."

Eva was not the first generation in her family to experience childhood abuse. "My mom had issues with her parents. She drank a lot and did drugs in high school. Her dad was physically abusive to her and her siblings. My dad was 14 years older than her. They met when she 17." Eva told me that she had been abstinent for several months since moving to my area. She never drank alone, but always with roommates or friends to help her overcome her sense of inadequacy. Her sexual acting out had begun the year before. "I'd get really drunk anytime I've hooked up with someone and some of those I don't remember. It was consensual. Some of them I'd remember bits and pieces. Some of them I don't remember any of it." She reported being able to have sex on a couple of occasions without drinking and denied any numbing or depersonalization during sex when she had not been drinking. Eva's memory seemed generally intact with the exception of periods in which she had been drinking and for the memories of childhood sexual abuse.

AN EXTENDED PREPARATION PHASE

Eva's preparation phase was extended for several sessions to address concerns over her recent history of alcohol abuse, her intense feelings of shame and mistrust, and some fears related to EMDR reprocessing. These sessions were devoted to mood stabilization, building the therapeutic alliance, gathering more history, and developing a treatment plan. By the fifth session, Eva had achieved more stability and a stronger therapeutic alliance. She had left her job at a bar in favor of a lower paying job at a gym to decrease exposure to alcohol consumption and to start working out again regularly. She was still wearing her baseball cap pulled low over her forehead, but she made more consistent eye contact in session. Her sleep hygiene had improved and she felt more positively about herself for taking better care of herself and making better choices. I had learned that she had a history of seizures in early childhood that ended by the time she was 8 years old. She denied ever being evaluated by a physician or taking medication for these seizures.

Over the course of those initial sessions, I had provided some orientation and information to Eva about the impact of childhood trauma in general and childhood sexual abuse. She had been anxious that stirring up her memories of childhood sexual abuse would be overwhelming. In the past, this had led her to "shutting down and sleeping a lot." I gave her information and metaphors about how we would pace our work with trauma-focused treatment with EMDR that helped lessen her concerns. When I led her through the calm place exercise, she had a minimal response. We then focused on installing a resource memory from a team sports activity in Junior High School when she had felt strong and capable. She had a stronger response to this.

EVA: SESSION 6–EMDR REPROCESSING BEGINS

At her sixth session, we began EMDR reprocessing on a memory from when Eva was about 3 years old. She remembered being in the bathtub with her father washing her with a washrag. Her image was, "Me being in the bathtub naked and dad being in there." Her negative cognition was, "I am disgusting." Her positive cognition was, "I am stronger." Her VoC was 1.5. Her emotion was, "Sick and sad." Her SUD was 8. For location, she reported, "Head and chest."

# SET	PATIENT REPORT AND [CLINICIAN RESPONSE]
28	Not as heavy. [Rocking in chair.]
29	I was starting to get a headache and now I'm not.
29	Just kind of the same, just not as tense. [Location] All over.
27	[Has stopped rocking.] Same.
T	Doesn't seem as dark. SUD: 5. [Worst.] Just thinking about my dad like that. [Who was responsible for what your dad did that day, you or him?] {Checking for generalization.} He was.
25	Some anger. [Tearful. Red in face.]
30	Um, just kind of "I'm over it, there's nothing I can do." [Even though you are over it, and there's nothing you can do, just notice if there are words you might like to have said or things you might like to have done during this next SEM.]
30	I'm getting a headache again. [Location] My head and my chest and my throat. [Stay with that and again notice if there are words you might wish to have said or things you might wish to have done.]
29	That I wish I could have said, "Stop" and told myself it wasn't my fault. [So imagine doing that now.]
30	I feel a lot easier. [Notice that change.]
25	Just the same.
T	Just sad. It was wrong. [Swallows hard several times.]
29	Um, that I was taken advantage of just like when I was in school and I did stuff with guys. {Makes the linkage spontaneously between child sexual abuse and adult reenactment.}
30	Just mad at myself for putting myself in those situations. [When you were doing that, did you know about the connection between what you were doing then and what happened to you as a little girl?] [Shakes head "no".] [Just notice that.]
31	I'm kind of grossed out by myself. {Self-disgust and self-blame.}
27	Just an overall sadness. [When you think about the little girl in the tub, I wonder what you as an adult might imagine saying to her to let her know it wasn't her fault what happened and that's she a good girl, a good person?] {This is both to redirect from later memories back to the original target and an interweave for self-compassion and adult responsibility from a healthy adult perspective.}
30	Um, I would tell her that, "He was sick and she wasn't the first one, so it wasn't her fault." {Here, Eva was referring to the fact that her older sister had previously reported sexual abuse by her father occurring long before this incident.}

43	Um, That I know that he should be in jail, but she still doesn't get it. {The "she" not "getting it" is the emotional part of Eva's personality or child ego state.}[Then, see what else you might say or do to let her know, to let her feel it wasn't her fault.]
40	Um, just thinking about my mom and thinking how I feel safe with her.
25	Anger because she didn't protect me.
27	That it wasn't my fault.
25	I think it was my dad's fault and he was wrong.
24	Um, I'm just tired.
T	SUD: 2–3. [Worst?] I just see my dad . . . just having him in that kind of memory . . . [I guess it kind changes some of the ways you see him and the ways you feel about him.] [Nods.] {My comment touches on grief over some possible loss of positive self-object representations from her positive, later memories of her dad.}
36	Just thinking about the happy times I remember with him. [Well, just notice both.]
25	That I do have more happy memories than sad memories with him.
T	Just disappointed that he would do that. [Sure.] SUD: 5. {Here the SUD had gone back up.}[What makes it more disturbing now?] I wonder if there were other times that he did it. And it just makes me sick. [And if there were other times; who was responsible for that happening?] Him.
22	Just, not wanting to think of him as a bad person for doing all that, but it was still wrong of him.
26	It just makes me wonder if he didn't care about any of that, because you don't do stuff like that to people you love.

At this point, we were nearly out of time for the session and I moved toward closure. I expressed appreciation to Eva for the work she had done and reminded her to keep her log. I commented, "It's hard to change the way you've thought about your dad, isn't it? To keep the positive thoughts about your dad and to stop blaming yourself for what happened." I then shared a metaphor about how leaving your house unlocked is not the same as an invitation to robbers to come in and steal what's yours.

EVA: SESSION 7

The next week, Eva cancelled her appointment on short notice. I took this as a sign that we needed to take a short break from further reprocessing. The following week, we returned our focus to stabilization. Eva expressed concerns over increased food cravings since she had moved to the area and stopped drinking. She was actually only eating two meals a day. She had gained weight due to a lack of exercise and eating junk food. Although she had started exercising most days at the gym, she still was not eating on a regular schedule. I cautioned her against meal and calorie restriction due to her history of an eating disorder. I told her that she would get better, more permanent results from regular eating and regular aerobic exercise to maintain an optimal metabolic level. We focused the rest of the session on identifying and restructuring her most frequent negative self-assessments and localized these beliefs as being related to residue from the impact of childhood sexual abuse on her self-concept. We agreed to return to reprocessing and doing more work on the childhood memory at the next session.

EVA: SESSION 8

At her eighth session, we returned to her memory of being in the bathtub with her dad washing her with a washcloth. When I asked what she noticed about it now, she said, "I don't get as scared and emotional." I asked her about the worst part of it and she said, "Realizing it's happening and not being able to stop it." I noticed how the use of the present tense indicated the memory was still being reexperienced intrusively. Normally, I would not obtain a new negative cognition, but it had been 2 weeks and a different theme seemed present than in the first reprocessing session on this memory. For her negative cognition, Eva said, "I am helpless." Her positive cognition was, "I am in control now." For her emotion, Eva said, "I feel a sadness, anger and sadness." Her SUD was 3. She again located these feelings in her chest and we resumed reprocessing.

# SET	PATIENT REPORT AND [CLINICIAN RESPONSE]
27	My chest isn't as heavy.
24	I just don't have any emotions about it at all.
27	Nothing really.
T	I think my dad was bad and sick.
29	Just an overall ease.
26	Just the same.
T	SUD: 2. [What part is still disturbing?] Just thinking about my dad in that context. Just knowing that I trusted and respected him and he could do that. It just makes me sad.
27	Nothing really. It doesn't really bug me anymore.
T	SUD: probably a 0 or 1. Just a feeling, just holding on to that last little bit of anger. [Imagine what you'd need to be able to say or do to be able to express that.]
26	Um, um, probably just telling him I don't want to carry around this hate anymore. [Seems to be feeling more: flushed in face slightly.]
27	[Wipes tears with face tissue.] Um, just I wish I could find a way to forgive him and just move on.
26	Um, I felt like, in order to forgive him, I just need to forgive myself and quit hating myself.
26	Um, kind of an ease again.
25	Just kind of the same.
T	SUD: probably about a 0.
28	That it's fine, there's no more tightness in my chest and I don't have a headache. [SUD] 0. [PC: I am in control now.] I'm at ease with myself. [You mean, "I am ok as I am?"] Yes, I don't blame myself, and I don't blame him. [Final PC] I can accept myself as I am. VoC: 6. [Install]
26	VoC: 7. [Install]
23	VoC: 7. [Body Scan] Nothing. There are no bad thoughts about anything and no bad feelings in my body.

In the closure phase, I said to Eva, "You didn't know you could do that, did you?" She said, "No." I added, "You didn't think you could, did you?" With a smile she said, "No. I didn't." I asked what she felt about the work she had done. She said, "There's a sense of relief. My chest doesn't feel tight. I don't have a headache." I asked, "Has that been there in the background pretty often?" She explained, "I get headaches pretty often. If I am working and I stress or if I don't drink enough water that day."

EVA: SESSION 9

At her ninth session, Eva seemed more at ease than I had ever seen her before. She reported working out regularly and starting weight training. She had no thoughts or feelings about the last session or about her dad since our previous session. During reevaluation, she said, "I just have some sadness for him. It's not overwhelming like it used to be. My heart's not racing and my head's not pounding. I think about what he's had to miss out on all our lives. I have some sadness for me because I don't get to see him anymore. My sister sent him a letter about what he did to her and he sent each of us a letter saying none of it was true. That was the last time any of us had any contact with him. I know my sister remembers what happened to her, and him denying it made her more mad."

We spent the bulk of that session exploring how Eva's drinking had evolved during her teen years and became an issue in high school and a crisis in college. "I started drinking when I was 12 or 13 and that was when I didn't see my dad anymore. The last time we saw him was for Christmas and he and my sister got in a big argument. She didn't want to see him anymore and she wouldn't let me go see him by myself." She went on, "If I got in an argument with mom, I'd threaten to go live with dad and I'd call him and he'd offer to let me come live with him, but mom wouldn't let me. I didn't really understand what was going on."

"When I drink, I make the excuse that my friends are doing it. I want to go hang out with them and I have to drink to hang out with them. I've been making that excuse forever. If I don't want to drink, I don't have to. They wouldn't care. Drinking is always what I've used for a socializing thing. I'm really shy and when I drink, I'm ready to open up and have a good time."

EVA: SESSION 10

At her tenth session, Eva reported that she was continuing to work out and eat more regularly. She was sleeping more efficiently, with much fewer awakenings, but still not enough hours. We explored her negative body image, the onset of anorexia in adolescence, and her beliefs that she was unattractive and disgusting. I gave her a homework assignment to practice looking in the mirror and say, "I am ok as I am. I am attractive. I like myself."

EVA: SESSION 11

At her eleventh session, Eva reported continuing to exercise and eat regularly. She said she was feeling better, stronger, and had more energy. She said she was ready to reprocess her worst episode of drinking to the point of blacking out while having sex with a guy she had just met and did not find attractive. The image was, "Waking up the next morning in the bed with that guy." Her first statement for a negative cognition was, "That was disgusting and slutty. I can't believe it happened." The selected negative cognition was, "I am disgusting and slutty." Her first statement for a positive cognition was, "I can have a healthy relationship, be sober, and hang with guys and have fun." The selected positive cognition was, "I can enjoy being with men while sober and have a healthy relationship." Her VoC was 2. The emotion was, "Disappointment and hurt." Her SUD was 8. She felt it in her "Chest, throat, head."

# EM/SET	PATIENT REPORT AND [CLINICIAN RESPONSE]
33	Gives me a headache.
28	Everything's not as tight.
28	Just the same. Everything's not as tight.
T	Still disappointed in myself. At the same time, I think that he would take advantage.
30	Nothing really. Just the same.
T	SUD: 4. [Worst?] Just having to live with that happened that I did that. {Here I began to consider an interweave along the lines of, "What would you tell a friend who confessed she'd done something like that and felt ashamed of herself?"}
30	I'm just kind feel some ease from the stress. {If a friend confessed she'd done something like that and felt ashamed of herself, would you tell her you were disgusted and thought she was a slut or would you help her focus on the fact she decided not to do it anymore?] To focus on deciding not to do it anymore.
34	Just kind of realizing I can change it. I can choose not to drink. I can make a difference if I want.
29	Nothing really. [How's your head feel now?] Fine. It's not pounding.
25	Just an overall ease.
T	[SUD] 1–2. [Which part?] Still the fact that it happened. [Location] Chest.
26	My chest was pounding a little bit harder and now its not.
27	Just feeling kind of calm again.
T	[SUD] 0. It's calm.
25	[SUD] The same. [PC check: I can enjoy being with men while sober and have a healthy relationship.] I also just want to be in control. I know every time I drink I'm not in control. {Selected PC} I can make good choices now. VoC: 4. [Install]
25	VoC: 6. [Install]
26	VoC: 7. BS: Nothing. [What do you notice in your body?] Stomach has some butterflies. That's about it.
25	I'm just kind of calm again.

In the closure phase, we discussed Eva's options for drinking, abstinence, or having a limit. She disclosed drinking two beers a couple of weeks ago with some friends over several hours. She said that's her limit now. This appeared to be a completed session, but it's always a good idea to check to make sure that the memory has been fully accessed and fully reprocessed.

EVA: SESSION 12

At her twelfth session, Eva reported continuing regular workouts. She was noticing changes in her body, feeling more fit, and being more slender. She also reported feeling a bit more confident and more talkative. In reevaluating the incident from the previous session, she reported the SUD to be between 1 and 2. The thought she had with this memory was, "I may always be disappointed in myself." I asked if there were other similar incidents that were more disturbing. Eva explained, "That was probably the worst because I blacked out. There are others I remember more about but this one bothers me more because I had gotten to that point and I wasn't in control." She described, "Waking up the next morning and not knowing what happened. I feel a little sick like I could throw up." For location she said, "Stomach and my throat." We resumed reprocessing.

# SET	PATIENT REPORT AND [CLINICIAN RESPONSE]
27	[Rocks her top ankle of her crossed legs.] Nothing really, just kind of sad.
26	Nothing. [In your body?] My heart is beating a little faster than it was. [Here I increased the EyeScan speed from 26 to 27.]
26	Um, just thinking if it happens again, if I go out and drink.
28	Everything is just kind of calm in my body.
T	It's not quite as upsetting. [What do you think you were doing?] I don't know, just being stupid to drink like that and let stuff happen. [Anything else besides just being stupid?] Being pretty reckless, not caring enough about myself to do something like that.] {I was probing current awareness for unconscious intention of reenactment and her history of CSA.}
33	Um, that I do want to have control and be in control.
28	Um, just an overall calm again.
T	It just doesn't have as strong as a presence. [What do you think you were doing then?] Being irresponsible. [Anything else?] Still just kind of not caring. [Imagine as you're sitting here now what you might want to say to that younger you.] {Unspoken words to invite self-care.}
29	That it's time to grow up and be responsible and care enough about myself to change. [Note both legs are resting on floor calmly.]
27	I think I can go out and not get drunk and still have a good time. {Imagines more responsible, self-control in future behavior.}
24	Just kind of an ease.
T	It won't happen again.
26	That headache I was getting isn't so bad. [Location] In the back of my head. [Here I changed the direction of the eye movements to an upper left diagonal.]
27	I'm not as tense. [Location.] All over. [Here I decreased the EyeScan speed from 27 to 26.]
31	My head doesn't hurt. Why do I get such bad headaches? [Do you?] Sometimes, I get real bad headaches and then they go away. [We don't know why that happens. It might be an unconscious psychological conflict or it might be the eye movements.]
T	SUD: 0–1. Just that I let it happen. [Is that going to happen again?] I don't want it to ever happen again. [Who's in control now?] I'm in control. I'll probably never get drunk like that because then I'm not in control.

25	That I don't need to drink to have fun.
T	That I can change. I don't have to repeat my past mistakes. That I am better than that. {Here, I moved to the installation phase and checked the PC.}[I'm in control. I've learned from it. I can change.] I'd say that, "I've learned from it". VoC: 7 [Install]
24	That I believe I can change. I can talk to a guy without being annihilated, without being totally drunk.

Due to time constraints, we stopped the session at that point. Eva had three more sessions after this one, but this was the last in which we did reprocessing. She told me she was ready to leave the area and return to her college. Her last three sessions focused on learning to cope with her shy temperament and how she was going to deal with drinking and men in the future. She had gone shopping both because her clothes no longer fit and she was ready to stop wearing baggy sweatshirts all the time and to start wearing clothes that showed the shape of her body. At her last session, she came in dressed for work with makeup and her hair up instead of in the tomboy clothes she had always worn to session. I think, before leaving, she wanted me to know how different her self-image had become. She barely looked like the same lost, young woman who had entered my office 4 months before. She requested referral resources in the area where she would be living because she was planning to continue treatment on her return. She admitted that when she came in, she was doing so just to please the supportive family who had recommended EMDR to her. She added that over the course of our sessions, she had realized that she was motivated to continue what she had started and to "make these changes permanent."

Research-Supported Standard EMDR Protocols for Other Disorders and Situations

Surely all art is the result of one's having been in danger, of having gone through an experience all the way to the end, where no one can go any further.
—Rainer Maria Rilke

To him who is in fear everything rustles.

—Sophocles

What is needed, rather than running away or controlling or suppressing or any other resistance, is understanding fear; that means, watch it, learn about it, come directly into contact with it. We are to learn about fear, not how to escape from it.

—Jiddu Krishnamurti (1994)

Curiosity will conquer fear even more than bravery will.
—James Stephens (1912)

… the emergence of the self requires more than the inborn tendency to organize experience. Also required is the presence of others… …who provide certain types of experiences that will evoke the emergence and maintenance of the self.
—Earnest S. Wolf (1988)

That which is feared lessens by association. This is the thing to understand.
—Nagarjuna

| Treating Specific Phobia

ADDITIONAL ISSUES FOR TREATING SPECIFIC PHOBIAS

OVERVIEW

In this chapter, we will examine additional issues to be considered when applying Eye Movement Desensitization and Reprocessing (EMDR) to the treatment of individuals with specific phobias. We will consider the nature of specific phobias both those of traumatic and nontraumatic origins. We will examine the similarities and differences of specific phobias of a traumatic origin with posttraumatic stress disorder (PTSD). We will discuss the absence of controlled research on all treatments for specific phobias of a traumatic origin. We will review the literature on case reports of EMDR treatment for specific phobias and discuss rationale for applying EMDR to the treatment of specific phobias. We will go through all eight phases of the standard protocol for EMDR treatment of specific phobias including how to identify targets, how to prepare patients, and the sequence of treatment for applying EMDR reprocessing. As we proceed, we will review a series of case vignettes that illustrate key aspects of applying EMDR to the treatment of specific phobias.

THE NATURE OF SPECIFIC PHOBIAS

Specific phobias involve marked anxiety or panic that disrupts personal or social functioning and leads to anxious anticipation, avoidance, or distress. People with specific phobias recognize their fears as excessive or irrational (American Psychiatric Association [APA], 1994). Specific phobias are common in the general population with lifetime prevalence rates reported in the range of 9.4%–12% (Becker et al., 2007; Magee, Eaton, Wittchen, McGonagle, & Kessler, 1996; Stinson et al., 2007). In spite of their adverse impact on people's lives, most specific phobias go untreated.

The *Diagnostic and Statistical Manual of Mental Disorders* (DSM-IV) (APA, 1994, 2000) identifies five subtypes of specific phobias. These are: (a) animal type—such as phobias of spiders, insects, snakes, dogs, or rodents; (b) natural environment type—such as phobias of heights, lightning, or water; (c) situational type—such as phobias of elevators, enclosed spaces, driving, flying, or bridges; (d) blood–injury–

injection type—such as phobias of getting injections, or seeing blood; and (e) other types—such as phobias of choking, vomiting, or contracting an illness. Individuals with specific phobias often have multiple fears. The greater the number of separate fears, the greater their severity tends to be (Magee et al., 1996).

TRAUMATIC AND NONTRAUMATIC ORIGIN FOR SPECIFIC PHOBIAS

From the perspective of the Adaptive Information Processing (AIP) model, it is essential to consider the etiology of specific phobias to conceptualize clinical cases, consider an appropriate role for EMDR reprocessing, and develop appropriate treatment plans. Specific phobias may be viewed as deriving from two distinct origins. Some phobias clearly have an identifiable traumatic origin. These include driving phobia after a motor vehicle crash, medical phobia after a traumatic medical procedure, or choking phobia after an experience of choking on food. In the AIP model, these traumatic experiences are viewed as being encoded in state-specific form in a maladaptive memory network. Current stimuli—such as thinking about or confronting the phobic situation—give rise to maladaptive perceptions, attitudes, and behaviors emerging from the maladaptive memory network. Specific phobias can also be viewed from the behavioral perspective of classical conditioning (Davey, 1997). For example, if the traumatic experience of the motor vehicle crash is the unconditioned stimulus (UCS), being in the car is the conditioned stimulus (CS).

On the other hand, many specific phobias derive from a nontraumatic origin. Some specific phobias of a nontraumatic origin begin with revulsion or disgust (De Jongh, Ten Broeke, & Renssen, 1999). These include fears of blood, spiders, rodents, snakes, and frogs and may involve innate disgust responses interacting with operant conditioning (Mulkens, de Jong, & Merckelbach, 1997, p. 1994). A tendency toward fainting in those with blood–injury phobia may lead to the onset of injection phobia independently of innate disgust (Gerlach et al., 2006). All of the published, randomized, controlled research on the use of EMDR for specific phobias has been with spider phobia, a phobia of a nontraumatic origin (Muris & Merckelbach, 1997; Muris, Merceklbach, Holdrinet, & Sijsenaar, 1998; Muris, Merckelbach, van Haaften, & Mayer, 1997). These studies have been criticized (De Jongh et al., 1999; Shapiro, 1999) for several limitations and weaknesses, including limited fidelity and lack of applicability to other types of phobias especially those of a traumatic origin.

History taking often reveals that these nontraumatic fears evolve over time. They may be shaped by social responses, such as a lack of compassion or overt social ridicule. Based on their clinical experience, De Jongh et al. (1999) believe that phobias without an identifiable traumatic component in their etiology respond less strongly to EMDR reprocessing. Answers to this question await further studies that examine nontraumatic phobias other than spider phobia and that would meet research standards for fidelity to full, published treatment protocols. De Jongh et al. (1999) suggest that specific phobias of a nontraumatic origin can generally be treated with prolonged exposure, and they point out that essentially all research on single specific phobias—not just EMDR related research—has been on phobias of nontraumatic origin. A search of the literature on specific phobias confirmed the paucity of controlled treatment outcome research on specific phobias of a traumatic origin. Thus, there is little guidance from controlled research for selecting treatments of specific phobias of a traumatic origin.

The Role of In Vivo Exposure in Treating Specific Phobias

As discussed by De Jongh and Ten Broeke (2007), in vivo exposure appears not to be as effective or appropriate for phobias of known traumatic origin. For example, with medical–dental phobias, initial treatment failure rates of 25% have been reported. Another 36% relapsed into avoidant behaviors (Van der Zijpp, Ter Horst, De Jongh, & Makkes, 1996). This poor tolerance for in vivo exposure in traumatic medical phobia leads us to consider other treatment options for most patients. In vivo exposure may not be the best received nor the most effective initial treatment for some specific phobias with a traumatic origin. However, as discussed below, in vivo exposure can be an important element in the later stages of EMDR treatment plans for many specific phobias with a traumatic etiology and is essential in treating specific phobias of a nontraumatic origin.

RATIONALE FOR APPLYING EMDR TO SPECIFIC PHOBIAS OF A TRAUMATIC ORIGIN

With some specific phobias of a traumatic origin, it is simply not practical to use in vivo exposure in structured treatment, such as for lightning phobia. With flying phobia, in vivo exposure requires several expensive airplane flights. In my own clinical experience, flying phobia can sometimes be resolved in four to eight 50-minute EMDR reprocessing sessions. Based on several published case reports, there appears to be an appropriate role for EMDR reprocessing for specific phobias with a traumatic etiology. Many of these case reports are reviewed below together with some cases of specific phobias of nontraumatic origin. For further reviews and comments on case reports of EMDR treatment of specific phobias, see De Jongh & Ten Broeke (2007), De Jongh et al. (1999), and Shapiro (2001).

Case Reports of EMDR Treatment of Specific Phobias

Marquis (1991) was the first to report EMDR to be effective as part of treatment of 10 patients suffering from specific fears including flying, high places, and animals. Kleinknecht (1993) reported a patient with a 16-year history of blood and injection phobia who was successfully treated with EMDR in four brief sessions. Lohr, Tolin, and Kleinknecht (1995) reported two other cases with blood–injury–injection phobia that both showed an initial decrease in Subjective Units of Disturbance (SUD) scale ratings, and in scores on the Symptom Checklist 90-R (SCL-90-R) (Derogatis, 1977). However, treatment was limited in its effectiveness because both of these patients were offered a single session, thus not following the comprehensive treatment plan proposed by Shapiro (1995, 2001). Nonetheless, both cases showed partial gains on treatment goals with this incomplete treatment. Young (1994) reported success in treating two female patients with multiple personality disorder with EMDR. One patient with a snake phobia was treated in one session, and the other with extreme fear of moths was treated in two sessions. Although Young reported the gains were maintained after 6 months, it appears from the report that neither the full standard EMDR procedure, nor the full phobia protocols were used.

Muris and Merckelbach (1995) reported using an abbreviated version of the EMDR phobia protocol in two subjects with spider phobia in a single, 1-hour session, which led to gains on self-reported fear and a behavioral measure. Next, both subjects were given 2.5 hours of in vivo exposure after which both were able to touch the spider. Muris and De Jongh (1996) reported treating a young girl with spider phobia of traumatic origin from age 2 years. Again, a single, 1-hour session of EMDR was offered after which her score on a self-report measure dropped close to zero with significant gains on a behavioral approach test. Then they provided 1 hour of in vivo exposure after which she allowed the spider to walk on her hand.

De Jongh and Ten Broeke (1994) reported success in using EMDR with a female patient with a fear of vomiting in a single session with stable gains maintained at 4-month follow-up. Ten Broeke and De Jongh also reported (1993) successful treatment of a mouse phobia in a 63-year-old woman whose fear had not resolved during prior in vivo exposure. After a single session of EMDR treatment, they reported that her fear was reduced, and had not returned at 6-month follow-up.

De Jongh, Ten Broeke, and Van der Meer (1995) describe the case of a man with dental phobia who avoided dental treatment for 12 years after an extremely painful tooth extraction. His phobic avoidance had not been alleviated by five sessions of graded exposure and coping skills training. After a single session of EMDR treatment, he resumed dental treatment with a level of distress he found acceptable. In another case, De Jongh and Ten Broeke (1996) describe a woman who avoided dental treatment for 30 years after a traumatic incident from age 8 of having her dentist restrain her arms to the dental chair with towels. One year of previous behavior therapy had failed to alleviate her symptoms. After two sessions of EMDR treatment, she was able to start dental treatment. They reported that at 2-year follow-up, she had completed her dental work and remained free of panic attacks.

Schurmans (2007) described treating a woman who developed a severe choking phobia following an allergic reaction to an herbal beverage. The severity of her avoidance led to her being hospitalized several times because of her inability to consume food and beverages. However, a diagnosis of choking phobia may be incomplete because this patient had a complex trauma history that included being adopted from an orphanage and was repeatedly hospitalized as a child. In addition, she had a chaotic home life growing up with verbal abuse and restricted access to food as well as adult traumatic exposures with a physically and emotionally abusive husband. The patient disclosed traumatic incidents of being choked by both her mother and her husband. Prior to treatment with EMDR, the patient had 4 years of a series of treatments including brief psychodynamic therapy, cognitive behavioral therapy, psychopharmacological, and eating disorder treatment. These prior treatments all failed to eliminate her disorder. Consistent with this more complex case presentation, Schurmans (2007) provided a series of 20 sessions of EMDR treatment addressing childhood etiological events. This led to a complete remission of the choking phobia.

The Need for Controlled Research on Specific Phobias of Traumatic Origin

With regard to phobias that include a traumatic etiology, controlled research is clearly needed to explore the issues of patient–treatment matching and differences in treatment effectiveness among EMDR, in vivo exposure, systematic desensitization, and prolonged imaginal or virtual reality exposure. To help guide clinical decision making, such body of research would need to compare active treatment methods. Until such controlled research becomes available, it is reasonable to consider the use of EMDR as an initial treatment intervention of specific phobias of a traumatic origin for two reasons. First, as summarized above, there is support from various published case reports (De Jongh & Ten Broeke, 2007; Schurmans, 2007; Shapiro, 2001). Second, with striking similarities in etiology between PTSD and specific phobias of a traumatic origin, the AIP model predicts that EMDR is likely to be an effective treatment for Specific Phobias of a traumatic origin.

DIFFERENCES BETWEEN PTSD AND SPECIFIC PHOBIAS

Although there are similarities between phobias of a traumatic origin and PTSD, these conditions differ in several ways. Patients with PTSD have greater general distress and a broader range of symptoms. They experience spontaneous intrusive memories and hyperarousal that generally interferes with sleep. Patients with specific phobias do not have chronic sleep disturbances associated with their fears and become anxious only when deliberately thinking of their feared situation or when confronted with cues that stimulate their fear.

THE TREATMENT PLAN FOR SPECIFIC PHOBIA

In broad outline, EMDR treatment planning for patients with specific phobia is similar to treatment planning for patients with PTSD. Follow the same eight-phase approach to treatment and the three-pronged treatment plan. Reprocess targets first from the past, then the present, and finally the future. The assessment phase (phase 3) of specific targets is the same as with PTSD. The reprocessing of targets follows the same basic procedural steps in the desensitization phase (phase 4) and the installation phase (phase 5) as for PTSD.

However, treatment plans for specific phobias differ in several ways from those for PTSD. One of these differences relates to an issue identified by Shapiro in both her 1995 (p. 222) and 2001 (p. 226) texts. Shapiro proposed a distinction between *simple phobias* and *process phobias*. This distinction focused on the role of anticipatory anxiety and the need to make deliberate choices to encounter the phobic object or situation. As pointed out by De Jongh et al. (1999, p. 73), nearly any specific phobia can function as a *process phobia*. Based on many years of clinical experience with EMDR, I agree with the suggestion made by De Jongh et al. (1999, p. 74) when using EMDR to treat all specific phobias as process phobias. This means that to achieve full treatment effectiveness in most cases of specific phobia, it is necessary to plan to incorporate in vivo exposure and more structured future templates into the later stages of the treatment plan. When treating PTSD with EMDR, it is not always necessary to include such fully structured future templates or to incorporate in vivo exposure.

Although such comprehensive phobia treatment plans may turn out to be more than what is needed, it is best to plan for comprehensive treatment. The treatment plan can always be simplified should the patient achieve a complete elimination of the phobia with more limited treatment. Next, we will examine how to apply

13.1 | Specific Phobia Protocol Summary

1) History Taking (Phase 1)
   A) Clinical assessment, diagnosis, and case formulation
   B) Selecting appropriate treatment goals
   C) Selecting and sequencing of targets

2) Preparation (Phase 2)
   A) Psychoeducation on fears (if indicated)
   B) Introduce EMDR and obtain informed consent to treatment
   C) Teaching and rehearsing self-control procedures
      i) Breathing exercises and other calming procedures for anxiety
      ii) Applied tension for fainting (Öst & Sterner, 1987)

3) Reprocessing of targets
   A) Past events
      i) Background stressors (if any were identified)
      ii) First event
      iii) Worst or representative event
      iv) Most recent event
   B) Current external and internal cues
   C) Future template

4) Commitment to action plan
   A) Positive template with mental rehearsal

5) In vivo exposure (generally done independently)

6) Reevaluation and further reprocessing, if indicated

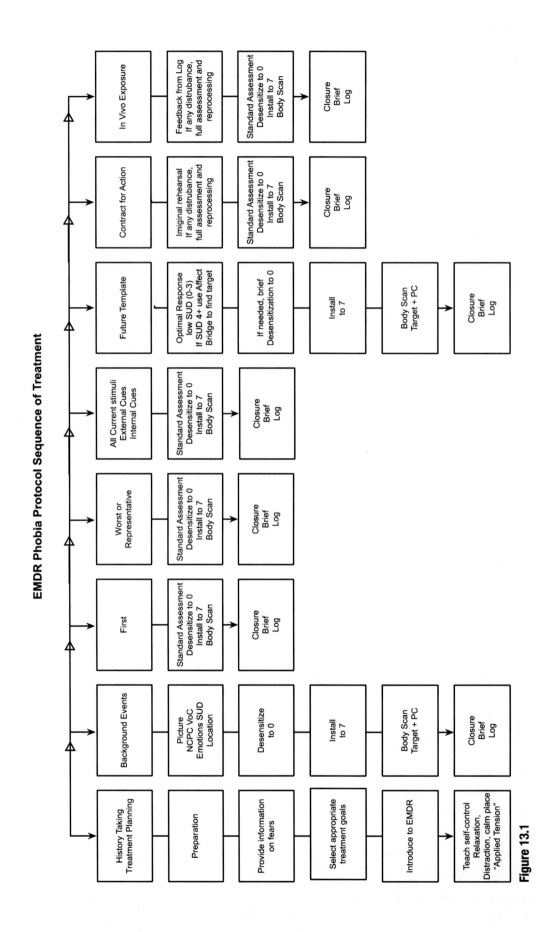

Figure 13.1

EMDR to specific phobias across all eight phases of treatment with an emphasis on features unique to the treatment of specific phobias.

PHASE 1: HISTORY TAKING AND TREATMENT PLANNING

As in the treatment of PTSD, when planning treatment for a specific phobia, begin with a comprehensive history, a clear diagnosis, and a strong case formulation. Many clinicians prefer to begin their information gathering with an open or unstructured clinical interview. When working within the AIP model, explore both the nature of the patient's problems and their etiology. Identify issues that were present at the onset of the phobic response and that serve to maintain it. It is helpful to identify patterns of response, including frequency, number, and severity of phobic episodes. Have these episodes increased in frequency or severity over time or remained stable? Have there been previous treatment episodes or self-directed attempts to overcome the phobia? What have been the results of these efforts? In exploring the issues surrounding the phobic responses, it is important to at least briefly explore the role of family of origin experiences, presence of anxiety disorders and other mental health issues in other family members, traumatic stressors, work and personal life stressors, life style, diet, and patterns of exercise.

Standardized Assessment with Structured Interview and Objective Instruments

In settings where a standardized assessment is required or desired, a structured interview can provide an efficient and comprehensive differential diagnosis. The Anxiety Disorders Interview Schedule for *DSM-IV* (ADIS-IV; Brown, DiNardo, & Barlow, 2004) is a structured interview designed to assess current episodes of anxiety disorders, and to permit differential diagnosis among the anxiety disorders according to DSM-IV criteria. The ADIS-IV also provides sections to assess current mood, somatoform, and substance use disorders, as well as medical and psychiatric treatment history. There are also screening questions for psychotic and conversion symptoms and familial psychiatric history.

Standardized assessment instruments can assist in determining the severity of anxiety symptoms, recognizing other possible problem areas, and documenting the course of treatment. Common self-report instrument for specific phobias include the Fear Survey Schedule (FSS; Wolpe & Lang, 1964, 1969), the Fear Survey Schedule-II (FSS-II, Geer, 1965), the Fear Questionnaire (FQ; Marks & Mathews, 1979), and the Symptom Check List-Revised (SCL-90-R; Derogatis, 1991).

Treatment plans for specific phobias must consider co-occurring disorders

Consider co-occurring disorders when developing a case formulation and a treatment plan. Specific phobias often co-occur with other anxiety disorders and with mood disorders (Barlow, 2002). In some cases, claustrophobia or another situational phobia may be the only anxiety symptom. In other cases, there may be a range of situational phobias linked by panic disorder. In such cases, the treatment plan must be for the broader issues of panic disorder. Panic disorder is covered separately in Chapter 14, as it often requires more extensive treatment than a specific phobia.

With other co-occurring disorders, when the memory networks for co-occurring disorders are substantially distinct, it is possible that each disorder can be approached and treated separately with EMDR. For example, it may be possible to provide focused and effective EMDR treatment for a patient with a specific phobia of a traumatic origin such as choking phobia after choking on food who also meets criteria for alcohol abuse. Of course, if an incident of choking occurred as a direct consequence of alcohol abuse, such as during an episode of intoxication, there could be overlaps between the memory networks for the two disorders that would lead to a more complex and interlinked treatment plan. In cases where there is no direct linkage between these two disorders, it may be possible to focus initially on the application of EMDR to the choking phobia and defer attention to the alcohol abuse, because there may be little or no overlap between the memory networks associated with these two conditions.

On the other hand, when memory networks for co-occurring disorders overlap to a significant degree, the treatment plan for the specific phobia may not be separable from the treatment for the second condition. For example, when a patient suffers from a second anxiety disorder such as chronic, complex PTSD (Herman, 1992a, 1992b) or obsessive–compulsive disorder and a situational specific phobia—such as fear of lightning after witnessing a nearby lightning strike—there may be too much overlap between memory networks and general difficulties in assessing threat cues.

For example, a clinician wanted to refer a patient for adjunctive, specific treatment with EMDR for lightning phobia who also suffered from complex PTSD related to childhood abuse and neglect. Her lightning phobia began when she first ran away from the family home at age 14. She had finally gathered the courage to disclose to her mother her sexual abuse at the hands of her stepfather. Her mother's response was to minimize and avoid the issue. The patient's traumatic experience of nearly being hit by lightning, alone on a rural road at night, was directly related to her attempt to flee from both her mother's failure to protect her and her stepfather's abuse. Any attempt to target and apply EMDR reprocessing to the memory of the near-lightning strike experience would likely involve the central issues of the larger childhood trauma. To use EMDR in such a case would likely require a more comprehensive treatment plan. Brief, focused, adjunctive treatment with EMDR on the lightning phobia alone might not be possible.

Identifying Targets for EMDR Reprocessing

When treating specific phobias, identify the earliest or first occurrence of a fearful experience related to the phobia. In most cases of traumatic onset, this first occurrence is a distinct vivid memory. In other cases of gradual onset with phobias that appear to begin with disgust or revulsion, there may not be a distinct first memory. In these cases, just select the earliest memory the patient can identify. You should also identify subsequent experiences related to this specific phobia with special attention to a worst experience—if there is one—as well as how the patient is currently affected. What kind of current situations does the patient avoid, and what are the specific situations that trigger the fear. This includes identifying external cues such as places, sounds, smells, objects, or animals and internal cues such as physical sensations—a racing heart beat, sweaty palms, tightness in the chest, or a large piece of food in the mouth. These events and cues can be written down on the master plan list of targets—Table 4.14—to guide the selection and sequencing of targets for reprocessing.

Treatment Goals

It is essential to identify the patient's treatment goals and to consider for what kind of future exposures to the phobic object or situation the patient wants to prepare. With medical, dental, or dog phobias, it may be essential to prepare for future encounters with the phobic situation. Required medical and dental procedures may be essential to the patient's health and well-being. It is likely impossible to avoid encountering dogs. In these cases, specific future targets need to be identified for future templates and for in vivo exposure. On the other hand, some more seldom and randomly encountered phobic objects and situations, such as spider and snake phobias, may not require that the patient prepare for deliberate planned future exposure. Nevertheless, these objects or situations can remain associated with persistent

13.2 | Questions to Identify Specific Phobia targets

Nature of phobia
What object or situation are you afraid of?
What is it about _____ (the object or situation) that you most fear?

First event
What was the first time you had this fear or the earliest time you can remember having this fear?

Background stressors
What other stressful experiences were going on in your personal, family, school, or work life at about time of that first occurrence?

Worst or representative event
What is the most intense or the most frightening experience of _____ (the object or situation) you have ever had?
If there is no "worst" experience, describe a significant, typical experience of your fear.

Most recent event
What is the most recent experience of this fear?

Current external and internal cues
What aspects of _____ (the object or situations) seem to stimulate your fear?
What bodily sensations or feelings do you associate with times you experience your fear?

Future template
Please describe a future situation where you would be able to do what you would like to do free of this fear.

Check for secondary gains
What would you get to do or have to do if this fear were resolved?
And how would that be?
What would you get to stop doing or have to give up if this fear were resolved?
And how would that be?

anxiety and avoidance of environments where they are more likely to be encountered; thus, treatment goals should still be identified and both future templates and in vivo exposure should still be included in the treatment plan to assure comprehensive, stable treatment results.

Secondary Gains

In considering treatment goals, be alert to potential issues of secondary gains. Phobic anxiety can provide an excuse to avoid a situation the patient prefers to avoid but is pressured to engage in by their spouse, family, or friends. Examples include a woman who does not want to participate in her husband's hunting trips and has a fear of snakes and insects, or a man who is unable to visit a demanding and controlling mother because she lives on the other side of the country because of his fear of flying. Although secondary gains are present infrequently, they need to be considered in each case. When present, secondary gains need to be explored sensitively and thoroughly, the patient's treatment goals need to be clarified. Where phobic anxiety serves a secondary, practical purpose, EMDR reprocessing cannot succeed until an alternate set of coping strategies for the stressor are identified and developed.

The simplest way to identify the possible presence of secondary gain is to ask: "What would you get to do or have to do if this fear were resolved?" Then ask, "And how would that be?" In some cases, it may be helpful to ask the follow up question, "What would you get to stop doing or have to give up if this fear were resolved?" Then ask, "And how would that be?"

Background Stressors may need to be Distinct Initial Targets

In the history-taking phase, explore whether there may be background stressors that were factors in the patient's vulnerability to developing a phobic response at the time of the first phobic reaction. Although some phobic reactions of traumatic origin—such as choking phobia after nearly choking to death—can be understood as deriving entirely from the nature of the initial experience, others appear to involve an interaction between background stressors and situations (conditioned stimuli – CS) without external threat—such as a bridge phobia that develops after an initial anxiety attack on a bridge. Consider what background factors or events may have led to the vulnerability to having that initial anxiety episode on the bridge.

Thomas presented with a specific phobia for bridges. History taking revealed his first anxiety attack took place on a bridge. The night before he had been out late, drinking to excess. He was young and engaged to be married for the first time. He was deeply involved with a technology business he had started that was struggling and about to fail. His financial situation was therefore strained and uncertain at a time he was getting ready to be married. He was facing the prospect of having to take a job and give up his dream of getting rich with his start-up company. Surprisingly, Thomas had never connected the effects of these significant background stressors as possible factors in his first anxiety attack on the approach to the bridge. The failure of his start up was a huge blow to his sense of identity and self-worth. He seldom drank and rarely to excess. Yet, the night before his first phobic bridge experience, his distress over recognizing that his business was failing had led him to drink to excess. Ultimately, his business did fail and he found a well-paying position based on his technical knowledge and skills.

Several years later, Thomas presented for treatment as he prepared to begin looking for a better, higher-paying job in another geographic location where he would have to drive across bridges on a daily basis. The background stressor of the collapse of his start-up business and its impact on his sense of self remained significantly disturbing. It needed to be included as a target and reprocessed before the target of the first occurrence of the phobic response. As a result, when treatment shifted to the first occurrence of the phobic response, the reprocessing of that experience was straightforward, without any complicating associations to the background stressors that led up to the first occurrence.

PHASE 2: PREPARATION PHASE

The preparation phase for treating specific phobia is parallel to treatment of PTSD. There are four main elements to be addressed: teaching self-control methods for reducing anxiety, providing psychoeducation about the phobic situation, obtaining informed consent to treatment, and introducing the bilateral stimulation with the calm place exercise or a resource installation.

Self-Control Methods for Reducing Anxiety

In cases of specific phobias, patients can be taught self-control methods for reducing the fear of fear. These methods were reviewed in Chapter 6. Although these methods for reducing anxiety cannot eliminate the phobic response itself, they can provide an increased sense of self-control and mastery that can help prepare the patient for EMDR reprocessing and for in vivo exposure in the later stages of the treatment plan. Only some specific phobia patients need to learn or practice self-control methods to reduce anxiety before starting EMDR reprocessing.

Applied Tension

As noted above, patients with blood–injury–injection type phobia often have a tendency toward fainting. This is referred to as *vasovagal syncope*. The self-control

13.3 | Applied Tension

Sit in a comfortable chair and tense the muscles in your arms, legs, and trunk for about 10–15 seconds. Hold the tension until you start to feel a warm sensation in your head. Then, relax for 20–30 seconds. Repeat this five times.

Practice this five times per day for at least a week.

If you develop a headache during or after practicing applied tension, use less tension when you practice.

exercise for a tendency toward fainting is not relaxation training but *applied tension*. This technique, first described by Öst and Sterner (1987), can help patients gain enough control over their tendency toward fainting to permit EMDR reprocessing and then graduated in vivo exposure. More recent research suggests that rhythmic tension may be as or more effective as applied tension especially at raising diastolic blood pressure (Bodycoat, Grauaug, Olson & Page, 2000).

With patients who have a blood–injury–injection type phobia, first provide an explanation of the purpose of the applied tension exercise. Applied tension does not reverse the drop in blood pressure caused by the vasovagal response. Instead, it prevents an excessive pooling of blood in the lower extremities and maintains enough blood supply in the head to prevent fainting. After giving the purpose of applied tension, then explain and demonstrate the exercise. Then have the patient practice applied tension. Give feedback or guidance to help the patient optimize the use of applied tension. Finally, request the patient to practice applied tension five times a day for at least a week. If the patient develops a headache when practicing applied tension, just encourage the patient to reduce the amount of tension during practice sessions.

Psychoeducation About the Phobic Situation

For some types of specific phobia, it can be helpful to make sure the patient has accurate information about the feared object or situation. A good example is with flying phobia, where patients often misperceive the discomfort caused by turbulence as a danger signal. Air turbulence is not a cause of forced landings or air disasters. It is more like rough seas in the ocean that pose no threat to passengers' safety on a modern ocean liner, in spite of causing motion sickness for some. Air turbulence causes injuries or death to airplane passengers only when they are not wearing their seat belts. Although providing accurate information about the safety of flying is not likely to lessen the severity of a flying phobia, it is important to correct any misinformation that patients have acquired about their phobic situation.

Obtaining Informed Consent to Treatment

Patients being treated for a specific phobia need the same essential information as was described in chapter 6 on the preparation phase for the treatment of PTSD. They need (a) an introduction and basic information about EMDR procedures and common responses to treatment, (b) a metaphor to enhance mindful noticing without expectations or judgments during the bilateral stimulation, (c) an acceptance of the nature of reexperiencing psychological, emotional, and somatic aspects of previous phobic encounters that may occur during reprocessing, and (d) the risk of other disturbing memories emerging during reprocessing.

As discussed earlier in this chapter, many patients with a specific phobia will have a co-occurring disorder and other disturbing or traumatic memories which they may not initially associate with their specific phobia during the intake and treatment planning process. Patients need to understand and *consent* to the possibility that they may associate to any other disturbing life experience during reprocessing. When a patient reports a history of witnessing domestic violence in childhood and claims, this is not related to their driving phobia, it remains essential that the patient consent to the possibility that memories and feelings related to these adverse childhood events may emerge spontaneously during reprocessing and may need to be directly addressed as part of the treatment plan.

When a patient indicates an unwillingness to have to think about or deal with these other adverse experiences in treatment, it is not possible or ethical to proceed with EMDR reprocessing. Whether these experiences may not emerge during or after reprocessing sessions cannot be guaranteed. Clinical assessment may suggest that such associations to adverse childhood experiences may be likely in such cases. Although such a refusal to deal with other possible adverse memories is infrequent, it is essential not to offer unwarranted reassurances that it will not occur. Instead, at that point, you have two options. First, explore the basis of the patient's concerns about the possibility of dealing with these other memories. It may be that with further discussion the patient will be able to identify potential solutions to these concerns and then develop sufficient trust, self-confidence, or resources to face the possibility of these other memories emerging. Second, offer the patient an alternate treatment strategy other than EMDR reprocessing.

Another major aspect of informed consent to treatment for phobic patients is agreement to reexperiencing aspects of the conditioning events that shaped the phobic response. Such reexperiencing can include mental images of sights, sounds, smells, and tastes from these memories as well as negative thoughts and dialogue. Often, reexperiencing will lead to emergence of emotional states such as fear, sadness, loneliness, grief, or shame. De Jongh and Ten Broeke (2007, p. 53) describe the case of Donald who had a water phobia and could not, at first, recall the origin of his fear during the history taking phase. As his earliest image of his fear, he initially selected an image, possibly from a movie, of a person swimming in the ocean with a shark out of sight below. Starting with this image, after many minutes of bilateral stimulation in the midst of reprocessing, Donald began to experience loneliness and then remembered an incident in which his younger brother nearly drowned and was saved by some passersby. Reprocessing of this remembered incident led to resolution of his phobic reactions to water. Informed consent to reexperiencing such emotional states and to the reemergence of such childhood memories is an essential aspect of preparing the patient for EMDR reprocessing.

Patients who had noxious or painful sensations during the adverse experiences that led to or shaped their phobic responses will commonly reexperience these sensations to some degree during EMDR reprocessing, and they need to be prepared for this possibility. Generally, the sensations will be experienced at a lower level of intensity than during the original experience and with successful reprocessing, these sensations will soon attenuate. After successful reprocessing, these memories will no longer be held in a form in the brain where they can be restimulated.

Emily had developed a fear of medical procedures and insomnia after a traumatic outpatient surgical experience. She had been traumatized by intensely painful sensations during the surgery because the anesthesia had not been effective. She remained awake but was unable to speak or move. In her case, informed consent had to include acceptance of the likely reexperiencing of the memory of these intensely painful sensations. During the reprocessing, she did reexperience these painful sensations for several minutes. However, they then faded away, and never returned. For Emily, more distressing than the memory of the painful sensations themselves, were feelings of helplessness and her inability to express the frustration and anger she felt when she was immobilized by the anesthesia. These emotional responses to the experience also resolved during the reprocessing when she spontaneously rehearsed verbalizing what she had been unable to say to the surgeon and anesthesiologist during the procedure.

In summary, providing informed consent includes describing the possibility of other memories emerging and reexperiencing incidents, emotions, or unpleasant sensations. Preparing patients for reprocessing includes providing metaphors—such as the train metaphor described in chapter 6—to help orient patients to the witnessing stance that facilitates effective reprocessing. Once you have obtained informed consent to treatment with EMDR reprocessing, proceed to introducing the mechanics of the bilateral stimulation.

Introducing Bilateral Stimulation with the Calm Place Exercise or RDI

As described in chapter 6, it is always a good idea to practice the eye movements or alternate form of bilateral stimulation before commencing reprocessing of the first disturbing memory. This demystifies the mechanical aspects of the procedure. It also gives some assurance that the patient can tolerate horizontal and diagonal eye movements without eyestrain or dizziness. Next, it is helpful to introduce abbreviated reprocessing with the calm place exercise or a resource installation. This provides two benefits. For the patient, it creates an initial positive set of associations with reprocessing. Because the unknown is nearly always slightly anxiety provoking, experiencing the calm place exercise—or a resource installation—offers the patient a psychophysiological experience of moving from initial anxiety to increasing calm and well-being associated with bilateral stimulation. This initial positive experience with reprocessing tends to create a pattern for future sessions in which patients will start with an even more anxiety-producing memory and then allow it to reprocess to a more neutral state. In addition, as an assessment intervention, when patients have a simple, positive response to the calm place exercise, it is more likely that they will experience effective reprocessing when working on their phobic memories begins.

PHASE 3: ASSESSMENT OF THE TARGET

When treating a specific phobia, the procedural steps for the assessment of the target selected for reprocessing are identical to those used when treating PTSD. These are described in detail in chapter 7. Begin with eliciting a picture that represents a sensory aspect of the specific incident to be reprocessed. Then help the patient identify the negative and positive cognitions and obtain a baseline Validity of Cognition (VoC). Next, using the picture and the negative cognition, ask for the specific emotion. Then get a baseline SUD rating on the experience and identify the body location where the patient feels it now.

When dealing with specific phobias of a traumatic origin, it is more likely to find negative self-appraisals reflecting the perception of danger in the environment—"I am not safe" or "I will be hurt"—or a lack of control—"I am helpless" or "I am weak." Even in cases of medical and dental phobia, where patients perceived themselves as having been mistreated, it is less likely that you will encounter negative beliefs reflecting defectiveness or shame—"I am worthless" or "I am unlovable"—as when working with memories of childhood abuse. In these cases, you may encounter beliefs reflecting guilt—"I should have known better" or "I did something wrong." With blood–injury type of specific phobias as well, negative beliefs tend to be focused on danger and lack of control.

PHASES 4-6: REPROCESSING PROCEDURES FOR SPECIFIC PHOBIAS

Procedures for reprocessing of targets for specific phobias are essentially identical to those for PTSD and are described in detail in chapters 8, 9, and 10. Reprocessing begins with the desensitization phase (phase 4) of the earliest identified conditioning experience. Criteria for deciding when to return to target and for how to deal with ineffective reprocessing are the same when treating specific phobia and PTSD. Continue the desensitization phase until the SUD is reported to be stable at zero. Then proceed to the installation phase (phase 5) checking to see if the patient still prefers the originally selected positive cognition or if a better positive cognition has emerged. Then have the patient rate the VoC and continue installation with sets of bilateral stimulation (BLS), checking the VoC after each set of BLS until the VoC is reported to be a 7 and is not getting any better.

Move to the body scan phase (phase 6), which involves asking the patient to hold the incident in mind, think of the positive cognition just installed, and then ask the patient to scan for any notable physical sensations. If negative sensations are reported, reprocess these down a channel of associations until they are gone. Then conduct the body scan again until the patient reports only neutral or positive sensations. If time remains and the patient reports positive sensations, provide more sets of BLS until the positive sensations are not getting any better.

PHASE 7: CLOSURE PROCEDURES

When treating patients for specific phobias, it is rare to encounter patients at risk for tension reduction, self-injurious, or threatening behaviors as you do when treating patients for PTSD and disorders of extreme stress not otherwise specified (DESNOS). The presence of such additional symptoms would indicate the presence of a co-occurring disorder and the need for a more comprehensive treatment plan. Therefore, even when treatment sessions for specific phobia are incomplete and the SUD level is still reported to remain significantly disturbing, it will seldom be necessary to provide containment, grounding, or anxiety management procedures. However, in some cases in the course of reprocessing, additional highly disturbing memories that the patient had previously forgotten or dissociated could emerge and bring the patient to the end of the session in a vulnerable, regressed, or agitated state. In these cases and in other cases where specific phobia patients become and remain significantly distressed at the end of the session, make use of the procedures described in chapter 6, The Preparation Phase, to assist the patient to return to a stable, grounded and well-oriented state.

During the closure phase, always offer the standard briefing reminders—described in chapter 10—to be mindful of new insights, memories, dreams, and new patterns of response and to keep a written log of these for the next session. Because patients often feel remarkably calm at the end of a successful EMDR reprocessing sessions, they may assume that their phobic anxiety has been completely eliminated from a single successful reprocessing session. Although this certainly occurs, it is unusual. It can be helpful to remind the patient that the treatment plan calls for reprocessing several incidents as well as current stimuli and finally mental rehearsal of future encounters over a series of sessions. It may be predicted that there may still be noticeable anxiety when confronting or thinking of confronting the phobic object until the treatment plan is complete. This avoids the patient developing unrealistic expectations and becoming discouraged when they experience residual, intersession phobic anxiety.

PHASE 8: REEVALUATION

In the subsequent session, we review information from the patient's log and check the status of the target from the previous session. The reevaluation steps are described in detail in chapter 11. If the previous session had been completed—SUD of 0, VoC of 7, and only neutral or pleasant sensations in the body scan—simply reconfirm the SUD and VoC on the previous target, then move to begin the assessment phase on the next target in your treatment plan. If the previous session was incomplete, return to the target memory and resume reprocessing.

MOVING THROUGH THE TREATMENT PLAN FROM PAST TO PRESENT

The sequence of treatment of a specific phobia—see Figure 13.1 or Table 13.1—follows the standard EMDR treatment sequence of selecting targets first from the past, then the present, and finally the future. After reprocessing any background events, the first occurrence and the worst or a representative phobic experiences, ask the patient to scan for memories of any other phobic experiences that remain disturbing. If any remain disturbing, these should be assessed and reprocessed until the patient has no further disturbance associated with any phobic memories.

Next, turn attention to the current stimuli that the patient identified during the history taking and treatment planning phase as well as those stimuli that the patient has reported in feedback from the log between treatment sessions. Occasionally, treatment effects will be generalized so completely to external cues during the reprocessing of the past memories that the patient reports no residual phobic anxiety. Any external or internal cues that remain sources of anxiety or distress should be reprocessed next.

INCORPORATING THE FUTURE TEMPLATE

James had developed a choking phobia after an incident of nearly choking during dinner in a restaurant. Although his near-choking experience was brief, during the reprocessing of this memory it turned out to have been associated with a highly disturbing childhood memory of witnessing his father nearly dying in a choking episode in a restaurant. His father had needed the Heimlich maneuver, which was promptly performed by another restaurant patron. As a 6-year-old boy, he recalled his own sense of helplessness and horror of witnessing his father being rendered helpless while eating. After reprocessing both the memory of witnessing his father choking and the memory of his own incident of choking, James reported an episode of anxiety when he had eaten out the next week by himself during a 1-day business trip. He had been preoccupied with the possibility of choking with no one there to rescue him if he needed assistance. During the assessment phase on his current anxiety, the SUD level was between 4 and 5. With reprocessing, this residual disturbance was quickly resolved, and he was able to achieve high confidence in a preferred belief, "I'm in control now." James was then asked to imagine eating alone in a restaurant. His SUD level on this future template was about a 2 and quickly dropped with further reprocessing to a 0. To further challenge James' scenario, his EMDR clinician then asked him to imagine that some food got briefly stuck in his throat while eating. He was able to imagine taking a few sips of water, easily dislodging the stuck food, and then swallowing it. He was then able to fully accept the preferred belief "I am in control now" to a VoC of 7. In the body scan, he then reported only positive physical sensations of ease, comfort, and a sense of confidence. These feelings were strengthened with further sets of bilateral stimulation. Follow up 4 weeks later indicated that he was eating alone on his occasional business trips with confidence and enjoyment.

In this case example, the initial SUD on the future template was low, indicating that the associated memories had been successfully reprocessed. It is always a good idea to challenge the patient with some plausible scenarios to probe for a residual material that needs further reprocessing and encourage further generalization of treatment effects. For example, when reprocessing the future template in treating a speaking phobia, ask the patient to imagine confronting problems with the audiovisual system, a disruption from an adjacent meeting room, or a difficult question from the audience. In treating a patient with a flying phobia, during the reprocessing of the future template, ask the patient to imagine encountering moderate turbulence or having the plane bypass the initial landing attempt and have to go around for a second landing attempt.

Visualizing the Future as a Movie

Some specific phobias involve the simple, unanticipated confrontation with the phobic situation as in the choking phobia described above. Other specific phobias require planning and a series of steps such as medical and flying phobias. For phobias for situations that require advance planning, a simple, single scene future template may fail to uncover residual anxiety. To assure comprehensive resolution of all aspects of these phobias, you can ask patients to visualize all the steps leading up to and through the target situations for their treatment goals.

This mental movie should have a series of scenes covering all the actions that require the patient to confront previously avoided or anxiety-provoking situations. Patients can visualize this series of scenes with their eyes open or closed, whichever best enables them to visualize. Instruct patients in advance to notice if they experience any part of their imagined future scenario as still disturbing. If so, ask them to pause at that point to briefly describe the aspect that is disturbing and where they feel it in their body. Then offer them further bilateral stimulation until the disturbance has been cleared. Then, ask them to resume their visualization until they can imagine all the facets of their future scenario with no further disturbance. Then, ask them to review this positive "mental movie" of the future and thinking of their preferred belief while providing further bilateral stimulation until patients reports their VoC on the future template is 7.

Evaluating and Responding to Feedback from In Vivo Exposure

At this point, patients need to make specific plans for in vivo exposure. In vivo exposure assures patients achieve their treatment goals by providing opportunities for discovering and mastering any residual anxiety as well as for consolidating gains made during in-office reprocessing. Patients should be instructed to self-monitor their level of comfort or anxiety with each of the requisite steps in their plan, so that they can report their gains and any residual issues that may be encountered during in vivo exposure. Occasionally, in vivo exposure will lead to uncovering of significant issues that would benefit from further reprocessing. You can then select appropriate current stimuli or past events as targets for reprocessing. In most cases, in vivo exposure itself will allow for direct resolution of any residual anxiety encountered.

SUMMARY

Published case reports indicate that EMDR treatment of specific phobias appears to hold great promise as an effective treatment for patients with phobias of a traumatic origin (De Jongh & Ten Broeke, 2007; De Jongh et al., 1999; Schurmans, 2007; Shapiro, 2001). These patients often have the most elevated levels of anxiety. These case reports suggest that EMDR provides the same type of efficient—rapid—treatment effects for phobias of a traumatic origin observed in the treatment of PTSD. These reports are consistent with the widespread, repeated, controlled research findings that EMDR is an effective treatment for those with both full and partial PTSD symptoms after traumatic exposure (Bisson & Andrew, 2007; van Etten & Taylor, 1998; Wilson, Becker, & Tinker, 1997).

Behavioral studies of exposure show that those with high levels of phobic anxiety appear to benefit more from distraction during exposure than from a pure exposure-focused condition (Johnstone & Page, 2004; Oliver & Page, 2008; Penfold & Page, 1999). EMDR is, in part, a method that intrinsically incorporates distraction as part of its dual attention condition. It is therefore reasonable to hypothesize that EMDR reprocessing will turn out to be an effective component in the treatment of nontraumatic phobias as well as those of traumatic origin.

EMDR treatment plans for patients with specific phobias share many similarities with treatment plans for PTSD. Both sets of treatment plans follow the basic eight-phase model with comprehensive history taking, development of a treatment plan, patient preparation, and reevaluation phases. Reprocessing is sequentially applied over a series of treatment sessions following the standard treatment sequence. This standard treatment sequence focuses first on targets from the past, then the present, and finally the future. Targets from the past are treated in sequence starting first with background stressors—when present—then to the first phobic exposure, then to the worst or a representative phobic experience, and finally to more recent phobic experiences. Only after targets from the past are no longer disturbing does reprocessing shift to current internal and external cues that remain sources of phobic anxiety. Finally, reprocessing is applied to mental rehearsal of future in vivo exposure. However, an essential difference from treatment plans for patients with PTSD is that when treating patients with specific phobia reevaluation follows actual in vivo exposure. In vivo exposure should be included as part of a comprehensive treatment plans for applying EMDR to specific phobias to assure and confirm consolidation and generalization of treatment gains from reprocessing sessions.

## 14

Treating Panic Disorder

OVERVIEW

In this chapter, we will examine additional issues that need to be considered when applying EMDR to the treatment of individuals with panic disorder (PD) and panic disorder with agoraphobia (PDA). We will review the literature on effective treatments for PD and PDA with a focus on cognitive and behavioral therapies, pharmacotherapy, and EMDR. We will review the case reports and controlled studies on the application of EMDR to PD and PDA to consider what lessons can be learned from these reports to guide EMDR clinicians. We will then go step by step through two model treatment plans for using EMDR for treating PD and PDA, one for simpler cases with PD without agoraphobia or other co-occurring disorders, and the other for more complex cases of PDA or PD with generalized anxiety disorder, avoidant personality disorder, and other co-occurring anxiety or axis II disorders. Then in chapter 15, we review case summaries for two patients treated with EMDR for PD. The first case is one of PD in a high school student. The second involves the onset of depersonalization disorder following a recent motor vehicle crash in a preexisting case of PD.

PANIC DISORDER WITH AND WITHOUT AGORAPHOBIA

Individuals with PD experience periods of extreme anxiety accompanied by intense somatic and cognitive distress. These episodes can be as brief as 1 to 5 minutes, but more commonly increase over a period of about 10 minutes. Some individuals experience episodes of panic that can wax and wane over an hour or longer. The symptoms of panic include palpitations, sweating, trembling or shaking, sensations of shortness of breath, sensations of choking, chest pain or discomfort, nausea or abdominal distress, dizziness or light-headedness, derealization or depersonalization, fear of losing control or "going crazy," fear of dying, tingling, and chills or hot flushes. Initial episodes of panic are frequently perceived as just as life-threatening as other experiences that meet criterion A for posttraumatic stress disorder ([PTSD]; American Psychiatric Association, 2000). Indeed, initial episodes of panic are a common cause of visits to hospital emergency rooms where they generally must be evaluated as potential heart attacks, thereby consuming resources that might be directed to those with medical conditions (Fleet et al., 1996).

To meet criteria for PD, panic attacks must recur and must initially be unexpected, rather than being linked to a specific situation as in specific phobia or social phobia. Subsequently, individuals may come to expect panic attacks in settings where they have occurred previously. This expectation may lead to avoidance of those settings and thus is associated with the development of agoraphobia—the fear of having panic in situations from which escape may be difficult. These settings can include bridges, public transportation, crowds, and lines of people. In extreme agoraphobia, individuals may become unwilling to leave their place of residence. About 2.7% of individuals older than the age of 18 experience PD each year (Kessler, Chiu, Demler, & Walters, 2005). About one in three of those with PD in the general population develop agoraphobia (National Institute of Mental Health, 2008). However, in clinical settings, the rate of agoraphobia is considerably higher (American Psychiatric Association, 2000).

THE LONGITUDINAL COURSE AND RELATIONSHIP OF AGORAPHOBIA AND PANIC DISORDER

The Baltimore Longitudinal Study of Panic and Agoraphobia (Bienvenu et al., 2006, p. 436) confirmed that "baseline spontaneous panic attacks (especially frequent ones, i.e. DSM III panic disorder) strongly predicted new-onset agoraphobia" but also found "base-line agoraphobia without spontaneous panic attacks also predicted first-onset panic disorder." Bienvenu et al. (2006, p. 436) ". . . suggest that DSM-V should de-emphasise the implied one-way causal relationship from spontaneous panic to agoraphobia and make agoraphobia itself a stand-alone diagnosis again, as in ICD–10 (World Health Organization, 1993)" and that "clinicians should keep in mind that agoraphobia without panic appears to be at least a marker of risk for later-onset panic disorder." (p. 437)

TREATMENTS FOR PANIC DISORDER

Research on treatments for PD, with or without agoraphobia, has focused on pharmacological and cognitive behavioral therapy (CBT) approaches, both of which are generally considered effective treatments (American Psychiatric Association, 1998; Sturpe & Weissman, 2002). Selective serotonin reuptake inhibitors (SSRIs), tricyclic antidepressants (TCAs), and benzodiazepines appear to be roughly equivalent in their efficacy (Campbell–Sills & Stein, 2006). Use of benzodiazepines "as needed" rather than on a regular schedule has been linked to poorer CBT outcomes (Westra, Stewart, & Conrad, 2002). While benzodiazepines may provide slightly faster benefits, patients receiving only SSRIs have been found to "catch up" within a few weeks.

A significant portion of patients find the side effects of benzodiazepines and SSRIs unacceptable. Benzodiazepine treatment has been associated with sedation, reduced coordination, cognitive impairments, increased accident proneness, and development of dependence. Rebound panic attacks sometimes occur during taper (Watanabe, Churchill, & Furukawa, 2007). Treatment with SSRIs is generally well tolerated, but has been associated with several side effects. These include nausea, drowsiness, headache, teeth clenching, vivid and strange dreams, dizziness, changes in appetite, weight loss or gain, changes in sexual function, increased depression or anxiety, tremors, autonomic dysfunction, including orthostatic hypotension, increased or reduced sweating, suicidal ideation or attempts, and triggering of manic episodes (Cohen, 2004). The combination of CBT plus SSRI has been found to be more effective than either treatment alone for early-phase treatment of PD or PDA; however, the combination produces more dropouts due to side effects from SSRI than psychotherapy alone (Furukawa, Watanabe, & Churchill, 2006).

CBT has been shown to be at least as effective as first-line pharmacotherapies (Campbell–Sills & Stein, 2006). Both interoceptive exposure—deliberately inducing physiological symptoms of panic—and cognitive therapy appear to be equally effective for treating PD without agoraphobia (Arntz, 2002). Both panic-control treatment and in vivo exposure have been shown to reduce panic-related fears and agoraphobia (Craske et al., 2002). Other therapies requiring minimal therapist contact, including bibliotherapy, computer-administered vicarious exposure, problem solving, and computer-administered therapy, have shown some positive results for the treatment of panic symptoms. However, patients with agoraphobia appear to need therapist-initiated exposure. See Newman, Erickson, Przeworski, and Dzus (2003) for a review.

LIMITATIONS OF EXISTING TREATMENTS

CBT is widely recognized as an effective treatment for PDs, yet few studies have examined the stability of its effectiveness over time. While some patients recover from a short course of treatment, it appears that most patients need prolonged additional treatment (de Beurs, van Balkom, Van Dyck, & Lange, 1999). Curiously, although it appears that CBT and pharmacotherapy are roughly equally effective, their combination appears to lead to greater risk of relapse after discontinuing CBT (Barlow, Gorman, Shear, & Woods, 2000). A 5-year follow up of pharmacotherapy studies indicated that only 45% of those treated achieved full remission (Woodman, Noyes Jr, Black, Schlosser, & Yagla, 1999). Ost, Thulin, and Ramnerö (2004) found that adding CBT to exposure alone did not appear to provide any additional benefit. They further note that, "there is still much room for further development of CBT methods for PDA [panic disorder with agoraphobia] because only 60% of the patients treated in RCTs [randomized controlled trials] published since 1990 have achieved a clinically significant improvement" (p. 1106).

CBT and exposure are not well tolerated by all patients with dropout rates as high as 24% for exposure (Marks, Kenwright, McDonough, Whittaker, O'Brien, & Mataix–Cols, 2004) and 26% for CBT (Bakker, van Dyck, Spinhoven, & van Balkom, 1999). Research also suggests that those who are more severely affected by PDA are more likely to refuse or drop out of these treatments (Hunt, 2000). The reasons for the limited results in the CBT and pharmacotherapy studies are not made clear in these review articles, but have been explored by some of the authors of EMDR studies and case reports that we will turn to in the next section. As we will see, part of the explanation may be found through the AIP model by examining the etiology and function of panic symptoms in the context of PD and PDA patient life histories.

RESEARCH ON EMDR TREATMENT OF PANIC DISORDER

Research on EMDR treatment of PD and PDA is considerably more limited than for EMDR treatment of PTSD. There is an early case series, (Goldstein & Feske, 1994), four individual case reports (Fernandez & Faretta, 2007; Goldstein, 1995; Nadler, 1996; Shapiro & Forrest, 1997), and two controlled studies (Feske & Goldstein, 1997; Goldstein, de Beurs, Chambless, & Wilson, 2000).

THE FIRST PANIC DISORDER CASE SERIES BY GOLDSTEIN AND FESKE (1994)

Goldstein and Feske published the first case series on seven cases of PD in 1994. Five of their patients also met criteria for agoraphobia. Most of their patients had comorbid generalized anxiety disorder or specific phobia. Their rationale for exploring the application of EMDR to PD was based on their observation that:

> Panic patients almost always report early panic episodes to have been traumatic and their subsequent symptoms are, in some ways, like those experienced by PTSD victims. Since fear of panic attacks is considered by cognitive-behavior therapists (e.g., Beck & Emery, 1985; Goldstein & Chambless, 1978) to be the core of panic disorder, we were intrigued enough to explore the possible effects of EMDR for panic-related memories on the clinical status of clients with panic disorder. (p. 353)

Goldstein and Feske used both standardized self-report data and daily self-monitoring records. Treatment consisted of one 60-minute treatment planning session and five 90-minute EMDR sessions. The second author, who was newly trained in EMDR, provided all sessions. Standard EMDR reprocessing was applied to targets such as the first and worst episodes of panic attacks, life events related to panic, and anticipated panic attacks. They reported that all seven patients experienced decreased fear of panic attacks and behavioral gains with an absence of further panic attacks or decreased frequency of panic attacks. The greatest gains were in the two patients without agoraphobia.

The authors reported surprise that these gains occurred in the absence of consistent changes in panic-related cognitions normally expected in cognitive behavioral treatment of panic (Chambless & Gillis, 1993). They also reported considerable variability in the content of patients' scenes with some being focused exclusively on past and future panic episodes and body sensations only, while others associated to events prior to the onset of their panic attacks. These other events were often childhood memories with themes of lack of trust, helplessness, and profound loneliness. While these observed differences might reflect random variations in reprocessing style, they may reflect differing contributions of early life deficits on whether patients develop complex forms of PDA with other co-occurring anxiety or mood disorders. Goldstein and Feske concluded that their results suggested that, "EMDR might be a powerful treatment for panic disorder" (p. 360). They emphasized none of the patients treated in their study was considered "cured" after five sessions of EMDR—implying that considerably more than five sessions would be needed to achieve complete resolution of PDA—and called for controlled research.

BREAKING THROUGH THE BARRIERS TO RECOVERY – GOLDSTEIN (1995)

In 1995, Goldstein followed up the case series with a key paper exploring the limitations of existing cognitive–behavioral treatments for PD and PDA. He proposed that a network theory of cognitive–affective meaning, together with EMDR, offered a way to understand and break through the "barriers to recovery" for PD and PDA. He stated that "behavior therapy with exposure to feared situations reduced avoidance behavior for only about 50% of those with agoraphobia" (p. 83) and cited a review by (Chambless & Gillis, 1994) indicating an average improvement rate of 58%, with only 27% of exposure participants ending treatment with little or no residual agoraphobic behavior. The current review of the existing CBT treatments for PD and PDA at the start of this chapter indicates that few gains were achieved in the decade after Goldstein's 1995 report.

"Knowing From the Heart": the Implicational Meaning Schema of Teasdale and Barnard

Goldstein stated that little was known about the barriers to further treatment gain and suggested that comorbid depression and avoidant personality disorder could play a role. He proposed that the barriers to further gains could be understood and overcome with a network theory of cognitive–affective meaning based on the work of Teasdale and Barnard (1993), together with EMDR. The Teasdale and Barnard model of associative networks bears many striking similarities to Shapiro's AIP model (1995, 2001). Both models build on the earlier work of Bower (1981). Teasdale and Barnard proposed that cognitive, emotional, physical, and behavioral patterns and stored memories form an associative network where every component of the network is connected to every other component and can trigger activation of some or all of the network. Teasdale and Barnard's associative networks include some elements of the "fear network" described by Foa & Kozak (1986) and by Lang (1977) that were hypothesized to be affected by cognitive behavioral treatment. Fear networks and their relationship to AIP are discussed in chapters 1 and 2.

Teasdale and Barnard further proposed that an "implicational meaning schema" (IMS)—a way of "knowing from the heart"—develops out of this associative network that is not responsive to cognitive behavioral interventions because the IMS does not rest on logic. In discussing Goldstein's work, I will use the term IMS—as Goldstein does—and the EMDR term *maladaptive memory network* interchangeably. This usage is not found in Goldstein's article. I take responsibility for any distortions this imposes on Teasdale and Barnard's, Goldstein's, or Shapiro's (2001) conceptualizations of their models.

While exposure is capable of reducing responsiveness to some threat cues in the fear network, according to Goldstein, neither exposure nor cognitive interventions, such as discussion and interpretation, seem to affect the maladaptive memory network in treatment resistant cases of PDA. Instead, Goldstein proposed that "affect-provoking interventions" are required and that "EMDR will provide us with just [such] an intervention" (Goldstein, 1995, p. 85).

Goldstein observed that as patients with PDA make initial progress in treatment, they often report a growing sense that behind their physical anxiety symptoms lies "an intense sense of isolation" (1995, p. 86). He indicates that they have a profound dread of this emotional experience. Goldstein claims that milder aspects of this dread of isolation can be addressed with support and CBT, but that when it is more intense, progress can only be made when the IMS is accessed and altered. Goldstein indicates that this can be difficult to achieve for two reasons, one dealing with the patient and the other with the clinician.

PANIC ATTACKS THAT CAN PERSIST FOR HOURS

First, Goldstein observes that these patents seem to have disconnected or disassociated the formative experiences from the affective component of the maladaptive memory network. When the maladaptive memory network of these formative experiences is triggered, patients can go into a state similar to a panic attack that goes on for hours. Since the associated formative memories are generally not being accessed during these prolonged episodes, PDA patients are left with no explanation for the source of these dread feelings. Instead, they "attribute these feelings to insanity, a biochemical disorder or signs of some disease" (Goldstein, 1995, p. 87).

Second, clinicians may be unable to tolerate the intensity of affect generated when patients with PDA access their central issues. Consistent with Bower's principles of state specific memory (Bower, 1981) and Shapiro's AIP (2001), Goldstein stated that change in the maladaptive memory network can only take place when it is being accessed. When this happens, clinicians can experience being torn between the goal of assisting the patient to learn to tolerate and resolve the material in the maladaptive memory network or the impulse to do something to bring about an immediate positive shift in the patient's state. Unfortunately, the later impulse may result in pulling the patient out of the maladaptive memory network. The result of such misguided interventions is to shift the patient's state before the patient has completed reprocessing of the maladaptive memory network. Goldstein suggests that less experienced clinicians are often tempted to move away from this challenging material before it is resolved.

Finally, Goldstein proposes that the formative experiences of this maladaptive memory network involve an early "parent-child role reversal" frequently reported by PDA patients (Goldstein, 1995, p. 87). Goldstein offers several examples of parent–child role reversals where children gain recognition primarily for meeting the needs of an impaired parent, while their own needs for nurturance and safety tend to go unmet. These include caring for an abused parent, one suffering from agoraphobia, alcohol abuse, or other mental or physical illness. When their parents were impaired, these PDA patients may have become primary caregivers for siblings at a very young age while their own needs for attention, recognition, and validation as a separate person went unmet. Goldstein directs his readers to the work of John Bowlby (1973) for a further discussion of the role of attachment issues in the development of agoraphobia.

Goldstein's description of the lack of association between PDA patients' prolonged states of anguish, dread, and fear of loneliness, and their childhood experiences of parent–child role reversal, as dissociation suggests that we might view PDA through the lens of the model of structural dissociation just as van der Hart, Nijenhuis, and Steele (2006) suggest we view PTSD. Goldstein's assertion that we should consider unresolved issues of insecure attachment as underlying the barriers to treatment gain in more complex cases of PDA is parallel to the assertions I have made (Leeds, 2001) that attachment theory provides a foundation for EMDR case conceptualization in cases of complex PTSD, or DESNOS.

It appears these prolonged states of anguish, dread, and fear of loneliness in patients with complex cases of PDA reflect structurally dissociated, maladaptive memory networks of unresolved, preverbal, infant experiences of chronic misattunement as described by Schore (1994, 1996, 1997, 2003a, 2003b) and others (Dozier, Stovall, & Albus, 1999; Solomon & George, 1999). This formulation strengthens the conceptualization that a prolonged exposure to misattunement in early childhood with insecure—disorganized—attachment should be considered a contributory foundation for cases of complex PDA. This leads to the rationale for considering EMDR as an approach in cases of complex PDA for accessing and resolving hypothesized issues with the IMS—maladaptive memory network—described by Teasdale and Barnard (1993) that fail to respond to exposure and CBT.

We should keep in mind Goldstein's observations on the challenges for clinicians in tolerating patients' intense affective states when treating cases of complex PDA. Clinicians need to be alert to the possibility that their urges to rapidly alleviate patient distress—or their own—may lead to interventions that prematurely shift the patient out of poorly tolerated, intense emotional states leading to incomplete resolution of the core material in the maladaptive memory network. On the other hand, clinicians should not necessarily press patients with PDA to address this core material in the maladaptive memory network in their initial EMDR reprocessing sessions. Most PDA patients will need both extended initial preparation and a carefully selected sequence of targets for reprocessing that builds mastery and symptomatic gains before addressing this core material. Goldstein illustrated his formulation of complex PDA with a case report on Ms. C. Over the course of approximately 25 sessions, he provided extended preparation with psychoeducation on anxiety and avoidance, coping skills training, several sessions of interoceptive exposure, 12 sessions of guided in vivo driving exposure in separate cars to extend independent activities, and 9 sessions of EMDR reprocessing.

It is unclear from the session summaries Goldstein provided to what degree treatment gains were the result of exposure, EMDR reprocessing, assertiveness training, or the therapeutic relationship since these different treatment elements overlapped and alternated. Many of the EMDR reprocessing sessions appear to have been incomplete with only limited use of interweaves. Target selection did not appear to follow a predetermined sequence, but instead tended to follow emerging material. In the strikingly similar PDA case of Adriana described later in this summary of the literature, Fernandez and Faretta (2007) report stable treatment gains in approximately the same total number of treatment sessions, but without the need to incorporate interoceptive or in vivo exposure. It appears that this may have been due to their greater confidence in their ability to access and reprocess the formative maladaptive memory networks without needing to resort to in vivo exposure and to a more well-developed sense of target selection and sequencing with a case conceptualization based firmly on the AIP model.

PSYCHODYNAMICALLY INFORMED EMDR TREATMENT OF PANIC DISORDER

Nadler (1996) presented a single case report of a woman in her late 20s whom he refers to as "Sarah" that summarized aspects of EMDR treatment of her PD and considered PD from both the behavioral and psychodynamic perspectives. Two sessions of EMDR reprocessing appeared to alleviate Sarah's panic attacks and reduced her anticipatory anxiety. Nadler acknowledged the contributions and limitations of cognitive and behavioral approaches in developing structured treatments that can be effective in "7 to 15 sessions but with reports of considerable residual anticipatory anxiety and a definite subset of patients with minimal or 'low level change' (Barlow, 1994; Clark, 1994; Klosko, Barlow, Tassinari, & Cerny, 1990; Telch et al., 1993)." Nadler referred to separation anxiety and attachment issues as central to the psychodynamic theory of the etiology of PD (Bowlby, 1973; Nemiah, 1984; Shear, Cooper, Klerman, Busch & Shapiro, 1993). He commented on the contrast between the extensive training needed to apply Davanloo's Intensive Short-Term Dynamic Psychotherapy (ISTDP) (Davanloo, 1989a, 1989b) and the potential power of EMDR to quickly elicit associated contributory material from patients' childhood issues with considerably less required training.

Nadler's approach to treatment in this case of panic was to initially target a recent experience of feeling lightheaded followed by panic. No indication or description of a preparation phase was included. Sarah was still living with her father 20 years after the death of her mother, and working at a job she loathed and had taken at her father's insistence. Nadler reported that during EMDR reprocessing, Sarah quickly associated to feelings of sadness over the death of her mother after a "deteriorating illness" early in her childhood. Deep emotions of grief over her unmet childhood needs for comforting and rage at her mother's childhood expectations of her to be "perfect and adultlike" emerged and were reduced in intensity from a SUD of 9 to 1 within a single session. No reassessment or further reprocessing of this target memory was reported.

A second EMDR reprocessing session focused on residual "odd sensations" at work in which the patient's dissatisfaction with her job emerged along with anger at her father, who was about to finally remarry. She had tried to please her father by taking a job that she loathed. She gained insights into her recent symptoms as an appeal for her father to take care of her just as she had found in childhood that symptoms of illness were "the only reliable way to gain attention." The patient decided to be more direct in expressing her emotions to her father and to take action to improve her living situation.

Nadler reported "occasional contact" with Sarah over the next 6 months. He indicated that she continued to be free of panic, but eventually reported a surge of anxiety over unnamed feelings. He then offered further EMDR reprocessing, which led to elaboration of her growing conflicts with her stepmother and a realization of her need to move out on her own. Nadler also commented on the two types of responses to EMDR reprocessing in PDA cases described previously by Goldstein and Feske (1994).

> As Goldstein [and Feske] found, some patients experience desensitization and the alteration of catastrophic cognitions without the emergence of underlying dynamic issues while others produce memories of earlier trauma or disturbance. In our clinic I have also found PDA patients who did not produce memories but became profoundly relaxed with an alteration of catastrophic beliefs. (Nadler, 1996)

Nadler does not offer a specific hypothesis to explain these two different kinds of responses to EMDR reprocessing, nor does he comment on the potential need to prepare patients with more complex cases of PDA for the intensity of the material that may emerge with EMDR reprocessing.

SHAPIRO AND FORREST: PANIC DISORDER IN A CASE OF UNRESOLVED TRAUMATIC LOSS

Shapiro and Forrest (1997, pp. 74–88) described the case of Susan, a woman with a lifelong fear of storms, who had her first panic attack while sitting at home with her second husband, listening to a blizzard outside just 6 years after the tragic death of her first husband in a tornado. When her panic attacks began, she tried treatment with biofeedback and a 30-day intensive stress-reduction program without success. She eventually met with an EMDR trained clinician, Beverly Schoninger, who provided two preparation and treatment planning sessions and three 90-minute sessions of EMDR reprocessing. In these three reprocessing sessions, she was able to complete the grieving process for her first husband, work through her irrational self-blame for the tornado that killed her first husband, and desensitize threat cues she associated with storms. This vivid, narrative case report suggests that brief treatment with EMDR for PD can be successful, but provides no standardized measures or follow-up information on stability of treatment effects.

FERNANDEZ AND FARETTA (2007): RESOLVING SEPARATION ANXIETY IN A CASE OF PANIC DISORDER WITH AGORAPHOBIA

Fernandez and Faretta (2007) described a case of a 32-year-old woman, Adriana, treated with EMDR for PDA that had started when she was 20 years old. Adriana's panic attacks occurred when driving alone and led to an avoidance of driving alone. Her panic symptoms included the feeling of choking, tachycardia, and sweating, feeling faint, tingling in her hands, leg tremors, visual disturbances, and a fear of dying. Her agoraphobia had evolved over the previous 8 years to include avoidance of places where it might be difficult to escape or receive help, such as traffic jams, shopping, and riding elevators. Eventually, she became afraid to be alone, even at home, and had to have a companion at all times.

Her history revealed several early contributory and recent etiological events that were addressed in the comprehensive treatment plan. These included being placed by her parents to live with her grandparents for an extended period when she was a few months old due to the parents work schedule. Her parents visited her in the evenings. She was reunited with her parents at the age of 8 when her mother was pregnant with her brother. The day of his birth, she was accidentally trapped in an elevator. The year of his birth there was a brief but frightening home invasion experience. Years later, her first anxiety attack was associated with an episode of cannabis intoxication. Her first panic attack while driving occurred soon after an appendectomy.

Adriana recorded behavioral data daily on frequency, severity, duration, and triggers for panic attacks as well as who was with her. Fernandez and Faretta (2007) indicated that Adriana received a total of 30 treatment sessions. Six sessions were devoted to history taking and preparation. This initial phase was followed by 12 sessions of EMDR reprocessing of targets selected from past events and triggers. Then three sessions were devoted to EMDR reprocessing of rehearsal of future behaviors. Finally, there were nine additional sessions reviewing results from the active treatment phase. Follow-up data was collected posttreatment at 3 months, 6 months, and 1 year. The follow-up data confirmed that Adriana achieved the following:

- Elimination of anxiety and panic attacks
- Elimination of avoidance behaviors
- Establishment of independent functioning through the ability to be alone and drive
- Resolution of agoraphobic symptoms
- Insight and understanding about symptoms and secondary gains
- Establishment of a new self-perception, which included an adjustment of interpersonal relationships, and return to normal daily life functioning

Fernandez and Faretta (2007) suggested that the positive outcome in this case of PDA was the result of several key factors. They emphasized the importance when treating agoraphobia of providing an extended preparation phase, and contrasted the six sessions of history taking, alliance building, and psychoeducation offered Adriana with the single session of history and preparation provided in the controlled study by Goldstein et al., (2000)—reviewed in the next section. Fernandez and Faretta observed successful within session reprocessing effects that led to an elimination of panic symptoms after just four reprocessing sessions. They emphasized the ability of EMDR reprocessing to assist in both the uncovering and resolving of key contributory and etiological events and maladaptive learning experiences. Like Goldstein (1995) and Nadler (1996), they drew attention to the need to identify and apply EMDR reprocessing to attachment related issues such as separations from parents, experiences of parental apprehension, overly strict parenting, and parental rigidity that reduce patients' "ability to explore independently and to achieve self-confidence (Parker, 1981)" (Fernandez & Faretta, 2007, p. 50). Later in this chapter, after the review of the literature, we will discuss the need to consider the impact of attachment-related experiences on the development of capacities for resilience, self-monitoring, and emotional self-regulation.

Fernandez and Faretta emphasized the role of "negative or stressful experiences" in the etiology of PD and the need for clinicians to take a thorough history "to identify and define the experiences that have created a vulnerability to these symptoms" (p. 50). They suggested that subclinical anxiety issues may have preceded the onset of the first panic attack. "The first panic attack is often the climax of a chain of stressful events, occurring once life circumstances are no longer conducive to escaping into avoidance (Fava & Mangelli, 1999)" (Fernandez & Faretta, 2007, p. 50). They stressed the importance in cases of agoraphobia of considering potential "secondary gain" issues where the maintenance of avoidant behaviors provides a buffer against fears of failure, anxiety about tolerating feeling good, or the loss of a highly dependent, unbalanced attachment relationship. They directed clinicians to develop treatment plans founded on the standard EMDR phobia protocol (Shapiro, 2001), including "a sufficient preparation phase" and EMDR reprocessing of targets related to "(a) events that set the foundation for the pathology; (b) first experience of fear, anxiety, or panic; (c) worst experience; (d) most recent experience; (e) current triggers; and (f) future templates" (p. 50).

CONTROLLED RESEARCH: FESKE AND GOLDSTEIN (1997)

In 1997, Feske and Goldstein published the first controlled study of EMDR treatment for PD. All but two of the participants also met criteria for agoraphobia. They randomly assigned 43 outpatients with PD to a waiting list, to receive six sessions of EMDR reprocessing, or six sessions of an EMDR-like treatment without eye movements called "eye fixation exposure and reprocessing" (EFER). In the EFER treatment, participants watched the therapist's index and middle fingers held stationary, approximately 12 inches away from their faces. Wait-list participants were later assigned to one of the treatment groups if they still met inclusion criteria. As we will see in examining this study—subtitled *A Controlled Outcome and Partial Dismantling Study*, the research design developed by Feske and Goldstein appeared to be focused on the question of the extent to which eye movements contribute to treatment effectiveness without adequately considering the question of what constitutes an adequate trial for EMDR treatment of PDA itself.

Participants were excluded if they met criteria for a personality disorder, current alcohol or substance abuse, depression with suicidal ideation or had more severe depression than panic symptoms, or if they were taking more than a specified amount of a benzodiazepine. Participants completed standard objective questionnaires 1 week before treatment, 1 week after treatment, and 3 months after treatment. Participants also completed self-monitoring records for 7 weeks of the treatment phase and for 2 weeks at the 3-month follow-up period.

In the active treatment groups, participants received one history-taking session followed by five EMDR or EFER sessions (one 2-hour and four 90-minute sessions) over 3 weeks. Participants were offered no other preparation or treatment interventions such as the calm–safe place, relaxation or breathing exercises, or in vivo exposure. Treatment plans focused on targets from participants' "anxiety-provoking memories, such as the first and worst panic attack, life events that the client identified as related to the panic disorder, and anticipated panic episodes" (Feske & Goldstein, 1997, p. 1028). It appears that deliberate targeting of current stimuli, such as unpleasant body sensations, was excluded to avoid procedures similar to in vivo exposure. It also appears that no specific effort was made to identify or target early adverse childhood experiences of separations, traumas, or stressful parental interactions.

Feske and Goldstein (1997) found EMDR to be more effective in alleviating panic and panic-related symptoms than the waiting-list procedure at posttest. Compared with EFER, EMDR led to greater improvement on two of five primary outcome measures at posttest. However, at the 3-month follow-up, EFER and EMDR showed statistically equivalent results. At posttest, eight of the EMDR participants had achieved medium to high end-state functioning compared to only one EFER participants and none of the wait-list participants. At follow-up, six EMDR participants and three EFER participants achieved medium or high end-state functioning, while 9 EMDR and 11 EFER participants were at low end-state functioning. Their discussion focused on the lack of difference in treatment effects at follow-up to suggest that EMDR was a placebo treatment or a ritual procedure with only short-term advantages over a wait-list control. While they cite their earlier case series, Goldstein & Feske (1994), they notably failed to cite or discuss the positive results or central issues discussed in Goldstein's 1995 case report. Thus, they omit from their discussion the possibility that they failed to offer a credible treatment plan based on the second author's most emphasized issues and concerns in his paper from just 2 years before for case formulation and treatment planning in cases of PDA.

In comparison with the positive results reported for PDA cases by Fernandez and Faretta (2007), Goldstein (1995), and Nadler (1996), these findings by Feske and Goldstein (1997) must be interpreted carefully to consider what significance they hold for the application of EMDR to PDA. While Feske and Goldstein provided good evidence for procedural fidelity within their EMDR reprocessing sessions, it appears that the overall treatment plan and number of sessions offered failed to meet the standards set by the authors of the successful single case reports and suggested by EMDR's developer (Shapiro, 2001). It appears that they did not offer the number of sessions needed for preparation and development of rapport. It appears that they did not uncover and reprocess maladaptive memory networks related to adverse attachment related childhood experiences or traumas. It appears that they did not reprocess current stimuli and triggers including unpleasant physical sensations associated with panic attacks—on the grounds that this would involve in vivo exposure—nor did they help participants prepare for future situations.

The behavioral literature suggests that 7 to 15 sessions of cognitive or behavior therapy are needed to achieve results with a significant portion of those with PDA (Nadler, 1996). From the descriptions and results in the single case reports on EMDR treatment of PDA cited above, it should hardly be surprising that the research design selected by Feske and Goldstein with no preparation sessions and only five sessions of EMDR reprocessing would prove insufficient to test EMDR's effectiveness for PDA.

GOLDSTEIN, DE BEURS, CHAMBLESS, AND WILSON (2000)

In 2000, Goldstein et al. published a controlled study of PDA essentially replicating Feske and Goldstein (1997). Like Feske and Goldstein, they randomly assigned 46 participants to a wait-list, EMDR or an alternate condition, but they replaced the eye fixation condition (EFER) with a credible placebo control condition known to be ineffective for PDA. At the end of the waiting period, wait-list participants were randomly assigned to one of the two treatment conditions. The credible placebo control treatment, referred to as "association and relaxation therapy" (ART), consisted of 30–45 minutes of progressive muscle relaxation training followed by 30–45 minutes of association therapy. Both of these treatments had been found to be inferior in their effects to cognitive–behavior therapy for PDA.

The authors acknowledged that, "Feske and Goldstein (1997) obtained positive results for EMDR's efficacy for panic disorder with agoraphobia (PDA)," but they expressed concern that "in light of the conflicting findings with earlier results for treatment of phobia, these effects require replication" (p. 948). The limitations of the research on EMDR treatment of specific phobia—especially of spider phobia—are discussed in chapter 13. Given the significant issues in the flawed spider phobia research and the differences in the nature and etiology of PDA and specific phobia, this does not appear to be a valid rationale for a replication study. Given the positive initial findings from both the uncontrolled case series in Goldstein and Feske (1994) and from the randomized controlled study by Feske and Goldstein (1997), a more useful study would have directly compared EMDR to a credible alternate known effective treatment such cognitive therapy or exposure.

Goldstein et al. (2000) used similar exclusion criteria as Feske and Goldstein (1997) for higher doses of benzodiazepines or recent medication changes, for substance dependence, for a more severe comorbid anxiety disorder, or for mood, thought, and certain axis II disorders—specifically paranoid, schizoid, schizotypal, antisocial, or borderline. Twenty of their participants had another anxiety disorder; three met criteria for obsessive–compulsive personality disorder; and four met criteria for avoidant personality disorder. They used similar standardized measures including structured interview measures, self-report questionnaires, and daily self-monitoring forms. They assessed treatment integrity with both credibility measures by participants and fidelity ratings of session audio or video recordings.

Treatment consisted of six 90-minute sessions over an average of 4 weeks. The first session focused on information gathering regarding symptoms, history, and course of the disorder, as well as details on the first and worst panic attacks and plausible rationales for the treatment being offered. Thus, participants received just five 90-minute sessions of treatment with either EMDR reprocessing or ART. Neither group received the kind of extended preparation or treatment, described as important in the earlier report by Goldstein (1995) or in the later report by Fernandez and Faretta (2007). Indeed, "Throughout treatment, therapists in both conditions were prohibited from using interventions outside the realm of the protocol such as anxiety management training, cognitive restructuring, in vivo exposure, and exploration of intrapsychic issues" (Goldstein et al., 2000, p. 949).

Results from Goldstein et al. (2000) showed less benefit from EMDR treatment than found in the earlier study by Feske and Goldstein (1997). This may have been due in part to the differences in selection criteria, which focused on frequency of panic attacks in Feske and Goldstein (1997) and on severity of agoraphobia in Goldstein et al. (2000). Thus, the Goldstein et al. (2000) participants had more severe agoraphobia. The authors cited several reasons that these weaker results could not be due to poor methodology including a randomized control group design with carefully diagnosed clients, the use of a treatment manual reviewed and approved by Shapiro, and EMDR trained therapists supervised weekly by Alan J. Goldstein, who was highly experienced in EMDR treatment for panic and agoraphobia. Their conclusion was that, "In light of the availability of treatments with solid efficacy evidence, the results of this investigation do not support the use of EMDR for treatment of panic disorder with agoraphobia." (p. 955)

However, we should be cautious about accepting this interpretation of the carefully gathered data in the Goldstein et al. (2000) study. This study suffers from the same treatment design issues as the study done 5 years earlier by Feske and Goldstein (1995). As described above, these include the following: (a) not offering the number of sessions needed for preparation and development of rapport, (b) not uncovering and reprocessing maladaptive memory networks related to adverse, attachment-related childhood experiences or traumas, (c) not reprocessing current stimuli and triggers including unpleasant physical sensations associated with panic attacks—on the grounds that this would involve in vivo exposure, and (d) not helping participants prepare for future situations.

As an explanation for the relatively weaker findings by Goldstein et al. (2000) compared with those of Goldstein and Feske (1994) or Goldstein (1995), Goldstein stated,

> … the question of how agoraphobic clients are different, from people with PTSD, for example, in ways that might affect the process and outcome of EMDR treatment. Possible explanations include observations that people with agoraphobia are more avoidant of intense affect, that they have highly diffused fear networks, and that they have difficulty making accurate cause-effect attribution for anxiety and fear responses. It is my belief that they often come into therapy feeling overwhelmed and confused by seemingly inexplicable forces. *The first order of business in therapy is to provide a lot of structure, reassurance and to focus on concrete anxiety management skills. In the early stage of therapy, perhaps they are not ready to engage in a process that is as emotionally provocative as is EMDR.* (Shapiro, 2001, p. 363)

CONTRASTING GOOD FIDELITY IN SINGLE SESSIONS WITH AN ADEQUATE TREATMENT PLAN

It is entirely possible to have good fidelity to the standard EMDR procedural steps when reprocessing each selected target and fail to offer an adequate treatment plan. This is a general issue seen by approved consultants working with clinicians being trained or recently trained in EMDR. In addition to the fact that all participants in the Goldstein et al. (2000) study met criteria for moderate to severe agoraphobia, 13 participants also met criteria for generalized anxiety disorder, social phobia, or obsessive–compulsive disorder and 7 of the participants met criteria for obsessive–compulsive personality disorder or avoidant personality disorder. Based on the individual PDA case reports cited in this chapter and other reports on the application of EMDR to the treatment of axis II disorders (Manfield, 2003) and generalized anxiety disorder (Gauvreau & Bouchard, 2008), a significantly more comprehensive and longer treatment plan would be needed to successfully treat patients with these comorbid conditions.

When patients have moderate to severe agoraphobia, the kind of treatment plan described by Goldstein et al. (2000), which merely identified and reprocessed memories of first, worst and recent panic attacks, will not yield adequate results on either the frequency or severity of panic attacks themselves nor on the avoidant behaviors of the agoraphobia. Many of the reasons for this are well described by the authors of the three PDA case reports first cited in this chapter (Fernandez & Faretta, 2007; Goldstein, 1995; Nadler, 1996). In the next section, we will take the lessons learned from the published reports on the EMDR treatment of PD and PDA and from my own clinical experiences to outline the elements of two model treatment plans, one for simpler cases of PD and one for more complex cases of PDA or PD with co-occurring disorders.

A SPECTRUM OF CASES FROM PD TO PDA TO PANIC SECONDARY TO PTSD

As we have seen in the review of the literature on EMDR treatment of PD and PDA, two different kinds of responses can occur when applying EMDR reprocessing to experiences of panic. In simpler cases, most commonly in PD without agoraphobia, EMDR reprocessing of memories of first, worst, or recent occurrences of panic attacks leads to simple associations within the memory of the panic experiences. During reprocessing in these cases, patients report changes in the vividness of the images, sensations, and emotions associated with the experience of panic without associations to deeper feelings of dread of loneliness, and without recall of distressing childhood attachment-related memories. In contrast to these simpler cases of PD, in more complex cases of PDA, to achieve successful resolution of the affective avoidance that underlies the agoraphobia, EMDR reprocessing of memories of panic attacks eventually leads to the uncovering of associations to childhood memories of parental separations, strict parenting, superficial parenting without "mindsight" (Siegel, 1999, p. 140), parental illness, or neglect or to experiences of parent–child role reversals. Guilt over feelings of anger and resentment, together with shame and self-doubt over worth and being deserving, can lead to conflicts in working through deep feelings of hurt, anger, and grief associated with early childhood maladaptive memory networks. These maladaptive memory networks can include preverbal material for which patients have no defined memories but which evoke intense affective states as well as later experience for which patients have discrete childhood memories. Patients may find these later, identifiable memories more disturbing than seems comprehensible to them in part because of the non-identifiable preverbal memories that underlie them. When present, these conflicts in working through the deep feelings of hurt, anger, and grief must be carefully and deliberately approached and worked through in a well-sequenced approach with judiciously selected interweaves. These interweaves will generally focus on the responsibility theme either to externalize responsibility for early parent–child reversals or to increase capacities for emotional self-soothing, self-validation, and self-worth (see chapter 9).

A more comprehensive history taking can often identify the presence of these adverse childhood experiences at intake. However, a treatment plan that initially targets these earliest life events for EMDR reprocessing may expose the patient to the full intensity of deep feelings of dread, loneliness, hurt, anger, or grief for which the patient may not feel adequately prepared. Instead, these patients need a structured approach that combines reassurance with a treatment plan that begins with concrete anxiety management skills, Resource Development and Installation for self-soothing and affect tolerance and then initially targets their panic attacks. These patients first need to achieve a sense of mastery and greater confidence in EMDR reprocessing and an adequate sense of trust in the therapeutic alliance through successfully completed, within session reprocessing of memories of first, worst, and most recent panic attacks. Only after some initial gains are these patients ready to address the central contributory memories holding the core painful affects that underlies their panic attacks and agoraphobia.

This approach, which begins with a highly structured treatment plan, including anxiety management skills building and an initial reprocessing sequence focused first on the first, worst, and most recent panic attacks before proceeding to deeper, earlier aspects of the maladaptive memory network bears some similarities to the "inverted protocol" described by Dr. Arne Hoffman (2004, 2005) for treatment of complex PTSD. In the inverted protocol for complex PTSD, the sequence of targets selected for reprocessing inverts the standard "past, present, future" treatment planning sequence proposed by Shapiro (1995, 2001). The inverted protocol begins with the future, then the present, and then moves to reprocessing the past. The earliest identifiable maladaptive memories are too intense for the level of affect tolerance and the availability of resources—also referred to by Dr. Hoffman as *positive channel ends*. Also, patients with complex PTSD often present with inadequate current day-to-day functioning and an impaired ability to tolerate current stressors. Instead, their treatment begins with a focus on skills and resource building. Early work in the inverted protocol model focuses on building a positive image of self in the future and on increasing current coping skills and resources to improve self-confidence and build a sense of hope and the resilience needed to gradually approach the maladaptive memory networks that ultimately need to be reprocessed.

In addition to their dread of confronting the core painful affects that underlies their agoraphobia, many patients with PDA have significant comorbid conditions that complicate the treatment process. For example, PD and PDA are commonly found in patients with histories of chronic exposure to traumatic events in childhood and emotional neglect. These patients also meet the proposed criteria set for DESNOS or complex PTSD (Herman, 1992a; Pelcovitz et al., 1997). In such cases, it may be more appropriate to consider PD and PDA not as separate diagnosable conditions but as part of the overarching condition of DESNOS. As van der Kolk and Pelcovitz (1999, p. 23) state: "We propose that in patients with PTSD these symptoms do not constitute separate 'double diagnoses,' but represent the complex somatic, cognitive, affective, and behavioral effects of psychological trauma, particularly trauma that is prolonged and starts early in the life cycle." For patients who meet criteria for DESNOS, the treatment plans described in this chapter are generally not sufficiently comprehensive to adequately meet the clinical needs of these patients. This can seem mysterious to patients and even to some referring clinicians less familiar with the AIP model and the literature on DESNOS who tend to view a condition like PD or PDA as a discrete set of symptoms that can be considered and treated separately from the overall life experience of the patient.

PHASE 1: HISTORY TAKING AND TREATMENT PLANNING ISSUES

It is important to consider potential medical and lifestyle factors that can contribute to the onset, frequency, and severity of panic attacks. Excess consumption of caffeinated beverages, especially coffee and sodas, as well as over-the-counter medications such as analgesics containing caffeine and pseudoephedrine hydrochloride—

a common cold remedy—can create anxiety states that make panic attacks more likely. Several prescription medications can cause anxiety as side effects. It is important to screen for any changes in prescription medication around the time frame of the onset of panic attacks as well as current prescriptions. Most common medication induced anxiety occurs with epinephrine and other sympathomimetics, theophylline and other neurostimulant bronchodilators, and corticosteroids (Beers, 2004, p. 608). Sleep deprivation can be a significant factor in anxiety states as well. A thorough screening should check on sleep hygiene (Foldvary–Schaefer, 2006). While medication and lifestyle factors are rarely the unique cause of panic, they should always be considered and addressed when appropriate with appropriate psychoeducation and guidance.

SCREENING FOR FORMATIVE EXPERIENCES THAT PRECEDED THE ONSET OF PANIC ATTACKS

When patients present for treatment of PD or PDA, they seldom spontaneously report the full range of early life, contributory experiences that may have contributed to the development of these conditions. Instead, they focus on their desire to get rid of their current frightening and embarrassing episodes of panic. EMDR-trained clinicians may decide to select a simple, symptom focused view of treatment planning. Since the patient reports panic attacks, the initial approach may be to just treat the memories of panic attacks. In many cases of PD without agoraphobia—and without co-occurring complex PTSD, generalized anxiety disorder, obsessive compulsive disorder, or a cluster C personality disorder—an approach based on the EMDR protocol for specific phobia may prove sufficient. However, the presence of agoraphobia and other comorbid disorders that often are not be spontaneously reported, may lead to treatment complications or outright failure of a simple treatment plan. This is more likely when patients were also exposed to persistent adverse childhood experiences and suffer from complex PTSD, generalized anxiety disorder, or a cluster C personality disorder. When present, these co-occurring conditions can lead to spreading activation of multiple, additional maladaptive memory networks and ineffective reprocessing.

Both a thorough history and comprehensive clinical assessment, which considers comorbid conditions, are essential to the formulation of the treatment plan in cases of PDA. Merely asking patients with PDA at intake to describe the stressors that were associated with the onset of their first panic attack or worst panic attack may not reveal the essential formative experiences that created the vulnerability to developing PD. Goldstein (1995) emphasized that PDA patients may have disassociated formative experiences from the affective component of the maladaptive memory network. As we have seen in the detailed case reports of Goldstein (1995), Nadler (1996), and Fernandez and Faretta (2007)—as well as in clinical case examples from my practice, we will review later in the chapter—some of these experiences involve very early parent–child role reversals that may emerge through EMDR reprocessing. PDA patients often have such a deep dread of reconnecting to these experiences that they may only be able to consciously identify them after they have achieved some mastery over their current panic symptoms and developed greater trust and confidence in the therapeutic alliance and in the benefits of EMDR reprocessing. Even when PDA patients can identify formative maladaptive experiences from childhood early in the treatment planning process, they may dissociate or minimize the relationship between these events and their panic attacks. In other cases, they may be able to recognize how these experiences have played a formative role, but may be too preoccupied with their current distress over current panic attacks to initially directly confront these early memories.

SCREENING FOR IMPAIRED CARE-GIVERS AND EXPERIENCES OF PARENT–CHILD ROLE REVERSALS

When patients present or are referred with a primary presenting complaint of panic attacks, clinicians need to explore for other past or present axis I and axis II disorders. History taking needs to consider adverse life events—both those that meet criterion A for PTSD as well as those that do not meet criterion A such as early life exposures to perceived and actual abandonments and impaired caregivers, especially in the first few years of life. Early experiences of persistent parental misattunement can create recurrent states of abandonment terror and episodes of disorientation and dissociation. When chronic, these experiences lead to insecure attachment and an increased vulnerability to adolescent and adult psychiatric disorders (Schore, 1996, 1997). As they develop, these children learn not to expect their caregivers to meet their needs for emotional regulation and support, but instead shift into a parent–child role reversal. They gain attention, not for their own emotional needs for nurturance and safety, but by meeting the needs of an impaired parent.

Parental impairments can be obvious and identifiable during history taking such as a parent who was abused or suffering from agoraphobia, alcohol abuse, or other mental or physical illness. When their parents were impaired, these PDA patients may have simply experienced outright neglect. In other cases, they may have become primary caregivers for siblings—or been taken care of by siblings—while their own needs for parental attention, recognition, and validation as a separate person went unmet. However, in many cases, the period of parental impairment may have been limited to an early portion of the patient's life and may not have persisted throughout the patient's childhood. Some patients with PDA or PD with co-occurring GAD, DESNOS, or an axis II disorder and an avoidant insecure attachment will minimize parental impairments and idealize one or both parents. In these cases, clinicians will have to look beyond patients' beliefs and claims of a "happy childhood" to discern evidence of unmet attachment or developmental needs at one or more phases in early life. A challenge in exploring these issues is to avoid creating the impression for the patient that the clinician is seeking to blame parents.

Some individuals may be genetically predisposed to developing PD or PDA. Research on twins shows that panic attacks are five times as likely to co-occur with an identical twin as with a fraternal twin (Torgersen, 1983). Childhood emergence of panic attacks or another anxiety disorder may occur in the absence of environmental factors. In their quest to be thorough, clinicians should not start from an assumption that formative life experiences involving impaired caregivers or parental misattunement are invariably involved in the etiology of PD or PDA. Until there are widely accepted tests for genetic vulnerability to PD (Philibert et al., 2007), clinicians have to rely on careful psychosocial assessment and history taking.

Due to the strong tendency to dissociate the painful formative life experiences that often underlie the vulnerability to the later development of PD and PDA, clinicians may not be able to overtly identify the presence of such formative life experiences during the early phases of the therapy. Instead, it may be preferable to postpone directly exploring or targeting these experiences for reprocessing until after patients have made gains in reducing the intensity and frequency of panic attacks and developing greater confidence in the therapeutic process with EMDR. As patients experience a growing sense of mastery over the current symptoms of panic, they often begin to make connections with memories of key formative experiences that can gradually be made the focus for further reprocessing. Clinicians need to exercise care when starting therapy with these patients to find the appropriate balance between obtaining sufficient history to be able to proceed with reprocessing without overwhelming these patients with what might initially seem an unrelated or overwhelming challenge to confront deeper issues.

 | Questions to Identify Panic Disorder Targets

Frequency of Current Panic Attacks
How often have you experienced panic attacks in the last two weeks?

Intensity and Duration of Current Panic Attacks
*How would you rate the intensity of your panic attacks in the last two weeks on a scale from 0
(none) to 10 (the worst it could possibly be)?*
How long do your panic attacks last?

Current Experience of Panic
What sensations do you experience during panic attacks?

Depersonalization and Derealization
*During panic attacks do you ever experience sensations of detachment or disconnection from your
body, numbness or a sense of the world being dreamlike or far away?*

Past Frequency, Intensity and Duration of Panic Attacks
How have the frequency, intensity and duration of your panic attacks changed over time?

Current Avoided or Feared Situations
What situations do you tend to avoid or fear because you might have a panic attack?
*Do you have periods where you avoid leaving home or can only leave home with someone you trust
or with whom you feel safe?*

First Event
What was the first time you had a panic attack or the earliest time you can remember having a panic attack?

Background Stressors
*What other stressful experiences were going on in your personal, family, school or work life at about
time of that first occurrence?*

Parental–Child Role Reversals
*Describe any childhood experiences where one or both of your parents needed you to care for them
because they were depressed, anxious, ill, or impaired by alcohol or substance abuse.*
How often did this happen? How long did it go on?
What are the earliest and most disturbing memories of this occurring?

Worst or Representative Panic Attack
When was the most intense or the most frightening panic attack you ever had?
If there is no "worst" experience, describe a significant, typical experience of panic attack.

Most Recent Event
What is the most recent experience of panic attack?

Current External and Internal Cues
What situations seem to stimulate your panic attacks?

Future Goal
Please describe a future situation and what you would like to be able to do free of the fear of panic attacks.

TWO MODEL TREATMENT PLANS FOR PANIC DISORDER

Model I: Cases of Panic Disorder without Agoraphobia or any other co-occurring anxiety disorder such as GAD, OCD, complex PTSD (DESNOS), or an axis II disorder
1) History taking (Phase 1)
   A. Clinical assessment, diagnosis, and case formulation
   B. Selecting appropriate treatment goals
   C. Selecting and sequencing of targets
2) Preparation (Phase 2)
   A. Psychoeducation on panic
   B. Teaching and rehearsing self-control procedures
      i. Breathing exercises and other calming procedures for anxiety
   C. Introduce EMDR and informed consent to treatment
3) Reprocessing of targets
   A. Past events
      i. Background stressors to first panic attack(s) (if any were identified)
      ii. First panic attack
      iii. Worst or representative panic attack
      iv. Most recent panic attack
   B. Current stimuli
      i. External cues (associated with panic attacks)
      ii. Internal (interoceptive) cues
   C. Future templates (for external and internal cues)
4) In vivo exposure to external cues (generally done independently)
5) Re-evaluation and further reprocessing, if indicated

Model II: Cases of Panic Disorder with Agoraphobia or with a co-occurring anxiety disorder such as GAD, OCD, complex PTSD (DESNOS), or an axis II disorder
1) History taking (Phase 1)
   A. Clinical assessment, diagnosis, and case formulation
   B. Selecting appropriate treatment goals
   C. Selecting and sequencing of initial targets
2) Preparation (Phase 2)
   A. Psychoeducation on panic
   B. Teaching and rehearsing self-control procedures
      i. Breathing exercises and other calming procedures for anxiety
      ii. Sensory focusing and other procedures for decreasing depersonalization
   C. Introduce EMDR and informed consent to treatment
      i. Explain the childhood experiences are likely to emerge as later targets
   D. Consider installing one or more resources for:
      i. Self-soothing, self-acceptance, or connection before or after beginning reprocessing core maladaptive memory networks of etiological experiences from childhood
3) Reprocessing of targets
   A. Past panic attacks
      i. Background stressors to first panic attacks (if any were identified)
      ii. First panic attack
      iii. Worst or representative panic attack
      iv. Most recent panic attack
   B. After some gains on reprocessing memories of panic attacks: contributory childhood experiences of perceived abandonment, misattunement, humiliation, fear, and early parent–child reversals
      i. These can be addressed in the order they emerge during reprocessing
      ii. When patients can tolerate it, these can be addressed in the order of central importance to core maladaptive memory network of avoided emotional material.
   C. Current stimuli
      i. External cues (associated with panic attacks)
      ii. Internal (interoceptive) cues
   D. Future templates
      i. For external and internal cues
4) In vivo exposure to external cues (generally done independently)
5) Re-evaluation and further reprocessing, if indicated
6) Install one or more resources to represent emergence and consolidation of new sense of self, free of avoidance of core maladaptive memory network

PHASE 2: PREPARATION PHASE ISSUES

One of the ways patients with PDA tend to differ from those who present as survivors of complex early relational trauma is in their dissociation of the role of the formative experiences with their caregivers. Goldstein emphasized that in the early phases of treatment clinicians need "…to provide a lot of structure, reassurance and to focus on concrete anxiety management skills…" (quoted in Shapiro, 2001, p. 363). Fernandez and Faretta (2007, p. 45) make the same point, "Thus, as the client is at risk of becoming overwhelmed, thoroughly preparing the client to tolerate the intense affect that often accompanies the processing phase of EMDR is an essential component of therapy."

In order for patients with PDA or PD with co-occurring GAD, DESNOS, or an axis II disorder to be able to make informed consent to treatment they need to know that formative childhood experiences may need to be addressed later in the treatment plan. Generally, the best way to do this is to be straightforward, simple and direct in describing the elements of the treatment plan you intend to offer them. Once you have completed enough history taking and clinical assessment to develop an initial case formulation and treatment plan, you can describe the approach you will take in helping the patient resolve their issues and achieve their treatment goals.

The first order of business is to provide basic psychoeducation on panic attacks, the physiological symptoms they experience, and to clarify that, while distressing, they pose no threat to their physical health. Next, patients need to learn and practice self-control and anxiety management procedures to help gain some control over their background anxiety states. If they experience depersonalization episodes, they need education about these experiences and how to gain control over them. Finally, patients need to be provided basic information about EMDR reprocessing itself and the likely sequence and stages of their treatment plan.

PSYCHOEDUCATION ON PANIC ATTACKS

Patients need to clearly understand that the complete range of symptoms they experience with panic attacks pose no direct threat to their physical health. Accepting this reassurance can be challenging when patients are caught up in beliefs that there really is something wrong with them physically, causing these symptoms, or that these symptoms can damage them physically. To help patients reduce their fear of panic, it is important to offer simple easy to understand information about what happens in their bodies and brains when they are having panic attacks.

One possible exception is for postmenopausal women where a 6-month history of PD has been identified as an independent risk factor leading to a fourfold greater risk of heart attack. However, these women were also more likely to have other risk factors for heart attack including smoking, high blood pressure, diabetes, and a history of cardiovascular problems. Existing research does not yet indicate whether panic attacks reflect autonomic instability that predisposes to cardiac events or whether the physiology of panic anxiety triggers latent coronary instability. Postmenopausal women having panic attacks should be evaluated for comorbid coronary heart disease (Smoller, Pollack et al., 2007).

As mentioned earlier in this chapter, patients frequently perceive their initial episodes of panic to be immediate, life-threatening experiences. They feel out of control and at risk of imminent death. Many have been traumatized by these experiences. The perceived life-threatening nature of these experiences often seems just as real to them as for those external events that meet criterion A for PTSD (American Psychiatric Association, 2000). However, the many symptoms of panic merely represent excessive activation of the sympathetic branch of the autonomic nervous system. In situations of actual danger, strong sympathetic activation prepares the body for such coping behaviors as scanning the environment for threat cues and the intense muscular activity to flee or fight danger.

14.3 | Psychoeducation on Symptoms of Panic

Symptoms of panic begin with strong activation of the sympathetic branch of the autonomic nervous system in the absence of actual external danger. In situations of actual danger, strong sympathetic activation prepares the body for coping behaviors such as scanning the environment for threat cues and strenuous physical activity to flee or fight danger. Strong sympathetic activation releases adrenaline (epinephrine). Adrenaline accelerates heart rate (tachycardia), leads to rapid breathing (hyperventilation)—sometimes perceived as shortness of breath (dyspnea), and promotes sweating—to increase grip and aid heat loss. Because strenuous activity rarely follows panic, hyperventilation leads to a drop in carbon dioxide levels in the lungs and then in the blood. This produces changes in blood pH (respiratory alkalosis).

More alkaline blood lowers the firing threshold for many nerves. This leads to other symptoms, including tingling or numbness, dizziness, burning, and lightheadedness. In extreme hyperventilation, this can lead to tonic–clonic spasms in the hands and lips. The release of adrenaline during a panic attack also causes vasoconstriction, resulting in less blood flow to the head, which can cause dizziness and lightheadedness. A panic attack can cause blood sugar to be drawn away from the brain and toward the major muscles.

In extremely elevated states of anxiety, the combination of high arousal in the brain stem and decreased blood flow and blood sugar to the brain can lead to dramatically decreased activity in the prefrontal region of the brain and a temporary lack of coordination between different regions of the brain. This produces a state of depersonalization or derealization in which the person feels disconnected from the normal sense of self. One's body and the world can seem far away and unreal. Without an understanding of the cause of all these symptoms, many people having panic attacks fear that they are dying or going crazy. In fact, in spite of how frightening these experiences are, they are not dangerous to physical well-being and are not a sign of serious mental illness.

For patients who have experienced symptoms of tetany from hyperventilation, a brief explanation of how overbreathing leads to these intense sensations of tingling or numbness in the hands and face and tonic–clonic spasms in the hands and lips can be demystifying. Breathing into a paper bag is a widely recommended technique for avoiding the side effects of over breathing during panic attacks. This technique works because it forces the patient to rebreathe excess excreted carbon dioxide. Over breathing decreases the carbon dioxide levels in the blood too rapidly for the body to maintain normal acid–alkaline balance. Overly, alkaline blood lowers the firing threshold for peripheral sensory and motor neurons producing the strange sensations and eventually peripheral muscle spasms.

ANXIETY MANAGEMENT METHODS IN THE PREPARATION PHASE

Anxiety management methods can be helpful in giving these patients some increased control over their autonomic nervous systems and can begin to reduce the intensity and frequency of panic attacks. These methods were described in some detail in chapter 6. The most useful of these methods for patients with PD and PDA are square breathing and heart rate coherence training. Square breathing can be learned by most patients in a few minutes. When practiced two or three times a day for 5 minutes, square breathing provides patients with a sense of internalized skill over their baseline level of psychophysiological arousal. For simple PD, just teaching diaphragmatic and square breathing can significantly reduce the frequency and severity of panic attacks. In some cases, it can eliminate them. However, for most patients, anxiety management methods do not eliminate either their panic attacks or their fear of further panic attacks.

INTRODUCING BILATERAL STIMULATION WITH THE CALM PLACE EXERCISE OR RESOURCE INSTALLATION

As described in chapter 6, it is always a good idea to practice the eye movements or alternate form of bilateral stimulation (BLS) before starting reprocessing of the first disturbing memory in the treatment plan. Next, introduce abbreviated reprocessing with the calm place exercise or a resource installation. For most patients with PD or PDA the calm place exercise will be appropriate and will provide an additional tool for self-regulation in the preparation phase. PD patients should be encouraged to practice the calm place exercise—without BLS—at least once or twice a day without waiting for another panic attack to occur. Rehearsing the calm place exercise regularly together with square breathing and other self-regulation methods can help lower baseline anxiety levels and build the patient's capacity to shift state from an anxious state to a calm state. Simple, uncomplicated, positive responses during the initial safe place exercise with BLS provide an early indication that the patient is likely to respond well to EMDR reprocessing of memories of past panic attacks and contributory experiences.

PHASE 3: ASSESSMENT OF THE TARGET

When treating a patient with PD or PDA, the procedural steps for the assessment of targets selected for reprocessing are identical to those used for treatment of PTSD. These are described in detail in chapter 7. You begin with eliciting a picture that represents a sensory aspect of the specific incident to be reprocessed. Then you help the patient to identify the negative and positive cognitions and obtain a baseline VoC. Next, using the picture and the negative cognition, you ask for the specific emotion. You then get a baseline SUD rating on the experience and identify the body location where the patient feels it now.

When treating memories of past panic attacks, it is more likely you will find negative self-appraisals reflecting the perception of extreme danger—"I am not safe" or "I am going to die"—or a lack of control—"I am helpless" or "I am not in control." However, if attention later shifts to contributory experiences from childhood involving parent–child role reversals you may find negative self-appraisals reflecting a lack of self-worth such as "I am worthless," or "My feelings do not matter," or "I am invisible."

PHASE 4: REPROCESSING REQUIRES DECISIONS ON WHEN TO MOVE TO CORE MATERIAL

Procedures for reprocessing of targets for PD and PDA are essentially identical to those for PTSD and are described in detail in chapters 8, 9, and 10. You will move through the desensitization, installation, and body scan phases in the standard manner. However, clinicians need to be prepared to make decisions on when to follow associations to earlier contributory experiences based on an appraisal of the patient's sense of trust and self-capacities for affect tolerance.

Reprocessing begins with phase 4. The first target will generally be the memory of the first panic attack (see Table 14.2). Criteria for deciding on when to return to target and for how to deal with ineffective reprocessing can be somewhat different when treating PD and PDA compared to treating PTSD. As described in the review of the published EMDR case summaries earlier in this chapter, patients with PD and PDA vary in the nature of the material they report during reprocessing. Some, generally those with PD without agoraphobia, remain narrowly focused on each specific memory of past panic attacks and primarily report descriptions of changing body sensations and emotions. Others, generally those with moderate to severe PDA, will at some point associate to events prior to the onset of their panic attacks. These other events are often childhood memories with themes of lack of trust, helplessness, and profound loneliness. Patients also vary considerably in the degree to which they are initially prepared to address the core affect in these memories.

Some patients, as in the cases described by Goldstein (1995) and Fernandez and Faretta (2007), will better tolerate an initial, narrow focus on just the memories of the first and worst panic attacks while postponing work on their early childhood memories of moments of parental misattunement, abandonment, or parent–child role reversals. For these patients, should associations to these early memories begin to surface during initial reprocessing sessions, you should acknowledge the importance of their associations and express appreciation to the patient for identifying these important memories. Clarify that you will return to directly address these memories in future sessions. Then return to the selected target memory and continue reprocessing with this narrowed focus.

After these patients have experienced successful, completed reprocessing on the memories of their first and worst panic attacks, they will have more confidence in EMDR reprocessing itself. By working on the memories of their panic attacks, they will also have begun to restructure elements—the affects, sensations, and beliefs—of the central maladaptive memory network that contributed to their vulnerability to developing panic attacks. This will tend to make the eventual work on their contributory memories more tolerable. Often their current symptoms of panic attacks will have become less frequent and/or less intense. They will become more motivated and less fearful about getting to the root of their issues and they will have better access to the capacities to work through this core material for a permanent resolution of their problems.

Other patients, such as in the case of Sarah described by Nadler (1996), appear to be ready to confront core material from their first reprocessing session. From Nadler's description of Sarah it is possible to identify a number of factors that supported a clinical decision to allow associations to early childhood material from their first reprocessing session. These included:

1) She did not feel traumatized or overwhelmed by her panic attacks.
2) She had reported only one major and numerous partial panic attacks.
3) She did not meet full criteria for agoraphobia.
4) She tolerated the anxiety she experienced when alone.
5) She was not sensitive to situations from which escape might have been difficult.
6) She had a good social support network and did well socially.
7) She was reading a book on panic, which she thought would help her cope.
8) She asked to be seen as needed and wanted to master the panic on her own.

All these factors indicated what appeared to be a generally milder case with only moderate anxiety, recent onset of panic attacks, and few, if any, behavioral avoidance symptoms. She presented with a self-perception of being resourceful and wanting to use treatment to support a move toward greater autonomy and independence. The presence of so many factors indicating general resilience, ego strength, and self-capacities together with the absence of significant agoraphobia all supported Nadler's decision to bypass the normally required preparation phase and allow immediate in depth reprocessing on spontaneous associations to core childhood material. If we were to put PD and PDA cases on a spectrum from mild, to moderate, to severe, the case of Sarah would be near the mild end of the spectrum. Yet even in this "mild" case of PD, Nadler correctly hypothesized that due to Sarah's life experiences, EMDR reprocessing would quickly open up "repressed feelings of loss and fears of imminent independence which would evoke unresolved attachment issues" (Nadler, 1996).

14.4 | When to Consider Pruning Early Associations to Core Material in PDA

The greater the presence of the following factors, the greater the need to consider planning to "prune" associations to core maladaptive childhood material and returning attention to the selected memory of a panic attack during the initial series of EMDR reprocessing sessions on memories of panic attacks.

1) Limited or negative responses to the calm place exercise during BLS
2) Reporting depersonalization or derealization just before or during panic attacks
3) Feeling traumatized or overwhelmed by panic attacks
4) Reporting current panic episodes that last for more than an hour
5) Sensitivity to situations from which escape might be difficult
6) Meeting full criteria for moderate to severe agoraphobia
7) Inability to tolerate anxiety when alone
8) Absence of a good social support network and or other social problems
9) Reluctance or refusal to practice anxiety management skills at home
10) Inability to benefit from practicing anxiety management skills
11) Requests to be seen at home or more often than once per week
12) Dependence on moderate to high doses of benzodiazepine medication
13) Co-occurring GAD, DESNOS, or an axis II disorder.

Not all cases of simple PD will need to address core issues from childhood. In many cases of simple PD, EMDR reprocessing will remain focused on the physical sensations and emotions directly associated with targeted memories of panic attacks. However, when you have reasons to hypothesize the presence of such core maladaptive memory networks from childhood, you must be alert to the potential need to narrow the focus of attention in early reprocessing sessions by "pruning" associations to this core material and refocusing back to the selected target memory.

PHASE 5: INSTALLATION PHASE

Normally, you continue the desensitization phase until the SUD is reported to be stable at a zero before proceeding to the installation phase. This generally remains true in cases of PD and PDA. However, with some patients with PDA you may elect to offer a modified form of installation of a modified positive cognition (PC) when the desensitization phase remains incomplete and the SUD has only dropped to a 2, 3, or 4. In these cases, when it is clear that the initial EMDR reprocessing session on the first panic memory will not be completed in one session, you can consider offering the following modified form of installation of a modified PC. "When you focus on the memory, as it seems to you now, what positive statement can you make about what you have learned or gained from our work on this memory today?" When electing to offer installation of a modified PC during an incomplete session, it is important not to press the patient to continue to a VoC of 7. Simply offer two or three standard sets of BLS checking the VoC on the modified PC after each set. Each time after you check the VoC, again link the memory "as it seems to you now" with the modified PC and add BLS. In this situation, you would not go on to do the body scan phase because this would clearly be an incomplete session. Instead you would use the procedures described in chapter 10 for closure of an incomplete session.

In most cases when doing initial work on memories of panic attacks, it will not be necessary to do anxiety reduction techniques as part of the closure phase.

However, if you have moved on to more intense core material from childhood, a more extended closure process may be needed to leave the patient in as stable a state as when they arrived for the session (see phase 7 below).

Assuming you have completed the desensitization phase for the selected target and have reached a stable zero SUD, you then proceed to the standard installation—phase 5 as described in chapter 10—checking to see if the patient still prefers the originally selected PC or if a better PC has emerged. You then have the patient rate the VoC and continue sets of BLS, checking the VoC after each set of BLS until the VoC is reported to be a 7 and is not getting any better.

PHASE 6: BODY SCAN PHASE

After the patient reports a VoC of 7 that is not getting any better, you then move to the body scan—phase 6. As described in detail in chapter 10, the body scan phase involves asking the patient to hold the incident in mind, then think of the positive cognition that was just installed, and scan for any notable physical sensations. If negative sensations are reported, you reprocess these until they are gone. Then you continue the body scan until the patient reports only neutral or positive sensations. If time remains and the patient reports positive sensations, provide more sets of BLS as long as the positive sensations are getting better.

PHASE 7: CLOSURE PROCEDURES

When treating PD and PDA it is rare to encounter patients at risk for tension reduction, self-injurious or threatening behaviors as is the case among some patients who meet criteria for PTSD, DESNOS, and borderline personality disorder. The presence of such symptoms would most likely indicate additional co-occurring disorders and the need for a more comprehensive treatment plan than covered in this chapter. When, during initial reprocessing work on memories of panic attacks, you move to the closure phase because the desensitization phase is incomplete, it is seldom necessary to use anxiety reduction techniques as part of the closure phase. When you have moved on to reprocessing more intense core material from childhood, a more extended closure process may be needed for some, to leave patients in as stable a state as when they arrived for the session. However, unless patients with PD or PDA are at risk for tension reduction behaviors or a relapse to substance abuse, the decision to offer anxiety management interventions during the closure phase should be based primarily on patients' own perceptions of their ability to tolerate any residual feelings or sensations that were activated during the session.

During the closure phase, clinicians should be alert to counter-transference urges to rescue PD and PDA patients from feelings that they are actually capable of tolerating. However, when patients indicate that they want or need assistance to feel calmer and more in control at the end of an intense EMDR reprocessing session, you should offer them assistance with the calm place, guided imagery, breathing, and other interventions that have been found to be most helpful in the preparation phase. On the other hand, a relatively small percentage of PD patients with more severe agoraphobia or with co-occurring generalized anxiety disorder or a cluster C personality disorder—notably avoidant or dependant personality disorder—may not be sufficiently aware of residual activated states of anxiety after an incomplete EMDR reprocessing session on core childhood material to express their need for assistance. If you have identified indications of patients' limited capacities for detecting activated states of anxiety during the treatment planning phase or in previous reprocessing sessions, you should be prepared to initiate extended closure procedures without depending on patients to identify their need for assistance.

When working with PDA patients on core maladaptive memory networks from childhood, it is helpful after completing extended closure interventions to allow additional time for patients to mentalize (Allen, 2003; Fonagy, Gergely, Jurist, & Target, 2002) about their experiences in the session. Typically, at the end of EMDR reprocessing sessions, it is easier for patients to have a greater sense of distance from and emerging new perspectives on what have previously been perceived as overwhelming states. Allowing time to support the process of reflection on what has occurred in session and on the new connections that are emerging makes it possible for patients to integrate greater self-understanding, self-compassion and self-regulation.

PHASE 8: RE-EVALUATION

After starting EMDR reprocessing, in subsequent sessions, review information from patients' logs and check the status of the target from the previous session. Standard re-evaluation steps are described in detail in chapter 11. If the previous session had been completed—SUD of 0, VoC of 7, and only neutral or pleasant sensations in the body scan—simply reconfirm the SUD and VoC on the previous target, then move on to begin the assessment phase for the next target in your treatment plan. If the previous session was incomplete, return to the target memory and resume reprocessing.

In cases of simple PD without agoraphobia or any other co-occurring anxiety disorder or an axis II disorder, clinicians will generally find that the model I treatment plan—described in Table 14.2 (Two models of treatment for PD and PDA)—will be sufficient. The model I treatment plan follows a simple version of the prototype "past, present, future" treatment protocol described by Shapiro (1995, 2001). In cases of PDA or PD with a co-occurring anxiety disorder or an axis II disorder, the two-layered model II treatment plan will generally be necessary. The model II treatment plan requires clinicians to assess emerging patient readiness based on treatment gains before making a transition from selecting targets based directly on panic attacks themselves to targets based on contributory memories from childhood.

MODEL I: MOVING THROUGH THE TREATMENT PLAN FROM PAST TO PRESENT TARGETS

When you are following the model I treatment plan for simple PD cases, re-evaluation will guide the decision as to when to make the transition from memories of past panic attacks to external and internal cues from current episodes of panic. When you have successfully reprocessed earliest, worst and more recent memories of past panic attacks, you will reach point when memories of past panic attacks are no longer disturbing. At this point you make the transition from targeting memories of past panic attacks to reprocessing external and internal cues.

PD patients may have fearful associations with certain locations or other external cues such as certain smells or sounds. For some patients such cues may involve places where "escape" is more difficult such as standing in the checkout line at the store or when riding in public transportation. After reprocessing past occurrences of panic attacks, these external cues also need to be reprocessed to make sure they are no longer perceived as threat cues or associated with rising anxiety.

When you make this transition, some patients may still be experiencing occasional panic attacks. Other may no longer be experiencing panic attacks. Continue reprocessing with all of the interoceptive cues that patients have associated with their panic attacks. These could include any of the common symptoms of panic such as palpitations, sweating, trembling, sensations of shortness of breath, sensations of choking, chest pain, nausea, dizziness or light-headedness, derealization or deper-sonalization, tingling, chills or hot flushes. Because most of these interoceptive cues can reoccur for various reasons, it is important that patients no longer fear a reoccur-rence of these sensations.

After both external and interoceptive cues have been reprocessed, reprocess-ing should shift to future templates in which the patient imagines being in for-merly avoided locations and experiencing formerly anxiety provoking internal cues. Then patients should be encouraged to confront previously avoided loca-tions and internal cues through in vivo exposure to verify these cues no longer trigger significant distress and to reprocess any that still do. Treatment is not complete until the patient reports stable treatment gains are maintained during and after in vivo exposure.

MODEL II: MAKING THE TRANSITION TO TARGETING CONTRIBUTORY CHILDHOOD EXPERIENCES

When you are following the model II treatment plan for PDA or PD with a co-occurring anxiety disorder or an axis II disorder, two indicators can help guide your decision as to when to make the transition from reprocessing memories of panic attacks to reprocessing contributory childhood experiences of perceived abandonment, misattunement, humiliation, fear, and early parent–child reversals. The first indicator is when the patient reports decreased frequency and inten-sity of current panic symptoms. While a complete elimination of current panic symptoms would be a strong signal for this transition, it is sometimes possible to make the transition to core childhood material before current panic symptoms have been completely eliminated. More commonly, you will observe a substantial decrease—often on the order of 50%–80%—in frequency, duration and intensity of current panic attacks. Parallel with these changes in overt panic symptoms is another significant indicator.

The second indicator of readiness for this transition is when you observe changes in patients' attitudes about interoceptive signals of anxiety and the asso-ciated underlying emotional states of loneliness, fear, or grief. As patients make progress in reprocessing memories of panic attacks, they gradually gain great-er confidence in their emerging capacities for self-acceptance and self-soothing. These growing self-capacities for self-regulation may be reflected in frequency, duration, and intensity of current panic attacks. They may also be directly sig-naled by verbalizations of less fear about current panic episodes and some con-fidence that with further progress on contributory experiences, episodes of panic could come to an end. As these indications of progress appear, discussions will naturally turn deciding when the patient is ready to directly address these early childhood memories.

In addition to shifts in their attitudes about the experience of panic attacks themselves, patients signal their readiness to transition to reprocessing contribu-tory childhood experiences by a growing *awareness* and increased verbalization of their *realization* that these experiences have been contributory and need to be addressed. These verbalizations often reflect patients' shifts in perception from a cognitive recognition that these experiences *may* have played a role in their vulner-ability to developing PD to a *felt-experience* of the ways in which these childhood experiences actually underlie their dread of panic.

The extent of patients' needs to reprocess contributory childhood experiences varies from needing to address only one or two incidents with a single caregiver to a number of experiences, involving more than one caregiver or siblings. As much as possible, it is better to complete reprocessing on a significant contributory memory before moving on to address other experiences. Principles for deciding when to shift between targets are described in detail in chapter 9. These same principles equally apply when working with the contributory memories of patients with PDA. Work on reprocessing contributory childhood experiences is complete when patients no longer report significant disturbance when focusing on these memories. Attention may then shift to any residual disturbances associated with current stimuli. These can involve external cues and situations or internal cues including interoceptive sensations and thoughts.

REPROCESSING CURRENT STIMULI

After successful reprocessing of past panic attacks and any contributory childhood experiences, turn your attention next to current external and internal cues that were identified during history taking and treatment planning or have been reported in during reassessment of feedback from current self-monitoring. Current stimuli can include external situations that have been associated with panic attacks such as driving alone in the car—often related to separation anxiety—or being on a bus, train or airplane—related to limited ability to escape, scrutiny fears, or concerns over lack of control. Internal cues can also need additional work after contributory childhood events have been successfully reprocessed. Internal cues can include any of the common interoceptive sensations associated with panic attacks as well as specific anxiety provoking thoughts. While reprocessing contributory childhood events generally will resolve most of the intensity from both external and internal cues, additional work on these cues is sometimes needed to fully resolve overly conditioned associations. It is helpful to maintain a matter-of-fact attitude of acceptance when patients report residual current stimuli remain distressing. If past panic attacks and contributory childhood experiences have been successfully reprocessed, simply continue to methodically work through the treatment plan. When current stimuli remain distressing, it is generally simply because these are overly conditioned threat cues that need further reorganization. Sometimes, it is helpful to consider whether current external stressors or current attachment issues are contributing to the persistence or recurrence of anxiety responses. In situations where current external stressors are contributing to persistent anxiety responses patients may need encouragement to target and reprocess these current stressors until they can identify and make use of more appropriate coping responses.

INCORPORATING THE FUTURE TEMPLATE

When, after resolving contributory childhood experience, past memories of panic and current cues, patients continue to experience anticipatory anxiety over the possible recurrence of certain interoceptive sensations or avoid certain situations due to residual anxiety, it can be helpful to incorporate reprocessing future templates. During reprocessing with the future template, patients rehearse reexperiencing the interoceptive sensations they still fear or imagine being in the feared situations to help further resolve associated anxiety. As described in chapter 11, initial SUD ratings should be low to moderate for these future template targets. When initial SUD ratings are elevated above a 4, you should probe for additional past targets by using the affect or somatic bridge technique described in chapter 4. It is also possible to use the positive template to help patients consolidate their treatment gains by successfully rehearsing functioning comfortably in previously avoided or dreaded situations. For patients with good visualization skills, they can be encouraged to visualize a sequence of events leading up to and through mastery of situations they previously could not tolerate or avoided due to fear of recurrence of panic attacks.

EVALUATING AND RESPONDING TO FEEDBACK FROM IN VIVO EXPOSURE

The only way to be completely certain that treatment has been successful is when patients expand their activities without reexperiencing symptoms of panic. At some point, patients need to make specific plans for in vivo exposure. In vivo exposure assures patients achieve their treatment goals by providing opportunities both for identifying residual targets that need further reprocessing and for mastery experiences that represent consolidation of their gains in treatment.

SUMMARY

While existing cognitive, behavioral, and pharmacotherapy treatments for PD and PDA are generally considered effective, a significant percentage of patients receiving these treatments either dropout or fail to achieve clinical goals. Published case reports suggest EMDR treatment of PD and PDA can help eliminate symptoms of panic and agoraphobia. Controlled EMDR treatment outcome studies of PDA have failed to show the same gains as the individual case reports. This may be due to the need to provide extended preparation phase interventions and apply the model II approach with a gradual transition to reprocessing contributory events. It is hoped that future controlled research will compare EMDR treatment of PDA with cognitive behavioral treatment and will incorporate the model II approach outlined here. Published case reports of EMDR treatment of simple PD without agoraphobia or other co-occurring disorders suggest it can be effective in a small number of sessions and that EMDR treatment of PDA can be effective when the model II approach is employed. Clinicians need to keep in mind the importance of offering sufficient preparation and trust building when treating cases of PDA or PD with other co-occurring anxiety or axis II disorders.

## 15

Cases Illustrating EMDR Treatment of Panic Disorder

INTRODUCTION

Next, we will explore two case examples: the first one, an adolescent girl named Hannah, and the other, a young man named Justin. Both were treated with Eye Movement Desensitization and Reprocessing (EMDR) for panic disorder without agoraphobia (PD). Clinicians who want to review a case example of EMDR treatment of panic disorder with agoraphobia (PDA) are referred to the detailed description of the case of Adriana, reported by Fernandez and Faretta (2007) that is summarized in chapter 14. Both Hannah and Justin presented with mild subclinical social anxiety, and both had contributory experiences in childhood involving chronically stressful experiences with a caregiver. Hannah had been suffering from panic attacks about 1 year, while Justin had experienced panic attacks and insomnia for 8 years. For both cases, record of treatment forms show session by session what happened over the course of their complete treatment. In the case of Hannah, I have included near-verbatim summaries for some of her EMDR reprocessing sessions. The case of Justin illustrates a treatment plan that needed to consider the interaction of a preexisting PD with a recent traumatic exposure that led to the onset of depersonalization disorder.

THE CASE OF HANNAH

Hannah was a 17-year-old junior in high school who presented with panic attacks primarily in the classroom and especially during exams. I saw her for a total of 12 sessions during a 3-month period. Through our work with EMDR, she quickly overcame her panic attacks, raised her grades significantly, and gained a new sense of strength to help her cope with the manipulative behaviors of her alcoholic mother. In her first session she explained that, in addition to classroom panic attacks, she experienced anxiety at other times when she was sitting alone at home just thinking about certain classes. Her anxiety would reach a peak when she was sitting in class, especially if she were seated away from the classroom doors in the middle of the class. She would start getting sweaty and dizzy and feel an overwhelming need to lie down.

 | Record of Treatment

List symptoms by name or letter from Master Treatment Plan. Indicate worsened: − 3, − 2, or − 1. Unchanged 0 or improved: + 1, + 2, to + 3.

For each session code activities with this key

Hx = History taking	RE = Reevaluation	SC = Structured Calming	RDI =Calm Place or Resource
Mem = Target Memory	CrS = Current Stimuli	Fut = Future Template	VT = Verbal Therapy
IVE = in vivo exposure	CBT = Cognitive	Art = Art Therapy	Hyp = Hypnosis
IM = Imagery			

Name: _____Hannah_____   Page: ___1___ of ___1___

Session	Date	GAF	Symptoms	Activity Target	Pre SUD VoC	Post SUD VoC	Selected Negative Cognition Final Positive Cognition	Outcome Homework
1	1/23	56	Panic	Hx Ed	N/A	N/A	History taking, Psychoeducation on Panic and EMDR	Treatment plan developed.
2	1/30	56	Panic 0	SC RDI	N/A	N/A	Diaphragmatic & Square Breathing Calm place - cue word: "Soothing"	Practice Square Breathing
3	2/6	58	Panic + 1	1st panic attack in class	8 3.5	2.5 N/A	I am weird and an outcast. I'm cool. I am a nice person.	Significant gains. Target incomplete.
4	2/20	59	Panic + 2	1st panic attack in class	3.5 N/A	0.5 N/A	Contributory memories identified. No installation.	Target resolved, technically incomplete.
5	2/27	59	Panic + 2	Worst panic attack in class	7–8 4	1.5 7	I'm weird. I'm normal. No BS.	Target resolved.
6	3/5	59	Panic + 2	Most recent panic attack in class.	7 1	0.5 7	I'm not in control. I'm in control now.	BS: excited instead of anxious.
7	3/12	60	Panic + 3	RE	N/A	N/A	No residual test taking anxiety. Positive images for future tests.	Hannah asks to focus on her mom next.
8	3/19	60	Panic + 3	RE Hx	N/A	N/A	History taking re mom's drinking behavior and angry outbursts.	Target selected. Worst incident.
9	3/26	61	Panic + 3	Mom's worst drinking & anger.	8 3	0.5 7	I'm a troublemaker. I am a rational person	Target resolved. BS: clear.
10	4/2	61	Panic + 3	VT	N/A	N/A	Changes in self-perception. A prior therapist supported mom's denials.	Greater confidence in self-perception.
11	4/9	63	Panic + 3	RE	N/A	N/A	Greater social ease. Tx to end. Refocus Tx to panic at movies.	Target selected.
12	4/16	65	Panic + 3	Panic in movie theatre.	7 3	0 7	Something is wrong with me. I am healthy and in control now.	Target resolved. BS: clear. Tx ended.

She told me that her anxiety symptoms had begun the previous spring when she was living in New York City with her mother and stepfather. The primary immediate stressor she identified from that time was telling her mother that she was going to move back to California to live with her father and stepmother at the end of the school year. Actually, she informed her mother and stepfather about her decision by writing them a note, because she was too apprehensive about their reactions to tell them face-to-face.

Hannah had been born and raised in Southern California. Her parents divorced when she was 3 years old. She continued to live with her father until she was 12, when her father informed her that she would start living with her mother and her mother's fiancée at the end of that school year. Her father did not offer her a specific reason, but Hannah gave me the impression that there was an ongoing power struggle between her parents that had continued long after the divorce. Over the course of several sessions, I pieced together more information about Hannah's troubled relationship with her mother. Hannah painted a picture of her mother as a maintenance drinker who drank to excess from time to time. She was generally narcissistic, arbitrary, and controlling, while remaining completely in denial about her dysfunctional behaviors. On the other hand, Hannah described her father as supportive and helpful to her. Hannah never said so directly, but she implied that her father was often worried about money and angry about the controlling and manipulative behaviors of Hannah's mother.

Hannah's father had remarried and lived with his second wife for several years. When Hannah had first gone to live with her mother she had been living nearby, so Hannah could continue to see her father on weekends and some holidays. A couple of years before, her mother's work had taken her to New York City and Hannah had reluctantly gone along with her. She had struggled at first to make friends and fit into the different culture in the big city, but she told me that she had made a reasonable adjustment. Her biggest difficulty in living in New York was with her mother's punitive and controlling behavior. She told me that her mother's fiancée was cold to her and always took her mother's side. Hannah also admitted that she was sometimes frightened by some of the violent criminal activity that happened in the big city. She told me about one violent public murder in a nearby neighborhood where one of her classmates lived. This gruesome event made the headlines and was the subject of discussion among her friends in school for several weeks. She told me that she saw the crime scene on TV. Afterward, she had trouble sleeping for a few nights and worried that she might not make it back to California.

None of these stressors seemed to explain why Hannah would have been more prone to panic attacks in the classroom during test taking. I asked her if anything else had happened in the classroom that led to her feeling more anxious there. Hannah then told me about a health problem that had affected her in the classroom. She said, "I got a stomach ulcer that really messed up my insides." She explained, "I would get really sick in the middle of class and have to go running to the bathroom. That's when I got into the habit of sitting by the classroom door, so I could get to the bathroom in time. My mom didn't believe there was anything really wrong with me. Eventually, the doctors found out what was wrong with me, and I was on some kind of antibiotics for a while. Afterward, I started to have these weird feelings and thoughts when I was in class that made it really hard for me to concentrate. I was still getting 'As' and 'Bs' on my homework, but I started to get like 'Ds' and 'Fs' on my tests."

After gathering this history and learning about the development of her anxiety symptoms, I gave Hannah some basic information about panic and explained the treatment plan I would offer her. I said that we would start the next week with methods to give her some control over the anxious feelings. After that, we would use EMDR to decrease the vividness of her memories of classroom panic attacks and help her brain readjust to being in a better living situation and being free of the ulcer. I gave a brief explanation of EMDR. I added that next week, we would start with using EMDR to enhance feelings of calm.

Hannah's Session 2

At her second session, I taught Hannah diaphragmatic breathing and then square breathing while monitoring her heart rhythm coherence with the emWave® PC. She was impressed by the large increases in her heart rhythm coherence as she was learning square breathing. I asked her to practice square breathing everyday at home when she was away from the stress of the classroom environment. As she got more skillful and confident with square breathing, I explained, she would be able to use square breathing when she started to get anxious in the classroom environment. Then I did the calm place exercise with her and added several sets of eye movement. She responded positively to the calm place exercise and said she was looking forward to getting started with using EMDR on the memories of panic attacks in our next session.

Hannah's Session 3

At her third session, Hannah said, "Today in my math test, I didn't have a panic attack. There was a little anxiety and then it went away. I was listening to music while I was waiting for the test. I've had a few anxious feelings here and there, but no huge ones." I asked about practicing square breathing. She reported, "I practiced the square breathing the same time after school at home everyday. It seems calming. I haven't tried it in class or before a test. At home, I'm already pretty relaxed."

We then went through the assessment phase of her memory of her first panic attack in the ninth grade. Hannah again told me, "When I had the ulcer, my mom didn't believe me. It got so bad that I wouldn't show up at class. They thought I was just 'ditching' class. Actually, I went to the library and the bathroom because I felt so sick. People asked me why I wasn't there. It was just that I didn't feel like puking in class, so I left." When I asked for her image for this memory, she replied, "The people were watching and asking me questions about it all the time. I'm a kind of shy person in school. It drew attention to me in front of so many people. It's not fun to have to run to the bathroom to puke. It was really uncomfortable. One day, I came back and they were watching a movie. I asked the teacher to be able to move my seat near the door, so it wouldn't be so obvious when I left." Her negative belief was, "I am weird and an outcast." Her preferred belief was, "I'm cool. I am a nice person." Her initial Validity of Cognition (VoC) rating was 3 to 4. When I asked what emotion she felt now, she replied, "Frustrated more than anything. When I think about it, which I try not to, it makes me upset because I wish I hadn't been so upset, because then I wouldn't be so anxious. It makes me frustrated and angry." Her initial Subjective Units of Disturbance (SUD) scale rating was 8. When I asked where she felt it, she replied, "I have no idea. It's more in my head." I then asked Hannah to, "Notice the image, that thought, 'I am weird and an outcast,' and where you feel it in your head, and follow the lights."

REPROCESSING TRANSCRIPT WITH HANNAH FROM SESSION 3

# EM SET	PATIENT REPORT AND [CLINICIAN RESPONSE]
23	Um, okay, that was really weird. I don't know. My mind definitely drifted though. That's for sure.
22	Um, I don't know. It's a weird feeling. I just started thinking about situations where this happened. How all those times I was frustrated with it. It's like, I don't know. Really annoyed by it.
23	There's like a weird sensation, a weird feeling in my head. I don't know.

23	I guess I'm kind of calmed down about it. I kind of have to let it go. Let it pass, I guess.
25	Um, I don't really know... It's hard to describe but I'm angry, but at the same time I'm relieved. [Notice them both, the anger and the relief.]
25	[Shakes head.] Hmm. My mind wandered to... I thought about a lot of people in my English class. I don't know why. I just did. I guess I just kind of... I realize in a way that they have more things they're concerned about than me and what I'm doing.
29	Embarrassment, because my mind flashed back to like one of the really bad experiences. [Which one?] Study hall. It was in ninth grade. I actually puked in the class. [Just notice that memory and see what happens next.]
30	Actually, I thought about the end of the year in that same class. I don't think anybody remembered or even cared that happened in that class.
28	Same thing. Just end of the year and everyone was happy. School was over and I was really happy because people had just forgotten about it. I was kind of relieved about it. I had thought it was unforgettable. But now that I am thinking about it, I realize it was unforgettable for me because it was my illness and I dwelled on it more than I needed to.
30	I started thinking about my grandparents and how comfortable I am around them, but ironically, they judge me more than the people at school. [That is ironic.] But in a weird way, I'm okay with it. I'm just happy to be around them.
T	[Let's go back to the event we started with when they were showing that film. What do you notice when you focus on it now?] I think that now that I think about it, more people were concerned than judgmental. The majority of people weren't even paying attention. I think that if I went and asked all those people today, I don't think they'd remember. I've never thought about like that before. I'm kind of content with that, I guess. [SUD] 2 to 3. [Worst] The actual feeling sick more than... before, it was a combination of feeling sick and being embarrassed with what everyone else was thinking. It's still traumatic in a way because of the actual ulcer.
28	Not exactly sure. [Drumming with fingers on arms of the chair.] I'm still angry or disappointed that I even got sick in the first place. Angry it happened at school rather than when I was at home or whatever. I'm also angry because that feeling probably wouldn't have been there that day if my mom had believed me sooner. Because a lot of these experiences progressively got worse. This was when it was at its worst and she didn't believe me. Of course, when I stopped going to class, she finally took me and I finally got some medicine.
25	Well, uh, I remember being anxious to finish school everyday because I wanted to end the feeling that everyone was watching me. So when I was at home, I wasn't being watched or being judged. I was just relieved when the day was over.
29	Thinking about the contrast. How happy I was at home compared with how I was at school and how they were opposite. How it wasn't really fair. I felt cheated or something like that. You just shouldn't feel so miserable at school. You shouldn't be overly excited to get home.

At this point, we were running out of time in the session. I praised Hannah for doing a good job of just noticing and reporting what she noticed. I explained that we would continue work on this memory the next session. Then, I asked her what her impressions of EMDR were from the session. She answered, "It's definitely helping me. Some of these feelings I haven't thought about in a long time. It's weird. It's mixed emotions. It definitely changed one view. Now that I've thought about it, people weren't thinking about me as much as I thought."

Hannah's Session 4

Hannah's father called to cancel her next scheduled appointment because Hannah had spent the night in the hospital with an elevated fever that turned out to just be a flu-like virus. By the next week, Hannah was fully recovered, back in school, and caught up on her schoolwork. I asked about any in-class panic or anxiety attacks, especially during exams. She reported, "I haven't had any anxiety on the last few tests. I had some anxiety when I got sick, maybe related to how much work I would have to do to get caught up. I was a bit anxious about whether I would have to throw up, but I never did." I asked Hannah what she noticed after the EMDR session 2 weeks ago. "I haven't had any anxiety at all. It's a good thing not to have anxiety. I did some square breathing in Spanish class when I was getting sick. I was feeling light headed. I did the square breathing and sat there a minute. It helped calm me down. My heart slowed down. I was still a little woozy. I haven't needed to use the square breathing in class except for that." With another positive report on Hannah's ability to use the square breathing when needed and with no new material emerging, I moved to resume reprocessing the incomplete target from our previous session.

I asked Hannah, "What do you notice when you focus on that memory we worked on last time from ninth grade, when you were sick with that ulcer?" She answered, "I wish it had not happened. I've come to terms with the fact I cannot change it. I don't think I can blame myself. No one was really paying attention to what I was doing. When we were doing the EMDR, my mind wandered to what someone else would be thinking. I realized no one else was concerned about what I was doing. I guess you could call me content." I checked the SUD level. Hannah reported it as, "3, 3 or 4 tops."

I asked, "What about the memory, is it still disturbing now?" She explained, "It's that you're always scared about what others are thinking. I think it's the fact of being uncomfortable and not. . . I don't know if I was worried about not making it to the bathroom and what if something worse happened,. What could have happened." I asked her to, "Notice that and follow the lights."

REPROCESSING TRANSCRIPT WITH HANNAH FROM SESSION 4

# EM SET	PATIENT REPORT AND [CLINICIAN RESPONSE]
27	Well, again I thought about what could have happened. I thought about when I was in that situation wanting to run out, and then I fall, and something embarrassing happens. That's what my mind went to.
27	Well, I thought about. . . the same time we were watching the movie and I was by the door. I was really nervous, nervous and angry.
26	My mind wandered to, have you ever seen that show, *Heroes*? I thought of my math class last year. I guess you'd call it happy, lonely, but happy. I get really entertained by that show, but when it's over, I'm like, "What now?" I kind of forget about everything else that's going on.
T	I don't really know. It's almost like I don't care. I'm just sort of over it in a sense. It happened, but I don't know. It's weird. It's not that I don't care. [SUD?] I got to think for a minute. Maybe like a 2, 2.5 or 2. [Worst?] I don't know actually. Something about it still bothers me. I don't know what. [Here, I read aloud the section from the previous session about Hannah being angry that her mother hadn't believed her earlier.] That's definitely an accurate statement.
24	Uh, kind of PO'd ["Pissed off"]. I guess you could say. That statement actually is, the sad thing about that is, it's true. It brought me back to all the times she's done something crazy or irrational. Or it doesn't make sense. I thought about the exact time the doctor called her and told her I had something, and she was like shocked like she didn't believe me. She seemed to think I did nothing all day and just wasted my time. It really frustrates me. After thinking all that, I'm pretty irritated.

26	Well, I thought about an argument we had, and then I thought about nothing. Around the time I was sick. . . It's weird. I wrote in English class about what I use to alleviate stress, because you can escape from your world like when I'm on my PlayStation. This argument with her was when I was stressed out about being sick. She took my PlayStation and threw it off the stairway, and it smashed into million pieces. That really heated me to the point I've never screamed so hard in my life. It's weird. It's like you're possessed when you're that pissed. I would not have acted like that if she had believed me. [So it was about her not believing you?] [Interweave: Responsibility.] She always had this thing about me faking things. She is a chronic liar. She claims I'm faking it being sick, but the reality is she is a chronic liar.
26	I'm still very upset. I'm thinking about other times she's lied. I guess it's hurtful that (a) she doesn't believe me and (b) that she is a hypocrite. It's not fair. I have to come to terms with, that is the way she is, and that's why I'm no longer living there. I guess it's better to know what she's really like than not to know what she's really like. I don't think the people I was in class with in ninth grade, I'll ever see again. Its been 2 years and you gotta move on and let go. One of my problems is I've been holding on to things from my past for too long. I have a precondition to hold onto things forever. [Maybe what you've been holding onto is anger with her, only it's been showing up as anxiety.] There's definitely a lot of anger. Fifty percent of my stored anger is about her. You hope the good times would outweigh the bad times, but with her, that's not true. That makes me mad. One thing that comforts me, she's made like ten other people feel that same way. I'm not the only one who has this whole deal. They've dealt with their anger in a different way. [Who do you mean, other kids or adults?] My sister who is 22, my dad, and other adults. [So they've had more growing-up time to learn to deal with someone like your mom.] [Here, I was (a) normalizing Hannah's anger, (b) offering an interweave to externalize responsibility, and (c) suggesting new choices that Hannah can develop skills for coping with her mother.] [So maybe in another session, we could focus on the stored anger you have with your mom and think about what events that it's linked to.] It started before I got sick. [Back to target.]
T	[SUD?] If mom's not part of it, I'd give it a 0 or a 1. The anxiety has been dealt with. The only other part of it is anger and irritation.

Normally, I would avoid returning to target and checking the SUD at the end of the session. In this session, I was confident that Hannah would report a near 0 SUD. There was not enough time left in the session to go on to the installation phase. Returning to target was a way to shift attention away from the contributory memories in which Hannah was angry with her mom for repeatedly accusing her of lying. By returning to target, I could help refocus Hannah's attention to the gains she had made in reprocessing the classroom anxiety and the situational cues with which her illness had led to fears of negative social attention from her peers.

Hannah's Session 5

At her fifth session the next week, Hannah reported that she had not felt any significant anxiety at school. She said, "I had a little anxiety in English for a test, but nothing major. It wasn't to the point that I had to leave or was really distracted. I was able to focus on the test. Sometimes, the anxiety flames up really bad, but I haven't had any of that." I then explored Hannah's thoughts about our focus of attention for the session. I mentioned the contributory experiences with her mom that Hannah referred to at the end of the previous session and asked where she wanted to focus her attention. She said, "I know that there's still a lot of stored anger with her, but I'd like to get past this test-taking anxiety so I can pull my grades up. Otherwise, I know she's going to be giving me a hard time. She's like maybe coming out to buy me a car. That's all she's going to be talking about. She'd say like, 'If you're too lazy to study, why should I get you a car?' So let's stay with the panic and test taking."

I then probed for the worst of the panic attacks Hannah had experienced since she had recovered from the ulcer. "The worst was during my last few days in New York. I couldn't sleep or eat. I got up at 1 AM. Mom asked, 'What are you doing up?' I'm too nervous. She said, 'Go back to bed.' I had the worst panic attack at home at nighttime. I wanted nothing to do with my mother and stepfather." With Hannah's request to focus on her classroom anxiety attacks, I was concerned that this memory of a panic attack at home would take us away from her school issues and directly into the material with her mother. So I said, "How about we think about dealing with that memory later and today, let's focus on the worst panic attack you had in school." Hannah then said, "That happened toward the end of tenth grade. During final tests, the last final in geography, I felt nauseous. I told the teacher I felt like throwing up. I had to leave. I told the teacher I had to sit outside the test because of anxiety feelings. I did really bad on the test. My mom was surprised because I had an 'A' in there, but then I flunked the final." When I asked for the picture, Hannah said, "I know for a fact everyone was watching me. I was in the middle of the class too and stood up. It builds up. I got sweaty hands. I got a sick feeling. I wanted to leave, but I couldn't leave without telling the teacher. Kids were saying if you throw up, throw up in the garbage back there." For the negative self-statement, Hannah identified, "I'm weird" and for her preferred self-statement, "I'm normal." Her initial VoC was 4. Her emotions were anger and frustration. Her SUD was 7 to 8. She located the feeling in her stomach. I asked her to, "Notice the image, that thought, 'I am weird,' and where you feel it in your stomach, and follow the lights."

REPROCESSING TRANSCRIPT WITH HANNAH FROM SESSION 5

# EM SET	PATIENT REPORT AND [CLINICIAN RESPONSE]
30	Just angry. . . or envious of other people who don't have it or don't understand.
26	Just thinking about people I know who don't have it. How I think before the whole incident when I first got anxiety, how much easier things were compared to now. I guess I took things for granted. You have to realize what you have.
28	Well, I was. . . I had a feeling of jealously, but then I kind of got, not sad, but just depressed or something like that.
28	I guess I'm kind of confused because I'm jealous of people who don't have it, I'm scared of how people judge me. Both those things.
29	I thought about the friends I have now. They understand my anxiety. I didn't make friends with bad people, but with people who would judge me the least. We all don't care about each other's problems.
T	I guess the people in there saw it as more of a joke, or a quirk, or something. They don't think of me negatively because of it. No one ever said anything negative about it. I don't think they even knew I had anxiety. Nobody judged me based on that. People could care less. Thinking back, what people might have thought at that exact moment, I know they get over it. I'm more scared of reliving it, even though I know I won't relive it. [When you notice the fear of reliving it, where do you feel that?] I'd have to say my stomach. When I get angry, I tense up. When I get fear, it's in my lower stomach. Like punched-in-the-stomach feeling.
31	Well, when I thought about the feeling, I got the feeling. Then I felt like punching someone. I got angry. That's about it. [Normally, my inclination would be to prompt here with the question, "Who do you feel like punching?" but this might have taken us back to issues with Hannah's mother. Instead, I refocused back to target and then checked the SUD.]
T	SUD: 2 or 3. [Worst?] Just the way. . . it's just frustration with the teacher who was very slow. . . He didn't understand what was going on. He said, "I'll write a pass. Hang on." The moment where I was waiting for him to write the pass and I was just waiting.

26	Well, just I'm excited, but it's hard to put it in words. Like you're irritated, but you're understanding. I was really pissed with him, but at the same time I understood why he was going so slow.
31	Just, not jealousy, but just irritated. It's not fair, but you have to move on.
T	SUD: 1.5. It always will probably be that because of the setting and you're always bound to be a little uncomfortable. Now that I've thought about how other people think about it, it didn't really affect their lives. I understand why the teacher was going so slow. If I thought someone was just sick and I didn't know they were anxious, I'd maybe be going slow with writing a pass. More kids make it funny. The more I think about each experience and I can reflect on what people think. I normally never think about things. I'm always preoccupied about things. [At this point, we were again nearly out of time for the session and even though the SUD was slightly elevated, I wanted to do at least one set of installation to strengthen Hannah's self-statement.] PC: I'm normal. VoC: 6. [Install.]
24	VoC: 7. Satisfied with it more. I know I'm normal. People wouldn't be talking to me on Facebook if I were weird.

Hannah's Session 6

At her sixth session, Hannah reported that she had missed school on Friday and Monday and had been sick over the weekend with a sore throat and swollen glands, but that she had been free of anxiety episodes since our last session. Her current lowest grade was in her toughest class, Mathematics. She confirmed she was getting "Bs" and "As" on her Math homework, but was currently earning a "D" because of failing some tests. She identified another recent anxiety attack when she showed up a few minutes late for class after lunch and had forgotten there was a test. "It was freezing cold. I was late. Normally, the teacher arranges the seats differently. I normally sit next to someone I am comfortable with. All the seats were taken except for one in the front–right corner. I sat down. I immediately started getting nervous and shaking. I don't know why. Everyone started the test. I started feeling physically sick. I asked the teacher to use the bathroom. She said okay. I went to the nurse, but she sent me back to class after 30 minutes. When I went back to class, I had to lay my head down. Then, when it was over, I felt fine."

The picture Hannah described was, "Walking in and seeing all the seats taken and being forced to sit next to someone I don't know and am not comfortable with." Her negative self-statement was, "I'm not in control." Her preferred self-statement was, "I'm in control now." Her initial VoC was 1. Her emotions were frustration and worry. Her SUD was a 7 with a felt location in her chest area. I asked Hannah to, "Notice the image, that thought, 'I'm not in control,' and where you feel it in your chest, and follow the lights."

REPROCESSING TRANSCRIPT WITH HANNAH FROM SESSION 6

# EM SET	PATIENT REPORT AND [CLINICIAN RESPONSE]
28	Um, I was not thinking, but... well there's one thing. I didn't have control, but I did because... like I was still able to leave. I'm confused because I don't know why I can sit next to certain people.
30	I thought about... actually, my mind drifted to English. Usually, I can't sit next to new people. I thought about one new girl. I thought I would be comfortable next to her, and I was fine. That's what I thought of. Just how that was weird that I could sit next to her. Maybe because she was quiet and didn't say anything.

23	Um, actually, I thought back to math again. I was thinking about the kid I was sitting next to that day. Because I don't put myself out there. I don't know a lot of people. Every time there's some change, I feel uncomfortable. Maybe if I put myself out there more, if I knew that kid, I would have felt more comfortable. [Here, Hannah begins to imagine being more socially outgoing.]
28	Um, I got kind of angry because I remember somebody actually made a remark about me not changing seats in English. [Location?] In my stomach.
27	Um, actually, I kind of got excited because. . . Well, I don't know. Well, nervous and excited. I was thinking, if I decided not to pick where I would sit to see if I could feel comfortable around other people. If I could, then that would stop me from having problems. I was totally nervous because if that doesn't work. . . you know. [Here, Hannah is spontaneously confronting how avoidant strategies have served to maintain her classroom anxiety, and she is imagining changing her behavior.]
22	Um, I went back to that experience in Math. I don't recall anytime that anyone noticed me leaving or coming back. I don't think anyone noticed, which I thought people did, but none of those people know me, so how would they care if I walked in or out.
26	Well, I noticed *I felt comforted.* Is that a word? Because I was thinking, at least I have a couple of people in that math class that I feel comfortable sitting next to. I'm fed up with the whole musical-chairs thing that I have to go through to be comfortable sitting to not have anxiety. It's kind of silly.
26	Well, I just got, not angry; I got tense. Because. . . no, actually, I felt like punching someone because I'm just so sick and tired of jumping through hoops over something so silly. "Oh, I have to sit here." I'm tired of it. I'm so focused on isolating myself somewhere in the class so I don't talk to anyone. It's not how it should be.
27	I am just coming to terms with the fact that if I don't . . . I think I'm causing some of this anxiety. I'm building this up in my head. The guy next to me doesn't care and doesn't mind. That's what they're focusing on. That I focus on other things, causes me to do badly on the tests, and stresses me out socially.
T	SUD: 1. Because I think nobody noticed. Everyone was focused on the test. I was late. You have to deal with it. That's just how it goes. I actually had some physical symptoms from the anxiety. Without all the physical stuff, it's all silly stuff. You think about all that and build it up in your head. I can't expect to live for another 70 years saying, "Oh, I can't sit in that spot." That has to end. If I do the opposite, maybe that will help. [That's an interesting experiment.] I have not had any anxiety for a while. I still am choosing my seats. [Worst?] The physical pain. My stomach hurts and I sweat. That part I can't do anything about. That's from my whole mindset. [Interweave: choices] [There are two things you can do. You can choose to sit next to people you don't know and you can do square breathing.] At that time, I didn't know square breathing. If I had, I would have gone to the bathroom and done square breathing instead of doing that fast breathing and making it worse.
25	Just that I'm prepared. I kind of just wish I had known the square breathing. That's it.
T	SUD: 0.5 PC: "I am in control now." I'd say I'm calm and ready to deal with any situation. I'm calm and ready to deal with it now. VoC: 6
25	VoC: 6.5
25	VoC: 7. I thought of something. In the beginning of the year, I took a lot of tests around people when I was brand new, and I was fine. It was freezing outside, and I was comfortable in the class. No matter who it is, bring it on. [Body Scan] I don't feel anything. I have a little something like butterflies. I think it's more of being excited to try something different. It's so daring.
24	Actually, this is going to sound really weird. My parents have been wanting me to get a job. I haven't wanted to do it because I'm afraid of having anxiety.,But I started thinking of applying for a job.

Hannah's Session 7

The next session focused on reevaluation of Hannah's test-taking anxiety and exploration of other settings in which she had had panic attacks. She reported no significant classroom panic episodes. She said, "I had one minor issue with some worries after changing seats in English, but I got over it quickly. In other classes, I went along with seat changes that the teacher imposed without any issues. I'm talking to different people. I went out Saturday and got a number of job applications, filled some in, and turned some in." Hannah described being back on track with homework and school projects. She was working harder on her homework as well. Her grades on her classroom tests had increased in all of her classes. I probed Hannah about her future test-taking attitude. She replied, "Neutral. I'm not worried. I'm in the middle." I asked her to imagine her next math exam. "I see myself taking the test along with everyone else. If I were anxious, I'd do the square breathing. If I were to get really anxious in the middle of the test, I could go to the bathroom and do the square breathing. Then I'd go back and finish." She was matter of fact and seemed quite confident of her ability to manage any residual anxiety and to complete her exams successfully.

With her in-class panic and test-taking anxiety substantially resolved, I explored for other settings in which Hannah had experienced panic attacks. In addition to the panic episode at her mom's house before leaving New York City, Hannah described having had panic attacks at one or two social functions and on a couple of transcontinental airplane flights. The panic attacks in social situations involved being with extended family members, who Hannah feared judging her for how she was doing in school. Now that her school functioning was so improved, she was less worried about recurrences of those issues. Hannah explained that she had realized that her panic on the transcontinental flights had to do with unresolved issues she had with her mother. She let me know that she wanted to reprocess some of the contributory experiences with her mother to be more prepared to deal with her during her upcoming visit. We agreed to discuss those experiences in the next session and to select experiences for reprocessing.

Hannah's Session 8

At her eighth session, Hannah continued to report an absence of panic attacks, increased ability to concentrate in class, and improving grades on her in-class examinations. She did have one minor anxiety episode during a mathematics exam that she was able to end quickly by practicing square breathing for 2 minutes while remaining in her seat. She was pleased that because of her improving ability to focus, she was able to earn a "B" on that exam. Hannah then began to describe the impact of some of her mother's strange behaviors. These included isolating herself in her bedroom for hours at a time, leaving the house without an explanation at all hours of the day and night, and being highly inconsistent in her treatment of Hannah. The most disturbing of these involved her mother drinking to excess and then becoming angry and yelling for an extended period on Christmas Eve. We agreed to reprocess this incident at the next session.

Hannah's Session 9

At the start of her ninth session, Hannah was excited to report on further progress with test taking. "I had the big 5-hour SAT test last Saturday. I think I did okay. There were all these people I didn't know. I went to sit by the door, but the proctor told me I had to sit where she told me to sit. I was fine for the first hour of the test. Then the anxiety started. I did the square breathing, and then it was okay. The rest of the test went fine. There was only one 5-minute break. I was amazed I got through without a panic episode. It was all strangers. It was all the circumstances that have triggered panic attacks in the past, but I was fine. I did fine in Spanish with an oral presentation today. That's about it as far as anxiety goes. I anticipated it to be worse than it was. If I had taken that test a year ago, no way I would have made it through. That was a long time to be in there. It was about 5 hours."

We then went through the assessment of the target memory that we had selected for reprocessing. This was her memory of her mother drinking to excess on Christmas Eve and yelling at Hannah and her sister. When I asked what picture represented the worst part of the experience, Hannah replied, "The fact that there was yelling on Christmas Eve. That really upset me. I'm a holiday person. You need to be happy on that day and enjoy it while it's there. She was screaming. That destroys the whole idea of it being Christmas." Her negative self-statement was, "I'm a troublemaker." Her preferred self-statement was, "I'm a good person." Her initial VoC was 3. Her emotions were "saddened and frustrated." Her initial SUD was an 8 with a location in her chest area. I asked Hannah to, "Notice the image, that thought, 'I'm a troublemaker,' and where you feel it in your chest, and follow the lights."

REPROCESSING TRANSCRIPT WITH HANNAH FROM SESSION 9

# EM SET	PATIENT REPORT AND [CLINICIAN RESPONSE]
26	I feel kind of little. When I look back on it, I feel like compared to my mom, emotionally I was nothing. I feel sympathetic to my sister. My sister was older and had to deal with it more often. I feel like I was powerless compared to my mother. There was nothing I could do to make her calm down or make the situation better.
29	Um. [Big sigh.] I'm just kind of shocked by how it all happened. It was over something really stupid. It became something really big. I'm just really disappointed that something so little became so big. It just doesn't make any sense to me.
26	I was thinking about wondering if every time I see her will there be an argument? Almost every time I see her, there's an argument. Will this continue on forever? It's really draining.
T	I notice if I look back on it, I didn't deal with things the right way. I need to take this and use it for the future like a reference. If something like this happens again, just calm down. I can't deal with her being irrational. I won't see her unless she can be rational. Now that I think about it, I think she was 90% at fault. She's the one who made the bad choices. I'd rather spend Christmas with my dad than her if she's going to be like that. [While Hannah was now old enough to make the choice for herself not to spend holidays with her mother, I was concerned that she was still holding self-blame for her mother's behavior. So I offered the following interweave.] [Who was the adult?] My mom. [Who was responsible for managing the situation?] My mom.
31	I'm just kind of disgusted because every time I think about this I'm upset that she would be drunk on Christmas Eve. That's what she does. When I think about her being the adult and her being in charge of managing it, I feel a lot better. She could have dealt with it better. I'm not her parent. I'm not responsible for managing her. When she wants to get a hold of her own life, she'll get a hold of it. I'm definitely disgusted with her being drunk on Christmas Eve. It really angers me. I think it's unfair. I didn't deserve it.
36	I don't notice anything different. What I was thinking the whole time was she should have managed it. Nothing else. I'm annoyed that she didn't. I'm hoping she remembers that. Basically the same feelings about it.
T	[SUD] 1.5 or maybe 2. [Worst?] The fact that my sister and I left to take a walk for 5 minutes to let my mother calm down. It was the fact we had to leave because her temper was so high. It kind of bothers me. She should have managed it better. She shouldn't have been drinking. She wouldn't have been irrational. [So focus on how it bothers you that you and your sister had to leave to wait for your mother to calm down.]

32	Well, I remember going outside and being really nervous and the butterfly thing [nervous feeling in her stomach]. I didn't know what she'd be like when we got back or on Christmas morning. Just nervousness from that. Because it's really unpredictable. It's like going into a cave with a flashlight. You don't know what you're going to find in there.
25	I kind of got, not anxiety, but an uneasy feeling just thinking about that. Course, when I got back everything was kind of weird. When we woke up Christmas morning, everything was supposedly fine and that was the end of that. She seemed to forget it even happened. I'm over here going "okay." {With the working hypothesis that bottled up emotion from experiences like this one that were contributory to Hannah's anxiety and panic episodes, I wanted to support her in experimenting with ways to express these feelings. So I offered her "unspoken words" as an interweave in support of new choices.} {So instead of going "okay," imagine with this next set of eye movements what you might have wanted to say then or would want to say to her now about what happened.}
29	I got some relief from that. I can picture myself on Dr. Phil yelling at her. Not yelling, but telling her what I really thought about that. I felt like I was really there telling her or trying it out in a way.
29	Like up here in my chest, I got kind of tight with an adrenaline thing. I pictured lashing out. It felt good. I pictured myself putting all that out there and saying, "It was your fault. How dare you ruin my Christmas and my sister's Christmas? It's unfair and selfish."
29	I just started thinking, "That's the end of it." I gave my piece and she can choose to listen or not. I just feel relaxed. That's about it.
T	[SUD?] I can't say 0. I think there's always going to be something about it that bothers me. I'd say 0.5. I know I wasn't at fault. I know I can express what I feel and maybe what I should have said Christmas morning. I guess knowing her temper can get triggered whenever she drinks. I can't control it. If she's going to drink, she's going to drink. That one thing, that her personality can be turned upside down like that is kind of amazing. [So, it's partially that the incident may always bother you a little, but also that as long as she has a drinking problem that will bother you.] Exactly. [PC?] I'd change it. I don't know if this works. Can you put it as, "It's not my fault." [And if "It's not my fault" then what positive statement can you make?] "It's her problem. I am a rational person." [VoC?] 7. A full on 7. No doubt in my mind.
28	VoC: 7. Body Scan: None.

During the closure phase, I asked Hannah to comment on her experience with the reprocessing. She said, "It's kind of amazing. A lot of these are things I've never thought about. It's cool getting a new perspective. It's kind of like a puzzle when you can figure it out. It makes you feel a lot better about the whole deal."

Hannah's Session 10

At her tenth session, Hannah continued to report an absence of further classroom panic or anxiety. She discussed changes in her self-perception since the previous session and described a few of the other incidents typical of her mom's unpredictable and bizarre behaviors. Hannah also discussed her disappointment with a previous therapist she had seen who had not validated nor acknowledged her expressed concerns about how her mom's drinking and odd behavior were affecting her.

Hannah's Session 11

At her eleventh session, Hannah continued to report an absence of panic attacks or anxiety episodes at school. She described mild anticipatory anxiety during a social occasion with her extended family. As soon as she started talking with one of her paternal uncles, it quickly faded, and she felt at ease. She told me more about the impact of her early life exposure to her mother's unpredictable behaviors. She told me, "Some days mom just wouldn't show up after work to pick me up from the library. I'd have to call my aunt to come and get me. I'd say, 'Don't I have a right to be angry?' She'd tell me it was my fault. It didn't make any sense. She'd say, 'You're only upset if you make yourself upset.' I realize now how bogus that was. Of course, I had a right to be angry with her for treating me like that. She just couldn't ever admit to any of her issues. She still doesn't."

She then remembered that her father had asked her to let me know that she would only be able to have one more session because of some financial issues that had come up for the family. Realizing that we would not be able to work through all the experiences with her mother that had contributed to her vulnerability to anxiety issues, I decided to probe for any residual settings in which she experienced panic attacks. Hannah described the panic episodes she had experienced in movie theatres. "I can't sit in the middle. I get too claustrophobic. I'm always pretty much on the end. That began in New York City last year. I'd get anxiety like I was going to puke or something. It happened after I got the ulcer. I got really bad anxiety from that. I felt like I was going to puke, but I didn't. I still have that occasionally with movie theatres." We agreed to reprocess this experience at our next and last session.

Hannah's Session 12

Hannah reported a complete absence of panic or anxiety in the classroom or during exams. She also said that she noticed she was experimenting with being more outgoing. She said she realized she could sit next to anyone. She reported starting conversations with students that she had not interacted with or spoken to before. She seemed to be experiencing herself as more socially acceptable. We then went through the assessment phase for the memory of her worst panic attack in the movie theatre. The picture that represented the worst part of the experience was sitting in the center of the row of seats when a group of people came and filled in the rest of the row of seats. "I realized I wouldn't be able to get out of the row quickly if I had to. All of a sudden, I got this wave of nausea, and I felt like I was going to puke." Her negative self-statement was, "Something is wrong with me." Her preferred belief was "I am healthy now." Her initial VoC was a 3. Her emotions were frustration and fear. Her SUD was a 7. She felt it in her stomach. I asked Hannah to, "Notice the image, that thought, 'Something is wrong with me,' and where you feel it in your stomach, and follow the lights."

REPROCESSING TRANSCRIPT WITH HANNAH FROM SESSION 12

# EM SET	PATIENT REPORT AND [CLINICIAN RESPONSE]
26	Um, I was actually remembering when I first got sick with the ulcer. It wasn't at the movie theatre. It was at home. When I realized that I had to puke, I barely made it to the bathroom.
28	Um, it's weird but I was thinking about how that happened at home and it happened at school a bunch of times, but it actually never happened at the movie theatre. It would always catch me by surprise at first. Then, I started like just being totally nervous that it would happen whenever I went anywhere.
27	Um, actually, I was thinking about how there are all these times I have been to the movies since I got over the ulcer, since I stopped being sick. Anyway, I haven't been nervous about getting sick every time I go to the movies. It would just pop up like at random times. Only like I'm sort of realizing now that it wasn't so random. It was maybe connected with things that had happened with mom being weird.

26	I was just thinking more about that it wasn't so random and feeling well irritated with her, but then I started to just calm down. She's the one who's always been out of control and I'm not responsible for managing her. That annoyance just faded when I started to think about it being her problem.
T	Actually, I was remembering when some of my friends were at a theatre with me watching *Pirates of the Caribbean*. The whole time I was excited about the movie and didn't think once about getting sick. It's actually kind of hard to really fixate on that the way I used to. [SUD?] 1.5 or 2. [Worst?] Maybe just a little of that irritation that it interfered with being able to kick back and relax for as long as it did. Fun should be fun.
26	It just faded away. I mean I had the flu 2 months ago and spent 1 night in the hospital. I don't worry about getting the flu again. It just seems like its history now. I can just sit where I want to sit.
24	Kind of the same. It just doesn't seem like a big deal now.
T	SUD: 0. PC: "I'm healthy and in control now." VoC: 6. [Install.]
25	[VoC] 7. It just feels true now. I know I'm healthy now. I'm not stressed about being sick or about being nervous at the movie theatre. I haven't been stressing about being nervous at school anymore. I can sit anywhere I need to sit, and it's just fine now. (Body Scan) Calm.

As we brought our last session to a close, Hannah and I reviewed her progress. She was completely matter of fact about the resolution of her panic attacks. She expressed confidence in being able to cope with her mother when she came to visit. She knew her mother would be controlling, critical, and arbitrary but, with her new perspective, she felt prepared to trust herself and not get caught up in her mother's manipulations. When I asked her to describe her thoughts about the EMDR reprocessing Hannah said, "It's kind of amazing. It makes you feel a lot better about the whole deal."

Hannah's case illustrates several of the issues described in chapter 14. First, her case shows the rapidity of treatment effects that can occur with EMDR reprocessing in cases of PD, or another co-occurring anxiety, or Axis II disorder. Second, her case illustrates the differences and interrelation between *etiological* and *contributory* experiences. Although she had many stressful experiences with her mother in her early years, Hannah had never suffered from panic attacks until she became ill with an ulcer that made her vulnerable to sudden unexpected bouts of nausea and vomiting. Clearly, her experiences when she had the ulcer were the direct *etiological* cause of her panic attacks. It was therefore possible to start treating her PD by targeting and reprocessing these *etiological* experiences and the cues associated with panic attacks without having to reprocess the *contributory* experiences with her mother. However, her mother's role in minimizing her illness and her mother's long-standing pattern of critical, blaming, and controlling behaviors were clearly contributory factors, both to Hannah's vulnerability to the development of a PD and to other impacts, such as some emerging social anxiety, fears of being judged and rejected by family members and peers, and Hannah's diminished sense of self-confidence and self-worth.

Her family's financial issues led to a somewhat abrupt decision to end her therapy before we could comprehensively address the full range of Hannah's contributory experiences in her relationship with her mother. While the contributory issues with her mother were often present in the background of our session and were a focus of several discussions, we only were able to devote one reprocessing session to a memory related to her issues with her mother. Because of her youth and a number of resiliency factors including her positive relationship with her father and stepmother, Hannah was able to make substantial and rapid gains both in eliminating panic attacks and in strengthening her self-confidence and sense of self-worth.

The Case of Justin: Panic Disorder With Depersonalization

When Justin presented for treatment, he was a 20-year-old junior college student. At his first session, he told me that he began having panic attacks 8 years earlier when he was in the seventh grade. He said that his first panic attack occurred when he was in bed and about to fall asleep. "I thought I was going to die." He continued to have panic attacks several nights a week over the next 8 years up to the time he came to see me. Understandably, he developed poor sleep habits by avoiding going to bed out of fear of having more panic attacks. By the time he came in to see me, he was averaging only 3 to 4 hours of sleep each night because of episodes of depersonalization in the middle of the night.

At his first session, I gathered basic information about Justin's family history. Justin told me that his mother and father divorced when he was 4 years old. He grew up with his mother and a stepfather with whom he described having a difficult relationship "for a while." "My stepfather was raised by a stern father and that's how he was with me. He didn't show emotions. He expected me to do everything for myself. He yelled at home a lot." He reported no traumatic events in his childhood and denied ever experiencing physical or sexual abuse. When I asked if his stepfather ever did anything more than yelling, Justin described two physical encounters with his stepfather. "He threw me up against the wall a couple of times, but nothing big." He described a positive relationship with his mother. "We talk everyday. Mom is really talkative, intelligent, nice, and understanding."

Justin described moving many times when growing up because of his parents being in military service. The year before he came to see me, Justin had moved away from the rural area where his mother and stepfather lived to attend the local junior college. He was living with a roommate in an apartment and working at a retail sales job at the mall. He received financial support from his mother to pay for school costs and to help him in months when his expenses exceeded his modest wages.

Regarding previous counseling or treatment for his panic symptoms, he reported only a brief period of counseling in high school when he was caught with marijuana paraphernalia on campus; however, they never discussed Justin's panic attacks. All of Justin's friends in the rural community where he attended high school smoked marijuana, and it seemed "stupid" to him to have to see a counselor for doing what all of his friends were doing. On the positive side, Justin had subsequently stopped smoking marijuana and did not drink alcohol at all. He was deeply involved with physical conditioning and went to the gym everyday. He has been in a relationship for more than a year with a girl who lived near his parents. Although she was several years younger than Justin, he reported that both her parents and his parents approved of their relationship. He hoped to marry her after he secured a job as a firefighter.

At his first session, I gave Justin basic information on panic attacks and sleep hygiene and taught him square breathing. I asked him to practice square breathing several times a day. I emphasized the importance of improving his sleep hygiene. I asked him to establish a consistent time to start getting ready to go to sleep and to get into bed. I asked him to practice square breathing before he started his going-to-bed rituals and right after he got into bed. Based on the information he gave me in his first session, I concluded that Justin was a good candidate for treatment with EMDR. My tentative treatment plan was to start EMDR reprocessing with his earliest memory of a panic attack at age 12 and then work our way forward. I planned to introduce EMDR at our 2nd session with the calm place exercise and develop a treatment plan with him.

At the second session, Justin stated that he had been practicing square breathing. He said, "It's been helping. Except for today in class I had a derealization episode. It felt like it wasn't me breathing." This was the first time he referred to experiencing a daytime derealization. He stated that in the week since his first session, he had 5 to 6 panic attacks per day with an average severity of 6 to 7 on a 0- to 10- point scale.

| Record of Treatment

List symptoms by name or letter from Master Treatment Plan. Indicate worsened: − 3, − 2, or − 1. Unchanged 0 or improved: + 1, + 2, to + 3.

For each session code activities with this key

Hx = History taking	RE = Reevaluation	SC = Structured Calming	RDI =Calm Place or Resource
Mem = Target Memory	CrS = Current Stimuli	Fut = Future Template	VT = Verbal Therapy
IVE = in vivo exposure	CBT = Cognitive	Art = Art Therapy	Hyp = Hypnosis
IM = Imagery			

Name: _____Justin_____   Page: ___1___ of ___1___

Session	Date	GAF	Symptoms	Activity Target	Pre SUD VoC	Post SUD VoC	Selected Negative Cognition Final Positive Cognition	Outcome Homework
1	2/19	50	a=0 b=0	Hx SC	N/A	N/A	History taking Psychoed on panic and sleep hygiene Sq breathing	Set bedtime Sq breathing 2–3x day
2	2/25	50	a=0 b=0 c=0 d=0	Hx	N/A	N/A	History taking: MVA Informed consent EMDR	Revised Tx Plan
3	3/06	50	a=0 b=0 c=0 d=+1	Mem #5 MVA	7 1	4.5 N/A	I'm helpless. I'm in control now.	Incomplete In session depersonalization
4	3/13	50	a=+1 b=0 c=+1 d=0	Mem #5 MVA	4.5 N/A	0 7	I'm in control now.	Complete BS clear
5	3/20	50	a=+2 b=0 c=+2 d=+1	CrS #c Anx in bed	7 1	7–8 N/A	I'm not safe. I am safe.	Incomplete Close w/ daytime nap on bed
6	3/26	50	a=+2 b=+1 c=+2 d=+1	CrS #c Anx in bed	6 N/A	1 6	I am safe now.	Complete Decreased fear of depersonaltion
7	4/10	52	a=+2 b=+1 c=+2 d=+1	RE Hx 12 y/o panic	N/A	N/A	Hx of onset panic 12 y/o + CrS	Plan to target early panic attacks
8	4/17	52	a=+2 b=+1 c=+2 d=+2	VT BT	N/A	N/A	VT: excess water, supplement, food intake, nighttime urinary pressure	Less H₂O Sq breathing Daily summary
9	4/24	53	a=+2 b=+1 c=+2 d=+2	CrS #a,c at gym	8 2	0 7	I am going to pass out and die. I am completely fine.	BS: clear Very tired Daily summary
10	5/1	53	a=+2 b=+1 c=+2 d=+2	CBT	N/A	N/A	Epworth Sleepiness Scale 12 Ref: Sleep study after Tx ends	Relax CD at bedtime for sleep onset.
11	5/8	55	a=+2 b=+1 c=+2 d=+2	VT	N/A	N/A	1 depersonalization after "breakup" with girlfriend Attachment insecurity	Increased mentalization
12	5/15	57	a=+3 b=+2 c=+2 d=+2	RE VT	N/A	N/A	Disoriented in nighttime 1x Current motorcycle-driving anxiety	Planned CrS for motorcycle driving

(continued)

 **15.2** | Record of Treatment *(continued)*

List symptoms by name or letter from Master Treatment Plan. Indicate worsened: − 3, − 2, or − 1. Unchanged 0 or improved: + 1, + 2, to + 3.

For each session code activities with this key

Hx = History taking	RE = Reevaluation	SC = Structured Calming	RDI =Calm Place or Resource
Mem = Target Memory	CrS = Current Stimuli	Fut = Future Template	VT = Verbal Therapy
IVE = in vivo exposure	CBT = Cognitive	Art = Art Therapy	Hyp = Hypnosis
IM = Imagery			

For RDI and EMDR sessions, you can list selected target memory, stimuli, or resource by ID # from Master Treatment Plan.

Name: _____Justin_____   Page: ___1___ of ___1___

Session	Date	GAF	Symptoms	Activity Target	Pre SUD VoC	Post SUD VoC	Selected Negative Cognition / Final Positive Cognition	Outcome Homework
13	5/22	58	a=+3 b=+3 c=+3 d=+2	CrS #d	7 2	1 7	I'm not in control. / I'm in control.	Completed CrS
14	5/29	58	a=+3 b=+3 c=+3 d=+3	HX VT	N/A	N/A	Reviewed Hx marijuana use with onset of mild social anxiety	Outlined steps to lessen social anxiety
15	6/5	61	a=+3 b=+3 c=+3 d=+3	RE VT	N/A	N/A	Reviewed sleep hygiene and diet No anxiety or depersonaltion episodes	End H_2O intake by 7 PM
16	6/12	60	a=+3 b=+3 c=+3 d=+3	RE CBT	N/A	N/A	Identified tendency to rumination and worry	Continue evening review
17	6/19	63	a=+3 b=+3 c=+3 d=+3	RE CBT	N/A	N/A	Reviewed coping skills to lessen rumination and worry	Practice problem solving
18	6/25	63	a=+3 b=+3 c=+3 d=+3	RE	N/A	N/A	Reviewed career goals and concerns	Follow-up scheduled
19	7.17	66	a=+3 b=+3 c=+3 d=+3	RE	N/A	N/A	Reviewed current functioning and treatment gains	Treatment ended

15.3 | Justin's Treatment Plan

MASTER TREATMENT PLAN CHART

List memories and resources from earliest (top) to most recent (bottom)

Name: _____ Justin _____   Page: _1_ of _1_

ID	AGE	TRAUMA MEMORY OR PERSISTENT STRESSOR DATE(S) OF TREATMENT AND POST-TX SUDS	ID	AGE	RESOURCE MEMORY DATE(S) OF TX AND POST RDI VOR
1	4	Parents divorced (N/A)	A		Being comfortable in bed for afternoon nap (without fears of depersonalization)
2	4–11	Frequent moves (military family) (N/A)	B		
3	6–14	Stern stepfather — thrown against wall 2x (N/A)	C		
4	12	Panic attacks in bed at night 3/20—SUD 7–8; 3/26—SUD 1	D		
5	20	Motorcycle crash 3/06—SUD 4.5; 3/13—SUD 0	E		
6	20	Depersonalization episodes 4/24: SUD 0	F		
7			G		
8			H		
9			I		
10			J		

List symptoms and associated current stimuli with Frequency (F) and Severity (S) 0–7

ID	SYMPTOMS	CURRENT STIMULI	INTAKE F AND S	DESIRED F AND S	DISCHARGE F AND S
a	Panic attacks	In bed and classroom	7/7	0/0	0/0
b	Insomnia	Nighttime in bed	7/7	0/0	0/0
c	Depersonalization episodes	In bed, classroom, gym	5/5	0/0	0/0
d	Motorcycle driving phobia	Parking lots / Freeway in country	1/5 / 5/5	0/0	0/0
e					
f					
g					

He added that, "I wake up every night and my heart is beating really fast. I have a derealization episode for a bit and go back to sleep. Sleep is still bad. I have had an episode every night for the last week or so." He then gave me some critical information that forced me to modify the tentative treatment plan I had been developing. Justin told me, "I forgot to mention that I was in a bad motorcycle accident at the end of last year." He then described unsafely driving his motorcycle in a parking lot at 40 miles per hour and crashing into a car that crossed in front of him. He flew though the air and landed on a shopping cart corral full of carts.

"I was taken to the trauma center. I had no broken bones. Everything was fine. My motorcycle was totaled. I was wearing a helmet." I asked, "How soon after the crash did your anxiety symptoms get worse?" Justin explained, "The first week or two, all I could think about was the accident everyday. About a month after that, my anxiety got worse. The depersonalization episodes just started in the beginning of February." Careful questioning then revealed that Justin had experienced peritraumatic dissociation after he hit the car and flew through the air. He also went into a state of shock and could not get up after he landed.

Once I understood that the depersonalization episodes were a new symptom and had only developed several weeks after the motorcycle crash, I realized that this new symptom was most likely connected to a reexperiencing of the derealization he experienced during and immediately after the crash. As we explored the changes in his symptoms after the motorcycle crash, it became apparent that Justin actually met the criteria for both preexisting PD and posttraumatic stress disorder related to the motorcycle crash. Justin was initially extremely frightened by the depersonalization episodes. Even after he had found out what depersonalization was through research on the Internet, he continued to feel helpless and frightened by these recent nightly episodes that had further eroded his ability to obtain restorative sleep. He also reported that he had developed motorcycle-driving anxiety that he had never experienced before the crash. I decided I needed to modify the treatment plan to begin reprocessing with the recent trauma of the motorcycle crash. The first treatment goal was to address the new and debilitating symptom of depersonalization that was interfering with his school functioning and disrupting his sleep. After reprocessing the motorcycle crash and eliminating or at least substantially reducing the depersonalization, we could then target the pre-existing panic attacks themselves.

During the second session, I introduced EMDR as a way to resolve his anxiety symptoms and obtained his informed consent to EMDR reprocessing. The idea that EMDR might stimulate the same parts of his brain active in random eye movement sleep appealed to Justin. I explained my proposed treatment plan and he said that it sounded good.

At the third session, I decided to move directly to reprocessing the motorcycle crash without doing the calm place exercise and without teaching Justin skills for reducing episodes of depersonalization. However, during the reprocessing, Justin experienced a major episode of depersonalization and gave the stop signal. To address the depersonalization, I directed Justin through a sensory-focusing exercise. (See Exhibit 6.7 – "External sensory focus exercise.") He began to reorient, so we resumed reprocessing. To strengthen the bilateral sensory stimulation, I resumed reprocessing with bimodal stimulation using both eye movements and the vibrating paddles, but the depersonalization returned with even greater intensity. I then offered Justin a choice of several essential oils to help him reorient. He chose lavender. This scent helped him reorient. With a lavender-scented face tissue in his hand to smell as needed, we resumed reprocessing with bimodal stimulation. He held the face tissue to his nose several times between sets of eye movements, but he was able to continue the reprocessing. As we reached the end of the session, reprocessing of this first target remained incomplete. Over the course of the session, Justin reported a decrease in the SUD from an initial rating of 7 to between 4 and 5.

At the fourth session, Justin reported that he had experienced a slight decrease in nighttime anxiety and derealization. Before resuming reprocessing, I offered him the essential oil to have on hand. He again selected lavender, but left the scented face tissue on his lap most of the session. We resumed reprocessing the memory of the motorcycle crash. This time, I offered Justin trimodal stimulation, adding earphones with synchronized beeping to the eye movements and vibrating paddles. Justin completed reprocessing this memory with a 0 SUD rating and a 7 VoC rating on his selected belief, "I am in control now." In the body scan, he reported feelings of calm.

At his fifth session, Justin reported that he had experienced no depersonalization episodes since his last session and only one panic attack during a daytime class. This dramatic decrease in frequency of both depersonalization episodes and panic attacks appeared to confirm the working hypothesis that the onset of depersonalization and the increase in frequency of panic attacks were secondary to intrusions of unresolved peritraumatic depersonalization from the memory network of the motorcycle crash. If Justin had presented only for symptoms that developed after the motorcycle crash, I would next have targeted current residual symptoms of motorcycle-driving anxiety. However, I wanted to help him make further progress on his panic attacks, as these were still threats to both his sleep hygiene and his school functioning. He had no anxiety on driving his car and I frankly thought that a few weeks of motorcycle-driving anxiety might temporarily keep him from driving his motorcycle at excessive speed. Not only had the motorcycle crash been caused by excessive speed, but he had also been cited for speeding on his motorcycle several times.

So we turned our attention to reprocessing his residual current fear of nighttime depersonalization episodes that had begun after the crash. We targeted the recent experience of being in bed late at night and being fearful of having a depersonalization episode. Reprocessing led to a moderate episode of depersonalization and an increase in the initial SUD rating from 7 to 8. Justin again used the lavender-scented facial tissue and sensory focusing to help him reorient. I then confirmed that Justin had continued to always felt at ease in his bed when he took occasional afternoon naps. We finished this incomplete session by having Justin focus on a memory of being in his bed for an afternoon nap in the absence of fear of depersonalization. I did a few short sets of eye movements to enhance positive associations to being in his bed. We then closed the session with a reminder to continue to practice square breathing and to keep his log.

At his sixth session, Justin reported decreased intensity and frequency of depersonalization episodes, decreased anticipatory anxiety about depersonalization episodes, and decreased reactive anxiety when they occurred. He dreamed of being in a motorcycle crash, but in the dream, when the car approached he flew over it without being hurt. He reported less overall anxiety. He said that he could look now down from the second floor railing at the mall without becoming anxious as he had at intake. During this sixth session, Justin reported improved sleep hygiene with an average of 6 hours of sleep per night—twice the amount he had been obtaining at intake. He also reported having had one minor, middle-of-the-night depersonalization episode after which he had been able to go back to sleep within 5 to 10 minutes. It was clear that he was already considerably less apprehensive about this residual depersonalization. However, I believed that this residual symptom merited further reprocessing. We therefore resumed reprocessing of the current stimuli of his being in bed at bedtime with anxiety about having a depersonalization episode. While this session was technically incomplete, Justin reached an SUD of 1. This was a dramatically different result than the previous reprocessing session on this target when his SUD had increased from 7 to 8. I considered this a major milestone for Justin. Near the end of the desensitization phase, he reported realizing that much of the depersonalization had been the result of extreme sleep deprivation. He said, "Now I'm telling myself it's just so much lack of sleep." To support this reorganization of his associations to moments of mild depersonalization, I told him to, "Stay with that. Let yourself enjoy that tired feeling." Near the end of the session, as a result of the substantial decrease in the SUD, I went ahead with the installation phase, installing the belief, "I am safe now," to a VoC of 6. In contrast to our previous sessions, he experienced no in-session depersonalization. While I did not do a formal body scan because of being out of time, he reported no residual sense of depersonalization or anxiety, only a pleasant sense of fatigue.

Justin missed 1 week because of illness with a cold virus. At his 7th session, he said that he had just one daytime anxiety episode on the day when he was coming down with the virus. Justin discussed his sleep hygiene over the previous 2 weeks, and we reviewed his early history of panic attacks that had started at age 11 or 12. As I had suggested, he had chosen a regular nightly bedtime and reported going to bed consistently at 10:30 PM—instead of 1 or 2 in the morning—and rising everyday at 7:30 AM—instead of sleeping in on the weekends. Justin expressed concern over the possibility that he might have been having nighttime depersonalization and panic episodes secondary to obstructive sleep apnea (OSA). I pointed out that he had never experienced middle of the night panic or depersonalization until after the motorcycle crash. Prior to his developing nightmares and nighttime depersonalization after his motorcycle crash, his nighttime panic had always been at sleep onset and not in the middle of the night. However, I encouraged him to schedule an evaluation at a local sleep medicine center if he still had concerns about the possibility of OSA after his treatment with me was complete.

During our discussions of sleep hygiene and the effects of sleep deprivation, I explained to Justin that after an extended period of sleep deprivation, he had built up quite a bit of sleep debt. I predicted that as he began to sleep regularly, he would go through a period of several weeks where he would feel even sleepier during the daytime until he began to catch up on his sleep debt. Justin reported not having depersonalization episodes during the previous 2 weeks—except for those that occurred during reprocessing. He had only one daytime panic attack from the week before, which he now realized was related to the onset of flu-like symptoms that had persisted for a few days. Even though the reprocessing session from the week before had been incomplete and led to an increased SUD rating, Justin reported that he had been noticing he was actually less anxious about possible nighttime depersonalization episodes. I indicated that if he remained free of nighttime depersonalization, we might resume reprocessing the next week focused on his earliest memory of a panic attack.

Justin's eighth session was focused on the discussion of residual dreamlike feelings and fatigue that he was continuing to experience throughout most days. Review of his sleep patterns revealed that he was unclear about how many hours of actual sleep he was experiencing during the 9 hours he was spending in bed each night. His best guess was between 6 and 7 hours. It then emerged that he was drinking remarkable quantities of water to compensate for an over-the-counter nutritional supplement he was taking at extremely high doses. As a result, he had to get up to urinate six to seven times a night. I asked him to consider cutting back on this supplement and to cutoff his water consumption by 7:30 PM, 3 hours before his selected bedtime. In response to my inquiries, he confirmed that he was also having racing thoughts when he was lying in bed at bedtime and after urinating. I asked him to continue to practice square breathing before preparing for bed and once he was in bed. I also asked him to write a nightly journal entry as part of his getting ready for bed ritual. In his journal, I asked him to write down three things: (a) a list of unresolved concerns that he would address the next day, (b) a list of what he had accomplished and felt good about from the day, and (c) what he was looking forward to for the next day. I thought that this journal would allow Justin to empty his mind of racing thoughts and would allow him to fall asleep more quickly and deeply.

At his ninth session, Justin reported having had a panic attack at the gym the evening before our session followed by derealization later in the evening at home. I asked him whether he had been keeping his evening record of concerns, accomplishments, and events he was looking forward to. He confirmed that he was doing that every night and that he had been sleeping better. "I'm not tossing and turning anymore." He added that he had figured out that the cause of his panic attack was that he had been procrastinating his schoolwork. He recognized that he had been feeling increasingly anxious about the impact this would have on his grades. This was the first time that Justin had ever connected anxiety or a panic attack to a current issue or concern. It represented a significant gain in his emerging capacity for mentalization. Recognition of the cause of the panic attack helped give Justin a sense of control. I went through the assessment phase on his memory of his first panic attack at age 12, but the SUD was a 0 and he felt no disturbing emotion. I then did an assessment of the panic attack from the evening before. His negative cognition (NC) was, "I am going to pass out and maybe die." The emotion was fear with a SUD level of 8. We then reprocessed this recent experience of panic at the gym to a completed session with a SUD of 0, a VoC of 7, and a clear body scan. During the installation phase, he reconfirmed and selected his initial statement, "I am completely fine." He told me he had been experiencing a growing sense that he was going to be okay.

At his tenth session, Justin complained of persistent daytime sleepiness, as well as a dry cough, sinus congestion, an intermittent sore throat, delayed sleep onset, and residual awakening at 12:30 AM and 2:30 AM. I suggested that he review his program of dietary supplements with his personal physician and request a check up for his sinus condition. I then administered the Epworth sleepiness scale. Justin scored a 12 (Johns, 1991), which was just into the clinical range that calls for referral to a sleep specialist. I again told him that he should consider requesting a referral from his primary care doctor to a sleep specialist if the sleepiness persisted after he completed his treatment with me for his panic attacks. I encouraged him to consider using a guided imagery CD to help him with his occasional sleep-onset issues.

At his eleventh session, Justin reported an episode of depersonalization after an argument with his girlfriend when he believed she was breaking up with him. We explored the issues in their relationship that had led to this episode. Justin reported a pattern of jealous and controlling behaviors toward his young girlfriend although she had given him no cause to be jealous over her behavior. A brief check of his past behavior indicated that his behavior with other women had been questionable. He was then able to recognize that he was projecting guilt and insecurity from his own inappropriate behaviors onto his girlfriend. I encouraged him to take responsibility for what had happened, apologize, and make amends to her. This session again furthered Justin's ability to mentalize about the connection between unresolved emotional issues and conflicts that could lead to panic or depersonalization. I told Justin that his growing ability to monitor, recognize, and deal proactively with his current issues was his best protection against recurrences of panic attacks and depersonalization episodes in the future.

At his twelfth session, Justin reported one minor depersonalization episode when getting out of bed in the middle of the night to urinate. This was not what had awoken him, but was more like a state of profound sleepiness and disorientation and was not significantly disturbing to him. He reported that he and his girlfriend were again on good terms. He also reported residual driving anxiety on his motorcycle in certain situations. As he had not had a recurrence of a panic attack, I agreed that we could refocus our attention to reprocessing these current stimuli of motorcycle-driving anxiety at his next session.

At his thirteenth session, Justin reported a continuing absence of any further panic attacks or episodes of depersonalization. He described noticing improved concentration in class and when doing homework with decreased daytime sleepiness. He again reported consistently good sleep hygiene. The only residual anxiety he experienced was when he started to feel "dreamy" during a low stimulus portion of his 1-hour motorcycle drive to visit his girlfriend. We selected this current stimulus for reprocessing. He selected the NC, "I am not in control." His initial VoC was a 2 for the belief, "I am in control." His emotion was fear with a SUD of 7 and anxiety in his chest. Reprocessing was essentially complete with a SUD of 1 and a VoC of 6 and no residual anxiety. This was the last session in which we used EMDR reprocessing.

At his fourteenth session, Justin discussed his recent visit to his primary care physician and presented some concerns about mild social anxiety that had started in sixth grade. This appeared to be related to the frequent moves his family made in his childhood and the strain in his relationship with his stepfather. It also appeared to have been related to the onset of his experimenting with marijuana. We discussed the effects of marijuana on a young person's emerging sense of self in the context of his frequent changes in residence and peer groups and the absence of closeness with his stepfather. We explored steps that he could take to strengthen his social relatedness and decrease his social anxiety. Justin reaffirmed his decision not to return to smoking marijuana.

At his fifteenth session, Justin reported waking only once the night before. He said that he was getting an average of 7 hours of sleep per night. He discussed the absence of significant findings from his recent blood tests as reported by his primary care doctor. He reported continuing to push his caloric and fluid intake all day long as part of his workout routine. He had no anxiety on his most recent long motorcycle ride to see his girlfriend.

At his sixteenth, seventeenth, and eighteenth sessions, Justin continued to report an absence of either panic attacks or depersonalization episodes. He still experienced some occasional episodes of mild anxiety when he was not using appropriate coping skills with a current concern or worry. We discussed problem solving and cognitive strategies to address the pragmatic aspects of these concerns as well as to address the automatic negative thoughts associated with habitual worry. At his eighteenth session, we scheduled a follow-up session for 1 month later when we would discontinue treatment unless there were additional issues needing attention. When Justin returned for his nineteenth session, he reported no further panic attacks or depersonalization episodes. His sleep hygiene remained generally good with an average of 7 hours of sleep per night. As I had predicted, his daytime sleepiness gradually decreased and was absent most days. He stated that he was confident that the panic attacks and depersonalization were no longer issues for him and that he did not fear their return.

Justin's case illustrates aspects of the symptom-informed model of treatment planning described in chapter 4. Rather than focus reprocessing initially on targets related to his earliest onset symptoms of panic attacks, we began reprocessing on targets associated with his most recent onset and most debilitating symptom of depersonalization from the trauma of the motor vehicle crash. Only after significant gains on the worst symptom of depersonalization did we focus attention on addressing the history of his panic attacks. Later, we returned to addressing his residual motorcycle-driving anxiety. The decision to sequence targets in this nonchronological way was derived entirely from a case formulation built on the Adaptive Information Processing model. This careful sequencing of targets allowed for consistent symptomatic gains and a growing sense of mastery for the patient.

Professional Development

Try to put well in practice what you already know. In so doing, you will, in good time, discover the hidden things you now inquire about.

—Rembrandt

A man's errors are his portals of discovery.

—James Joyce

## 16

Professional Development in Clinical Application

GETTING STARTED—INTEGRATING EMDR INTO CLINICAL PRACTICE

SYSTEMS ISSUES: INFORMING YOUR SYSTEM

Clinicians currently being trained or recently trained in Eye Movement Desensitization and Reprocessing (EMDR) face a range of issues when introducing EMDR into their practice settings. Graduate students and pre-licensed and licensed clinicians employed in organized settings are generally required to discuss their treatment plans and choice of methods with clinical supervisors. In most cases, they will be restricted to using methods that have been approved by medical or clinical directors. Although licensed clinicians in independent practice do not face these requirements and restrictions, they do face issues of informed consent with patients—discussed in chapters 5 and 6. They will need to inform their referral sources that they are offering a new method of treatment and may need to deal with constraints from third-party payors. Patients who are being seen in long-term psychotherapy and who have become accustomed to one set of procedures and clinical experiences will have a range of reactions to the introduction of a new method especially when their clinician has hesitations or doubts about procedural skills and clinical integration.

Ethical guidelines and practical considerations dictate that these issues be addressed directly, openly, and frankly. Often, such a direct approach will be quickly successful at obtaining understanding and support, but it should come as no surprise that in some settings there may be opposition to change. Many clinicians have succeed in overcoming systemic barriers to the use of EMDR in organized settings by taking proactive steps to educate their system.

In most cases, barriers to the use of EMDR are based on ignorance, misinformation, or preferential adherence to one model of treatment independent of evidence of efficacy. One helpful strategy is to begin by determining the criteria by which methods of treatment are approved for use by the agency, employer, or third-party payor. Only after these criteria have been identified does it make sense to present evidence about the empirical status or other characteristics of EMDR. If the barrier to the acceptance is based on a claim that EMDR is not effective or not as effective as some other method, recent meta-analyses can then be offered showing EMDR to be equally effective as cognitive and behavioral therapy methods. Treatment guidelines can be cited showing EMDR to receive the highest ratings for efficacy. See Appendix C for listings of meta-analyses and treatment guidelines. If the barrier to acceptance is that EMDR is a form of hypnosis, evidence can be offered that EMDR does not induce a hypnotic state (Nicosia, 1995) nor does it require the use of hypnotic suggestion.

To support clinicians in educating their systems, resources are available from both the EMDR International Association (EMDRIA) and the EMDR Humanitarian Assistant Programs (EMDR HAP) online stores. EMDRIA offers brochures, articles, DVDs, and PowerPoint presentation packages and, in some cases, sends letters to medical directors of major PPO or HMO plans. EMDR HAP offers introductory DVDs and other materials.

COORDINATION OF CARE WITH OTHER HEALTH CARE PROFESSIONALS

Coordination of care with other professionals involves educating them about your approach and the methods that you use. Educating other professionals about EMDR often requires introducing basic information about EMDR as well as correcting misinformation. When other professionals have heard about EMDR, they may believe that it can only be applied to the treatment of posttraumatic stress disorder (PTSD). They often may not understand that EMDR can be applied to a wide range of diagnoses, where there are symptoms of anxiety or depression and maladaptive perceptions, attitudes and behaviors that are the result of unresolved adverse life experiences. Thus, they might not think about referring for EMDR for complex grief reactions, chronic pain, reactive depressions, or patients facing life-threatening illnesses such as cancer. Yet, as discussed in chapter 1, EMDR has been shown to be an effective and efficient treatment for patients in these situations. They may believe that EMDR is only effective for adults and not for children and adolescents. Although there is not yet as much controlled research for children and adolescents as for adults, the literature base is growing rapidly and shows evidence of effectiveness as described in the recent review in *EMDR and the Art of Psychotherapy with Children* (Adler–Tapia & Settle, 2008, pp. 6–17). On the other hand, other professionals may have unrealistic expectations such as believing that survivors of even complex, prolonged trauma can be treated in three or four sessions. Educating other professions about the range of cases where EMDR can be considered takes time, but it is well worth the effort.

ADJUNCTIVE REFERRALS AND EMDR

As your system become educated about your ability to offer treatment with EMDR, you may get requests for treatment with EMDR as an adjunct to another clinician's ongoing treatment. Although adjunctive treatment with EMDR is possible and can be beneficial, there are several issues to be considered. The first is to that such referrals tend to work out better when you have a well-established relationship with the referring clinician. In this way, you are already familiar with the referring clinician's level of training, experience, and clinical acumen. You are therefore more likely to avoid issues where your diagnosis and case formulation turn out to be substantially different than the referring clinician's. Some kinds of cases are more suitable for brief adjunctive treatment. An example would be a specific phobia that had a clear traumatic onset in a case otherwise free of complex trauma or structural dissociation. Cases where there is a complex trauma history, long-term relational trauma, significant borderline personality disorder features, or structural dissociation are extremely challenging to address on an adjunctive basis. Such complex cases are generally more appropriately addressed by accepting the case as a regular referral, rather than attempting adjunctive treatment.

Whenever you consider accepting an adjunctive referral, establish in advance the frequency and the means by which you will exchange information. Where you do not have a well-developed relationship with clinicians requesting to refer for adjunctive treatment with EMDR, it is essential to make sure that the referring clinician and the potential patient have appropriate knowledge and expectations for EMDR treatment prior to accepting the referral. This includes issues of informed consent—discussed in chapters 5 and 6—and your need to obtain an appropriate history and determine readiness for EMDR before you consider offering EMDR reprocessing. If you accept adjunctive referrals, you will eventually have cases where your diagnosis and case formulation differ from the referring clinician's. This should be addressed and resolved directly with the referring clinician before you proceed with EMDR reprocessing on an adjunctive basis. In some cases, after some initial positive experiences with EMDR reprocessing, patients may want to transfer their treatment to you and to expand the issues they are addressing with you. It is wise to establish in advance with the referring clinician and the patient whether this is an option.

LENGTH OF REPROCESSING SESSIONS

Decisions on scheduling the length of each treatment session depend on treatment setting, stage of therapy, stability of the patient, experience of the clinician, and the treatment plan. Shapiro (2001, pp. 101) recommends 50-minute sessions for history taking and 90 minutes for EMDR reprocessing sessions. Clinicians who are newly trained in EMDR should strongly consider offering EMDR reprocessing within extended treatment sessions lasting 75–90 minutes. Extended sessions allow clinicians with less experience with EMDR extra time for the check in and assessment of the target to be reprocessed, for the reprocessing phases, and for the closure phase. With extended sessions, 45–70 minutes can be devoted to EMDR reprocessing in the desensitization, installation, and body scan phases. In some organized health care settings such as staff model HMOs or Community Mental Health departments, sessions may be standardized at 45–50 minutes, and there may be little or no flexibility for longer sessions. Clinicians with adequate experience and skills in clinical use of EMDR have been able to achieve positive outcomes in patients with PTSD in such settings as demonstrated by the treating clinicians in Marcus, Marquis, and Sakai (1997) where all sessions were completed in 50 minutes at an HMO treatment center. Less experienced EMDR clinicians have sometimes dealt with this dilemma by completing the assessment phase (phase 3) on the selected target in one session and in the subsequent session starting reprocessing promptly. This is not an ideal solution, but it can allow greater time for EMDR reprocessing when it would otherwise be impractical. It is important to provide adequate containment and closure when conducting the assessment phase without going on to reprocessing in that session. During the intervening time, aspects of the target memory may have shifted, and it may prove necessary to recheck the Subjective Units of Disturbance (SUD) scale or modify the selected negative cognition (NC) and positive cognition (PC).

More seasoned EMDR clinicians may continue to find extended sessions helpful when offering EMDR reprocessing to patients with complex histories of trauma and neglect whose capacities for emotional self-regulation are less developed. These patients will generally require more than one reprocessing session for each selected reprocessing target especially early in the treatment plan. They will tend to have incomplete treatment sessions more frequently and need extended time for the closure phase. The closure phase for these patients may require more than one containment and stabilization intervention to help the patient return to a stable psychophysiological state and to put the material activated during reprocessing into perspective.

In some cases, even 90 minutes may not be sufficient time. Sessions conducted at in-patient treatment facilities and in some outpatient situations may be lengthened to 2 hours or more when clinical judgment indicates that this would permit completion of a unit of work best done within a single session. Such lengthy sessions can be tiring for the patient and the clinician and can be destabilizing if they continue to open up more traumatic memories without fully resolving them. Thus, longer sessions should be offered only when patients show clear evidence of adequate stability and gains following each longer session. Not all patients—or clinicians—have the mental energy required for more lengthy sessions. In many cases, narrowing the focus of attention to one aspect of the target memory and providing sufficient containment and closure for incomplete reprocessing may turn out to be better tolerated and just as efficient as 2-hour sessions.

Structure of Reprocessing Sessions

When you offer EMDR reprocessing within a standard 45- to 50-minute session, reprocessing with bilateral stimulation should begin within 10–12 minutes of the start of the session. Because completing the assessment of the target is likely to take at least 5 minutes, the check-in should last no more than 5 minutes. Closure and confirming the next appointment will also take at least 5 minutes. This leaves a maximum of 30–35 minutes for EMDR reprocessing. For experienced, skillful EMDR-trained clinicians, 30 minutes of reprocessing is probably the minimum duration needed to complete reprocessing for a single target. Clinicians choosing or required to work within a traditional 45- to 50-minute session will have incomplete sessions more frequently and will need a larger number of sessions to complete their treatment plans than those who are able to use extended sessions. However, other considerations such as organizational policies, scheduling issues, professional fees, and reimbursement sometimes make extended sessions impractical.

STAGES IN CLINICAL SKILL DEVELOPMENT

During the course of initial training in EMDR, clinicians need to begin applying EMDR to actual cases (EMDRIA, 2007). Because of their early stage of EMDR knowledge and skills development, clinicians at this point in their professional development with EMDR should expect a larger percentage of incomplete sessions than after they have more experience. As a result of this concern, some clinicians conclude they should not start using EMDR at all until after they have completed training; however, this is not the optimum strategy for most clinicians. In cases where patients meet readiness criteria—described in chapter 5—and when reprocessing sessions follow the standard procedural steps with reasonable fidelity, the vast majority of the time incomplete reprocessing sessions will still advance clinical outcomes better than nonspecific interventions such as traditional talk therapy. Patients will be appreciative of their gains, and these initial experiences are essential to clinicians' professional development. These initial experiences reveal areas of knowledge and confusion, skills that can be relied on or are in need of more development. They provide the content for required consultation with an EMDRIA Approved Consultant during basic training in EMDR. As discussed in the next chapter, even after completing basic training in EMDR, consultation remains essential to professional development with EMDR.

The EMDR procedural steps and the standard EMDR PTSD protocol are sufficiently robust that most technical errors in treatment fidelity—as opposed to substantial deviations—do not prevent patients from achieving significant gains. Rather, most technical errors in treatment fidelity tend to make reprocessing less efficient or directly consume extra clinical time. By getting started applying EMDR reprocessing early in their EMDR training and continuing to apply EMDR reprocessing as often as possible, clinicians strengthen their skills and clarify areas of knowledge and skills in need of attention. It can be helpful to keep in mind that research indicates that the degree of confidence in one's EMDR skills is not correlated with clinical gains as much as is degree of fidelity to the procedural steps (Edmond, Rubin & Wambach, 1999).

Selecting Cases for Initial Use of EMDR Reprocessing

When getting started with standard EMDR reprocessing, clinicians should consider three groups of patients for initial case selection. These patients are most likely to respond positively to the basic EMDR procedures often taught earlier in training and are least likely to require use of the advanced EMDR skills covered in later stages of basic EMDR training or in advanced EMDR workshops.

1) Patients with mild symptoms and Global Assessment of Functioning (GAF) ratings above 63 (American Psychiatric Association [APA], 2000) whose histories reflect a generally sound childhood, can benefit with enhanced self-esteem, self-confidence, and greater freedom to pursue their goals by reprocessing adverse or contributory memories using the standard EMDR PTSD protocol.

2) Patients with specific phobias who do not suffer from another significant disorder—such as generalized anxiety disorder, social phobia, agoraphobia, or an Axis II disorder—and whose history shows a generally sound childhood can benefit from the phobia protocol described in chapter 13.

3) Patients with single-episode PTSD with GAF ratings above 45 whose history shows a generally sound childhood and a good premorbid history are good candidates for the standard EMDR PTSD protocol.

In addition, for patients with more prolonged or complex forms of PTSD who do not meet readiness criteria described in chapter 5, clinicians can begin by focusing on enhancing stabilization with the methods described in chapter 6 including Resource Development and Installation (RDI). (See Exhibits B.6 and B.7.) In some cases, as few as two or three sessions of RDI will decrease symptoms and improve functioning to the point where it is possible to begin EMDR reprocessing (Korn & Leeds, 2002).

After clinicians have some initial positive experiences, they should continue to expand the range of cases in which they offer EMDR reprocessing. Clinicians should keep in mind that PTSD symptom severity by itself does not predict ineffective reprocessing or the need for advanced EMDR reprocessing skills. As discussed in chapter 4, case formulation involves many other factors beyond the severity of PTSD symptoms. Patients with severe PTSD symptoms—and who meet readiness criteria—can generally benefit from the application of EMDR reprocessing within the first two or three treatment sessions.

Understanding the AIP Model

An understanding of the Adaptive Information Processing (AIP) model (Shapiro, 2001)—described in chapter 2—is essential to applying EMDR in actual cases. When most clinical issues arise during EMDR reprocessing, the AIP model informs the selection of standardized procedures. When clinical challenges arise that cannot be resolved through use of standardized EMDR procedures, clinicians need to be able to think within the AIP model to adapt EMDR procedures within the framework of AIP to meet the needs of individual patients. Clinicians learning to apply EMDR benefit from regularly returning to review the AIP model to deepen their understanding of the model because it relates to each of their early cases. Discussions in consultation sessions should examine clinical cases in light of the AIP model to assist clinicians in learning to conceptualize cases within the framework of the AIP model.

Knowledge of Procedural Steps

Clinicians currently being trained or recently trained in EMDR should work to memorize the sequence of the standard EMDR procedural steps and the standard phrases used in each step as soon as possible. Until these steps and standard phrases are memorized, clinicians can read from a prepared script. A version of the standard script is provided in Exhibit B.9. Many years of observing both live practice sessions during EMDR training sessions and behavioral work samples during consultation sessions have led me to the firm conviction that clinicians should abstain from demonstrating creativity with the standard procedural steps and standard phrases until after they have learned to consistently use the standard procedural steps and phrases and have achieved results comparable with the best of the treatment outcome literature.

Observational Skills

Observational skills are crucial to the clinical application of EMDR. Most psychotherapy clinical training programs emphasize paying attention to patient verbalization. During EMDR reprocessing sessions, there tends to be dramatically less verbalization than in verbal therapy. In addition, there are many nonverbal process indicators that can indicate a need to slightly modify the speed or direction of bilateral eye movements, activation and accessing of additional maladaptive memory networks or defenses such as dissociative numbing or ego state shifts, or activation and accessing of adaptive memory networks and effective reprocessing. Experienced, skillful EMDR clinicians make use of these indicators to discern what is happening and how to intervene efficiently.

EMDR clinicians need to develop and hone their observational skills. Changes in facial expression, microexpressions, skin color, patterns of breathing, gestures, postural changes, and voice tones should all be noted as possible indicators of shifts in activation and reprocessing of memory networks. Studying videotapes of reprocessing sessions from one's own work or of others' work in consultation groups or workshops is an invaluable way to learn to detect information that may not be noticed or may not be understood as sessions unfold. EMDR-trained clinicians may find supplemental training in some types of body-focused training that include an emphasis on observation of nonverbal expression helpful. Ekman and Friesen's (2003) *Unmasking the Face: A Guide to Recognizing Emotions from Facial Clues* describes how emotion is displayed in each part of the face and is illustrated with over 100 photographs. Online training in recognizing microexpressions is available at http://www.mettonline.com/. Annotations in near-verbatim session notes should, as much as possible, include references to observations of nonverbal elements to assist clinicians in learning to recognize and grasp the significance of these important process indicators.

Session Notes and Recordkeeping

Clinicians will strengthen their skills in EMDR more quickly by creating and maintaining good written records for the cases where they are applying EMDR. A selection of forms for this purpose is provided in Appendix B and includes:

Exhibit B.1—Treatment goals and concerns

Exhibit B.2 and B.3—Assessing stability and readiness for reprocessing

Exhibit B.4—Master treatment plan list of targets

Exhibit B.5—Record of treatment

Exhibit B.10—Session summary

Case Formulation and Treatment Planning Skills

In addition to applying EMDR procedural skills with good fidelity within each reprocessing session, clinicians need to be sure they are sequencing and selecting targets appropriately within a good overall treatment plan. Consultation with an EMDRIA-Approved Consultant is essential to achieve the ability to develop and formulate appropriate EMDR treatment plans, follow the standard procedural steps, and develop strong reprocessing skills. Less experienced EMDR-trained clinicians may seek consultation about problems that emerged in a specific session but may only be prepared to discuss the details of that one session. A good case overview is essential for a consultant to be able to comment effectively on the specifics of what happened in a given reprocessing session. A case inquiry form— Exhibit 17.1—is provided in chapter 17 to assist patients with summarizing their case formulation for consultation.

The Need for Peer Support and Consultation

Chapter 17 provides a comprehensive discussion of the role of consultation and supervision in EMDR training. In addition to consultation, peer-led groups can be an important source of support to clinicians integrating EMDR into their clinical practice. These groups can help clinicians who are new to EMDR to feel more at ease with the learning process by connecting with colleagues at different stages of their professional development with EMDR. The EMDR Institute maintains a comprehensive list of contacts for peer-led groups throughout the United States on their Web site.

Continuing Education in EMDR

Although the standard EMDR PTSD protocol and standard procedural steps are mature and widely recognized as empirically supported, effective treatments for adult posttraumatic syndromes, EMDR as an approach to psychotherapy continues to evolve. Research continues to explore additional clinical applications as well as EMDR's mechanism of action and the psychological and neurological foundations for the AIP model. As clinicians have positive experiences applying EMDR to cases of PTSD, many clinicians observe that basic training in EMDR does not adequately prepare them for the full range of clinical cases where they are interested in applying EMDR and where they suspect or have read that it may be helpful. Fortunately, there are now abundant opportunities for continuing education in EMDR.

EMDRIA and the EMDR Associations of Canada and Europe provide annual conferences with a diverse range of research and clinical programs selected by peer review. EMDRIA offers a process for approving advanced workshops in EMDR for EMDRIA Credit at EMDRIA regional meetings and commercial workshops. These EMDRIA Credit programs are listed on their Web site along with information on how to obtain audio recordings and handouts from past EMDRIA Conferences. Since 2007, EMDRIA has published the *Journal of EMDR Practice and Research* four times a year as well as listing since 2005 peer-reviewed journal articles in the EMDRIA newsletter and on its Web site. Through the remarkable efforts of Dr. Barbara J. Hensley, former president of EMDRIA and Philip Yannarella, documents librarian at the Steely Library, a comprehensive EMDR reference list known as *The Francine Shapiro Library* is now hosted by Northern Kentucky University as a service to the EMDR International Association. More information on these resources is listed in Appendix C.

Confidence in Treatment Effects

One of the most challenging aspects of integrating EMDR into one's clinical work is overcoming initial doubts and fears about asking patients to deliberately access and activate their most disturbing traumatic memories. Required practice sessions in basic training sessions are intended to help clinicians have initial, supervised experiences and gain enough confidence to get started. But back in one's clinical setting, with no training supervisor at hand, even seasoned clinicians can feel like rank beginners all over again as they move from the familiar terrain of their customary ways of providing verbal psychotherapy and begin to use EMDR.

Starting EMDR reprocessing with a patient with pronounced symptoms of PTSD can feel a bit like a first solo parachute jump. One has to have confidence that the EMDR procedures you have learned will guide you and your patient to a safe landing. The impulse to stop and talk about painful material that is emerging can feel so tempting. Continuing from one set of bilateral stimulation to another with only the standard—but minimal—phrases for verbal encouragement and clinical responses can leave new EMDR clinicians feeling anxious and filled with a sense of self-judgment as if they were abandoning patients at the moments of their greatest distress. However, these standard but minimal clinical verbal statements have proved effective for patients all over the world in every kind of clinical setting. During these early clinical experiences with EMDR, clinicians new to EMDR need to trust the research and the body of work of the tens of thousands of clinicians who have gone before you. Follow the treatment plan, follow the standard procedures, and watch your patients recover in ways that will often amaze you.

You cannot increase your confidence, knowledge, and skills in EMDR while practicing in isolation. Fortunately, there are many resources available to support you in your professional development. Next, in chapter 17, we will turn to the most important of these—the role of supervision and consultation.

Supervising and Consulting on EMDR Treatment

ADVANCING CLINICAL SKILLS IN EMDR THROUGH CASE DISCUSSION

Learning to use Eye Movement Desensitization and Reprocessing (EMDR) safely and effectively requires clinicians to integrate a wide range of knowledge and skills. You need to learn to think within the Adaptive Information Processing (AIP) model. You need fundamental knowledge and understanding about psychotraumatology, structural dissociation, attachment theory, and childhood development. You need to be able to keep track of a large amount of information about complex patient histories. You need to be able to form a clear diagnostic picture. You need to understand when to consider the use of EMDR reprocessing and to be able to select an appropriate EMDR treatment protocol. You need skills in case conceptualization and treatment planning and to be able to think strategically about target selection and sequencing. You need to memorize the sequence of the standard EMDR procedural steps and the standard phrases used in each step. You need to be able to discern when reprocessing is proceeding effectively. When it is not, you need to be able to select skillfully from a range of possible interventions to restore effective reprocessing.

Studying a treatment manual helps you acquire essential knowledge. Participating in supervised training exercises as part of basic training in EMDR is a crucial first step to developing essential skills. However, to achieve consistent, positive treatment outcomes, you must also continue to discuss your clinical experiences in using EMDR with other, more experienced EMDR clinicians through consultation or—in the case of prelicensed clinicians—supervision that continues after completing basic didactic and practical training in EMDR. As your knowledge, skills, and clinical experiences deepen over time, you may decide to expand your professional services to share your knowledge and skills with other clinicians by providing consultation or supervision. The decision to move toward offering consultation or supervision begins another rewarding journey, but one that requires developing another set of skills and careful consideration of several issues. These include potential legal, regulatory, risk management, business, ethical, and record-keeping questions.

In this chapter, we will examine the role of consultation and supervision in completing the requirements established by the EMDR International Association (EMDRIA) for basic training in EMDR and for achieving advanced recognition as an EMDRIA-Certified Clinician in EMDR and as an EMDRIA-Approved Consultant. Slightly different standards apply to clinicians practicing in Europe, Australia, South America, and in other countries that have their own EMDR professional associations, but the issues and principles discussed in this chapter still apply to meeting the challenges and making the most of the opportunities of consultation and supervision. We will discuss how those who are seeking consultation can select qualified Approved Consultants who will provide a "best fit" with their needs for extending their understanding and skills in EMDR. We will also touch on some of the issues of professional development, ethics, and recordkeeping that those wanting to move toward and those who already are providing EMDR consultation should consider.

Although many clinicians look forward to the collaborative learning process in consultation and supervision, others experience apprehension, self-doubt, and trepidation over the prospect of having their work evaluated and discussed. To help make this a supportive experience for everyone, we will explore several strategies and different formats for structuring EMDR consultation and supervision. There are significant legal and ethical issues that arise in participating in consultation and supervision. We will clarify what these issues are and how to organize consultation and supervision agreements and procedures to manage these issues skillfully.

THE CENTRAL ROLE OF CONSULTATION AND SUPERVISION IN CLINICAL TRAINING

The central role of supervision in achieving minimal acceptable standards of knowledge and skill is consistently recognized by state licensure boards requirements. They typically require 3,000 hours of supervised experience to obtain a license to practice psychotherapy. After licensure, the need for periodic, professional consultation by clinicians is recognized in nearly all professional codes of ethics such as those of the American Psychological Association ([APA], 2002) and the American Association for Marriage and Family Therapy (2001). Although widespread recognition of the benefits of consultation clearly exists, not all clinicians seek consultation when learning a new method of psychotherapy. The avoidance of consultation may be particularly problematic when integrating EMDR into clinical practice. The early literature on EMDR treatment outcome studies is marked by several studies in which those providing EMDR to study subjects had only partial training. In both these and in some other studies where research clinicians had completed 2 weekends of basic training, results consistently showed smaller treatment effect sizes when there was limited fidelity to the standard EMDR procedures and protocols (Perkins & Rouanzoin, 2002; Shapiro, 2001; Maxfield & Hyer, 2002).

The need for consultation on EMDR clinical experiences to achieve mastery was recognized early in the history of the EMDR International Association (EMDRIA). When setting standards in 1999 to achieve the designation of EMDRIA-Certified Therapist in EMDR, EMDRIA specified a requirement of 20 hours of consultation after completing basic training in EMDR (EMDRIA, 2008b). An additional 20 hours of "consultation on consultation" were specified to earn the designation of Approved Consultant in EMDR. Hours of consultation to meet both of these standards are to be provided by an EMDRIA-Approved Consultant in EMDR or, in some cases, by a consultant-in-training (CIT). The standards for achieving both EMDRIA Certification and Approved Consultant status are discussed in this chapter. More recently, EMDRIA further recognized the central role of consultation for clinicians being trained in EMDR in its first major revision of basic training curriculum requirements (EMDRIA, 2007) effective June 2007 by requiring 10 hours of consultation as part of basic training in EMDR.

Maxfield and Hyer (2002) examined the relationship between effect size and methodology ratings in EMDR treatment outcome studies using the Gold Standard Scale (GS Scale) adapted from Foa and Meadows (1997). They reported, "Results indicated a significant relationship between scores on the GS Scale and effect size, with more rigorous studies according to the GS Scale reporting larger effect sizes" (Maxfield & Hyer, 2002, p. 23). Their research further underscores a point emphasized in this chapter. When clinicians do seek consultation, presenting verbal summaries of what takes place in EMDR treatment sessions may provide only limited benefits. Maxfield and Hyer conclude, "This study of methodological features suggests that methodological rigor influences outcome, and that meticulous attention to detail can result in more clearly defined outcomes" (2002, p. 39). The phrase "meticulous attention to detail" indicates that consultants and supervisors need to directly observe behavioral work samples of actual EMDR treatment sessions through live observation, video or audio recordings, or near-verbatim transcripts.

DEFINITION OF TERMS: DIFFERENCES BETWEEN CONSULTATION AND SUPERVISION

Although consultation and supervision share essential elements in their focus on an educational framework, they differ in fundamental ways. Some clinicians use these terms in ways that make them seem equivalent or interchangeable. They are not. It is important that clinicians do not confuse these terms when discussing their professional relationships and when drafting written agreements that define their professional relationship. The differences between consultation and supervision have significant ethical and legal implications and consequences.

Before discussing some of the professional, legal, and ethical issues in consultation and supervision, I need to make clear that I am not an attorney. The information in this chapter is based on reviews of books and journal articles and consultation with representatives of professional associations. None of the materials in this chapter should be considered legal advice. Before obtaining or offering consultation or supervision, clinicians should obtain appropriate legal advice specific to your licensure and jurisdiction about how to structure your professional relationships.

Supervisees are required to function under supervision because they are not yet legally entitled to practice independently or, in some cases, as part of rehabilitation imposed by a licensing board. The nature and duration of the supervision is determined not by the supervisee but by an external legal entity, generally a licensing board. The most important distinction between consultation and supervision is that *clinical supervisors are legally responsible for the services provided by their supervisees.*

> Clinical supervision is an ongoing relationship between a senior member and an apprentice or junior member of the profession in which the supervisor monitors the quality of the treatment given by the apprentice or junior member, enhances professional functioning, and may also be used to ensure the qualifications of the junior member to become an independently practicing professional (Watkins, 1997). (Knapp & VandeCreek, 2006, p. 217)

In contrast, *consultees retain full professional autonomy and legal responsibility for their services* when they voluntarily enter into consultation in order to meet ethical or professional standards—as opposed to legal requirements—or to obtain advanced certification. Therefore, the essence of consultation is a collaborative process between peers that examines available professional standards, research findings, and clinical experience to enhance the knowledge and application of skills by the consultee. In general, consultees remain uniquely responsible for the services they provide. From a risk management perspective, consultants should be diligent to maintain an educational role that references scholarly knowledge, professional and community standards, and research findings, while avoiding a proscriptive role.

"An individual may seek consultation to develop expertise in some new area of practice or as a strategy to enhance his or her professional development. The duration is determined by the needs of the consultee, and the ultimate responsibility for clinical decisions rests with the consultee" (Thomas, 2007, p. 221). Although consultants can be named in civil lawsuits and licensure board complaints, they generally will not be held responsible for the actions of consultees, unless they have become aware of the specific identities of patients or have assumed a stance of directing choices and actions for consultees. However, there are circumstances in which consultants may be found responsible for the actions or inactions of consultees by a court or a licensing board.

RELEVANT ETHICAL MODELS AND PRINCIPLES

The American Association for Marriage and Family Therapy (AAMFT) *Code of Ethics* identifies the central role of supervised experience as part of an obligation to maintain competence and pursue knowledge. "Marriage and family therapists pursue knowledge of new developments and maintain competence in marriage and family therapy through education, training, or supervised experience" (AAMFT, 2001, Principle 3.1). However, with this choice of terminology, it is unclear whether the principle is intended to include voluntary "consultation" or only legally required "supervised experience."

The ethics code of The National Board for Certified Counselors (NBCC) refers explicitly to consultation with a more permissively stated principle that "Certified counselors may choose to consult with any other professionally competent person about a client and must notify clients of this right" (NBCC, 2005, p. 3). The California Association for Marriage and Family Therapy (CAMFT) is more specific on the need to consult for professional development, stating that: "While developing new areas of practice, marriage and family therapists take steps to ensure the competence of their work through education, training, consultation, and/or supervision." (CAMFT, 2008, section 3.9) Consultation is clearly described as a central responsibility of psychologists in principle B, Fidelity and Responsibility, of the American Psychological Association's "Ethical Principles of Psychologists and Code of Conduct." "Psychologists consult with, refer to, or cooperate with other professionals and institutions to the extent needed to serve the best interests of those with whom they work" (APA, 2002, p. 3).

STANDARDS OF THE EMDR INTERNATIONAL ASSOCIATION FOR BASIC TRAINING IN EMDR

In May 2006, EMDRIA issued revised basic training in EMDR curriculum requirements for training starting in June 2007. These standards (EMDRIA, 2007) require at least 20 hours of instruction, 20 hours of "supervised practicum," and 10 hours of consultation as part of the basic training in EMDR. The curriculum, which can be obtained at the EMDRIA Web site, specifies instructional content, faculty qualifications, and format for consultation in basic training. Note that although EMDRIA refers to supervised practicum, this use of the term "supervised" should not be confused with legally required supervision. *Supervised practicum* in basic training refers to a focus on assisting training participants to learn and follow standard procedures rather than assuming legal liability for the outcomes of training exercises. EMDRIA-Approved Providers of basic training generally require participants to sign a participant agreement acknowledging that training exercises are not intended to be psychotherapy. Training providers generally request participants to select personal material for practicum exercises that is suitable for the training environment and to avoid dealing with issues more suitable to personal psychotherapy.

Eligibility for Basic Training in EMDR

EMDRIA and EMDR associations in other countries limit eligibility for training in EMDR to those with an appropriate graduate education in a mental health field and a license to practice psychotherapy or those working under qualified supervision of a licensed mental health professional. In the United States and in other countries operating under EMDRIA standards, to be eligible to enroll in EMDR training with a provider approved by EMDRIA, you must hold a state-issued license or a national credential from one of several categories as a mental health professional or be in a qualifying graduate or internship program.

The list of qualifying credentials is carefully defined. To be eligible, medical doctors must have specialist training in psychiatry and must hold a current license. Registered nurses must have a master's degree in psychiatric nursing and must have a current state license or national nursing board registration. All other mental health clinicians must have a master's or doctoral degree in one of several specific disciplines (social work, counseling, marriage, family therapy, or psychology) and must be licensed or certified by a state or national credentialing board. Because of inconsistent standards from state to state, clinicians who have completed programs in art therapy or drug and alcohol counseling have to submit detailed information to EMDRIA about the program that they completed and a copy of a current license or certification through a state or national board to determine eligibility for registering for EMDRIA-Approved Basic EMDR Training.

To encourage graduate students to be trained in EMDR, EMDRIA provides eligibility criteria for students enrolled in a master's or doctoral level program in one of the mental health fields listed above. Qualifying graduate students must be currently enrolled in a licensing track program. They must be in a second year or later practicum or internship program and must be working under the supervision of a licensed mental health professional. Qualifying graduate students and pre-licensed, postgraduate clinicians must submit a letter from their supervisor to their provider of EMDR basic training.

Note that EMDRIA does not require that supervisors of qualifying graduate students and pre-licensed, postgraduate clinicians have been trained in EMDR. EMDRIA has not directly addressed the professional issues or proposed standards for EMDR specific supervision for qualifying graduate students and pre-licensed postgraduate clinicians during EMDR basic training or while earning hours towards EMDRIA Certification. This has been left to the standards of the setting in which pre-licensed graduate students and post-graduate interns are employed. The hours of consultation required in EMDR basic training and for EMDRIA Certification generally cannot address licensing board requirements for required supervision. First, they are defined as consultation not supervision. Second, as they are normally organized they do not provide sufficiently detailed oversight. Under optimal conditions, supervisors of graduate students and post-graduate interns are trained in EMDR and are EMDRIA Certified or Approved Consultants. When supervisors are not trained in EMDR, this book provides a guide to principles, procedures and forms than can assist supervisors in obtaining information on patient preparation, readiness, and treatment sessions.

STANDARDS FOR CONSULTATION AS PART OF BASIC TRAINING IN EMDR

Consultation as part of basic training in EMDR is intended to support trainees to be able "to safely and effectively integrate the use of EMDR into their clinical setting" (EMDRIA 2007, p. 9). EMDRIA permits either individual or group settings to meet the consultation requirement. In group settings, the minimum group duration is set as the number of participants times 15 minutes. Participants receive credit for the entire duration of each group session in which they are present whether or not they present case material or actively participate. Consultation as part of the basic training in EMDR may be provided only by an EMDRIA-Approved Trainer, Approved Consultant, or a CIT "under the supervision of an Approved Consultant" (EMDRIA, 2007).

Different providers of basic training organize their training programs in quite different ways and integrate consultation in various formats and sequences. Some basic trainings follow a weekend workshop format. Some are offered as weekly classes in university settings. Consultation sessions may be offered interspersed between didactic teaching segments in a manner entirely predetermined and pre-scheduled by the provider of training or these sessions may be scheduled individually by trainees with consultants selected from a list of faculty approved by the provider according to a more open and flexible schedule.

EMDRIA describes consultation in basic training as involving "teaching, practicum" and review of "clinical use" of EMDR. However, EMDRIA emphasizes that consultation should focus on individualized feedback and specifies that "Consultation is about real cases and not experiences that occur in practicum" (EMDRIA, 2007, p. 10). This suggests that although some portion of the 10 hours may be devoted to practicum exercises, clinicians need to be actually applying EMDR in a clinical setting between consultation sessions. Thus, trainees must review with their consultants their clinical use of EMDR with actual patients seeking treatment and not merely what they have done in supervised or unsupervised practice sessions with other clinicians or with non-patients such as friends, neighbors, or family members. EMDRIA standards further requires that consultation provide opportunities "to *assess the strengths and weaknesses* [italics added] of each trainee's overall understanding and knowledge of EMDR, and the practice of EMDR skills, and the opportunity to tailor further learning experiences to address deficits" (EMDRIA, 2007, p. 10).

EMDRIA has not specified any objective standards for minimum knowledge or skills to be achieved by trainees in order to complete basic training in EMDR nor a minimum number of clinical sessions in which trainees have used EMDR reprocessing. For trainees obtaining consultation in a group setting, EMDRIA has not specified a minimum number of hours of presenting their own case material. To assess each trainee's strengths and weaknesses and give individualized feedback, the consultant must review clinical experiences from each trainee's work setting. This raises the question of how to implement an adequate review of actual clinical application during basic training.

Standards for Individualized Feedback during consultation

EMDRIA has not specified objective criteria that require trainees to demonstrate any specific level of knowledge or skill during consultation. However, trainees are to receive individualized feedback and instruction in the areas of case conceptualization, client readiness, target selection, treatment planning, and specific application of skills. While EMDRIA does not require consultants to review a behavioral sample for each trainee, EMDRIA recognizes that providers of Basic Training may choose to require it (EMDRIA, 2007, p. 10, lines 426–427). *Without a review of at least one work sample and case presentations from each clinician during these 10 hours of consultation, it would be difficult for the consultant to offer the individualized feedback and instruction called for in the current EMDRIA standards for consultation in basic training.*

In the spirit of advocating for aspirational standards, here are proposed additional minimum standards for consultation as part of basic training in EMDR. Over the course of the 10 hours of consultation, each trainee would need to present case material using some form of behavioral work sample on at least two different cases in which the standard EMDR procedural steps were employed. Case presentations and discussion would need to be at least 20 minutes in duration.

The consultant would need to document the duration of each trainee's case presentations and evidence of strengths and weaknesses in knowledge and skills.

Methods for Individualized Feedback on Clinical Application of EMDR

Various methods can be employed for providing individualized feedback on clinicians' application of EMDR. The degree of detailed information that consultants can obtain and respond to is inversely correlated with increasing costs in terms of time, effort, and logistics. In order of degree of rigor, these include:

- Observing trainees responding to written or videotaped vignettes
- Direct observation of practicum exercises between a pair of trainees
- Listening to verbal summaries of actual clinical interactions and reprocessing sessions with patients
- Review of near-verbatim transcripts of actual reprocessing sessions or other EMDR related clinical interactions with patients
- Review of audio or video recordings of actual reprocessing sessions or other EMDR related clinical interactions with patients
- Observing actual reprocessing sessions or other EMDR related clinical interactions with patients through a one-way mirror

Using Written or Videotaped Vignettes

Consultants can observe trainees responding to prescribed written or videotaped vignettes. This method offers the advantage that the consultant can directly observe trainees' abilities to perceive, conceptualize, and respond to selected clinical challenges. This method has the further advantage that the consultant can present trainees with a graduated range of simple to more complex vignettes that provide common challenges encountered by newly trained clinicians. Although trainees cannot hide or distort what they actually do in responding to these prepared vignettes, their responses under such artificial circumstances, while being observed by peers and a consultant, may not accurately reflect their level of perceptual, conceptual, or practical skills when they are at ease with an actual patient in their customary clinical setting. Most importantly, this method fails to address the requirement for a review of the clinical application of EMDR from *actual cases*. Therefore, if used, this method can only be a supplement to actual case review. With only 10 hours of consultation required, if significant time were devoted to vignette exercises, it could be difficult to provide each trainee with more than one review of actual clinical application of EMDR. If considered at all, it might best be used only for an initial group session, when some trainees have yet to prepare work samples for review.

Practicum Exercises between a Pair of Trainees

Consultants can directly observe practicum exercises between a pair of trainees. This is equivalent to the format used in the supervised practicum portion of basic training, only with more observers. Whereas practicum supervisors are typically expected to supervise up to three triads or five pairs of trainees simultaneously, during consultation, the consultant would ideally be observing only one pair of "clinician" and "patient" at a time. Other trainees in the group would observe this practicum exercise and hear the consultant's feedback and instruction during and after the practicum. The use of practicum exercises is clearly endorsed as one facet of consultation for basic training by EMDRIA along with teaching and discussion of the use of EMDR in actual clinical cases (EMDRIA, 2007, p. 10, lines 450–451).

This method offers the advantage that the consultant has access to all the same perceptual and clinical information available to the trainee. The consultant can directly observe how the trainee gathers, organizes, and makes use of the information offered by the trainee playing the role of "patient." The consultant can choose to give real time or delayed feedback. Other trainees may find that these exercises give them opportunities to learn from others' skills and mistakes.

However, this method creates potential issues with the requirement for multiple relationships by being peers in consultation and then entering into a therapeutic relationship. Practicum exercises are not generally done as mere role playing. Significant clinical issues may emerge that go beyond the scope of what is suitable for a consultation group exercise. Although these issues would be addressed fully in an actual clinical setting, in the basic training consultation setting these issues will typically be set aside, often with encouragement for the "patient" to address them in private EMDR therapy sessions with a qualified clinician. Peers from a practicum exercise may decide to enter into a private therapeutic relationship while continuing in the group consultation. Although these therapeutic relationships may prove quite helpful, the existence of multiple relationships by being in the same consultation group creates a potential increased risk of harm or exploitation. If one trainee offers another private EMDR therapy sessions, there may be additional issues in whether these sessions are to be included for case discussion in the consultation group. Doing so would violate the principle of omitting identifying information from case discussion. This would raise two ethical issues for the consultant. First would be knowledge of the existence of multiple roles between trainees. Second would be discussion of case material for an identified patient. Consultants may want to address these potential issues in written agreements and discussion with trainees entering group consultation.

During practicum exercises in consultation sessions, the trainee in the role of "patient" could uncover issues that could be embarrassing or undermining to their stature in their community. More commonly, the issues being addressed and the level of functioning of the "patient" in this practicum exercises are not likely to be as challenging or complex as the clinical material that trainees encounter in their clinical settings. Most importantly, practicum exercises fail to meet the requirement for review of clinical application by each trainee with actual cases. Therefore, like the use of vignette exercises, if practicum exercises are used, they can only be a supplement to actual case review.

Verbal Summaries of Clinical Interactions and Reprocessing Sessions

Reviewing verbal summaries of clinical interactions or reprocessing sessions is the easiest method for implementing actual clinical case review. It requires the least amount of preparation by trainees and consultant. It also offers the least amount of detail and is subject to the limitations of incomplete and distorted recall. The absence of a documented record limits the ability of both the consultant and other trainees to perceive directly what the consultee perceived and did. It also fails to provide the consultee with an objective summary of what occurred. Whether in the form of written summaries or audio or video recording, reviews of trainees' own work samples help trainees to examine their work objectively and learn from it. Also, because trainees often do not yet know what to look for in their clinical work to guide their case conceptualization, treatment planning, target selection, and reprocessing interventions, their verbal summaries often fail to provide critical perceptual and behavioral information consultants need to determine what a more experienced EMDR clinician might perceive or do in a given situation. This method has the one strength that it focuses on clinical application with actual patients as required by EMDRIA.

Review of Written Case Summaries and Near-Verbatim Transcripts

Review of written case summaries and near-verbatim transcripts of clinical interactions and reprocessing sessions offers several advantages over the methods described above. Although they can be time consuming to prepare, written case summaries can provide concise, well-organized information on patient history, diagnoses, mental status, treatment goals, medical issues, and interventions used in an actual course of treatment. In many clinical settings, some of these materials may already be required to be prepared. In these cases, trainees would merely have to remove, redact, or alter identifying information from copies of existing records to present them for review in consultation. Table 17.1 provides a format for preparing a case summary.

Near-verbatim transcripts of sessions, where standard EMDR procedures were used, provide an objective record for discussion of actual case material. Although they offer several distinct advantages over all the other methods for review of actual case material, near-verbatim transcripts suffer from several disadvantages. Many clinicians do not have the keyboarding speed and accuracy to prepare near-verbatim transcripts during sessions. Some would be uncomfortable with the idea of doing so as an intrusion into the therapeutic relationship. However, it does appear from anecdotal reports that patients tolerate clinicians taking notes on a keyboard as well as clinicians making handwritten notes. Before being presented for case discussion, keyboarded notes must still be reviewed to remove or alter potentially identifying information. When prepared from audio recordings or hand-written notes, near-verbatim transcripts require clinicians to devote additional time to their preparation. Although this investment of time may appear at first to be an onerous burden, many clinicians are surprised by how much they learn from the process of preparing and reviewing these transcripts, even before they present them for discussion in consultation. Of course, clinicians can also pay for a transcription. This requires an additional person—who is probably not a clinician—to have access to confidential case material and would require a further signed release from the patient.

As with written case summaries, near-verbatim transcripts offer members of consultation groups a time-efficient format to discuss rich case material. Being able to visualize the sequence of an entire session allows for discussion of some facets of clinical decision making that can be much more challenging and certainly more time consuming when reviewing audio or video recordings. However, compared with audio or video recordings, this ease in review comes at a cost. Near verbatim notes cannot directly capture the timing of interactions, nor the voice tones, facial expressions, body posture, and other nonverbal communication expressed by both the patient and the clinician. Although some of these nonspoken elements of the session can be annotated, most that would be easily captured by an audio or video recording will be omitted.

Finally, use of written case summaries and near-verbatim transcripts of sessions is an ideal way to ground case discussions that take place remotely via telephone or video chat. Nearly all clinicians have access to the Internet. These written materials can be distributed ahead of time as email attachments or placed onto online Web servers with access protected by a password known only to members of the consultation group. The consultant—and other members of the group—can verbally comment on and annotate comments into the shared document. If group members are all able to access the Internet during group sessions, these materials can be distributed and even annotated by the consultant in real time in an online working space. These case summaries and near-verbatim transcripts, together with annotated comments, provide a documentary record of both the clinician's case work and the feedback received with ideas and directions for clarifying case conceptualization, treatment planning, and specific strategies for enhancing clinical outcomes.

 | EMDR Case Inquiry Format

When consulting on clinical cases related to the application of EMDR, please provide the relevant portions of the following information. Keep in mind that you are responsible for obtaining your patient's written permission for the release of any confidential information and for disguising any identifying data.

CLINICIAN DATA

1.) Please indicate your work setting and licensure: _____

2.) Please indicate your theoretical orientation before EMDR training:

_____

3.) EMDR training status. Please specify: in training; completed basic training; additional advanced EMDR training; EMDRIA Certified.

_____

4.) Duration of EMDR experience: year completed training; amount of experience.

_____

Please describe the issue(s) you want to address through consultation on this case:

_____
_____

PATIENT DATA

Presenting problem(s) including duration, severity, and any remission:

_____
_____

Patient's treatment goal(s): _____

_____

Age: _____   Gender: _____   Marital status: _____   Ethnicity: _____
Current family system:

_____
_____

Social support system:

_____
_____

Synopsis of patient history including past and present life issues, traumatic events, childhood attachment status, legal issues, health history.

_____
_____
_____
_____

Resources including ego strengths, coping skills, self-capacities:

_____
_____

Past treatment episodes and diagnoses: _____

Past responses to treatment both positive and negative _____
_____

Current diagnoses and medical health conditions (Axis I, II, and III)
Axis I: _____
Axis II: _____
Axis III: _____
Current Global Assessment of Functioning (GAF): _____

SCREENING FOR DISSOCIATION

DES II and DES Taxon scores: _____ SDQ20 or SDQ 5 score: _____
Dissociative symptoms: _____
_____

Other testing data: _____
Defenses: _____

PAST AND CURRENT STABILITY
Note any impulse control problems with alcohol, drugs, violent urges or behaviors, self-injurious behaviors, suicidal thoughts, urges or plan, compulsive sexual behavior, compulsive spending, etc.: _____

_____

TREATMENT PLAN:
Please describe your overall treatment plan and estimated duration of treatment:

_____

_____

Responses to stabilization and ego strengthening
Please describe methods of stabilization used and responses: _____

_____

RESPONSES TO THE CALM (SAFE) PLACE EXERCISE AND RDI:
Resource 1: _____
Response to bilateral stimulation: _____
Resource 2: _____
Response to bilateral stimulation: _____

RESPONSES TO EMDR REPROCESSING
Please indicate how many targets have been reprocessed and with what outcome. Copy this section if necessary for additional targets.
Target: _____ *past;* _____ *present;* _____ *future.*
Target situation: _____
Image: _____
NC: _____
PC: _____
VoC: _____ Emotion(s): _____ SUDs: _____
Location of body sensations: _____
End of session: SUDs: _____ VoC: _____ Body scan: _____
Session was: complete _____; incomplete _____.
PC: (final): _____

REASSESSMENT (FOLLOW-UP SESSION):
Please describe any observed or reported changes in patient functioning following session(s) in which reprocessing was used:

_____

_____

Adapted from Forgash and Leeds (1999)

Review of Audio or Video Recordings

For retrospective review of general clinical interactions in the history taking and preparation phases as well as of specific reprocessing sessions, video recordings clearly provide the most rigorous and comprehensive documentation. Video recordings provide the greatest information on facial expressions and other nonverbal elements of patient communications such as voice tones, gestures, and body postures. They capture exactly what is said along with the timing of responses. Most importantly, they capture nonverbal information the clinician may have failed to notice or understand at the time of the session, which can then be highlighted and discussed to improve perceptual and conceptual skills. For example, when patients report that the selected target is no longer disturbing, newly trained EMDR clinicians may have difficulty differentiating between situations where the material has been reprocessed and those where the patient has disconnected from the material through dissociative processes. Although a near verbatim text may reveal sufficient information to identify these moments, these situations can often be directly observed in video recordings. Strategies for clarifying and addressing these moments can then be discussed more readily.

The richness of video recordings cannot be matched by any other form of retrospective review. However, they do have several limitations that need to be considered. For group case discussions, it is often too time consuming to review video recordings of an entire treatment session. Clinicians can be encouraged to select key portions of a treatment session for review and discussion. In this way, near-verbatim transcripts provide a more time efficient and comprehensive review of the verbal portions of sessions that can be more quickly scanned, reviewed, and returned to for further review. In a group discussion, different members of the group can independently highlight and comment on selected passages of their own copy of the document.

With a video recording, there is generally only a single copy being reviewed in part during the group session. This limits members of a group to reviewing only the portions of the session selected for review and prevents them from interacting with the record directly. The technology does exist for placing complete video recordings into private- and password-protected online video storage for complete and independent review by members of a consultation group. However, at present, few clinicians have the technical knowledge to take advantage of such services. Even with secure, independent online access, complete review of video recordings remains much more time consuming and therefore limits the amount of clinical material consultants can review for each member of a consultation group.

Video recordings have several other limitations for use in consultation. These include the cost of video recording equipment, the difficulty of obtaining a specific written release for video recording for case consultation purposes, and the challenges of masking the identity of the patient. Although the costs of video recording equipment and storage media have fallen dramatically in recent years, not all clinicians have video recording equipment available to them. Many patients, especially those in private practice settings, are unwilling or reluctant to be video recorded. Patients are often concerned about the security of the highly confidential material being captured. They can be concerned that the original recording may not be destroyed after it has been reviewed or that copies may be made and released to unauthorized persons. Reassuring them about how the recordings will be safeguarded may help overcome these concerns, but doing so can take time away from the primary purpose of the sessions.

Finally, a major dilemma with video recordings is the protection of the patient's identity. Even if the patient is willing to have their face shown to other clinicians, doing so identifies a specific individual to those viewing the video recording. This alters the nature of case discussions and changes the risk management issues by involving the consultant with an identified patient. A patient whose face had been video recorded during treatment could later decide to name the consultant in a civil lawsuit or board complaint. The argument could be made that because the consultant knew the patient's identity, the consultant was, in effect, directing a specific course of treatment for a specific, identified patient and thus was responsible for any inadequacies in that treatment. If, in order to avoid this identification of the patient, the video recording excludes the face of the patient, then a great deal of the richness of the video recording is lost.

In addition, when video taping their sessions, consultees need to instruct their patients to avoid referring to domestic partners and family members or perpetrators by name. Clinicians also need to avoid saying the patient's name as they normally do during sessions. Should names or other identifying information be verbalized during the video recording, the recording would have to be edited prior to showing to the consultant or other consultees to remove the identifying information from the recording. Not all clinicians have the skills or the access to the necessary equipment to perform this kind of video editing. This would necessitate paying a video editor with the equipment and skills to perform the required editing.

Audio recordings do not capture any of the visual information found in video recordings; however, they can capture exactly what was said along with voice tones and the timing of verbal interactions. Reviewing audio recordings can be even more time consuming than reviewing video recordings, because it is generally harder to locate specific moments quickly by fast forwarding to them. With video recordings, there are visual cues that help identify the sequence of what took place in the session. These visual cues make it easier to skip to key moments in the session for review. Audio recordings can capture more complete information about what is verbalized than most clinicians' near-verbatim transcripts. For clinicians who do not want to make comprehensive notes during sessions, audio recordings can be transcribed after the session is over to provide a transcript to be presented for case consultation.

There are many challenges associated with the use of video recordings in consultation. However, because of the richness of the information they can provide, they remain an important alternative to be considered for reviewing consultees' work samples and providing consultees with detailed feedback on their implementation of EMDR knowledge and skills. Video recordings are a rich source of material for case discussions and will continue to be used in both consultation and supervision settings. The use of video recordings requires the use of appropriate written releases and safeguards to protect patients' confidentiality. A sample form is provided as a starting point for clinicians in preparing their own consent forms. Consultants and consultees should make sure that they have reviewed any draft consent forms for video recording and release of information forms as well as their security measures, with an ethics representative of their professional association and with an attorney familiar with the standards of their licensing board and the laws of the state in which they practice.

Observing Actual Clinical Sessions through a One-Way Mirror

Observing actual clinical sessions through a one-way mirror provides an opportunity for comprehensive review of trainees' clinical application of EMDR. The consultant and any consultation group members are able to observe all the information available to the clinician being observed and all of the clinician's responses. Although this method for observing the trainee's work is robust and detailed, it has several limitations and issues. With video recordings, trainees have the freedom to select which recordings will be presented for retrospective review. With live observation, licensed clinicians going through EMDR training have no way to know what might occur next in the session. This increased uncertainty is more likely to create a greater sense of performance anxiety while being observed in real time than when clinicians know they can select or omit any particular recording after the fact.

With live observation, it is extremely difficult to maintain the anonymity of the patient's identity. Observers will see the patient's face and are more likely to become aware of identifying information. As discussed above, the consultant's awareness of the patient's identity increases the risk that the patient could hold the consultant responsible for any issues that might arise during the course of treatment. A consultant who is physically present, even in a passive observer role during treatment sessions, is much more likely to be viewed by third parties as responsible for treatment outcomes regardless of written agreements to the contrary. Patients may also feel uneasy about having other clinicians observing their treatment sessions. They may be less able or less willing to allow challenging material to come to the surface. This may increase the risk of ineffective reprocessing.

Direct observation through the one-way mirror is more commonly used in therapy training programs where clinicians being observed are not yet licensed for independent practice. In these situations, the observer is in fact a supervisor who is legally responsible for the quality of the treatment being provided and who is both permitted and expected to know the identity of the patient. Graduate training programs and postgraduate internship settings may provide the most likely settings where direct observation could be implemented without undue complications or additional risk management issues for nonsupervisor consultants.

 Sample Consent to Video Record and Show Recordings for Consultation

I, _____, give my permission for video recording of my sessions with my therapist _____, for the purpose of assisting my therapist in obtaining consultation to support professional development.

In giving my consent, I understand that:

I am under no obligation to provide this consent.

I may withdraw this consent at any point in the future by giving my therapist a signed and dated note withdrawing this consent.

I understand that refusing to give my consent or withdrawing my consent will have no effect on the services being provided to me.

I understand that my face will not be filmed, and my name will not be revealed.

I understand that video recordings of my sessions will be reviewed by my therapist and will be shown to:

[ ] _____ An Approved Consultant in EMDR _____
[ ] _____ A Consultant-in-Training _____
[ ] _____ Other clinicians in a consultation group with my therapist.

I understand that video recordings of my sessions will remain in the control of my therapist at all times, and will not be reproduced or shown for any other purpose unless I were to agree at some future date in a separate written consent.

I understand that this consent will be retained in my file and will remain valid while I remain in treatment.

After my therapist has completed consultation and review of video recorded sessions, my therapist and I agree that my therapist will do the following with these video recordings:

[ ] _____ Video recordings are to be retained in my file.
[ ] _____ All existing video recordings are to be destroyed and disposed of.

I understand that I may withdraw this consent whenever I choose. If I withdraw my consent, any and all video recordings will be secured from any further showing or destroyed at my discretion after discussion with my therapist.

I am initialling below to indicate:

_____ I received a copy of this consent. _____ I waived receiving a copy of this consent.

I have read all of this consent form, and I consent freely.

| _____ | _____ | _____ |
| Patient Name | Signature | Date |

| _____ | _____ | _____ |
| Therapist Name | Signature | Date |

WITHDRAW CONSENT TO VIDEO RECORD AND SHOW RECORDINGS FOR CONSULTATION

I, _____, hereby withdraw my permission for video recording of my sessions with _____.

[ ] _____ I want all existing video recordings to be secured from further showing, and to be retained in my file.
[ ] _____ I want all existing video recordings to be destroyed and disposed of.

| _____ | _____ | _____ |
| Patient Name | Signature | Date |

| _____ | _____ | _____ |
| Therapist Name | Signature | Date |

STANDARDS FOR CONSULTATION TOWARD BEING AN EMDRIA-CERTIFIED CLINICIAN IN EMDR

The EMDRIA Program for Certification in EMDR provides an important acknowledgment of professional achievement that is recognized by a growing number of hospitals, national and local mental health centers, and third party payors in their credentialing of EMDR clinicians. Clinicians who are applying to become an EMDRIA-Certified Clinician in EMDR are required to have completed 20 hours of consultation with an EMDRIA-Approved Consultant or consultant-in-training. A maximum of 15 hours can be earned with a consultant-in-training. The remaining 5 hours must be earned with an Approved Consultant. These hours of consultation must have been obtained after completing basic training in EMDR.

Prelicensed clinicians cannot earn the designation of certification until they receive a license to practice independently. However, prelicensed clinicians can complete basic training in EMDR and earn all 20 hours of consultation toward certification. The application for certification requires a notarized statement that the applicant has "at least 2 years of experience in your field of license, certification, or registration" (EMDRIA, 2008c). The application does not state that these 2 years must be postlicensure. Most licenses or credentials for independent practice require at least 2 years of experience before licensure. If they have met all other requirements, as soon as certification applicants receive their licenses to practice independently they may submit their applications for certification and be recognized as Certified in EMDR. For this reason, you will note that the sample written agreements for consultation for certification include optional language addressing issues related to the supervisors of prelicensed clinicians. See Exhibit 17.3, "Sample Consultation Agreement toward EMDRIA Certification" and Exhibit 17.4, "Sample Consultation Agreement with a CIT" further below.

Of the required 20 hours, up to 10 hours can be "group hours" obtained during group consultation with a maximum of eight consultees in attendance. Unlike consultation to meet the basic training requirement for 10 hours, there is no minimum group duration based on the number of participants. A group with up to eight participants could be of any duration, for example, from 1 hour to 3 hours. In addition, unlike the standards for consultation for basic training in EMDR, there is no explicit requirement that these hours of consultation be developmentally structured and spread over time. Theoretically, they could be earned en masse in an intensive consultation program over 3 or 4 days. In addition, it is possible to earn some or all individual hours of consultation during group consultation sessions.

EMDRIA requires applicants for EMDRIA certification to submit with their application a notarized statement in which they attest to having 2 years of clinical experience and having conducted "50 EMDR sessions with no less than 25 clients" (EMDRIA, 2008c). However, there is no minimum standard for how many cases each consultee must present during the required 20 hours of consultation.

Evaluating Consultees' Readiness for Certification

Since first formulating standards for certification in 1997, EMDRIA has provided a "consultation packet" which includes a "certification in EMDR evaluation form" (EMDRIA, 2008a, 2008b, 2008f). However, this evaluation form is labeled as "sample." Although the use of the sample evaluation form is clearly not a requirement, it seems to suggest the knowledge and skills EMDRIA believes Approved Consultants should address during consultation toward EMDRIA Certification. EMDRIA requires Approved Consultants to base their letters of recommendation for Certification on applicants' "utilization of EMDR" (EMDRIA, 2008a). Yet, EMDRIA has not established any specific objective standards by which Approved

Consultants are to determine whether applicants should be recommended for Certification. With the 2007 Basic Training Curriculum, EMDRIA provided specific descriptions of what Approved Consultants should do during consultation as part of basic training. It would be helpful if EMDRIA would provide guidance to Approved Consultants that is more detailed regarding what is to be covered during consultation toward Certification in the standards for consultation toward EMDRIA certification beyond what is indirectly suggested by the "Sample Evaluation Form" in the "Consultation Packet."

The Sample Evaluation Form in the "Consultation Packet" includes 17 scaled items and 2 summary statements for "strengths" and "weaknesses." There is a space for the Approved Consultant to sign and date the form suggesting that it could be submitted to EMDRIA or retained in the consultee's file as part of the Approved Consultant's records of consultation. The Sample Evaluation Form represents a good foundation for evaluating candidates for Certification. Approved Consultants may want to consider at least three broad issues not explicitly assessed in the Sample Evaluation Form:

- Applicants' knowledge of EMDR's principles, protocols, and procedures as described in Shapiro's basic text (2001)
- Applicants' ability to apply the standard reprocessing procedural steps— from memory—with good fidelity
- Applicants' ability to achieve treatment outcome results consistent with the scientific literature on EMDR

In evaluating candidates for certification, Approved Consultants should consider incorporating the use of standard fidelity rating scales, session summary forms, and treatment summary forms such as those provided in this treatment manual. Fidelity rating scales, such as those found in Appendix A, can be used both for self-evaluation by consultees and by the Approved Consultant to rate behavioral work samples provided by consultees. Session summary and record of treatment forms— found in Appendix B—help provide evidence of consultees' ability to achieve treatment outcome results consistent with the scientific literature on EMDR.

Accredited, graduate level university courses that meet standards for EMDRIA's basic training in EMDR generally require objective tests to assess fundamental knowledge of EMDR theory and procedures. EMDRIA does not presently require such examinations in EMDRIA approved basic training programs in EMDR. It is possible to develop a scientifically valid and reliable written objective proficiency examination to assess professional knowledge and skills in a postgraduate credentialing program such as the EMDRIA's certification program (McGhan, Stimmel, Gilman & Segal, 1982; Vu, Baroffio, Huber, Layat, Gerbase & Nendaz, 2006). A scientifically valid and reliable objective EMDR professional examination could be used as part of the credentialing process for becoming EMDRIA Certified in EMDR. Such an instrument could provide a more flexible approach to the consultation component of the requirements for EMDRIA certification. After completing Basic Training in EMDR some applicants might be capable of demonstrating appropriate knowledge and skills in the use of EMDR with less than 20 hours of consultation after completing basic training in EMDR. Approved Consultants could be freed from their dual role as both educators and evaluators to be able to focus on the educational component. Until EMDRIA or another respected EMDR association develops a scientifically validated objective examination for assessing EMDR knowledge and skills, Approved Consultants need to review and evaluate clinicians' *work samples*. The kinds of *work samples* Approved Consultants can consider were reviewed and discussed above in the section on the consultation portion of basic training in EMDR. *Of those methods reviewed above, video recordings and near-verbatim transcripts of sessions provide the most relevant and accessible information about what clinicians have actually done in their EMDR reprocessing sessions.*

Aspirational Standards for Consultation toward EMDRIA Certification in EMDR

In the spirit of advocating for aspirational standards, here are *proposed* minimum standards for consultation toward EMDRIA certification in EMDR that Approved Consultants can consider. Some Approved Consultants have already embraced some or all of these standards. For consultees obtaining group consultation, over the course of 10 hours of *group consultation*, each consultee would need to present case material on at least three different cases in which the standard EMDR procedural steps were employed. Case presentations and discussion would need to be at least 20 minutes in duration. Approved Consultants would need to document in writing the duration of each consultee's case presentations along with ratings of specific strengths and weakness in knowledge and skills for each case presentation.

During 10 hours of *individual consultation*, each consultee would need to present case material and behavioral work samples on at least five EMDR reprocessing sessions covering at least three different cases in which the standard EMDR procedural steps were employed. If all 20 hours of consultation were earned in individual consultation, each consultee would need to present case material and behavioral work samples on at least eight EMDR reprocessing sessions covering at least five different cases in which the standard EMDR procedural steps were employed. These behavioral work samples would need to achieve at least an "adequate" to "good" score on applicable standardized, fidelity rating scales. See Appendix A for a set of standardized, fidelity rating scales that could be used for this purpose.

Responding to Identified Weaknesses in Consultees' Knowledge and Skills

The consultation process toward EMDRIA certification requires Approved Consultant to play two roles. In one role, Approved Consultant are educators, reviewing concepts, principles, and techniques covered in the EMDR basic training and in scholarly publications on EMDR in the context of specific clinical cases. In their second role, Approved Consultants are required to evaluate applicants for EMDRIA certification before providing a letter of recommendation. EMDRIA has made this clear by stating that Approved Consultants are to communicate ". . .concerns about the applicant's readiness for Certification early in the consultation process so appropriate corrective measures can be taken by the applicant" (EMDRIA, 2008a).

In most cases, these two roles can be smoothly blended together in a supportive, collegial process. Issues can and do arise in some instances when Approved Consultant identify significant and persistent weaknesses in consultees' knowledge or skills that affect their use of EMDR. Outside of organized settings where clinicians may obtain hours of consultation from qualified supervisors, most consultees pursuing EMDRIA certification pay professional fees for required hours of consultation. They often have the expectation that when they have completed the minimum 20 hours of consultation, their Approved Consultant will write a letter of recommendation for EMDRIA certification. However, no matter how well Approved Consultants fulfill their responsibilities, 20 hours of consultation will not always be enough to address identified issues for every consultee.

EMDRIA has not provided guidelines for Approved Consultants and consultees to follow when the 20 hours of consultation have been completed, but the Approved Consultant has identified unresolved weaknesses in a consultee's understanding and use of EMDR that indicate the applicant is not ready for certification. EMDRIA has also not specified what an Approved Consultant's responsibilities are should an applicant withdraw from consultation with less than 20 hours of consultation after demonstrating unresolved weaknesses in knowledge or skill in the use of EMDR that would prevent the Approved Consultant from recommending that candidate for certification. Although such circumstances may be encountered infrequently, they do occur.

When the required consultation hours remain incomplete, the Approved Consultant is still required to provide a letter documenting hours of consultation earned, but only if asked to do so by the applicant. Two related issues not spelled out in EMDRIA's Philosophy of Consultation (EMDRIA, 2008a) may need to be addressed in the written agreement for consultation. The first arises when the applicant asks for documentation of completed hours. In this first case, is the Approved Consultant required, encouraged, or permitted to include in this required documentation reservations about an applicant at the time the applicant withdrew from consultation? The second arises when the applicant withdraws from consultation and does not request a letter of documentation. In this second case, is the Approved Consultant required, encouraged, or permitted to correspond with EMDRIA and to provide documentation that has not been requested to disclose reservations about an applicant at the time the applicant withdrew from consultation?

When an applicant's initial Approved Consultant has identified unresolved issues regarding a consultee's readiness for certification, this first Approved Consultant is likely to refuse to provide a letter of recommendation. The Approved Consultant may be required by professional standards to withhold such recommendation. The applicant may then elect to find another Approved Consultant. If most hours of consultation have been fulfilled with the first Approved Consultant, it may be difficult in the few remaining hours of consultation for the final Approved Consultant to identify the unresolved issues identified by the first Approved Consultant. In some cases, a consultee may search for an Approved Consultant who has different, and, perhaps more lax, subjective standards for recommending candidates for certification. This is an issue that experienced Approved Consultants have confronted. To address this issue, Approved Consultants may decide to inform consultees in advance how they address this issue when it arises by including it in the written agreement between the Approved Consultant and consultees.

When the applicant withdraws from consultation and does not request a letter of documentation, that applicant may abandon pursuing certification. It is also possible that the applicant will continue to pursue certification with a different Approved Consultant who holds different, perhaps less rigorous, standards than the first Approved Consultant. An explicit clause in a written agreement for consultation can provide clarification of the actions to be taken by the Approved Consultant when an applicant withdraws from consultation without completing all required hours. This can be more important when the Approved Consultant has identified significant concerns about the applicant's readiness for certification. Although these concerns may be fully mitigated by the applicant's subsequent corrective actions, they may not be. With an explicit prior written agreement,, the first Approved Consultant may appropriately disclose these concerns in a letter sent to both the applicant and to EMDRIA when the applicant withdraws from further consultation. Such correspondence strengthens the certification program by assuring that appropriate feedback is provided to all applicants and to EMDRIA regarding all applicants.

Since the aim of consultation is to help consultees achieve readiness for Certification in a supportive educational format, Approved Consultants may recommend a variety of measures beyond consultation to applicants who demonstrate weaknesses in knowledge or skills. These can include reading specific EMDR-related books or journal articles, taking the basic EMDR training a second time, attending EMDRIA approved continuing education programs, or studying handouts and recordings of EMDRIA Conference presentations. Other recommendations could include watching video recordings of EMDR sessions demonstrating good treatment fidelity or obtaining EMDR treatment to strengthen learning by experience or to address countertransference issues.

Elements of a Contract for Consultation toward EMDRIA Certification

EMDRIA does not explicitly state a requirement for a written contract for consultation for applicants for EMDRIA certification. However, EMDRIA does provide a sample contract (EMDRIA, 2008a). Prudent risk management and the importance of clarifying issues in advance make a written consultation agreement a wise idea. Several of the issues raised in this chapter go beyond those addressed in the sample contract provided by EMDRIA (EMDRIA, 2008a). Some of the key issues to be addressed in a consultation agreement toward EMDRIA certification include:

1) Specifying the nature of the relationship—consultation not supervision
2) Describing the financial arrangements
3) Listing the responsibilities of the consultee
4) Listing the responsibilities of the Approved Consultant.

The responsibilities of the consultee include the following:

1) Obtaining written consent for the release of information to the Approved Consultant from each patient prior to presenting case material during consultation.
2) Keeping a completed written release form in the patient's chart.
3) Avoiding disclosure of patients' names or other identifying information in verbal presentations, written documentation, or recordings of patient sessions.
4) Presenting case summaries, treatment plans, session summaries, behavioral work samples of sessions, and self-assessments that assist both the consultee and the Approved Consultant to assess the consultee's knowledge of EMDR theory, principles, and skills in the use of EMDR.
5) Honoring the financial agreement with the Approved Consultant.
6) Relying on the consultee's own discretion in selecting and using key information, principles, and methods the approved consultant brings to the consultee's attention.
7) Considering the need for additional reading, education, consultation, or training to meet minimum standards for knowledge and skills based on community and professional standards and as recommended by the approved consultant.

Responsibilities of the Approved Consultant include the following:

1) To have a completed, written agreement with consultees prior to starting consultation.
2) If a consultee is working under legally required supervision, to have the supervisor's name, contact information, and written acknowledgement that the consultee is obtaining consultation on their clinical use of EMDR.
3) To keep accurate records and to provide documentation of hours of consultation to the consultee and to the EMDRIA Education and Training coordinator.
4) To remain current on EMDR-related research, books, EMDRIA standards, and resources.
5) To be aware of the consultant's own limits of knowledge and competence for specific patient populations and, when warranted, to refer consultees to other Approved Consultants
who are more familiar with the population being treated by the consultee.
6) To encourage consultees to create appropriate written records and behavioral work samples of their clinical application of EMDR and to engage in self-evaluation of these records through the use of fidelity rating scales.
7) To provide clear, specific, and objective feedback on consultees' knowledge and application of EMDR theory, principles, and skills based on consultees' self-report, behavioral work samples, and the use of fidelity rating scales.
8) To review, clarify, and, where appropriate, instruct the consultee in knowledge and skills covered in the EMDRIA-required curriculum of the basic training in EMDR and in the relevant professional literature that supports the clinical use of EMDR.

9) To communicate concerns about areas where the consultee is in need of further development and the consultee's readiness to meet standards for EMDRIA certification periodically and as early in the consultation process as possible.

10) To recommend additional specific reading, education, training, and/or consultation to help consultees address areas in need of further development.

11) To provide the EMDRIA Education and Training coordinator a written recommendation or, if warranted, expression of concern about areas in need of further development when consultees complete their consultation requirement or withdraw from consultation.

To assist Approved Consultants and clinicians seeking consultation, two sample written agreements for consultation toward EMDRIA certification in EMDR are provided. One is for consultation provided by an Approved Consultant. The other is for consultation provided by a CIT. Approved Consultants and CITs should develop their own consultation agreements based on their own standards and understanding of evolving EMDRIA, professional, and statutory requirements. This sample agreement may be more detailed than what some approved consultants or consultees may prefer. The sample consultation agreement is as comprehensive as possible to assist clinicians in reviewing all the issues that need to be considered when entering into consultation toward EMDRIA certification. Approved Consultants and CITs should check with their professional associations and an attorney when drafting their own written agreements for consultation.

Selecting an Approved Consultant

The decision to select an Approved Consultant is important. The Approved Consultant you select will not only be your instructor and coach but also your evaluator. To select a consultant who will be a good fit, you need to consider your own learning style and potential consultants' teaching style, theoretical orientation, professional standards, and goals. EMDRIA leaves much to the discretion of Approved Consultants in determining how to structure consultation sessions and what standards to apply when recommending candidates for certification. Therefore, you need to be aware of how Approved Consultants you are considering working with have chosen to organize their consultation approach.

EMDRIA requires you to earn a total of 20 hours of consultation. As described above, EMDRIA permits up to 10 hours of group consultation to be earned during group sessions with up to eight participants. Many certification applicants chose to earn 10 hours of individual consultation in one-to-one consultation and 10 hours of group consultation during group sessions. During these 10 hours of group consultation, you are not always presenting your own case material. Instead, you are often listening or participating in discussions of other clinicians' case material. However, EMDRIA permits you to earn individual hours of consultation during group sessions when you are presenting case material. There is no specified limit to how many individual hours of consultation you can earn during group consultation. If you and your consultant agree, you could potentially present 10 hours of your case material over a series of group consultation sessions. Because the cost per hour of group sessions is generally significantly less than the cost of individual sessions, this can be a highly cost-effective way to earn all the required 20 hours. However, it will probably take significantly longer to earn the 10 individual hours of consultation through group sessions than it would in one-to-one sessions.

In addition to considering financial costs and length of time needed to accrue all 20 hours, many clinicians find the feedback and encouragement of other clinicians in the group setting can make presenting individual case material a more supportive and broader-based experience. During group consultation sessions, other clinicians give encouragement, discuss similar cases, raise additional questions, and offer additional resources. If you prefer the give-and-take group consultation, you may want to find an Approved Consultant who will allow you to earn

17.3 | Sample Consultation Agreement Toward EMDRIA Certification

This agreement is made between _____ (an EMDRIA-Approved Consultant—referred to in this agreement as "Consultant") and _____ ("Consultee"). Consultant agrees to provide Consultee with clinical case consultation in the use of EMDR consistent with EMDRIA's standards for consultation toward the designation of EMDRIA-Certified Clinician in EMDR.

Nature of Service: Consultee is seeking consultation services to increase Consultee's skills in the use of EMDR. In addition, Consultee requests Consultant to evaluate Consultee's fidelity in application of EMDR methods and procedures. Specific learning objectives include perceptual, conceptual, and functional skills with the theoretical, practical, and technical application of EMDR as a method of psychotherapy. EMDR case formulation and treatment planning skills will also be addressed.

Limits of Service: It is expressly understood that no supervision or employment relationship exists between Consultant and Consultee. Consultee affirms that he or she is independently licensed or credentialed to practice psychotherapy in his or her jurisdiction, maintains professional liability insurance, and that Consultee remains solely responsible for the nature and quality of the services provided to Consultee's clients. Consultant agrees to provide Consultee information based on available research, scholarly consensus, and Consultant's experience for Consultee to consider. At all times, Consultee will rely on his or her own judgment and discretion in offering psychotherapy services to Consultee's clients. Consistent with the professional standards of Consultee's licensure or certification, jurisdiction and professional membership's, Consultee will consider the need to obtain separate, additional consultation from another consultant(s) for any significant clinical, ethical, legal, or professional issues which either Approved Consultant or Consultee believe merit it.

(Alternate **Limits of Service** language when Consultee is working under legally required supervision as a prelicensed clinician: It is expressly understood that no supervision or employment relationship exists between Consultant and Consultee. Consultee acknowledges not being independently licensed or credentialed to practice psychotherapy in his or her jurisdiction. Consultee is providing psychotherapy services under the legally required supervision of _____ [referred to as "Supervisor"]. In signing below, Supervisor acknowledges that Supervisor remains solely responsible for the nature and quality of the services provided to Consultee's clients. Consultee agrees to review information received from Consultant during case discussions with Supervisor. Both Consultee and Supervisor affirm that they are covered by professional liability insurance. Consultant agrees to provide Consultee information based on available research, scholarly consensus, and Consultant's experience for Consultee to consider. At all times Consultee will work closely with Supervisor and rely on Supervisor's judgment in offering psychotherapy services to Consultee's clients. When significant clinical, ethical, legal, or professional issues arise which merit it, Consultee and/or Supervisor will consider the need to obtain additional consultation from another consultant in accord with the professional standards of Consultee's internship requirements and Supervisor's licensure or certification, jurisdiction and professional membership.)

Confidentiality: Consultee will notify his or her clients and obtain written informed consent prior to presenting any confidential case material to Consultant. Consultee agrees not to disclose any identifying information to Consultant and to take steps to alter or omit any potentially identifying information from case material being presented orally, in writing, or in audio or video recordings.

Evidence of fidelity in the use of EMDR: To assist Consultant in evaluating Consultee's knowledge and skill, Consultee will provide Consultant with behavioral work samples from actual clinical sessions. These can be in the form of audio or video recordings or near verbatim transcripts. One or more work samples must demonstrate satisfactory fidelity to standard EMDR principles, procedures, and protocols. More than one review may be needed to provide evidence of satisfactory fidelity. Consultee will present at least one behavioral work sample to Consultant by the 5th hour of consultation. If Consultant identifies significant issues that would prevent Consultant from being able to recommend Consultee for certification in EMDR, Consultant will notify Consultee as soon as possible. Consultant will then recommend possible corrective actions to Consultee.

(continued)

17.3 | Sample Consultation Agreement Toward EMDRIA Certification *(continued)*

Records and correspondence: Consultant will maintain a record of hours of consultation completed by Consultee. Consultee will maintain completed release of information forms in each individual case file authorizing Consultee to release information to Consultant. Consultee agrees that Consultant will submit a letter to EMDRIA describing the number of hours of consultation Consultant has provided when Consultee either completes required hours of consultation or discontinues consultation. Consultee may discontinue sessions at any time with the understanding that Consultant will submit a letter to EMDRIA documenting number of hours of consultation completed. If the Consultee discontinues consultation with significant issues identified by Consultant that remain unresolved, Consultant will describe these issues in correspondence to EMDRIA along with Consultant's suggestions for corrective action. If Consultee has completed required hours of consultation and provided evidence of satisfactory knowledge and skills in the application of EMDR, then Consultee will write a letter recommending Consultee for the designation of EMDRIA-Certified Clinician in EMDR.

Fees: Consultee will pay Consultant a fee of $_____ per hour of service for consultation. If consultee requests consultant to review work samples, such as videotapes or audiotapes without Consultee in attendance, Consultee agrees to pay a fee of $_____ per hour for review of work samples. Hours of consultation time may be counted for review of work samples only when both Consultee and Consultant are present. Consultee or Consultant will give at least ___ hours' notice of cancellation of scheduled sessions.

Resolution of issues: Consultant and Consultee agree to follow their respective professional organizations' code of ethics. If any professional or ethical issues arise related to the consultation relationship, Consultant and Consultee will make every effort to resolve them informally and with good will.

Approved Consultant   Consultee

Signed: _____   Signed: _____
Name: _____   Name: _____
Date: _____   Date: _____

(Name and signature below are only needed if Consultee is working under supervision.)

Supervisor

Signed: _____
Name: _____
Date: _____

some or all of your individual consultation hours during group sessions. On the other hand, you may prefer to have more individualized attention or may wish to avoid the need to disclose confidential case material to anyone other than a single Approved Consultant. You may want to schedule individual consultation sessions more frequently to get support with certain challenging cases or to complete certification requirements more quickly. In this case, you will want to focus on finding an Approved Consultant with whom you can earn all your hours of consultation in individual sessions.

You need to consider several issues when selecting your approved consultant. How important are the speed and cost of completing the process to you? Do you want to work face-to-face with a local consultant in your area? Are you willing—or do you need— to consider obtaining consultation by telephone or videoconference? Do you want to develop your knowledge and skills with a specific, specialty population? Do you prefer small group learning situations with three or four consultees, larger group situations with eight consultees, or individual sessions? Are you willing and able to video record reprocessing sessions or prepare near-verbatim transcripts?

 Sample Consultation Agreement With a Consultant-in-Training Toward EMDRIA Certification

This agreement is made between _____ (an EMDRIA Consultant-in-Training—referred to in this agreement as "CIT") and _____ ("Consultee"). CIT agrees to provide Consultee with clinical case consultation in the use of EMDR consistent with EMDRIA's standards for consultation toward the designation of EMDRIA-Certified Clinician in EMDR. CIT is in consultation with _____ (an EMDRIA-Approved Consultant—referred to in this agreement as "Consultant"). CIT and Consultant acknowledge that EMDRIA will allow a maximum of 15 of the required 20 hours of consultation to be obtained from a Consultant-in-Training. The additional 5 individual hours must be obtained from an EMDRIA-Approved consultant.

Nature of Service: Consultee is seeking consultation services to increase Consultee's skills in the use of EMDR. In addition, Consultee requests CIT to evaluate Consultee's fidelity in application of EMDR methods and procedures. Specific learning objectives include perceptual, conceptual, and functional skills with the theoretical, practical, and technical application of EMDR as a method of psychotherapy. EMDR case formulation and treatment planning skills will also be addressed.

Limits of Service: It is expressly understood that no supervision or employment relationship exists between CIT and Consultee. Consultee affirms that he or she is independently licensed or credentialed to practice psychotherapy in his or her jurisdiction, maintains professional liability insurance, and that Consultee remains solely responsible for the nature and quality of the services provided to Consultee's clients. CIT agrees to provide Consultee information based on available research, scholarly consensus, and Consultant's experience for Consultee to consider. At all times, Consultee will rely on his or her own judgment and discretion in offering psychotherapy services to Consultee's clients. Consistent with the professional standards of Consultee's licensure or certification, jurisdiction and professional membership's, Consultee will obtain separate, additional consultation from another consultant(s) for any significant clinical, ethical, legal, or professional issues which merit it.

(Alternate **Limits of Service** language when Consultee is working under legally required supervision as a prelicensed clinician: It is expressly understood that no supervision or employment relationship exists between CIT and Consultee. Consultee acknowledges not being independently licensed or credentialed to practice psychotherapy in his or her jurisdiction. Consultee is providing psychotherapy services under the legally required supervision of _____ [referred to as "Supervisor"]. In signing below, Supervisor acknowledges that Supervisor remains solely responsible for the nature and quality of the services provided to Consultee's clients. Consultee agrees to review information received from CIT during case discussions with Supervisor. Both Consultee and Supervisor affirm that they are covered by professional liability insurance. CIT agrees to provide Consultee information based on available research, scholarly consensus, and CIT's experience for Consultee to consider. At all times, Consultee will work closely with Supervisor and rely on Supervisor's judgment in offering psychotherapy services to Consultee's clients. When significant clinical, ethical, legal, or professional issues arise which merit it, Consultee and/or Supervisor will obtain additional consultation from another consultant in accord with the professional standards of Consultee's internship requirements and Supervisor's licensure or certification, jurisdiction and professional membership.)

Confidentiality: Consultee will notify his or her clients and obtain written informed consent naming both CIT and Consultant prior to presenting any confidential case material to Consultant. Consultee agrees not to disclose any identifying information to CIT and to take steps to alter or omit any potentially identifying information from case material being presented orally, in writing, or in audio or video recordings.

Evidence of fidelity in the use of EMDR: To assist CIT in evaluating Consultee's knowledge and skill, Consultee will provide CIT with behavioral work samples from actual clinical sessions. These can be in the form of audio or video recordings or near verbatim transcripts. One or more work samples must demonstrate satisfactory fidelity to standard EMDR principles, procedures, and protocols. More than one review may be needed to provide evidence of satisfactory fidelity.

(continued)

 | Sample Consultation Agreement With a Consultant-in-Training Toward EMDRIA Certification *(continued)*

Consultee will present at least one behavioral work sample to CIT by the 5th hour of consultation. If CIT identifies significant issues that would prevent CIT from being able to recommend Consultee for certification in EMDR, CIT will notify Consultee as soon as possible. CIT will then recommend possible corrective actions to Consultee. Consultee expressly gives permission for CIT to present verbal and written summaries of their consultation sessions to Consultant and to review all behavioral work samples with Consultant. Consultee expressly gives permission to CIT to provide a copy to Consultant of this agreement and all correspondence with EMDRIA regarding Consultee.

Records and correspondence: CIT will maintain a record of hours of consultation completed by Consultee. Consultee will maintain completed release of information forms in each individual case file authorizing Consultee to release information to CIT and Consultant. Consultee agrees that CIT will submit a letter to EMDRIA describing the number of hours of consultation CIT has provided when Consultee either completes required hours of consultation or discontinues consultation. Consultee may discontinue sessions at any time with the understanding that CIT will submit a letter to EMDRIA documenting number of hours of consultation completed. If the Consultee discontinues consultation with significant issues identified by CIT that remain unresolved, CIT will describe these issues in correspondence to EMDRIA along with CIT's suggestions for corrective action. If Consultee has completed required hours of consultation and provided evidence of satisfactory knowledge and skills in the application of EMDR, then CIT will write a letter recommending Consultee for the designation of EMDRIA-Certified Clinician in EMDR.

Fees: Consultee will pay CIT a fee of $_____ per hour of service for consultation. If Consultee requests CIT to review work samples, such as videotapes or audiotapes without Consultee in attendance, Consultee agrees to pay a fee of $_____ per hour for review of work samples. Hours of consultation time may be counted for review of work samples only when both Consultee and CIT are present. Consultee or CIT will give at least ___ hours' notice of cancellation of scheduled sessions.

Resolution of issues: CIT and Consultee agree to follow their respective professional organizations' code of ethics. If any professional or ethical issues arise related to the consultation relationship, CIT and Consultee will make every effort to resolve them informally and with good will.

Consultant-in-Training   Consultee

Signed: _____   Signed: _____
Name: _____   Name: _____
Date: _____   Date: _____

(Name and signature below are only needed if Consultee is working under supervision.)

Supervisor

Signed: _____
Name: _____
Date: _____

If you live in a rural area, there are likely to be few or no approved consultant or CITs in your immediate geographic area. This could necessitate time- and fuel-consuming trips to be able to meet with an Approved Consultant or CIT. However, EMDRIA makes provisions for telephone consultation for those who live in rural areas and have no Approved Consultant easily accessible for face-to-face consultation (EMDRIA, 2008c). No prior approval is needed in advance. Although EMDRIA may have created the option of telephone consultation for those with "no easily accessible" approved consultant, this option is actually available to any applicant. Therefore, clinicians can select an Approved Consultant from another region based on other factors in addition to accessibility. You may want to consider telephone consultation because of differences in fees, areas of expertise, methods and standards for certification, teaching style, or other factors.

Telephone consultation toward EMDRIA certification does not have to be by traditional telephone. Any real-time voice-only or videoconference communication would be equivalent including computer-based "voice chat" or "video chat" using an online service such as Skype. This makes even international consultation a readily viable option. Technology advances in recent years have led to increased ease of use and dramatically lower costs that make the use of voice-over-internet protocol (VOIP)-based communication widely accessible. These technologies make file sharing and video conferencing easy to use methods for advancing EMDR case discussions.

When clinicians prepare case summaries and behavioral work samples in handwritten form, these can be faxed to the Approved Consultant in advance. This method works fine for individual consultation or for a small group. For a group larger than three or four clinicians, faxing becomes less convenient. When clinicians prepare their materials on a computer, these can easily be emailed as attached files or can be placed in a free online file sharing service such as Box.net—with access limited to those you invite or in a password protected folder on file hosting service—such as the free skydrive.live.com or fee-based services such as fileburst.com. Electronic file distribution can be just as easy and secure when eight clinicians need access as when only the Approved Consultant needs access.

You can locate Approved Consultants in your geographic area through the main page of the EMDRIA Web site's "find a therapist" option by specifying, "Yes" in the Approved Consultant search field. You can then search by various geographic variables. Some of the Approved Consultant who offer telephone consultation advertise their availability in the *EMDRIA Newsletter*. EMDRIA members can access past and current newsletter issues through the members area of the EMDRIA Web site.

BECOMING AN APPROVED CONSULTANT

After achieving the designation of EMDRIA Certified Clinician in EMDR, as you gain more experience and confidence in your knowledge and skills in the use of EMDR, you may want to consider advancing professionally to the designation of Approved Consultant. Becoming an Approved Consultant gives you the opportunity to assist other clinicians in their process of professional development through consultation. As an Approved Consultant you are able to supervise the practice portion of the basic training in EMDR. Becoming an Approved Consultant is also the pathway for becoming an EMDRIA instructor for basic training in EMDR.

The process for becoming an Approved Consultant begins with familiarizing yourself with the standards for becoming an Approved Consultant. These include an experience requirement of having "conducted at least 300 EMDR sessions with no less than 75 clients" (EMDRIA, 2008d). Then find an Approved Consultant to serve as your mentor by providing you "consultation on your consultation." Enter into an agreement to discuss with your Approved Consultant the consultation you are providing to consultees. After establishing this agreement with your Approved Consultant, you are then considered a CIT. CITs do not have to submit an application or to register with EMDRIA to begin providing consultation. Apparently, EMDRIA considers the Approved Consultant providing consultation to each CIT sufficient representation for EMDRIA.

As a CIT, you have all the same responsibilities and many of the same privileges as an Approved Consultant. There are three primary differences. First, you may only provide 15 of the 20 hours of consultation required for certification.

Second, you must be receiving consultation from an Approved Consultant when you are providing consultation toward certification, and, when working in the basic training in EMDR, you must be "under the supervision of an Approved Consultant" when providing consultation or leading the practicum (EMDRIA, 2007, p. 10). However, the frequency of required consultation or "supervision" by an Approved Consultant is not specified by EMDRIA. Third, you may not provide consultation on consultation toward becoming an Approved Consultant. As a CIT, you do not have to pay an application fee or submit an application to be an Approved Consultant until you have completed all of the requirements to be an Approved Consultant. However, you do have to maintain your status as certified in EMDR.

STANDARDS FOR CONSULTATION TOWARD BEING AN APPROVED CONSULTANT

EMDRIA provides no explicit standards regarding frequency, documentation, structure, or focus for "consultation on consultation," or for evaluation of services provided by CITs. There is a sample "Consultant-in-Training Evaluation Form" in the "Consultation Packet" (EMDRIA, 2008a). However, EMDRIA has not established a requirement for a formal or informal evaluation process nor has EMDRIA established performance standards. The content of the CIT evaluation form not only suggests potential guidelines to Approved Consultant, providing consultation on consultation for CITs and evaluation of their services, but it also appears that EMDRIA gives wide latitude to Approved Consultant to determine their own standards. The consultant-in-training evaluation form is discussed further below. No surveys of the practices of Approved Consultant have been published or presented at EMDRIA conferences to date. Therefore, little is known about the methods or standards Approved Consultant use in working with CITs.

Aspirational Standards for Consultation on Consultation for EMDRIA CITs

In the spirit of advocating for minimum aspirational standards, here are some *proposed standards* for Approved Consultant to consider when providing consultation on consultation for CITs. Some Approved Consultants have already embraced some or all of these standards.

1) Establish a written agreement between the Approved Consultant and the CIT. Proposed elements for this agreement are listed in the next section below.
2) Notify EMDRIA that the CIT is starting to provide consultation services.
3) Have the CIT commit to meeting the proposed, aspirational standards for consultation toward EMDRIA certification described in the section above.

Elements of a Contract for Consultation for EMDRIA Consultant in Training

As with consultation toward certification, EMDRIA does not explicitly require a written contract for consultation with CITs. EMDRIA does provide a sample contract (EMDRIA, 2008a), which may be applicable to one model for *group consultation* to meet the CIT requirements for consultation, but which does not address other options such as individual consultation between the CIT and the Approved Consultant. This chapter addresses additional issues beyond those in the sample contract provided by EMDRIA. Issues to be addressed in a consultation agreement for CITs toward EMDRIA-Approved Consultant status include the following:

1) Specifying the nature of the relationship—consultation not supervision
2) Describing the financial arrangements
3) Listing the responsibilities of the CIT
4) Listing the responsibilities of the approved consultant

The responsibilities of the CIT include:

1) Establishing a written agreement with each consultee prior to commencing consultation toward certification.
2) Assuring that each consultee of the CIT obtain written consent for the release of information to both the CIT and the Approved Consultant from each patient prior to presenting case material during consultation.
3) Assuring that consultees keep a completed written release form in each patient's chart whose case is reviewed.
4) Instructing consultees to avoid disclosure of patients' names or other identifying information in verbal presentations, written documentation, or recordings of patient sessions and to avoid such disclosures in consultation with the CIT.
5) Presenting documentation for how they have reviewed case summaries, treatment plans, session summaries, behavioral work samples of sessions, and self-assessments that assist both consultees and the CIT to assess consultees' knowledge of EMDR theory, principles, and skills in the use of EMDR.
6) Honoring the financial agreement with the Approved Consultant.
7) Relying on the CIT's own discretion in selecting and using key information, principles, and methods the Approved Consultant brings to the CIT's attention.
8) Considering the need for additional reading, education, consultation, or training to meet minimum standards for knowledge and skills in providing consultation on EMDR based on community and professional standards and as recommended by the Approved Consultant.

Responsibilities of the Approved Consultant include the following:

1) To have a completed, written agreement with the CIT prior to the CIT starting consultation and prior to providing consultation to the CIT.
2) To keep accurate records and to provide documentation of hours of consultation to the CIT and to the EMDRIA education and training coordinator.
3) To remain current on EMDR-related research, books, EMDRIA standards, and resources.
4) To be aware of the consultant's own limits of knowledge and competence for specific patient populations and, when warranted, to refer CIT to other Approved Consultants who are more familiar with the population being treated by a consultee.
5) To make sure that the CIT understands the difference between consultation and supervision and to encourage the CIT to work from an instructional and consulting framework when providing consultation.
6) To encourage CIT to create appropriate written records and behavioral work samples of their consultation services on clinical application of EMDR and to engage in self-evaluation of these records.
7) To provide clear, specific, and objective feedback on CIT's knowledge and application of EMDR theory, principles, and skills based on CIT's self-report and behavioral work samples.
8) To review, clarify, and, where appropriate, instruct the CIT in knowledge and skills about consultation on the clinical use of EMDR.
9) To communicate concerns about areas in need of further development and the readiness of CIT to meet standards for EMDRIA-Approved Consultant status periodically and as early in the consultation process as possible.

10) To recommend additional specific reading, education, training, and/or consultation to help CIT address areas in need of further development.
11) To provide the EMDRIA education and training coordinator a written recommendation for the designation of Approved Consultant or, if warranted, written expression of concern about areas in need of further development when CIT completes the consultation requirement or withdraws from consultation.
12) To assist in providing consultees of CIT documentation of hours of consultation obtained from CIT and, if necessary and appropriate, letters of recommendation for certification should CIT withdraws from consultation without providing documentation of consultation hours to consultees.

Possible Formats for Providing "Consultation on Consultation"

Consultation on consultation can be provided in private sessions between the CIT and the Approved Consultant in person, over the telephone, or by computer voice chat or videoconference. It is also possible to provide group consultation on consultation sessions. The EMDRIA application for Approved Consultant (EMDRIA, 2008d) states that documentation of the required 20 hours of consultation from the Approved Consultant must specify how many hours were individual and how many were group. In this application, EMDRIA states that consultation of consultation groups should contain no more than four CITs.

To provide meaningful consultation on consultation, CITs need to be able to present behavioral work samples from their consultees together with their own consultative responses. The form of behavioral work samples Approved Consultant and CITs select for review shapes the format. CITs can provide verbal summaries of their consultation on consultees' verbal summaries of clinical interactions and reprocessing sessions. The verbal summary format requires the least preparation time by CITs and their consultees, and challenges the Approved Consultant to absorb and integrate a great deal of self-reported information that has no objective anchors. This is the weakest format for consultation, because it gives CITs and Approved Consultant the least amount of directly observable material from which to work.

Some CITs may offer group consultation sessions that include direct observation of practicum exercises between a pair of trainees. These practicum exercises could be video recorded to capture the consultative dialogue between consultees and the CIT. Excerpts of these video recordings could then be discussed with the Approved Consultant. Although this format provides some objective work samples for review, as discussed earlier in this chapter, the use of practicum exercises limits the relevance of clinical material being reviewed. Practicum exercises are fundamentally different from actual clinical cases. EMDRIA standards clearly call for consultation toward certification regarding actual clinical cases (EMDRIA, 2008a). At best, this format should have a limited role, if any, in consultation on consultation.

CITs can provide consultation based on a review of written case materials prepared by consultees. These can include case history and case formulation summaries and near-verbatim transcripts of clinical interactions and reprocessing sessions. CITs can then annotate these written materials with their observations and feedback. This method provides behavioral work samples of both consultees' underlying clinical work and CIT's consultative responses. As discussed earlier in this chapter, written case history, case formulation summaries, and near-verbatim transcripts provide a concise and easily reviewed set of objective material. Although written materials omit all of the timing and nearly all of the nonverbal elements of clinical sessions, their use anchors consultation on consultation to meaningful and objective work samples in a time-efficient manner.

In rare situations, CITs may be able to provide consultation after observing actual clinical sessions through a one-way mirror. These sessions and

 | Sample Consultation Agreement Toward EMDRIA-Approved Consultant

This agreement is made between _____ (an EMDRIA-Approved Consultant–referred to in this agreement as "Consultant") and _____ (an EMDRIA Consultant-in-Training—referred to in this agreement as "CIT"). Consultant agrees to provide CIT with clinical case consultation in how to provide consultation on the use of EMDR for applicants (referred to in the agreement as "Consultees") pursuing the designation of EMDRIA-Approved Consultant in EMDR.

Nature of Service: CIT is seeking consultation services to increase CIT's skills in providing consultation on the use of EMDR by qualified clinicians. Specific learning objectives can include perceptual, conceptual, and functional skills involving the theoretical, practical, and technical application of EMDR as a method of psychotherapy. EMDR case formulation and treatment planning skills as well as consultation strategies and evolving standards of consultation will also be addressed.

Limits of Service: It is expressly understood that no supervision or employment relationship exists between Consultant and CIT. CIT affirms that he or she is independently licensed or credentialed to practice psychotherapy in his or her jurisdiction, maintains malpractice insurance and that CIT remains solely responsible for the nature and quality of the consultation services provided to clinicians obtaining consultation from CIT. Consultant agrees to provide CIT information based on available research, scholarly consensus, EMDRIA standards, and Consultant's experience for CIT to consider. CIT will rely on his or her own judgment and discretion in offering consultation services to clinicians obtaining consultation from CIT.

Confidentiality: CIT will make sure that clinicians who obtain consultation from CIT will obtain written informed consent from their clients naming both Consultant and CIT for any disclosures prior to Consultees' patients presenting any confidential case material to CIT and Consultant. CIT agrees not to disclose any identifying information to Consultant and to take steps to alter or omit any potentially identifying information from case material and behavioral work samples being presented orally, in writing, or in audio or video recordings.

Evidence of ability to evaluate and increase fidelity in the use of EMDR: It is agreed that before Consultant will write a letter in support of EMDRIA-Approved Consultant status for CIT, CIT will provide Consultant with documentation that CIT is able to recognize when EMDR-trained clinicians are meeting or failing to meet reasonable standards of satisfactory fidelity to standard EMDR principles, procedures, and protocols, and that CIT is able to provide effective consultation services that assist clinicians in meeting those standards. This documentation will include: (a) one or more behavioral work samples (such as near verbatim transcripts or recordings) of EMDR treatment sessions that CIT has annotated with feedback for clinicians consulting with CIT; and (b) case summary forms for evaluation of EMDR treatment planning or treatment review that CIT has annotated with feedback for clinicians consulting with CIT. If Consultant identifies significant issues that would prevent Consultant from being able to recommend CIT for the designation of Approved Consultant in EMDR, Consultant will notify CIT as soon as possible. Consultant will then recommend possible corrective actions to CIT.

Records and correspondence: Consultant will maintain a record of hours of consultation completed by CIT. CIT will notify EMDRIA that CIT has begun providing consultation for EMDR-trained clinicians toward EMDRIA Certification. CIT agrees that Consultant will submit a letter to EMDRIA describing the number of hours of consultation Consultant has provided to CIT when CIT either completes required hours of consultation or discontinues consultation. CIT may discontinue sessions at any time with the following two agreements: (a) Consultant will submit a letter to EMDRIA documenting number of hours of consultation completed. (b) To enable Consultant to document hours of consultation for the Consultees of CIT, CIT will provide Consultant a list of hours of individual and group consultation CIT had provided to each EMDR-trained clinician who obtains consultation from CIT during the period of consultation covered by this agreement. If CIT discontinues consultation with significant issues identified by Consultant that remain unresolved, Consultant will describe these issues in correspondence to EMDRIA along with Consultant's suggestions for corrective action. If CIT has completed required hours of consultation and provided evidence of satisfactory knowledge and skills in the providing of consultation on application

(continued)

17.5 | Sample Consultation Agreement Toward EMDRIA-Approved Consultant *(continued)*

of EMDR, then Consultant will write a letter recommending CIT for the designation of EMDRIA-Approved Consultant in EMDR.

Fees: CIT will pay Consultant a fee of $____ per hour of service for consultation. If CIT requests Consultant to review work samples, such as videotapes or audiotapes without CIT in attendance, CIT agrees to pay a fee of $____ per hour for review of work samples. Hours of consultation time may be counted for review of work samples only when both CIT and Consultant are present. CIT or Consultant will give at least ___ hours' notice of cancellation of scheduled sessions.

Resolution of issues: Consultant and CIT agree to follow their respective professional organizations' code of ethics. If any professional or ethical issues arise related to the consultation relationship, Consultant and CIT will make every effort to resolve them informally and with good will.

Approved Consultant   Consultant-in-Training

Signed: _____   Signed: _____

Name: _____   Name: _____

Date: _____   Date: _____

the consultation sessions could be video recorded. The Approved Consultant could review excerpts of these recordings. These video recordings provide a dense record of the work samples of the actual clinical and consultative process. Again, because of time constraints, in most cases, only excerpts will be reviewed. This format provides a rich basis for consultation on consultation but, precisely because of the richness of video recordings, limits the amount of material that can be reviewed.

Evaluating Consultants-in-Training

EMDRIA clearly expects Approved Consultants to evaluate CITs before recommending applicants for acceptance as Approved Consultant. Their sample contract for CITs states that, "The Approved Consultant maintains the right to evaluate the applicant's performance and the amount of work deemed necessary for a positive outcome" (EMDRIA, 2008a, p. 5). The implication of this statement is that the required 20 hours is a minimum requirement, and that CITs are to reach EMDRIA's standards of readiness to serve as Approved Consultants. In the absence of an explicit statement of standards, it appears that EMDRIA gives wide discretion to Approved Consultants to determine what these standards are and to evaluate CIT's readiness.

EMDRIA provides some guidance on how to evaluate CIT readiness with a sample "Consultant-in-Training Evaluation Form" (EMDRIA, 2008a). EMDRIA does not require the use of this form or any other specific method of evaluation. This sample evaluation form has seven scaled items, one checklist for type of consultation offered by the CIT and two descriptive summaries, one for strengths and one for concerns and weaknesses. The first scaled item asks about the frequency of use of the sample certification in EMDR evaluation form that is found in the same consultation packet. The inclusion of this item suggests that EMDRIA considers it advisable to use the certification in EMDR evaluation form or a similar form to evaluate consultees.

Although the consultant-in-training evaluation form represented a useful starting point for developing an evaluation form when it was made available in 1999, it has never been updated. It is missing items for several key areas that

Approved Consultant should probably consider before recommending CITs to be approved as Approved Consultant. These include the following:

- Ability to teach the principles of case formulation and the rationale for procedural steps from the Adaptive Information Processing model.
- Ability to consistently recognize and appropriately correct technical errors or omissions in the standard EMDR procedural steps.
- Ability to recognize when reprocessing is effective or ineffective and suggest appropriate interventions—especially use of interweaves—to restore effective reprocessing.
- Whether the CIT appropriately encourages consultees to limit preparation time in cases that meet readiness for reprocessing with the standard EMDR procedural steps and to extend preparation time only as much as is needed to reach readiness for reprocessing.
- Whether the CIT makes effective use of appropriate fidelity rating scales.
- Whether the CIT refers consultees to appropriate professional books, journal articles, and other educational resources to supplement professional development for special populations and clinical issues.
- Whether the CIT deals appropriately with ethical, professional, and risk-management issues that arise in the consultative process.

In evaluating CITs, Approved Consultants bear the full responsibility for fulfilling EMDRIA's mission that is "dedicated to the highest standards of excellence and integrity in EMDR" (EMDRIA, 2008g). Approved Consultant provide the instruction, guidance, evaluation, and recommendations that prepare consultees and CITs for advanced recognition as EMDRIA Certified Clinician in EMDR and Approved Consultant. This makes Approved Consultant the guardians of EMDRIA's future. If their guidance is too vague or too idiosyncratic, if their standards are too permissive, they risk advancing applicants who will provide ineffective EMDR treatment or weak EMDR consultation and supervision. If their guidance is too dogmatic, if their standards are too rigid, they risk discouraging applicants and the clinical creativity needed to support the gradual evolution of a scientifically grounded clinical application of EMDR and consultation. More work needs to be done to develop additional resources to support Approved Consultant as well as to provide clearer standards to guide the consultative process.

SUMMARY

Consultation on the use of EMDR provides a crucial element in the training and development of clinicians, supervisors, consultants, and researchers. The consultative experience is a richly rewarding one. It provides clinicians a rare opportunity to discuss the challenging work that they do behind closed doors. It allows clinicians to reflect on their "successes" and "failures." Consultation provides a forum for intellectual stimulation, emotional support, and acknowledgement of professional achievement. Consultation carries with it additional requirements for the development of knowledge and skills, for reflection on professional and ethical standards, and the recognition and management of risk. EMDRIA-Approved Consultants assist in the delivery of basic training in EMDR, in the development and evaluation of treatment outcome research, and they play an essential role in the professional advancement of EMDR-trained clinicians.

Fidelity Checklists, Forms, Resources

Few clinicians like to have their work evaluated. However, such evaluations are often essential to advancing scientific knowledge or individual clinical skills. The degree to which a manualized method is applied as intended is referred to as a fidelity rating. Having a system for fidelity rating is one component of what has been described as the "gold standard" (Foa & Meadows, 1997) for treatment outcome studies of posttraumatic stress disorder. Clinicians who are serving as Approved Consultants need to have an objective set of criteria for evaluating the clinical work of those seeking the designation of being EMDR International Association (EMDRIA) Certified in Eye Movement Desensitization and Reprocessing (EMDR). Training supervisors may also be called on to assess the work of prelicensed clinicians in applying EMDR.

Until recently (Adler-Tapia & Settle, 2008), there were no published fidelity rating scales for assessing the application of EMDR. After reviewing the existing published fidelity rating scales (Adler-Tapia & Settle, 2008), EMDR Readiness Questionnaires (Sine & Vogelman-Sine, 2004), the "EMDR Implementation Fidelity Rating Scale" available from the EMDRIA Research Committee (Korn, Zangwill, Lipke, & Smyth, 2001), and the EMDRIA Consultation Packet (Standards and Training Committee, 2001), a set of six fidelity rating scales were developed for this manual.

This set of rating scales can be used by clinicians for self-rating. They can be used in clinical supervision by supervisees and clinical supervisors to clarify the use of EMDR. They can be use in conjunction with consultation as part of basic training in EMDR and toward the advanced designation of EMDRIA certification. Researchers should be aware that in addition to the scales in this chapter, the "EMDR Implementation Fidelity Rating Scales" (Korn, Zangwill, Lipke, & Smyth, 2001) are available from the EMDRIA Research Committee as described on the EMDRIA Web site (EMDRIA, 2008e). What follows is an overview of the six fidelity rating scales developed for this manual.

1) There is one fidelity scale covering history taking, case formulation, and treatment planning.
2) The preparation phase has three fidelity scales. The first scale covers general preparation issues including informed consent issues. A separate fidelity scale covers the use of calm place exercise. A third scale addresses the use of Resource Development and Installation (RDI)—including both appropriate use and avoiding excessive or inappropriate use. This scale can be skipped as not applicable in many treatment situations. When applicable, it can be used repeatedly if necessary to cover installation of resources during more than one treatment session.
3) A single reprocessing session rating scale is used repeatedly as necessary for as many targets as there are to be rated. It includes a reassessment section at the start that is skipped and not scored for the first reprocessing session for the patient.
4) The sixth rating scale provides an assessment of overall treatment including adjustments to the treatment plan based on previous reprocessing sessions and feedback from log; whether targets related to past, present, and future were identified and reprocessed appropriately; whether treatment goals were achieved.

Each of the six scales in this system uses a 3-point numeric rating:

a. "0" signifies missing or no adherence.

b. "1" signifies adherence is identified but is weak or flawed.

c. "2" signifies adherence is good.

Average rating scores are to be calculated for each scale as a whole and for each of the six sections of the reprocessing scale. Note that because some items are only scored when applicable, the total number of items to be averaged has to be counted for sections containing such items. There are a few critical items that, when applicable, are counted as two items. These doubled items contain two sets of rating numbers for ease in counting the number of items to be averaged.

Finally, there is a summary chart where average ratings from each applicable fidelity rating scale can be listed and a global adherence score can be computed. There is space on this summary chart for up to three applications of RDI and up to eight EMDR reprocessing sessions. The interpretation of the average ratings is as follows. An average rating of below 1 signifies inadequate adherence. An average rating of above 1 signifies weak adherence. An average rating above 1.25 signifies adequate adherence. An average rating above 1.5 signifies good adherence. An average rating of 1.75 signifies superior adherence.

EMDR FIDELITY RATING SCALE FOR HISTORY TAKING, CASE FORMULATION, TREATMENT PLANNING

Subject Code:		Date of Session:	
Rater:		Date of Review:	
Comments:		Average Rating:	

Rating scale: no adherence 0, weak 1, good 2.

1	Did the clinician obtain a list of presenting complaints (symptoms)?	0	1	2
2	Did the clinician identify the subject's treatment goals regarding desired behavioral, somatic, affective, and cognitive changes as well as any treatment related concerns or fears?	0	1	2
3	Did the clinician identify current external and internal stimuli and patterns of response associated with symptoms?	0	1	2
4	Did the clinician obtain a life history of adverse and traumatic events?	0	1	2
5	Did the clinician identify childhood and current attachment patterns?	0	1	2
6	Did the clinician rule out medical and other risk issues for EMDR reprocessing?	0	1	2
7	Did the clinician identify nature and degree of structural dissociation (primary, secondary, or tertiary) using tools and clinical assessment?	0	1	2
8	Did the clinician identify specific Axis I diagnoses and identify or rule out Axis II diagnoses?	0	1	2
9	Did the clinician assess history and current substance abuse?	0	1	2
10	Did the clinician assess history and current danger to self and others?	0	1	2
11	Did the clinician assess history and current tension reduction, self-injurious, and therapy interfering behaviors?	0	1	2
12	Did the clinician assess skills needed and provide a preparation phase of appropriate length, (i.e., long enough while not needlessly delaying or avoiding reprocessing)?	0	1	2
13	Did the clinician develop a collaborative treatment plan and sequence of targets?	0	1	2
14	Did the clinician develop an overall case formulation?	0	1	2
	History-taking phase average score: Total of 14 items.			

EMDR FIDELITY RATING SCALE FOR PREPARATION PHASE SESSION

Subject Code:		Date of Session:	
Rater:		Date of Review:	
Comments:		Average Rating:	

Rating scale: no adherence 0, weak 1, good 2.

1	Did the clinician provide psychoeducation on trauma and recovery?	0	1	2
2	Did the clinician provide psychoeducation on subject's role in sessions?	0	1	2
3	Did the clinician provide informed consent to treatment with EMDR?	0	1	2
4	Did the clinician assess subject's tolerance for bilateral eye movements?	0	1	2
5	Did the clinician have subject rehearse a stop signal?	0	1	2
6	Did the clinician provide a metaphor to enhance mindful noticing?	0	1	2
7	Did the clinician assess, teach, and reassess anxiety-reduction skills as needed?	0	1	2
8	Did the clinician assess, teach, and reassess dissociation reduction skills as needed?	0	1	2
9	Did the clinician utilize calm (safe) place or RDI before reprocessing?	0	1	2
	Preparation phase average score: Total of 9 items.			

EMDR FIDELITY RATING SCALE FOR CALM PLACE - SAFE PLACE EXERCISE

Subject Code:		Date of Session:	
Rater 1:		Date of Review:	
Comments:		Average Rating:	

Rating scale: no adherence 0, weak 1, good 2.

1	Did the clinician provide an explanation and purpose for the exercise?	0	1	2
2	Did the clinician assist in identifying an appropriate memory or image?	0	1	2
3	Did the clinician elicit additional sensory details?	0	1	2
4	Did the clinician add brief sets (4–12 cycles) of bilateral stimulation?	0	1	2
5	Did the clinician ask subject to report feelings and observations after each set of stimulation?	0	1	2
6	Did the clinician ask subject to identify a cue word or phrase and rehearse it with the imagery and additional sets of stimulation?	0	1	2
7	Did the clinician ask subject to rehearse the imagery and cue word(s) without guidance?	0	1	2
8	Did the clinician ask subject to remember a disturbing incident or situation and then rehearse the exercise again with guidance?	0	1	2
9	Did the clinician ask subject to remember another disturbing incident or situation and then rehearse the exercise again without guidance?	0	1	2
10	Did the clinician ask subject to identify an alternate memory or image if the first led to negative associations? (*Skip if not applicable.*)	0	1	2
	Calm (safe) place exercise average score: One item can be skipped. Possible total of 10 items.			

EMDR FIDELITY RATING SCALE FOR RESOURCE DEVELOPMENT AND INSTALLATION

Subject Code:		Date of Session:	
Rater:		Date of Review:	
Comments:		Average Rating:	

Rating scale: no adherence 0, weak 1, good 2.

1	If RDI was used for stabilization, did the clinician identify the presence of one of the following four criteria before using RDI? (*Skip if RDI was not used for stabilization. **Counts as two items if applicable.***) a. The subject shows impaired self-regulation skills, engages in maladaptive tension reduction behaviors, substance abuse, self-injurious, or therapy interfering behaviors, or has expressed fears of starting EMDR reprocessing, and standard methods for self-control (progressive relaxation, breathing exercises, or calm place exercise) have proven insufficient. b. The clinician identified a substantial risk the subject would terminate treatment prematurely if EMDR reprocessing were started because of borderline shifts from idealizing to devaluing the clinician, weak ego strength, or intolerable shame over acting out or tension reduction behaviors, or reexperiencing incompletely reprocessed or other intrusive, painful memories. c. The subject has episodes of being overwhelmed by affect, is confused, and is unable to express thoughts, concerns, or affects about events in a coherent narrative. d. EMDR reprocessing has led to chronically incomplete treatment sessions or to adverse impacts on subject's day-to-day functioning.	0 0	1 1	2 2
2	Did the clinician provide an explanation and purpose for the exercise?	0	1	2
3	Did the clinician identify an appropriate, current, challenging target situation from a behavioral chain analysis or a chronically incomplete reprocessing target?	0	1	2
4	Did the clinician assist in identifying one or more qualities or skills needed for the target situation?	0	1	2
5	Did the clinician assist in identifying one or more appropriate memories or images for the qualities or skills needed for the target situation?	0	1	2
6	Did the clinician prompt the subject (if needed and appropriate) to consider mastery memories, role models, supportive others, and symbols as potential sources for adaptive responses? (*Skip if not applicable.*)	0	1	2
7	Did the clinician elicit additional sensory details?	0	1	2
8	Did the clinician repeat these sensory details to enhance recollection and vividness of the memory or image?	0	1	2
9	Did the clinician add brief sets (4–12 cycles) of bilateral stimulation?	0	1	2
10	Did the clinician ask the subject to report feelings and observations after each set of stimulation?	0	1	2
11	If needed, did the clinician repeat the sensory details to restore access to the resource memory or imagery before subsequent sets of stimulation?	0	1	2
12	Did the clinician ask subject to identify cue words or linking imagery and rehearse with the resource and additional sets of stimulation?	0	1	2
13	Did the clinician ask subject to identify an alternate memory or image if the first led to negative associations? (*Skip if not applicable.*)	0	1	2
14	Did the clinician verify the subject was able to mentally rehearse making use of one or more resources with adequate confidence in a future occurrence of the target situation?	0	1	2
15	Did the clinician verify in a follow-up session that the subject was better able to manage the target situation? (*Skip if not applicable.*)	0	1	2
	Resource Development and Installation average score: Up to four items can be skipped. Fifteen items, one can be doubled.			

EMDR FIDELITY RATING SCALE FOR REPROCESSING SESSION

Subject Code:		Date of Session:	
Rater:		Date of Review:	
Comments:		Average Rating:	

Rating scale: no adherence 0, weak 1, good 2.

Reevaluation phase average score (items 1–5):		
Assessment phase average score (items 6–13):		
Desensitization phase average score (items 14–27):		
Installation phase average score (items 28–33):		
Body scan phase average score (items 34–37):		
Closure phase average score (items 38–43):		

	Reevaluation phase			
1	Did the clinician assess the subject's experience since the last session with attention to feedback from the log, presenting complaints, responses to current stimuli, and additional memories or issues that might warrant modifications to the treatment plan?	0	1	2
2	Did the clinician check the SUD and VoC on the target from the last session? (*Skip if this is the first reprocessing section.*)	0	1	2
3	Did the clinician check for additional aspects of the target from the last session that may need further reprocessing? (*Skip if this is the first reprocessing section.*)	0	1	2
4	If the target from the last session had been incomplete or if in this session the subject reported the SUD were now a 1 or above or the VoC were a 5 or below, did the clinician resume reprocessing on the target from the last session? (*Skip if this is the first reprocessing section or if a more appropriate, disturbing, earlier or related memory was identified and selected as the next target.*)	0	1	2
	Reevaluation phase average score (items 1–4):			
	Possible total of four items. Three can be skipped.			

	Assessment phase			
5	Did the clinician select an appropriate target from the treatment plan?	0	1	2
6	Did the clinician elicit a picture (or other sensory memory) that represented the entire incident or the worst part of the incident?	0	1	2
7	Did the clinician elicit an appropriate negative cognition (NC)?	0	1	2
8	Did the clinician elicit an appropriate positive cognition (PC)?	0	1	2
9	Did the clinician obtain a valid VoC by referencing the felt confidence of the PC in the present while the subject focused on the picture (or other sensory memory)?	0	1	2
10	Did the clinician elicit the present emotion by linking the picture and the NC?	0	1	2
11	Did the clinician obtain a valid SUD (i.e., the current level of disturbance for the entire experience)?	0	1	2
12	Did the clinician elicit a body location for current felt disturbance?	0	1	2
13	Did the clinician follow the standard assessment sequence listed above?	0	1	2
	Assessment phase average score (items 5–13):			
	Total of nine items.			

	Desensitization phase			
14	Before beginning bilateral stimulation, did the clinician instruct subject to focus on the picture, NC (in the first person) and the body location?	0	1	2
15	When beginning desensitization, did the clinician provide bilateral stimulation of at least 24–30 repetitions per set as fast as could be tolerated comfortably?	0	1	2

16	During bilateral stimulation, did the clinician give some periodic nonspecific verbal support (perhaps contingent to nonverbal changes in subject) while avoiding dialogue?	0	1	2
17	At the end of each discrete set of bilateral stimulation, did the clinician use appropriate phrases to have the subject, "Rest, take a deeper breath, let it go," then make a *general* inquiry ("What do you notice now?") and then resume bilateral stimulation?	0	1	2
18	After each verbal report, did the clinician resume bilateral stimulation without excessive delay for discussion and without repeating subject's verbal report?	0	1	2
19	If verbal reports and nonverbal observations indicated reprocessing was effective, after reaching a neutral or positive channel end, did clinician return attention to the selected target and check for additional material in need of reprocessing (i.e., "What's the worst part of it now?")	0	1	2
20	If verbal reports or nonverbal observations indicated reprocessing was ineffective, did the clinician vary characteristics of the bilateral stimulation (speed, direction, change modality, etc.)? (*Skip if not applicable.* Counts as two items if applicable.)	0 0	1 1	2 2
21	If verbal reports or nonverbal observations indicated reprocessing was ineffective, did the clinician do any of these? (*Skip if not applicable.* Counts as two items if applicable.) 1) Explore for an earlier disturbing memory with similar affect, body sensations, behavioral responses, urges, or belief. 2) Explore for a negative belief, fear or concern, and a related memory. 3) Explore target memory for more disturbing images, sounds, smells, thoughts, beliefs, emotions, or body sensation. 4) Invite subject to imagine expressing unspoken words or acting on unacted urges. 5) Offer an interweave.	0 0	1 1	2 2
22	If subject showed extended intense emotion, or if reprocessing was ineffective, did clinician show appropriate judgment in selecting and offering an interweave from among the categories of responsibility, safety, and choices while avoiding excess verbiage? (*Skip if not applicable.* Counts as two items if applicable.)	0 0	1 1	2 2
23	If subject showed extended intense emotion, did clinician continue sets of bilateral stimulation with increased repetitions per set, remain calm, detached, compassionate, and provide verbal cueing paced with the bilateral stimulation to encourage the subject to continue to "just notice" or "follow." (*Skip if not applicable.* Counts as two items if applicable.)	0 0	1 1	2 2
24	If a more recent memory emerged, did the clinician acknowledge its significance, offer to return to the more recent memory later, and redirect the subject back to the selected target memory within one or two sets of bilateral stimulation? (*Skip if not applicable.*)	0	1	2
25	If an earlier (antecedent) memory emerged, did the clinician continue bilateral stimulation on the earlier memory until it was resolved before redirecting the subject back to the selected target memory? (*Skip if not applicable.*)	0	1	2
26	If it became clear it was not possible to complete reprocessing in this session, did clinician show appropriate judgment to avoid returning subject's attention to residual disturbance in target, skip installation and body scan phases and go directly to closure? (*Skip if not applicable.*)	0	1	2
27	If it appeared the desensitization phase may have been complete, did clinician show appropriate judgment to return subject's attention to target to confirm the SUD was 0 (or an "ecological" 1) before going to the installation phase? (*Skip if not applicable.*)	0	1	2

Desensitization phase average score (items 14–27):

Up to eight items can be skipped. Fourteen items, plus four can be doubled.

Installation phase

If the desensitization phase were completed (and item 27 above was scored) proceed to score installation phase items. If the desensitization phase was incomplete, skip both the installation and body scan phases and proceed to score the closure phase. However, if the desensitization was incomplete and the clinician incorrectly proceeded to the installation or body scan phases, these phases should be scored and down rated accordingly.

28	Did the clinician confirm the final PC by inquiring whether the original PC still fit or if there were now a more suitable one?	0	1	2
29	Before offering bilateral stimulation, did the clinician obtain a valid VoC (i.e., by having subject assess the felt confidence of the PC while thinking of the target incident)?	0	1	2
30	Did the clinician offer more sets of bilateral stimulation after asking each time that the subject focus on the target incident and the final PC?	0	1	2

31	Did the clinician obtain a valid VoC after each set of bilateral stimulation?	0	1	2
32	After sets of bilateral stimulation, if the VoC did not rise to a 7, did the clinician inquire what prevents it from rising to a 7 and then make an appropriate decision to target the thought or move to body scan or closure? (*Skip if not applicable.*)	0	1	2
33	Did the clinician continue sets of bilateral stimulation until the VoC was a 7 and no longer getting stronger (or a 6 if "ecological") ? (*Skip if not applicable.*) (Note that unless there were (a) insufficient time to complete the installation phase or (b) a new issue emerged that prevented completing the installation phase, either item 32 or 33 should be scored.)	0	1	2
	Installation phase average score (items 28–33): Up to two items can be skipped. Possible total six items.			
	Body scan phase			
34	Did the clinician obtain a valid body scan (asking subject to [a] report any unpleasant sensation while focusing on [b] the final PC and [c] the target incident with eyes closed)?	0	1	2
35	*If any unpleasant sensations were reported,* did the clinician continue with additional sets of bilateral stimulation until these sensations became neutral or positive? If unpleasant sensations were reported and bilateral stimulation was not offered, was there an appropriate clinical rationale (i.e., linkage to a different memory)? (*Skip if not applicable.*)	0	1	2
36	*If a new memory emerged,* did the clinician make an appropriate decision to continue by targeting the new memory in the session or later as part of the treatment plan? (*Skip if not applicable.*)	0	1	2
37	*If pleasant sensations were reported,* did the clinician target these and continue with additional sets of bilateral stimulation until these sensations became more positive? (*Skip if not applicable.*)	0	1	2
	Body scan phase average score (items 34–37): Up to three items can be skipped. Possible total of four items.			
	Closure phase			
38	Did the clinician make an appropriate decision to move to closure?	0	1	2
39	Did the clinician offer appropriate empathy, psychoeducation, and statements to normalize and help put into perspective the subject's experience?	0	1	2
40	Did the clinician assure subject was appropriately reoriented to the present by (a) *assessing* the subject's residual distress and need to change state and (b) *if needed* then offer appropriate and sufficient structured procedures (such as guided imagery, breathing exercises) for decreasing anxiety, distress, dissociation, and for containment?	0	1	2
41	Did the clinician brief the subject on the possibility between sessions of continuing or new, positive or distressing thoughts, feelings, images, sensations, urges, or other memories or dreams related to the reprocessing from this session?	0	1	2
42	Did the clinician request that the subject keep a written log of any continuing or new material or other changes to share at the next session?	0	1	2
43	Did the clinician remind the subject to make use of a self-control procedure daily or as needed?	0	1	2
	Closure phase average score (items 38–43): Total of 6 items.			

EMDR FIDELITY RATING SCALE FOR OVERALL TREATMENT

Subject Code:		Date of Session:	
Rater:		Date of Review:	
Comments:		Average Rating:	

Rating scale: no adherence 0, weak 1, good 2.

1	Did the clinician assess the degree to which the subject achieved treatment goals regarding desired behavioral, somatic, affective, and cognitive changes?	0	1	2
2	Did the clinician assess the degree to which adverse and traumatic events from subject's history were resolved and offer further EMDR reprocessing as indicated?	0	1	2
3	Did the clinician assess the degree to which maladaptive patterns of response to current external and internal stimuli were resolved and offer further EMDR as indicated?	0	1	2
4	Did the clinician assess the degree to which the subject could benefit from exploring new behavioral choices (such as overcoming previous avoidant behaviors) or integrating new skills or a new self-image for the future and offer further EMDR reprocessing on a future template or Resource Development and Installation to consolidate a new self-image as indicated?	0	1	2
	Overall treatment average score:			
	Total of 4 items.			

EMDR FIDELITY SUMMARY CHART		
FIDELITY RATING SCALES	AVERAGE SCORES RATER 1	AVERAGE SCORES RATER 2
History-Taking phase		
Preparation phase		
Calm (safe) place Exercise		
Resource Development and Installation 1 (optional)		
Resource Development and Installation 2 (optional)		
Resource Development and Installation 3 (optional)		
Reprocessing session 1		
Reprocessing session 2		
Reprocessing session 3		
Reprocessing session 4		
Reprocessing session 5		
Reprocessing session 6		
Reprocessing session 7		
Reprocessing session 8		
Overall Treatment		
Average across all charts		

Rater 1 Comments

Rater 2 Comments

Average rating	Adherence interpretation
0–0.99	Inadequate
1.0–1.25	Weak
1.26–1.50	Adequate
1.51–1.75	Good
1.76–2.00	Superior

Appendix B
Procedural Scripts and Forms for Planning and Documenting EMDR Treatment

B.1 | Treatment Goals and Concerns

Name: _____   Date: _____

BEHAVIORAL: WANTS MORE	WANTS LESS	CONCERNS

AFFECTIVE: WANTS MORE	WANTS LESS	CONCERNS

COGNITIVE: WANTS MORE	WANTS LESS	CONCERNS

SOMATIC: WANTS MORE	WANTS LESS	CONCERNS

 **B.2** | Assessing Stability and Readiness for Reprocessing

Name: _____   Date: _____

For *history* indicate severity of worst episode.
For *current situation* indicate severity on date of assessment.
Impact of factor on stability: 0 absent; 1 minimal; 2 moderate; 3 severe.

ISSUE	HISTORY INCLUDES	SEVERITY	CURRENT SITUATION	SEVERITY
Secondary gain/loss		0 1 2 3		0 1 2 3
Trust or truth absent		0 1 2 3		0 1 2 3
External crises		0 1 2 3		0 1 2 3
Financial instability		0 1 2 3		0 1 2 3
Health risk		0 1 2 3		0 1 2 3
Bipolar Depression		0 1 2 3		0 1 2 3
Suicidal ideation		0 1 2 3		0 1 2 3
Suicide attempts		0 1 2 3		0 1 2 3
Self-injury		0 1 2 3		0 1 2 3
Injury to others		0 1 2 3		0 1 2 3
High-risk behaviors		0 1 2 3		0 1 2 3
Denial of diagnosis		0 1 2 3		0 1 2 3
Accident-prone self		0 1 2 3		0 1 2 3
Substance abuse		0 1 2 3		0 1 2 3
Compulsive sex		0 1 2 3		0 1 2 3
Compulsive acts ($)		0 1 2 3		0 1 2 3
Alexithymia		0 1 2 3		0 1 2 3
Flooded by affect		0 1 2 3		0 1 2 3
Depersonalization		0 1 2 3		0 1 2 3
Amnesia or fugue		0 1 2 3		0 1 2 3
DID or DDNOS		0 1 2 3		0 1 2 3

| | Notes on Assessing Readiness and Stability for Reprocessing |

Secondary gain/loss	When current secondary gain is moderate or severe, reprocessing is more likely to be incomplete and may require problem solving. Reprocessing may be attempted unless incomplete reprocessing would lead to premature discontinuation of treatment.
Trust or truth absent	When the patient lacks sufficient trust to be truthful *and* there are other dangerous or therapy-interfering behaviors, reprocessing may need to be postponed. Even without overt evidence of dangerousness, attempts to reprocess targets with inadequate trust or disclosure (truth telling) can lead to dangerous acting out or complications that might prevent future consideration of reprocessing.
External crises	When external work, personal, or family crises require patient's full attention, reprocessing may need to be postponed. Other patients may benefit from prompt reprocessing of associated early memories.
Financial instability	Inability to complete treatment or realistic fears of impending loss of basic financial security may need to be addressed before reprocessing.
Health risk	Any life threatening health risk that could be exacerbated by emotional reprocessing, and any history of eye problems should be evaluated and cleared by a physician before starting reprocessing. (Examples: risk of stroke, heart attack). Also potential risk to pregnancy requires informed consent and physician ok.
Bipolar depression	Bipolar depression carries greater risk of suicide attempts.
Suicidal ideation	Suicidal ideation requires careful assessment and ongoing monitoring for intent, plan, and lethality.
Suicide attempts	Past suicide attempts need to be fully understood to assess current risk. Risk factors need ongoing monitoring during treatment. When risk remains present, clinicians should be cautious in considering reprocessing. Clarify treatment contract and mandated actions to protect patient.
Self-injury	Self-harming behaviors need to be carefully assessed for dangerousness to life and risk of self-mutilation. Dangerous self-harm should be fully stabilized before reprocessing and carefully monitored during reprocessing. Clarify treatment contract and mandated actions to protect patient.
Injury to others	Past- and current-acts and urges need to be carefully assessed and monitored for risk and lethality. Clinicians should be cautious in considering reprocessing when risks factors are present. Clarify treatment contract with patient and that mandated reports may become necessary.
High-risk behaviors	Current vulnerability to high-risk behaviors should be carefully assessed and addressed to protect patient from dangerous self-injury, revictimization, or harm to others.
Denial of diagnosis	Attempts to proceed with reprocessing when the patient is in denial of a major diagnosis—such as substance abuse, dissociative identity disorder, bipolar disorder, or any psychotic disorder—can put the patient at risk.
Accident-prone self	Accident proneness can indicate unconscious acts of self-injury or assault and should be assessed carefully for current risk.
Substance abuse	For types of substance abuse that can be threats to life or health, reprocessing should be postponed until stable recovery is achieved. With limited published EMDR research for this population, clinical issues require careful consideration and informed consent.
Compulsive sex	Dangerousness to self and others needs to be carefully considered.
Compulsive acts ($)	Compulsive spending or gambling could remain unstable or be worsened by emotional reprocessing. Absence of controlled research needs to be part of informed consent. Stabilizing interventions should be considered.
Alexithymia	Mild alexithymia (such as problems naming emotions) should not interfere with reprocessing. Moderate to severe alexithymia—no access to affect—is more likely to interfere with reprocessing and may require modifications in procedure. Alexithymia by itself is seldom a reason to withhold EMDR, but it may be when present with other factors.
Flooded by affect	Prolonged intense weeping, anger, terror, or shame during verbal therapy may predict inability to reprocess. Affect tolerance and management skills building may need to be the focus. Standard reprocessing should not be withheld unless a failure at reprocessing would lead to a refusal to consider reprocessing in the future.
Depersonalization and derealization	Depersonalization and derealization experiences can be intensely painful, frightening, and shameful for some patients. Patients who frequently experience depersonalization or derealization in verbal therapy are more likely to do so and more intensely during reprocessing. Strategies for self-control and affect management may need to be practiced before reprocessing can succeed.
Amnesia or fugue	Evidence of past or current fugue or current amnesia episodes—loss of time—indicates a need for more complete assessment of dissociation before reprocessing to avoid risk of harm to patient.
DID or DDNOS	A possible current diagnosis of dissociative identity disorder or dissociative disorder not otherwise specified indicates a need for more careful assessment of dissociation before reprocessing to avoid risk of harm to patient. Lack of stabilization in DID or DDNOS such as uncontrolled rapid switching, uncontrolled flashbacks, and poor cooperation and communication among parts of the personality indicate a need to postpone reprocessing. ISST-D and EMDR Treatment Guidelines should be followed.

Master Treatment Plan List of Targets

MASTER TREATMENT PLAN CHART		

List memories and resources from earliest (top) to most recent (bottom)

Name: _____   Page: _____ of _____

ID	AGE	TRAUMA MEMORY OR PERSISTENT STRESSOR DATE(S) OF TREATMENT AND POST-TX SUDS	ID	AGE	RESOURCE MEMORY DATE(S) OF TX AND POST RDI VOR
1			A		
2			B		
3			C		
4			D		
5			E		
6			F		
7			G		
8			H		
9			I		
10			J		

List symptoms and associated current stimuli with Frequency (F) and Severity (S) 0–7

ID	SYMPTOMS	CURRENT STIMULI	INTAKE F & S	DESIRED F & S	DISCHARGE F & S
a					
b					
c					
d					
e					
f					
g					

 Record of Treatment

List symptoms by name or letter from Master Treatment Plan. Indicate worsened: −3, −2, or −1. Unchanged 0 or improved: +1, +2, to +3.

For each session code activities with this key

Hx = History taking	RE = Reevaluation	SC = Structured Calming	RDI =Calm Place or Resource
Mem = Target Memory	CrS = Current Stimuli	Fut = Future Template	VT = Verbal Therapy
IVE = in vivo exposure	CBT = Cognitive	Art = Art Therapy	Hyp = Hypnosis
IM = Imagery			

For RDI and EMDR sessions, you can list selected target memory, stimuli, or resource by ID # from Master Treatment Plan.

Name: _____   Page: _____ of _____

SESSION	DATE	GAF	SYMPTOMS	ACTIVITY TARGET	PRE SUD VOC	POST SUD VOC	SELECTED NC FINAL PC	OUTCOME HOMEWORK
1								
2								
3								
4								
5								
6								
7								
8								
9								
10								
11								
12								

B.6 | Basic Procedural Steps and Script for Resource Development and Installation

1) *Describe an incident or stressful situation:* _____

   How disturbing does it feel to you right now, from 0 to 10 where 0 is no disturbance or neutral and 10 is the highest disturbance you can imagine?

   SUD: 0   1   2   3   4   5   6   7   8   9   10

2) *Which positive resource, skill, or strength will help you to deal better with this stressful situation?* (Identify up to three of these if possible. It is fine to just identify one initially and go through step 4. Then return to step 2 to identify a second resource, and later return to step 2 to identify a third. Note: When possible select resources that will assist both with the current stressful situation and with subsequent reprocessing of etiological experiences.)

   a. _____

   b. _____

   c. _____

   Describe a moment or situation in your life when you experienced that resource, skill, or strength.

   a. _____

   b. _____

   c. _____

3) *What image best represents this situation?*

   a. _____

   b. _____

   c. _____

   Where do you feel it in your body?

   a. _____

   b. _____

   c. _____

4) *Now focus on the image and notice where you are feeling in your body. Then follow my fingers (lights, taps, or tones).*

   (Add one set of 6–12 movements.)

   What do you notice in your body now?

   a. _____

   b. _____

   c. _____

   (If the experience stays positive or gets stronger, do a second set of 6–12 movements.)

   Stay with that and follow again.

   What do you notice in your body now?

   a. _____

   b. _____

   c. _____

   Tell me a word or phrase that can help identify this resource.

   a. _____

   b. _____

   c. _____

   (Do a third set of 6–12 movements.)

   Focus on where you feel it in your body and repeat that word or phrase and follow again.

(continued)

5) Repeat steps 2–4 with two other resources. Then go on to step 6.

6) *Focus on all the resources that we found during our session. Notice where you feel them in your body. Repeat the word or phrase for each one.*

   (Add one set of 6–12 movements.)

   Follow again.

   What do you notice in your body now? _____

   Now, notice these positive feelings as you think of the stressful situation you described at the beginning.
   (Add one set of 6–12 movements.)

   Follow again.

   What do you notice in your body now? _____

   Focus on the stressful situation you identified at the beginning. How disturbing does it feel to you right now, from 0 to 10 where 0 is no disturbance or neutral and 10 is the highest disturbance you can imagine?

   SUD: 0   1   2   3   4   5   6   7   8   9   10 _____

7) At the next session check on the patient's ability to cope with the identified stressful situation. Repeat steps 2–6, as needed, on this or other target situations.

 | Detailed Procedural Steps and Script for Resource Development and Installation

Select from the bold phrases listed in each step those appropriate for each client

Target situation

1A) The clinician should select a target situation from a current situation that triggers maladaptive urges, overwhelming emotion (such as shame, fear, or anger), or depersonalization. This target situation is generally selected using a behavioral chain analysis. It can also be a reprocessed memory that is chronically incomplete.

Target situation: _____

Worst part

1B) *As you to think about _____ (the target situation), what is the worst part of it now?*

Worst part: _____

Initial SUD or LOU
(Optional step)

1C) *SUD: As you hold that situation in mind, how disturbing does it feel to you now on a scale from 0 to 10, where 0 represents neutral or no disturbance and 10 represents the most disturbing you can imagine.*

OR

1D) *LOU: As you hold that situation in mind, how strong does that urge feel to you now on a scale from 0 to 10, where 0 represents neutral or no urge and 10 represents the strongest urge you can imagine.*

SUD or LOU level: 0   1   2   3   4   5   6   7   8   9   10

To identify a resource, select phrases from *either* 2A, *or* 2B and 2C, and 2D.

Identifying a Resource (abstract)	Identifying a Resource (concrete)
2A) *When you think about this situation, what qualities, or strengths do you need?* Desired qualities or strengths:	2B) *What would you like to be able to do in this situation?* Desired behavior: 2C) *What would you like to believe about yourself in this situation?* Desired belief: 2D) *What would you like to feel in this situation?* Desired emotion:

Select one resource from 2E, F, G *or* H at a time and continue to 4F. Then return to the start of step 2 for as many resources as needed until the patient achieves stability. When possible select resources that will assist both with the current stressful situation and with subsequent reprocessing of etiological experiences.

Exploring Memories and Images of Resource Experiences

Mastery Experiences

2E) *Think of a time when you were able to _____.* (Say client's desired behavior or quality).

Think of a time when you were able to believe _____. (Say client's desired belief).

Think of a time when you felt _____. (Say client's desired emotion).

Mastery Experience: _____

Relational Resources – Models

2F) *Think of people in your life who possess or embody this quality.*

Think of people in the world who can serve as a role model for you.

Think of people who made a difference in your life by showing you other choices.

Model: _____

Relational Resources – Supportive Figures

2G) *Think of who you would want helping you, coaching you to do what is best for you, to think what is best for you, and helping you to feel* _____. (Say client's desired emotion).

Think of any friends, relatives, teachers, caregivers, animals, or pets who encouraged or sustained you?

Think of a spiritual guide, someone who gives you hope or strength.

Supportive Figure:

Metaphors and Symbolic Resources

2H) *Close your eyes if you'd like (or leave them open if you'd prefer) and allow an image (or symbol) to come to you that would help you to be able to* _____ (Say client's desired behavior or quality) *or help your to believe* _____ (Say client's desired belief) *or help you to feel* _____ (Say client's desired emotion).

Symbol:

Resource Development – Accessing More Sensory and Affective Information

(Working with one resource memory or image at a time.)

3A) *As you focus on* _____ (i.e., that experience, person, symbol, etc.), *what do you see? What do you hear? What do you smell? What sensations do you notice in your body? What emotions do you feel as you focus on this image or memory?*

Where do you notice these feelings in your body

(Write *verbatim* client's words and phrases.)

Images:

Sounds:

Emotions & Sensations:

Location of Sensations:

Checking the Ecology and Validity of the Resource (VoR)

3B) *As you focus on* _____ (repeat words for resource image) *and notice the* _____ (repeat words for resource sounds, smells, sensations, feelings), *how do you feel now?*

Assess the VoR

3C) *As you focus on the picture that represents the worst part of* _____ [the target situation,] *how true or helpful do* _____ (repeat descriptions of the resource image and feelings) *feel to you now from one, completely false or not helpful to seven, completely true or helpful?* (Initial VoR of 1 is a caution.)

VoR: 1   2   3   4   5   6   7

Reflecting the Resource

3D) *Close your eyes if you'd like (or leave them open if you'd prefer) and let yourself be aware of* _____ (repeat words for resource image) *and notice the* _____ (repeat description of resource feelings, sensations, smells, sounds).

(Repeat and vary the order of client's words for the image, sounds, emotions, and sensations.)

Verify the resource has positive associations or affects

3E) *What do you notice or feel now?*

When client reports positive feelings and associations, continue to step 4A, Installation.

If the client reports negative associations or affect, do *not* continue with this resource. Instead, start over with another resource.

Resource Installation

4A) *Now, as you continue to focus on* _____ (say client's words for the resource image, emotions and sensations), *follow my fingers* (or tones, lights, taps).

Do the first set of 6–12 movements. Then: *What are you feeling or noticing now?* _____

Stop bilateral stimulation if client reports negative associations or affect. Neutralize and set these aside and start over with an alternate resource. With positive responses continue.

Do a second set of 6–12 movements. Then: *What are you feeling or noticing now?* _____

Do a third set of 6–12 movements. Then: *What are you feeling or noticing now?* _____

(continued)

 | Detailed Procedural Steps and Script for Resource Development and Installation *(continued)*

Linking verbal or sensory cues (occurs spontaneously sometimes).

Select one or more phrases from 4 B, C, D or E, then add two more sets of stimulation

- -

(For mastery experiences)

4B) *As you focus on that experience* (if needed repeat client's words of the image, emotions and sensations), *think of the most positive words you can say about yourself now.*

___

(For models)

4C) *Imagine seeing and hearing* _____ (name model person) *being as you would most like to be. If you would like to, imagine step-ping right into* _____'s (name model person) *body, so you can see through their eyes and feel how it is to be able to act, feel and think like that.*

___

(For supportive figures)

4D) *Imagine* _____ (supportive figure) *standing near you and offering you what you need. Imagine that he or she knows exactly what to say to you, exactly what you need to hear. Image a reassuring touch in just the way you need it.*

___

(For metaphoric or symbolic resources)

4E) *Imagine seeing* _____ (name the symbol). *Imagine holding* _____ (name the symbol) *in your hands. Imagine being sur-rounded by* _____ (name the image or feeling). *Breathe in* _____ (name the feeling). *Notice where you feel the positive feelings in your body.*

4F) Continue with two more sets of stimulation as long as processing appears helpful.

Do a fourth set of 6–12 movements. Then: *What are you feeling or noticing now?* _____

_____

Do a fifth set of 6–12 movements. Then: *What are you feeling or noticing now?* _____

_____

Install additional resources for the same or additional needed qualities or capacities

5) Repeat steps 2A to 4F with as many additional resources for the same or other needed qualities or capacities until the patient can successfully complete the Future Template below.

Future Template

Select one or more phrases from 9 A, B, C or D, then add two more sets of stimulation.

6A) *Think about* _____ (being able to act, think or feel as in the resource experience or possessing this quality) *in the future as you next face* _____ (the target situation).

___

(For mastery experiences)

6B) *Imagine being able to act with* _____ (name their mastery action) *as you remember doing in* _____ (say client's mastery memory). *Imagine thinking* _____. (Say client's mastery belief). *Imagine feeling* _____ (say client's master emotion) *in the future as you next face* _____ (the target situation).

Select from the bold phrases listed in each step those appropriate for each client

___

(For models)

6C) *Imagine seeing and hearing* _____ (say client's model) *being as you would most like to be. Or, if you would like to, imagine step-ping right into* _____'s body, so you can see through their eyes and feel how it is to be able to act, feel and think like that in the future as you next face* _____ (the target situation).

___

(For supportive figures)

6D) *Imagine feeling connected with* _____(say client's supportive figure) *as you face this situation. Notice what that would be like for you. Hear* _____ (name supportive person) *saying exactly what you need to hear in the future as you next face* _____ (the target situation).

(For symbolic resources)

6E) See and feel your symbol in just the way you need to. Be aware of this symbol in just the way you need to experience it in the future as you next face _____ (the target situation).

Continue with two more sets of stimulation as long as processing appears helpful.

Do the first set of 6–12 movements on the future template. Then ask: *What are you feeling or noticing now?*

Do a second set of 6–12 movements on the future template. Then ask: *What are you feeling or noticing now?*

Checking the Validity of the Resource (VoR):

6F) *And now as you imagine being in* _____ [the target situation], *in the future, how true or helpful does* _____ (name the resource(s) and self-statement or say client's words for the image, sensation, feelings) *feel to you now from one, completely false or not helpful to seven, completely true or helpful?*

VoR: 1   2   3   4   5   6   7

Repeat for each quality or resource

6G) Repeat this process with additional resources until the VoR rises to a 6 and the SUD or LOU on the presenting target situation falls to a five or lower.

Reassess the target issue

SUD or LOU

6H) *And now as you think of* _____ (name each of the installed resources) *and imagine being in* _____ [the target situation] *in the future, how disturbing does it feel to you now on a scale from 0 to 10, where 0 represents neutral or no disturbance and 10 represents the most disturbing you can imagine.*

OR

6I) *And now as you think of* _____ (name each of the installed resources) *and imagine being in* _____ [the target situation] *in the future, how strong does that urge feel to you now on a scale from 0 to 10, where 0 represents neutral or no urge and ten represents the strongest urge you can imagine.*

SUD or LOU level: 0   1   2   3   4   5   6   7   8   9   10

Verify stability in the target situation with feedback from patient log

7) Review the patient's log to verify the patient is now able to cope adequately with the target situation without giving in maladaptive urges, overwhelming emotion, depersonalization, or is now able to successfully reprocess a previously, chronically, incompletely reprocessed memory.

 | Log

Making brief log entries provides important information on your experiences and your responses to treatment. Your log helps us monitor and adjust your treatment plan. Write a word or two or a short phrase in each box to summarize your experience.

Name: _____   Week: _____ of _____

DATE	TRIGGER OR INCIDENT	IMAGE OR SOUND OR SMELL	BELIEF OR SELF-STATEMENT	EMOTION	LOCATION OF SENSATION	SUD 0–10	NOTES

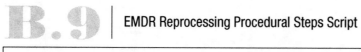

EMDR Reprocessing Procedural Steps Script

Target selected from Master Treatment Plan List Targets:
_____

Phase 3: Assessment of the Target
Image:
"What image represents the worst part of the incident?"
If the patient has no image, elicit another aspect of *sensory* memory: *"When you think of the incident, what part of the incident do you notice?"*

Negative Cognition (NC):
"What words go best with that image" (if there is no image, say—*"with that incident"*) *"that express your negative belief about yourself now?"*

Positive Cognition (PC):
"When you think of that image, what would you like to believe about yourself now?"

Validity of Cognition (VoC):
"When you think of that image" (if there is no image, say—*"with that incident"*), *"how true do those words* _____ *"* (repeat the PC—as an "I" statement) *"feel to you now, on a scale of 1 to 7, where 1 means they feel completely false and 7 means they feel completely true?"*

                            0   1   2   3   4   5   6   7
                        completely false   completely true

Emotions:
"When you focus on that image," (if there is no image, say—*"on that incident"*) *"and think of those words* _____ *"* (repeat the negative cognition—as an "I" statement), *"what emotions do you feel now?"*

SUD scale:
"On a scale from 0 to 10, where 0 is no disturbance or neutral and 10 is the highest disturbance you can imagine, how disturbing does the incident feel to you now?"

                        0   1   2   3   4   5   6   7   8   9   10
                    (no disturbance–neutral)   (highest disturbance)

Location of Body Sensation:
"Where do you feel it in your body?"

Orientation to reprocessing:
"We'll start reprocessing now. As we do sets of eye movements (taps or tones), sometimes, things will change and sometimes they won't. You may notice other images, thoughts, emotions, or body sensations. Other memories may come up. Other times, you may not be aware of anything but the eye movements (taps or tones). Remember what we discussed with the metaphor of riding the train. There are no right or wrong responses. Just notice whatever happens. If you need to stop at any point, just show me the stop sign we rehearsed."

Phase 4: Desensitization
"I'd like you to focus on that image" (if no image—*"on that incident"*) *"and those negative words* _____ *"* (repeat the negative cognition—as an "I" statement). *"Notice where you are feeling it in your body, and follow my fingers"* (Or *"notice the lights,"* *"the taps,"* or *"the sounds"*).
After a set of 24–30 complete movements:
"Rest. Take a deeper breath. Let it go. What do you notice now?"

After patient reports, continue reprocessing:
"Focus on that and notice what happens next."

Continue sets of eye movements down a channel of associations using the instructions above as long as patient reports indicate reprocessing is occurring. If patient reports the same content without change after two sets of BLS, change the direction, height, speed, and/or width of the eye movements. If using auditory stimulation, change the speed or type of sound. If using kinaesthetic stimulation, change the speed, intensity, or location of the stimulation.

(continued)

B.9 | EMDR Reprocessing Procedural Steps Script *(continued)*

Returning to target:
Continue additional sets of bilateral stimulation until the patient reports no further disturbing material and reports only neutral or positive material. Also return to target if associations become so remote from the original target that clinical judgment suggests reprocessing of the selected target is no longer occurring. Then, to return to the target, say:
"When you bring your attention back to the original experience, what do you notice now?"

If the patient reports additional disturbing material:
"Focus on that and notice what happens next."
When you return to target, if the patient reports ambiguous, or apparently neutral or positive associations on the target, check the SUD rating.

Check SUD scale:
"Focus on the original experience. On a scale from 0 to 10, where 0 is no disturbance or neutral and 10 is the highest disturbance you can imagine, how disturbing does it feel to you now?"

After checking the SUD scale:
If the SUD rating is a 1 or higher, say:
"What's the worst part of it now?" _____.
Then say: *"Focus on that and notice what happens next."*
Or
Where do you feel that in your body? _____.
"Focus on that and notice what happens next."
If the SUD rating is 0, say:
"Focus on how the incident seems to you now, and notice what happens next."
When the patient reports a SUD rating of 0 a second time, continue to the installation phase.

Phase 5: Installation

Check for a better PC:
"Do the words _____ " (repeat the positive cognition – as an "I" statement) *"still fit, or is there another positive statement that would be more suitable?"*

Check the VoC on the selected PC:
"Think about the original experience and those words _____ " (repeat the selected Positive Cognition in the first person). *"On a scale from 1 to 7, where 1 means they feel completely false and 7 means they feel completely true, how true do those words feel to you now?"*

1   2   3   4   5   6   7
completely false   completely true

Before each set of BLS in the installation phase, link the original experience and the PC:
"Focus on the original experience and those words _____ " (repeat the selected Positive Cognition in the first person) *"and follow."*
Offer another set of BLS.

After each set of BLS in the installation phase, check the VoC again.

Check the VoC on the selected PC:
*"Think about the original experience and those words _____ * (repeat the selected Positive Cognition in the first person). *On a scale from 1 to 7, where 1 means they feel completely false and 7 means they feel completely true, how true do those words feel to you now?"*

1   2   3   4   5   6   7
completely false   completely true

When the VoC is rising:
Continue the installation phase as long as the patient continues to report growing confidence in the selected positive cognition or other more positive material.

When the VoC does not rise to a 7:
After several sets of BLS, if the reported material is not getting more positive and rising up to a VoC of 7, change the direction or type of BLS. If the patient continues to report a VoC of 6 or less—even after changing the direction or type of BLS—check for a blocking belief.
"What thought or concern keeps these words from feeling completely true?"
This blocking belief can sometimes be directly targeted and resolved in a few more sets of BLS. Then, return to standard installation phase instructions above to complete the installation phase.
In other cases, starting from the patient's expressed blocking belief, you may need to use an affect bridge or somatic bridge to identify an associated memory and target that for reprocessing in this session or in the next session. This generally will mean the originally selected target will remain incomplete for this session until the source of the blocking belief can be reprocessed.

Completing the installation phase
When the patient reports a VoC of 7 and the material is no longer becoming more positive, go on to the body scan phase.

Phase 6: Body Scan
"Close your eyes. Hold in mind the original experience—as it seems to you now—and those words _____" (repeat the selected positive cognition). *"Then bring your attention to all the different areas of your body, starting with your head and continuing down to your feet. Any place you feel any tension, tightness, or unusual sensations, tell me."*
For any reported negative sensations, offer additional sets of BLS until the patient reports only neutral or positive sensations. Then return to target again, and use the instructions above to do the body scan again to check for any new, residual sensations.
For reported positive sensations, continue BLS to enhance the positive sensations until they are no longer getting more positive. In the body scan phase, use the same standard directions between sets of BLS as in the desensitization phase.
*"Rest. Take a deeper breath. Let it go. What do you notice now?"*_____
"Focus on that and notice what happens next."

Phase 7: Closure

Procedures for an incomplete session:
An incomplete session is one where: the SUD rating is above a 1; the VoC rating is less than a 6; or there are residual negative sensations reported in the body scan that were not reported before the session began and that appear to be linked to the targeted material.
Explain the need to stop. Offer encouragement for the patient's work in the session. When the desensitization phase is incomplete, skip the installation of positive cognition and the body scan. Explore the patient's somatic, emotional and cognitive state. Assess the patient's need for structured containment or stabilization procedures.
"We are almost out of time and we will need to stop soon. You have done good work today. I appreciate the effort you have made. How are you feeling?"
If needed, offer one or more containment, calming or sensory orienting exercises.
When the patient is in a stable state, review the briefing statement below.

Closure procedures for a complete session:
Offer acknowledgment for the patient's work in the session. If time remains encourage the patient to discuss their observations about what occurred in the session. If appropriate, briefly mention any significant observed shifts or gains the patient does not mention.
You have done good work today. How are you feeling?"

Brief the patient and request a log report:
"The processing we have done today may continue after the session. You may or may not notice new insights, thoughts, memories, or dreams. You may notice changes in how you are functioning. To help us evaluate your responses to today's session, notice what you experience and make entries in your log. Remember to practice the _____ exercises we worked on to help you manage disturbances this week. We will review your log report and continue our work next time. If you have something urgent to report or need additional support before our next session, call me."

 | Session Summary

| Patient Name: | | Session Date: |
| Clinician: | | Session #: |

Test scores before today's session

| Test: | Test: |
| Score: | Score: |

General notes and log report

Target selected for session

Assessment of Target

Picture:

NC:

PC:

| VoC: | Emotion: | SUD: | Location: |

POST-SESSION SUMMARY				
Patient Name:		Session Date:		
Clinician:		Session #:		
Target complete ☒	Target Incomplete ☒	Last SUD:		Back of Head Scale:

VoC: Final PC (if different):

Final sensations and location at end of body scan phase:

Neutral ☒   Positive ☒   Unpleasant ☒

Stabilization methods used during closure:

Not needed ☒

Issues identified in session that may need further attention:

Patient status, orientation, and attitude about session at closure:

Meta-analyses of EMDR

Bradley, R., Greene, J., Russ, E., Dutra, L., & Westen, D. (2005). A multidimensional meta-analysis of psychotherapy for PTSD. *American Journal of Psychiatry*, *162*, 214–227.

Davidson, P.R., & Parker, K.C.H. (2001). Eye movement desensitization and reprocessing (EMDR): A meta-analysis. *Journal of Consulting and Clinical Psychology*, *69*, 305–316.

Maxfield, L., & Hyer, L.A. (2002). The relationship between efficacy and methodology in studies investigating EMDR treatment of PTSD. *Journal of Clinical Psychology*, *58*, 23–41.

van Etten, M., & Taylor, S. (1998). Comparative efficacy of treatments for posttraumatic stress disorder: A meta-analysis. *Clinical Psychology and Psychotherapy*, *5*, 126–144.

Treatment Guidelines Listing for EMDR

US Guidelines

American Psychiatric Association. (2004). *Practice Guideline for the Treatment of Patients With Acute Stress Disorder and Posttraumatic Stress Disorder*. http://www.guideline.gov/summary/summary.aspx?ss = 15&doc_id = 5954&nbr = 3920

Department of Veterans Affair & Department of Defense. (2204). *VA/DoD Treatment Guidelines: Post Traumatic Stress Disorder*. http://www.oqp.med.va.gov/cpg/PTSD/PTSD_Base.htm

Therapy Advisor. (2004). *Effective Treatments for Posttraumatic Stress Disorder*. http://www.therapyadvisor.com/taDisorder.aspx?disID = 11#4

International Guidelines

Australian Centre for Posttraumatic Mental Health. (2007). *Australian Guidelines for the Treatment of Adults With Acute Stress Disorder and Posttraumatic Stress Disorder*. Melbourne, Victoria: ACPMH. http://www.acpmh.unimelb.edu.au

The Cochrane Database of Systematic Reviews. (2007). *Psychological Treatment of Posttraumatic Stress Disorder (PTSD)*. Issue 4.

Clinical Resource Efficiency Support Team (2003). *The Management of Post Traumatic Stress Disorder in Adults*. Belfast: Northern Ireland Department of Health, Social Services, and Public Safety.

Dutch National Steering Committee for Mental Health Care. (2003). *Multidisciplinary Guideline Anxiety Disorders*. Utrecht, Netherlands: Quality Institute Health Care CBO/Trimbos Institute.

Foa, E. B., Keane, T. M., Friedman, M. J., Cohen, J. A., & International Society for Traumatic Stress Studies. (2009). *Effective Treatments for PTSD: Practice Guidelines From the International Society for Traumatic Stress Studies* (2nd ed.). New York: Guilford Press.

Institut National de la Santé et de la Recherche Médicale. (2004). *Psychotherapy: An Evaluation of Three Approaches.* Paris, France: French National Institute of Health and Medical Research.

National Institute for Health and Clinical Excellence. (2007). *Post-traumatic Stress Disorder.* http://www.nice.org.uk/CG026NICEguideline

Sjöblom, P.O., Andréewitch, S. Bejerot, S., Mörtberg, E., Brinck, U., Ruck, C., & Körlin, D. (2003) *Regional Treatment Recommendation for Anxiety Disorders.* Stockholm, Sweden: Medical Program Committee/Stockholm City Council.

United Kingdom Department of Health. (2001). *Treatment Choice in Psychological Therapies and Counseling: Evidence Based Clinical Practice Guideline.* London, England.

Databases on EMDR Research and Publications

The *Francine Shapiro Library (FSL)* is the repository for scholarly articles and other important writings related to the Adaptive Information Processing (AIP) model and EMDR. The Library is hosted by Northern Kentucky University as a service to EMDR International Association (EMDRIA), available at: http://library.nku.edu/emdr/emdr_data.php

The *Trauma Information Pages* includes a comprehensive listing of all published journal articles related to EMDR from 1989 through 2005, available at: http://www.trauma-pages.com/s/emdr-refs.php.

The *EMDRIA Newsletter* publishes a column listing current research on EMDR compiled by Andrew M. Leeds, Ph.D.. Each quarterly column includes citations, abstracts, and preprint/reprint information when available on all EMDR-related journal articles. Previous columns from 2005 to the present are available on the EMDRIA Web site at: http://emdria.org/displaycommon.cfm?an = 1&sub articlenbr = 18

Standardized Assessment Tools

The *Trauma Assessment Packet* is available from
The Trauma Center at Justice Resource Institute
1269 Beacon Street, 1st Floor
Brookline, MA 02446, USA
Telephone: (617) 232-1303 × 204.
Price and ordering information is available on their Web site at:
http://www.traumacenter.org/products/instruments.php

A summary of *The Adult Attachment Interview (AAI) Protocol* by Mary Main including the 20 questions used in the AAI has been made available by Everett Waters, Ph.D. of Department of Psychology at Stony Brook University at: http://www.psychology.sunysb.edu/attachment/measures/content/aai_interview.pdf

Extensive additional resources on attachment research is available at: http://www.psychology.sunysb.edu/attachment/

The *Adult Attachment Projective (AAP)* is available at: http://www.attachment projective.com/

The *Clinician Administered PTSD Scale (CAPS)* is available on request from The National Center for PTSD, as well as from Western Psychological Services (WPS), available at: http://www.mentalhealth.va.gov/MENTALHEALTH/ptsd/Assessment_instrument_request_form.asp
www.wpspublish.com/

The *Dissociative Disorders Interview Schedule (DDIS)* is available at: http://www.rossinst.com/dddquest.htm

The *Dissociative Experiences Scale–II* (DES–II; Carlson & Putnam, 1993) is available from several sources:

The University of Oregon Scholars' Bank hosts all back issues of the journal Dissociation as a free public service. The DES–II is included as an appendix to Carlson & Putnam (1993). Available at: https://scholarsbank.Uoregon.Edu/xmlui/bitstream/handle/1794/1539/diss_6_1_3_Ocr.Pdf?Sequence = 1

The Sidran Foundation sells the DES–II and other assessment tools for a nominal fee, available at: http://www.sidran.org/store/index.cfm?fuseaction = category. display&category_id = 3

The *DES taxon calculator*, described by Waller & Ross (1997), can be obtained without charge from the International Society for the Study of Trauma and Dissociation (ISST–D), available at: http://isst-d.org/education/des-taxon-portal.htm

The *Impact of Events Scale Revised (IES-R)* is a 22-item self-report scale for assessing the intrusion, avoidance, and hyperarousal symptoms of PTSD. Available at: http://www.swin.edu.au/victims/resources/assessment/ptsd/ies-r.html

The *Multidimensional Inventory of Dissociation (MID)*, Paul F. Dell, Trauma Recovery Center, 1709 Colley Avenue, Ste. 312, Norfolk, VA 23517. Those who request a copy of the MID will receive (a) the MID, (b) its Excel-based scoring program, (c) the directions for using that scoring program, and (d) the MID mini-manual. The MID is in the public domain; it is freely available upon request—without charge—to all mental health professionals from PFDell@aol.com. Members of the International Society for the Study of Trauma and Dissociation can request it or can download it directly from the members' area at: http://www.isst-d.org/

The *Psychotherapy Assessment Checklist (PAC) Forms* (McCullough, 2001), a *PAC Summary Form* (McCullough, 1998), and directions (McCullough, 2003b) are available at: http://www.affectphobia.org/pacforms.html

The *Multimodal Life History Inventory*, Arnold A. Lazarus and Clifford N. Lazarus (1991), Research Press, 2612 North Mattis Avenue, Champaign, IL, 61821. Telephone: (800) 519-2707. Web site: http://www.researchpress.com/product/item/4250/

A set of *Schema Questionnaires* developed by Jeffrey Young, Ph.D. are available for download or purchase along with reference citations at: http://www.schema-therapy.com/

The *Somatoform Dissociation Questionnaire* is available at: http://www.enijenhuis. nl/sdq.html

The *Structured Clinical Interview for DSM-IV Dissociative Disorders-Revised (SCID-D-R)* is available at American Psychiatric Publishing Inc. (703) 907-7322, toll-free order telephone number (800) 368-5777, and on their Web site at: http://www.appi. org/set.cfm?id = 8862

The *Symptom Checklist 90-R (SCL90R)* and the *Brief Symptom Inventory (BSI)* are available at Pearson Assessments, telephone number (800) 627-7271. Web sites: http://www.pearsonassessments.com/tests/scl90r.htm http://www.pearsonassessments.com/tests/bsi18.htm

ISST–D. Treatment Guidelines of the International Society for the Study of Trauma and Dissociation. Web site: http://www.isst-d.org/education/treatmentguide lines-index.htm

Professional Associations

EMDR International Association
   5806 Mesa Drive, Suite 360, Austin, Texas 78731
   Telephone: 512-451-5200, toll free in the United States: 866-451-5200
   Fax: 512-451-5256
   Email: info@emdria.org
   Web site: http://www.emdria.org/
EMDR Europe Association
   PO BOX 784, Hertfordshire AL2 3WY, UK
   Web site: http://www.emdr-europe.org/
International Society for the Study of Trauma and Dissociation
   8201 Greensboro Drive, Suite 300, McLean, VA 22102
   Telephone: 703/610-903   Fax: 703/610-9005
   E-mail: info@isst-d.org
   Web site: http://isst-d.org

International Society for Traumatic Stress Studies (ISTSS)
60 Revere Drive, Suite 500, Northbrook, IL 60062
Telephone: 847-480-9028   Fax: 847-480-9282
Web site: http://www.istss.org/
American Psychological Association (APA)
750 First Street, NE, Washington, DC 20002-4242
Telephone: (800) 374-2721 or (202) 336-5500
Web site: http://apa.org/

Equipment Suppliers

Genogram-Maker Millennium Software to accompany *Genograms: Assessment and Intervention* by McGoldrick, Gerson & Petry, 2008 (3rd ed.). New York: W.W. Norton & Company is available at: http://www.genogram.org/
Institute of HeartMath®
Devices and software that collect pulse data through a finger or ear sensor and display heart rhythm coherence information on a computer screen or a pocket-sized mobile device.
14700 West Park Ave. Boulder Creek, CA 95006
Telephone: (831) 338-8500
Fax: (831) 338-8504
Email: ihminquiry@heartmath.org
Web site: http://www.heartmath.org/
Neurotek Corporation
EyeScan, LapScan, Tac/AudioScan, and CATScan products provide bilateral visual, auditory, and kinesthetic stimulation for qualified EMDR-trained clinicians.
12100 W. 52nd Ave. Unit 116, Wheat Ridge, CO 80033
Telephone: (303) 420-8680
Fax: (303) 422-9440
Email: emdrtools@neurotekcorp.com
Web site: http://neurotekcorp.com

Services for Consultation Groups

Skype.com
Free voice or video conferencing with Skype users and low cost telephone service for telephone-based conference calls. Works with all computer-operating systems.
Free telephone conference calling services
FreeConferenceCall.com
FreeConference.com
Online sharing of text, audio, and video files
Box.net (free file-sharing services available)
Skydrive.live.com (free file-sharing services available)
Fileburst.com (fee only file-sharing service)
Motionbox.com (video sharing with access control)

Resources on Trauma and Treatment

Adverse Childhood Experiences Study
Free print and audio resources on the effects of adverse childhood experiences on adult health and well being from the ongoing collaboration between Kaiser Permanente's Department of Preventive Medicine in San Diego, California, and the US Centers for Disease Control and Prevention. Available at: http://www.acestudy.org/publications.php

The Child Trauma Academy

    Provides a range of resources related to childhood trauma recognized by the Office of Disease Prevention and Health Promotion of the US Department of Health and Human Service as a trusted source of information. Available at: http://childtraumaacademy.org/default.aspx

    Free online courses on attachment and the effects of childhood trauma on the brain, the person, and the society. Available at: http://www.childtrauma academy.com/

The National Child Traumatic Stress Network

Learning Center for Child and Adolescent Trauma

    Free online courses with Continuing Education Units (CEU) credit on assessment and treatment of complex trauma, developmental impact of childhood trauma, and treatment of children and families after natural disaster. Funded by the Center for Mental Health Services (CMHS), Substance Abuse and Mental Health Services Administration (SAMSHA), US Department of Health and Human Services and jointly coordinated by University of California, Los Angeles and Duke University. Available at: http://learn.nctsn.org/

The Sidran Traumatic Stress Institute, Inc.

    The Sidran Traumatic Stress Institute, Inc. (formerly The Sidran Foundation) helps people understand, recover from, and treat traumatic stress (including PTSD), dissociative disorders, and co-occurring issues, such as addictions, self-injury, and suicidality. They publish and distribute books, videos, assessment tools, newsletters, and home study CE and CME programs. They provide excellent, free Web site-based resources for professionals and survivors. Through their help desk, they provide information and referral to treatment resources.

    200 East Joppa Road, Suite 207, Baltimore, MD 21286-3107

    Web site: http://www.sidran.org

The Trauma Information Pages

    An award-winning Web site that provides a wealth of both scholarly and support resources for clinicians, patients, and their families including a bibliography on EMDR research, full text articles, and links to other high-quality Web sites. Available at: http://www.trauma-pages.com/

abreaction—Refers to reliving an experience to purge it of its emotional intensity.

Adaptive Information Processing model—The theoretic model developed by Francine Shapiro (2001) to explain observed effects of the EMDR procedure and to predict treatment effects.

affect bridge—A hypnoanalytic technique first described by Watkins (1971, 1990) for identifying an earlier etiological or contributory experience by associating from a current emotional experience.

alexethymia—Difficulty identifying and describing feelings to other people.

bilateral stimulation—The use of alternating, generally left–right, neutral, sensory stimulation via eye movements, gentle kinesthetic, or auditory stimulation during EMDR treatment.

BLS—See bilateral stimulation.

blocked responses—See ineffective reprocessing.

cognitive interweaves—See interweaves.

completed session—An EMDR reprocessing session that reaches completion with a SUD of 0, a VoC of 7, and a body scan with only neutral or positive sensations.

consensus model—Models of posttraumatic treatment that are based on Janet's *phase oriented model*.

contingent responses—Responses by a caregiver or other person that are attuned in time to the affective expressions of a person.

contributory experiences—Experiences that may not have led to an immediate onset of clinical symptoms, but which have contributed to the development of vulnerability factors or to the nature of maladaptive responses to later-occurring *etiological experiences*.

emotional processing—Concept first described by Rachman (1979) in which the increased vividness of imagery resulting from relaxation leads to fear reductions by first producing stronger physiological responses to phobic imagery.

etiological experiences—Traumatic and other adverse life experiences that produce maladaptive memory networks and lead to immediate and overt clinical signs and syndromes.

fear structures—A model for defining anxiety, first described by Lang (1977, 1979), involving behavioral responses in three systems: physiological activity, overt behavior, and subjective report.

future template—The third prong of the standard EMDR–PTSD protocol that focuses on a future scene generally after memories and current threat cues have been resolved.

incomplete session—The SUD rating is above a 1; the VoC rating is less than a 6; or there are residual negative sensations reported in the body scan that were not reported before the session began and that appear to be linked to the targeted material.

index trauma—A discrete traumatizing experience that is followed by the onset of overt symptoms of acute stress disorder or posttraumatic stress disorder. Symptoms related to this experience are a primary focus of concern of presenting complaints at intake. See also etiological experiences.

ineffective reprocessing—When reprocessing fails to move spontaneously to an adaptive resolution and the clinician needs to make an additional intervention beyond the basic EMDR procedural steps.

interweaves—The deliberate accessing of an adaptive memory network, generally an adult perspective, during reprocessing to facilitate integration of memory networks and a positive treatment outcome.

inverted protocol—A general approach to treatment planning for complex PTSD described by Hoffman (2004, 2005) that emphasizes initial ego strengthening and stabilizing applications of EMDR by starting with targets in the future, later the present and only addresses etiological experiences from the past after significant treatment gains have been achieved.

memory networks—An aspect of Shapiro's (2001) AIP model describing how information is stored in five aspects in memory: image, thought and sound, physical sensation, emotion, and belief. Leeds (2001) proposed a sixth element of memory networks: "acts, urges, and states."

peritraumatic dissociation—Peritraumatic dissociation involves depersonalization and/or derealization at the time of a traumatic experience.

phase-oriented approach—A general model for treating posttraumatic syndromes first proposed by Janet (1889, 1977) that consists of the following phases: (a) stabilization and symptom reduction, (b) uncovering and modifying traumatic memories, and (c) personality integration.

prolonged exposure—PE is based on flooding or implosion therapy (Stampfl & Levis, 1967) and the principle of extinction that nerves can only be stimulated for limited periods of time.

state-specific memory—The model proposed by Bower (1981) that specific memories (a) are encoded in association with the specific emotional or physiological state at the time they are laid down and (b) are more easily retrieved when in the same emotional or physiological state.

somatic bridge—A hypnoanalytic technique first described by Watkins (1971, 1990) for identifying an earlier etiological or contributory experience by association with a current somatosensory experience.

threat cues—Current external sensory cues and internal somatosensory perceptions that trigger dysfunctional responses linked to maladaptive memory networks for adverse early life experiences.

Abreaction. (2007, November 10). In *Wikipedia, the free encyclopedia*. Retrieved 15:42, December 1, 2007, from http://en.wikipedia.org/w/index.php?title = Abreaction&oldid = 170595413

Adler-Tapia, R., & Settle, C. (2008). *EMDR and the art of psychotherapy with children*. Springer Publishing: New York.

Adshead, G. (2000). Psychological therapies for post-traumatic stress disorder. *The British Journal of Psychiatry, 177*, 144–148.

Ahmad, A., Larsson, B., & Sundelin-Wahlsten, V. (2007). EMDR treatment for children with PTSD: Results of a randomized controlled trial. *Nordic Journal of Psychiatry, 61*(5), 349–354.

Ainsworth, M. D., Blehar, M. C., Waters, E., & Wall, S. (1978). *Patterns of attachment: Assessed in the strange situation and at home*. Hillsdale, NJ: Lawrence Erlbaum.

Allami, N., Paulignan, Y., Brovelli, A., & Boussaoud, D. (2008). Visuo-motor learning with combination of different rates of motor imagery and physical practice. *Experimental Brain Research, 184*(1), 105–113.

Allen, J. G. (2003). Mentalizing. *Bulletin of the Menninger Clinic, 67*, 91–112.

Alpert, J. E., Brown, L. S., Ceci, S. J., Courtois, C. A., Loftus. E. F., & Ornstein, P. A. (1996). *Working group on investigation of memories of childhood abuse final report*. Retrieved October 27, 2007, from http://www.apa.org/pi/memories_report/homepage.html

Altmaier, E. M. (2002). EMDR: Past, present and future. *Clinician's Research Digest, 20*(6), 5.

American Association for Marriage and Family Therapy (2001). AAMFT Code of Ethics. Retrieved April 28, 2008, from http://www.aamft.org/resources/LRM_Plan/Ethics/ethics code2001.asp

American Psychiatric Association. (1980). *Diagnostic and statistical manual of mental disorders* (3rd ed.). Washington, DC: Author.

American Psychiatric Association. (1994). *Diagnostic and statistical manual of mental disorders* (4th ed.). Washington, DC: Author.

American Psychiatric Association. (1998). Practice guideline for the treatment of patients with panic disorder. *American Journal of Psychiatry, 155*(5 Suppl), 1–34.

American Psychiatric Association. (2000). *Diagnostic and statistical manual of mental disorders* (4th ed.). Washington, DC: Author.

American Psychiatric Association (2004). *Practice guideline for the treatment of patients with acute stress disorder and posttraumatic stress disorder*. Arlington, VA: American Psychiatric Association Practice Guidelines.

American Psychological Association. (1992). Ethical principles of psychologists and code of conduct. *American Psychologist, 57*, 1597–1611.

American Psychological Association. (2002). Ethical principles of psychologists and code of conduct. *American Psychologist, 57*(12), 1060–1073.

Amundsen, J. E., & Kårstad, K. (2006). Om bare Jeppe visste - EMDR og rusbehandling. [Integrating EMDR and the treatment of substance abuse.]. *Tidsskrift for Norsk Psykologforening, 43*(5), 469.

Anderson, G., Yasenik, L., & Ross, C. A. (1993). Dissociative experiences and disorders among women who identify themselves as sexual abuse survivors. *Child Abuse and Neglect, 17*(5), 677–686.

Andrade, J., Kavanagh, D., & Baddeley, A. (1997). Eye-movements and visual imagery: A working memory approach to the treatment of post-traumatic stress disorder. *British Journal of Clinical Psychology, 36*, 209–223.

Armstrong, N., & Vaughan, K. (1994, June). An orienting response model for EMDR. Paper presented at the meeting of the *New South Wales Behaviour Therapy Interest Group*. Sydney, Australia.

Armstrong, M. S., & Vaughan, K. (1996). An orienting response model of eye movement desensitization. *Journal of Behavior Therapy and Experimental Psychiatry, 27*, 21–32.

Arntz, A. (2002). Cognitive therapy versus interoceptive exposure as treatment of panic disorder without agoraphobia. *Behaviour Research and Therapy, 40*, 325–341.

Australian Centre for Posttraumatic Mental Health. (2007). *Australian guidelines for the treatment of adults with acute stress disorder and posttraumatic stress disorder*. Melbourne, Victoria: Author.

Baddeley, A. D., & Hitch, G. J. (1974). Working memory. In G. A. Bower (Ed.), *The psychology of learning and motivation* (pp. 47–89). New York: Academic Press.

Bakker, A., van Dyck, R., Spinhoven, P., & van Balkom, A. J. (1999). Paroxetine, clomipramine and cognitive therapy in the treatment of panic disorder. *Journal of Clinical Psychiatry, 60*, 831–838.

Baldwin, D. V. (revised April 9, 2002) EMDR Bibliography: 1989 through 2001, Published journal articles, by year. Retrieved July 7, 2002, from Trauma Information Web site: http://www.trauma-pages.com/emdr-2001.htm

Barach, P. M. (1991). Multiple Personality Disorder as an Attachment Disorder. *Dissociation, 4*, 117–123.

Barber, B. (1961). Resistance by scientists to scientific discovery. *Science, 134*, 596–602.

Barlow, D. H. (1994). Effectiveness of behavior treatment for panic disorder with and without agoraphobia. In B. Wolfe & J. Maser (Ed.), *Treatment of panic disorder: A consensus development conference*. Washington: American Psychiatric Press.

Barlow, D. H. (2002). *Anxiety and its disorders: the nature and treatment of anxiety and panic* (2nd ed.). New York: Guilford Press.

Barlow, D. H., Gorman, J. M., Shear, M. K., & Woods, S. W. (2000). Cognitive-behavioral therapy, imipramine, or their combination for panic disorder: a randomized controlled trial. *The Journal of the American Medical Association*, 283:2529–2536

Barrowcliff, A. L., Gray, N. S., MacCulloch, S., Freeman, T. C., & MacCulloch, M. J. (2003). Horizontal rhythmic eye movements consistently diminish the arousal provoked by auditory stimuli. *British Journal of Clinical Psychology, 42*(Pt 3), 289–302.

Barrowcliff, A. L., Gray, N. S., Freeman, T. C. A., & MacCulloch, M. J. (2004). Eye-movements reduce the vividness, emotional valence and electrodermal arousal associated with negative autobiographical memories. *Journal of Forensic Psychiatry and Psychology, 15*, 325–345.

Barrowcliff, A. L., MacCulloch, M. J., & Gray, N. S. (2001). *The de-arousal model of Eye Movement Desensitization and Reprocessing (EMDR), Part III: Psychophysiological and psychological concomitants of change in the treatment of Post-Traumatic Stress Disorder (PTSD) and their relation to the EMDR protocol*. Paper presented at the EMDR Europe 2nd Annual Conference "EMDR innovations in theory and practice," London, UK.

Barrowcliff, A. L., Macculloch, M. J., Gray, N. S., MacCulloch, S., & Freeman, T. C. A. (2001). *The de-arousal model of Eye Movement Desensitization and Reprocessing (EMDR), Part II: An investigation of the mechanisms underlying treatment effects in EMDR*. Paper presented at the EMDR Europe 2nd Annual Conference "EMDR inovations in theory and practice," London, UK.

Barrowcliff, A. L., Gray, N. S., & MacCulloch, M. J. (2002). *Eye movements reduce the vividness, emotional valence and electrodermal arousal associated with autobiographical memories*. Unpublished manuscript.

Bartholomew, K. (1990). Avoidance of intimacy: An attachment perspective. *Journal of Social and Personal Relationships, 7*, 147–178.

Bartholomew, K. (1997). Adult attachment processes: individual and couple perspectives. *British Journal of Medical Psychology, 70* (Pt 3), 249–263; discussion 281–290.

Bartholomew, K., & Horowitz, L. M. (1991). Attachment styles amoung young adults: A test of a four category model. *Journal of Personality and Social Psychology, 61*, 226–244.

Beck, A. T., & Emery, G. (1985). *Anxiety disorders and phobias*. New York: Basic Books.

Beck, A. T., Emery, G., & Greenberg, R. L. (2005). *Anxiety disorders and phobias: a cognitive perspective* (15th anniversary ed.). Cambridge, MA: Basic Books.

Becker, E. S., Rinck, M., Turke, V., Kause, P., Goodwin, R., Neumer, S., et al. (2007). Epidemiology of specific phobia subtypes: findings from the Dresden Mental Health Study. *European Psychiatry, 22*(2), 69–74.

Becker, L., Todd-Overmann, T., Stoothoff, W., & Lawson, P. (1998). *Ironic memory, PTSD and EMDR: Do eye movements hinder the avoidance process leading to greater accessibility of traumatic memories?* Paper presented at the EMDRIA Annual Conference, Baltimore, MD.

Beers, M. H. (2004). *The Merck manual of health & aging*. Whitehouse Station, NJ: Merck Research Laboratories.

Benson, H. (1975). *The relaxation response*. New York: Morrow.

Bergmann, U. (1998). Speculations on the neurobiology of EMDR. *Traumatology, 4*(1), 4–16. Retrieved January 31, 2009, from http://www.fsu.edu/~trauma/contv4i1.html

Bergmann, U. (2001). Further thoughts on the neurobiology of EMDR: The role of the cerebellum in accelerated information processing. *Traumatology, 6*(3), 175–200. Retrieved January 31, 2009, from www.fsu.edu/~ trauma.

Bergmann, U. (2008). Hidden selves: Treating dissociation in the spectrum of personality disorders. In C. Forgash & M. Copeley (Eds.), *Healing the heart of trauma and dissociation with emdr and ego state therapy* (pp. 227–266). New York, NY: Springer Pub. Co.

Bernstein, E. M., & Putnam, F. W. (1986). Development, reliability and validity of a dissociation scale. *Journal of Nervous and Mental Disease, 174,* 727–735.

Besson, J., Eap, C., Rougemont-Buecking, A., Simon, O., Nikolov, C., & Bonsack, C. (2006). [Addictions]. *Revue Médicale Suisse, 2*(47), 9–13.

Bienvenu, O. J., Onyike, C. U., Stein, M. B., Chen, L. S., Samuels, J., Nestadt, G., & Eaton, W. W. (2006). Agoraphobia in adults: incidence and longitudinal relationship with panic. *The British Journal of Psychiatry, 188,* 432–438.

Bisson, J., & Andrew, M. (2007). Psychological treatment of post-traumatic stress disorder (PTSD). *Cochrane Database of Systematic Reviews* 2007, Issue 4.

Black, D. W. (2007). Compulsive buying disorder: a review of the evidence. *CNS Spectrum, 12*(2), 124–132.

Blake, D. D., Weathers, F. W., Nagy, L. M., Kaloupek, D. G., Gusman, F. D., Charney, D. S., et al. (1995). The development of a clinician-administered PTSD scale. *Journal of Traumatic Stress, 8*(1), 75–90.

Bodycoat, N., Grauaug, L., Olson, A., & Page, A. C. (2000). Constant Versus Rhythmic Muscle Tension in Applied Tension. *Behaviour Change, 17*(2), 97–102.

Bower, G. (1981). Mood and Memory. *American Psychologist, 36,* 129–148.

Bowlby, J. (1973). *Separation: Anxiety and anger.* New York: Basic Books.

Bowman, E. S. (2006). Why conversion seizures should be classified as a dissociative disorder. *Psychiatric Clinics of North America, 29*(1), 185–211.

Bowman, E. S., & Coons, P. M. (2000). The differential diagnosis of epilepsy, pseudoseizures, dissociative identity disorder, and dissociative disorder not otherwise specified. *Bulletin of the Menninger Clinic, 64*(2), 164–180.

Bradley, R. T., McCraty, R., Atkinson, M., Arguelles, L., Rees, R. A., & Tomasino D. (2007). Reducing test anxiety and improving test performance in American's schools: Summary of results from the TestEdge National Demonstration Study. Retrieved August 22, 2008, from Institute of HeartMath Publication Web site: http://www.heartmath.org

Bremner, J. D., Elzinga, B., Schmahl, C., & Vermetten, E. (2008). Structural and functional plasticity of the human brain in posttraumatic stress disorder. *Prog Brain Res, 167,* 171–186.

Bremmer, J. D., Randal, P., Scott, T. M., Bronen, T. A., Seibyl, J. P., Southwick, S., et al. (1995). MRI-based measurement of hyppocampal volume in patients with PTSD. *American Journal of Psychiatry, 152,* 973–981.

Breuer, J., & Freud, S. (1955). Studies on hysteria. In J. Strachey (Ed. & Trans.), *The standard edition of the complete psychological works of Sigmund Freud* (Vol. 2, pp. 1–335). London: Hogarth Press. (Original work published 1895)

Briere, J. (1995) *Trauma Symptom Inventory (TSI)*, Psychological Assessment Resources, PO Box 998, Odessa, FL, 33556. (800) 331-TEST. Retrieved January 31, 2008, from http://www.parinc.com/products_search.cfm

Briere, J. (1996). *Therapy for adults molested as children: Beyond survival* (2nd ed.). New York: Springer Publishing Company, Inc.

Briere, J. (2000) Inventory of Altered Self-Capacities (IASC), Psychological Assessment Resources, PO Box 998, Odessa, FL, 33556. (800) 331-TEST. Retrieved January 31, 2008, from http://www.parinc.com/products_search.cfm

Brown, D., & Fromm, E. (1986). *Hypnotherapy and hypnoanalysis.* Hillsdale, NJ: Lawrence Erlbaum Associates.

Brown, M. Z., Comtois, K. A., & Linehan, M. M. (2002). Reasons for suicide attempts and non-suicidal self-injury in women with borderline personality disorder. *Journal of Abnormal Psychology, 111*(1), 198–202.

Brown, K. W., McGoldrick, T., & Buchanan, R. (1997). Body dysmorphic disorder: Seven cases treated with eye movement desensitization and reprocessing. *Behavioral and Cognitive Psychotherapy, 25,* 203–207.

Brown, S., & Shapiro, F. (2006). EMDR in the Treatment of Borderline Personality Disorder. *Clinical Case Studies, 5*(5), 403–420.

Brown, S., & Gilman, S. (2007). Integrated trauma treatment program for co-occurring PTSD and substance abuse in a drug court program. Retrieved October 25, 2008, from www.nadcp.org/postcon/agendadocs/clinic%206%20HO1.pdf

Brown, S., Gilman, S. G., & Kelso, T. (2008). *Integrated trauma treatment program: A novel EMDR approach for PTSD and substance abuse.* Paper presented at EMDRIA Conference, Phoenix, AZ.

Brown, T. A., DiNardo, P., & Barlow, D. H. (2004). *Anxiety disorder interview schedule ADIS-IV and ADIS-IV-L combination specimen set*. New York: Oxford University Press, USA.

Brunstein Klomek, A., & Stanley, B. (2007). Psychosocial treatment of depression and suicidality in adolescents. *CNS Spectrum, 12*(2), 135–144.

Bryan, C. J., & Rudd, M. D. (2006). Advances in the assessment of suicide risk. *Journal of. Clinical Psychology, 62*(2), 185–200.

California Association for Marriage and Family Therapy (2008). *Ethical standards*. Retrieved December 20, 2008, from http://www.camft.org/scriptcontent/index.cfm?displaypage = ../CamftBenefits/EthicalStandards1.html

Campbell-Sills L., & Stein, M. B. (2006). Guideline watch: Practice guideline for the treatment of patients with panic disorder. Retrieved December 12, 2008, from American Psychiatric Association Web site: http://www.psych.org/psych_pract/treatg/pg/prac_guide.cfm

Cardeña, E., Maldonado, J., van der Hart, O., & Spiegel, D. (2000). Hypnosis. In E. B. Foa, T. M. Keane, & M. J. Friedman (Eds.), *Effective treatments for PTSD: Practice guidelines from the International Society for Traumatic Stress Studies*. New York: The Guilford Press.

Carlson, E. A., & Sroufe, L. A. (1995). Contribution of attachment theory to developmental psychopathology. In D. Cicchetti & D. J. Cohen (Eds.), *Developmental psychopathology* (Vol. 1, pp. 581–587). New York: Wiley.

Carlson, E. B. (1997). *Trauma assessments: a clinician's guide*. New York: The Guilford Press.

Carlson, E. B., & Putnam, F. W. (1993). An update on the Dissociative Experiences Scale. *Dissociation, 6*, 16–27.

Carnes, P. J. (2000). Sexual addiction and compulsion: recognition, treatment, and recovery. *CNS Spectrum, 5*(10), 63–72.

Cassidy, J., & Shaver, P. R. (Eds.). (1999). *Handbook of attachment: Theory, research, and clinical applications*. New York: Guilford Press.

Chambless, D. L., & Gillis, M. M. (1993). Cognitive therapy of anxiety disorders. *Journal of Consulting and Clinical Psychology, 61*, 248–260.

Chambless, D. L., & Gillis, M. M. (1994) A review of psychosocial treatments for panic disorder. In B. F. Wolfe & J. D. Maser (Eds.), *Treatment of panic disorder: A consensus development conference* (pp. 149–173). Washington, DC: American Psychiatric Press.

Chemali, Z., & Meadows, M. E. (2004). The use of eye movement desensitization and reprocessing in the treatment of psychogenic seizures. *Epilepsy & Behavior, 5*(5), 784–787.

Chemtob, C. M., Nakashima, J., & Carlson, J. G. (2002). Brief treatment for elementary school children with disaster-related Posttraumatic Stress Disorder: A field study. *Journal of Clinical Psychology, 58*(1), 99–112.

Christman, S. D., Garvey, K. J., Propper, R. E., & Phaneuf, K. A. (2003). Bilateral eye movements enhance the retrieval of episodic memories. *Neuropsychology, 17*(2), 221–229.

Chu, J. A. (1998). *Rebuilding shattered lives: Treating complex post-traumatic and dissociative disorders*. New York: John Wiley & Sons.

Clark, D. M. (1994). Cognitive therapy for panic disorder. In Wolfe, B. & Maser J. (Eds.), *Treatment of panic disorder: A consensus development conference*. Washington, DC: American Psychiatric Press.

Clarkin, J. F., Levy, K. N., Lenzenweger, M. F., & Kernberg, O. F. (2007). Evaluating three treatments for borderline personality disorder: a multiwave study. *Am J Psychiatry, 164*(6), 922–928.

Cloitre, M., Koenen, K. C., Cohen, L. R., & Han, H. (2002). Skills training in affective and interpersonal regulation followed by exposure: A phase-based treatment for PTSD related to childhood abuse. *Journal of Consulting and Clinical Psychology, 70*(5), 1067.

Coffey, S. F., Gudmundsdottir, B., Beck, J. G., Palyo, S. A., & Miller, L. (2006). Screening for PTSD in motor vehicle accident survivors using the PSS-SR and IES. *Journal of Traumatic Stress, 19*(1), 119–128.

Cohen, J. S. (2004). The underlying cause of suicides and homicides with SSRI antidepressants: Is it the drugs, the doctors, or the drug companies? Retrieved July 1, 2008, from http://www.medicationsense.com/articles/april_june_04/underlying_cause.html

Comtois, K. A., & Linehan, M. M. (2006). Psychosocial treatments of suicidal behaviors: a practice-friendly review. *Journal of ClinicalPsychology, 62*(2), 161–170.

Connor, D. F., Melloni, R. H., Jr., & Harrison, R. J. (1998). Overt categorical aggression in referred children and adolescents. *Journal of the American Academy of Child Adolescent Psychiatry, 37*(1), 66–73.

Connors, R. (1996). Self-Injury in Trauma Survivors: 1. Functions and Meanings. *American Journal of Orthopsychiatry, 66*(2), 197–206.

Conrad, A., & Roth, W. T. (2007). Muscle relaxation therapy for anxiety disorders: it works but how? *Journal of Anxiety Disorders, 21*(3), 243–264.

Cooper, N. A., & Clum, G. A. (1989). Imaginal flooding as a supplementary treatment for PTSD in combat veterans: A controlled study. *Behavior Therapy, 20*, 381–391.

Corrigan, F. M. (2004). Psychotherapy as assisted homeostasis: activation of emotional processing mediated by the anterior cingulate cortex. *Medical Hypotheses, 63*(6), 968–973.

Courtois, C. (1988). *Healing the incest wound: Adult survivors in therapy*. New York: Norton.

Courtois, C. A. (1999). *Recollections of sexual abuse: Treatment principles and guidelines.* New York: W. W. Norton.

Craske, M. G., Rowe, M., Lewin, M., & Noriega-Dimitri, R. (1997). Interoceptive exposure versus breathing retraining within cognitive-behavioural therapy for panic disorder with agoraphobia. *Br J Clin Psychol, 36 (Pt 1)*, 85–99.

Craske, M. G., Roy-Byrne, P., Stein, M. B., Donald-Sherbourne, C., Bystritsky, A., Katon, W., & Greer, S. (2002). Treating panic disorder in primary care: A collaborative care intervention. *General Hospital Psychiatry, 24*, 148–155.

Crouch, J. L., & Behl, L. E. (2001). Relationships among parental beliefs in corporal punishment, reported stress, and physical child abuse potential. *Child Abuse and Neglect, 25*(3), 413–419.

Crowell, J. A., Fraley, R. C., & Shaver, P. R. (1999). Measurement of Individual Differences in Adolescent and Adult Attachment. In J. Cassidy & P. R. Shaver (Eds.), *Handbook of attachment: Theory, research, and clinical applications* (pp. 434–465). New York: Guilford Press.

Curcio, G., Ferrara, M., & De Gennaro, L. (2006). Sleep loss, learning capacity and academic performance. *Sleep Medicine Reviews, 10*(5), 323–337.

Dalenberg, C. J. (2000). *Countertransference and the treatment of trauma* (1st ed.). Washington, DC: American Psychological Association.

Dannon, P. N., Lowengrub, K., Gonopolski, Y., Musin, E., & Kotler, M. (2006). Pathological gambling: a review of phenomenological models and treatment modalities for an underrecognized psychiatric disorder. *Primary Care Companion to the Journal of Clinical Psychiatry, 8*(6), 334–339.

Davanloo, H. (1989a). The technique of unlocking the unconscious in patients suffering from functional disorders. Part I. Restructuring ego's defenses. *International Journal Short-Term Psychotherapy, 4*(2), 93–116.

Davanloo, H. (1989b).The technique of unlocking the unconscious in patients suffering from functional disorders. Part II. Direct view of the dynamic unconscious. *International Journal Short-Term Psychotherapy, 4*(2), 117–148.

Davey, G. (1997). *Phobias: a handbook of theory, research, and treatment.* Chichester; New York: Wiley.

de Beurs, E., van Balkom, A. J., Van Dyck, R., & Lange, A. (1999). Long-Term outcome of pharmacological and psychological treatment for panic disorder with agoraphobia: A 2-year naturalistic follow-up. *Acta Psychiatrica Scandinavica, 99*(1), 59–67.

De Jongh, A., & Ten Broeke, E. (1994). Opmerkelijke veranderingen na één zitting met eye movement desensitization and reprocessing: Een geval van angst voor misselijkheid en braken. [Remarkable changes after one session of EMDR: Fear of nausea and vomiting]. *Tijdschrift voor Directieve Therapie en Hypnose, 14*, 89–101.

De Jongh, A., & Ten Broeke, E. (1996). Eye movement desensitization and reprocessing (EMDR): een procedure voor de behandeling van aan trauma gerelateerde angst. [Eye movement desensitization and reprocessing (EMDR): A procedure for the treatment of trauma- related anxiety]. *Tijdschrift voor Psychotherapie, 22*, 93–114.

De Jongh, A., & Ten Broeke, E. (2007). Treatment of Specific Phobias With EMDR: Conceptualization and Strategies for the Selection of Appropriate Memories. *Journal of EMDR Practice and Research, 1*(1), 46–56.

De Jongh, A., Ten Broeke, E., & Renssen, M. R. (1999). Treatment of specific phobias with Eye Movement Desensitization and Reprocessing (EMDR): Protocol, empirical status, and conceptual issues. *Journal of Anxiety Disorders, 13*(1–2), 69–85.

De Jongh, A., Ten Broeke, E., & Van der Meer, K. (1995). Eine neue entwicklung in der behandlung von angst und traumata: Eye movement desensitization and reprocessing (EMDR). *Zeitschrift für Klinische Psychologie, Psychopathologie und Psychotherapie, 43*, 226–233.

Dell, P. F. (2006a). The multidimensional inventory of dissociation (MID): A comprehensive measure of pathological dissociation. *Journal of Trauma and Dissociation, 7*(2), 77–106.

Dell, P. F. (2006b). A new model of dissociative identity disorder. *Psychiatric Clinics of North America, 29*(1), 1–26.

Dell, P.F., & Lawson, D. (2009). Empirically delineating the domain of pathological dissociation. In P. F. Dell, & J. A. O'Neil (Eds.), *Dissociation and the dissociative disorders: DSM–V and beyond* (pp. 667–692). New York: Routledge.

Demos, E. V. (1988). Affect and development of the self: A new frontier. In A. Goldberg (Ed.), *Frontiers in self psychology* (pp. 27–53). Hillsdale NJ: The Analytic Press.

Department of Veterans Affairs & Department of Defense. (2004). *VA/DoD Clinical practice guideline for the management of post-traumatic stress.* Veterans Health Administration, Department of Veterans Affairs and Health Affairs, Department of Defense: Office of Quality and Performance Publication.

Derogatis, L. R. (1991). *Symptom checklist revised.* Minneapolis: NCS Professional Assessment Services.

Dolan, Y. M. (1991). *Resolving sexual abuse: solution-focused therapy and Ericksonian hypnosis for adult survivors* (1st ed.). New York: Norton.

Dozier, M., Stovall, K. D., & Albus, K. E. (1999). Attachment and psychopathology in adulthood. In J. Cassidy & P. R. Shaver (Eds.), *Handbook of attachment: Theory, research and clinical applications* (pp. 497–519). New York: Guilford.

Dunn, A. L., Trivedi, M. H., Kampert, J. B., Clark, C. G., & Chambliss, H. O. (2002). The DOSE study: a clinical trial to examine efficacy and dose response of exercise as treatment for depression. *Control Clin Trials, 23*(5), 584–603.

Dutch National Steering Committee Guidelines Mental Health Care (2003). *Multidisciplinary guideline anxiety disorders.* Utrecht: Quality Institute Heath Care CBO/Trimbos Institute.

Dyck, M. J. (1993). A proposal for a conditioning model of eye movement desensitization treatment of posttraumatic stress disorder. *Journal of Behavior Therapy and Experimental Psychiatry, 24,* 201–210.

Dziegielewski, S., & Wolfe, P. (2000). Eye movement desensitization and reprocessing (EMDR) as a time-limited treatment intervention for body image disturbance and self-esteem: A single subject case study design. *Journal of Psychotherapy in Independent Practice, 1,* 1–16.

Edmond, T., & Rubin, A. (2004). Assessing the long-term effects of EMDR: results from an 18-month follow-up study with adult female survivors of CSA. *Journal of Child Sexual Abuse, 13*(1), 69–86.

Edmond, T., Rubin, A., & Wambach, K. (1999, June). The effectiveness of EMDR with adult female survivors of childhood sexual abuse. *Social Work Research, 23*(2), 103–116.

Egan, K. J., Carr, J. E., Hunt, P. P., & Adamson, R. (1988). Endogenous opiate system and systematic desensitization. *Journal of Clinical and Consulting Psychology, 56*(2), 287–291.

Ehrsson, H. H. (2007). The experimental induction of out-of-body experiences. *Science, 317*(5841), 1048.

Eifert, G. H., & Heffner, M. (2003). The effects of acceptance versus control contexts on avoidance of panic-related symptoms. *Journal of Behavior Therapy and Experimental Psychiatry, 34*(3–4), 293–312.

Eisen, M. R., & Fromm, E. (1983). The clinical use of self-hypnosis in hypnotherapy: tapping the functions of imagery and adaptive regression. *International Journal of Clinical and Experimental Hypnosis, 31*(4), 243–255. EMDR International Association. (2000, June) The EMDRIA Newsletter, 5(2), 8.

Ekman, P., & Friesen, W. V. (2003). *Unmasking the face: A guide to recognizing emotions from facial clues.* Cambridge MA: Malor Books.

Ellis, A. (1994). *Reason and emotion in psychotherapy* (Rev. and updated ed.). Secaucus, NJ: Carol Pub. Group.

Elofsson, U. O., von Scheele, B., Theorell, T., & Sondergaard, H. P. (2008). Physiological correlates of eye movement desensitization and reprocessing. *Journal of Anxiety Disorders, 22*(4), 622–634.

EMDRIA (2007). *Basic training curriculum.* Retrieved March 11, 2007, from http://www.emdria.org/displaycommon.cfm?an = 1&subarticlenbr = 281

EMDRIA (2008a). EMDR International Association consultation packet. Retrieved May 3, 2008, from http://www.emdria.org/displaycommon.cfm?an = 1&subarticlenbr = 45

EMDRIA (2008b). History. Retrieved May 5, 2008, from http://www.emdria.org/displaycommon.cfm?an = 1&subarticlenbr = 72

EMDRIA (2008c). Certification criteria; application for EMDRIA certification in EMDR; frequently asked questions. Retrieved May 23, 2008, from http://www.emdria.org/displaycommon.cfm?an = 1&subarticlenbr = 41

EMDRIA (2008d). Application for EMDRIA approved consultant. Retrieved May 30, 2008, from http://www.emdria.org/associations/5581/files/2007%20AC%20Application.pdf

EMDRIA. (2008e). Resources for researchers. Retrieved May 31, 2008, from EMDRIA Web site: http://www.emdria.org/displaycommon.cfm?an = 1&subarticlenbr = 34

EMDRIA (2008f). EMDR International Association consultation packet. Revised July 2008. Retrieved December 12, 2008, from http://www.emdria.org/displaycommon.cfm?an = 1&subarticlenbr = 45

EMDRIA (2008g). Mission. Retrieved December 12, 2008, from http://www.emdria.org/displaycommon.cfm?an = 1&subarticlenbr = 8

Fairbank, J. A., & Keane, T. M. (1982). Flooding for combat-related stress disorders: Assessment of anxiety reduction across traumatic memories. *Behavior Therapy, 13,* 499–510.

Fava, G. A., & Mangelli, L. (1999). Subclinical symptoms of panic disorder: New insights into pathophysiology and treatment. *Psychotherapy and Psychosomatics, 68,* 281–289.

Feldman, G. (2007). Cognitive and behavioral therapies for depression: overview, new directions, and practical recommendations for dissemination. *Psychiatric Clinics of North America, 30*(1), 39–50.

Felitti, V. J., Anda, R. F., Nordenberg, D., Williamson, D. F., Spitz, A. M., Edwards, V., et al. (1998). Relationship of childhood abuse and household dysfunction to many of the leading causes of death in adults: The Adverse Childhood Experiences (ACE) study. *American Journal of Preventative Medicine, 14*(4), 245–258.

Fernandez, I. (2008). EMDR after a critical incident: Treatment of a tsunami survivor with acute posttraumatic stress disorder. *Journal of EMDR Practice and Research, 2*(2), 156–159.

Fernandez, I., & Faretta, E. (2007). EMDR in the treatment of panic disorder with agoraphobia. *Clinical Case Studies, 6*(1), 44–63.

Ferreira, C., Deslandes, A., Moraes, H., Cagy, M., Basile, L. F., Piedade, R., et al. (2006). The relation between EEG prefrontal asymmetry and subjective feelings of mood following 24 hours of sleep deprivation. *Arquivos de Neuro-Psiquiatria, 64*(2B), 382–387.

Ferrie, R. K., & Lanius, U. F. (2001) *Opioid antagonists and EMDR.* Paper presented at EMDR International Association, Austin, TX.

Feske, U., & Goldstein, A. J. (1997). Eye movement desensitization and reprocessing treatment for panic disorder: a controlled outcome and partial dismantling study. *J Consult Clin Psychol, 65*(6), 1026–1035.

Fine, C. G., Paulsen, S., Rouanzoin, C., Luber, M., Puk, G., & Young, W. (1995). EMDR dissociative disorders task force recommended guidelines: A general guide to EMDR's use in the dissociative disorders. In F. Shapiro (Ed.), *Eye movement desensitization and reprocessing, basic Principles, protocols and procedures* (pp. 365–369). New York: The Guilford Press.

Fine, C. G., Paulsen, S., Rouanzoin, C., Luber, M., Puk, G., & Young, W. (2001). EMDR dissociative disorders task force recommended guidelines: A general guide to EMDR's use in the dissociative disorders. In F. Shapiro (Ed.), *Eye movement desensitization and reprocessing, basic principles, protocols and procedures* (2nd ed., pp. 441–445). New York: The Guilford Press.

Fleet, R. P., Dupuis, G., Marchand, A., Burelle, D., Arsenault, A., & Beitman, B. D. (1996). Panic disorder in emergency department chest pain patients: prevalence, comorbidity, suicidal ideation, and physician recognition. *American Journal of Medicine, 101*, 371–380

Foa, E. B., Hembree, E. A., & Rothbaum, B. O. (2007). *Prolonged exposure therapy for PTSD: emotional processing of traumatic experiences: therapist guide.* New York: Oxford University Press.

Foa, E. B., Keane, T. M., Friedman, M. J., Cohen, J. A., & International Society for Traumatic Stress Studies. (2009). *Effective treatments for PTSD: practice guidelines from the International Society for Traumatic Stress Studies* (2nd ed.). New York: Guilford Press.

Foa, E. B., Keane, T. M., & Friedman, M. J. (2000). *Effective treatments for PTSD: Practice guidelines from the International Society for Traumatic Stress Studies.* New York: Guilford Press.

Foa, E. B., & Kozak, M. J. (1985). Treatment of anxiety disorders: Implications for psychopathology. In A. H. Tuma & J. D. Maser (Eds.), *Anxiety and the anxiety disorders* (pp. 451–452). Hillsdale, NJ: Erlbaum.

Foa, E. B., & Kozak, M. J. (1986). Emotional processing of fear: exposure to corrective information. *Psychological Bulletin, 99*(1), 20–35.

Foa, E. B., & Meadows, E. A. (1997). Psychosocial treatments for posttraumatic stress disorder: a critical review. *Annual Review of Psychology, 48*, 449–480.

Foa, E., & Riggs, D. (1995). Posttraumatic Stress Disorder Following Assault: Theoretical Considerations and Empirical Findings. *Current Directions in Psychological Science, 4*, 61–65.

Foa, E. B., & Rothbaum, B. O. (1998). *Treating the trauma of rape: cognitive-behavioral therapy for PTSD.* New York: Guilford.

Foldvary-Schaefer, N. (2006). *Getting a good night's sleep.* Cleveland, OH: Cleveland Clinic Press.

Follette, V. M., & Ruzek, J. I. (2006). *Cognitive-behavioral therapies for trauma* (2nd ed.). New York: Guilford Press.

Fonagy, P., Gergely, G., Jurist, E. L., & Target, M. (2002). *Affect regulation, mentalization, and the development of the self.* New York: Other Press.

Forgash, C., & Copeley, M. (2008). *Healing the heart of trauma and dissociation with EMDR and ego state therapy.* New York, NY: Springer Pub. Co.

Forgash, C., & Leeds, A. M. (1999). *Case inquiry format.* Unpublished manuscript.

Foster, S., & Lendl, J. (1995). Eye movement desensitization and reprocessing: Initial application for enhancing performance in athletes. *Journal of Applied Sport Psychology, 7* (Supplement), 63.

Foster, S., & Lendl, J. (1996). Eye movement desensitization and reprocessing: Four case studies of a new tool for executive coaching and restoring employee performance after setbacks. *Consulting Psychology Journal, 48*, 155–161.

Frederick, C., & McNeal, S. (1999). *Inner strengths: Contemporary psychotherapy and hypnosis for ego-strengthening.* Mahwah, New Jersey: Lawrence Erlbaum Associates.

Freud, S. (1955). Beyond the pleasure principle. In S. Freud & J. Strachey (Eds.), *The standard edition of the complete psychological works of Sigmund Freud.* London: Hogarth Press.

Freyd, J. J., & DePrince, A. P. (Eds.). (2001). *Trauma and cognitive science: A meeting of minds, science and human experience.* New York: The Haworth Maltreatment & Trauma Press.

Fried, R., Fox, M. C., & Carlton, R. M. (1990). Effect of diaphragmatic respiration with end-tidal CO_2 biofeedback on respiration, EEG, and seizure frequency in idiopathic epilepsy. *Annals of the New York Academy of Sciences, 602*, 67–96.

Fromm, E., & Kahn, S. (1990). *Self-hypnosis: the Chicago paradigm.* New York: Guilford Press.

Furukawa, T. A., Watanabe, N., & Churchill, R. (2006). Psychotherapy plus antidepressant for panic disorder with or without agoraphobia: systematic review. *Br J Psychiatry, 188*, 305–312.

Gauvreau, P., & Bouchard, S. P. (2008). Preliminary evidence for the efficacy of EMDR in treating generalized anxiety disorder. *Journal of EMDR Practice and Research, 2*(1), 26–40.

Geer, J. H. (1965). The development of a scale to measure fear. *Behaviour Research and Therapy, 3*, 45–53.

Gelinas, D. J. (2003). Integrating EMDR into phase-oriented treatment for trauma. *Journal of Trauma and Dissociation, 4*(3), 91–135.

George, C., & West, M. (2001). The development and preliminary validation of a new measure of adult attachment: The adult attachment projective. *Attachment and Human Development, 3*(1), 30–61.

George, C., Kaplan, N., & Main, M. (1996). *Adult attachment interview* (3rd ed.). Unpublished manuscript, Department of Psychology, University of California, Berkeley.

Gerlach, A. L., Spellmeyer, G., Vogele, C., Huster, R., Stevens, S., Hetzel, G., et al. (2006). Blood-injury phobia with and without a history of fainting: disgust sensitivity does not explain the fainting response. *Psychosomatic Medicine, 68*(2), 331–339.

Giesen-Bloo, J., van Dyck, R., Spinhoven, P., van Tilburg, W., Dirksen, C., van Asselt, T., et al. (2006). Outpatient psychotherapy for borderline personality disorder: randomized trial of schema-focused therapy vs transference-focused psychotherapy. *Archives of General Psychiatry, 63*(6), 649–658.

Gil, E. (1988). *Treatment of adult survivors of childhood abuse.* Walnut Creek, CA: Launch Press.

Gold, S. N. (2000). *Not trauma alone: Therapy for child abuse survivors in family and social context.* Philadelphia, PA: Brunner/Routledge.

Goldstein, A. (1995). Treatment of panic disorder with agoraphobia: Going beyond the barrier. *In Session: Psychotherapy in Practice, 1*(3), 83–98.

Goldstein, A., & Chambless, D. L. (1978). A reanalysis of agoraphobia. *Behavior Therapy, 9*, 47–59.

Goldstein, A. J., de Beurs, E., Chambless, D. L., & Wilson, K. A. (2000). EMDR for panic disorder with agoraphobia: comparison with waiting list and credible attention-placebo control conditions. *Journal of Consulting and Clinical Psychology, 68*(6), 947–956.

Goldstein, A., & Feske, U. (1994). Eye movement desensitization and reprocessing for panic disorder: a case series. *Journal of Anxiety Disorders, 8*(4), 351–362.

Goldstein, J. (1994). *Insight meditation: The practice of freedom.* Boston: Shambhala Publications.

Grand, D. (2003). Emerging from the coffin: Treatment of a masochistic personality disorder. In P. Manfield (Ed.), *EMDR casebook* (pp. 69–94). New York: Norton.

Greenwald, R. (2007). *EMDR: within a phase model of trauma-informed treatment.* New York: Haworth Press.

Gunter, R. W., & Bodner, G. E. (2008). How eye movements affect unpleasant memories: Support for a working-memory account. *Behavior Research and Therapy, 46*, 913–931.

Guralnik, D. B. (1970). *Webster's New World dictionary of the American language* (2nd college ed.). New York: World Pub. Co.

Hammond, D. C. (1990). *Handbook of hypnotic suggestions and metaphors.* New York: Norton.

Hansen, P. A. (1991). *Survivors and partners: Healing the relationships of sexual abuse survivors.* Longmont, CO: Heron Hill Publishing Co.

Harris, A. H., Cronkite, R., & Moos, R. (2006). Physical activity, exercise coping, and depression in a 10-year cohort study of depressed patients. *Journal of Affective Disorders, 93*(1–3), 79–85.

Hase, M., Schallmayer, S., & Sack, M. (2008). EMDR Reprocessing of the Addiction Memory: Pretreatment, Posttreatment, and 1-Month Follow-Up. *Journal of EMDR Practice and Research, 2*(3), 170–179.

Haskell, W. L., Lee, I. M., Pate, R. R., Powell, K. E., Blair, S. N., Franklin, B. A., et al. (2007). Physical activity and public health: updated recommendation for adults from the American College of Sports Medicine and the American Heart Association. *Medicine & Science in Sports & Exercise, 39*(8), 1423–1434.

Hassett, A. L., Radvanski, D. C., Vaschillo, E. G., Vaschillo, B., Sigal, L. H., Karavidas, M. K., et al. (2007). A pilot study of the efficacy of heart rate variability (HRV) biofeedback in patients with fibromyalgia. *Applied Psychophysiology and Biofeedback, 32*(1), 1–10.

Hazan, C., & Shaver, P. (1987). Romantic love conceptualized as an attachment process. *Journal of Personality and Social Psychology, 52*(3), 511–524.

Heber, R., Kellner, M., & Yehuda, R. (2002). Salivary cortisol levels and the cortisol response to dexamethasone before and after EMDR: A case report. *Journal of Clinical Psychology, 58*(12), 1521–1530.

Heide, F. J., & Borkovec, T. D. (1983). Relaxation-induced anxiety: Paradoxical anxiety enhancement due to relaxation training. *Journal of Consulting and Clinical Psychology, 51*(2), 171–182.

Heide, F. J., & Borkovec, T. D. (1984). Relaxation-induced anxiety: Mechanisms and theoretical implications. *Behaviour Research and Therapy, 22*(1), 1–12.

Hekmat, H., Groth, S., & Rogers, D. (1994). Pain ameliorating effect of eye movement desensitization. *Journal of Behavior Therapy and Experimental Psychiatry, 25*(2), 121–129.

Hembree, E. A., Foa, E. B., Dorfan, N. M., Street, G. P., Kowalski, J., & Tu, X. (2003). Do patients drop out prematurely from exposure therapy for PTSD? *Journal of Traumatic Stress, 16*(6), 555–562.

Hemingway, R. B., 3rd, & Reigle, T. G. (1987). The involvement of endogenous opiate systems in learned helplessness and stress-induced analgesia. *Psychopharmacology (Berl), 93*(3), 353–357.

Henry, S. L. (1996). Pathological gambling: Etiologic considerations and treatment efficacy of eye movement desensitization/reprocessing. *Journal of Gambling Studies, 12*(4, Winter), 395–405.

Herman, J. L., & van der Kolk, B. A. (1987). Traumatic origins of borderline personality disorder. In B. A. van der Kolk (Ed.), *Psychological trauma*. Washington, DC: American Psychiatric Press.

Herman, J. L. (1992a). Complex PTSD: A syndrome in survivors of prolonged and repeated trauma. *Journal of Traumatic Stress, 5*, 377–391.

Herman, J. L. (1992b). *Trauma and recovery: The aftermath of violence - from domestic abuse to political terror*. New York: Basic Books.

Hoffman, A. (2004). *EMDR in the Treatment of Complex PTSD*. Paper presented at the EMDR International Association Conference, Montreal, Quebec.

Hoffman, A. (2005). *EMDR in der Behandlung psychotraumatischer Belastungssyndrome [EMDR therapy with posttraumatic stress syndromes]*. Stuttgart, Germany: Thieme.

Hogberg, G., Pagani, M., Sundin, O., Soares, J., Aberg-Wistedt, A., Tarnell, B., et al. (2007). On treatment with eye movement desensitization and reprocessing of chronic post-traumatic stress disorder in public transportation workers - A randomized controlled trial. *Nordic Journal of Psychiatry, 61*(1), 54–61.

Högberg, G., Pagani, M., Sundin, O., Soares, J., Aberg-Wistedt, A., Tarnell, B., et al. (2008). Treatment of post-traumatic stress disorder with eye movement desensitization and reprocessing: Outcome is stable in 35-month follow-up. *Psychiatry Research, 159*, 101–108.

Horowitz, M. J. (1979). Psychological response to serious life events. In V. Hamilton & D. M. Warburton (Eds.), *Human stress and cognition*. New York: Wiley.

Horowitz, M. J. (1986). *Stress response syndromes* (2nd ed.). Northvale, New Jersey: Jason Aronson Inc.

Horowitz, M., Wilner, M., & Alvarez, W. (1979). Impact of event scale: A measure of subjective stress. *Psychosomatic Medicine, 41*, 209–218.

Horvarth, A., Gaston, L., & Luborsky, L. (1993). The therapeutic alliance and its measures. In N. E. Miller, L. Luborsky, J. P. Barber, & J. P. Docherty (Eds.), *Psychodynamic treatment research* (pp. 247–273). New York: Basic Books.

Hunt, C. (2000). The unmet need for treatment in panic disorder and social phobia. In G. Andrews & S. Henderson (Eds.), *Unmet need in psychiatry: Problems, resources, responses* (pp. 277–289). New York: Cambridge University Press.

Hyman, J. W. (1999). *Women living with self-injury*. Philadelphia, PA: Temple University Press.

Ichii, M. (2003). *Effect of RDI for ameliorating depression in college students*. Poster session presented at the EMDR International Association, Denver, CO.

Institute of Medicine (IOM). (2007). *Treatment of posttraumatic stress disorder: An assessment of the evidence*. Washington, DC: The National Academies Press.

International Society for the Study of Dissociation. (2005). Guidelines for treating dissociative identity disorder in adults. *Journal of Trauma and Dissociation, 6*(4), 69–149. Retrieved September 9, 2006, from http://www.isst-d.org/education/treatmentguidelines-index.htm

Ironson, G. I., Freund, B., Strauss, J. L., & Williams, J. (2002). A comparison of two treatments for traumatic stress: A pilot study of EMDR and prolonged exposure. *Journal of Clinical Psychology, 58*(1), 113–128.

Iyengar, B. K. S. (1981). *Light on pranayama: The yogic art of breathing*. New York: Crossroad.

Jaberghaderi, N., Greenwald, R., Rubin, A., S., D., & Zand, S. O. (2004). A comparison of CBT and EMDR for sexually abused Iranian girls. *Clinical Psychology and Psychotherapy, 11*(5), 358–368.

Jacobs, D. G., & Brewer, M. L. (2006). Application of The APA Practice Guidelines on suicide to clinical practice. *CNS Spectrums, 11*(6), 447–454.

Jacobson, E. (1938). *Progressive relaxation*. Chicago: University of Chicago Press.

Jacobson, N. S., Dobson, K. S., Truax, P. A., Addis, M. E., Koerner, K., Gollan, J. K., et al. (1996). A component analysis of cognitive-behavioral treatment for depression. *Journal of Consulting and Clinical Psychology, 64*(2), 295–304.

Jacobson, N. S., & Gortner, E. T. (2000). Can depression be de-medicalized in the 21st century: scientific revolutions, counter-revolutions and the magnetic field of normal science. *Behaviour Research and Therapy, 38*(2), 103–117.

Janet, P. (1889). *L'Automatisme psychologique*. Paris: Felix Alcan.

Janet, P. (1977). *The mental state of hystericals*. In D. N. Robinson (Ed.), C. R. Corson (Trans.), Washington, DC: University Publications of America.

Janoff-Bulman, R. (1992). *Shattered assumptions: Toward a new psychology of trauma*. New York: Free Press.

Janoff-Bulman, R. (1992). *Shattered assumptions: Toward a new psychology of trauma*. New York: Free Press.

Jobes, D. A., Wong, S. A., Conrad, A. K., Drozd, J. F., & Neal-Walden, T. (2005). The collaborative assessment and management of suicidality versus treatment as usual: a retrospective study with suicidal outpatients. *Suicide and Life Threatening Behavior, 35*(5), 483–497.

Johns, M. W. (1991). "A new method for measuring daytime sleepiness: the Epworth sleepiness scale". *Sleep* 14(6), 540–545.

Johnstone, K. A., & Page, A. C. (2004). Attention to phobic stimuli during exposure: the effect of distraction on anxiety reduction, self-efficacy and perceived control. *Behaviour Research and Therapy, 42*(3), 249–275.

Joseph, R. (1998). Traumatic amnesia, repression, and hippocampus injury due to emotional stress, corticosteroids and enkephalins. *Child Psychiatry and Human Development, 29*(2), 169–185.

Karavidas, M. K., Lehrer, P. M., Vaschillo, E., Vaschillo, B., Marin, H., Buyske, S., et al. (2007). Preliminary results of an open label study of heart rate variability biofeedback for the treatment of major depression. *Applied Psychophysiology and Biofeedback, 32*(1), 19–30.

Kavanagh, D. J., Freese, S., Andrade, J., & May, J. (2001). Effects of visuospatial tasks on desensitization to emotive memories. *British Journal of Clinical Psychology, 40*(Pt 3), 267–280.

Keane, T. M., Fairbank, J. A., Caddell, J. M., & Zimering, R. T. (1989). Implosive (flooding) therapy reduced symptoms of PTSD in Vietnam combat veterans. *Behavior Therapy, 20*, 245–260.

Kelley, S. D. M., & Selim, B. (2007). Eye movement desensitization and reprocessing in the psychological treatment of trauma-based psychogenic non-epileptic seizures. *Clinical Psychology and Psychotherapy, 14*(2), 135.

Kessler, R. C., Chiu, W. T., Demler, O., & Walters, E. E. (2005). Prevalence, severity, and comorbidity of twelve-month DSM–IV disorders in the National Comorbidity Survey Replication (NCS-R). *Archives of General Psychiatry, 62*(6), 617–627.

Kessler, R. C., Sonnega, A., Bromet, E., Hughes, M., & Nelson, C. B. (1995). Posttraumatic stress disorder in the National Comorbidity Survey. *Archives of General Psychiatry, 52*(12), 1048–1060.

Kessler, R. C., Sonnega, A., Bromet, E. J., Hughes, M., Nelson, C. B., & Breslau, N. (1999). Epidemiological risk factors for trauma and PTSD. In R. Yehuda (Ed.), *Risk factors for posttraumatic stress disorder* (pp. 23–59). Washington: American Psychiatric Press.

Killgore, W. D., Kahn-Greene, E. T., Lipizzi, E. L., Newman, R. A., Kamimori, G. H., & Balkin, T. J. (2007). Sleep deprivation reduces perceived emotional intelligence and constructive thinking skills. *Sleep Med, 8*(3), 215–221.

Killgore, W. D., Killgore, D. B., Day, L. M., Li, C., Kamimori, G. H., & Balkin, T. J. (2007). The effects of 53 hours of sleep deprivation on moral judgment. *Sleep, 30*(3), 345–352.

Kim, D., Bae, H., & Park, Y. C. (2008). Validity of the Subjective Units of Disturbance Scale in EMDR. *Journal of EMDR Practice and Research, 2*(1), 57–62.

Kim, D., & Kim, K.-I. (2004). A case series of Eye Movement Desensitization and Reprocessing (EMDR) in 30 psychiatric patients: Korean experience. *Journal of the Korean Neuropsychiatric Association, 43*(1), 113–118.

Kirsch, I., & Lynn, S. J. (1995). The altered state of hypnosis: Changes in the theoretical landscape. *American Psychologist, 50*(10), 846–858.

Kleinknecht, R. A. (1993). Rapid treatment of blood and injection phobias with eye movement desensitization. *Journal of Behaviour Therapy and Experimental Psychiatry, 24*, 211–217.

Klosko, J., Barlow, D., Tassinari R., & Cerny J. (1990). A comparison of alprazolam and behavior therapy in treatment of panic disorder. *Journal of Consulting and Clinical Psychology, 58*(1), 77–84.

Kluft, R. P. (1993). Basic principles in conducting the psychotherapy of multiple personality disorder. In R. P. Kluft & C. G. Fine (Eds.), *Clinical perspectives on multiple personality disorder* (pp. 19–50). Washington, DC: American Psychiatric Press.

Kluft, R. P. (1999). An overview of the psychotherapy of dissociative identity disorder. *American Journal of Psychotherapy, 53*(3), 289–319.

Knapp, S., & VandeCreek, L. (2006). *Practical ethics for psychologists: a positive approach* (1st ed.). Washington, DC: American Psychological Association.

Kneff, J. C., & Krebs, K. (2004). Eye movement desensitization and reprocessing (EMDR): Another helpful mind-body technique to treat GI problems. *Gastroenterology Nursing, 27*(6), 286–287.

Knipe, J. (2003). "it was a golden time". Treating narcissistic vulnerability. In P. Manfield (Ed.), *EMDR casebook* (pp. 296–319). New York: Norton.

Knipe, J., & Forgash, C. (2001). *Safety focused EMDR/Ego state treatment of severe ego state disorders*. Paper presented at EMDR International Association Conference, Austin, TX.

Knipe, J. (2002). A tool for working with dissociative clients. *The EMDRIA Newsletter, 7*(2), 14–16.

Koerner, K., Miller, A. L., & Wagner, A. W. (1998). Dialectical behavior therapy: Part I. Principle based intervention with multi-problem patients. *Journal of Practical Psychiatry and Behavioral Health, 4*, 28–36.

Konuk, E., Knipe, J., Eke, I., Yuksek, H., Yurtsever, A., & Ostep, S. (2006). The effects of eye movement desensitization and reprocessing (EMDR) therapy on posttraumatic stress disorder in survivors of the 1999 Marmara, Turkey, Earthquake. *International Journal of Stress Management, 13*(3), 291.

Korn, D. L., & Leeds, A. M. (1998). Clinical Applications of EMDR in the Treatment of Adult Survivors of Childhood Abuse and Neglect, *EMDR International Association*. Baltimore, MD.

Korn, D. L., & Leeds, A. M. (2002). Preliminary evidence of efficacy for EMDR resource development and installation in the stabilization phase of treatment of complex posttraumatic stress disorder. *Journal of Clinical Psychology, 58*(12), 1465–1487.

Korn, D. L., Weir, J., & Rozelle, D. (2004). *Looking beyond the data: Clinical lessons learned from an EMDR treatment outcome study, Session 321*. Paper presented at EMDR International Association Conference, Montreal, Quebec.

Korn, D. L., Zangwill, W., Lipke, H., & Smyth, M. J. (2001). *EMDR Fidelity Scale*. Unpublished monograph, The Trauma Center, Brookline, MA.

Krause, R., & Kirsch, A. (2006). [On the relationship between traumatization, amnesia and symptom stress—an empirical pilot study]. *Zeitschrift für Psychosomatische Medizin und Psychotherapie, 52*(4), 392–405.

Krystal, S., Prendergast, J., Krystal, P., & Fenner, P., Shapiro, I., & Shapiro, K. (2002). Transpersonal psychology, eastern nondual philosophy, and EMDR. In F. Shapiro (Ed.), *EMDR as an integrative psychotherapy approach: Experts of diverse orientations explore the paradigm prism* (pp. 319–339). Washington: American Psychological Association.

Kuhn, T. S. (1996). *The structure of scientific revolutions* (3rd ed.). Chicago, IL: University of Chicago Press.

Kuiken, D., Bears, M., Miall, D., & Smith, L. (2001–2002). Eye movement desensitization reprocessing facilitates attentional orienting. *Imagination, Cognition and Personality, 21*(1), 3–20.

Kutz, I., Resnik, V., & Dekel, R. (2008). The Effect of Single-Session Modified EMDR on Acute Stress Syndromes. *Journal of EMDR Practice and Research, 2*(3), 190–200.

Ladd, G. (2007). Treatment of psychological injury after a scuba-diving fatality. *Diving and Hyperbaric Medicine, 37*(1), 36–39.

Lamprecht, F., Köhnke, C., Lempa, W., Sack, M., Matzke, M., & Munte, T. F. (2004). Event-related potentials and EMDR treatment of post-traumatic stress disorder. *Neuroscience Research, 49*(2), 267–272.

Lang, P. J. (1968). Fear reduction and fear behavior: Problems in treating a construct. In J. M. Shlien (Ed.), *Research in psychotherapy* (Vol. 3, pp. 90–102). Washington, DC: American Psychological Association.

Lang, P. J. (1977). Imagery in therapy: An information processing analysis of fear. *Behavior Therapy, 8*, 862–886.

Lang, P. J. (1979). A bioinformational theory of emotional imagery. *Psychophysiology, 16*, 495–512.

Lanius, U. F. (2004, September 11, 2004). *PTSD, information processing and thalamo-cortical dialogue*. Paper presented at the EMDR International Association Conference, Montreal, Quebec.

Lanius, U. F. (2005). EMDR Processing with Dissociative Clients: Adjunctive Use of Opioid Antagonists. In R. Shapiro (Ed.), *EMDR solutions: Pathways to healing* (pp. 121–146). New York: W.W. Norton.

Lankton, S. R. E. (1987). *Central themes and principles of Ericksonian therapy (Ericksonian Monographs, No 2)*. New York: Brunner-Routledge.

Lansing, K., Amen, D. G., Hanks, C., & Rudy, L. (2005). High-resolution brain SPECT imaging and eye movement desensitization and reprocessing in police officers with PTSD. *The Journal of Neuropsychiatry and Clinical Neurosciences, 17*(4), 526–532.

Lansing, K. M., Amen, G. G., & Klindt, W. C. (2000, November). *Tracking the neurological impact of CBT and EMDR in the treatment of PTSD*. Paper presented at the annual meeting of the Association for the Advancement for Behavior Therapy, New Orleans.

Lazrove, S., & Fine, C. G. (1996). The Use of EMDR in Patients with Dissociative Identity Disorder. *Dissociation, 9*(4), 289–299.

Lazarus, A., & Lazarus, C. (1991). *Multimodal life history inventory*. Champaign, IL: Research Press.

Lazarus, A. A. (1989). *The Practice of Multimodal Therapy: Systematic, comprehensive, effective psychotherapy*. Baltimore, MD: John Hopkins University Press.

LeDoux, J. E. (1996). *The emotional brain: the mysterious underpinnings of emotional life*. New York: Simon & Schuster.

LeDoux, J., Romanski, L., & Xagoraris, A. (1989). Indelibility of subcortical emotional memories. *Journal of Cognitive Neuroscience, 1*(3), 238–243.

Lee, C. W., & Drummond, P. D. (2008). Effects of eye movement versus therapist instructions on the processing of distressing memories. *Journal of Anxiety Disorders, 22*(5), 801–808.

Lee, C. W., & Schubert, S. (2009). Omissions and errors in the institute of medicine's report on scientific evidence of treatment for posttraumatic stress disorder. *Journal of EMDR Practice and Research, 3,* 32–38.

Lee, C., Gavriel, H., Drummond, P., Richards, J., & Greenwald, R. (2002). Treatment of PTSD: stress inoculation training with prolonged exposure compared to EMDR. *Journal of Clinical Psychology, 58*(9), 1071–1089.

Lee, C., Gavriel, H., & Richards, J. (1996, Nov). Eye movement desensitisation: Past research, complexities, and future direction. *Australian Psychologist, 31*(3), 168–173. Lee, C., Taylor, G., & Drummond, P.D. (2006). The active ingredient in EMDR: Is it traditional exposure or dual focus of attention? *Clinical Psychology and Psychotherapy, 13,* 97–107.

Leeds, A. M. (1997, July,). *In the eye of the beholder: reflections on shame, dissociation, and transference in complex posttraumatic stress and attachment related disorders. Principles of case formulation for EMDR treatment planning and the use of Resource Installation.* Paper presented at the EMDR International Association, San Francisco, CA.

Leeds, A. M. (1998a). Lifting the burden of shame: Using EMDR resource installation to resolve a therapeutic impasse. In P. Manfield (Ed.), *Extending EMDR: A case book of innovative applications* (pp. 256–282). New York: W. W. Norton.

Leeds, A. M. (1998b). *EMDR safe place survey.* Unpublished manuscript.

Leeds, A. M. (2001). *Strengthening the self: Principles and procedures for creating successful treatment outcomes for adult survivors of neglect and abuse.* (Cassette Recording and Manual). Available from Andrew M. Leeds, Ph.D., 1049 Fourth Street, Suite G, Santa Rosa, CA 95404.

Leeds, A. M. (2006, September 9). *Learning to feel good about positive emotions with the positive affect tolerance and integration protocol.* Paper presented at the EMDRIA Conference, Philadelphia, PA.

Leeds, A. M., & Shapiro, F. (2000). EMDR and resource installation: Principles and procedures for enhancing current functioning and resolving traumatic experiences. In J. Carlson & L. Sperry (Eds.), *Brief therapy strategies with individuals and couples* (pp. 469–534). Phoenix, AZ: Zeig, Tucker, Theisen, Inc.

Lehrer, P. M., Carr, R., Sargunaraj, D., & Woolfolk, R. L. (1994). Stress management techniques: are they all equivalent, or do they have specific effects? *Biofeedback & Self Regulation, 19*(4), 353–401.

Lehrer, P. M., Woolfolk, R. L., & Sime, W. E. (2007). *Principles and practice of stress management* (3rd ed.). New York: Guilford Press.

Lendl, J., & Foster, S. (2003). *EMDR 'Performance Enhancement' for the workplace: A practitioners' manual* (2nd USA Edition ed.). San Jose, California: Performance Enhancement Unlimited.

Lenggenhager, B., Smith, S. T., & Blanke, O. (2006). Functional and neural mechanisms of embodiment: importance of the vestibular system and the temporal parietal junction. *Rev Neurosci, 17*(6), 643–657.

Lenggenhager, B., Tadi, T., Metzinger, T., & Blanke, O. (2007). Video ergo sum: manipulating bodily self-consciousness. *Science, 317*(5841), 1096–1099.

Levin, P., Lazrove, S., & van der Kolk, B. (1999). What psychological testing and neuroimaging tell us about the treatment of posttraumatic stress disorder (PTSD) by eye movement desensitization and reprocessing (EMDR). *Journal of Anxiety Disorders, 13*(1–2), 159–172.

Linehan, M. M. (1993). *Cognitive-Behavioral treatment of borderline personality disorder.* New York: Guilford Press.

Lipke, H. (1992). *Manual for the teaching of Shapiro's EMDR in the treatment of combat-related PTSD.* Pacific Grove, CA: EMDR Institute.

Lipke, H. (1995). EMDR Clinician survey. In F. Shapiro (Ed.), *Eye Movement Desensitization and Reprocessing, Basic Principles, Protocols and Procedures* (1st ed., pp. 376–386). New York: The Guilford Press.

Lipke, H. (1996). A four-activity model of psychotherapy and its relationship to Eye Movement Desensitization and Reprocessing (EMDR) and other methods of psychotherapy. *Traumatology, 2*(2). Retrieved June 5, 1998, from http://www.fsu.edu/~trauma/art1991v1992i1992.html

Lipke, H. (1999). *EMDR and psychotherapy integration: theoretical and clinical suggestions with focus on traumatic stress.* Boca Raton: CRC Press.

Liotti, G. (1992). Disorganized/disoriented attachment in the etiology of the dissociative disorders. *Dissociation, 5*(4), 196–204.

Liotti, G., Pasquini, P., & The Italian Group for the Study of Dissociation. (2000). Predictive factors for borderline personality disorder: patients' early traumatic experiences and losses suffered by the attachment figure. *Acta Psychiatrica Scandinavica, 102*(4), 282–289.

Loewenstein, R. J. (1991). An office mental status examination for complex chronic dissociative symptoms and multiple personality disorder. *Psychiatric Clinics of North America, 14*(3), 567–604.

Lohr, J. M., Tolin, D. F., & Kleinknecht, R. A. (1995). Eye movement desensitization of medical phobias: Two case studies. *Journal of Behavior Therapy and Experimental Psychiatry, 26,* 141–151.

MacCulloch, M. J., & Barrowcliff, A. L. (2001, May). *The de-arousal model of eye movement desensitization and reprocessing (EMDR), Part I: A theoretical perspective on EMDR.* Paper presented at the EMDR Europe 2nd Annual Conference "EMDR innovations in theory and practice," London, UK.

MacCulloch, M. J., & Feldman, P. (1996). Eye movement desensitization treatment utilizes the positive visceral element of the investigatory reflex to inhibit the memories of post-traumatic stress disorder: A theoretical analysis. *British Journal of Psychiatry, 169,* 571–579.

Magee, W. J., Eaton, W. W., Wittchen, H. U., McGonagle, K. A., & Kessler, R. C. (1996). Agoraphobia, simple phobia, and social phobia in the National Comorbidity Survey. *Archives of General Psychiatry, 53*(2), 159–168.

Main, M. (1996). Introduction to the special section on attachment and psychopathology: 2. Overview of the field of attachment. *Journal of Consulting and Clinical Psychology, 64*(2), 237–243.

Main, M., & Solomon, J. (1986) Discovery of a new, insecure-disorganized/disoriented attachment pattern. In T. B. Brazelton & M. Yogman (Eds.), *Affective development in infancy* (pp. 95–124). Norwood, New Jersey: Ablex.

Manfield, P. (2003). *EMDR casebook: Expanded* (2nd ed.). New York: Norton.

Marcus, S., Marquis, P., & Sakai, C. (1997). Controlled study of treatment of PTSD using EMDR in an HMO setting. *Psychotherapy, 34,* 307–315.

Marks, I., & Mathews, A. (1979). Brief standard self-rating for phobic patients. *Behaviour Research and Therapy, 17,* 59–68.

Marks, I., Kenwright, M., McDonough, M., Whittaker, M., O'Brien, T., & Mataix-Cols, D. (2004). Saving clinicians' time by delegating routine aspects of therapy to a computer: a randomised controlled trail in panic/phobia disorder. *Psychological Medicine, 34,* 9–17.

Martinsen, E. W., Hoffart, A., & Solberg, O. (1989). Comparing aerobic with nonaerobic forms of exercise in the treatment of clinical depression: a randomized trial. *Comprehensive Psychiatry, 30*(4), 324–331.

Marquis, J. N. (1991). A report on seventy-eight cases treated by eye movement desensitization. *Journal of Behavior Therapy and Experimental Psychiatry, 22,* 187–192.

Mathews, A. M. (1971). Psychophysiological approaches to the investigation of desensitization and related procedures. *Psychological Bulletin, 76*(2), 73–91.

Maxfield, L. (2003). Clinical implications and recommendations arising from EMDR research findings. *Journal of Trauma Practice, 2,* 61–81.

Maxfield, L. J. (2004). A working memory analysis of the dual attention component of eye movement desensitization and reprocessing (Doctoral dissertation, Lakehead University). *Dissertation Abstracts International, 64*(10-B).

Maxfield, L., & Hyer, L. (2002). The relationship between efficacy and methodology in studies investigating EMDR treatment of PTSD. *Journal of Clinical Psychology, 58*(1), 23–41.

McCann, I. L., & Pearlman, L. A. (1990). Psychological trauma and the adult survivor: theory, therapy and transformation. New York, New York: Brunner/Mazel, Inc.

McCraty, R., Atkinson, M., Tomasino, D., & Bradley, R. T. (2001) The science of the heart: exploring the role of the heart in human performance. Institute of HeartMath Publication. Boulder Creek, CO. Retrieved August 22, 2008, from http://www.heartmath.org

McCraty, R., Atkinson, M., Tomasino, D., & Stuppy, W. P. (2001). Analysis of twenty-four hour heart rate variability in patients with panic disorder. *Biological Psychology, 56*(2), 131–150.

McCullough, L. (1996). *Changing character: Short-term anxiety-regulating psychotherapy for restructuring defenses, affects, and attachment*: Basic Books.

McCullough, L. (1998). *PAC summary form.* Retrieved November 20, 2008, from http://www.affectphobia.org/pacforms.html

McCullough, L. (2001). *Psychotherapy assessment checklist.* Retrieved November 20, 2008, from http://www.affectphobia.org/pacforms.html

McCullough, L. (2003, February 13, 2003). *Directions for the Psychotherapy Assessment Checklist (PAC Forms).* Retrieved November 20, 2008, from http://www.affectphobia.org/pacforms.html

McCullough, L., Kuhn, N., Andrews, S., Kaplan, A., Wolf, J., & Hurley, C. (2003). *Treating affect phobia: A manual for short-term dynamic psychotherapy.* New York: Guilford Press.

McEwan, T., Mullen, P. E., & Purcell, R. (2007). Identifying risk factors in stalking: a review of current research. *International Journal of Law and Psychiatry, 30*(1), 1–9.

McEwen, B. S. (2006). Protective and damaging effects of stress mediators: central role of the brain. *Dialogues in Clinical Neuroscience, 8*(4), 367–381.

McGhan, W. F., Stimmel, G. L., Gilman, T. M., & Segal, J. L. (1982). Pharmacists as drug prescribers: validation of certification exams and evaluation instruments. *Evaluation & the Health Professions, 5*(2), 115–129.

McGoldrick, M., Gerson, R., & Petry, S. S. (2008). *Genograms: assessment and intervention* (3rd ed.). New York: W.W. Norton & Company.

McLeod, J. (1997). *Narrative and psychotherapy.* London: Sage Publications.

McNally, V. J., & Solomon, R. M. (1999). The FBI's critical incident stress management program. *FBI Law Enforcement Bulletin, 68*, 20–26.

Meichenbaum, D. (1985). *Stress inoculation training.* New York: Pergamon Press.

Merckelbach, H., Hogervorst, E., Kampman, M., & de Jongh, A. (1994). Effects of "eye movement desensitization" on emotional processing in normal subjects. *Behavioural and Cognitive Psychotherapy, 22*, 331–335.

Merluzzi, T. V., Taylor, C. B., Boltwood, M., & Götestam, K. G. (1991) Opioid antagonist impedes exposure. *Journal of Clinical and Consulting Psychology, 59*(3), 421–430.

Merrill, R. M., Aldana, S. G., Greenlaw, R. L., Diehl, H. A., & Salberg, A. (2007). The effects of an intensive lifestyle modification program on sleep and stress disorders. *Journal of. Nutrition, Health & Aging, 11*(3), 242–248.

Mick, T. M., & Hollander, E. (2006). Impulsive-compulsive sexual behavior. *CNS Spectrum, 11*(12), 944–955.

Miller, P. (2007). *A case series detailing phenomenology, EMDR protocol and clinical outcome of EMDR in severe depression, with psychosis, delusional dysmorphobia and Schizophrenia.* Paper presented at the 8th EMDR Europe Conference, Paris, France.

Mol, S. S., Arntz, A., Metsemakers, J. F., Dinant, G. J., Vilters-van Montfort, P. A., & Knottnerus, J. A. (2005). Symptoms of post-traumatic stress disorder after non-traumatic events: evidence from an open population study. *British Journal of Psychiatry, 186*, 494–499.

Mulkens, A. A. N., De Jong, P., & Merckelbach, H. (1997). Disgust sensitivity and spider phobia. *Journal of Abnormal Psychology, 105*, 464–468.

Muris, P., & De Jongh, A. (1996). Eye movement desensitization and reprocessing. Een nieuwe behandelingstechniek voor trauma-gerelateerde angstklachten: Over de behandeling van kinderen. [Eye movement desensitization and reprocessing. A new treatment method for trauma-related anxiety complaints: About the treatment of children]. *Kind en Adolescent, 17*, 159–217.

Muris, P., & Merckelbach, H. (1995). Treating spider phobia with eye movement desensitization and reprocessing: Two case reports. *Journal of Anxiety Disorders, 9*, 439–449.

Muris, P., Merceklbach, H., Holdrinet, I., & Sijsenaar, M. (1998) Treating phobic children: effects of EMDR versus exposure. *Journal of Clinical and Consulting Psychology, 66*(1), 193–198.

Muris, P., Merckelbach, H., Van Haaften, H., & Mayer, B. (1997). Eye movement desensitisation and reprocessing versus exposure in vivo. A single-session crossover study of spider-phobic children. *British Journal of Psychiatry, 171*, 82–86.

Muzina, D. J., Colangelo, E., Manning, J. S., & Calabrese, J. R. (2007). Differentiating bipolar disorder from depression in primary care. *Cleveland Clinic Journal of Medicine, 74*(2), 89, 92, 95–89 passim.

Nadler, W. (1996). EMDR: Rapid treatment of panic disorder. *International Journal of Psychiatry, 2*, 1–8. Retrieved November 8, 2008, from http://www.priory.com/emdr.htm

Najavits, L. (2002). *Seeking safety: A treatment manual for PTSD and substance abuse.* New York: Guilford Press.

Najavits, L. M., Gallop, R. J., & Weiss, R. D. (2006). Seeking safety therapy for adolescent girls with PTSD and substance use disorder: a randomized controlled trial. *Journal of Behavioral Health Services & Research, 33*(4), 453–463.

Najavits, L. M., Schmitz, M., Gotthardt, S., & Weiss, R. D. (2005). Seeking Safety plus Exposure Therapy: an outcome study on dual diagnosis men. *Journal of Psychoactive Drugs, 37*(4), 425–435.

Najavits, L. M., Weiss, R. D., Shaw, S. R., & Muenz, L. R. (1998). "Seeking safety": outcome of a new cognitive-behavioral psychotherapy for women with posttraumatic stress disorder and substance dependence. *Journal of Traumatic Stress, 11*(3), 437–456.

Nathanson, D. L. (1998, July). *Locating EMDR: Affect, scene and script.* Paper presented at the EMDR International Association Conference, Baltimore, MD

Nathanson, D. L. (1992). *Shame and pride: Affect sex and the birth of the self.* New York: W.W. Norton.

National Board for Certified Counselors (2005). *Code of ethics.* Retrieved April 28, 2008, from http://www.nbcc.org/extras/pdfs/ethics/nbcc-codeofethics.pdf

National Institute for Clinical Excellence. (2005). *Posttraumatic stress disorder: The management of PTSD in adults and children in primary and secondary care.* London, UK: National Institute for Clinical Excellence.

National Institute of Mental Health (2008). *The numbers count: mental disorders in America.* Retrieved June 14, 2008, from National Institute of Mental Health Web site http://www.nimh.nih.gov/health/publications/the-numbers-count-mental-disorders-in-america.shtml

Nemiah, J. C. (1984). The psychodynamic view of anxiety. In R.O. Pasnace (Ed.), *Diagnosis and treatment of anxiety disorders* (pp. 117–137). Washington, DC: American Psychiatric Press.

Newman, M. G., Erickson, T., Przeworski, A., & Dzus, E. (2003). Self-Help and minimal-contact therapies for anxiety disorders: Is human contact necessary for therapeutic efficacy? *Journal of Clinical Psychology, 59*(3), 251–74.

Nicosia, G. (1994, March). *A mechanism for dissociation suggested by the quantitative analysis of electro-encephalograpy.* Paper presented at the International EMDR Annual Conference, Sunnyvale, CA.

Nicosia, G. (1995). Eye movement desensitization and reprocessing is not hypnosis. *Dissociation, 9*(1), 69.

Nijenhuis, E. R., Spinhoven, P., Van Dyck, R., Van Der Hart, O., & Vanderlinden, J. (1996). The development and psychometric characteristics of the somatoform dissociation questionnaire (SDQ-20). *The Journal of Nervous and Mental Disease, 184*(11), 688–694.

Nijenhuis, E. R., Spinhoven, P., van Dyck, R., van der Hart, O., & Vanderlinden, J. (1997). The development of the somatoform dissociation questionnaire (SDQ-5) as a screening instrument for dissociative disorders. *Acta Psychiatrica Scandinavia, 96*(5), 311–318.

Ogden, P., & Minton, K. (2000). Sensorimotor psychotherapy: One method for processing traumatic memory. *Traumatology, VI*(3). Retrieved October 24, 2008, from http://www.fsu.edu/~trauma/v6i3/v6i3a3.html.

Oh, D.-H., & Choi, J. (2004). Changes in the regional cerebral perfusion after eye movement desensitization and reprocessing: A SPECT study of two cases. *Korean Journal of Biological Psychiatry, 11*(2), 173–180.

Oliver, N. S., & Page, A. C. (2008). Effects of internal and external distraction and focus during exposure to blood-injury-injection stimuli. *Journal of Anxiety Disorders, 22*(2), 283–291.

Oquendo, M. A., Currier, D., & Mann, J. J. (2006). Prospective studies of suicidal behavior in major depressive and bipolar disorders: what is the evidence for predictive risk factors? *Acta Psychiatrica Scandinavia, 114*(3), 151–158.

Oquendo, M. A., Galfalvy, H., Russo, S., Ellis, S. P., Grunebaum, M. F., Burke, A., et al. (2004). Prospective study of clinical predictors of suicidal acts after a major depressive episode in patients with major depressive disorder or bipolar disorder. *American Journal of Psychiatry, 161*(8), 1433–1441.

Oras, R., Ezpeleta, S. C., & Ahmad, A. (2004). Treatment of traumatized refugee children with eye movement desensitization and reprocessing in a psychodynamic context. *Nordic Journal of Psychiatry, 58*(3), 199–203.

Osuch, E. A., Benson, B., Geraci, M., Podell, D., Herscovitch, P., McCann, U. D., et al. (2001). Regional cerebral blood flow correlated with flashback intensity in patients with posttraumatic stress disorder. *Biological Psychiatry, 50*(4), 246–253.

Öst, L. G., & Sterner, U. (1987). Applied tension: A specific behavioural method for treatment of blood phobia. *Behaviour Research and Therapy, 25*, 25–30.

Öst, L. G., Thulin, U., & Ramnerö, J. (2004). Cognitive behaviour therapy vs. exposure in vivo in the treatment of panic disorder with agoraphobia. *Behaviour Research and Therapy, 42*, 1105–1127.

Pagani, M., Hogberg, G., Salmaso, D., Nardo, D., Sundin, O., Jonsson, C., et al. (2007). Effects of EMDR psychotherapy on 99mTc-HMPAO distribution in occupation-related post-traumatic stress disorder. *Nuclear Medicine Communications, 28*(10), 757–765.

Panksepp, J. (1998). *Affective neuroscience: The foundations of human and animal emotions.* New York: Oxford University Press.

Parker, G. (1981). Reported parental characteristic of agoraphobics and social phobics. *British Journal of Psychiatry, 135*, 555–560.

Parrish, I. S. (1999). *Military veterans PTSD reference manual.* Bryn Mawr: Infinity Publishing.

Paulsen, S. (1995). Eye movement desensitization and reprocessing: Its cautious use in the dissociative disorders. *Dissociation, 8*(1), 32–44.

Pavlov, I. P. (1927). *Conditioned reflexes: An investigation of the physiological activity of the cerebral cortex.* New York: Dover Publications, Ind.

Pearce, S. S. (1996). *Flash of insight: metaphor and narrative in therapy.* Boston: Allyn and Bacon.

Perkins, B. R., & Rouanzoin, C. C. (2002). A critical evaluation of current views regarding eye movement desensitization and reprocessing (EMDR): Clarifying points of confusion. *Journal of Clinical Psychology, 58*(1), 77–97.

Pearlman, L. A., & Courtois, C. A. (2005). Clinical applications of the attachment framework: Relational treatment of complex trauma. *Journal of Traumatic Stress, 18*(5), 449–459.

Pelcovitz, D., van der Kolk, B. A., Roth, S., Mandel, F., Kaplan, S., & Resick, P. (1997). Development of a Criteria Set and a Structured Interview for Disorders of Extreme Stress (SIDES). *Journal of Traumatic Stress, 10*, 3–16.

Penfold, K., & Page, A. C. (1999). The effect of distraction on within-session anxiety reduction during brief in vivo exposure for mild blood-injection fears. *Behavior Therapy, 33*, 607–621.

Philibert, R. A., Crowe, R., Ryu, G. Y., Yoon, J. G., Secrest, D., Sandhu, H., et al. (2007). Transcriptional profiling of lymphoblast lines from subjects with panic disorder. *American Journal of Medical Genetics Part B: Neuropsychiatric Genetics, 144B*(5), 674–682.

Piquero, A. R., Brame, R., Fagan, J., & Moffitt, T. E. (2006). Assessing the offending activity of criminal domestic violence suspects: offense specialization, escalation, and de-escalation evidence from the Spouse Assault Replication Program. *Public Health Rep, 121*(4), 409–418.

Pitman, R., Altman, B., Greenwald, E., Longre, R. E., Macklin, M. L., Poire, R. E., et al. (1991). Psychiatric complications during flooding therapy for posttraumatic stress disorder. *Journal of Clinical Psychiatry, 52*, 17–20.

Pope, K. S., & Brown, L. S. (1996). *Recovered memories of abuse: assessment, therapy, forensics* (1st ed.). Washington, DC: American Psychological Association.

Popky, A. J. (2005). DeTUR, an urge reduction protocol for addictions and dysfunctional behaviors. In R. Shapiro (Ed.), *EMDR solutions: pathways to healing* (pp. 167–188). New York: W.W. Norton.

Power, K., McGoldrick, T., & Brown, K. (2002). A controlled comparison of EMDR versus Exposure plus cognitive restructuring versus wait list in the treatment of post traumatic stress disorder. *Clinical Psychology and Psychotherapy, 9,* 299–318.

Propper, R. E., Pierce, J., Geisler, M. W., Christman, S. D., & Bellorado, N. (2007). Effect of bilateral eye movements on frontal interhemispheric gamma EEG coherence: implications for EMDR therapy. *Journal of Nervous and Mental Disease, 195*(9), 785–788.

Putnam, F. (1989). Pierre Janet and modern views of dissociation. *Journal of Traumatic Stress, 2*(4), 413–429.

Putnam, F. W., Zahn, T. P., & Post, R. M. (1990). Differential autonomic nervous system activity in multiple personality disorder. *Psychiatric Research, 31*(3), 251–260.

Raboni, M. R., Tufik, S., & Suchecki, D. (2006). Treatment of PTSD by eye movement desensitization reprocessing (EMDR) improves sleep quality, quality of life, and perception of stress. *Annals of the New York Academy of Sciences, 1071,* 508–513.

Rachman, S. (1980). Emotional processing. *Behaviour Research and Therapy, 14,* 125–132.

Rauch, S. L., van der Kolk, B. A., Fisler, R. E., Alpert, N. M., Orr, S. P., Savage, C. R., et al. (1996). A Symptom Provocation Study of Posttraumatic Stress Disorder Using Positron Emission Tomography and Script-Driven Imagery. *Archives of General Psychiatry, 53*(May), 380–387.

Reiser, M. F. (1990). *Memory in mind and brain: What dream imagery reveals.* New York: Basic Books.

Resick, P. A., & Schnicke, M. K. (1993). *Cognitive processing therapy for rape victims: A treatment manual.* Newbury Park, CA: Sage.

Ricci, R. J., & Clayton, C. A. (2008). Trauma resolution treatment as an adjunct to standard treatment for child molesters: A qualitative study. *Journal of EMDR Practice and Research, 2*(1), 41–50.

Ricci, R. J., Clayton, C. A., & Shapiro, F. (2006). Some effects of EMDR on previously abused child molesters: Theoretical reviews and preliminary findings. *The Journal of Forensic Psychiatry & Psychology, 17*(4), 538–562.

Rogers, S., & Lanius, U. F. (November, 2001). *Phobia, PTSD, endogenous opioids and EMDR treatment response.* Paper presented at the Annual Meeting of the Association for the Advancement of Behavior Therapy, Philadelphia, PA.

Rogers, S., & Silver, S. M. (2002). Is EMDR an exposure therapy? A review of trauma protocols. *Journal of Clinical Psychology, 58*(1), 43–59.

Ross, C. A., & Joshi, S. (1992). Schneiderian symptoms and childhood trauma in the general population. *Comprehensive Psychiatry, 33*(4), 269–273.

Rossi, E. L. (1980a). *The collected papers of Milton H. Erickson on hypnosis:* Vol. 1. *The nature of hypnosis and suggestion.* New York: Halsted Press.

Rossi, E. L. (1980b). The collected papers of Milton H. Erickson on hypnosis, Volume II - Hypnotic alteration of sensory, perceptual and psychophysiological processes. New York: Halsted Press.

Rossi, E. L. (1999, June). *Does EMDR facilitate new growth in the brain? Immediate-early genes in optimizing human potentials.* Paper presented at the EMDR International Association Conference, Las Vegas, NV.

Rossi, E. L. (2000). In search of a deep psychobiology of hypnosis: visionary hypotheses for a new millennium. *American Journal of Clinical Hypnosis, 42*(3-4), 178–207.

Rossman, M. L. (2000). *Guided imagery for self-healing: an essential resource for anyone seeking wellness* (2nd ed.). Novato, CA: New World Library.

Roth, S., & Friedman, M. (1997). *Childhood trauma remembered: A report on the current scientific knowledge base and its applications.* Retrieved October 27, 2007, from http://istss.org/publications/ChildhoodTraumaRemembered.pdf

Rothbaum, B. O., Astin, M. C., & Marsteller, F. (2005). Prolonged Exposure versus Eye Movement Desensitization and Reprocessing (EMDR) for PTSD rape victims. *Journal of Traumatic Stress, 18*(6), 607–616.

Rothbaum, B. O., Foa, E. B., & Hembree, E. A. (2007). *Reclaiming your life from a traumatic experience: workbook.* Oxford; New York: Oxford University Press.

Rudd, M. D., Berman, A. L., Joiner, T. E., Jr., Nock, M. K., Silverman, M. M., Mandrusiak, M., Van Orden K, Witte, T., (2006). Warning signs for suicide: theory, research, and clinical applications. *Suicide & Life Threatening Behavior, 36*(3), 255–262.

Russell, M. C. (1992). *Towards a neuropsychological approach to PTSD: An integrative conceptualization of etiology and mechanisms of therapeutic change.* Unpublished doctoral dissertation, Pacific Graduate School of Psychology, Palo Alto, CA.

Russell, M. C. (2006). Treating combat-related stress disorders: A multiple case study utilizing eye movement desensitization and reprocessing (EMDR) with battlefield casualties from the Iraqi War. *Military Psychology, 18*(1), 1–18.

Russell, M. C. (2008a). *Meeting military mental health needs in the 21st century and beyond: A critical analysis of the effects of dualism, disparity and scientific bias.* Paper presented at EMDRIA Conference, Phoenix, AZ.

Russell, M. C. (2008b). Treating traumatic amputation-related phantom limb pain: a case study utilizing eye movement desensitization and reprocessing (EMDR) within the armed services. *Clinical Case Studies, 7*(1), 136–153.

Russell, M. C. (2008c). Scientific resistance to research, training and utilization of eye movement desensitization and reprocessing (EMDR) therapy in treating post-war disorders. *Social Science & Medicine, 67*(11), 1737–1746.

Sack, M., Lempa, W., & Lamprecht, F. (2001). [Study quality and effect-sizes - a metaanalysis of EMDR-treatment for posttraumatic stress disorder.][Article in German] *Psychotherapy, Psychosomatic Medicine & Psychology, 51*(9–10), 350–355.

Sack, M., Lempa, W., Steinmetz, A., Lamprecht, F., & Hofmann, A. (2008). Alterations in autonomic tone during trauma exposure using eye movement desensitization and reprocessing (EMDR)-results of a preliminary investigation. *Journal of Anxiety Disorders. 2*(7), 1264–1271.

Salter, A. C. (1995). *Transforming trauma: A guide to understanding and treating adult survivors of child sexual abuse.* Thousand Oaks, CA: Sage Publications.

Sanders, S. (1991). *Clinical self-hypnosis: The power of words and images.* New York: Guilford.

Santos, R. V., Tufik, S., & De Mello, M. T. (2007). Exercise, sleep and cytokines: is there a relation? *Sleep Medicine Reviews, 11*(3), 231–239.

Sartory, G., Rachman, S., & Grey, S. J. (1982). Return of fear: the role of rehearsal. *Behavior Research and Therapy, 20*(2), 123–133.

Schacter, D. L. (1987). Implicit Memory: History and Current Status. *Journal of Experimental Psychology, 13*(3), 501–518.

Schmidt, N. B., Woolaway-Bickel, K., Trakowski, J., Santiago, H., Storey, J., Koselka, M., et al. (2000). Dismantling cognitive-behavioral treatment for panic disorder: questioning the utility of breathing retraining. *Journal of Consulting and Clinical Psychology, 68*(3), 417–424.

Schneck, C. D. (2006). Treatment of rapid-cycling bipolar disorder. *Journal of Clinical Psychiatry, 67*(Suppl 11,) 22–27.

Schneider, G., Nabavi, D., & Heuft, G. (2005). Eye movement desensitization and reprocessing in the treatment of posttraumatic stress disorder in a patient with comorbid epilepsy. *Epilepsy & Behavior, 7*(4), 715–718.

Schneider, J., Hofmann, A., Rost, C., & Shapiro, F. (2008). EMDR in the treatment of chronic phantom limb pain. *Pain Medicine, 9*(1), 76–82.

Schore, A. N. (1994). *Affect regulation and the origin of the self: the neurobiology of emotional development.* Hillsdale, New Jersey: Lawrence Erlbaum Associates, Publishers.

Schore, A. N. (1996). The experience-dependent maturation of a regulatory system in the orbital prefrontal cortex and the origin of developmental psychopathology. *Development and Psychopathology, 8*, 59–87.

Schore, A. N. (1997). Early organization of the nonlinear right brain and the development of a predisposition to psychiatric disorders. *Development and Psychopathology, 9*, 595–631.

Schore, A. N. (2000). Attachment and the regulation of the right brain. *Attachment & Human Development, 2*, 23–47.

Schore, A. N. (2001a). Effects of a secure attachment relationship on right brain development, affect regulation, and infant mental health. *Infant Mental Health Journal, 22*(1), 7–66.

Schore, A. N. (2001b). The effects of early relational trauma on right brain development, affect regulation, and infant mental health. *Infant Mental Health Journal, 22*(1), 201–269.

Schore, A. N. (2003a). *Affect dysregulation & disorders of the self* (1st ed.). New York: W.W. Norton.

Schore, A. N. (2003b). *Affect regulation & the repair of the self* (1st ed.). New York: W.W. Norton.

Schottenbauer, M. A., Glass, C. R., Arnkoff, D. B., Tendick, V., & Gray, S. H. (2008). Nonresponse and dropout rates in outcome studies on PTSD: review and methodological considerations. *Psychiatry, 71*(2), 134–168.

Schultz, J. H., & Luthe, W. (1959). *Autogenic training; a psychophysiologic approach in psychotherapy.* New York: Grune & Stratton.

Schurmans, K. (2007). EMDR treatment of choking phobia. *Journal of EMDR Practice and Research, 1*(2), 118–121.

Scurfield, R. M. (1985). Post-traumatic stress assessment and treatment: Overview and formulations. In C. R. Figley (Ed.), *Trauma and its wake* (Vol. 1, pp. 219–256). New York: Brunner/Mazel.

Segal, Z. V., Williams, J. M. G., & Teasdale, J. D. (2002). *Mindfulness-based cognitive therapy for depression.* New York: Guilford Press.

Seligman, M. E. (1995). The effectiveness of psychotherapy. The Consumer Reports study. *American Psychologist, 50*(12), 965–974.

Servan-Schreiber, D. (2004). *The instinct to heal: curing stress, anxiety, and depression without drugs and without talk therapy.* Emmaus, Pa.: Rodale; Distributed to the book trade by St. Martin's Press.

Servan-Schreiber, D., Schooler, J., Dew, M. A., Carter, C., & Bartone, P. (2006). Eye movement desensitization and reprocessing for posttraumatic stress disorder: a pilot blinded, randomized study of stimulation type. *Psychotherapy and Psychosomatics, 75*(5), 290–297.

Shalev, A. Y. (1996). Stress versus traumatic stress: From acute homeostatic reaction to chronic psychopathology. In B. A. van der Kolk & A. C. McFarlane & L. Weisaeth (Eds.), *Traumatic Stress: the effects of overwhelming experience on mind, body, and society*. New York: The Guilford Press.

Shapiro, F. (1989a). Efficacy of the eye movement desensitization procedure in the treatment of traumatic memories. *Journal of Traumatic Stress Studies, 2,* 199–223.

Shapiro, F. (1989b). Eye movement desensitization: A new treatment for post-traumatic stress disorder. *Journal of Behavior Therapy and Experimental Psychiatry, 20,* 211–217.

Shapiro, F. (1991a). Eye movement desensitization and reprocessing procedure: from EMD to EMD/R-a new treatment model for anxiety and related traumata. *The Behavior Therapist, 14,* 133–135.

Shapiro, F. (1991b). Eye movement desensitization and reprocessing: A cautionary note. *The Behavior Therapist, 14,* 188.

Shapiro, F. (1995). *Eye movement desensitization and reprocessing, basic principles, protocols and procedures*. New York: The Guilford Press.

Shapiro, F. (1996). Errors of context and review of eye movement desensitization and reprocessing research. *Journal of Behavior Therapy & Experimental Psychiatry, 27*(3), 313–317.

Shapiro, F. (1998a). Eye Movement Desensitization and Reprocessing (EMDR): Historical Context, Recent Research, and Future Directions. In S. Knapp, T. L. Jackson, L. Vandecreek (Eds.), *Innovations in clinical practice: A source book* (Vol. 16, pp. 143–161). Sarasota, FL: Professional Resource Press.

Shapiro, F. (1999). Eye movement desensitization and reprocessing (EMDR) and the anxiety disorders: clinical and research implications of an integrated psychotherapy treatment. *Journal of Anxiety Disorders, 13*(1–2), 35–67.

Shapiro, F. (2001). *Eye movement desensitization and reprocessing, basic principles, protocols and procedures* (2nd ed.). New York: The Guilford Press.

Shapiro, F. (2002a). EMDR 12 years after its introduction: Past and future research. *Journal of Clinical Psychology, 58*(1), 1–22.

Shapiro, F. (Ed.). (2002b). *EMDR and the paradigm prism*. Washington DC: American Psychological Association Press.

Shapiro, F. (2004). *Adaptive information processing: EMDR clinical application and case conceptualization*. Paper presented at EMDRIA Conference 2004. Montreal, QC, Canada.

Shapiro, F. (Ed.). (2008). *EMDR Institute basic training course, weekend 1* (January 2008 ed.). Watsonville, CA: EMDR Institute.

Shapiro, F., & Forrest, M. S. (1997). *EMDR: The Breakthrough Therapy for Overcoming Anxiety, Stress and Trauma*. New York: Basic Books.

Shapiro, F., Kaslow, F. W., & Maxfield, L. (2007). *Handbook of EMDR and family therapy processes*. Hoboken, NJ: John Wiley & Sons Inc.

Shear, M., Cooper, A., Klerman, G., Busch, M., & Shapiro, T. (1993). A psychodynamic model of panic disorder. *The American Journal of Psychiatry, 150*(6), 859–866.

Shearin, E. N., & Linehan, M. M. (1994) Dialectical behavioral therapy for borderline personality disorder: theoretical and empirical foundations. *Acta Psychiatrica Scandinavica 89*(suppl. 379): 61–68.

Shedler, J., Mayman, M., & Manis, M. (1993). The illusion of mental health. *American Psychologist, 48*(11), 1117–1131.

Siegel, D. J. (1999). *The developing mind: Toward a neurobiology of interpersonal experience*. New York: Guilford.

Sifneos, P. E. (1975). Problems of psychotherapy of patients with alexithymic characteristics and physical disease. *Psychotherapy and Psychosomatics, 26*(2), 65–70.

Sifneos, P. E. (1988). Alexithymia and its relationship to hemispheric specialization, affect, and creativity. *Psychiatric Clinics of North America, 11*(3), 287–292.

Silver, S. M., & Rogers, S. (2002). *Light in the heart of darkness: EMDR and the treatment of war and terrorism survivors* (1st ed.). New York: W.W. Norton.

Sine, L. F., & Vogelman-Sine, S. (2004) *EMDR Questionnaires Facilitating EMDR Treatment*. New Hope, PA: EMDR-HAP.

Slade, A. (1999). Attachment theory and research: Implication for the theory and practice of individual psychotherapy with adults. In J. Cassidy & P. R. Shaver (Eds.), *Handbook of attachment: Theory, research, and clinical applications* (pp. 575–594). New York: Guilford Press.

Smoller, J. W., Pollack, M. H., Wassertheil-Smoller, S., Jackson, R. D., Oberman, A., Wong, N. D., et al. (2007). Panic attacks and risk of incident cardiovascular events among postmenopausal women in the Women's Health Initiative Observational Study. *Archives of General Psychiatry, 64*(10), 1153–1160.

Sokolov, E. N. (1990). The orienting response, and future directions of its development. *Pavolovian Journal of Biological Sciences, 25*(3), 142–150.

Solomon, J., & George, C. (Eds.). (1999). *Attachment disorganization*. New York: Guilford Press.

Solomon, S. D., Gerrity, E. T., & Muff, A. M. (1992). Efficacy of Treatments for Posttraumatic Stress Disorder: An Empirical Review. *Journal of the American Medical Association, 268*(5), 633–638.

Spector, J., & Kremer, S. (2009). Can I use EMDR with clients who report suicidal ideation?. *Journal of EMDR Practice and Research, 3*(2), 107–108.

Spector, J., & Read, J. (1999). The Current Status of Eye Movement Desensitization and Reprocessing (EMDR). *Clinical Psychology and Psychotherapy, 6*, 165–174.

Spinhoven, P., Giesen-Bloo, J., van Dyck, R., Kooiman, K., & Arntz, A. (2007). The therapeutic alliance in schema-focused therapy and transference-focused psychotherapy for borderline personality disorder. *Journal of Consulting and Clinical Psychology, 75*(1), 104–115.

Sprang, G. (2001). The use of eye movement desensitization and reprocessing (EMDR) in the treatment of traumatic stress and complicated mourning: Psychological and behavioral outcomes. *Research on Social Work Practice, 11*(3), 300–320.

Sroufe, L. A., & Waters, E. (1977). Heart rate as a convergent measure in clinical and developmental research. *Merrill-Palmer Quarterly, 23*(1), 3–27.

Stampfl, T. G., & Levis, D. J. (1967). Essentials of implosive therapy: a learning-theory-based psychodynamic behavioral therapy. *Journal of Abnormal Psychology, 72*(6), 496–503.

Standards and Training Committee, EMDR International Association. (2001). *Consultation packet* (pp. 10). Austin, TX: Author.

Stapleton, J. A., Taylor, S., & Asmundson, G. J. (2006). Effects of three PTSD treatments on anger and guilt: Exposure therapy, eye movement desensitization and reprocessing, and relaxation training. *Journal of Traumatic Stress, 19*(1), 19–28.

Stein, H., Jacobs, N. J., Ferguson, K. S., Allen, J. G., & Fonagy, P. (1998). What do adult attachment scales measure? *Bulletin of the Menninger Clinic, 62*(1 [Winter 1998]), 33–82.

Steinberg, M. (1994). *Structured clinical interview for DSM–IV dissociative disorders-revised (SCID-D-R)*. Washington, DC: American Psychiatric Press.

Steinberg, M. (2000). Advances in the clinical assessment of dissociation: the SCID-D-R. *Bulletin of the Menninger Clinic, 64*(2), 146–163.

Stickgold, R. (2002). EMDR: A putative neurobiological mechanism of action. *Journal of Clinical Psychology, 58*(1), 61–75.

Stickgold, R. (2008). Sleep-Dependent Memory Processing and EMDR Action. *Journal of EMDR Practice and Research, 2*(4), 289–299.

Stinson, F. S., Dawson, D. A., Patricia Chou, S., Smith, S., Goldstein, R. B., June Ruan, W., et al. (2007). The epidemiology of DSM–IV specific phobia in the USA: Results from the National Epidemiologic Survey on Alcohol and Related Conditions. *Psychological Medicine, 37*(7), 1047–1059.

Stowasser, J. (2007). EMDR and family therapy in the treatment of domestic violence. In F. Shapiro, F. W. Kaslow & L. Maxfield (Eds.), *Handbook of EMDR and family therapy processes* (pp. p. 243–264). Hoboken, N.J.: Wiley.

Sturpe, D. A., & Weissman, A. M. (2002). Clinical inquiries. What are effective treatments for panic disorder? *The Journal of Family Practice, 51*(9), 743.

Summers, R. F., & Barber, J. P. (2003). Therapeutic alliance as a measurable psychotherapy skill. *Academic Psychiatry, 27*(3), 160–165.

Suzuki, S., & Dixon, T. (1970). *Zen mind, beginner's mind* ([1st ed.]). New York: Walker/Weatherhill.

Taylor, G. J., Ryan, D., & Bagby, R. M. (1985). Toward the development of a new self-report alexithymia scale. *Psychotherapy Psychosomatic, 44*(4), 191–199.

Teasdale, J. D. (1999). Emotional processing, three modes of mind and the prevention of relapse in depression. *Behaviour Research and Therapy, 37 Suppl 1*, S53–77.

Teasdale, J. K., & Barnard, P. J. (1993). Affect, cognition and change: Re-modeling depressive thought. Hillsdale, JN: Lawrence Erlbaum Associates.

Teicher, M. H. (2000). Wounds that time won't heal: The neurobiology of child abuse. *Cerebrum, 2*(4), 50–67.

Teicher, M. H. (2002). Scars that won't heal: The neurobiology of child abuse. *Scientific American, 286*(3), 68–75.

Teicher, M. H., Glod, C. A., Surrey, J., & Swett, C., Jr. (1993). Early childhood abuse and limbic system ratings in adult psychiatric outpatients. *Journal of Neuropsychiatry and Clinical Neurosciences, 5*(3), 301–306.

Teicher, M. H., Ito, Y., Glod, C. A., Andersen, S. L., Dumont, N., & Ackerman, E. (1997). Preliminary evidence for abnormal cortical development in physically and sexually abused children using EEG coherence and MRI. In R. Yehuda & A. C. McFarlane (Eds.), *Psychobiology of posttraumatic stress disorder* (Vol. 821, pp. 161–175). New York: The New York Academy of Sciences.

Telch, M. J., Lucas, J. A., Schmidt, N. B., Hanna, H. H., LaNae Jaimez, T., & Lucas, R. A. (1993). Group cognitive-behavioral treatment of panic disorder. *Behaviour Research and Therapy, 31*(3), 279–287.

Ten Broeke, E., & De Jongh, A. (1993). Eye movement desensitization and reprocessing (EMDR): Praktische toepassing en theoretische overwegingen [Eye movement desensitization and reprocessing (EMDR): Practical applications and theorethical considerations]. *Gedragstherapie, 26*, 233–254.

Thomas, J. T. (2007). Informed consent through contracting for supervision: Minimizing risks, enhancing benefits. *Professional Psychology: Research and Practice, 38*, 221–231.

Tinker, R. H., & Wilson, S. A. (2005). The phantom limb pain protocol. In R. Shapiro (Ed.), *EMDR solutions: Pathways to healing* (pp. 147–159). New York: W. W. Norton.

Todder, D., & Kaplan, Z. (2007). Rapid eye movements for acute stress disorder using video conference communication. *Telemedicine Journal and e-Health, 13*(4), 461–463.

Tomkins, S. S. (1962a). *Affect imagery consciousness. The positive affects* (Vol. 1). New York: Springer Publishing.

Tomkins, S. S. (1962b). *Affect imagery consciousness. The negative affects* (Vol. 2). New York: Springer Publishing Company.

Tomkins, S. S. (1991). *Affect imagery consciousness. The negative affects: anger and fear* (Vol. 3). New York: Springer Publishing Company.

Torgersen, S. (1983). Genetic factors in anxiety disorders. *Archives of General Psychiatry, 40*(10), 1085–1089.

Trull, T. J. (2001). Relationships of borderline features to parental mental illness, childhood abuse, Axis I disorder, and current functioning. *Journal of Personality Disorders, 15*(1), 19–32.

Tufnell, G. (2005). Eye movement desensitization and reprocessing in the treatment of pre-adolescent children with post-traumatic symptoms. *Clinical Child Psychology and Psychiatry, 10*(4), 587.

Tully, E. C., Iacono, W. G., & McGue, M. (2008). An adoption study of parental depression as an environmental liability for adolescent depression and childhood disruptive disorders. *American Journal of Psychiatry, 165*(9), 1148–1154.

van Balkom, A., de Beurs, E., Koele, P., Lange, A., & van Dyck, R. (1996). Long-term Benzodiazepine use is associated with smaller treatment gain in panic disorder with agoraphobia. *Journal of Nervous & Mental Disease, 184*(2),133–135.

van den Hout, M., Muris, P., Salemink, E., & Kindt, M. (2001). Autobiographical memories become less vivid and emotional after eye movements. *British Journal of Clinical Psychology, 40*(Pt 2), 121–130.

van der Hart, O., & Friedman, B. (1989). A reader's guide to Pierre Janet on dissociation: A neglected intellectual heritage. *Dissociation, 2*(1), 3–15.

van der Hart, O., Nijenhuis, E. R. S., & Steele, K. (2006). *The haunted self: structural dissociation and the treatment of chronic traumatization.* New York: W. W. Norton.

van der Hart, O., & Horst, R. (1989). The dissociation theory of Pierre Janet. *Journal of Traumatic Stress, 2*(4), 397–411.

van der Kolk, B. A. (1996). The body keeps the score: Approaches to the psychobiology of posttraumatic stress disorder. In B. A. van der Kolk, A. C. McFarlane, & L. Weisaeth (Eds.), *Traumatic stress: The effects of overwhelming experience on mind, body, and society* (pp. 214–241). New York: The Guilford Press.

van der Kolk, B. A., Burbridge, J. A., & Suzuki, J. (1997). The Psychobiology of traumatic memory: Clinical implications of neuroimaging studies. In R. Yehuda & A. C. McFarlane (Eds.), *Annals of the New York Academy of Sciences: Psychobiology of Posttraumatic Stress Disorder* (Vol. 821, pp. 99–113). New York: New York Academy of Sciences.

van der Kolk, B., & Fisler, R. (1995). Dissociation and the fragmentary nature of traumatic memories: Overview and exploratory study. *Journal of Traumatic Stress, 8*(4), 505–525.

van der Kolk, B. A., McFarlane, A. C., & Weisaeth, L. (Eds.). (1996). *Traumatic Stress: The effects of overwhelming experience on mind, body, and society.* New York: The Guilford Press.

van der Kolk, B. A., & Pelcoitz, D. (1999). Clinical applications of the structured interview for disorders of extreme stress (SIDES). *National Center for PTSD Clinical Quarterly, 8*(2), 21–26.

van der Kolk, B. A., Pelcovitz, D., Roth, S., Mandel, F. S., McFarlane, A., & Herman, J. L. (1996). Dissociation, somatization, and affect dysregulation: the complexity of adaptation of trauma. *American Journal of Psychiatry, 153*(7 Supplement), 83–93.

van der Kolk, B. A., Spinazzola, J., Blaustein, M. E., Hopper, J. W., Hopper, E. K., Korn, D. L., et al. (2007). A randomized clinical trial of eye movement desensitization and reprocessing (EMDR), fluoxetine, and pill placebo in the treatment of posttraumatic stress disorder: treatment effects and long-term maintenance. *Journal of Clinical Psychiatry, 68*(1), 37–46.

van der Kolk, B. A., & van der Hart, O. (1989). Pierre Janet and the Breakdown of Adaptation in Psychological Trauma. *American Journal of Psychiatry, 146*(12), 1530–1540.

Van der Zijpp, A. T., Ter Horst, G., De Jongh, A., & Makkes, P. C. (1996). Angst voor de tandheelkundige behandeling. Evaluatie van behandeling van patiënten met angst [Treatment of dentally anxious patients evaluated]. *Nederlands Tijdschrift voor Tandheelkunde, 103*, 213–215.

van Etten, M. L., & Taylor, S. (1998). Comparative efficacy of treatments for post-traumatic stress disorder: A Meta-analysis. *Clinical Psychology and Psychotherapy, 5*, 126–144.

Vogelmann-Sine, S., Sine, L., Smyth, N. J., & Popky, A. J. (1998). *EMDR chemical dependency treatment manual.* New Hope, PA: EMDR-HAP.

Vu, N., Baroffio, A., Huber, P., Layat, C., Gerbase, M., & Nendaz, M. (2006). Assessing clinical competence: a pilot project to evaluate the feasibility of a standardized patient- based practical examination as a component of the Swiss certification process. *Swiss Medical Weekly, 136*(25–26), 392–399.

Walker, E. A., Newman, E., Dobie, D. J., Ciechanowski, P., & Katon, W. J. (2002). Validation of the PTSD Checklist in an HMO sample of women. *General Hospital Psychiatry, 24*(6), 375–380.

Waller, N. G., & Ross, C. A. (1997). The prevalence and biometric structure of pathological dissociation in the general population: Taxometric and behavior genetic findings. *Journal of Abnormal Psychology, 106*(4), 499–510.

Walsh, B. W. (2006). *Treating self-injury: a practical guide.* New York, NY: Guilford Press.

Watanabe, N., Churchill, R., & Furukawa, T. A. (2007). Combination of psychotherapy and benzodiazepines versus either therapy alone for panic disorder: a systematic review. *Biomedcentral Psychiatry, 7,* 18.

Watanabe, N., Hunot, V., Omori, I. M., Churchill, R., & Furukawa, T. A. (2007). Psychotherapy for depression among children and adolescents: a systematic review. *Acta Psychiatrica Scandinavia, 116*(2), 84–95.

Watkins, C. E. (1997). Defining psychological supervision and understanding supervisor functioning. In C. E. Watkins (Ed.), *Handbook of psychotherapy supervision* (pp. 3–10). New York: Wiley.

Watkins, J. G. (1971). The affect bridge: A hypnoanalytic technique. *Journal of Clinical and Experimental Hypnosis, 19*(1), 21–27.

Watkins, J. G. (1990). Watkins' affect or somatic bridge. In D. C. Hammond (Ed.), Handbook of hypnotic suggestions and metaphor (pp. 523–524). New York: Norton

Watkins, J. G. (1992). Hypnoanalytic techniques: The practice of clinical hypnosis (Vol. 2). New York: Irvington.

Webert, D. R. (2003). Are the courts in a trance? Approaches to the admissibility of hypnotically enhanced witness testimony in light of empirical evidence. *American Criminal Law Review, 40*(3), 1301–1327.

Wegner, D. (1994). Ironic processes of mental control. *Psychological Review, 101,* 34–52.

Weiss, D., & Marmar, C. (1997). The Impact of event scale - Revised. In J. Wilson & T. Keane (Eds), *Assessing psychological trauma and PTSD.* New York: Guilford.

Westra, H. A., Stewart, S. H., & Conrad, B. E. (2002). Naturalistic manner of benzodiazepine use and cognitive behavioral therapy outcome in panic disorder with agoraphobia. *Journal Anxiety Disorders, 16,* 233–246.

Whalen, J. E., & Nash, M. R. (1996). Hypnosis and dissociation: Theoretical, empirical and clinical perspectives. In L. K. Michelson & W. J. Ray (Eds.), *Handbook of dissociation: Theoretical empirical and clinical perspectives.* New York: Plenum Press.

Wildwind, L. (1994, March 4). *Chronic Depression.* Paper presented at the EMDR Conference "Research and Clinical Applications", Sunnyvale, California.

Wilson, S. A., Tinker, R., Becker, L. A., Hofmann, A., & Cole, J. W. (2000, September). *EMDR treatment of phantom limb pain with brain imaging (MEG).* Paper presented at the annual meeting of the EMDR International Association, Toronto, Canada.

Wilson, D., Silver, S. M., Covi, W., & Foster, S. (1996). Eye movement desensitization and reprocessing: Effectiveness and autonomic correlates. *Journal of Behavior Therapy and Experimental Psychiatry, 27,* 219–229.

Wilson, S., Becker, L. A., & Tinker, R. H. (1995). Eye movement desensitization and reprocessing (EMDR) treatment for psychologically traumatized individuals. *Journal of Consulting and Clinical Psychology, 63*(6), 928–937.

Wilson, S. A., Becker, L. A., & Tinker, R. H. (1997). Fifteen-month follow-up of eye movement desensitization and reprocessing (EMDR) treatment for posttraumatic stress disorder and psychological trauma. *Journal of Consulting and Clinical Psychology, 65*(6), 1047–1056.

Wilson, S., Tinker, R., Becker, L., & Logan, C. (2001). Stress management with law enforcement personnel: A controlled outcome study of emdr versus a traditional stress management program. *International Journal of Stress Management, 8*(3), 179–200.

Winson, J. (1990). The meaning of dreams. *Scientific American, 263*(5), 86–88, 90–82, 94–86.

Winson, J. (1993). The biology and function of rapid eye movement sleep. *Current Opinion in Neurobiology, 3*(2), 243–248.

Wittmann, L., Schredl, M., & Kramer, M. (2007). Dreaming in posttraumatic stress disorder: A critical review of phenomenology, psychophysiology and treatment. *Psychotherapy and Psychosomatics, 76*(1), 25–39.

Wolpe, J. (1954). Reciprocal inhibition as the main basis of psychotherapeutic effects. *American Medical Association Archives of Neurology and Psychiatry, 72,* 205–226.

Wolpe, J. (1958). *Psychotherapy by reciprocal inhibition.* Stanford, CA: Stanford University Press.

Wolpe, J., & Lang, P. J. (1964). Fear survey schedule for use in behavior therapy. *Behaviour Research and Therapy, 2,* 27–30.

Wolpe, J., & Lang, P. J. (1969). The fear survey schedule. San Diego, CA: Educational and Industrial Testing Service.

Woodman, C. L., Noyes Jr, R., Black, D. W., Schlosser, S., & Yagla, S. J. (1999). A 5-year follow-up study of generalized anxiety disorder and panic disorder. *Journal of Nervous and Mental Disease, 187*(1), 3.

World Health Organization (2004). *The ICD-10 classification of mental and behavioural disorders: Clinical descriptions and diagnostic guidelines* (2nd ed.) Geneva: World Health Organization, 2004.

Yerkes, R. M., & Dodson, J. D. (1908). The relation of strength of stimulus to rapidity of habit-formation. *Journal of Comparative Neurology and Psychology, 18,* 459–482.

Yoo, S. S., Hu, P. T., Gujar, N., Jolesz, F. A., & Walker, M. P. (2007). A deficit in the ability to form new human memories without sleep. *Nature Neuroscience, 10*(3), 385–392.

Young, J. E. (1999). *Cognitive therapy for personality disorders: a schema-focused approach* (3rd ed.). Sarasota, FL.: Professional Resource Press.

Young, J. E., Zangwill, W. M., & Behary, W. E. (2002). Combining EMDR and schema-focused therapy: The whole may be greater than the sum of the parts. In F. Shapiro (Ed.), *EMDR and the paradigm prism* (pp. 181–208). Washington DC: American Psychological Association Press.

Young, W. (1994). EMDR treatment of phobic symptoms in multiple personality. *Dissociation, 7,* 129–133.

Zaghrout-Hodali, M., Alissa, F., & Dodgson, P. W. (2008). Building Resilience and Dismantling Fear: EMDR Group Protocol With Children in an Area of Ongoing Trauma. *Journal of EMDR Practice and Research, 2*(2), 106–113.

Zlotnick, C., Najavits, L. M., Rohsenow, D. J., & Johnson, D. M. (2003). A cognitive-behavioral treatment for incarcerated women with substance abuse disorder and posttraumatic stress disorder: findings from a pilot study. *Journal of Substance Abuse Treatment, 25*(2), 99–105.

Index